The Dark Side of Church/State Separation

The Dark Side of Church/State Separation

The French Revolution, Nazi Germany, and International Communism

STEPHEN STREHLE

Transaction Publishers
New Brunswick (U.S.A.) and London (U.K.)

This book is printed on acid-free paper that meets the American National Standard for Permanence of Paper for Printed Library Materials.

Library of Congress Catalog Number: 2013008855
ISBN: 978-1-4128-5271-5
Printed in the United States of America

Library of Congress Cataloging-in-Publication Data
Strehle, Stephen, 1952-
The dark side of church-state separation : the French revolution, Nazi Germany, and international Communism / Stephen Strehle.
pages cm
Includes bibliographical references and index.
ISBN 978-1-4128-5271-5
1. Church and state. 2. France--History--Revolution, 1789-1799--Religious aspects. 3. National socialism--Germany. 4. National socialism--Religious aspects. 5. Communism and Christianity. I. Title.
BV630.3.S77 2013
322'.109--dc23

2013008855

"God grant that in America true religion and civil liberty may be inseparable and that the unjust attempts to destroy the one, may in the issue tend to the support and establishment of both."

—John Witherspoon, Fast Day Sermon, May 17, 1776

Contents

Introduction

The concept of church/state separation developed different nuances throughout its history in Western civilization. The early church followed its own version of the concept by centering its mission upon liberating individuals from a fallen world, ignoring social problems, and planting a cosmopolitan church, which was able to thrive under different cultural conditions and governmental policies by accepting the status quo. In scripture, Jesus tells the Pharisees to unburden their lives with the concerns about the things of the world and "render to Caesar the things of Caesar," leaving the problem of oppressive taxation to those who care about material possessions (Matt 22:21). He tells Pilate, "My kingdom is not of this world," refusing to fight or even protest his unjust arrest and execution (John 18:36). Paul alludes to the words of Jesus in Romans 13 and develops a general policy of church/state relations out of them, telling the church to accept its role in society under the government (ὑποτάσσω) and not rebel against it (ἀντιτάσσω) as if longing for another mission. One should accept the social structure of the day or whatever policy comes down from the government as a matter of indifference to the high calling of God in Christ Jesus and the separate role of the church in society (1 Cor 7:20–24).

After the initial phase, the position of the early church changed from treating political concerns as a matter of indifference, deteriorating into a more rancorous polemical relationship with the empire as subordination gave way to a call for complete separation from the evils of society. Already within the scripture, one detects a darker tone in 1 John, where loyalty to the kingdom of God means forsaking the "world" of temptation outside the confines of the church as a realm of demonic activity.[1] "Love not the world, neither the things that are in the world. If anyone loves the world, the love of the Father is not in this particular person. For all that is in the world, the lust of the flesh, the lust of the eyes, and the pride of one's possessions is not of the Father but of the world" (1 John 2:15–16). This dark view of society expressed the fundamental attitude of the church during the first three centuries of its existence and was most consistently presented in the works of Tertullian, the third-century father of Latin theology, who called Christians to reject military and government service, Greco-Roman philosophical thought, and the many decadent amusements of the time, including the games, tragedy, and music.[2] The call for separation was meant to preserve the purity of the church from worldly pleasures, but it also brought unintended consequences and produced a considerable and equally sanctimonious backlash within the society at large, as citizens of the empire accused Christians of harming the social fabric through unpatriotic behavior and paving the way for its ultimate destruction by spreading pacifism among the people.[3] The emperors tried to stop the spread of the religion by implementing periodic persecutions but ultimately failed in this endeavor, eventually caving into the religion through the conversion of Constantine and witnessing the dissipation of the empire's former glory through the invasion of barbarian hordes in the next century. Even when Christianity absorbed the empire and compromised the original message of the gospel with the exercise of temporal powers, it still preserved a remnant of the New Testament (NT) approach to social issues in its overall orientation, always constrained by its founding documents to exalt the spiritual over the temporal. During the Reformation, it gave birth to radical separatist groups like the Anabaptists, who called for a return to the *radices* (roots) of the faith and condemned involvement in society altogether, based upon the example of the NT church and the sole authority of scripture.[4] Christianity's proclivity toward the NT and its doctrine of church/state separation brought considerable scorn from social critics in the modern world, who thought of the religion as little more than a form of opium, anesthetizing the people and preventing any serious attempt to resolve social problems in a culture dominated by its teachings.

Some segments of the church responded to the accusations by developing a less polemical relationship with the state, while trying to preserve the basic dichotomy between the two realms. These Christians accepted the responsibility of a dual citizenship, which sanctioned the place of spiritual and secular loyalties as separate and irreconcilable realms of service. Martin Luther expressed a form of the position at the beginning of the Reformation when he spoke of the God of the Bible possessing two hands: the left-hand exhibiting severity and justice, the right-hand showing mercy and grace to a certain few. Through this dichotomy, Luther gave expression to the genuine difficulty of reconciling the spiritual commission of the church in bringing the gospel of grace and forgiveness to the vilest of sinners with the temporal commission of the government, which must protect the citizenry and punish criminals through the strict enforcement of the law. The dichotomy between the law and the gospel created a need to recognize some sense of church/state separation, or duality between private religious practice and the public need for justice.[5]

The most literal followers of this position were Roger Williams and the Baptists, who sanctioned the participation of Christians in the church and government but erected a wall between the two realms, not allowing any communication between the two, or letting the left hand know what the right hand was doing.[6] The position certainly recognized the difficulty of translating the Mosaic economy or the private admonitions of Jesus into a contemporary message with an obvious social application in our day and age. It showed the problematic nature of partisan political activity in the church: where left-wing Socialists transform the message of individual spiritual salvation into a social gospel of physical deliverance through the state, or right-wing conservatives, like the reconstructionists, make the laws of the Bible eternal and unchanging and readily applicable to all realms of modern society.[7] It recognized the need for "relative justice" in a fallen world, where the believer must refrain from imposing the absolute will of God upon society and accept the possibility of depraved institutions, like slavery or divorce in certain cultures, as a necessary matter of *Realpolitik* (Mark 10:1–9; 1 Cor 7:20–22). However, the position was criticized for exaggerating the dichotomy and containing once again the same basic problem as the former Anabaptist doctrine of separation, except this time resigning society to a similar fate by participating in the world without trying to reform it into a more perfect image. It was accused of encouraging spiritual laxity among the faithful, allowing them to lead a duplicitous life away from the faith toward antinomian behavior and justifying the abusive nature of present institutions and their role in it through cultural conservatism.[8] Within this framework, no roomed existed for the progressive social policies of a reformer like William Walwyn, who challenged the Machiavellian policy of his day as justifying the depravity of worldly institutions and helped pave the way for the development of a more tolerant, egalitarian, and democratic society, admonishing the believers to follow the polity of the NT church in all walks of life.[9]

In the secular world, the Baptist position was adopted by those who expressed concern about the power of the church in society oppressing freedom of religious opinion and disturbing the public peace. The early church and the later Anabaptists promoted church/state separation as a means of preserving the purity of the church from the evil influence of the world and the temptations of power; the modern secular position represented the exact opposite motivation in wanting to promote church/state separation as a means of protecting the state from the church and the limits and bigotry of narrow-minded dogma. In America, the position was first enshrined in the *Virginia Statute for Religious Freedom* (1786), which rejected the coercive practices of the Anglican Church in imposing specific creeds upon the people, exacting religious tests for office, compelling church attendance, collecting taxes from the citizens to support its activities, and guaranteeing to it or any other denomination a special place of privilege. The position helped inspire the First Amendment of the US Constitution and its clear rejection of following the practice of Mother England and establishing the Anglican Church or any other denomination on the national level. Americans generally accepted this position as a fair and just arrangement in allowing all religious groups to compete for the affections of the citizens on an equal playing field, but they became deeply divided when the Supreme Court went far beyond the narrow limits of the First Amendment in 1947 and wanted to extend the program by deconstructing its simple intendment into a broader doctrine, calling for a wall of separation between church and state, which meant to eliminate all religious influence on the government and representation in the public square and establish a completely secular or nonreligious state. The new interpretation was developed out of a letter Thomas Jefferson wrote to the Danbury Baptist Association of Connecticut, while serving as the president of the United States, justifying his decision to overturn the policy of his two predecessors in the office and eliminate the national day of fasting and prayer. In general, those who defended the wall considered it the best way of guaranteeing neutrality of the government in regard to religious practice, while those who questioned the broader interpretation found a trace of a darker motive indelibly etched within the policy—a motive that came from the French Enlightenment/Revolution in its war against the Judeo-Christian tradition and unfortunately made its way into the writings of Jefferson. It is clear that Jefferson was more devoted to the principles of the French Enlightenment/Revolution than the other Founding Fathers, that he developed anti-Semitic/anti-Christian sentiments from this source in following the religion and biblical criticism of the day, and that he wanted to use public education as a means of weaning the people off the Christian faith, following the same exact program of the Jewish emancipators and the Jacobins in this specific regard.[10] It is also clear that other cultures have used the secular French model of church/state separation as a means of conducting a war upon the Judeo-Christian tradition and reeducating the citizens through the power of the state into a new image—at the very least pointing to the possible temptations and latent problems with the position.

This dark side of church/state separation serves as the basic concern of our present study. The plan is to exhibit certain cases in Western civilization, where political movements used the power of government to promote the French concept in forwarding an extreme secular agenda and destroy the Jewish and Christian community. The study first discovers the darker spirit working in France and emanating from the French Enlightenment and the proceeding Revolution at the end of the eighteenth century. The new spirit permeated western European civilization in varying degrees during the subsequent era and brought a visceral and irrational form of intense hatred toward the Judeo-Christian tradition, exaggerating the sins of the *Ancien Régime* and hoping to substitute a new etatism in the place of the former religious communities. The spirit wanted to unify its citizens by providing a new identity within the state and making war against the former religious passions as a divisive factor or rival for the loyalty of its people, preaching religious toleration, while transmuting the message into intolerance by treating the traditional faith as a form of bigotry, marginalizing its participation in society, and expanding the power of the secular state as the new focus of attention. In the process, the spirit proceeded to deny the significance of the church in developing the positive aspects of modern society and to exaggerate its own secular contribution in creating a better world at the church's expense—a claim that our previous study, *The Egalitarian Spirit of Christianity*, countered by demonstrating that much of the credit actually belongs to the Reformed community in bringing fundamental concepts, such as liberty, equality, democracy, and federal government, to the forefront in the seventeenth century—long before the sons of the Enlightenment. In many ways, the present study represents a continuation of that work, hoping to place another question mark upon the exalted status of the Enlightenment in present day society and exhibit a darker side of its ideology this time in serving as the root of modern anti-Semitism and anti-Christianity. The emphasis may seem negative, but the ultimate purpose is not to discount the positive and considerable achievements of the Enlightenment, which are well documented and well discussed in restoring some sense of free thought and autonomy in human inquiry, free from the extensive power of priestly authority in the *Ancien Régime*. The purpose is merely to question its exalted status in the modern world and the problematic nature of its clear bigotries, which assaulted the Judeo-Christian tradition and helped inspire a culture of hate toward Jews and Christians as a common enemy and the subsequent political tactics of the French Revolution, Nazi Germany, and Communist Russia in attempting to destroy these religious communities.

The study is divided into three basic sections, beginning with a discussion of the French Enlightenment, the Revolution of 1789, and the modern *état*. The study starts with Voltaire and the philosophes laying the foundation for etatism by creating an extreme caricature of the Judeo-Christian tradition and visceral hatred toward the old religious order, inflating the ability of reason to discover first principles outside of divine revelation, and encouraging human beings to live apart from faith and dependence upon God in complete secular autonomy. Instead of providing the tradition with much needed criticism and reform, the philosophes laid the foundation for modern anti-Semitism and anti-Christianity by exaggerating its weaknesses and blaming it for all the ills of European society. The French Revolution soon followed and represented this animosity of the philosophes by rejecting the need for reform and conducting a civil war against the *Ancien Régime* of ecclesiastical and royal order. Robespierre and the National Assembly replaced the need for time-tested tradition with a new emphasis upon the general will of the people as the "voice of God," using the utilitarian method of the philosophes as a way to justify their many atrocities in serving this one voice. They demanded the Jews leave their individual religious communities behind to find a new identity as members of the French fraternity or state. They conducted a direct assault upon the church as a divisive element, nationalizing its property, desecrating its buildings, secularizing the clergy, and replacing the former allegiance to the Pope with a new civil oath. This direct assault failed in the short term, but it succeeded over the course of the next century, as the state increased in power and intelligentsia adopted the ideals of the Enlightenment and Revolution as the basic paradigm. Eventually, the Third Republic established French etatism at the turn of the nineteenth and twentieth centuries, separating the church from the state and creating a secular citizenry through its doctrine of *laïcité*, which keeps religion out of the public view.

The next section shows the ramifications of this ideology in Nazi Germany. Hitler praised the work of Voltaire and followed the atmosphere of hate created by the French Enlightenment in his attempt to destroy the Jews and Christians of Europe,[11] particularly displaying intense animosity toward their doctrine of egalitarianism, which he considered unscientific and destructive to his superior race and culture. He launched his most direct attack upon the Jews as the weaker of the two people, enacting anti-Semitic laws in the 1930s and then trying to exterminate all of them in the 1940s during the horrors of World War II. Against the more powerful opponent, he chose to bide his time, using the French tactic of separating church and state to limit the place of Christianity in German society, giving the state control over education, and planning to exterminate the religion in Germany after the successful completion of the war. His methods were more zealous and brutal than most enlightened Germans were prepared to go in ending the Judeo-Christian tradition, but his ideology was not unusual for the time and reached the highest levels of academia in post-Enlightenment Germany, with many professors and student organizations adopting a similar view of life. This cultural and intellectual matrix influenced Hitler's ideology and promoted many of the same Nazi-like themes: Pan-German nationalism, scientific racism, antipathy toward Jews, radical biblical criticism, and atheistic/voluntaristic philosophies—all following the Enlightenment and all meant to undermine the egalitarian message of the church and synagogue.[12] Hitler's ideology had no specific or fundamental relation to the historic teaching of the church. In fact, the Catholic Church was his most strident opponent early on, forbidding its members to join the Nazi party and pointing out the hostility of the group to fundamental doctrines of the faith. The Protestant Church was divided between the traditional or Neo-Orthodox faction, who repudiated anti-Semitism and overall Nazi ideology, and the liberal German Christians, who embraced Hitler's point of view—demonstrating clearly, graphically, and unequivocally the point of our study that the roots of anti-Semitism came from the Enlightenment or those liberals who were compromised by its message, not the traditional teachings of the church.

The third section discusses the ramifications of this ideology during the first three stages of International Communism in Europe. It looks at the overall philosophy of Karl Marx and Friedrich Engels and shows the emergence of their revolutionary ideology out of the antithetical spirit of Georg Hegel, the atheistic concepts of Ludwig Feuerbach, the anti-Semitic/anti-Christian writings of Bruno Bauer, and the assault upon the *Ancien Régime* in the French Revolution, which serves as the basic historical paradigm for all three Internationals of the Communist Party. Marx and Engels followed the Revolution in its desire to absorb all aspects of society under the state and provide a total "human emancipation" from outside forces like religion, which alienate the people from controlling their lives through the state. The Second and Third Internationals agreed with them on the need to eliminate the Judeo-Christian tradition and bring all aspects of society under the control of an atheistic state but disagreed over the precise method of achieving the ultimate goal, both emphasizing different sides of Marx's work. Karl Kautsky and the Second International preferred a more gradual and less violent method of reform, working within the democratic process of Germany, respecting the dignity and freedom of individual citizens, and believing that German higher criticism of scripture and scientific progress would eventually destroy religious superstition. Lenin and the Third International were more faithful to the revolutionary passions of the young Marx, employing utilitarian principles to justify violent tactics against the opposition, imposing a "dictatorship of the Proletariat" against all bourgeois elements remaining in society, conducting a continuous civil war against their own people and party, and proclaiming their rational and scientific ideas as an absolute dogma against other points of views—all echoing the revolutionary side of Marx and his infatuation with the ideals and tactics of the French Revolution. Of course, Lenin employed this revolutionary policy against the Russian Orthodox Church as an early bastion of opposition to his regime, arresting, exiling, and murdering those priests who resisted the state. He also used the typical French tactic of church/state separation, claiming religion was a private matter, while using the state to conduct an aggressive campaign of propaganda against the church and religion in general. Stalin only escalated the policies during much of his regime, gripping the whole nation with fear and paranoia over the capricious nature of his many purges and leaving few churches open to serve the spiritual needs of the people when the Germans invaded the country on June 22, 1941.

All three sections of our study show the dark side of a certain concept of church/state separation that received its initial inspiration from the French Enlightenment. The political apparatus of each culture use the French concept as a means of replacing the Judeo-Christian tradition with the new ideology of the state and exhibits the anti-Semitic/anti-Christian roots of the concept through direct political measures designed to destroy the Jewish and Christian community. Nazism and communism have their own unique ways of developing the policy, which each section discusses at length and places within the overall ideology of the respective system, but they both share a common heritage within the French concept and enact the program with the literal and brutal force of a totalitarian regime. In both cases, the analysis confirms the thesis of Arthur Hertzberg that the roots of modern anti-Semitism are found within the Enlightenment, except this time extending the thesis to include anti-Christianity, showing the relationship between the two religious communities and uniting Jews and Christians together as brothers and sisters in the same struggle.[13]

The postscript mentions the more subtle approach to the French position that was established in America in the middle of the last century. The approach shares a common heritage with the other case studies, finding its fundamental inspiration in the writings of Thomas Jefferson and the exaltation of his enlightened point of view by the Supreme Court in *Everson v. the Board of Education* (1947), although the overall culture still exhibits a strong religious heritage and the proponents of the wall try to distance the position from any historical roots in anti-Semitism and anti-Christianity. Whether this is possible remains a matter of further discussion, but our case studies certainly raise a red flag by showing the problematic nature of a "high and impregnable" wall separating the church from the state, given its dubious background in the bigotries of the French philosophes and those nefarious political movements that implemented the policy with the most literal force. Our previous study followed this same type of historical analysis and also placed a question mark upon the wall by showing the importance of religious ideas in developing the most sacred political institutions and concepts of the modern world, making it difficult to discriminate between religious and secular ideas, and so erect a simple wall between them. This study follows the same methodology as the *Egalitarian Spirit of Christianity* in using genealogy as a means of critique, or questioning our present values based upon a detailed analysis of their development in history—a method most associated with the monumental work of Michel Foucault.

Notes

1. H. Richard Niebuhr, *Christ and Culture,* (New York: Harper San Francisco, 2001) 46–47.
2. Tertullian, *De Praesciptione Haereticorum,* vii (PL 2.19–21); *De Anima,* ii (PL 1.649, 650); *De Spectaculis,* xxx (PL 1.735–38); *De Idolatrria,* xix (PL 1.767–68); *Apologeticus adversus Gentes pro Christianis,* xlvi–xlvii (PL 1.565–81); Niebuhr, *Christ and Culture,* 51–55; Adolf Harnack, *Militia Christi,* David Gracie (trans.) (Philadelphia: Fortress Press, 1981) 76–81; Jean Daniélou, *The Origins of Latin Christianity,* David Smith and John Austin Baker (trans.) (London and Philadelphia: Darton, Longman & Todd, 1977) 209. PL represents J.-P. Migne's *Patrologia Latina.*
3. Celsus, *On the True Doctrine,* R. Joseph Hoffman (trans.) (New York and Oxford: Oxford University Press, 1987) 124–25; Harnack, *Militia Christi,* 73.
4. Ernst Troeltsch, *Protestantism and Progress,* W. Montgomery (trans.) (Boston: Beacon Press, 1966) 49. Here we are referring to the particular strain of Anabaptism that became most identified with the movement over

time, having its origin in Switzerland (Conrad Grebel), Southern Germany (Balthasar Hubmaier), and the Netherlands (Menno Simons). The term Anabaptism can refer to other groups with a varied relationship to the sword. James Stayer, *Anabaptism and the Sword* (Lawrence, KS: Coronado Press, 1972); James Stayer, Werner Packull, and Klaus Depperman, "From Monogenesis to Polygenesis: The Historical Discussion of Anabaptist Origins," *MQR* (April 1975) 83–121.

5. WA 46.667–72 (LW 22.150–57); WA 18.389 (LW 46.49–50); Paul Althaus, *The Theology of Martin Luther*, Robert C. Schultz (trans.) (Philadelphia: Fortress Press, 1975) 19; Niebuhr, *Christ and Culture*, 170–171. WA is *Luthers Werke* (Weimarer Ausgabe), and LW is *Luther's Works* (Concordia Publishing House/Fortress Press).
6. Roger Williams, *Mr. Cottons Letter Lately Printed, Examined and Answered* (London, 1644) 45; *The Bloudy Tenent of Persecution for Cause of Conscience*, Richard Groves (ed.) (Macon, GA: Mercer University Press, 2001) 83, 153, 239; *The Writings of John Leland*, L. F. Greene (ed.) (New York: Arno Press and The New York Times, 1969) 181, 184; Philip Hamburger, *Separation of Church and State* (Cambridge, MA: Harvard University Press, 2002) 43–45, 51–52, 59.
7. Karl Barth says the earthly state is not a simple repetition of the church or the kingdom of God. *Community, State, and Church: Three Essays* (Gloucester, MA: Peter Smith, 1968) 168. For those Christian Socialists who bring the two together, see Gustavo Gutiérrez, *A Theology of Liberation*, Sister Caridad Inda and John Eagelson (trans.) (Maryknoll, NY: Orbis Books, 1973) 72, 150–51, 160; Jürgen Moltmann, *The Crucified God*, R. A. Wilson and John Bowden (trans.) (New York: Harper & Row Publishers, 1974) 23–24, 319–21. Cf. Harvey Cox, *Religion in the Secular City* (New York: Simon & Schuster, 1984) 148; Reinhold Niebuhr, *Christianity and Power Politics* (New York: Archon Books, 1969) ix, x, 42; *The Nature and Destiny of Man* (New York: Charles Scribner's Sons, 1943) 2.87–88, 180. For the reconstructionists' merger of the two, see Rousas John Rushdoony, *Law and Liberty* (Fairfax, VA: Thoburn Press, 1977) 40–41; Greg L. Bahnsen, *Theonomy in Christian Ethics* (Nutley, NJ: The Craig Press, 1979) 35, 217, 457; *By This Standard* (Tyler, TX: Institute for Christian Economics: 1985) 37, 52, 66, 140–42. Bahnsen even advocates the biblical penology (e.g., stoning) as the proper, eternal method of penology. *By this Standard*, 278.
8. Niebuhr, *Christ and Culture*, 184–88.
9. *The Writings of William Walwyn*, Jack R. McMichael and Barbara Taft (ed.) (Athens, GA, and London: The University of Georgia , 1989) 207ff., 259–62.
10. Stephen Strehle, "Jefferson's Opposition to the Judeo-Christian Tradition," in *Faith and Politics in America: From Jamestown to the Civil War*, Joseph Prud'homme (ed.) (New York: Peter Lang, 2011) 59–90.
11. Arthur Schopenhauer provides a scintillating analysis demonstrating the importance of fundamental appetites like hate in motivating or skewing our judgment. Rationalizations are only secondary. *The World as Will and Representation*. E. F. J. Payne (trans.) (New York: Dover Publications, Inc., 1969) 2.212–17, 229–37, 255.
12. Voltaire and many of the philosophes imbibed racial theories. The French concept of *egalité* did not originally exclude racism. Even in America,

Thomas Jefferson and Abraham Lincoln can emphasize their belief that "all men are created equal" (i.e., they have equal rights in nature), while accepting the racism of the day.

13. Following Hertzberg's work, a number of conservative Jewish scholars are now beginning to recognize this relationship. See Hertzberg's *The French Enlightenment and the Jews* (New York and London: Columbia University Press, 1968) and chap. 4, p. 70.

I

France and the Modern État

1

Voltaire and English Deists

The eighteenth century brought with it a strong reaction to the dogmatic and polemical struggles of the church during the age of orthodoxy. A fresh spirit of toleration swept across Western civilization among those who experienced the intolerance of dogmatic religion and preferred a more general religion to replace the many details of orthodoxy, which served as the root cause of civil strife—at least in their eyes. During the age of orthodoxy, the various factions of the church pronounced anathema upon each other, cursing and damning anyone who deviated from the many subtle and debatable points of their creeds. The sons of the Enlightenment found all this rancor unsettling and destructive to the fabric of society as a whole. They responded by attacking the dogmatic nature of Christendom and helped to produce a more civil discourse and inclusive society by disestablishing the hegemony of certain religious groups in their respective regions and promoting freedom of religious inquiry among all. They deserved and received much credit in the history of religious toleration for the important and crucial role they played in developing a more humane world, but their position clearly involved a paradox, which caused them to represent much the opposite in too many instances. Their zeal in promoting toleration involved a polemic against intolerance and too often transmuted into its opposite, labeling others as bigots and creating extreme caricatures of their opponents' shortcomings or intolerance.[1] Even John Locke provided testimony to this paradox and temptation in his famous *Letter concerning Toleration* by exhorting society to practice intolerance toward those who reject the message of tolerance![2]

No kingdom proceeded faster in this direction and experienced more dramatic changes in its attitude toward religion in general than the nation-state of France. Immediately after the Reformation the kingdom achieved a national unity above and beyond the principalities of Germany confessing "one faith, one law, one king," but dissident groups like the Huguenots often disrupted the verisimilitude of a formula and brought considerable debate over the relationship between church and state.[3] In the course of time, the Huguenots experienced the many vicissitudes of French policy, marked by some of the most telling events in its history—the Massacre of St. Bartholomew's Day (1572), the Edict of Nantes (1598), the revocation of the edict (1685), and the reinstatement of toleration under Louis XVI (1788). By the time of the Enlightenment, the Huguenots had suffered so much hardship that the natural sympathy of many French people switched sides and turned against their own church as responsible for the plight of these dissidents. The sympathy for the oppressed transformed into a deep-seated hatred for ecclesiastical authorities and dogmatic religion in general as the main sponsors of bigotry. Many of the leading lights decided to abandon traditional religion at the time, reacting to the antithesis of their "self-incurred tutelage," making a mass exodus from the church, and gaining a reputation throughout Europe for developing agnostic and cynical attitudes in its place. Rather than reform the church, much of French intelligentsia chose to work for its elimination altogether, much to the horror of English and American sensibilities.

Voltaire

The spirit of the French Enlightenment centered much of its devotion upon the life and teachings of one man. Many of the other great figures of the Enlightenment, like Diderot or d'Alembert, afforded their own unique contribution to the times, but they often deferred to this one man as if serving his own personal legacy.[4] Toward the end of his life, the Parisians crowned a bust of him and celebrated the man with godlike accolades.[5] His life and work seemed to embody all that was fashionable among the social elite of the day—the cynicism, the satire, and the wit—the love of toleration and the hatred of the church.[6] He led his people down the path of irreverence, demeaning the Christian piety of simple peasants, encouraging impious blasphemy among those who were capable of mastering the art of cynicism, and extolling the power of human reason to establish its own divine truth. Born François-Marie Arouet, his stature only grew throughout his life, beginning with the success of his first tragedy in 1718. Thereafter he adopted the enigmatic name of Voltaire and developed along with it an enormous ego and reputation in becoming the leading philosophe of human prowess and reaching godlike immortality upon the occasion of his death. His influence upon the French Revolution and its Civil Constitution of the Clergy (1790) was immortalized when his body was exhumed and enshrined as the first and foremost deity in the Panthéon of leading Enlightenment figures. The apotheosis was accompanied with a cavalcade of "military and civil organizations carrying banners and flags, a model of the Bastille, busts of Rousseau and Mirabeau, a statue of Voltaire surrounded by pyramids bearing the titles of his works, and a golden casket containing the seventy volumes of the edition published by Beaumarchais at Kehl."[7]

Voltaire and the French had a pretext within the many transgressions of their church to develop this extreme and blasphemous aversion to the religion. The revocation of the Edict of Nantes haunted the liberal sensibilities of the philosophes during the era and brought considerable justification for those who wished to turn against the church and heap aspersions upon it.[8] The hatred of this policy and others like it seemed to well up in Voltaire from his youth, forming a deep-seated resentment toward the faith, but what drove him over the edge and shocked him into action was a particular event: the unjust execution of a kind and benevolent man from Toulouse. His name was Jean Calas. A Protestant cloth merchant, he was accused by his fellow citizens of murdering his son for converting to Catholicism, even though all the evidence pointed to an apparent suicide. Voltaire successfully helped to overturn the verdict in the Council of State and clear the name of the father and his family, even if no one could change the initial wrongdoing. Out of the experience he wrote the widely distributed and esteemed *Treatise upon Toleration* (1763), which recounts the episode in detail at the beginning of the work and proceeds to develop a broad theory on the subject, filled with much anti-Christian venom.[9]

His work launches into a tirade against sectarian religious fanaticism. Any religion that divides the human race against itself is wicked and false. He thinks that all religions contain the same basic concept of God, and whatever differences arise over the course of time are the product of the nonessential speculations of dogmatic theologians. There is no reason why Jews, Muslims, and the many sects of Christianity cannot live in harmony under a general theism or Deism and a basic code of ethics, which is the most important matter in religion, not doctrine.[10] Religion is essential in creating social order and providing moral orientation through its belief in the ultimate judgment, but it deteriorates into a destructive force when its theologians engage in sectarian disputes over nonessential matters of faith. Ethics unites people together under one God, while doctrine divides them into warring factions.[11]

Of course, Voltaire's own beliefs are much in harmony with what he wants all others to believe in order to obtain coalescence. True religion is confined to a belief in the goodness of one, true God, the unity of the human race through acts of kindness, and the expectation of divine judgment, which discriminates between the good and the bad.[12] Religion consists of heartfelt reverence and basic acts of justice, not trips to a holy land or an altar, where mystical graces descend from the utterance of magical formulas.[13] True religion is based upon a most rational belief in the order and design of the cosmos and does not require a childlike act of faith in mythical stories, miraculous events, and the contradictory doctrines of biblical revelation. Faith is based upon the power of the human intellect and its ability to discover what is revealed for all to see in nature.[14] No grace or special revelation is needed.

The Bible receives much criticism in Voltaire's later writings, when it was safer for him to vent his wrath against the entire Christian faith and its sources. He believes that the miraculous nature of the biblical account drives many honest scholars to atheism, who simply find it incredible to believe in talking serpents and donkeys or prophets eating excrement and marrying prostitutes.[15] The Old Testament (OT) is described as a mingle-mangle of teachings that withstand all purity, charity, and reason.[16] The NT is described as a mishmash of inept reason, outright lies, and contradiction in "almost every fact," and its stories are considered juvenile, superstitious, and fanatical.[17] The Bible is a book of wickedness and inferior literary style, leading Voltaire to deprecate its authors by expressing the typical anti-Semitic epithets of the Enlightenment in general. The Jews are denigrated as a cruel and barbarous enemy of the whole human race, hopelessly alienated from others, filled with antisocial behavior and xenophobic practices, and yet much inferior to other people in cultural, artistic, and scientific achievement.[18] They are denigrated as an evil people, who never reconciled righteous living with ultimate judgment, never developed a firm concept of the afterlife in the OT, and ever remain on a materialistic level without genuine spirituality and moral fervor. The only Jewish or biblical figure who is spared the tirade is Jesus of Nazareth, and he receives a favorable review through Voltaire's reduction of his message to liberal toleration and rejection of many other elements in the church's miraculous account.[19] His portrait of the historical Jesus is set in contrast with the account of the canonical Gospels, which were written after the fall of Jerusalem and used Platonic categories to turn the simple carpenter from Nazareth into the eternal Son of God.[20]

The severe criticism of the Bible is a by-product of Voltaire's contempt for what the Christian faith represented in his society. The Church of France had supplied its enemies with many reasons to hate it: Dominican Inquisitions, the massacre of Huguenots, Jesuit and Jansenist polemics, and so on. During the last year of *l'Ancien Régime* (1789), the French government employed 178 censors to control publications and make sure all of them were compatible with sound faith, public order, and good morality. Voltaire himself had some of his works censored for unsound theological opinions, and he spent eleven months in the Bastille.[21] No wonder that Voltaire could describe Christians as "the most intolerant of all men."[22] Their religion should be the most tolerant of all others, considering the words and deeds of its benevolent founder, but instead of following the example of Jesus, it became much the opposite—"a virulent infection, a terrifying madness, a bloodthirsty monster."[23] Voltaire sees the history of Christianity as filled with little more than "fraud," "errors," and "disgusting stupidity," and so "every sensible man . . . must hold the Christian sect in horror. . . . It is a tree that has only borne rotten fruit."[24] In his *Sermon des Cinquante* (1762), he declares war upon *l'infâme*. He wishes to "terminate and destroy the idol from top to bottom."[25] This solution is summarized in his famous cry *écrazer l'infâme* (crush the filth), which he incessantly repeats throughout his later works. The self-professed man of tolerance is now willing to have certain enlightened despots develop a final solution and destroy the infamous religion as a necessary step in creating a better world.[26]

Throughout his analysis, Voltaire never seems to blame the despots for their own policies. He was too much of a sycophant to go after the real source or proximate cause of oppression and become a martyr for the cause of liberty. He supported democracy late in his life, only after it was safe to do so and his career was insured.[27] Instead, Voltaire preferred to blame the Christian religion and its clergy for much of the bloodshed spilled over the previous six centuries in Europe. He wanted national independence from the Christian religion in general and the political impotence of the clergy in particular. He wanted the priestly aristocracy removed from any position of authority in the state. After all, they only prey upon the superstitions of the multitude in his mind and fill the king's ear with their ambitious plans and petty sectarian disputes, causing continual turmoil within the land.[28] It is the fault of the clergy, not the king, that intolerance fills the land.

His antipathy toward Christianity is displayed most graphically in his revisionist history of the world. In his account, he tries to contrast the bigotry and intolerance of Christian civilization with the freedom of thought that was celebrated by all civilized nations in antiquity. These nations emphasized multiculturalism and diversity, recognizing one supreme deity under a host of names and theological systems.[29] The Romans in particular were "great friends of toleration." Nero, Diocletian, and the Roman emperors did not really persecute the early Christians for religious reasons, even if the exact nature of their martyrdom remains obscure.[30] Religious persecution developed when Christianity assumed the reins of power, and "the blood of the subjects has flown in torrents [ever since] either on the scaffold or in the field, from the fourth century to the present."[31] Christianity stands for the assassination of rulers and the massacre of the innocent. It must be held in contempt and destroyed by responsible powers. It possesses no redeeming qualities, and Voltaire finds no room to amend these comments by mentioning anything positive on the other side. He prefers to ignore any virtues in Christendom and highlight the eras that surround enlightened despots like Alexander the Great, Julius and Augustus Caesar, the Medici family, and Louis XIV as the greatest centuries of human achievement.[32]

Of course, Voltaire only wants to accentuate the negative and speak of the specific atrocities within the religion, but certain positive influences are found in his own life and tell a much different story. One of the major influences was an early visit to England, where he noted the great freedom of the society and became an instant Anglophile, like many others in his generation. He later writes his famous *Philosophical Letters*, celebrating the English way of life, but he fails to appreciate in all his writings the important role of the Protestant faith in the society, except through some scattered and muted comments.[33] When Voltaire thinks of Christianity, he invariably identifies it with the atrocities of the Catholic Church in his country and the ambitions of its priestly aristocracy, seldom mentioning any other expression of the faith or the many blessings of his own church.

English Deists

The pervasive Anglomania of the era brought Voltaire and the philosophes into contact with English Deism and provided the fundamental matrix for their religious/antireligious sentiments.[34] The Deists bequeathed to the sons of the Enlightenment a reverence for the revelation of God, as witnessed in the laws of nature and emulated by those who follow its universal moral duties, as well as a distinct aversion for the special revelation of the Judeo-Christian tradition, with its talk of divine miracles and the sacramental powers of priestcraft.[35] Norman Torrey has afforded the most in-depth study of this influence through a meticulous examination of Voltaire's library in Leningrad, making detailed observations about his usage, markings, and notes within specific deist texts. Torrey warns scholars against following a more facile approach, which prefers turning to Voltaire's work and accepting prima facie the references to deist authors or texts in an uncritical manner, since the overall corpus of Voltaire contains a mixture of "false and true attributions."[36] Torrey is able to develop a more exacting list of influences by comparing the library's notations with the attributions of the corpus.

Torrey uses the method to correct what he considers a gross exaggeration in scholarship, which wants a simple origin of ideas and stresses the relationship of Voltaire with Viscount Bolingbroke, as if Voltaire was a mere product or pupil of a single mentor. Voltaire certainly contributes to this image by referring to this English lord incessantly in his work—often falsely, perhaps to lend some credence to problematic ideas or "cover his borrowings from [Bolingbroke and] the most varied sources."[37] Torrey uses the evidence of false attribution to challenge the notion of a simple etymology, but not even this line of argumentation can dismiss the significance of Bolingbroke in the development of Voltaire's ideas altogether. The two enjoyed a direct personal relationship for a number of years, discussing a whole range of enlightened ideas, and Voltaire read the *Philosophical Works* of Bolingbroke, which was published later on and embodied the essence of their many conversations.[38] One discerns a great amount of affinity and spiritual kinship on a number of issues in the *Philosophical Works*, including anti-Semitism and anti-Christianity.[39] The two speak of Jewish hubris in calling themselves the chosen people of God;[40] Jewish avarice and immorality in failing to develop a concept of immortality and ultimate judgment; the unscientific nature of the Torah and the cruelty of its God and people; the salvific quality of Jesus's teaching and the perversion of it in Paul and the Hellenistic church; the menace of theological systems, which transformed the simple carpenter into a mystical divine Savior, satisfying the demands of an angry Jewish God for blood; and the exaltation of reason and its ability to find God in nature, outside of any special revelation in the scripture.[41] Torrey explains that Voltaire marks these types of anti-Semitic/anti-Christian comments throughout Bolingbroke's work.[42]

Torrey also points to Matthew Tindal as exerting a direct and profound influence upon Voltaire, especially through the work entitled *Christianity as Old as Creation*. Voltaire marks up and reiterates in his own writings the sections that appeal to the revelation of God in nature as the ultimate judge of any special word from heaven given to a certain people, as well as the parts that provide a specific and unrelenting criticism of the Bible as a most irrational and unethical body of writings when compared to the dictates of right reason.[43] Abbé Guénée noted the relationship at the time and describes Voltaire as a "poor copier of a poorer writer [Tindal]."[44]

In *Christianity as Old as Creation*, Tindal identifies his faith as Deism and extols the power of an all-sufficient reason to examine every truth claim throughout the work. Following the basic outline of this system, he sees all human beings possessing a God-given capacity to reason and judge any external claim of divine revelation coming from an Apostle or Prophet of old. The power of reason is given "antecedent to any external Revelation" and able to serve as a "sufficient means" in assessing the validity of a special revelation and judge what is worthy of God.[45] Reason can judge metaphysical matters as an autonomous capacity within human beings and discover through its own prowess whether the external Word is consistent with its understanding and verdict as an autonomous umpire. Within this capacity, it is able to develop unequivocal proofs for the existence of God and come to a general knowledge of the divine will and essence. Reason comes to know God as possessing an immutable nature and recognizes the "duty to God and man" in terms of universal and unchangeable laws, which are "plain and perspicuous" and the same for all others.[46]

One might expect Tindal to produce at this point a deontological list of eternal laws for the human race to appropriate and follow, but he ends up surprising us, much like Voltaire and the philosophes, and develops specific duties out of a utilitarian calculation. The basis for his utilitarianism resides within a metaphysical presupposition, which thinks of God as perfect and content within the God-self and creating people for their own happiness as an act of selfless love. The eternal God is complete from all eternity and derives no benefit from those who follow the divine will, or deficit from those who do not follow what is intended to serve their own need as if transgressions require satisfaction or reparation to a lost honor. The true end of religion is "human happiness," not the glory of God or a supralapsarian justification of divine justice and mercy, and God has provided people with the liberty to meet that end and develop their own rational means in the midst of different and evolving circumstances in fulfilling it. Tindal speaks of good and evil as possessing an absolute distinction in the law of nature, but then he makes its immutability superfluous by overturning the force of the natural law in special circumstances and providing a "large Field," in which God "leaves Men at Liberty to act as they please in all indifferent matters," reducing individual and civil matters to a utilitarian or reasonable calculation. In all this, he leaves little room to experience an antecedent judgment of God in declaring what is right or wrong through a special act of revelation and prefers submitting ethical conduct to the rational acuity and verdict of human beings in a given circumstance. He wants a religion free from "tyrannical impositions" of outside authority, spurning any message from the heavens above, beyond the realm of human and earthly possibilities, and prefers to exclude any need for special revelation a priori.[47] In other words, Tindal wants people to "know God apart from God,"[48] as if human reason is capable of providing transcendent/metaphysical perspectives on its own. This position will permeate the community of English Deists and philosophes as a simple truism, even if modern philosophy and theology questions this ability of the human mind to transcend its own experience in the world.[49] It will serve as a basis of separating one's life from the church or revealed religion in those who wish to build a wall between the two.

Tindal uses much of his inflated concept of human reason to deprecate the Bible as filled with contradictions and irrational assertions, withstanding all ethical and metaphysical judgments. The God of the Bible is judged as a capricious monster, who defies the natural law of "right reason" and any logical consistency or fidelity to immutable divine truth and behavior. The Jewish people are deprecated as a "most cruel" and "superstitious" race, who spewed their "hatred" upon all those who refused to follow their fanatical cult. Their priests are condemned for leading the way in depraved behavior, inculcating superstitious beliefs and enslaving the people to the useless performance of ceremonies and rites, as if God would "damn Men for things not Moral." Like most sons of the Enlightenment, Tindal finds the true essence of religion in morality and excoriates priests for transforming it into rituals of sacramental sorcery and theological dogmas, meant to enhance and empower their position over rival authorities and leading the Jews to hate other people as godless reprobates. The clergy of Christendom brought the same "Animosity, Enmity, and Hatred" to the world as the Jewish priesthood, corrupting kings through their spiritual powers, leading them to persecute infidels in the name of orthodox teaching, and creating continuous doctrinal polemics over nonsensical issues as a false pretense to gain more power. The history of the church "contains a continued scene of Villany" against people of true virtue and piety, who are "hated and persecuted as a most dangerous Enemy." The evil of the church results from the emphasis upon orthodoxy ("correct teaching") in its historical confessions and the failure to recognize the true essence of religion in morality and the service of humankind. Tindal rejects any relation between orthodoxy and orthopraxis and believes people can know the will of God and emulate it in their moral conduct, without knowing much about God,[50] as if the divine will is divided from its essence!

Torrey also mentions the importance of a couple of works by Peter Annet, which are filled with the same anti-Semitic/anti-Christian invective as Tindel's work and used by Voltaire in developing his own ideas on the subject. Voltaire particularly finds a pretext for his anti-Semitism in the short work of Annet on the *Life of David,* which he uses extensively, displaying exact parallels in his drama on *Saül.*[51] Annet acknowledges the controversial nature of his comments at the beginning of the work and recognizes that a number of people will despise it, receiving no profit from its message, but he is hoping his criticisms will find an audience among those who really care about virtue and seek the truth with an open mind, just like he later finds in Voltaire. Annet hopes in the meantime for the same modicum of toleration that Voltaire will desire in his day, that those who question the work will act like "true Protestants" and respect the freedom of an individual conscience in developing personal convictions.[52]

With this plea for toleration, Annet feels free to proceed with his intolerant, anti-Semitic tirade in trashing the Jews as the "most vicious and detestable of mankind." The extreme nature of the comment might sound harsh to the unenlightened, but it is confirmed "beyond a possibility of doubt" through the testimony of "all historians of credit," the "whole series of facts which constitute their history," and even acknowledged by "their own historians." The assessment makes sense when one recognizes that the Jews had "more religion" and "more priests" than other people, and so "became so much more depraved than their neighbors." Religion permeated every aspect of their lives with incessant rituals, ceremonies, and legal observances—much in contrast to other nations, who were satisfied with practicing a few solemn festivals, observing some important occasions, and maintaining a few dozen priests at most. The Jewish cult was an enormous machinery and managed by a large priesthood, who represented one-twelfth of the nation and consumed one-tenth of its produce, "without contributing anything to productive labour."[53] "It is probable that the Jewish nation alone . . . had more priests than the rest of the then known World collectively, and were consequently more vicious and more enslaved than any other people."[54]

It is within this understanding of the Jewish people that Annet relates his account of the life of David, ever mindful of the power of priests in the culture and their bias in portraying and spinning events in the present biblical history. The text reveals to Annet and the discerning reader that the real power behind the fortunes of Saul and David was Samuel, the high priest and last judge of Israel, despite the attempt of the biblical account to exalt David because of his superior virtue. Samuel only wanted to find a person who would serve his bidding and so decided to anoint David and reject Saul as king over Israel (1 Sam 13:8–13, 15:22–23). There was certainly nothing laudable about the character of David that would commend him to the priest or make him the paradigm for the future kings of Israel according to the later accounts of priests and prophets; in fact, he was the "worst and wickedest man" of the "most depraved of all nations": He was chosen by Samuel to be the "instrument of revenge on an untractable king." He spent much of his early career conniving and contriving to obtain power as a rebellious subject. He assembled a lawless band of ruffians to withstand the king of Israel and plunder neighboring countries. He allied his "mighty men" with the Philistines' armies to wage war against his own country and father-in-law. He usurped the throne of Israel by persecuting Ishbosheth to the grave. He continued to plunder and massacre the surrounding nations in his role as king. He defiled the wife of a leading officer and murdered him to cover up the crime when she was found with child. He betrayed some of his most loyal subjects like Joab (2 Sam 19:13; 1 Kgs 2:5–6), and he sought vengeance to his last breadth, "dictating two posthumous murders to his son Solomon" and leaving behind as a testimony of his character imprecatory psalms, filled with venom toward his enemies (Ps 68:22–24, 69:24–27). Of course, he "clothed his actions with most consummate hypocrisy, professing all along the greatest regard for every appearance of virtue and holiness," all for the service of priests and his glory in their historical accounts.[55]

Annet provides the same type of excoriating analysis of another biblical hero in his examination of the *Life of Paul* (*Examen Critique de la Vie & des Ouvrages de Saint Paul*).[56] He hopes to discredit Paul's immense reputation among Christians as an irrational product of extreme prejudice, just like he did in the previous work on David. He categorically rejects any claim of Paul and the rest of the apostles to the inspiration of the Holy Spirit and basically thinks of them as corrupt, inspired by the "spirit of pride, ambition, obstinacy, vengeance, avarice, and rebellion." Paul began his career as a tentmaker, who left the business because he grew weary of working for a living and wanted to live off of the new sect of Christians, just like the other disciples. His ambition soon swelled into enormous hubris, desiring to gain ascendency above the others, making up fantastic "miracles, visions, [and] revelations" to establish his position, and even claiming direct access to the Almighty in his ascension to the Third Heaven (2 Cor 12:2–4). He presented his teaching as the "only veritable doctrine" and "infallible Word," setting a horrid precedent for the extreme haughtiness of the church to "curse, excommunicate, damn, or deliver unto Satan whoever has the temerity to understand the Gospel in another way." Paul brought this hubris to Rome as the "true founder of the see," which developed a hierarchical system out of his aristocratic bearing, with all its divine rights and special privileges, causing much intolerance and turmoil throughout the world, making even kings tremble before the spiritual and temporal power.[57]

Of course, Annet claims that no one can verify Paul's claim to spiritual exaltation and finds it safer to trust the verdict of reason, which invariably brings truth and goodness and never leads people astray. Paul wants his followers to denounce reason and trust him, preferring to inculcate "stupid credulity" in his mysterious enigmas than promote a genuine search for the truth through philosophical and scientific inquiry.[58] Paul makes wisdom "foolishness," reason "unbelief," common sense "useless," and contradictions "impenetrable mysteries, which the faithful must adore in silence (1 Cor 1–2)." Annet finds his letters filled with "inconsistencies, contradictions, mistakes, false reasoning . . . bearing all the character of delirium, ignorance, and fraud." In fact, Annet thinks of his whole theology as a massive contradiction, as an affront to the immutability of truth, reason, and God, since it overturns the revelation of old, rather than fulfilling it in accordance with the concept of Jesus and the Gospels, deigning to destroy the Mosaic economy and create a new system in its place.[59]

Another important source of Voltaire's attack upon Christianity was Thomas Woolston and his *Discourses on the Miracles,* which he continually cites and uses in his work, often making explicit reference to the author and giving him much credit for stimulating an enlightened way of thinking. "Direct borrowings from [Woolston's] discourses on the miracles appear in nearly every work Voltaire wrote against Christianity from *Sermones des Cinquante* [1762] to the *Bible en fin expliquée* and *l'Établissement du Christianisme* [of 1777]," including the article upon "Miracles" in his *Philosophical Dictionary* as perhaps the most noteworthy.[60] During the last fifteen years of his life, Voltaire makes continuous use of the same list of miracles as Woolston, displaying the same mockery and ridicule when interpreting these so-called miracles with any literal force.[61]

Woolston spends much of his time in the *Discourses* preoccupied with this type of cynicism, trying to demonstrate that any "literal History of the Miracles of Jesus . . . imp[lies] Absurdities, Improbabilities and Incredibilities" in each particular pericope, without showing much interest in pointing out contradictions between the parallel accounts of the Gospels—a matter that will obsess David Strauss and later critical scholarship. He prefers to find the absurdity of the Gospels within the letter of each individual account and the many petty reasons he relates to each and every detail.[62] Because of this particular obsession, he finds it necessary to abandon the literal interpretation of the text and look for a deeper meaning in a "mystical, figurative, and parabolical" sense, in order to make it edifying for the enlightened reader.[63] For example, the "ridiculous" story of Jesus healing the woman with the issue or spirit of infirmity has a rich allegorical meaning.

> As the Woman was bow'd together; so the Church, as the Fathers do interpret, may be said to be bow'd down to the Earth, when she is prone and bent to, and intent on the literal or earthly Interpretations of the Scriptures; and can in no wise lift up her self, like the Woman, that is, can't raise her Thoughts to the Contemplation of the caelestial, spiritual, and sublime Sense of them. Hence we see the Propriety of the Name of the Woman's Disease, call'd πνευμα αθενειας [sic], a Spirit of Weakness, which is not properly

> significative is of any bodily Distemper, but succinctly is very expressive of the Church's Weakness at the Spirit of Prophecy, which at this Day she labours under.
>
> As it was eighteen Years that the Woman was griev'd with her Spirit of Infirmity, for so long had her Distemper been growing on her; so it is almost eighteen (hundred) Years, that this Infirmity of the Church at the Spirit of Prophecy has been coming on her; And she is now so bent to the Earth of the Letter, that nothing less than the Hand and Power of Jesus, that erected the Woman, can raise her to mystical, divine, and sublime Contemplations on the Law and Prophets.[64]

This method of interpretation he finds consonant with the exegetical approach of the church fathers, who also abandoned the literal level of scripture for a spiritual journey into the heavenly realm. He expresses much confidence that these fathers would endorse his work, even if he recognizes the anachronistic nature of his method, given the general tenor of the Reformation toward a more plain and simple reading of the text.[65] However, it is difficult to accept the sincerity of his claim to piety, given the intensity of his vitriolic preachments against the clergy of the church and its traditional orthodox teachings.[66] He spends much time libeling the clergy as the "Bane of Society and the Pest of Mankind," bringing about "unspeakable Mischief to the World" through their "Avarise, Ambition, and Power," and then after preaching a message of vicious intolerance, he turns around and professes to want nothing but tolerance and peace to reign among the religious community, expressing much disgust with the bloodshed of the church, experiencing much calumny in regard to his own work, and eventually serving time in prison, much like Voltaire.[67] He tries a preemptive strike to ward off further criticism by professing a semblance of Christian piety,[68] but one must wonder about the sincerity of his faith—whether he is just a Deist, using the guise of Christian faith to mock its teachings, or merely employing the subterfuge of mystical interpretation to undermine its fundamental integrity.[69]

This type of cynical analysis was all-too-characteristic of English Deism and led to the deification of cynicism in the work of Voltaire and the philosophes of France in their treatment of the Judeo-Christian tradition. Both the Deists and philosophes accentuated the power of reason and considered their analysis objective for the most part but lost perspective against their polemical opponents, too often creating dark caricatures of the Bible and its people out of a visceral prejudice toward a tradition that needed more objective criticism and reformation, not vilification and enmity. They deserve the infamous label of anti-Semitic and anti-Christian due to their unbalanced treatment, accenting only the negative, twisting almost every aspect of the tradition, and creating an atmosphere of extreme hate. Much of the rancor relates to their inflated belief in reason: their belief that reason could stand in judgment of God as it contains the metaphysical wherewithal to know what is worthy of divine revelation a priori; their belief that God must submit to consistent rational analysis, with no variations or mysteries to defy human expectations;[70] their belief that reason could address metaphysical concerns and destroy the faith of others without equivocation;[71] their belief that morality consists of a simple calculating sum, with no need of the transcendent, metaphysical judgment of faith; and their belief that reason is certain about ethics, as if it can exist outside of metaphysical dogma and find the will of God apart from the knowledge of God. This concept of reason led to an emphasis upon the autonomy of human beings and the blasphemy of the biblical deity and those who depended upon revelation and needed a touch of divine grace. When Cromwell witnessed the rise of profane and anti-Christian groups like the Ranters, showing them a modicum of toleration during the Puritan Revolution,[72] he had no idea how far the blasphemy would permeate England in the decades to come, challenging the very foundation of the church. The growing toleration was used by Voltaire and the Deists to attack the Judeo-Christian tradition with the most vicious libels and criticisms and lay the foundation for a modern form of anti-Semitism and anti-Christianity as a political force—all in the name of a "universal toleration" that must destroy the enemies of toleration. The hypocrisy and danger was evident at the time and raised concern among those who perceived the threat, especially a vulnerable group like the Jews, who wrote to Voltaire sharing their concerns.

> We have been persuaded that we shall always find more protection and humanity among true Christians than among the greatest part of deists, notwithstanding their pretended *universal toleration*. . . . What was our surprise, when, in a work that announces gentleness and humanity, and whose design seems to be to bind still faster those cords of love which should unite men, we found you once more treating our people, our sacred writings, and every thing that is dear to us, in a manner so different from that character of equity and moderation you assume! Could we expect to find so much prejudice and so much hatred against an unhappy people in the works of a philosopher who passes for the friend and reconciler of the human race?[73]

Notes

1. Even David Strauss, a radical left-wing intellectual, sees Voltaire and his disciples as living between God and the devil. David Friedrich Strauss, *Voltaire: Sechs Vorträge* (Leipzig: S. Hirzel, 1870) 345.
2. John Locke, *A Letter Concerning Toleration*, in *Great Books of the Western World*, Robert Maynard Hutchins (ed.) (Chicago: Encyclopaedia Britannica, Inc., 1978) 35.17–18.
3. Joseph Lecler, *Toleration and the Reformation* (New York: Association Press, 1960) 2.3, 32.
4. A. J. Ayer, *Voltaire* (New York: Random House, 1986) 171– 72.

5. Daniel Mornet, *Les Origines intellectuelles de la Révolution française 1715–1787* (Paris: Librairie A. Colin, 1967) 225–226; R. O. Rockwood, "The Legend of Voltaire and the Cult of the Revolution, 1791," in *Ideas in History*, R. Herr and H. T. Parker (ed.) (Durham: Duke University Press, 1965) 111; Peter Gay, *Voltaire's Politics: The Poet as a Realist* (New York: Vintage Books, 1965) 334–35.
6. Gay, *Voltaire's Politics*, 243, 310; Rockwood, "The Legend of Voltaire," 113.
7. M-M. H. Barr, *Voltaire in America 1744–1800* (Baltimore: The John Hopkins Press, 1941) 55; Rockwood, "The Legend of Voltaire," 132; Charles A. Gliozzo, "The Philosophes and Religion: Intellectual Origins of the Dechristianization Movement in the French Revolution," *Church History* 40/3 (Sept. 1971) 275. Voltaire was massively popular in the next few decades; his works sold millions of copies. Ralph Gibson, "Why Republicans and Catholics Couldn't Stand Each Other in the Nineteenth Century," in *Religion, Society and Politics in France since 1789*, Frank Tallet and Nicholas Atkins (ed.) (London and Rio Grande: The Hambeldon Press, 1991) 113–14.
8. Jürgen von Stackelberg, "1685 et l'idée de la tolérance," *Francia* 14 (1986) 230. Pierre Bayle wrote one of the first negative reactions to the revocation. He wrote two pamphlets in 1686: "Ce que c'est que la France toute Catholique sous le règne de Louis le Grand" and "Commentaire philosophique sur ces paroles de Jésus-Christ: 'contrain-les d'entrer.'" Ibid., 230–31; G. Adams, "Myths and Misconceptions: The Philosophe View of the Huguenots in the Age of Louis XV," *Historical Reflections* 1/1 (1974) 65–66.
9. *Traité sur la Tolérance*, in *Oeuvres Complètes de Voltaire* (Paris: Garnier Frères, 1877–85) 25.18–26; *The Works of Voltaire* (Paris: E. R. DuMont, 1901) 4.118–34; Strauss, *Voltaire*, 213, 219; Barr, *Voltaire in America*, 119; Zagorin, *Religious Toleration*, 295–96. Hereafter the French edition of Voltaire's work is designated OCV and the English edition WV.
10. OCV 20.494, 495 (WV 12.154–56); OCV 24.439; OCV 25.32 (WV 4.145). Theological disputes are "the most terrible scourge of the world." Atheism is a monstrous evil, but there is nothing worse than the fanaticism of meaningless, speculative dogma. Voltaire enjoys mocking doctrines like the Trinity, transubstantiation, supralapsarianism, etc. OCV 17.359–61 (WV 4. 20–23); OCV 17.475, 476 (WV 6.126); OCV 20.467 (WV 14.36–37); OCV 18.412–413 (WV 8.153–154); Ayer, *Voltaire*, 136–38; Gay, *Voltaire's Politics*, 268.
11. OCV 19.549 (WV 11.29); OCV 18.413 (WV 8.154–55); R. I. Boss, "The Development of Social Religion: A Contradiction of French Free Thought," *Journal of the History of Ideas* 34/4 (Oct.–Dec. 1973) 582–84. Voltaire sees the necessity of religion in society, unlike some radicals who want religion expunged entirely. God is useful for providing the multitude with the compulsion to lead a moral life. Ibid., 586–89; OCV 21.573; Strauss, *Voltaire*, 229–31. Voltaire's famous quip speaks to the importance and utility of religion in society. "If God did not exist, it would be necessary to invent him." OCV 10.403 (Éiptre 104). His tendency is to reduce religion to morality, believing the human race has basically the same concept of right and wrong. He accepts the fact that those who espouse a different religion from the prince might be treated as second class. OCV 25.33 (WV 4.147–48); Strauss, *Voltaire*, 255.

12. OCV 24.453. The basic rule of thumb is the fewer the dogmas the better. OCV 25.102 (WV 4.269). He expresses the typical doubts of a Deist concerning the belief in an afterlife and divine judgment. Gay, *Voltaire's Politics,* 266–67.
13. OCV 20.507– 8 (WV 14.82–83).
14. OCV 17.476 (WV 6.126); OCV 18.105 (WV 9.87–88); OCV 19.155, 156 (WV 8.326, 327): Strauss, Voltaire, 231–33. The emphasis upon natural religion came early in Voltaire (e.g., *La Pour et le contre* [Epître à Uranie], 1722; OCV 9.358–62).
15. OCV 17.476 (WV 6.127); OCV 20.355 (WV 13.84–85). Voltaire does not find God embodied in history or performing miracles, but he rejects those who categorically dismiss the possibility of the supernatural in the name of science. OCV 20.77ff. (WV 11.272ff.); Gay, *Voltaire's Politics,* 266.
16. OCV 24.439ff.
17. OCV 24.449–50; OCV 20.186–87 (WV 12.146–48).
18. OCV 12.159–64; 20.517–18, 525–26; 26.220 (WV 14.102, 112–14; 26.178ff.); Ayer, *Voltaire,* 70–71, 97; *Letters of Certain Jews to Monsieur Voltaire,* Philip Lefanu (trans.) [Antoine Guénée, *Lettres de qulelques Juifs Potugais, Allemands et Polonais a M. Voltaire* (Paris, 1769)] (Paris and Covington, KY: G. G. Moore and J. L. Newby, 1845) 44–46, 311–12; Arthur Herzberg, *The French Enlightenment and the Jews* (New York and London: Columbia University Press, 1968) 10, 37–41, 55, 286, 302–5. Claude Antoine Thiéry, a later advocate for Jewish emancipation, refers to Voltaire as one of the principle enemies of the Jews, who often prostituted his genius to take particular delight in denigrating them. *Dissertation sur cette Question: Est-il des moyens de rendre les Juifs plus heureux et plus Utiles en France?* [1788] (Paris: EDHIS, 1968) 49. The Jews write a series of somewhat respectful letters to Voltaire but complain that his writings are hateful to the Jews. *Letters of Certain Jews,* 20, 24, 64. He speaks of the OT people in the most vile manner as practicing human sacrifice, bestiality, etc., without much proof. Ibid., 156–69, 355.
19. OCV 20.521 (WV 14.104); Strauss, *Voltaire,* 245–46, 268–70. His head seems to reject the existence of an immortal soul, but his heart finds immortality useful. Strauss, *Voltaire,* 240–42, 247.
20. OCV 20.523 (WV 14.108), OCV 24.451; Strauss, *Voltaire,* 271–72; Ayer *Voltaire,* 132; Zagorin, *Religious Toleration,* 297.
21. Gay, *Voltaire's Politics,* 70–78; Strauss, *Voltaire,* 23.
22. OCV 20.517ff., 521 (WV 14.100ff., 104).
23. Ibid., Gay, *Voltaire's Politics,* 271–72; Strauss, *Voltaire,* 270, 274.
24. OCV 26.298; Strauss, *Voltaire,* 279; Ayer, *Voltaire,* 99.
25. OCV 24.252; Norman L. Torrey, *Voltaire and the English Deists* (Hamden, CT: Archon Books, 1967) 8.
26. OCV 42.186 [A Letter to Damilaville on July 26, 1762, where he says, "I finish all my letters by saying: Écr. L'inf. . . ."]; Gay, *Voltaire's Politics,* 170, 239, 244–46, 252; Strauss, *Voltaire,* 277–78; Ayer, *Voltaire,* 27; Gliozzo, "The Philosophes and Religion," 275 (note 12). There is some controversy over the precise interpretation of the phrase *écraser l'infâme,* but the apparent meaning is to extirpate Christianity. He says in his *Notebooks* (324) that if Frederick of Prussia, his patron, was more daring he could have destroyed the religion.

27. Ibid., 89, 225–26, 236; Peter Gay, *The Enlightenment: An Interpretation* (New York: Alfred A. Knopf, 1967–69) 2.462–63; Strauss, *Voltaire*, 109–11; Ayer, *Voltaire*, 27–28. Peter Gay says,

    When Voltaire launched his unscrupulous campaigns for admission to the *Académie française*, even hardened worldlings professed to find his self-abasement distasteful, and when he tried to consolidate his connections with Russian court by writing *Pierre le grand*, a collection of gross complements disguised as history, d'Alembert said that the book made him want to vomit. . . .

    It was in 1736, while he was still crown prince, that Frederick had begun a correspondence with Voltaire, and as Voltaire never failed to tell his friends, it was significant that it was Frederick that had taken the initiative. In his long and uncomfortable intercourse with the Prussian king, Voltaire, always ready with a pleasing comparison, found many synonyms calculated to please; as one patient scholar has discovered, Voltaire likened Frederick to Caesar, Augustus, Marcus Aurelius, Trajan, Antonius Pius, Titus, Julian, Vergil, Pliny, Horace, Maecenus, Cicero, Catullus, Homer, La Rochefoucauld, La Bruyère, Boileau, Solomon, Prometheus, Apollo, Socrates, Alcibiades, Alexander, Henri IV and Francis I (*The Enlightenment*, 2.67, 483–84).

    In his own country, he accepted Louis XV's claim to absolute power over the *parlements* and thinks of the Huguenots/Calvinists as seditious, calling for law and order against their conscientious objection to legitimate authority. David D. Bien, "Religious Persecution in the French Enlightenment," *Church History* 30/3 (1961) 330; Gay, *The Enlightenment*, 2.476–77.

28. OCV 20.195, 272 (WV 12.155–56, 303); Rockwood, "The Legend of Voltaire," 116; Stackelberg, "1685 et l'idée de la tolérance," 236–39; Gay, *Voltaire's Politics*, 108, 269, 354–55, 455. He finds Jesuits a most depraved lot. They cause civil wars wherever they go, and he favors a government policy to disband them. OCV 25.35, 96–97 (WV 4.151, 158).
29. Celsus, the anti-Christian apologist of the second century, makes this same point against Jews and Christians. He complains that the religions quibble too much over the precise name of God. He also has difficulty understanding their vehement rejection of idolatry, since this practice never involved the worship of the image itself. Celsus, *On the True Doctrine: A Discourse against the Christians*, R. Joseph Hoffman (intro. and trans.) (New York: Oxford University Press, 1987) 56, 118–19. The Jews find Voltaire's position astonishing and challenge his notion of the Greeks and Romans tolerating any kind of philosophy/religion with a number of counterexamples. *Letters of Certain Jews*, 198–99, 201, 255. The Jews think all religions and philosophies show moments of intolerance. Ibid., 21.
30. OCV 25.41–49, 54, 58 (WV 4.162, 165–77, 184, 192). He finds the accounts of Christians about their martyrs to be little more than works of fiction.
31. OCV 25.27, 64 (WV 4.136–37, 203–4).
32. Ayer, *Voltaire*, 92–93. He wants to blame intolerance upon religious groups and their ideas, while excusing every act of barbarism by rulers. He exalts Louis XIV as a great patron of the arts but fails to explain his revocation of

the Edict of Nantes. OCV 25.30; Ayer, *Voltaire,* 94; Stackelberg, "1685 et l'idée de la tolérance," 235.

33. OCV 22.99, 103, 109 [Voltaire, *Letters Concerning the English Nation* (New York: Burt Franklin Reprints, 1974) 34, 41–42, 52–53)]; Ayer, *Voltaire,* 15–16, 43, 49; Strauss, *Voltaire,* 6, 47–48; Gay, *Voltaire's Politics,* 42–44, 51–52; *The Enlightenment,* 387; Torrey, *Voltaire and the English Deists,* 12–13. At times he recognized that Protestants are more tolerant than the Catholics of his land. He finds the Quakers the most consistent with the teachings of Jesus on this issue. OCV 25.523 (WV 14.107). Cf. Strauss, *Voltaire,* 275–76.
34. Strauss, *Voltaire,* 224, 259. Of course, there are many other influences one could mention beside the English Deists. Pierre Bayle and Jean Meslier are worth a special mention. Bayle (1647–1706), the editor/author of the famous *Dictionnaire historique et critique,* served as a particular hero to Voltaire and the philosophes for his skepticism, anti-clericalism, criticism of Protestant scholasticism and dogma, trust in enlightened despots, and acceptance of civil toleration, even toward atheists. Elisabeth Labrousse, "The Political Ideas of the Huguenot Diaspora (Bayle and Jurieu)," in *Church, State, and Society under the Bourbon Kings of France,* Richard M. Golden (ed.) (Lawrence, KS: Coronado Press, Inc., 1982) 235–40, 255–58, 263; Strauss, *Voltaire,* 2; Abbé Yvon, "Athées," in *Encyclopédie de Diderot et d'Alembert* [Paris, 1751–1772] (F. M. Ricci, 1970–) A, 13.230ff.; Diderot, "Pyrrhonienne ou Sceptique," in *Encyclopédie,* P, 17.233, 234. Meslier was a priest but died in 1729/33 leaving an atheistic "Testament" that deprecated the Bible as filled with errors, contradictions, and fables; spoke of Jesus as filled with fanatical hubris; extolled materialism; promoted skepticism and nationalism; recommended tyrannicide; and denounced private property. *Testament: Memoirs of the Thoughts of Jean Melier,* Michael Shreve (trans.) (Amherst, NY: Prometheus Books, 2009); Charles Gliozzo, "The Philosophes and Religion: Intellectual Origins of the Dechristianization Movement in the French Revolution," *Church History* 40 (1971): 279–80; Strauss, *Voltaire,* 261–63, 395–424.
35. Gay, *The Enlightenment,* 1.375, 383–85.
36. Torrey, *Voltaire and the English Deists,* 8–13.

> No generalization can be formed concerning Voltaire's honesty in referring to English deists as authorities. When he has grouped them in lists he is usually, to use Abbé Guénée's expression, throwing dust in the eyes of his readers. Bolingbroke he mentions the most often, and with the least justification. Toland and Collins were accorded an almost even break between true and false attributions. Tindal is never mentioned in connection with particular details which Voltaire borrowed from his work, even after Guénée had charged Voltaire with copying from him. On the other hand, Woolston is almost always correctly referred to, and although the name of Annet does not appear in all of Voltaire's work, the pseudonym "M. Hut" or "Huet" which Voltaire chose for him is properly used in almost every case. Ibid., 203, 204.

37. Ibid., 4, 5, 130, 135–39, 151–53; Jacob Katz, *From Prejudice to Destruction: Anti-Semitism, 1700–1933* (Cambridge, MA, and London: Harvard University Press, 1980) 35. Cf. Strauss, *Voltaire,* 31.

38. Ibid., 142. The *Philosophical Works* was published posthumously and read by Voltaire in 1758–59. Voltaire says he gained little fruit from reading it, and Torrey agrees with this assessment, but it is clear that the eventual rift in their relationship tends to skew his judgment. (Much like Nietzsche's assessment of Wagner's influence after their falling-out, which will be discussed in a subsequent chapter.) Ibid., 137–40, 201.
39. Shmuel Ettinger, "*Jews and Judaism as Seen by the English Deists of the Eighteenth Century*," *Zion* 29 (1964): 204; Strauss, *Voltaire*, 224, 258.
40. Henry St. John, Viscount Bolingbroke, *Philosophical Works 1754–77* (New York and London: Garland Publishing, Inc., 1777) 2.220–21, 230–32; 5.333.
41. Ibid., 2. 223–24, 233, 248–49, 256, 328, 332; 4.147–48, 153–54, 268–71; 5.216–17, 332, 356, 359; Kramnick, *Bolingbroke and His Circle*, 84–87; D. G. James, *The Life of Reason: Hobbes, Locke, Bolingbroke* (London, Toronto, and New York: Longmans, Green and Co., 1949) 41.
42. Torrey, *Voltaire and the English Deists*, 144–45.
43. Ibid., 110–11, 117–22, 128–29.
44. *Letters of Certain Jews to Monsieur de Voltaire*, Philip Lefanu (trans.) (Dublin: William Watson, 1777) 1.328 (n. 1); *Letters of Certain Jews* [1845], 85, 153, 154; Torrey, *Voltaire and the English Deists*, 112, 113, 120–21. *Letters of Certain Jews* associates Voltaire with Tindal, Collins, Bolingbroke, and other English Deists, saying he is not original. See, for example, 13, 85, 102, 133, 141, 152–54, 173.
45. Matthew Tindal, *Christianity as Old as Creation*, reprint of 1730 edition (New York & London: Garland Publishing, Inc., 1978) 4, 179, 189. Hereafter cited as COC.
46. COC 2, 3, 6, 14, 20, 65–66, 179, 189, 283–84, 365, 368, 379, 424–26. Voltaire specifically underscores these ideas. Torrey, *Voltaire and the English Deists*, 111.
47. COC 14, 35, 38, 58ff., 104–5, 115, 125.
48. Stephen Strehle, *The Separation of Church and State: Has America Lost Its Moral Compass?* (Lafayette, LA: Huntington House Publishers, 2001) 94.
49. Karl Barth, *Church Dogmatics* (Edinburgh: T. & T. Clark, 1975) I/1, 29, 30, 42–43, 255–56, 259–61; I/2, 4, 29, 30, 62–63; II/1, 333, 400, 522, 537; Ludwig Wittgenstein, *Tractatus Logico-Philosophicus*, D. F. Pears & B. F. McGuinness (trans.) (London & Henley: Routledge & Kegan Paul, 1977) 3, 5 (1, 2, 2.01), 19 (4.003), 25–26 (4.112–4.1212), 56–57 (5.6, 5.61, 5.632, 5.633), 67–74.
50. COC 23, 24, 50–52, 107–8, 152–55, 164, 273, 285–86, 328–29, 337.
51. Torrey, *Voltaire and the English Deists*, 187–98.
52. [Peter Annet], *The Life of David; or, the History of the Man after God's own heart* (London: J. Carlile, 1820 vi, 68.
53. Ibid., xii, xiii.
54. Ibid., xiii, xiv.
55. Ibid., ix, xii–xiv, 26–29, 36–38, 45–50, 62–67. Annet's deprecation of David's character found a precedent in Bayle's critical article on David in the *Dictionnaire*.
56. Voltaire was influenced by Annet's work on Paul through the likes of Holbach and Fabricus, if not directly. Torrey, *Voltaire and the English Deists*, 183ff., 202.

57. *Exam de la Vie & des Ouvrages de Saint Paul* (Londres, 1770) Epitre Dédicatoire, 65–74, 78–86, 94–95, 173–74.
58. Ibid., 139–42, 166–68, 175–76. Paul particularly targeted women because they are credulous and talkative; i.e., they are easily duped and spread the message through their incessant chatter. EVC 45, 46.
59. Ibid., 3–5, 12, 15–16, 165. Paul uses "mystical, cabalistic, [and] allegorical" techniques to destroy the literal context of OT prophecies. Ibid., 45.
60. Torrey, *Voltaire and the English Deists*, 59, 73ff. A couple of other influences upon Voltaire are worth mentioning from the world of English Deism. Voltaire read and marked up the work of Conyers Middleton, using it most famously in his article on "Miracles." Ibid., 156, 159ff., 163, 202. He also had four works by Anthony Collins in his library and mentions them in his writings. Collins is most famous for attacking the NT's use of typology as a misuse of the OT scripture, trying to feign their fulfillment in Christ, although Voltaire displays little interest in this specific argument. Voltaire shows more affinity in other areas: Collins's deprecation of the OT God and the Jewish people, his hatred of Christianity, his belief in determinism and free will, and his concept of morality in terms of pleasure. Anthony Collins, *A Philosophical Inquiry Concerning Human Liberty* (London: Golden Lion, 1717) 69, 83–90; Hans Frei, *The Eclipse of the Biblical Narrative* (New Haven, CT: Yale University Press, 1974) 76–77; Torrey, *Voltaire and the English Deists*, 25–26, 31–38, 51.
61. Ibid., 59, 96–99. E.g., OCV 20.86–89 (WV 11.288–94).
62. Thomas Woolston, *Six Discourses on the Miracles of Our Savior and Defences of His Discourses*, 1727–1730 (New York & London: Garland Publishing, Inc., 1979) 1.19–20; 2.6, 62. Hereafter cited as SDM. He considers the story of the paralytic in Mark 2 the "most monstrously absurd, improbable and incredible of any [miracle] according to the letter."

    > [It] was next to impossible for the poor Man and his Couch to be heav'd over their Heads, and rais'd to the top of it: More unreasonable yet to think, the master of the House would suffer the Roof of it to be so broken up: But most of all against Reason to suppose, Jesus would not give forth the healing word, and prevent all this Labour, or by his divine Power disperse the People, that the Paralytick might have present and early access to him.
    >
    > Whether all this be not absolutely shocking of the Credit of this Story, let my Readers judge. In my Opinion, no Tale more monstrously romantick can be told." SDM 4.62.

63. SDM 1.8, 59.
64. SDM 2.32–33. Another good example is the healing of the invalid at Bethesda Pool. SDM 3.58–62. The first three discourses cover the cleansing of the temple, the Geresene demoniac, the Transfiguration, the healing of the woman with an issue of blood, the woman at the well, cursing of the fig tree, and the healing of the man at the Pool of Bethesda. The last two discourses cover the resurrections of Lazarus, the window of Nain's son, Jairus's daughter, and Jesus.

65. SDM 1.6–9, 21–22, 59, 63–64; 2.48; 4.3–4; Torrey, *Voltaire and the English Deists*, 60–61. Of course, Origen is his favorite church father, but he includes many others who follow the same method. He thinks the allegorical method goes all the way back to Moses and the ancient Hebrews, and was adopted later by the Greeks. *Defences of his Discourses*, 2.34–37.
66. Voltaire says, "Never was Christianity so daringly assailed by a Christian." OCV 20.86 (WV 11.288).
67. *Defences of his Discourses*, 1.21–24; SDM 2.vi, vii, 22–23; 3.67–68; 6.62–71; Torrey, *Voltaire and the English Deists*, 60–61.
68. E.g., SDM 4.63, 64.
69. Torrey, *Voltaire and the English Deists*, 62–66, 90, 91.
70. Ludwig Feuerbach will follow this line of reasoning and say that "man is the real God." "What a man declares concerning God, he in truth declares concerning himself." Barth is the most consistent opponent of Feuerbach and challenges the sons of the Enlightenment and religious liberals like Friedrich Schleiermacher to reconsider the ramifications of their own thinking as leading to this type of atheism. God is the Lord of revelation and opposes any glorification of human prowess in its attempt to find what is holy (or wholly other) outside of divine initiative. Ludwig Feuerbach, *The Essence of Christianity*, George Eliot (trans.), Karl Barth (intro.), H. Richard Niebuhr (foreword) (New York: Harper & Row, Publishers, 1957) vii, xxii, 29, 230: Barth, *Church Dogmatics*, I/1.42–43, 128, 193, 194, 220; I/2.4–5, 29–30.
71. Modern philosophers tend to find metaphysics off limits for rigorous philosophical analysis as defying the logic of language. Ludwig Wittgenstein, *Tractatus Logico-Philosophicus*, trans. by D. F. Pears & B. F. McGuinness (London and Henley: Routledge & Kegan Paul, 1977) 3, 5 (1–2, 2.01), 19 (4.003), 25–26 (4.112–4.1212), 56–57 (5.6–5.61, 5.632–5.633), 67–74; *Philosophical Investigations*, trans. by G. E. M. Anscombe (New York: Macmillan Publishing Co., 1968) 103ff. (308ff.); *On Certainty*, edit. by G. E. M. Anscombe and G. H. von Wright (New York: Harper & Row, Publishers, 1969) 24–26, 32–33 (245), 68 (520–521), 81 (612), 88 (669).
72. Stephen Strehle, *The Egalitarian Spirit of Christianity: The Sacred Roots of American and British Government* (New Brunswick, NJ, and London: Transaction Publishers, 2009) 248. Holland provides a list of the blasphemous teachings that circulated among the Ranters: personal identification with God, belief in reincarnation, promiscuous sexual relations, and the rejection of the incarnation, virgin birth, vicarious atonement, and Judgment Day. The Ranters excoriated the Bible as a "bundle of contradictions," the "greatest curse" upon humankind, and the "cause of all blood, that hath been shed in the world." There would be "no peace in the world, til all the Bibles in the world were burned." J. Holland, porter, *The Smoke of the bottomlesse pit* (London, 1651) 1–6.
73. *Letters of Certain Jews*, 61, 64.

2

The Philosophes

Any history of the Enlightenment is told from the perspective of a certain ideology. History suffers this deficit and too often becomes little more than the chronological rendition of a person's prejudices, distilling a moral lesson from the past and disseminating a sermon to the present. In his famous "definition" of the Enlightenment, Immanuel Kant discloses much of this problem with bias by depicting the period in heroic terms as the "exodus of human beings from their self-incurred tutelage" (*Ausgang des Menschen aus seiner selbst verschuldeten Unmündigkeit*) and exhorts the audience to follow its lead with the simple motto, "Dare to know" (*Sapere aude*).[1] Kant clearly reveals his bias by mixing together the study of the past with present-day exhortation in the definition, telling his audience to follow the moral lesson of the times, or take responsibility just like a son of the Enlightenment and risk the security of immature self-understanding with the adventure of new discovery; but this type of bias is not unique to Kant. It is endemic to the study of history and particularly acute when evaluating/valuating the Enlightenment. Subjectivity arises at the very beginning of the study when trying to identify the precise contours and individual figures of the times, since any attempt to define the period and its people involves an anachronistic procedure of capricious choices, creating a Platonic form within the cacophony of existence or congealing the "flowing stream" of life into "blocks of ice."[2] Peter Gay, the most celebrated scholar of the Enlightenment, recognizes the problem and speaks of the figures or objects of his study as a "loose, informal, wholly unorganized coalition of cultural critics," providing a "clamorous chorus" of "discordant voices," but even he tends to cherry pick the sources of his focus from the wide swath of individuals, times, and ideas, "from Edinburgh to Naples, Paris to Berlin, Boston to Philadelphia."[3] He ends up creating a favorable image of this loose, diverse confederation, conceiving of the Enlightenment as the fundamental impulse of modernity and accenting what is consonant with this interpretation—all answering to his own modern ideology. Of course, this problem also permeates the present study, which chooses to focus upon the French philosophes as the epicenter of the Enlightenment and to accent the dark side of their work from a particular religious perspective that is admittedly sympathetic with the Judeo-Christian tradition.

Within this limitation, the study remains bold enough to find the bias of modern culture toward the virtues of the Enlightenment overbearing and detrimental to understanding the positive place of the Judeo-Christian tradition in developing its past and present society. The very exaltation of the philosophes often carries with it a decisive hostility toward the tradition, inflating their contributions to the modern world, forwarding their prejudice and negative evaluation of the church, and diminishing the significance and merit of faith in shaping the past and present. The sons of the Enlightenment speak often of their place in history at the expense of the church and would bask in all the attention of modern times:

> The only signs which appeared of the spirit of liberty during those periods [before the French Revolution], are to be found in the writings of the French philosophers, . . . Montesquieu by his judgment and knowledge of laws, Voltaire by his wit, Rousseau and Raynal by their animation, and Quesney and Turgot by their moral maxims and systems of economy.[4]
>
> Although the detail of the formation of the American governments is at present little known or regarded either in Europe or in America, it may hereafter become an object of curiosity. It will never be pretended that any persons employed in that service had interviews with the gods, or were in any degree under the inspiration of Heaven, more than those at work upon ships or houses, or laboring in merchandise or agriculture; it will forever be acknowledged that these governments were contrived merely by the use of reason and senses. . . .[5]

Modern authors tend to concur with this estimate and patronize the age of reason, overemphasizing the isolated significance and genius of a handful of philosophes in developing the vital elements of modern government.[6]

> The three authors of *The Federalist*, known by their collective signature, "Publius," sound all the great themes of the Enlightenment, if often by implication only: the dialectical movement away from Christianity to modernity. . . . It will perhaps appear less quixotic if we recall that there was a time when tough-minded men looked to the young republic in America, saw there with delight the program of the philosophes in practice, and found themselves convinced that the Enlightenment has been a success.[7]

There are several basic problems with this general assessment of the Enlightenment as possessing such a decisive significance in creating the modern view of government—problems that should bring some pause to even the most zealous advocates. One, the fundamental concepts of liberty, equality, democracy, and federal government already permeated much of England

and New England during the seventeenth century, long before any son of the Enlightenment adopted these notions and wielded them together into a system of governance. Much of the credit actually belongs to the Puritans or Reformed community, which led the way in reforming all aspects of society, using the polity of their own church as the fundamental paradigm of the reform. The church emphasized democracy, the autonomy of each fellowship, and the power to depose ministers and officials who violated their federal responsibilities or covenant (*foedus*).[8] Even the area of toleration saw a number of monumental works produced on the subject during the times of the Puritan Revolution, despite the checkered history on this issue and the many ups and downs in the years to come. The year 1644 alone produced such classical works as William Walwyn's *The Compassionate Samaritane*, Roger Williams's *The Bloudy Tenent*, Henry Robinson's *Liberty of Conscience*, and John Milton's *Areopagitica*. Two, all the philosophes were Anglophiles, admiring British freedoms, intellectual life, and social/political relationships, and resting their hope within this land, that "liberal regimes were not fantasies but possibilities."[9] They were hardly alone in promoting liberal policies and deeply influenced by the reforms taking place in England since the seventeenth century. Even Montesquieu and his celebrated discussion upon checks and balances within the government only exposited a doctrine that permeated the Puritan community over a century earlier and expressly looked to the interactions of the British government as the basic model and impetus for the teaching.[10] Three, the politics of the philosophes tended to follow the nuanced discussions of Montesquieu, which never advocated democracy as the single, best form of government or any system of governance without equivocation. Montesquieu might criticize the oppression of an absolute despot and encourage the rule of law, but he never proscribed the possibility of monarchical regimes ruling wisely and preferred to understand the specific form of government as a matter of indifference relative to the situation or contingent upon a number of circumstances—the climate of the region, the size of the country, and the spirit of the people.[11] After all, most of the philosophes were part of a political order and developed a flexible approach to politics accordingly, often neglecting the social dimension of their ideas, seldom risking cozy arrangements with the state to challenge the status quo or becoming martyrs of a greater liberty at the expense of their careers. Most received pensions from the state, held government posts, and considered themselves conscientious servants of kings, foreign and domestic, spending much of their time flattering despots and groveling in distasteful obeisance for special royal favor:[12]

> In his long and uncomfortable intercourse with the Prussian king [a brutal dictator], Voltaire, always ready with a pleasing comparison, found many synonyms calculated to please; as one patient scholar has discovered, Voltaire likened Frederick to Caesar, Augustus, Marcus Aurelius, Antoninus Pius, Titus, Julian, Vergil, Pliny, Horace,

> Maecenas, Cicero, Catullus, Homes, La Rochefoucauld, La Bruyère, Boileau, Soloman, Prometheus, Apollo, Patroclus, Socrates, Alcibiades, Alexander, Henri IV, and Francis I—a rather miscellaneous but shrewdly conceived list.[13]

On occasion, a few of the philosophes resisted the system of courtiers and provided real guidance for substantive change within the power structure. Denis Diderot composed an influential and famous article in the first volume of the *Encyclopedia*, entitled "Political Authority" (1751), which helped lay the groundwork for the coming revolution, even if his ideas are not revolutionary or groundbreaking. In this article, he challenges the official view of the court as possessing unlimited authority through entitlement or natural endowment and speaks of individual liberty as a God-given right, sounding much like Locke and his *Two Treatises Concerning Civil Government*. He continues the Lockean themes by placing all princes under the natural law and promoting the social contract, which sets the conditions for exercising proper authority through the "choice and consent" of the governed.[14] In a subsequent article on "Natural Equality" (1755), he emphasizes more the democratic element by placing everyone under the "general will" of the people as the final arbiter of what is right and wrong and exhorting the audience to live in conformity with its demands and duties. This article sounds more left-wing and atheistic in its concept of government than the previous one and seems to represent more the spirit of the French Revolution with its emphasis upon democratic and utilitarian rule; rather than the old Lockean concept, which bases society upon the revelation of God's will in nature.[15]

The classic statement of this democratic view of government and law is found in Jean-Jacques Rousseau's great work, *The Social Contract* (1762). Rousseau and his work received much contempt from the philosophes, but his stature grew after his death and his concept of the general will exerted an enormous influence upon Robespierre and the French Revolution, as seen in Louis-Sébastien Mercier's work *De J. J. Rousseau considéré comme l'un des premiers auteurs de la Révolution* (1791).[16] Rousseau starts out the book with a famous paradox, "Man is born free, and he is everywhere in chains."[17] He sees no real limit on the exercise of freedom in nature, where no state, no general will, and no property rights exist to inhibit the desires of a person from possessing any object, beyond the limits of one's natural capacities to acquire it;[18] but all this changes when one enters society. The natural freedom is lost once one enters a social contract, pledging allegiance to the general will of a people and agreeing to follow their rules.[19] Rousseau might spend some time equivocating about *iura* (laws/rights) already present in nature,[20] but his overall direction tends to emasculate the traditional meaning of individual or inalienable rights and understand the law as a product of society and its common interests. The law first develops within the state as a necessary means to promote the "common good."[21] Virtue is first established in the state and "is nothing more than conformity of the particular wills with the general will."[22] Rousseau rejects the existence of the individual in the state and wants public education to inculcate the common bond of citizenship, instructing the students to "be aware . . . of their own existence merely as a part of the state, . . . to feel themselves members of their country, . . . to love it with the exquisite feeling which every isolated person only have for himself, . . . [and] to regard their individuality only in its relation to the body of their state."[23] The general will is justice; the "voice of the people" is the "voice of God."[24] As long as "sectarian associations" are left out of the process, the citizen can trust the decisions of the general will as "always good" and representative of the new common humanity and its interests within a unified nation, and leave behind all concerns about the diminished rights of the individual or the tyranny of the majority.[25] Even if the "opinion contrary to my own prevails, this only proves that I was mistaken all along."[26] Within this concept of the state, Rousseau sets the basic agenda for the French Revolution and its left-wing political tendencies, defining the individual in terms of the state, equivocating over property rights, subsuming all citizens under a central government, and prescribing utilitarian or revolutionary means to inculcate the common interest, often at the expense of individual liberty. This is the tendency of the French Revolution and the etatism of the world to come.

One of the reasons behind the exalted status of Rousseau and the philosophes is the secular texture of their presentation. In the previous two centuries, the scripture filled the pages of books and served as an ultimate authority in matters of religion, politics, and economics,[27] but now the Western world made a dramatic move away from religious authority toward a more secular way of thinking or justifying its ideas and chose to identify its culture with those who led the way in creating this "freedom of thought." The philosophes rejected the reign of "fanaticism and superstition" in the church and the dependence of believers upon faith and grace to establish their lives. They rejected the Augustinian/Anselmic formula of "faith seeking understanding" and preferred to trust in their own autonomous abilities to discover first principles in nature or develop a rational and ordered culture, where *honnête hommes* and philosopher-kings ruled society, free from the dogma of the *corpus Christianum*.[28] They saw Descartes as the herald of a new era in "shaking off the yoke of scholasticism, public opinion, and authority," implementing a new *modus operandi* from the strictures of reason and skepticism and "laying the foundation" for the autonomy and freedom of the enlightened way of thinking.[29] They employed his use of reason in developing metaphysical arguments, while expressing some concern about the nature of Cartesian idealism, theological dogmatism, or any abstract system-building, wanting a more solid empirical basis to verify the results.[30] Again they looked to England for inspiration, seeking to align their philosophy with the prestige of British empiricism, and they particularly exalted the experimental method of Bacon, the epistemology of Locke, and the physics of Newton.[31] Much of the relationship was manufactured in order to gain credence for their religious, political, and social criticisms, as if their opinions were grounded within material, objective, and scientific research and contained the imprimatur of British intelligentsia. Much of their work spent time praising the modern scientific progress coming from Britain,[32] without ever acknowledging any Puritan elements in this scientific revolution and cultural perspective,[33] preferring to think of it as a simple liberation from the dark ages of religious stagnation and to extol the present time as an unprecedented century of light and great thinkers. Of course, they added their own names to the list of enlightened thinkers and produced some important works, including Montesquieu's *Spirit of the Laws*, Buffon's *Natural History*, Voltaire's *Philosophical Dictionary*, Rousseau's *Emile* and *Social Contract*, and the *Encyclopedia* of Diderot and d'Alembert; but none of them were great scientists, and few of them were even remotely comparable to the greater philosophers of the Western canon—Plato, Aristotle, Descartes, Locke, Kant, Hume, and Hegel.[34]

The great philosophers of the time were not filled with such hubris concerning their own rational acuity and its ability to destroy or build metaphysical propositions. They tended to avoid and transcend the childish tirades of Voltaire and his followers, and saw difficulties for all human beings in using reason to discuss or dismiss metaphysical matters, displaying a greater sense of humility toward their abilities and results. David Hume conducted his life and meditations as a true gentleman and genuine human being,[35] without exhibiting undue belligerence toward adversaries, simply relating a number of serious doubts about the capacity of reason to establish metaphysical statements concerning the existence of God, or the truth or falsehood of any religion, whether it is Christianity or Deism.[36] In one of his most piquant arguments, he shows the inability of pure reason to analyze an effect in mundane experience and derive its cause without resorting to the custom or habit that views the two together, or taking a metaphysical leap. This problem he applies to cosmological proofs a fortiori, showing how difficult it is for reason to argue from the experience of the world (the effect) to the existence of God (the cause). It is difficult to argue this way in the everyday world of mundane casualty, let alone in regard to a universe, whose phenomena exceed the ability to comprehend and prevent people from rising above the present day experience around them and finding an ultimate, transcendent cause.[37] Immanuel Kant, the greatest of all modern philosophers, agreed with the "Scottish skeptic" about the limits of reason and emphasizes the importance of making metaphysical assumptions in his *Critique of Pure Reason* if reason is to justify its agenda in bringing unity and meaning to human existence. Metaphysical assumptions are necessary in order to justify the continuance of ethical questions, cosmic theories, and the quest for the ultimate purpose in life, but they also transcend the human ability to establish their existence or speak of them in a definitive way.[38]

The typical *philosophe* was far more dogmatic than Hume or Kant when it came to metaphysical propositions and considered reason more than capable of establishing the existence of God, discovering the ultimate purpose of life or moral means of divine service, and trashing other viewpoints. Thomas Paine provided a stereotypical portrait of this enlightened way of thinking about religion in his classic work *The Age of Reason*. Here he spends much time discrediting Christianity as an irrational religion, for withstanding the rational capacity of all human beings to know the things of God in nature and propagating a special revelation, filled with mythological nonsense about talking snakes and forbidden fruit and illogical mathematical formulas like the doctrine of the Trinity, "that three is one, and one is three."[39] The Jewish people who produced the sacred writings of the religion were an ignorant and illiterate race, far inferior to the Gentiles in artistic accomplishments, philosophical prowess, and scientific achievement. They were a "nation of ruffians and cutthroats," who imitated such "monsters and imposters as Moses and Aaron, Joshua, Samuel and David," and so produced a "book of lies, wickedness, and blasphemy," filled with "obscene stories" about "unrelenting vindictiveness" and "wickedness," "assassinations, treachery, and wars," inspiring the "most detestable wickedness, the most horrid cruelties, and the greatest miseries that have afflicted the human race" and "laid Europe in blood and ashes." Paine exhorts his readers to abandon all trust in the Bible or a revelation given to another person and rely on one's own rational capacity to discover the knowledge and nature of God through "visible facts." "My own mind is my own church"; "the creation is the bible of the true believer." Through the proper use of reason, it is easy to find divine wisdom all around by contemplating the design of the universe or the order of this "great machine."[40]

Paine goes on to speak of the Almighty as a "great mechanic" or "first Cause" and identifies the "true religion" with Deism, describing the faith in stereotypical terms. This religion is said to know God exists and to follow the dictates of the divine will as a means of service in this life, without possessing specific details about the divine essence (or knowing exactly what it discovers and imitates). Paine thinks of his religion as scientific but expresses much consternation over the growing propensity of modern science to provide matter with eternal principles, leaving God out of the equation altogether. He attributes motion to the activity of God in nature, and he cannot conceive of any other explanation or even understand those who impute its law-abiding character to an innate property in matter, outside an ultimate rational force;[41] but his religion clearly has a real problem at this point. It seems as if this increasing tendency toward scientism is an aspect of his own deist religion, which follows the metaphysical understanding of Galileo and Newton in a most literal way, conceiving of the material world as a machine, providing it with self-perpetuating autonomy or force (entelechy), and eventually crowding God out of the process. Newton certainly saw the difficulty but made the same sort of compromise when he made the ridiculous suggestion of turning the "ground of all being" into a *deus ex machina*, which was needed to stabilize astronomical irregularities in planetary motions and his equations through miraculous intervention. Many lambasted this *argumentum ex ignorantia* and the need to postulate the existence of God when Laprange and Laplace explained the planetary perturbations through their own mathematical calculations.[42] Paine, Newton, and most of the philosophes tried to spurn atheism as a pernicious idea,[43] but they were advocating ideas that seemed to proceed in this direction and clearly losing the battle, as secularism was on the rise and gaining more and more territory, with some abandoning faith in God altogether. Both Bayle and Diderot wrote articles making an appeal for toleration in regard to atheism, arguing that an atheist can be moral, that "morality can exist without religion" and that theism is not necessary in society.[44] Most philosophes agreed, for all practical purposes, when they abandoned the emphasis upon the natural law of God and replaced it with utilitarian calculations, centered upon human needs and man-made solutions, without making reference to God or ultimate ends and values.[45] Even those who saw God as a vital part of society—like Voltaire, Rousseau, and Robespierre—often couched their argument in utilitarian terms, seeing the cult of the Supreme Being as a necessary opium of the people, to keep them in line, or merely a useful tool of the state.[46] Deism enabled the philosophes to live outside of God within their own separate sphere of power, proceeding to the antithesis of the church's radical dependence upon God for revelation and grace, and many chose to use the new found power by extending Deism's domain, excising any need for God, creating a secular world of absolute autonomy, and laying the foundation for a complete separation between church and state.

The atheism of the times expressed the strongest reaction against the doctrine and practice of the Christian church. The criticisms often became nothing more than an exercise in extreme belligerence,[47] leaving behind all sense of objectivity that was so much associated with reason and the high standards of objective analysis. Diderot saw his differences with the church as a war between two camps, consisting of "us" and "them."[48] He associated intolerance with religion and saw Christianity as the worst of all religious expressions, hoping the "reign of the Anti-Christ" would come and destroy the "great whore of Babylon."[49] Philosophes who followed Diderot and proceeded in his direction toward atheism and materialism also tended to produce the same type of strident rhetoric and showed a willingness to advocate and incite the process of dechristianization—so much a part of the coming revolution.[50]

Holbach provides a disturbing illustration of this extreme animosity in his *Christianity Unveiled* (1761), putting down in the boldest and most extensive terms what the philosophes felt about the religion in general. In a "letter to a friend," Holbach seems to recognize a developing constituency of enlightened individuals who sympathize with the position of his book but remain reticent to speak out knowing the power of the church and the oppression of dangerous ideas in contemporary society. Holbach dismisses the reluctance of his constituents and plainly states, as his basic thesis, what they only imply in less caustic language: Christianity is evil and must be eliminated from society. According to his thesis, religion is responsible for despotism; Christianity has brought more evil into the world than "all the superstitions of heathendom"; it has brought the persecution of infidels, and it has "cost the human race more blood than all other religions of the earth taken collectively"; no reform is possible for the religion since its "spirit of intolerance and persecution" is "founded on the Bible"; and so, it is necessary to excise the religion from society in order to create a world of justice and peace free from "fanatic enthusiasm and bigotry."[51]

He hopes that reason will triumph over the ignorance of superstition one day and recreate society into its perfect image of truth and justice. "Fanatics and ignorant people are the disturbers of society. Sensible, enlightened, and disinterested persons are ever the friends of peace." The church has served Western culture for eighteen centuries as the breeding ground of stultifying ignorance and scientific poverty, developing a constituency of the "poor and ignorant"—those who blindly follow the dictates of priests and their culture. "No religion ever placed its sectaries in more complete dependence on priests . . . making all contribute to their power, riches, and dominion," enslaving the kings and people alike, subjecting them to metaphysical nonsense and "superstitious education," and creating "innumerable practices and duties," which openly violate "all the laws of morality and reason." The religion of these priests is "injurious to the welfare of the state" because it opposes all "progress of the human mind" and "principles of true morality" and prefers to inculcate practices of personal piety and salvation, dependent upon priestly occultism, possessing no social utility whatsoever. All this mystical piety destroys the essence of true virtue, which uses reason to calculate what is right or wrong and considers the effect of an action upon the felicity of concrete human beings in society, not religious mumbo jumbo.[52]

Holbach proceeds with the assault by underscoring the many internal contradictions within the scripture. The Old Testament breathes with the spirit of a capricious deity, who "blows hot and cold and contradicts himself every moment," commanding and condemning the same course of actions at different times, without insisting upon a uniform code of conduct. The text breathes this type of delirium throughout its many pages and contains a wealth of material, covering almost anything and everything "except good sense, good logic, and reason." It gives birth to a people who exhibit the same capriciousness and cruelty as their deity in dealing with their neighbors, stealing the possessions of Egypt, annihilating the city-states of Canaan, and treating all others as aliens and infidels, overturning the basic laws of decency whenever their extreme xenophobia arises. The Christians only continue and advance this type of irrational religious expression within the New Testament by canonizing the same capricious behavior and worshiping the same "terrible God of the Jews," who damns the majority of the human race out of despotic cruelty. Both religions try to defend the ridiculous nature of their special revelation by appealing to the impossible and unsubstantiated. Both religions "discredit experience and reject reason" by using miraculous events in the past as a vindication of their message and making an appeal once again to a God who "contradicts himself and the laws which he has prescribed to nature," but only end up defending irrationality with more irrationality. Holbach is unable to accept any mystery in life that exists outside of his uniform way of thinking about nature and its absolute laws.[53] Life affords no tensions or paradoxes to defy simple logical categories, and offers no suggestions or room to believe in a transcendent being, who lives above and beyond the universe and the ability of philosophes to comprehend what is feasible.

The philosophes went on to inscribe this animosity toward the Judeo-Christian tradition into a new analysis of history, which involved the vicious circle of re-presenting the past as a fundamental lesson for the present. Voltaire thought of history as a "recital of facts represented as true"[54] and used this weakness in historical analysis to run roughshod over the complexity of real life and insert his considerable prejudice in skewing events. The philosophes followed Voltaire and possessed the same moralistic outlook on life, often reducing religion to morality and proceeding to use history as a personal platform to vent their moral fervor, showing little concern for the actual details of real historical research and the complexity of its multifaceted events.[55] History was strictly a political matter, used as a means of pointing out the abysmal record of the Christian past and exalting the virtues of the pagan sector as a proleptic model for the future construction of civilization. History was used as a stage to present current polemical interests in terms of an epic battle of the ages, divided between the tolerant forces of reason and the intolerant forces of superstition, pitting the multiculturalism of the ancient world against the exclusive monotheism of the Judeo-Christian tradition and its rejection of other names and images for God.[56] The philosophes gave much credit in their history to Greek philosophers for spurning the authority of religious dogma and bringing critical reasoning to the Western world, even if they were not so fluent in the Greek language and its literature.[57] They tended to know Greek culture as it developed in later Latin authors like Cicero and Lucretius and thought of Rome as a "City on a Hill" shining its light upon the age of reason and providing the paradigm for a future of state.[58] The modern exaltation of Greco-Roman culture was born within the historical focus of French philosophes, who learned the Latin language from the church and preferred to use it in studying classical pagan literature, rather than continue the typical ecclesiastical interests that concentrated on the theology of the church fathers and medieval scholastics. The spread of Christianity and the incursions of "German barbarians" were blamed for the sacking of the Roman Empire and ushering in a millennium of Christian culture known as the Dark Ages.[59] The Renaissance was exalted as a rebirth of humanity, rescuing Western civilization from the darkness of ecclesiastical rule by rediscovering the "masterpieces of antiquity," purifying them from medieval usage, and proceeding to use their own enlightened reason, inspiring all.[60]

The philosophes proceeded to embellish this "historical" account by willfully choosing to demonize the Jewish people as the underlying spiritual force behind the church and the plight of Western civilization. The atrocities of church history were understood only in terms of its inception within the cultural milieu of ancient Palestine and dissemination of a message that was rooted within that culture. The primary target of attack remained the church,[61] but the philosophes felt an additional onus to deprecate its mother as the origin of the religion and rid Western civilization of the culprit once and for all by various ways and means. The French Enlightenment and Revolution proceeded to solve the Jewish question (*Judenfrage*) by advocating church/state separation to wall off the religious community and destroy it through the increasing power of the state. They offered the Jewish community a new existence as full citizens within a secular state, bribing its people with the benefits of citizenship at the price of their souls, while revealing a dirty secret, that the hatred of Jews in the Enlightenment and the emancipation of Jews in the French Revolution were one and the same,[62] that the proponents of this form of toleration only wished to destroy what they professed to tolerate. This "final solution" to the Jewish problem finds its deepest roots within the obsession of philosophes to end the reign of the Judeo-Christian tradition, which they condemned as responsible for all the evils of society,[63] rejecting any halfway measure to reform its shortcomings or lift it up to a higher plateau (*Aufhebung*) and preferring to create a new humanity *ex nihilo*. The attitude is found throughout the philosophes and illustrated with its varying levels of intensity in many books and articles. A representative sample must include the following significant works: Diderot's article on the "Juifs" in the *Encyclopedia*, Mirabaud's *Opinions des Anciens sur des Juifs*, and Holbach's magnum opus of hate, *L'esprit du Judaïsme ou Examen Raisonne*.

The first work of Diderot is rather sedate in comparison with the other two. It shows some deference to Christianity and affords a mixed review of the Jewish people and their religion down through the ages, sometimes speaking positively about certain sectarian groups and a few of its important leaders. The disparaging comments are rather tame considering the vitriol of the times and the rhetoric of many others, but the overall negative tone opens the way toward a more severe anti-Semitism, and some of the specific comments are disturbing enough to deserve a brief mention. One, at certain points Diderot emphasizes the hatred of Jews for groups inside and outside their religious community,[64] even though he never characterizes them as hatemongers per se like many other philosophes and anti-Semites. He particularly chastens the Jews for their teachings in the Talmud, which sanction the hatred of Christians by permitting the deprecation of their name, the stealing of their goods, and the killing of their people, and he says the work lacks all sense of decency and charity because of this. Two, he shows much disdain for many of the developments in Judaism since the fall of Jerusalem in 70 CE. He considers the editor of the Mishnah, Judah the Prince, as nothing more than a pompous ass and authoritarian bully for exalting his piety above the law and exhibiting a ridiculous proclivity toward pomp and circumstance—a criticism that holds true for many of the academic leaders who followed Judah and exerted enormous power over the people as experts of the law and tradition in the next few centuries. Three, he considers the next stage of rabbinic learning that completed the Gemara to be filled with complete "foolishness," and he thinks the Babylonian edition of the Talmud debases the Jewish people in numerous ways. Many rabbis tend to exalt it above the laws of Moses, making it worse to violate the wisdom of its sages than the prophets of old. Four, he denounces rabbinic learning in the Middle Ages that forsook the literal reproduction of meaning in a text for a more allegorical or mystical sense and disparages all Kabalistic spirituality as so much double-talk and obscurantism. Five, he denigrates the "infinite" number of metaphysical speculations that occur among rabbinic scholars, repeating for a number of pages fantastic discussions about angels, demons, humans, and all of creation, meant to characterize and debase the Jewish quest for wisdom.[65] At this point, he speaks of the Jewish intellect with great disdain:

> One cannot find any rightness of ideas, exactness of reasoning, or precision within the style of the Jews—in a word, all that which ought to characterize a sane philosophy. One finds only what is contrary—a confused mixture of principles of reason and revelation, an affected and often impenetrable obscurity, using principles that lead to fanaticism, [including] a blind respect for their teachers—in a word, all the faults that manifest an ignorant and superstitious nation.[66]

The next work of Mirabaud was republished in 1769 from an earlier version in order to intensify the burgeoning anti-Semitic feelings of the times, beyond what is seen in Diderot's presentation. It was promulgated by the Holbach Circle because of its scholastic approach using ancient historical sources to document the bigotries of the day toward the indelible depravity and problems of the Jewish community.[67] The book starts out trying to buttress a typical anti-Semitic argument of Deists and philosophes alike: the Jewish religion owes its origins to Egyptian influence and has no right to claim a unique relationship with God. Classical sources from Greek and Roman authorities are used to undermine the claim and show that Moses and his people merely forged a new religion out of their experiences in Egypt, placing the imprimatur of Jehovah upon customs like circumcision and dietary laws about meats that were actually borrowed from their surroundings.[68] Even the religious festivals are said to come from Egypt, and that is why they seem so dreary and lack the exuberant spirit and inspiration of Roman celebrations. In fact, the Jews became the real curmudgeons of antiquity by accenting the deficits of Egyptian life, living in an isolated environment along the banks of the Nile River, developing the dismal religious outlook of a desolate land, and exhibiting the same acrid spirit toward neighboring people. The Jews learned to hate others in this environment and forged a new religion to justify their ethnocentricities, where Jehovah possessed a unique love for them and a burning hatred for others, even ordering the extermination of those who withstood their will to power. This is why so many historians in antiquity despised and ridiculed them as a sanctimonious people, possessing no merit whatsoever, and why the Romans were forced to banish them from the land of Israel as an irascible people who hated the presence of others and refused to submit unto foreign rule—a problem that remains today in the places of their sojourn. Mirabaud says the Jews have no interest in living among the Gentiles and await, with increasing expectation, the coming of a Messiah, who will deliver them from their wretched condition and make them rulers over all nations. Throughout history, they refused to accept the normal course of events, placing their hope in a God who intervenes on their behalf in a miraculous way, and they continue with this foolishness to this day, longing for deliverance from the heavens through a supernatural act, embodied within the present messianic expectation.[69] The pagan writers of antiquity mocked their fantastic stories of divine intervention and ethnic pride, and all rational people today should join in the age-old chorus of ridicule.[70]

The last work of Holbach reaches the zenith of this type of ridicule and hate-literature, losing all sense of fairness and balance. The work focuses upon all things negative, interpreting the Jews and their religion in pejorative terms and accusing them of creating a culture of hate, but Holbach never seems to deconstruct the analysis or pause to reflect upon the type of hate-filled soul that makes scurrilous accusations to begin with.[71] As such, the work remains blinded to its own demons and unable to fulfill its ostensible purpose in searching out the historical roots of Christianity and seeing whether the religion has a sufficient foundation in the Jewish faith.[72] This purpose is skewed by the typical prejudices of the philosophes toward the church, which serve as the real motivation of the study, and forces it to hate the Jews because it hates Christians.[73]

In this culture of hate, it is not surprising that Holbach imputed his own subjective defect to the object of his study and finds the essence of the Jews and their religion within his own hatred of others. He says Jews developed a religion of hate by refusing to mix with others and embodied this teaching into a special doctrine of revelation, which excludes others from participating in the knowledge of God outside the limits of their community. He accuses them of developing this religion out of their own depravity and creating God in their own provincial image—a God who is now circumscribed within their community, less universal in nature, and more local, partial, jealous, and wicked than all other concepts of the divine within the world of religions. Their God commands "rape, treason, rebellions, fraud, . . . [and] the most basic violation of natural and human rights," and bestows special blessings upon the most wicked of OT lore, turning the "soiled monsters of the most revolting cruelty and frightful crimes" into its heroes. The religion of Moses came to justify the things most contrary to justice and right reason and annihilate every idea of moral decency as a consequence.[74]

Holbach begins the history of religion with Moses, describing him as a "cruel," "sanguinary," and "ambitious" man who duped the Israelites into following him. Moses knew that the Israelites were devoid of all knowledge of secondary causality, and he was able to use the magical arts of his Egyptian background to gain power over them, making these "stupid people" think that he actually controlled nature and was able to change the course of its immutable laws to meet their every need. Holbach goes on to characterize the Jews in general as the "most ignorant, most stupid, most superstitious people who ever lived on earth," utterly devoid of "light, morality, . . . true science, and sound reason." Moses was able to exploit this grotesque stupidity using "marvels, fables which he invented, as well as the credulity of the Hebrews to make them submit to his yoke, and eventually to the Levites [his own family], who . . . aided him during his lifetime to establish his power."[75]

Holbach says the whole purpose of the Mosaic economy is the "well-being of the priesthood. . . . All its laws, institutions, dogmas, [and] ceremonies have no other purpose than serving the incessant needs of the priests . . . [and] procuring for them offerings, gifts, sacrifices, and unlimited power above all else." This lust for power and riches served as the real underlying motive behind the numerous xenophobic measures in the Mosaic economy and the subsequent religious development. This is why all other forms of worship are so displeasing to Jehovah and bring swift retribution, including the death penalty for all idolaters. This is why the priests proscribe all alliances with surrounding nations, foment constant hostility toward foreign influence, and stir up conflict with rival religious expressions, sometimes sending the king and the people to war, hoping to prevent any intrusion on their territory. These policies led to the ruin of the people over time and caused them to suffer more from the authority of priests than any other bondage they endured under the Pharaohs of Egypt or the later kings of Israel. In fact, the priests were the real power before the thrones and exalted secular rulers like David, who followed their orders by destroying all rival cults and exalting Jerusalem as the only place for legitimate sacrifice. A few of the kings tried to end the tyranny and bring religious toleration to the religion, but these virtuous kings were treated like Ahab and sentenced to live under a curse forever within the biased account of priests and prophets contained in holy scripture.[76]

Holbach thinks his overview of Judaism is beneficial in understanding Christianity as its depraved offspring. Christians came to worship the same provincial God as the Jews, but they exhibit even greater intolerance in their account and cruelty than before, electing only a few individuals out of the whole human race to participate in the glories of heaven and damning the rest to an eternity in hell. Christians also placed the OT within their sacred canon and revered its saints as providing pious and efficacious examples to follow in serving the one, true God of both Testaments. Its priests continued to follow the same legacy as their Jewish prototype, preying upon the "stupidity of the people and the weakness of princes," devouring their incomes through a number of magical ceremonies, hating those who see God from a different perspective, persecuting infidels, exciting torrents, and spilling "great streams of human blood" through religious fanaticism—"barbarities unknown" to the human race—all to enhance the "grandeur, riches, and power" of their kingdom. Holbach thinks the Western world can no longer afford to close its eyes to the insidious nature of the Judeo-Christian tradition if it wishes to find deliverance from the true "enemy of liberty" and live in peaceful coexistence. The tradition has brought nothing but tyranny to the world and must be stopped as the great obstacle of all scientific, moral, and social progress.[77]

In this type of analysis, Holbach and the philosophes lost all sense of objectivity in their criticisms of the Judeo-Christian tradition. Their criticisms lacked balance and perspective, too often exaggerating darker elements or dubious events, in the most deviant way imaginable, and turning these stumbling blocks into the essence of the faith in general. The Bible was interpreted and characterized through the imprecatory Psalms; the church, through the evils of the Spanish Inquisition. The church was responsible for ushering in the Dark Ages, extinguishing the light of Greco-Roman learning and virtue, and destroying Western civilization until the Italian Renaissance recovered classical culture and founded modern scientific inquiry. This history culminated in the Enlightenment or age of reason, which threw off the shackles of ecclesiastical dependence upon revelation, faith, and grace from the heavens above and exalted the autonomous abilities of humankind in its quest for truth. The philosophes saw the outcome of history as justifying their own ideology, which also happened to trust in its own philosophical prowess in leading them to the portals of heaven, rather than receive any message from on high or depend upon outside authority. They rejoiced in their own freedom but clearly inflated their own independent ability in the process to establish first principles through the mere exercise of reason, often exaggerating their place in forging the basic elements of the modern world. None of them proved or disproved the existence of God; few of them dared to leave their privileged position in the old political order or challenge the *Ancien Régime* with a radical new paradigm; and practically all of them committed the naturalistic fallacy in trying to turn morality into a calculating sum and confusing the need for a divine imperative (oughtness) with a simple description of human desires.[78] Instead of displaying humility with the results, the philosophes continued to use reason as a sledgehammer to bludgeon the Judeo-Christian tradition as an irrational and immoral faith, based upon their rational concept of what is worthy of God and consonant with sound ethical behavior. They used their reason to disprove the authority of scripture by pointing to the odd and immoral behavior of its God and people, unwilling to accept the possibility of any paradoxes or mysteries within the uniform ways of divine activity, revealed in nature and its universal laws. Jews and Christians were simply dismissed as stupid and credulous ignoramuses for believing in miraculous stories of divine intervention into the uniform course of nature and deprecated as immoral for thinking that God acted in a special way on their behalf. For these and other beliefs, the philosophes went on to demonize Jews and Christians for producing a religion of hate and emphasizing its special relationship with God to the exclusion of all other members of the human race. Their specific analysis proceeded to justify this harsh judgment by searching for weaknesses and underscoring problematic teachings and episodes, but they often exaggerated the findings and revealed much of their own prejudice and hate in deconstructing the material from the most negative possible point of view. Instead of providing much needed criticism and reform,[79] they sought to destroy the faith and developed a culture of hate toward it, blaming the tradition for all social ills and seeking total emancipation from its devices. Their hatred provided the fundamental atmosphere for much of the anti-Semitism and anti-Christianity in the Western world and laid the foundation for its secular cultures, all made in the image of the philosophes and intended to achieve "human emancipation" from the tradition through the increasing power of the state[80]—a state that rejected the need for revelation and professed to live in secular autonomy, just like the philosophes.

Notes

1. Immanuel Kant, *Werke* (Wiesbaden: Insel-Verlag, 1958) 6.53.
2. Miguel de Unamuno, *The Tragic Sense of Life in Men and Nations*, Anthony Kerrigan (trans.) (Princeton, NJ: Princeton University Press, 1977) 100.
3. Gay, *The Enlightenment*, 1.8–9. For example, Gay basically ignores Thomas Paine and his age of reason, since it might provide a darker portrait of the era. He includes and accents the work of Hume and Kant, which might provide a more favorable image of the times, but their work clearly rises above the philosophes and their typical themes and prejudices.
4. Thomas Paine, *The Rights of Man* (Albany, NY: Dolphin Books, 1961) 332–33.
5. *The Works of John Adams* (Freeport, NY: Books for Libraries, 1969) 4.292–93.

6. Gay, *The Enlightenment,* 2.559–61.
7. Ibid., 563, 568.
8. Strehle, *The Egalitarian Spirit of Christianity,* chaps. 1–3.
9. Gay, *The Enlightenment,* 1.11–12, 387; 2.73–74, 451. The many influences include the French Protestant refugees from England, the many journals and journalists of the day who praised the British way (Michel de la Roche, Armand de la Chapelle, Jean Leclerc, etc.), the author of *Lettres sur les matieres du temps* (end of the seventeenth century), and a number of other authors, especially Rabin-Thoyras, who made the parliamentary system palatable in France and mixes the three powers together in his *Histoire d'Angleterre* (1723). Joseph Dedieu, *Montesquieu et la tradition politique anglaise en France* (New York: B. Franklin, 1970) 4–7, 12, 35–39, 41ff., 55ff., 67–68, 76ff., 84–102; M. J. C. Vile, *Constitutionalism and the Separation of Powers* (Oxford: Clarendon Press, 1967) 79–80.
10. Montesquieu, *De l'Esprit des Lois* (Paris, Garner Frères, 1961) I, v, 12 (63); II, xi, 2–3 (162); M. P. Bergman, "Montesquieu's Theory of Government and the Framing of the American Constitution," *Pepperdine Law Review* 18, no. 1 (1990): 19, 33; Scott Gordon, *Controlling the State* (Cambridge, MA: Harvard University Press, 1999) 309; Vile, *Constitutionalism and the Separation of Powers,* 92, 93, 124; J. R. Loy, *Montesquieu* (New York: Twayne Publishers, Inc., 1968) 109; G. Turdbet Delof, "La Theorie des Pouvoirs avant 'De l'Esprit des Lois'," *Mondes et Cultures* 47, no. 3 (1987): 585; *Records of the governor and company of the bay in New England,* N. B. Shurleff (ed.) (Boston: W. White, 1853) 2.92–93; P. M. Spurlin, *Montesquieu in America* (1760–1801) (Baton Rouge, LA: Louisiana State University, 1940) 30, 151; Strehle, *The Egalitarian Spirit of Christianity,* 98–103, 150–52.
11. Montesquieu, *De l'Esprit des Lois,* I, I, 3 (10, 11); II, v, 11 (63); viii, 19–20 (126); III, xiv, 1 (239); xix, 14 (326); 21 (331–32); Linda S. Frey and Marsha L. Frey, *The French Revolution* (Westport, CT, and London: Greenwood Press, 2004) 18; Paul R. Hanson, *Contesting the French Revolution* (Malden, MA, and Oxford: Wiley-Blackwell, 2009) 14.
12. Daniel Brewer, *The Enlightenment Past: Reconstructing Eighteenth-Century French Thought* (Cambridge: Cambridge University Press, 2008) 44–45; Peter Gay, "The Social History of Ideas: Ernst Cassirer and After," in *The Critical Spirit: Essays in Honor of Herbert Marcuse,* Kurth H. Wolff and Barrington Moore (ed.) (Boston: Beacon Press, 1967) 117–19; *The Enlightenment,* 1.25, 67, 462–63, 477. Voltaire's *Le Siècle de Louis XIV* provides some criticism of the monarch for his love of war, inhumane campaigns, and intolerance in revoking the Edict of Nantes. *The Enlightenment,* 2.472.
13. Gay, *The Enlightenment,* 2.483–84.
14. Diderot, *Oeuvres Complètes* (Nendeln, Liechtenstein: Kraus reprint LTD., 1966) 13.392–94; Dale K. Van Kley, *The Religious Origins of the French Revolution: From Calvin to the Civil Constitution, 1560–1791*(New Haven, CT, and London: Yale University Press, 1996) 191, 245, 246. Diderot does not proceed in the extreme direction of Locke and the Puritans, who advocate revolution. He calls the people to remove their obedience from an oppressive royal family but endure injustice without resorting to violent opposition.
15. Ibid., 14.299–301.

16. Gliozzo, "The Philosophes and Religion," 277; Kley, *Religious Origins of the French Revolution*, 294–95; Hanson, *Contesting the French Revolution*, 14–15; Gay, *The Enlightenment*, 1.7, 25.
17. Jean-Jacques Rousseau, *The Social Contract*, Maurice Cranston (trans.) (New York: Penguin Books, 2006) 2.
18. Ibid., 8, 20–21.
19. Ibid., 7, 15, 19.
20. Rousseau often speaks of rights in nature, but no specific meaning is attached to it beyond a liberty to do whatever. Elsewhere he can speak of the natural law and the need to protect life, liberty, and property through the government, but this asseveration is immediately undermined by other statements and the overall weight of his view of government. Rousseau, "Economie ou Oeconomie," *Encyclopédie de Diderot et d'Alembert*, E, 14.49–50. Jacques Derrida finds his view of nature and society filled with hopeless contradictions, providing Derrida with a classic example of his method of deconstruction, which shows the tensions within authors and the problematic nature of interpretation. *Of Grammatology*, Gayatri Chakravorty Spivak (trans.) (Baltimore and London: The Johns Hopkins University Press, 1976) 145, 239, 255. In *Émile*, Rousseau thinks of society in a negative way as deforming human beings and finds all truth and reality in nature. "Everything is good as it comes from the hand of the Author of Nature; but everything degenerates in the hands of man." *Émile*, William H. Payne (Amherst, NY: Prometheus Books, 2003) xix, 1, 10–11, 212, 253–54. He thinks it is best to start with the senses, not books or a priori dogmas, before listening to the prejudices of others. "Nature never deceives us." Ibid., 90, 127, 185–86. He thinks Émile is designed to live in society since other human beings are needed in exchanging services, but instruction in society and its moral code must come later in Émile's maturation and education. Ibid., 96, 165, 173–74, 240. Of course, this individual maturation is similar to what Rousseau envisions for the entire human race in his *Social Contract* as it develops moral relations. Elsewhere, in *Discourse on the Origin of Inequality*, he thinks humans were meant to remain in nature. *Origin of Inequality*, in *Great Books of the Western World*, Robert Maynard Hutchins (ed.) (Chicago: Encyclopaedia Britannica, Inc., 1978) 351, 352.
21. Rousseau, *Social Contract*, 26, 34–35, 41.
22. Rousseau, "Economie ou Oeconomie," E, 14.52.
23. Ibid., 54.
24. Ibid., 50. Rousseau provides some tension with this absolute belief in democracy in other sections of his work, providing another good case in point for deconstructionism. Elsewhere, he cites Montesquieu and argues that one size and type of government does not fit all circumstances. For example, democracy is better suited for poor countries, and monarchy for rich; democracy is better suited for small states, and monarchy for large. *Social Contract*, 51ff., 74–77, 91–93.
25. Rousseau, *Social Contract*, 31.
26. Ibid., 127.
27. Christopher Hill, *The English Bible and the Seventeenth-Century Revolution* (London: Allen Lane/Penguin Press, 1993) 7, 26–31.
28. Diderot, *Complètes Oeuvres*, 16.276–77; Gay, *The Enlightenment*, 1.231, 523–26. Only the superstitious multitude need to fall back on religion as a crutch.

29. Arnold Ages, "The Dark Side of the French Enlightenment," 139; D'Alembert, "Discours Preliminaire des Editeurs," in *Encyclopédie,* 13.xxvi; Brewer, *The Enlightenment Past,* 36–37. Descartes represents the burgeoning French Spirit that is challenging the *Ancien Régime.* Before Descartes, Peter Ramus (1515–1572) challenged the hierarchical structure of his day and especially the authority of Aristotle by developing a new system of logic. Montaigne (1533–1592) also rejected conformity to the teachings of Aristotle, along with dogmatism and authoritarianism in general, believing that one should learn from a wide variety of sources. *Essais* (Paris: Garnier Frères, 1962) 1.158–67 (I, xxvi—"De l'instruction des enfans"); Charles Waddington, *Ramus: sa vie, ses écrits et ses opinions* (Paris: Libraire de Ch. Meyrueis et ce, 1855; "Bèze à Pierre Ramus" (Dec. 1579), in *Correspondance de Théodore Bèze,* recueillie par Hippolyte Aubert (Genève: Droz, 1983) 11.295 (810); James Veazie Slalnik, "Ramus and Reform: The End of the Renaissance and the Origins of the Old Regime" (PhD diss., University of Virginia, 1990) 8, 38–39, 71, 126ff., 134, 145, 148; Frank Pierrepont Graves, *Peter Ramus and the Educational Reformation of the Sixteenth Century* (New York: The Macmillan Co., 1912) 24–26, 30.
30. Henri Coulet, "Réflexions sur les *Meditationes* de Lau," in *La Matérialisme du XVIII*[e] *Siècle et la literature Clandestine,* Olivier Bloch (ed.) (Paris: Libraire Philosophique J. Vrin, 1982) 37; Rolf Geissler, "Boureau-Deslandes lecteur de manuscits clandestine," in *Matérialisme du XVII*[e] *Siècle,* 233; Jean-Louis Lecercle, "Le matérialsime du sage, selon Rousseau," in *Être Matéterialiste à l'Âge des Lumières. Hommage offert à Roland Desné,* Béatrice Fink et Gerhardt Stenger (ed.) (Paris: Presses Universitaires de France, 1999) 177–78; Brewer, *The Enlightenment Past,* 36–37, 51; Strauss, *Voltaire,* 228–29; OCV 36.44. Gay stresses the empiricism, eclecticism, and skepticism of the philosophes, but recent studies point to their Cartesian moments of rationalism as much more pervasive than Gay suggested in his monumental work. Diderot, *Oeuvres Complètes,* 16.274; Kley, *The Religious Origin of the French Revolution,* 236. Cf. Gay, *The Enlightenment,* 1.141–45, 160–61, 189–91. The problem with the philosophes is that they are dogmatic about their skepticism; much in contrast to Augustine, who felt that he had treated his uncertainties as if they were certainties before finding faith. *Confessionum* (PL 32), VI, iv, 5.
31. D'Alembert, "Discours Preliminaire des Editeurs," 13.xxiv–xxviii; OCV 7.335; 22.401–2; Hans M. Wolff, *Die Weltanschauung der deutschen Aufklärung in geschichtlicher Entwicklung* (Bern und München: Franke Verlag, 1963) 179 [This work contains Friedrich von Hagedorn's poem about science being supported by the wealthiest citizens of England.]; Gay, *The Enlightenment,* 2.18, 25, 128ff., 139, 145ff.
32. They inculcate progress in their works. OCV 7.213; Condoret, *Esquisse d'un Tableau Historique des Progrès de l'Esprit Humain* (Paris: Editions Sociales, 1966) passim [253ff.]; Gay, *The Enlightenment,* 2.98–99, 120.
33. See Strehle, *The Egalitarian Spirit of Christianity,* 213–28. Gay is right to see the philosophes enamored with the idea of scientific and social progress but wrong in exaggerating their importance in developing this concept. Cf. *The Enlightenment,* 2.9, 10, 127–28.
34. Strauss, *Voltaire,* 139; Kley, *The Religious Origins of the French Revolution,* 235.

35. Gay, *The Enlightenment*, 1.345, 400–401, 405–6, 454. Hume recognizes the anti-Christian nature of France and expresses concern about the propensity of the Revolution to destroy everything old, even what is valuable. He finds Holbach's atheism much too dogmatic.
36. David Hume, *An Enquiry Concerning Human Understanding* (Chicago: Henry Regnery Co., 1965) 135ff.; *Dialogues Concerning Natural Religion and the Natural History* (Oxford and New York: Oxford University Press, 1993) 130. Those who believe in God must rest this conviction on faith, not reason.
37. Hume, *Dialogues*, 36–37, 46, 50, 53, 78–79, 84; *Enquiry*, 24ff., 64, 147ff.
38. Immanuel Kant, *The Critique of Pure Reason*, in Great Books of the Western World, R. M. Hutchins (ed.) (Chicago: Encyclopaedia Britannica, Inc., 1978) 9, 49–50, 89, 112–13, 117, 119–20, 128, 133, 178, 192, 200, 233.
39. *Age of Reason*, in *The Complete Religious and Theological Works of Thomas Paine* (New York: Peter Eckler, 1954) 1.43. Paine discounts the Mosaic authorship of the Pentateuch, following the work of Baruch Spinoza (*Theologico-Political Treatise*, 1670) and Richard Simon (*Histoire Critique de Vieux Testament*, 1678). He recognizes elements of the later JEDP theory (e.g., maintaining that Gen 1:1–2:3 and 2:4ff. were written by two different authors and thinking the laws of Moses were composed during the time of Josiah's Revival in the seventh-century BCE by some scribe or priest). Ibid., 1.79ff., 274ff., 310. Jesus was a good moral teacher, but was also misconceived by his followers and deified in its later and contradictory accounts of him in the Gospels. Ibid., 1.9–12, 14ff., 23–26.
40. Ibid., 1.6, 8, 18, 19, 29–31, 103–4, 176, 185, 355–56, 378, 398.
41. Ibid., 1.33–34, 49, 159, 183, 302–3, 308, 415–16.
42. Paul Tillich, *Systematic Theology* (Chicago: The University of Chicago Press, 1975) 1.4, 6, 205–6, 235–36, 238–39; Gay, *The Enlightenment*, 2.143–45, 150, 160. Descartes's system also helped withdraw God from the machine and lead to complete materialism. Laplace follows the mechanistic understanding of Descartes/Galileo/Newton and tells Napoleon that his physics no longer needs God to explain the universe. For Tillich, this way of thinking is wrongheaded. God cannot be made an object alongside of other beings. God is being itself, truth itself, goodness itself, and so on. This is why one cannot argue for the existence of God.
43. Thomas Kselman, "State and religion," in *Revolutionary France 1788–1800* (Oxford: Oxford University Press, 2002) 67; Gay, *The Enlightenment*, 1.397; Gliozzo, "The Philosophes and Religion," 279. Prominent atheists included Jean Meslier, Claude Helvétius, Paul d'Holbach, Julien la Mettrie, and Denis Diderot. Diderot was the most famous. He was particularly famous for his encyclopedia, which he began in 1746. He was a strident critic of Christianity and was imprisoned in the Chateau Vincennes for unorthodox and subversive opinions on religion and morality. P. France, *Diderot* (Oxford and New York: Oxford University Press, 1983) 7–9, 35–36.
44. Yvon, "Athées," A, 13.230–31; Diderot, *Oeuvres Complètes*, 15.253–54. Science was proceeding toward moral neutrality. Gay, *The Enlightenment*, 2.163.
45. Kingsley Martin, *The Rise of French Liberal Thought* (New York: New York University Press, 1954) 177–91; Gliozzo, "The Philosophes and Religion,"

283; Gay, *The Enlightenment*, 2.459. E.g., Helvétius, *De l'Esprit*, Guy Besse (intro. et notes) (Paris: Éditions Sociales, 1959) 115–16.

46. Rousseau, *Social Contract*, 159–61; *Oeuvres Complètes de Robespierre* (Paris: E. Leroux, 1910–) 10.453; Gliozzo, "The Philosophes and Religion," 278. Thus, Voltaire's famous quip, "If God did not exist, it would be necessary to invent him."
47. Gay, *The Enlightenment*, 1.38, 358–62. Christian intellectuals were much more hospitable to the philosophes but received animosity in return for the most part, even if the philosophes recognized that many of their intellectual heroes, including Newton and Locke, were Christians. Gay, *The Enlightenment*, 1.316–21.
48. Denis Diderot, *Correspondance*, Georges Roth (ed.) (Paris: Les Éditions de Minuit, 1958) 4.55.
49. Ibid., 5.117–18; 8.234–35; Gay, *The Enlightenment*, 1.371–73. In 1762, Diderot greets Voltaire as a "dear Anti-Christ (*cher Antéchrist*)." *Correspondance*, 8.178. Diderot also complains about the enormous cost of churches and their ornate rituals, believing the money should go to feeding the poor. Diderot, *Ouevres Complètes*, 16.184–86.
50. Gliozzo, "The Philosophes and Religion," 279–80. See note 52.
51. Holbach, *Christianity Unveiled*, W. M. Johnson (trans.) (New York: Gordon Press, 1974) 1–4, 21, 57, 60, 91, 94.
52. Ibid., 3–19, 55, 63, 70–75, 82, 94, 98. Diderot [d'Holbach], *Oeuvres Complètes*, 16.406–9. Of course, the abuse of priestly power is a major theme of the philosophes. See Voltaire's *Sìecle de Louis XIV*, chap. 37, and Jaucourt's "Constitution Unigenitus," in *Encyclopédie*, where Father Tellier, the king's confessor, is blamed for the shortcomings of Louis XIV.
53. Ibid., 12–15, 24–25, 31, 34, 37, 43–44, 51–52, 58–59, 72. Christians also delude themselves by finding the Messiah in the most vague OT passages and feigning a fulfillment in Jesus of Nazareth through allegorical interpretation. Following the Reformation, the English Deists, French philosophes, and German liberals accented literal interpretation as the only valid approach to scripture.
54. Voltaire, "Histoire," in *Encyclopédie*, H, 15.34.
55. Diderot, *Correspondance*, 3.156. Diderot writes to Voltaire on November 28, 1760, and says, "Other historians recount for us some facts so we can comprehend those facts. You do it to excite in the depth of our souls a strong indignation against lying, ignorance, hypocrisy, superstition, fanaticism, tyranny." *Correspondance*, 3.275. Rousseau writes to Monsieur Du Parc on June 25, 1761, saying that "the truth that I love is not so much metaphysical as moral." *Correspondance complètes de Jean Jacques Rousseau*, R. A. Leigh (ed.) (Genevè: Institut et Musée Voltaire, 1969) 9.28.
56. Condorcet, *Esquisse*, 120–21; OCV 11.13–14, 147; Deleyre, "Fanatisme," in *Encyclopédie*, F, 15.20– 21; Gay, *The Enlightenment*, 1. 31–33, 166–69. Celsus is one of the most infamous opponents of Christianity in antiquity and disparaged Christianity for a number of matters, including its lack of patriotism toward the Roman Empire and hostility toward other religious forms of worship. Celsus, *On True Doctrine: A Discourse against the Christians*, R. Joseph Hoffmann (New York and Oxford: Oxford University Press, 1987) 56, 118–19, 124, 126.

57. Diderot, *Oeuvres Complètes*, 15.63–64; Gay, *The Enlightenment*, 72–73, 80.
58. Gay, *The Enlightenment*, 1.39–58, 95, 98–109.
59. Ibid., 1.216; 2.388. Of course, Edward Gibbon's *History of the Decline and Fall of the Roman Empire* (1776–1788) is the most famous account from this perspective. Protestants had an unwitting hand in creating this secular view of history and image of the church. John Foxe's *Actes and Monumentes* (1563) is one of the first great works among Protestants to speak of the church as almost losing its candlestick in the Middle Ages and deserving complete annihilation except for a small remnant of true believers. The Anabaptist's *Martyrs Mirror* (1562) is also a good example of this type of Protestant perspective on the Middle Ages. Foxe, *The First Volumes of Ecclesiastical history containing the Actes and Monumentes* (London: Iohn Daye, 1570) "A Protestation to the Whole Church of England"; *The Bloody Theater or Martyrs Mirror of the Defenseless Christians . . . From the Time of Christ to the Year A. D. 1660*, Thielman J. van Braght (compiler) and Joseph F. Sohm (trans.) (Scottsdale, PA: Herald Press, 1950) 12–13, 17, 19, 24, 63, 153, 202, 208, 271, 301, 334.
60. D'Alembert, "Discours Preliminaire des Editeurs," 13.xxii–xxiii; Gay, *The Enlightenment*, 1.36–37, 207–9, 261–63, 388. They saw the Italian Renaissance as the birth of modern science.
61. According to Herbert Solow and Peter Gay, Voltaire (and the philosophes) only "struck at the church to strike at the Christians." Gay, *The Party of Humanity* (New York: W. W. Norton & Company, Inc., 1963) 103–8; *Voltaire's Politics*, 353–54; Solow, "Voltaire and Some Jews," *Menorah Journal* 13 (1927) 189, 197; Hertzberg, *The French Enlightenment and the Jews*, 283–84.
62. See chap. 4; Hertzberg, *The French Enlightenment and the Jews*, 8, 179–87, 279. Mendelssohn rejected the idea that Jews should obtain equality at the cost of their religion.
63. Ibid., 10, 286–90; Thiéry, *Dissertation sur cette Question: Est-Il des moyens de rendre les Juifs plus heureux et plus utiles en France?* [1788] (Paris: EDHIS, 1968) 49. Of course, Voltaire remains the major figure in promulgating modern anti-Semitism.
64. Diderot, *Oeuvres Complètes*, 15.322, 328, 333–37. Included with the Jewish hate are the Egyptians, Samaritans, and Sadducees.
65. Ibid., 356–64, 370, 372, 381, 386ff.; Hertzberg, *The French Enlightenment and the Jews*, 311.
66. Ibid., 378.
67. Hertzberg, *The French Enlightenment and the Jews*, 308.
68. Jean Baptiste de Mirabaud, *Opinions des Anciens sur des Juifs* (Londres, 1769) 4–5, 16–17.
69. Ibid., 6–14, 36, 51–52, 55, 58, 93–100, 103, 126–27. The Jews remain obstinate in this expectation. Their obstinacy has led to considerable gullibility throughout their history in accepting any messianic imposter with "unbelievable stupidity" (48–49). This messianic expectation was not found in OT times and only grew after 70 CE, despite the NT's false and anachronistic report about an earlier expectation (93ff.). It was only later on that the Jews created messianic promises out of obscure words in the prophets of old (38). Christians also developed this ridiculous method of interpretation, going

against the plain sense of OT texts and forcing a bizarre meaning into these "prophesies" (107, 110–12, 124).

70. Ibid., 11–14, 20; Hertzberg, *The French Enlightenment and the Jews,* 308–9.
71. Of course, it is fair game to deconstruct the author of this present study as hating Holbach for hating the hatred of the Jews, but hopefully the bias is not so overpowering as to lose all sense of decency and balance. At least the study admits bias and has no pretense of creating an overall portrait of the Holbach and philosophes out of its dark accents, unlike Holbach's treatment of the Jews.
72. Paul H. T. d'Holbach, *L'Esprit du Judaïsme ou Examen Raisonné de la Loi de Moyse, et de son Influence sur la Religion Chrétienne* [1770] (London: Elibron Classics, 2005) i. Hereafter cited as PHLJ.
73. Hertzberg, *The French Enlightenment and the Jews,* 309.
74. PHLJ v–ix, 1, 4, 13, 35, 150–54. Of course, he claims to know what is worthy of God and true morality.
75. PHLJ ii–iii, xiv, 25, 31–34, 43–48, 167, 196–97.
76. PHLJ iii–v, xiii–xiv, 76–79, 84, 95–97, 100–101, 115, 188. He follows much of Annet's account of David's life. He speaks of Samuel placing David on the throne to serve the priesthood and spends time deprecating the character of David as a "rebel, thief, assassin, [and] monster of avarice and cruelty."
77. PHLJ xxi–xxii, 55, 75, 96–97, 154–55, 169–74, 177, 180–82, 186–87, 190, 193, 201.
78. This is the infamous mistake J. S. Mill makes in his book on *Utilitarianism,* equating what is desired with what is desirable. *Utilitarianism,* in *Great Books of the Western World,* Robert Maynard Hutchins (ed.) (Chicago: Encyclopaedia Britannica, Inc., 1978) 446–48, 461. According to Einstein, "science can only ascertain what *is,* but not what *should be.*" Morals, values, and goals come outside the realm of science and belong to the domain of religious revelation. *Ideas and Opinions* (New York: The Modern Library, 1994) 33, 45, 48, 54.
79. Ernst Troeltsch, *The Absoluteness of Christianity and the History of Religions,* David Reid (trans.) (Richmond: John Knox Press, 1971) 29, 45–47.
80. The phrase "human emancipation" comes from Marx. "On the Jewish Question," in *Collected Works* (New York: International Publishers, 1975) 3.52–55, 160, 174 [*Werke* (Berlin: Dietz, 1964) 1.352–56, 361, 377].

3

The French Revolution

Etatism and the General Will

During the French Revolution, the people recast their identity, uniting together into a large secular fraternity and redefining their basic loyalty in terms of citizenship and its responsibilities within a state.[1] The leaders of the Revolution followed the work of Rousseau upon the social reconstruction of individuals and thought of the general will of the people, within this human and social contract, as representing the voice of God and symbolizing its massive and irresistible force through the pagan demigod Hercules.[2] The most celebrated motto of the Revolution spoke of *fraternité* as the essential feature of the new humanity, equating this man-made confederation of citizens with the Lockean emphasis upon God-given order of creation, which spoke of the *liberté* and *egalité* of all individuals in nature.[3] The French people were now destined to find their fundamental identity within the collective terms of the state.

A good example of this new identity is the *Catéchisme du Citoyen* (1775), which was written by Guillaume-Joseph Saige during the time of Chancellor Maupeou's anti-parliamentary policies in the 1770s. The work was immediately condemned by responsible authorities in Bordeaux and then Paris, but it reappeared in several editions just before the Revolution, exerting a significant influence upon the upcoming events as the most popular and radical expression of the prerevolutionary pamphlets in challenging the *Ancien Régime*.[4] Saige incites the radicals of the day by defending the ultimate legislative authority of the people against the powers that be, pointing to the historical rights of Francs from time immemorial, and complaining about the nobles, barons, and kings who usurped this prerogative in the past.[5] He says the social contract forges society into a unified body only through the free consent of the governed and serves to meet their needs as the beginning, middle, and end of government. The contract comes from the people and finds its sole purpose in serving the common good or interests of the nation as a whole, operating in a utilitarian manner to meet this general goal without consideration of any external authority. The contract rejects the divine rights of a privileged hierarchy and even minimizes the role of any antecedent authority coming from the will of God in nature, as if laying the foundation of government in a Lockean sense. Saige might display some inconsistency at this point and pay some lip service to the tradition of natural rights, but he really emasculates much of its force through his overall understanding and continues to assign ultimate authority to the general will of the people as the true essence of the body politic—much the same as Rousseau, who serves as his mentor in this and other matters of government. The law remains an expression of the people's will that is designed and calculated to meet their needs apart from any preexisting standard, including any divine standard implanted in nature or discovered within the human psyche. The voice of the people determines the voice of God through a utilitarian calculus, which views everything as an instrumental means of fulfilling their desires. The Third Estate serves the general will of the people as representing the vast majority of the nation in developing the laws of the land, and the king and senate merely execute the laws as instruments of the legislative branch. All magistrates and nobility receive their position from the will of the people and serve the nation at their behest, which is "able to create, destroy, and change all magistrates of the states, modify or change the constitution" in accordance with its good pleasure. The people even have authority over their own Catholic Church—at least in matters of "exterior polity" or "civil order," including the "administration of the sacraments" and "external constitution of the hierarchy," as well as "the goods that the [clergy] possess in society and the rank that they occupy in it." Saige follows the precedent set by the Conciliar Movement and Assembly of 1684 in creating a French Church, submitting papal decisions and appointments to the will of the people, and rejecting the temporal powers of the church over the state.[6] He mentions the term *rights* several times within the discussion, but he seems to have little interest in protecting this space in his overall system and prefers to submit everything to the collective will of the people for its civil use, including the rights of the church, the many associations throughout the land, and the individual members of society.

Saige's *Catéchisme* is just a short step away from the most famous and influential pamphlet of the Revolution, written by Abbé Sieyès at the end of 1788 and published in January of the following year under the title *Qu'est-ce que le Tiers Etats?* (or What is the Third Estate?). The work promulgated many of the same themes as Saige's pamphlet but developed the egalitarianism and nationalism of the Revolution in starker terms, demanding the end of the old system of hierarchical privileges and accenting the absolute sovereignty of the central government in representing the general will of the people. Sieyès helped forward much of this agenda through his own personal involvement as a deputy from Paris to the Estates-General, and he proved instrumental in the transformation of the Third Estate into the National Assembly in June of 1789, even if his specific schemes often failed to garner the same kind of support from his colleagues throughout the rest of his career.[7]

Sieyès work finds its prophetic calling within the modern spirit of egalitarianism and foments with righteous indignation against the order of privileges in French society. He claims the nobility has no special right to its present position in society because of certain events in the past, where it bludgeoned and subjected the people to slavery against their will. He hopes "The Third Estate will become noble again by becoming a conqueror in its own turn," ending the system of privileges forever and basing the future exaltation of individuals on merit, rather than laws that create special advantages for certain citizens. Sieyès argues that the nobles who rule in the Estates-General have no sense of justice and no ability to empathize with the underprivileged or represent them in any meaningful way. They speak the vocabulary of feudalism and denigrate those who work for a living, preferring to consume what others produce with their hands and lead a corpulent and frivolous lifestyle with no substantial benefit to society, burdening and weakening the nation as a whole. They only use their positions to enhance their own worthless privileges by creating more and better positions for those who govern, and they block any attempt at reforming the system, refusing to share any real power with the people or to even pay their fair share of the tax burden that supports them. This old system must be abolished in toto, along with the First and Second Estate that support it.[8]

In this excoriating analysis, Sieyès spares no one and finds nothing redeemable within the *Ancien Régime*, including his own Catholic Church. He displays no special empathy for the First Estate of clergy and their place in society, and he proceeds to demonize them just like the rest of the nobility in the eyes of the French as responsible for the old order of hierarchical privilege, helping to set off the wave of anti-clericalism to come. Sieyès is clearly far removed from the vows of his ordination in 1773 and seems like an irreligious man in the work, calling himself a philosophe in the text and looking for the triumph of reason in society.[9] Even the texture of his writing displays this secular agenda, with constant references to the Enlightenment and the use of its vocabulary, the neglect of any biblical passages or references to God, and the discussion of moral issues in purely secular terms. The church seems to have no place in his thought or his future conception of society.

Sieyès proceeds to make the Third Estate represent the entire nation and determine its law.

> The Third Estate then contains everything that pertains to the nation while nobody outside the Third Estate can be considered as part of the nation. What is the Third Estate? *Everything.*[10]

The Third Estate creates a new identity and subsistence for the people, wielding them together into a single nation. It has no specific interest in the life of the individual but subsumes all of the individual parts and associations in France into a "single whole, uniformly submitted . . . to the same legislation and a common administration,"[11] making "one nation, one representation, one common will." Of course, he uses Rousseau's concept of the general will throughout the work to express the "common concern" of all, and he identifies it in a bold and direct manner with the decisions of the National Assembly and the majority opinion of the public, which is described as the "one force alone that can be of use to a free nation." He says, "The nation is prior to everything. It is the source of everything. Its will is always legal; indeed it is the law itself. . . . The national will . . . never needs anything but its own existence to be legal. It is the source of all legality." Sieyès seems to mitigate the absolute force of these statements when referring to natural law within the discussion, but he equivocates like most of the philosophes and revolutionaries over the precise meaning and significance of this law, preferring to emphasize the will of the people as the real source of all governmental and legislative acts. The only inalienable right subsists within the power of the people to alter the government and its laws—a right he emphasizes and repeats with consistent clarity and conviction.[12]

Sieyès's dream of a National Assembly came to fruition on June 17, 1789, basically due to the crippling poverty in the land and the complete financial collapse of the former government. The Bourbon dynasty had incurred an enormous debt due to its extensive global policies and lackluster performance in a series of foreign conflicts—the War of Austrian Succession (1740–48), the Seven Years' War (1756–63), and the American War of Independence (1778–83). In the process, the regime lost much of its credibility, and the country became a second-rate power on the world stage—at least in comparison to the success of the British Empire, its most bitter rival. The regime had to settle for small victories, like helping America gain independence from Britain, but this act of revenge returned little for the effort and only drove the country into further financial ruin.[13] Louis XV and XVI tried to finance the debt by raising revenue, hoping to make the nobility pay their fair share of the tax burden, but the Parlement of Paris blocked any attempt at major reform, creating resentment among the people for the government in general.[14] According to the tax system, the clergy and most of the nobility were exempt from paying the *taille*, which served as the primary source of revenue and was paid by the peasants as a direct form of taxation. The church and its clergy owned approximately 10 percent of the land and just made freewill offerings to the king at their discretion as a "gift." The nobles owned over a fifth of the land and paid some additional taxes, like the *capitation* and *vingtièmes*, but they often escaped these and other obligations by invoking certain privileges.[15] According to Annie Moulin, the peasants were saddled with much of the financial burden, paying anywhere from a fourth to a half of their household income when all the taxes and fees were added together, such as the direct tax, the indirect tax on commodities like salt (the *gabelle*), the ecclesiastical tithes, and the seignorial taxes and dues, which the peasants paid to their feudal lords.[16] This burden only escalated when a series of natural disasters brought the bad harvests of the late 1780s, and the price of basic commodities like bread skyrocketed, leaving approximately 30 percent of the peasants on the edge of starvation and producing deep-seated resentment among the multitudes for the policies of the government and the opulent lifestyle of those in charge.[17] The Parlement of Paris responded by calling together the Estates-General (or all three estates of the people), which had not met in 175 years, hoping to settle the problems among the clergy, the nobles, and the remaining population.[18] After the initial meeting on May 5, 1789, the Third Estate eventually assumed power, swearing a month and a half later to write a new constitution and act as a National Assembly representing the entire nation.[19]

Much of its ascension was the direct result of the continuous threat and implementation of violence by unruly mobs and their rabble-rousers. In the most dramatic moment of the Revolution, a mass of some eighty thousand protesters stormed the Bastille on July 14, 1789, seizing guns and canons, fearing the king was preparing a military coup d'état against the National Assembly, asserting once again the sovereignty of the people and legitimizing the use of revolutionary violence.[20] In October of the same year, the people grew even more restless when Louis XVI refused to sign the Declaration of Rights and abolish seigniorial dues; nearly seven thousand women stormed the palace in Versailles, forcing the king to flee the grounds and sign the legislation in Paris.[21] The press picked up the mood of the day and began to foment violent threats against the king, the nobles, and the clergy. The journalist Jean-Paul Marat helped radicalize the anger to include those who sympathized with the *Ancien Régime* and its privileged estates, stirring up much of the furor against counter-revolutionaries and even moderates like the Girondins, promoting an internal war against "enemies of the people," and leading the country into a civil war, where no distinct lines were drawn to determine the sides.[22] In one brutal episode, during the first week of September 1792, Marat's sanguinary outbursts prompted the massacre of over 1,200 inmates in several Paris prisons, including some two hundred priests and a number of political prisoners.[23] The violence of the civil war only seemed to beget more violence, finally escalating into the Reign of Terror the following summer—a predictable outcome of the revolutionary tactics, which had no means of stopping the bloodshed or determining the enemy. The violence was regrettable for all sides of the conflict, but it was also a necessary component of the republican factions, who had to purge royalist elements if they wanted to succeed and impose this new form of government on the people. (Unlike Puritan England, no reformation had purified the church of hierarchical Romish practices, preparing the people and the culture through a change in ecclesiastical polity to accept egalitarian and democratic reform within the state. The revolutionaries had few willing subjects and ended up creating a civil Leviathan of coercive forces and agents interfering in the lives of the people in order to develop purity of thought[24]—much like the infamous case of Lenin and Stalin in the former Soviet Union, who used the French Revolution as their fundamental paradigm in conducting a continuous civil war against their own people. The Jacobins and Bolsheviks were impatient revolutionaries, unwilling to wait for the culture to develop at its own pace and more than willing to use violence and to force the issue, bringing much suffering and misery upon their own people.)

One might think that the Declaration of the Rights of Man and of the Citizen (August 26, 1789) would prevent the government from committing these atrocities. The articles speak of many good things associated with modern values: the "free communication of ideas and opinions" as "one of the most precious rights of man" (a.11), the equality of all human beings and the desire to create an equitable distribution of taxes (a.1, 13), and the "natural and inalienable rights" of all, including property rights (a.2, 17).[25] However, these rights are qualified or counterbalanced by other statements that emphasize the general will of the people as the source of law (a.6), the absolute sovereign authority of the nation (a.10), and the proscription of opinions that "disturb the public order established by law" (a.10)[26]—all providing a possible means of undermining the rights through the power of government. In fact, the rights lack any absolute force or serious metaphysical justification. The Declaration contains no reference to God and leaves the origin of these rights inexplicable, making one wonder whether their existence is a mere phantasm or rhetorical flourish lacking any substantial reality whatsoever. Duquesnoy, a delegate of the Third Estate, expressed some displeasure about the absence of religious language within the Declaration to undergird its moral statements,[27] and one must wonder whether the rights have a sufficient ontological basis to withstand the legislative power of the people or the discretionary power of the executive branch to assign or take away what is granted in accordance with its own good pleasure.

As it turns out, this concern is more than justified in light of the subsequent history of the Revolution. The noble sentiments of the Declaration were undermined in the course of events by zealous left-wing advocates of Rousseau's general will, who used the utilitarian tactics of the philosophes to impose this will and justify the most egregious violations of basic human rights—all in the name of the people. This tendency dominated the Revolution with its zeal to impose egalitarian and democratic principles at the expense of all else, reaching its zenith when the Jacobins dominated the National Assembly and ushered in the Reign of Terror.

Robespierre and the Jacobins

The Jacobin Club began as a gathering of certain deputies, who represented Breton in the Estates-General and developed radical revolutionary ideas in response to the nobles and clergy of Brittany and their negative reaction to the convention. When the National Assembly moved from Versailles to Paris, the club set up headquarters in a Dominican monastery and absorbed the nickname of the specific order that managed the building and first met on *Rue St. Jacques* (or Jacob in Hebrew).[28] Within the National Assembly, their members were perched high on elevated benches, earning these members the additional nickname of Montagnards (or Mountains) and beginning the Western tradition of referring to their overall political ideology as left-wing. The numbers of the club saw a meteoric rise at this time, starting with a thousand members of the "mother society" in Paris and numbering over nine hundred chapters throughout the country by the summer of 1791.[29] Their influence permeated the society with the spirit of revolution and incited Parisian mobs into massive demonstrations and violent outbursts of rage against the *Ancien Régime*, helping to sweep the Jacobins into power and forcing the convention to accept their reign of terror, wittingly or unwittingly.[30] The Jacobins continued their idealistic rhetoric while in power and even passed a constitution in 1793, filled with the typical staple of modern rights and a number of left-wing promises about universal suffrage, government aid to the poor, and public education for all citizens, but they also found it necessary to suspend their own constitution until the revolutionary government completed its mission of leveling society and destroying all counter-revolutionaries, which now included moderates like the Girondins, who favored gradual reform.[31]

The ideological and rhetorical leader of the Jacobins was Maximilien Robespierre. The Jacobins were stoked by his fiery speeches, and elected him the president of the Parisian Club in March of 1790, transforming a marginal member of the Assembly into a national figure.[32] In many ways, Robespierre served as the perfect choice for the Jacobins, embodying all the virtues and vices of the Enlightenment and inflaming the spirit of an era with considerable conviction and prejudice, like most left-wing ideologues. Robespierre served the era by extolling the "Encyclopedists" in his speeches as providing the "preface" of the Revolution with their renunciation of the church and support of human rights, even if he also chided them for cowardice in continuing to serve within the *Ancien Régime*, like the current men of letters, and refusing to make sacrifices on behalf of the people. He served the era by giving homage to Voltaire as the national demigod, extolling him for providing the fundamental impetus toward the coming Revolution and "distinguishing himself through his career of letters and philosophy, by the elevation of his soul and majesty of his character, . . . as worthy of the office of preceptor of the human race."[33] Of course, he added some other important names to the Panthéon and particularly followed Rousseau as the greatest political pundit of the Enlightenment, commending his virtuous example in serving the "good of his fellow-men," in spite of the many criticisms, and turning his doctrine of the general will into the centerpiece of all revolutionary ideology, without appreciating the tensions in Rousseau's overall work.[34] In all this, Robespierre served as the perfect demagogue of the era by appealing to the prejudices of the Jacobins and the growing constituency of citizens, who were more than willing to follow the prevailing mood of the enlightened culture—all caught up in a certain space and time and creating a caricature of the latest ideas.

Once in power Robespierre proved willing to implement his ideals and use whatever means necessary to establish the new era and destroy the old. On October 10, 1793, the National Assembly suspended the implementation of the Jacobin Constitution, declaring the government as "provisional" and "revolutionary until peace," and so sanctioned a number of extraordinary measures to ensure ultimate victory.[35] Robespierre justified these measures as necessary to accomplishing the objective, using the current utilitarian approach to ethical thinking as the basic rationalization.

> The function of government is to direct the moral and physical force of the nation toward the goal for which it was established.
>
> The goal of constitutional government is to maintain the Republic; the object of revolutionary government to establish it. . . .
>
> The revolutionary government needs an extraordinary activity precisely because it is at war. It is subject to less uniform and less rigorous rules because the circumstances in which it finds itself are tempestuous and shifting, and especially because it is forced to constantly deploy new and rapid resources to meet new and pressing dangers.
>
> Constitutional government is preoccupied with civil liberty; and revolutionary government public liberty. Under a constitutional regime, it suffices to protect individuals against the abuse of public power; under a revolutionary regime, the public power is obliged to defend itself against all factions which attack it.[36]

He says the revolutionary government or "despotism of liberty" has no constant laws and must act with swift and immediate brutality toward the enemies among us, mandating death as the one penalty for those who withstand the future welfare of the nation. This "prompt, severe, and inflexible . . . terror" is a positive form of virtue and justice in these extraordinary times, absolutely essential in accomplishing the goals of the Revolution.[37]

One of the first matters of business was the execution of the king on January 21, 1793. Louis XVI's commitment to the Revolution fell into question after he fled to Varennes in the dead of night on June 20, 1791, ostensibly to gather émigré forces and restore his power, but he was captured and sent back to an angry public in Paris, leaving the people deeply suspicious of his motives, with some calling for the end of the monarchy and others for his head. The suspicion only grew over the next year and a half and was confirmed in the minds of many citizens when royal letters were discovered in a cache that revealed a request for foreign aid and contempt for the Revolution in general.[38] Robespierre inflamed the growing animosity in his incendiary speeches by exaggerating the transgressions of the king, inflating royal expenditures, and overestimating the ability of the monarch to thwart legislative reform,[39] but he ultimately resorted to a utilitarian approach once again when it came to justifying the final sentence, maintaining that the king should die without trial or evidence for the sake of the nation, whether he is guilty or innocent.[40] With this type of ethical thinking in mind, the vote for execution won by a comfortable margin, and the Montagnards proceeded to stage another purge the very night of the sentence, targeting all those moderates who expressed reservations about the execution on the Executive Council, as another expedient gesture.[41]

This Jacobin policy of using utilitarian reason to purge political enemies led to the establishment of the Committee of Public Safety in the spring of 1793. The committee coordinated government activity in conducting the political inquisition and extended the scope of the operation, sending deputies on missions throughout the country and terrorizing the entire population for over a year until the purges dissipated with the fall of Robespierre and the Jacobins on July 27, 1794.[42] During the Reign of Terror, the Law of Suspects was enacted on September 17, 1793, which called for arrests and marked for extermination those who were working against the objectives of the Revolution in a covert manner, no longer limiting the focus of the operation to those who cultivated a direct or explicit relationship with counter-revolutionary activities and its ideology. The law called for the creation of specific lists of suspects and provided a brief profile to guide the inquisitions, asking them to focus in particular on some rather esoteric traits, such as those who fail their civic duties and display insufficient enthusiasm for the Revolution or those who emigrated between July 1, 1789, and April 8, 1792, as possible "enemies of liberty," perhaps coming to overthrow the Revolution.[43] The desperation only increased the following summer when the Assembly passed the infamous Law of 22 Prairial on June 10, 1794—the most extreme and draconian measure of the Revolution, which denied the right of counsel and the calling of witnesses to the accused and exacted the death penalty as the only punishment for those convicted of the new crime of "enemy of the people."[44] During this time of "Great Terror," Robespierre spoke incessantly about conspirators (*conjurés*) permeating all levels of society, recognizing the stark reality of the situation: many opposed his methods and ideology throughout the land, others were subject to bribery and corruption from domestic and foreign sources, no uniform could identify the opposition, and no simple list of criteria could uncover the "enemies among us." Robespierre's paranoia grew as he started accusing moderates of conducting a "perfidious strategy" by allowing positive measures to pass only for the sake of a greater evil. His attention focused upon the "bureux" and developed into an obsessive desire to purge it of those who wore patriotic masks, secretly working to undermine the Revolution and restore the monarchy to its former glory, while trying to maintain a difficult balancing act and display a modicum of toleration toward those who opposed specific Jacobin policies out of principle.[45]

These hypocrites represented an imminent danger to him and must be purged, but they were also difficult to identify. Robespierre was forced to use such nebulous criteria as becoming *plus Robespierrste que Robespierre,* or displaying too much left-wing zeal and so undermining the credibility of the Revolution through fanatical behavior, but he never seemed to admit the tenuous nature of his evidence or even acknowledge the loss of innocent lives during the ordeal, unlike others in his circle.[46] In fact, the typical trial was a complete farce, caring little about evidence and displaying much haste in rushing to judgment. It might parade anywhere from fifty to seventy prisoners before the Revolutionary Tribunal, ask a few questions for the sake of appearance, display ostensible clemency by exonerating a few of the accused for making indiscreet comments, and wrap up the trial in two or three hours, condemning the rest of the poor souls to death and executing them the same day.[47] This method produced more than forty thousand victims during the brief period, with another four hundred thousand dying in the civil war that wracked the land. The victims of execution were mainly the lower class, but they included a disproportionate number of the upper nobility and clergy, as well as a succession of political groups: "first the Girodins, then the *enragés,* followed by the Hébertistes, the Dantonists, . . . and finally, in Thermidor, Robespierre and his closest Jacobin supporters."[48]

Despite all the bloodshed, Robespierre interpreted his actions in moral and religious terms. He followed the philosophes in reducing religion to morality, thinking of God as inscribing the noble ideals of liberty and equality upon the hearts of all humankind and so providing justification for his own enlightened point of view. He constantly referred to *vertu* as the motivating factor in all of his activity and continually spoke in moralistic and absolute categories, identifying truth, reason, and virtue together into one self-evident reality, treating his imperious opinions as the voice of God, dismissing his opponents as the incarnation of evil, and condemning them with the utmost rigor of a sanctimonious brutality. Of course, morality became the basis of society in his scheme, but he also reversed the field, and like most left-wing ideologues, he made the state the basis of moral living by directing each individual and institution toward public service, rather than private concerns. The state was the ethical ideal as it absorbed everything under it, making each person serve its moral purposes. The state was responsible for education as its "sole right" and must claim the moral high ground in rearing the next generation as *citoyens,* not the *messieurs* of an aristocratic family or the *abbés* of an ecclesiastic order. It must make the church hierarchy submit to its will, empowering the people to elect the bishops and priests and transforming the mission of its clergy into the service of society or the "welfare of the people."[49]

Robespierre's ultimate goal was to absorb all religion and morality into the unity of the state. In bringing the church and state together, he followed the vision of Rousseau in his work on the *Social Contract,* which thinks of religion as subservient to the state and useful to enhancing patriotism if properly developed from its true principles. Rousseau extols religion as providing a necessary foundation for a well-constituted society but expresses considerable reservations about Christianity, thinking it might be more "injurious than serviceable to a robust constitution of the state," since it creates "two contradictory obligations" and "destroys social unity." It is better for the state to have a religion that follows basic deist principles, emphasizing belief in a "Supreme Being," the "eternal obligations of morality," and the "immorality of the soul," as an incentive to serve the divine will in society.[50] Robespierre wanted to move the nation along this direction but recognized more than others in his circle the difficulty of weaning the culture from its historic Christian roots. He thought the people were not ready to comprehend the profound depths of the philosophes and the metaphysics of present intelligentsia. On November 21, 1793, he began a blistering attack on the extreme methods of Jacobins involved in the dechristianization process, denouncing their blasphemy, their spoliation of churches, and their attempt to secularize the culture through a republican calendar. He felt that some of them were trying to establish a "religion of atheism" under the "pretence of destroying superstition." He felt that their tactics were also stupid from a utilitarian point of view in alienating moderates, undermining the unity of the Revolution in the provinces, and maybe turning the church into a bastion of resistance. Rather than attacking the church so directly, he preferred working with it for the time being, since the people's loyalty and morality were entangled within its traditions and contained some useful teachings, such as giving to the poor and rejecting oppression and the hoarding of wealth.[51]

In due time, he decided to take a bolder course of action and announced the establishment of a new state religion to encourage faith in his metaphysical principles and to undermine Christian superstition, without acts of violence. He denounced materialism by breaking a bust of Helvétius, and he decreed on May 7, 1794, that the "French people recognize the existence of the Supreme Being and the immortality of the soul." He then announced the establishment of a new annual festival of the Supreme Being, in which he will torch a monument of atheism and proclaim the dawning of a new state religion based on reason, alienating Catholics and atheists alike. At the initial festival on June 8, 1794, some five hundred thousand spectators were gathered in the *Champs de Mars* to experience a couple of grandiose columns, an awe-inspiring mountain, the singing of patriotic hymns, and symbols of the Revolution like a liberty tree and statue of wisdom. Robespierre, the newly elected president of the Convention, appeared at the head of the procession of deputies, all dressed in blue regalia and bearing a bouquet of berries, grain, and flowers, causing some to grumble about the new *pontifex maximus* and wondering about his new powers.[52] Robespierre went on to address the sacred gathering invoking the name of God to justify the principles of the Revolution, declaring that the Creator made everyone free and equal and had given a sacred mandate to bring "our wrath against tyrannical plots" and destroy the "impious league of kings" by using the "death sentence." He particularly encouraged the people to follow the heroes and the martyrs of liberty in giving their lives to the cause, believing that those who die for the sake of freedom will live forever with God and receive the eternal gratitude of humankind.[53]

Robespierre clearly wished to be numbered among the martyrs and received the fulfillment of this morbid passion a month and a half later. He continually spoke of his imminent death near the end and interpreted it in sacred language as a sacrifice for the sake of the nation and its liberty,[54] but he also became a self-fulfilling prophesy in arousing the hostile reactions of others through his own tyrannical and reckless behavior. At the Festival of the Supreme Being, he alienated many of his own party, receiving considerable criticism from those who derided religion in general and those who wondered about the sudden increase of temporal and spiritual powers in one man.[55] With derision all around him, he remained rigid in his convictions, calling for the Jacobins to accept the new religion and enacting the Law of 22 Prairial, which threatened the deputies of the entire Assembly with swift and final retribution before the Revolutionary Tribunal.[56] On July 26, 1794, he delivered his last speech, which envisioned a "criminal coalition in the heart of the convention" and called for a purge of the Committee of Public Safety, without identifying specific individuals, which left the deputies to wonder who was next.[57] Some of the deputies saw an urgent need to act first and proceeded to summon a couple columns of troops that day to arrest Robespierre, along with his cohorts. In the process of the arrest, his jaw was shattered with a bullet, but he managed to survive the injury long enough to experience the horror of the national razor the following evening and to "let out a scream which has echoed down through the centuries."[58] After his demise, the government proceeded to close the Jacobin clubs around the country and executed some of the leading members to bring a semblance of closure to this dark period. The process of purging royalists and instilling a republican agenda continued for some time, but the bloodletting was reduced significantly and a modicum of civility was returned to the legal system.[59]

Burke's Critique

The most famous and scintillating review of the French Revolution came from the British statesman Edmund Burke and his *Reflections on the Revolution in France* (1790). When it was first published, the book represented a notable exception to the initial enthusiasm over the Revolution in Britain and much of Europe, and it brought to the public a number of deep concerns through its careful analysis of the real situation, particularly when a few of its dire predictions came to fruition.[60] Burke had no particular ax to grind against the general idea of a popular revolt and even favored American colonists in their struggle to obtain liberties and rights against the British government, but he considered a full-scale revolution the last resort and expressed considerable reservations about any movement that deigns to overthrow and level the existing order with extreme measures and a radical new vision.[61]

In the work, Burke thinks the French Revolution makes its first serious mistake by abandoning the wisdom of the past, the common tradition of Western civilization, and the respect for all those who represent it in authority—God, king, priest, and nobility. He thinks the Revolution has accomplished little more than the destruction of its own society out of an insatiable appetite for change, based upon mere speculative thinking and the desire to try the latest and most extreme unproven solutions. This appetite for change and disrespect for authority develops out of cultural tastes in France for the "declamation and buffooneries of satirists," who seem to set the agenda and control the opinions of the present legislature in Paris. Satirists might have a place in society, but they are particularly "unqualified for the work of reformation," since they delight in "hating the vices [of people and leaders] too much" and display little ability to weigh the nuances of a matter for serious contemplation. The philosophes led the culture into this pit of cynicism by exaggerating the sins of the *Ancien Régime*, causing its leaders to be hated by the masses and inspiring the French to disavow the institutions of old, thus creating a present without a past. Burke rejects this type of antithetical thinking and remains thankful that Britain chose a slower path of reform and continued to evolve as a culture through its time-tested traditions, resisting the ultraisms of English free thinkers and the current crop of French cynics—men like Collins, Toland, Tindal, Bolingbroke, Voltaire, Rousseau, and Helvétius.[62]

Burke prefers a gradual reform of existing institutions to the French appetite for deprecating predecessors and authorities and manufacturing all things new from the most "extravagant and presumptuous speculations." He recognizes the need of hearing grievances and redressing past abuses, as long as reform remains the goal of the complaints and the oppressive nature of the society and ill-treatment of peasants are not turned into a ridiculous caricature of evil to deprecate the character of the king and the first two estates. He expresses particular consternation over the religious cynicism and atheism of leading French circles as the "most horrid and cruel blow that can be offered to civil society." Out of this cynicism, Burke believes the French have chosen to exaggerate the sins of religious leaders and use past transgressions to punish the present church, pillaging its estates and driving the clergy into poverty. Rather than reforming the institution, the French have chosen to destroy it, without having anything to replace its ethical teachings and provide a serious metaphysical foundation for the society.[63]

He thinks the French have forsaken the sacred moorings of their society and have chosen to place their faith in the capricious will of the people and the National Assembly, which feigns to represent it. As a pure democracy, the government must submit to the wantonness of the people, and the Assembly often finds this will in the streets of Paris, succumbing to the continuous threats of violence and mob rule. This type of government has no serious restraints, no fixed constitution to limit its power, no tradition of common law coming from the inherited wisdom of forefathers, and no antecedent rights existing outside the contrivances of the masses and their desire to possess the property of those who live in the unequal privileges of "luxury and pride." The Third Estate equates might with right and shows little interest in traditional law or the experience, wisdom, and gravitas of an elite class to guide the process, only the changing appetites of the people to determine what is right and wrong. Burke sees tyranny as the only possible outcome of the present political ideology and its fixation upon the will to power. Already the National Assembly has obtained an exalted authority over the rest of the country, as it relates the will of the people to the local districts and prescribes the law to judges scattered throughout the provinces. Burke fears the new high tribunal will represent the interests of Paris and the members of the Assembly, and so "extinguish the last spark of liberty in France and settle the most dreadful and arbitrary tyranny ever known in any nation." He also expresses concern over the vacuum of continuous leadership in the Assembly as providing the pretext for a popular general to gain the affection of his troops and establish a military dictatorship over the whole Republic.[64] Many have seen the rise of Robespierre and Napoleon in these last two predications, although it is possible to overstate his prescience.

At the very least, Burke's right-wing criticisms provide some pungent insights into the French Revolution, helping people to understand some of the incipient problems within extreme left-wing concepts and their relationship with later atrocities. Much of these problems developed from the obsession of Robespierre and the National Assembly with the general will of the people, making this one aspect of modern government represent the voice of God and the end of life itself. This emphasis made the leaders of the Revolution subsume individual and natural rights under a national *fraternité*, where the utilitarian thinking of the philosophes prevailed in justifying the suspension of constitutional government, the execution of the king and political enemies, the Law of Suspects, the Law of 22 Prairial, and the pillaging of ecclesiastical and seigniorial property—all for the sake of the people. The Revolution thought of the people as a Herculean force and often ceded the general will to the violent protest of the raging mobs in Paris. Their power engendered a "revolutionary government," which conducted a civil war—a continuous battle for power within the country—trying to impose a new political ideology upon the people (i.e., the real people, who were not so prepared through significant changes in their religion and culture to accept the new way of thinking and never represented the general will).[65] The power play of the Parisian Assembly mostly represented an expression of the leading philosophes and satirists, spewing their hatred and outlandish criticisms upon the *Ancien Régime* and purging elements that displayed a modicum of respect for the old order through a more sober-minded belief in the possibility of reform. The later Communists will follow the same left-wing concept of empowerment and use the French Revolution as the basic paradigm for social change, extending the egalitarian spirit in a more economic direction and employing many of the same violent tactics in conducting the revolution and civil war in Russia.[66] Marx and his followers will force an economic interpretation upon society, reading bourgeois capitalism into preindustrial France and Russia, expressing much chagrin over the outcome of the struggle within the French Revolution and the inability to end property rights and empower the nascent proletarian movement,[67] but gaining great success later on in the Russian Revolution with its continuous civil war against the real people.

Notes

1. Marcel David, *Fraternité et Révolution Française 1789–1799* (Paris: Aubier, 1987) 68; Claude Geffré and Jean-Pierre Jossua, *1789: The French Revolution and the Church* (Edinburgh: T. & T. Clark LTD, 1989) 19.
2. Lynn Hunt, "Hercules and the Radical Image of the French Revolution," in *The Revolution and Intellectual History*, Jack R. Censer (ed.) (Chicago: The Dorsey Press, 1989) 177. Hannah Arendt believes the concept of revolution changed at this time from a backward, cyclical movement into an irresistible force or historical destiny, which now withstood the status quo of nature and the power of the king. *On Revolution* (New York and Middlesex, UK: Penguin Books, 1979) 42–48, 55.
3. Locke thinks the purpose of government is to protect the inalienable rights that God has given to humankind in nature. These rights include "life, liberty, and possessions." The rights are so sacred that the government is dissolved if it acts against them. *Concerning Civil Government, Second Essay*, in *Great Books of the Western World*, Robert Maynard Hutchins (ed.) (Chicago: Encylcopaedia Britannica, Inc., 1978) 26, 56, 75–76 (6, 135, 221–22). For Locke, the king has no right to the throne through hereditary privilege, since all human beings are created equal in nature. His temporary exaltation is based on the will of the people and the laws established by God in nature. Ibid., 25–26 (4). And so, *liberté* and *egalité* are a part of the God-given order but not *fraternité*.
4. Keith Michael Baker, *Inventing the French Revolution* (Cambridge: Cambridge University Press, 1994) 128–29, 141–44. Maupeou tried to deprive the *parlements* (high courts of justice) of the power to block royal reforms. He lost the battle when Louis XVI came to the throne and restored the power in August of 1775.
5. Joseph Saige, *Catéchisme du Citoyen* (Geneve, 1787) 39, 61. He particularly extols Charles Martel for accenting the freedom and will of the people. Hereafter designated as CC.
6. CC 2, 3, 6–9, 26–28, 33, 102–4, 114,120–26, 129–30, 136–37, 152–56; Baker, *Inventing the Revolution*, 136. He hedges on sanctioning revolution, but the

citizens have the right to refuse obedience to a magistrate who acts against the law, as well as the right to wage war against a tyrant who overturns the republic. CC 13–14

7. Emmanuel Joseph Sieyès, *What is the Third Estate?*, M. Blondel (trans.), S. E. Finer (ed.), Peter Campbell (intro.) (New York, Washington, and London: Frederick A. Praeger, Publishers, 1964) 1, 6, 10, 24–25, 33–34; Baker, *Inventing the French Revolution*, 149.
8. Ibid., 56–67, 98–99, 104–7, 141, 161–62, 172–73. He says the Third Estate represents 25 million people, while the other two estates represent only about two hundred thousand. The clergy total anywhere from 80,400 to 81,400 individuals. Ibid., 81ff., 146.
9. Ibid., 95–96, 172–73.
10. Ibid., 58.
11. Glyndon G. Van Deusen, *Sieyes: His Life and His Nationalism* (New York: Columbia University Press, 1932) 85–86. See Ibid., 77, note 10; 95–96.
12. *What is the Third Estate?*, 18, 124–27, 146–47, 151, 157, 170. See William Scott, "The Pursuit of 'Interests' in the French Revolution: A Preliminary Survey," *French Historical Studies* 19/3 (Spring 1996): 823, 826. Like the National Assembly, he never renounced property rights and even contributed to the bourgeois distinction between active and passive citizens, which gave the right to vote to male property owners.
13. Paul R. Hanson, *Contesting the French Revolution* (Maiden, MA, and Oxford: Wiley-Blackwell, 2009) 27; Malcolm Crook, "The French Revolution and Napoleon, 1788–1814," in *Revolutionary France 1788–1800*, Malcolm Crook (ed.) (Oxford: Oxford University Press, 2002) 10; Gwynne Lewis, *The French Revolution: Rethinking the Debate* (London and New York: Routledge, 1997) 3–4; John Hardman, *Robespierre* (London and New York: Longman, 1999) 3. At the time, contemporary critics liked to castigate the court and its lavish lifestyle as somehow responsible for the debt, particularly Marie-Antoinette as being a spendthrift, but the real problem resided elsewhere.
14. Hardman, *Robespierre*, 5.
15. Lewis, *French Revolution*, 5, 74; Linda Frey and Marsha Frey, *French Revolution* (Westport, CT: Greenwood Press, 2004) 19. The nobles were anywhere between three and four hundred thousand and the clerics around 170,000.
16. Annie Moulin, *Peasantry and Society in France since 1789*, M.C. and M. F. Cleary (trans.) (Cambridge: Cambridge University Press, 1991) 14–15. Almost half of the *cahiers de doléances* of 1789 wanted to abolish the *casuel* fees and a third the tithes. Timothy Tackett, *Religion, Revolution, and Regional Culture in Eighteenth-Century France: The Ecclesiastical Oath of 1791* (Princeton, NJ: Princeton University Press, 1986) 12–13.
17. *The French Revolution and Napoleon: A Sourcebook*, Philip G. Dwyer and Peter McPhee (ed.) (London and New York: Routledge, 2002) 21; William Doyle, *Origins of the French Revolution* (Oxford: Oxford University Press, 1980) 194–95.
18. Norman Hampson, *The Life and Opinions of Maximilien Robespierre* (London: Duckworth, 1974) 28; Cook, "The French Revolution and Napoleon," 12–13.
19. *French Revolution and Napoleon*, 16–18.

20. Lewis, *French Revolution*, 45; Hardman, *Robespierre*, 19; Hanson, *Contesting the Revolution*, 43. Robespierre approved of the violence, saying there was "not much blood spilt, a few heads stuck off, but guilty ones." Hampson, *Life and Opinions of Maximilien Robespierre*, 56–57.
21. Hanson, *Contesting the Revolution*, 48–50.
22. Hampson, *Life and Opinions of Maximilien Robespierre*, 71, 123, 145–46; *French Revolution and Napoleon*, 21. Robespierre thought of Marat as bloodthirsty and later objected to his entombment within the Panthéon, but Marat praised Robespierre in his paper as the "only true patriot sitting in the senate." The Girodins brought Marat before the revolutionary tribunal, but he was acquitted. On July 13, 1793, Marat was assassinated by a Girodin sympathizer, Charlotte Corday.
23. Lewis, *French Revolution*, 38; Hardman, *Robespierre*, 51; *French Revolution and Napoleon*, 66. See *French Revolution and Napoleon*, 20, 112, 120 for lurid examples of extreme cruelty and bloodlust among the people in killing and torturing their victims.
24. Frey and Frey, *French Revolution*, 79. The central administration employed seven hundred men in the 1780s and six thousand in 1794 (with a total of 250,000 officers).
25. The National Assembly hedges on property rights but never completely abandons the concept. It ends up recognizing the peasants' demands and abolishes seignorial fees and feudalism on August 25, 1792. It also confiscates all church property. *French Revolution and Napoleon*, 52, 80–81, 121–22. In regard to capitalism, it vacillated between free-trade policies early on to partial control of the economy after 1792. Lewis, *French Revolution*, 64, 107; *French Revolution and Napoleon*, 32–34.
26. Later on article 10 is used to make religion a private matter of the conscience. Jean Baubérot, *Histoire de laïcité en France* (Paris: Presses Universitaires de France, 2004) 7.
27. Claude Langois, "Religion, culte ou opinion religieuse: la politique de révolutionnaires," *Revue Française de Sociologie* 30 (1989): 474.
28. Michael L. Kennedy, *The Jacobin Clubs in the French Revolution: The First Years* (Princeton, NJ: Princeton University Press, 1982) 3ff.; Hardman, *Robespierre*, 26.
29. Ibid., 3ff., 20ff.; Hanson, *Contesting the French Revolution*, 82.
30. Hampson, *Life and Opinions of Maximilien Robespierre*, 223.
31. Ibid., 130–31; *French Revolution and Napoleon*, 93–95. The Jacobins wanted a compulsory public education for children, which meant replacing church instruction and inculcating patriotic and republican values. They enacted a law on December 19, 1793, to this effect. Lewis, *French Revolution*, 98; *French Revolution and Napoleon*, 58, 89.
32. Frey and Frey, *French Revolution*, 98; Hampson, *Life and Opinions of Maximilien Robespierre*, 72; Hardman, *Robespierre*, 68.
33. *Oeuvres Complètes de Robespierre* (Paris: E. Leroux, 1910–) 10.454–56. Hereafter designated as OCR.
34. Hector Fleischmann, *Charlotte Robespierre et ses Mémoirs* (Paris: Albin Michel, 1909) 290–92; Gliozzo, "The Philosophes and Religion," 277; Hardman, *Robespierre*, 14; Hanson, *Contesting the French Revolution*, 14–15. He was familiar with Montesquieu and l'Esprit *des lois* but rejects his doctrine

of the separation and balance of powers. Hampson, *Life and Opinions of Maximilien Robespierre,* 169.

35. OCR 10.353; *French Revolution and Napoleon,* 66, 105.
36. "Rapport de Robespierre sur les principes de government revolutionnaire" (Dec. 25, 1793), in *La Pensée Révolutionnaire en France et en Europe 1780–1799,* Jacques Godechot (ed.) (Paris: Armand Colin, 1964) 191; Hampson, *Life and Opinions of Robespierre,* 162.
37. Robert R. Palmer, *The Age of the Democratic Revolution* (Princeton, NJ: Princeton University Press, 1964) 2.164; Jeremy Popkin, *A Short History of the French Revolution* (Upper Saddle River, NJ: Prentice Hall, 2002) 82–85; Frey and Frey, *French Revolution,* 128, 129; OCR 10.353, 357.
38. Frey and Frey, *French Revolution,* 10; Hanson, *Contesting the French Revolution,* 32.
39. Hardman, *Robespierre,* 32; *French Revolution and Napoleon,* 71.
40. *Oeuvres de Maximilien Robespierre* (Paris: Presses Universitaires de France, 1950) 9.121–130; Hampson, *Robespierre,* 135–36; Frey and Frey, *French Revolution,* 122–23. Hereafter *Oeuvres de Maximilien Robespierre* is designated OMR. Louis-Antoine de Saint-Just, a member of the Committee of Public Safety, said the king should be condemned to death as a public enemy and not judged through a legal procedure. A king is guilty *de facto.* "One cannot reign innocently." Simon Schama, *Citizens: A Chronicle of the French Revolution* (New York: Alfred A. Knopf, 1989) 651.
41. Hardman, *Robespierre,* 75.
42. Crook, "The French Revolution and Napoleon," 21–22; Frey and Frey, *French Revolution,* 28–29; Hampson, *Life and Opinions of Maximilien Robespierre,* 264. Hanson lists some examples: "Jean-Baptiste Carrier ordering the drowning of Vendéan rebels in Nantes; Jean-Marie Collot d'Herbois commanding the execution by cannon of federalist rebels in Lyon; Claude Javogues terrorizing the people of Loire department; or Joseph Fouché aggressively pursuing dechristianization in the Nièvre." *Contesting the French Revolution,* 113. See Frey and Frey, French *Revolution,* 30–31.
43. P.-J.-B. Buchez et P.-C. Roux, *Histoire Parlementaire de la Révolution* (Paris: Libraire Paulin, 1836) 29.109; OMR 9.524–27; Hanson, *Contesting the French Revolution,* 174; Frey and Frey, *French Revolution,* 130–31; Hampson, *Life and Opinions of Maximilien Robespierre,* 95, 146–47.When Robespierre assumed power on August 12, 1792, he shut down the royalist press and a demanded a certificate of good citizenship from the people. Frédéric Bluche, *Septembre 1792: Logiques d'un massacre* (Paris: Éditions Robert Laffon, 1986) 79.
44. *French Revolution and Napoleon,* 107–8; Frey and Frey, *French Revolution,* 31; Hardman, *Robespierre,* 126–27. The pretext for the law was an assassination attempt upon the life of Collot d'Herbuis, a member of the Committee of Public Safety. Robespierre and Georges Couthon coauthored the legislation and pushed it through the Assembly. From the establishment of this law to the end of July, the "Revolutionary Tribunal sentenced 1,594 people to death, roughly 500 more than in the previous fourteen months of its existence." Hanson, *Contesting the French Revolution,* 124, 127; Frey and Frey, *French Revolution,* 31. Hardman's estimate is slightly lower but still finds the majority of the executions during the last month and a half. *Robespierre,* 127.

45. OCR 10.361–65, 449; Hampson, *Life and Opinions of Robespierre*, 42, 64–65, 215, 231; Albert Mathiez, *Études sur Robespierre (1758–1794)* (Paris: Editione Sociales, 1973) 226–27; OMR 6.515–17; 10.544–45; E.B. Courtois, *Rapport fait au nom de la commission chargée de l'examen des papiers trouvés chez Robespierre et sex complices* (Paris: Maret, [1795]) 180; OCR 10.360, 448–49; Hampson, *Life and Opinions of Maximilien Robespierre*, 140–41, 226–27, 232–33.
46. Hampson, *Life and Opinions of Maximilien Robespierre*, 108–9; Handman, *Robespierre*, 117–18. Claude Payon participated as a juror in the show trials and thought it was expedient that the innocent should die for the good of the country as a whole.
47. Nicolas Ruault, *Gazette d'un Parisien sous la Révolution: Letters à son frère. 1783–1796*, Anne Vassal (ed.) (Paris: Librairie Académique Perrin, 1976) 354–55.
48. R. Bienvenu, "The Terror," in *Historical Dictionary of the French Revolution, 1789–1799*, Samuel F. Scott and Barry Rothaus (ed.) (Westport, CT: Greenwood Press, 1985) 2.442–46; Frey and Frey, *French Revolution*, 11–12, 27; Hanson, *Contesting the French Revolution*, 109; Crook, " The French Revolution and Napoleon," 21. Around 70 percent were from the lower class. Cf. Hanson, *Contesting the French Revolution*, 173.
49. OCR 6.386–88, 397–400; 10.350–53, 446–47, 458; OMR 5.116–20; *Robespierre vu par ses contemporains*, Louis Jacob (ed.) (Paris: Librairie Armand Colin, 1938) 82–83; Hampson, *Life and Opinions of Maximilien Robespierre*, 42–43, 82–83. He is more than willing to pillage the property of the church to feed the poor, since the church has raped the poor of their goods in the past. He also wants the stipends of the bishops reduced to promote more equality within the hierarchy. He says that God does not want rich ministers. OCR 6.193, 407–409. If anything, he wants to make legislators more important in society than ministers of religion. OCR 6.406. Of course, he speaks of priests in the typical irreverent tone of a *philosophe*, as those who enslave humanity with their superstitions, sacramental powers, and theological dogmas and polemics. He believes the age of reason is finally breaking their power. OCR 5.117; 10.239.
50. Rousseau, *The Social Contract*, 159–63; Gliozzo, "The Philosophes and Religion," 278–79; Pierre-Maurice Masson, *La Religion de Jean-Jacques Rousseau* (Genève: Slatkine Reprints, 1970) 1.169ff.; 2.178ff.; 3.226ff.
51. OCR 5.117–20; R. Douglas Ord, "The Catholic Church in the French Revolution," *The London Quarterly and Holborn Review* 179/23 (Jan.–Oct. 1954): 64; Hardman, *Robespierre*, 96; R. R. Palmer, *Twelve Who Ruled: The Year of the Terror in the French Revolution* (New York: Atheneum, 1966) 121–22; *Age of the Democratic Revolution*, 2.115.
52. OCR 10.442, 463–64, 480; 101–2.
53. OCR 10.442, 463–64, 480–83; Baubérot. *Histoire de la laïcité en France*, 15; John McManners, *The French Revolution and the Church* (New York and Evanston, IL: Harper & Row, Publishers, 1969) 102; Hardman, *Robespierre*, 122–24; Lewis, *French Revolution*, 97, 101–2. There were a number of festivals throughout the land dedicated to reason, liberty, Deism/atheism, etc., and the Directory will continue to sponsor/tolerate them. Jacques-Louis David, the friend of Robespierre and director of art during the Jacobin

Republic, was put in charge of this particular festival. Robespierre provided for special commissions to write hymns in honor of the heroes/martyrs of liberty. OCR 10.459–61, 464, 480; Lewis, *French Revolution*, 97; McManners, *French Revolution and the Church*, 101–2.

54. OCR10.445; OMR 8.157–64; Hampson, *Life and Opinions of Maximilien Robespierre*, 104, 181.
55. OMR 10.562 (Note original under 1); Hampson, *Life and Opinions of Maximilien Robespierre*, 281. Vadier expressed concern that Robespierre was identifying his own personal idiosyncrasies with the Revolution and thinking an attack upon one was an attack upon the other. Vadier particularly mocked his new religion, comparing it to Catherine Théot, a mystical prophet, who predicted a divine manifestation at Pentecost. Buchez et Roux, *Histoire Parlementaire de la Révolution*, 24.32; Hardman, *Robespierre*, 177, 187, 196.
56. OCR 10.466, 467; Hardman, *Robespierre*, 170, Hampson, *Life and Opinions of Maximilien Robespierre*, 242.
57. OMR 10.542–82; *French Revolution and Napoleon*, 110; Hanson, *Contesting the French Revolution*, 129–30; Hardman, *Robespierre*, 188–89; Hampson, *Life And Opinions of Maximilien Robespierre*, 279, 294–96. In his private papers, Robespierre "jotted down notes on deputies whom he suspected: Dubois-Crancé, Delmas, . . . Thuriot and the two Bourdons." Ibid., 279; Courtois, *Rapport*, 189–92.
58. Hardman, *Robespierre*, 201–3; Hampson, *Life and Opinions of Maximilien Robespierre*, 300.
59. Crook, "The French Revolution and Napoleon," 25–27; Frey and Frey, *French Revolution*, 34, 118–20.
60. Edmund Burke, *Reflections on the Revolution in France*, Thomas H. D. Mahoney (ed. and intro.) (New York: The Liberal Arts Press, 1955) xvii–xxii.
61. Ibid., xxi, 12, 35.
62. Ibid., xv, 39ff., 72–73, 97–98, 101, 126, 129, 198–99.
63. Ibid., xv, 42, 103–4, 117–21, 136, 145ff., 155–60, 181. He accuses Necker and the Jacobins of confiscating more property than was actually owed in taxes. He says the Assembly has destroyed the economy of France and run up an even larger deficit since they must support the clergy now.
64. Ibid., xxvi, 8–9, 36–38, 46–48, 51, 57, 68, 71, 78, 106–7, 230, 244–45, 249, 256–63. He thinks of government as a complex matter of balancing differences. He prefers the Aristotelian model of a mixed government, not an absolute monarchy or democracy. Hairdressers and tallow-chandlers are not meant by nature to rule the republic. Ibid., 56, 63–64, 70–71, 106–7, 143. In his *Rights of Man*, Thomas Paine affords the most famous rebuttal of Burke's position rejecting the notion of hereditary government as if the people abdicated their right to choose a government forever by an act of Parliament in 1688. Paine also provides a different interpretation of the French Revolution, commending its revolt against hereditary despotism and justifying the brutalities in light of the citizens' outrage. *Rights of Man*, in *Complete Works of Thomas Paine* (New York: Freethought Press Assoc., 1954) 2.12ff., 16, 19–22, 31ff., 109. See also, "Common Sense," in *Complete Works*, 13.

65. Scott, "The Pursuit of 'Interests' in the French Revolution," 831, 847–48. Robespierre and the Jacobins centralized government authority, hating divisions and destroying local communities. Arendt, *On Revolution*, 245.
66. Arendt, *On Revolution*, 66, 99–100.
67. Dale Van Kley, "Christianity, Christian Interpretation, and the Origins of the French Revolution," *Fides et Historia* 11/2 (S 1979): 9–10; Hanson, *Contesting the French Revolution*, 4. The typical Marxist interpretation first pits the bourgeoisie against the old aristocratic powerbase and then the bourgeoisie against the nascent form of proletarianism. The twentieth-century historian Alfred Cobban provided a major criticism of this position, noting that the leaders of the Revolution tended to be lawyers, landowners, and other professionals, not captains of industry. He also noted that France was 85 percent rural at the time and lagged behind Britain in industrialization; most of the wealth was in land. Alfred Cobban, *The Social Interpretation of the French Revolution* (Cambridge: Cambridge University Press, 1964) passim; Kley, "Christianity, Christian Interpretation, and the Origins of the French Revolution," 12–13, 18–19; Hanson, *Contesting the French Revolution*, 6, 42, 195–96; Lewis, *French Revolution*, 11–13, 72–73.

4

The Process of Secularization

Jewish Emancipation

The French Revolution faced one of its greatest challenges in trying to assimilate the Jews into the modern state. Many writers depicted the Jews as a "state within a state" during the last half of the eighteenth century, finding them to be an "alien" race of people in their "ritual, manner, customs, habits, and prejudices," and suggesting Jews preferred to live in a separate community outside the world of non-Jewish influence, rather than merge into the landscape of their present existence.[1] The situation brought the "wandering Jews" considerable hardship and hostility from the Gentile environment,[2] but these authors tended to blame Judaism for turning self-purity and segregation into a fundamental religious principle, thus creating the conditions of their own misery. This position found a general acceptance among a wide audience, but other voices began to question its complete honesty and preferred assigning the majority of the responsibility to the surrounding nations for the wretched conditions of the Jewish people, blaming Europeans for impoverishing the Jews by limiting their livelihood to certain occupations and viewing the money-making schemes of the community as a product of their neighbor's policies, rather than a sign of some innate depravity subsisting among them.[3] These authors were more empathetic with the plight of the Jews and felt that even their most infamous vices, like the selling of usury, were capable of finding redemption through social engineering, leading many of the authors to speak of the real possibility of a Jewish *régénération*, beginning as early as Pierre Louis Lacretelle in 1775 and becoming a more and more dominant theme later on with the work of the great emancipator, Abbé Henri Grégoire. As the culture moved toward secularism, these authors interpreted the *régénération* in non-Christian terms, shifting the focus away from the earlier and literal call for a born again experience through the power of the Holy Spirit to a more secular vocation of service within the new state as a means of securing citizenship.[4] Their analysis understood the Jewish propensity toward a separate communal identity as the one unpardonable sin of modern etatism and offered the Jews a new status of complete emancipation from their present condition, but only at the cost of losing their cultural identity. Grégoire says that the "plan which we are developing entails the dissolution of Jewish communities.... We must deny everything to the Jews as a Nation, and grant everything to Jews as individuals."[5] The plan went on to spell out specific measures in reaching the goal, including the end of self-government and communal privileges; the reeducation of all children into a new cultural identity through the state; the abolition of dialects and languages, such as Yiddish and Hebrew; the exhortation to wear cockades or dress like the *sans-culotte* to represent the spirit of the Revolution; and the shedding of distinctive Jewish garments or shaving of beards and sidelocks.[6] Most Jews ended up taking the deal in the course of time, succumbing to this process of secularization within the new *fraternité*, although it took a much longer time to affect this type of cultural transformation than the Revolution originally envisaged for the Jews and the French people in general.[7] Most Jews struggled to maintain their identity long after the Revolution, but eventually the Jews began to outpace their Christian neighbors in accepting the new secular way of life, preferring the benefits of the new professional mobility and participation in society as high-ranking officials to their former status and meager existence as a chosen people, separated from this type of worldly involvement.[8] Today the secular Jews tend to celebrate the many benefits of the emancipation and laud the process of secularization in general, while a growing minority of religious and conservative Jews are beginning to have second thoughts, especially after the monumental work of Rabbi Arthur Hertzberg and his recognition of the deep-seated anti-Semitic nature of Enlightenment thought and the dubious nature of the Jewish deal.[9] This present study certainly agrees with these scholars and endorses the basic thesis of Hertzberg, which finds the roots of modern anti-Semitism within the Enlightenment. In fact, the study proposes to go even farther and demonstrate the veracity of the thesis beyond the limits of his work by showing the direct and unequivocal relationship between the Enlightenment and the development of modern anti-Semitism, which led to the Holocaust and the destruction of the Jewish faith in Germany, Russia, and secular Western culture.

In looking for the seeds of the problem, it is instructive to explore the works of the early apologists for Jewish emancipation in some detail. The most significant of these works are published for the convenience of scholars in the eight-volume *Editions d'histoire socials* under the title *La Révolution Francaise et l'emancipation des Juifs* (1968), and I have chosen to relate the material in the first four volumes: (1) Mirabeau: *Sur Moses Mendelssohn, Sur la Reforme Politique des Juifs* (1787); (2) Thiéry, *Dissertation sur cette Question: Est-IL des moyens de rendre les Juifs plus heureux et plus utiles en France?* (1788); (3) Grégoire, *Essai sur la régénération physique, morale et politique des Juifs* (1789); and (4) Zalkind Hourwitz, *Apologie en Réponse; Est-il des moyens de rendre les Juifs plus heureux & plus utiles en France?* (1789). Volumes two, three, and four represent prizewinning works, written in response to an essay contest of the Royal Society of Arts and Sciences in Metz, answering an important question of the day, "Are there means of rendering the Jews more happy and more useful in France?" All these works display a sincere commitment to promoting toleration toward the Jews and their faith but also reveal the darker side of emancipation, which wants to absorb elements of the Jewish community into mainstream French culture and lays the foundation for Deists/atheists/secularists to use the power of the state to attack the Judeo-Christian tradition in a more brutal manner.

The first volume presents the work of le Comte de Mirabeau, a famous politician, writer, and revolutionary figure. His study of Jewish history leads him to the typical conclusion of the emancipators, that the faults of the Jewish people are more a result of their deprivation at the hands of Europeans than a necessary by-product of their culture, religion, or innate depravity. He strongly reproaches the European nations for preventing their pursuit of an honest subsistence in the Middle Ages and so mistreating and corrupting them, although he exonerates the papacy and the church in this and other means of oppression. The Jews were sentenced to certain professions, like commercial business (*négociant*), which brought an agitated lifestyle of sordid competition, self-interest, sumptuous greed, and sagacious manipulation to their way of life and developed a certain set of characteristics in them, just like any other profession.[10] He argues that these characteristics are entrenched within the psyche of Europeans as a stereotype of Jewish businessmen, serving as a constant source of friction between the people, but none of this is necessary or inevitable; much of the problem would subside in due time if the circumstances of the Jews changed, and they enjoyed the same rights and privileges to pursue other avenues of making a living. He sees nothing within the Jewish character or religion that prevents them from experiencing regeneration and merging with the rest of the French people into a united country. The Jews can honor the country just like the rest of us; they can defend the land against foreign invasion, even on the Sabbath day; they can be useful subjects and productive citizens, even if they practice a certain amount of separation like many other religious groups. He thinks it is possible to exaggerate the isolated tendencies of any religion, create a slanted image, and turn all of its members into bad citizens through ignoring the total picture of what the religion represents and offers to the culture in general. Often this type of hatchet job is performed by anti-Semites like Johann David Michaelis, the "most dreadful adversary" of emancipation, who exaggerates the hatred and xenophobia of the OT, relates false reports about antisocial and criminal behavior among the Jews, and ignores the problem of oppression in creating the present circumstances.[11]

The second volume of *La Révolution Francaise et l'emancipation des Juifs* presents the work of Claude-Antoine Thiéry, the Protestant advocate of the Nancy Parlement. Thiéry is a son of the Enlightenment and wants to combat the prejudice of all people through the consistent use of reason. He wants to reason with the Jews about religious fanaticism and superstitious prejudice, which cause them to practice separation from other people and relish in their suffering as the unique people of God, refusing neighborly acts of kindness from those who wish to help their community. He wants to use reason against the same fanaticism in Christians, who tried to convert the Jews and led to much persecution during the Middle Ages. However, he wishes to indict Europeans most of all for corrupting the chosen people, turning Jews into merchants and bankers and making the love of wealth dominate their lives, while providing no other means of enriching their souls and intellect. Others might want to blame the Jews and point to their indelible character or religious/cultural beliefs as a way of understanding their vices, but none of this explains the facts with full integrity, which point to our deep complicity in creating the problems and our responsibility to fix them. Thiéry says the nations of Europe have a responsiblity to redress these past wrongs, and France in particular must help the Jews make the transition to a new life through specific government action, which includes opening up useful and honest occupations to them, abolishing restrictions on Jewish access to towns, eliminating laws that sentence them to live in separate quarters, and taking away education from the prejudice of Jewish parents by letting the state mold their children as good citizens. Other nations have succeeded by developing similar policies of "toleration," and Thiéry sees no reason why the Jews cannot be remolded through government policies in France and the patient application of enlightened reason (*raison eclairée*) in order to become full citizens of the civil state.[12]

The fourth volume presents the work of a Polish Jew named Zalind Hourwitz. It provides the unique and significant perspective of a person who lived within the Jewish community and had enough experience in Paris to know the situation and afford an effective defense for his people, even if he personally appreciates the effort of sympathetic Christians and names, in particular, the two previous prizewinning entries of Grégoire and Thiéry in the Royal Society's contest as making important contributions. In the work, he exhibits familiarity with the cultural climate in Paris by expressing concern over contemporary anti-Semitic currents within the social elite: the hatred Voltaire and his followers had for the Jews, especially their wont to turn the chosen people into misanthropes because of a few OT passages, and the absurd charges of Michaelis, who identifies the Jews with half of the criminal element in Germany, using this ridiculous statistic to promote anti-Semitic measures. He responds to the charges using a number of counterarguments to show how anti-Semites exaggerate the vices of Jews, how Jews are far removed from the hatred of other people, and why Jews are actually better than others. Far from commanding hatred, the OT admonishes its people to treat strangers with dignity and compassion and never advocates complete separation from foreign influence, as it permits dining with others and even marrying them, except in the case of a few nations like the Moabites, Ammonites, and some Edomites and Egyptians. This tradition continues with the writings of the

Talmud, which underscore the importance of practicing *charité* to all human beings, even if it could make a stronger case against those who profit off the errors of others and so defraud their neighbors. The tradition might not be perfect, but it provides enough edification to produce a moral race of people, who should be praised for their good behavior with a *macte virtute* (well done), rather than condemned by those who treat them with so much cruelty. Jews are actually the "most peaceable, sober and industrious of all people," committing much less crime than others, and they have no inherent depravity or need of *régénération*, unlike Christians. Those who deprecate the Jews usually manufacture "pretended vices," exaggerate the deeds of a few fanatics, or center upon a few stereotypical vices like "usure & la fraude," which are not so bad and basically the result of their oppressed condition. Of course, he thinks full citizenship and equal rights will help eliminate the cruel and bizarre condition of his people, and he suggests some affirmative government measures to accelerate the process, including a prohibition on speaking Hebrew during commercial transactions, a ban on rabbinic teaching that restricts intercourse with Gentiles or forbids the cutting of the beard, and a mandate for Jewish children to attend public schools, learn French, and build relations with other people. He only rejects destroying the Jewish communities in the process but clearly remains obtuse to the problem of the growing etatism and the future existence of his culture under its increasing domain.[13]

The third volume presents the work of Abbé Grégoire, the great champion of Jewish emancipation at the National Assembly. Grégoire's work displays many of the tensions with the left-wing position of the times, as it recognizes the Jewish complicity in their isolation from others, while blaming the Gentiles for turning their segregated existence into a ghetto. He advocates the full rights of citizenship and the toleration of their religion, while devising means of integrating Jews into French culture and changing them into something else. Grégoire works for emancipation on behalf of the people but ever remains a critic of their religious/cultural milieu, hoping to expunge certain elements that contribute to their plight and inhibit the process of assimilation. Grégoire admits that the Mosaic law created a people who lived in isolation from pagans and their idolatrous practices, refusing to join with them in the sacred bonds of marriage, outside of a few notable exceptions like Solomon and Esther. Their religious isolation caused Jews to shun daily intercourse with other people, refuse simple neighborly acts of kindness, and view other nations as odious, allied against them, inviting non-Jewish people to reciprocate and view them with equal contempt. The reciprocal hostility only brought further isolation for the Jewish people, the weakening of their bodies through inbreeding, and the degeneration of their lives through a long saga of misery and persecution, which Grégoire relates in the typical exaggerated terms of the Enlightenment's moralistic style. He talks much about the Dark Ages (*siècles ténébreux*) and the ridiculous accusations that circulated during the time. Even if some of the stories about medical malpractice or the sacrifice of Christian infants were true, he argues Europeans were wrong to punish the entire Jewish community for the sins of a few isolated individuals and wrong to create fantastic tales about the Jews poisoning wells in finding a scapegoat for the Black Death.[14]

Grégoire proceeds to place most of the blame upon European nations for creating the miserable state of past and present Jewish existence, although he exonerates the church in this matter, denouncing the present fashion in Paris of blaming the church's hierarchy for all the intolerance of Europeans and the ills of the past, pointing to the zeal of the papacy and clergy in protecting the Jews throughout its history. National practices of discrimination receive most of the blame for leading Jews into a life of business and the handling of money, which brought vices like graft and extortion into the community, even though most avoided the evils of usury. He also argues this situation will never change without the states changing policies and improving the conditions of the Jews, allowing their business practices to adjust accordingly.[15]

Grégoire sees the Jews as capable of changing their lives in these and other areas. They are not limited to commerce or idle material speculation through some biological necessity and incapable of tilling the soil; they show an ability to discard ancient regulations, including Levirate marriage, the Sabbatical year, and the stoning of idolaters, and to adapt their lives to their host countries; they are more than willing to become patriotic citizens and defend their country whenever their relation to a country changes into the rights of equal citizenship; and they will no longer look for a Messiah and long for Jerusalem when their interests reside in their homeland. The Jews are capable of receiving a full *régénération* through the power of the state controlling public education, limiting the power of rabbis, mandating the use of the French language in religious texts and rituals, breaking up communication between Jews, scattering Jews among the Christian populace, and setting quotas for the number of Jews in each village. His plan "entails the dissolution of the Jewish communities" and sees the real possibility of religious reform or conversion to Christianity in the process, although most of his agenda and concept of *régénération* involves the adoption of French ways and customs. In the meantime, Grégoire announces complete freedom and toleration of religion to rule the country, believing the Jews will blend into the culture in due time, but this concept of toleration contains all the typical chicanery of left-wing ideologues, who define religion as a private matter, unrelated to the political world, and then use the power of the state to transform the individual beliefs of its citizens. His concept of toleration finds no problem with the state obliging Jewish children to undergo Christian instruction and listen to rational arguments ridiculing Jewish "absurdities" with the expressed purpose of dissipating their faith. While the government cannot meddle into the private affairs of the synagogue, it has the right to use the public forum for its own purposes and transform the Jews and all citizens into a new enlightened image serving the new state and culture of France.[16]

Abbé Grégoire was the most significant of the emancipators in the Estates-General and National Assembly. He was a *curé* and representative of the lower clergy from Lorraine, who developed compassion for the dispossessed through his Jansenist upbringing and personal familiarity with rural Jewish communities in Alsace-Lorraine, Switzerland, and the Vosges. He led the charge for emancipation from the very beginning of the Estates-General, presenting over three hundred *chahiers de doléances* on behalf of the Jews in the opening sessions, complaining about their unjust circumstances, and demanding their right to full and equal citizenship.[17] The Assembly was making strides in this direction, granting freedom to all religious opinions in the Declaration of the Rights of Man (a.10) and eventually providing the half-million Protestants of the land with the fundamental rights of citizenship on December 24, 1789, but still ignoring the Jewish question.[18] At this time, Grégoire stood up and issued his famous "Motion in favor of the Jews," in which he reiterates many of the same themes found in his essay for the Royal Society. He speaks of Jewish persecution in the same exaggerated terms of his essay, trying to create a guilty conscience among the delegates and gain sympathy for his constituency.

> Since the capture of Jerusalem, there are few countries in Europe where the Jews have not been continually stabbed and murdered, hunted, ransacked, massacred, and consumed with fire. The universe is driven with madness over the corpse of this nation; almost always the best they could do is cry and their blood made the universe red. We can only speak of horror about the massacre on St. Bartholomew's Day, but the Jews have been 200 times the victims of scenes just as tragic, and who were their murderers? For seventeen centuries the Jews struggled, remaining steadfast through carnage and persecution. All the nations have allied in vain to destroy a people who continue to exist with all nations.[19]

He challenges the growing anticlericalism in the Assembly by exonerating the papacy and clergy from any complicity in this evil and underscoring the accommodation and protection of the Jews throughout the vast majority of church history. Instead, he focuses much of the blame upon France and other European nations for creating the wretched condition of the Jews and making them a byword by limiting their occupations, interdicting the exercise of the creative arts, crushing them with inordinate taxes, and making them turn to unseemly occupations for the purpose of survival. He thinks it is time to end their separate status as a people and integrate them into society as full citizens before the law. Making them live in isolation or creating ghettos like Italy only brings suspicion and hatred from the Christian populace, and it is time to end this pretext for antagonism by providing them with an opportunity to spread out and live among the rest of the people as full citizens. If the Assembly adopts this policy, the French people will soon give up their prejudice and learn that Jews are not innately evil; they do not hate others; and their restrictions on diet and marriage do not prevent them from enjoying a lively and edifying mixture with other people. Those who have particular objections about granting the Jews full citizenship underestimate the power of the state to "shake all individuals" out of their present existence and transform them into patriotic citizens through education and legislation. Of course, Grégoire quickly adds a number of exhortations about practicing toleration toward Judaism and other cults, and he references the example of Jesus to provide the message with authority, but he ends up ascribing all real authority to the general will of the state, hoping it will transform all individuals and private communities and tolerate what it destroys, and assuring the National Assembly that their problems with Jews will no longer exist. Grégoire gives the state the power to set up its own public form of worship and develop its own judicial and civil system of laws, creating a dichotomy between private and public life unknown to the Mosaic economy, or any other religion for that matter, and sure to transform all religious expressions into its image.[20]

The Assembly remained divided for the next couple years over the issue. Robespierre called for the Jews to receive the "inalienable rights of man" and reiterated many of the same arguments as Grégoire and the emancipators, blaming the nation for debasing these people and excluding them from honorable professions.[21] Jean-François Rewbell, a Jacobin deputy from Alsace, rejected the call for assimilation as unrealistic, given his experience with the Ashkenazim in the region and the separatist tendency of their traditional Jewish community with its special laws, courts, and jurisdiction over its own affairs, including the rejection of French influence and the contemptuous treatment of outsiders.[22] At first, the Assembly forged a compromise in January of 1790 by making a dichotomy between the Jews, granting full citizenship to the small population of Sephardic Jews from the southwest because of their full commitment to the process of integration into French society, but refusing to extend the same right to the much larger population of Ashkenazim.[23] Then, on September 27, 1791, the Assembly decided to end the dichotomy through the ceaseless effort of Grégoire and other delegates and grant the same right to all Jews, as long as they took the oath of citizenship and renounced "all the special privileges and exceptions previously in their favor," ending the peculiar status of their communities.[24]

The subsequent era witnessed many ups and downs for the new Jewish members of *la grande famille française* as they experienced the various ramification of voluntary and involuntary *fusion sociale*.[25] During the Reign of Terror, their faith was tested with great tribulation at the hands of the Jacobins, who adopted the philosophes' hatred for the religion as the source of Christianity.[26] The Jacobins made a concerted effort to eliminate all remnants of the Judeo-Christian tradition and develop their version of an ideal social homogeneity, where "there are no longer in the Republic Jews, nor Protestants, nor Anabaptists, nor Catholics; there are only French republicans."[27] Many synagogues were closed or nationalized, Jewish communal properties seized, sacred articles confiscated, Torah scrolls burned, cemeteries desecrated, and Sabbath observance punished. Judaism was subject to attack as a part of the dechristianization process, but its people were never targeted personally for their religion or ethnicity, and they seemed to suffer less desecration of their religious symbols than the Catholic Church, which was decimated in a systematic way as the main religious pillar of the *Ancien Régime*. After the Reign of Terror, the Directory relaxed the direct nature of the religious persecution, bringing a slower and more unobtrusive approach to the process of secularization and allowing a number of synagogues to be reopened and new ones built. The Napoleonic era saw the spread of Jewish citizenship throughout western and central Europe, expanding the process of secularization to the Jewish community at large, which was now beginning to outpace the Christian community in leaving their religious past for a new life of nationalism. Perhaps, the zenith of the early process was reached on February 8, 1831, when the rabbis were made civil servants and salaried employees of the French government,[28] insuring state control of the synagogues as its willing subjects.

Dechristianization

The anticlerical/anti-ecclesiastical culture of the philosophes reached a crescendo in the iconoclastic days of the French Revolution, especially within the epicenter of Parisian culture and power.[29] During the Reign of Terror, Joseph Fouché, a fiery orator and deputy from Nantes, developed an infamous reputation in history as leading an all-out assault upon the church, denouncing all priests as hypocrites, inciting violent iconoclastic uprisings, and announcing on October 10, 1793, that the French people must renounce ecclesiastical dogma and recognize no other religion than what was necessary for morality.[30] A process of dechristianization soon escalated throughout the country, varying in degree from region to region, depending upon the capricious nature of the *représentants en mission*,[31] but receiving all along the primary impulse from the National Assembly in Paris and its basic anti-Christian policies. In the summer and fall of 1789, the Assembly initiated the process by ending ecclesiastical tithes and voting to place "all church property, at the disposal of the Nation" and sell it at auction to reduce the enormous debt, while promising to sustain the clergy out of the state treasury.[32] The government proceeded to confiscate chalices, ciboria, candlesticks, statues, vestments, crosses, stained-glass windows, and church bells, often using the precious metals for military purposes[33] and leaving few churches open to perform an Easter service by the spring of 1794.[34] Churches were ransacked and desecrated with national symbols like the *cocarde tricolore* of the French flag and the bonnet of liberty replacing the cross of Christ.[35] In Paris, Notre Dame was reconsecrated to the female goddess of reason with an accompanying pagan festival on November 10, 1793.

Robespierre inaugurated his feast of the Supreme Being, using the pageantry of the same cult of reason,[36] and the church of Sainte Genevierre was rededicated as a mausoleum or Panthéon of national heroes.[37] Modes of speech were changed from *monsieur* and *madame* to *citoyen* and *citoyenne,* from *vous* to the egalitarian *tu,* from the *Place Royal* to the *Place de la Liberté* or *Place de la Republique,* from *Notre-Dame* to the *Temple de la Raison.*[38] In the fall of 1793, the Assembly voted to remove the Gregorian calendar and substitute a new one based on revolutionary values, ending saints' days and Sundays, replacing the Sabbatical cycle with a decimal system, and making the most crucial day of human history the founding of the Republic on September 22, 1792—day one and year one of the new calendar, not the birth of Christ.[39]

The Assembly focused much of its attention upon the clergy in trying to undermine the authority of the church and gain complete ideological power over the Republic. The Revolution transferred the administration of birth, marriage, and death away from the sacramental control of the priests and made these special times a civil and secular matter.[40] It pressed the clergy to forgo the vow of celibacy as enervating the virtues of marriage and actually voted to end monastic vows altogether on February 13, 1790, because of its concern about the power of monasteries over local communities and their loyalty to Rome.[41] On July 12, 1790, the Parisian Assembly went far beyond the will of the people and passed its most controversial measure, the so-called Civil Constitution of the Clergy, daring to make the church a ward of the state. Through this measure, the Assembly conglomerated districts and redrew diocesan boundaries, reducing the number of bishops from 130 to 83; it subjected all church officials to local elections, allowing all citizens to participate in the process, regardless of their religious background, and divesting Rome of its authority; and finally it made bishops and priests salaried employees of the state and bound them to swear an oath of allegiance to the nation (a.21), causing a deep conflict in ultimate loyalty.[42]

The oath of allegiance was a monumental decision and brought a major crisis within the church and civil war within the country at large.[43] All but seven of the bishops refused to take the oath, and almost half of the priests followed their example.[44] The *réfractaires,* or nonjuring priests, often had the loyalty of the people in their decision and used the stance to foment popular dissent toward government for imposing the oath.[45] On November 27, 1790, the Assembly responded by threatening the refractory priests with the loss of their position and worse, and then added the specific charge of treason a couple years later as matters deteriorated, issuing ultimatums with more dire consequences, such as internment, exile, or the possibility of the death sentence.[46] Of course, the papacy expressed general disapproval of the French government and stoked the crisis over the oath by condemning the Civil Constitution and threatening those who swore allegiance to the state with excommunication,[47] but the government refused to back down.

On August 26, 1792, the nonjuring priests were blamed for causing defeat on the battlefield by spreading disloyalty among the people, and they were ordered to "leave the borders of their district and department of residence within eight days and the kingdom within a fortnight."[48] Anywhere between thirty thousand and forty thousand nonjurors were forced to leave France during the crisis, and another three thousand were executed defending the faith,[49] leaving some areas or dioceses with virtually no clergy and eliminating as many as three-fifths of the ecclesiastics from the *Ancien Régime*.[50] After the Reign of Terror, the majority of bishops were gone—"ten were dead (six on the scaffold), twenty-three had apostatized, and another twenty-four had renounced their letters of priesthood," leaving maybe twenty active bishops of the original eighty-three.[51] However, the dechristianization program was largely unsuccessful in its immediate goal of destroying the church, and it never gained the popular support of the majority of the peasants around the country[52]—perhaps, displaying the inherent difficulty for any government to change the religious fabric of a culture overnight, even through coercive militant policies. Montesquieu says, "[It is much] easier for the vanquisher to bend slowly to the vanquished people than the vanquished people to bend to the vanquishers."[53] Republican names were not adopted in general; the revolutionary calendar was suppressed a decade later; the new religious cults soon faded by the end of the eighteenth century; and Napoleon reconciled his country with the Catholic Church by signing a Concordat.[54] The coercive policies failed to change the culture and bring the type of immediate impact demanded by the impatience of revolutionary activity, but the ideology of the times still remained to fight another day, eventually prevailing over the church in the long run as the Enlightenment and its revolution became the dominant symbols of intelligentsia, when a new secular government and public educational system began to trumpet its virtues at the end of the nineteenth century and turn the citizens slowly and surely into secular subjects.

Jansenism

The Catholic Church was not a simple monolith in resisting democratic reform and the secularization of society. Dale Van Kley, a professor from The Ohio State University, has led a group of recent scholars who see a deep division within the Catholic Church over these emerging aspects of the modern world already transpiring within the French culture before the Revolution and providing inspiration for what will occur during and after that time. These scholars particularly focus their attention upon the Jansenist movement of seventeenth- and eighteenth-century France as providing a key to understanding the subsequent Revolution in its polemical struggles with the Jesuits, and other ultramontanist factions of the church, who looked to Rome for authority. The Jansenists were critical to the development of modernity in challenging the hierarchical and authoritarian structure of the *Ancien Régime* and paving the way toward a new social order, which emphasized modern concepts like nationalism, secularism, democracy, equality, and the tolerance/intolerance of religion.

The Jesuits first referred to this group as Jansenists in the 1640s because of their reverence for a Dutch-born theologian named Cornelius Jansen, who spent some time as a professor of theology at the University of Leuven and as a bishop over the newly founded diocese of Ghent in his later years, inspiring a following of like-minded disciples in northern France and southern Netherlands. His most significant work was a prodigious three-volume tome entitled *Augustinus* (1641), which was published after his death and promoted Augustine's doctrine of sin and grace.[55] On May 31, 1653, Pope Innocent XI issued the bull *Cum occasione* condemning the work in five points, denouncing in particular its concept of irresistible grace, the absolute sovereignty of God in human merit and demerit, the insufficiency of present grace to fulfill all divine precepts, and the limitation of the divine intent within the sacrifice of Christ.[56] The Pope rejected the Jansenist attempt to revisit a more conservative reading of Augustine on these and other matters, which the church already condemned long ago at the Synod of Orange (529). The Jansenists responded to the suppression of their ideas by expressing a concern for religious toleration in the church, and they became an integral part of developing a more liberal society, helping to secure freedom of conscience for the minority of like-minded Protestants and to enact Louis XVI's Edict of Toleration in 1788.[57] The Jesuits opposed them every step of the way on theological and political issues, inculcating the doctrine of free will and defending the old authoritarian structure of society in church and state as "soldiers of Jesus" and his vicar.[58] Unfortunately, the Jesuits gained an infamous reputation in France over time as purveyors of intolerance and despotism, and they were finally kicked out of the country in November of 1764 through an act of Parlement as antisocial and anti-French,[59] although they were successful in reducing the size of enemy forces as the number of Jansenists dwindled to a small remnant at that time through years of ecclesiastical struggle and persecution.[60]

The struggles of the Jansenists had a profound effect upon the spiral of events leading to the year 1789 and determining the future course of French history. Perhaps, the most significant incident took place on September 13, 1713, when Pope Clement XI issued a bull condemning Pasquier Quesnel's commentary of the *New Testament, with moral reflections upon every verse* . . . (1692, first complete French edition)—a condemnation that backfired as the papacy pressed the issue and brought an extreme cultural backlash among the French people, cascading toward the Revolution. Quesnel was a French theologian, who suffered throughout his life for refusing to comply with anti-Jansenist decrees, preferring to accept expulsion from his homeland, imprisonment in Brussels, and death as an exile in Amsterdam. In his commentary, he expresses much consternation over the willingness of the church to persecute its own kind through the imperious and capricious decisions of a few. He speaks of his respect for the traditions of the church, but he clearly follows the more democratic understanding of those traditions, as seen in the Conciliar Movement of France (or the Congregationalists of Puritan England), where the whole church must come together with its leaders in making authoritative decisions about the discipline of its members, the reformation of its practices, and the interpretation of scripture.[61]

Quesnel's commentary is filled with pious devotion to the Word of God and the teachings of Augustine, the greatest theologian of the church, but it receives condemnation from Rome for interpreting these sources outside the typical semi-Augustinian framework of the later church, which was determined by the Synod of Orange and reaffirmed in the Council of Trent (1545–1563). In fact, the work sounds similar to what was condemned at the Synod of Chiercy (853) in the teaching of Gottschalk, the ninth-century Augustinian monk, and recently revived among the Calvinists at the Synod of Dordrecht (1618–1619).[62] Quesnel speaks of human depravity in the same absolute terms, maintaining that nothing good comes from those who have fallen in Adam, outside the work of Christ in us.[63] He thinks of divine election as an unconditional act of grace, based solely upon the mercy of God and given to the unworthy, outside of anything found within those who are chosen. This grace dominates the human will with irresistible force as the "operation of [God's] own omnipotence," which works salvation and all good things in the hearts of the elect, apart from any disposition they possess in their own right. The elect "owes all to grace. . . . The call, the admission to, and the faithful discharge of the ministry, the thoughts, the desires, the choice of ecclesiastical labors, the beginning, the progress, and the perfection of the work, all is of God, from whom every thing proceeds, by whom every thing is completed and consummated."[64] With these and other comments, Quesnel proceeds toward a concept of predestination that exceeds the parameters of the mainline church, even broaching the Calvinist concept of the doctrine with its special emphasis upon limited atonement and perseverance of the saints (eternal security) at times,[65] although he never leaves the obscurity of his devotional language or clarifies his comments with scholastic erudition, and sometimes he appears to back down.

The Jesuits found the work offensive to their orthodox sensibilities and wanted Louis XIV's help in obtaining an official condemnation of its heretical teachings from the papacy in Rome. The Holy Office obliged the king with the bull *Unigenitus* and listed a hundred and one offensive propositions in the work, answering to many of the Jesuits' concerns.[66] The bull centered upon its view of salvation, condemning the emphasis upon the all-sufficiency of grace (2), the irresistible nature of grace (10–13), the absolute necessity of grace to do good works (40), the place of faith as the first grace and root of all others (27), and the limitation of the divine will and atonement of Christ in bringing salvation to the elect (31–32).[67] The bull also condemned the ecclesiology of the work, especially its attempt to encourage lay participation in the interpretation of scripture and the exercise of discipline (79–81, 84), along with its deprecation of the present church leadership for persecuting the pious (99–100). Of course, the Jansenists used the same ecclesiology to dismiss the papal pronouncement as a matter of further discussion and confirmation within the French Church. They participated in the heated debate without serious ramifications during the period immediately following the pronouncement until the Jesuits gained the upper hand and *Unigenitus* was made the law of the church and state on March 24, 1730, leading to the ascension of authoritarian rule and the purge of Jansenists from the priesthood and Protestants from France.[68] Thereafter, the Jansenists ceased to exist as a serious spiritual rival to the Jesuits within the church, but in destroying Jansenism, the Jesuits and their heavy-handed hierarchical church sustained considerable collateral damage for practicing intolerance as the public perceived them as bigoted, the hatred of priests grew exponentially, and church attendance plummeted by the middle of the century.[69] The resentment of the public erupted into open rebellion when the hierarchy refused to administer the viaticum and last rites unto those who opposed *Unigenitus*, denying comfort to them and their loved ones during this desperate hour of need.[70] The king recognized the discontent and the problem with his own participation in the debacle; on September 2, 1754, he decided to cave into the mounting pressure, ordering the administration of last sacraments to those who opposed *Unigenitus* and obtaining official authorization from Rome a couple years later for this change in policy.[71]

The Parlement of Paris and its various branches around the country emerged triumphant during the crisis. They sided with the Jansenists all along and served as the fundamental political force behind the king's sudden reversal, defending the rights of all Catholics to receive the sacraments against him and the episcopacy and ordering arrests of *curés* who refused to comply with them. The controversy pitted the will of Parlement against the spiritual and temporal authority in the country and provided the Jansenists with a powerful voice within the government, which they influenced and exploited to their advantage.[72] The Jansenists looked to Parlement as representing the nation and used its power as a willing ally and stronghold during the crisis in forwarding their basic religious/political agenda.[73] However, their use of secular power helped move the country down a slippery slope, providing a precedent and sanction for the later National Assembly to exploit the church and secularize society through the power of the state, using Jansenist juridical arguments but hoping to destroy the church, not just resolve one administrative issue or purge one of its factions.[74] Saige speaks of this fundamental Jansenist understanding in his *Catéchisme du Citoyen.*

> The church is enclosed in the state, and the citizen exists prior to the Christian. The Republic and its magistrates have a right to inspect the

> church, not in regard to its truth or dogma, because in that case the spiritual authority would be subjected to them; but over the exterior administration as it concerns civil order. . . . This jurisdiction extends itself over the administration of the sacraments and the exterior constitution of its hierarchy. . . . Who has defended our liberties with most courage against the pretentions of the court of Rome? [It is] the Parlement, the Court of France. It is its untiring vigilance that has preserved us from slavish superstitions which has engulfed all the Catholic nations.[75]

The Jansenists set the precedent for much of this, justifying Parlement's meddling into the sacramental affairs of the church and then seizing the property of Jesuits in the 1760s[76]—all without recognizing the full extent of the problem on the immediate horizon with giving the state too much power to secularize everything and decimate the whole church.

This political interest of Jansenism was an important aspect of the movement at the beginning of the eighteenth century. The Oratorian Seminary at Saint-Magloire provided early inspiration for the developing interest by producing thousands of books, pamphlets, and essays lampooning the established order in the French language and disseminating the message of democracy to a wide audience.[77] Vivien de Laborde helped to set much of the early agenda in his *Temoignage de la Vérité dans l'Eglise* (1714), where he made a determined effort to reach the public, seeing the voice of the people within the church and society as a means to affect political change.[78] In February of 1728, some of their theologians started publishing a highly successful eight-page periodical called *Nouvelles Ecclésiastiques* to serve as the basic organ of the new lay Jansenist constituency, using it to spread the antiauthoritarian/ anti-*Unigenitus* message throughout the country, defying the many attempts of successive regimes to close it down and punish those responsible.[79] For the next half century, the Jansenist lay movement, the *Nouvelles Ecclésiastques*, and its other publications provided the most consistent and significant attack upon the *Ancien Régime* and its hierarchical form of government within France, and coupled with the pervasive influence of Protestant countries and their churches in French culture, they brought division within the church and state over democratic principles, while the philosophes stood by and still wavered over the issues throughout the period.[80] What started as a polemical struggle within the church now reached outside its walls, developing into a contentious set of problems for the culture at large and soon devolving into a battle against the church, as Jansenism became a lay movement and reached a secular or anti-Christian audience, who possessed the same lack of nuance in their criticisms of Christendom as the philosophes. This audience preferred to blame the whole church and all the priests for every sin of the past, and was unwilling to recognize their significant debt to part of the tradition. Even the Jansenists tended to lose much of their spiritual focus and moorings in the process and display less interest in the historical theological polemics of the church, often finding their public voice in politicians and lawyers, who were influenced by the movement and championed the power of the people and elected assemblies against the despotism of the *Ancien Régime* without much reference to scripture or the metaphysical basis of their beliefs.[81] With their clergy significantly diminished through the Jesuit policies of the past, Jansenism tended to take on a worldly mission and talk within the terms of this world, causing Pidansat de Mairobert to comment, "Jansenism has lost its great merit, its genuine interest; through the extinction of Jesuits in France, it has transformed itself into a party of patriotism."[82]

The growing secular posture only belied the considerable debt of Jansenism and the revolutionary culture to the rich history of French Catholicism.[83] In many ways, the modern political order grew out of the Gallican Church and its special insistence upon its own individual or national identity and adherence to the authority of ecumenical church councils as representing the will of God, rather than listening and submitting to the power of Rome. This independent and democratic tendency came to the forefront during the Conciliar Movement and the Council of Constance (1414–1418), which unified the church under a single pope after a time of schism, wringing a number of concessions out of the Vatican and reducing its authority. Much of the controversy started as a struggle for power between France and Rome: Philip IV of France and Boniface VIII were each vying for more control over the church and state, with the king finally defeating his former enemy and eventually replacing him with a new pope, Clement V, who moved the Holy See from Rome to Avignon in 1309. The see remained there under French domination for the next seventy years until a great schism arose in 1378, where two candidates, Urban VI and Clement VII, staked their claim to the throne. A council met at Pisa in 1409 hoping to reconcile the church by electing Alexander V and deposing the other two. Instead the consecration of a third pope only created more confusion that would take six more years to end the schism at the Council of Constance and anoint a single pope, Martin V, to rule over a unified church. Jean Gerson led the successive effort at reconciliation, which insisted upon the authority of the church in establishing and judging the pope as a condition for allowing him to continue exercising his fullness of power—but only in conjunction with the church and never to the detriment of his subjects, or to usurp the natural rights or property of the clergy, laity, or state.[84] Through this way and means, Gerson and the Conciliar Movement diminished the authority of the pope but retained the basic episcopalian polity as representing the church and proceeded no farther.[85] The movement had the potential to develop in more radical directions but did so only with the advent of Protestantism and its concept of the priesthood of the believers, causing groups like the Huguenots of the sixteenth century[86] and Jansenists of the seventeenth and eighteenth century to proceed toward a democratic and egalitarian polity—truly empowering the church as a whole. The radical pamphlets of the Jansenists often showed this mixture of historical influence, constantly comparing the Estates-General to the General Council of the church in its relation to the nation, retaining the language of the Conciliar Movement and combining it with the natural rights tradition of the Decretalists, Holland, and Puritan England.[87] The Jansenists just took French Catholicism a step farther by extending their proclivity toward Calvinism into another area, proceeding beyond the Conciliar Movement and following a Congregationalist-like model, emphasizing the authority of simple believers, not just a small number of bishops at an ecumenical council.[88] Saige once again shows this same type of Jansenist argument in his *Catéchisme*, while keeping it a French affair and making no specific reference to the Protestants—typical of any French Catholic, including the Jansenists, who wish to remain within their church and conceal any connection with heretical or outside groups. The *Catéchisme* rejects the authority of papal bulls outside the reception of the church and commends the Parlement of Paris for protecting the freedom of the Gallican Church against the Vatican, referring specifically to the Council of Constance, the Parisian assembly of French clergy in 1684, and the Council of Basel (1431–1449) as supporting its view[89]—all in accordance with Jansenist argumentation. Saige writes:

> What are the principle articles of liberty for the Gallican Church? The first, and the principle is the superiority of the General Council or Assembly, which represents the entire church, all the members of the church, both the simple believers and pastors, without exempting from the first among them, namely the bishop of Rome, who must submit his person and decisions to the decisions of this assembly. The most important item after this, we teach that the infallibility of decision in a matter of faith belongs to the church alone, not to any of its pastors in particular, and that by consequence, the pretentions from the court of Rome, which assigns it to its bishop, are absurd and contrary to the constitution of the church.[90]

The Jansenists played a crucial role in radicalizing the society and shaping the fundamental ideology of the National Assembly, although they became less and less visible after 1730 as an organized religious faction with a simple identity. The oppressive measures of the church had reduced their numbers within the church to a small minority of prelates and clergy by the dawning of the Revolution, but much of their influence continued to exist in the form of a loose confederation of lay Jansenists, or at least the many individuals who were influenced by the movement directly or indirectly, without forming a specific association with the actual group.[91] Some of its members, like Abbé Grégoire, still remained to play a key and effective role in the Assembly.[92] but fewer and fewer identified their political or spiritual interest in any literal or direct way with the Jansenist system of belief.[93] In many ways, the Jansenists were the victims of their own ideology, which facilitated the secularization of their own group and society in general. They helped make etatism the alternative to religious affiliation by extending the French preoccupation with Gallicanism, patriotism, and nationalism over against the international designs of Rome.[94] By mid-century, they looked more and more to the state as a means of resolving problems within the church and facilitated the ascendency of the temporal over the spiritual by denying the property rights of the church and allowing the state to tax, seize, and own all church property.[95] They even advocated an early form of the Civil Constitution, or making the clergy a ward of the state, supporting its passage in the *Nouvelles Ecclésiastiques* during the early years of the National Assembly, when the anti-Christian designs of this body were coming to the forefront.[96]

Like the Jansenists, much of the Revolution looked to the power of the state or the general will of the people for solutions that ended up overturning individual life within religious communities. The Jansenists found Parlement a useful ally in the battle to obtain a measure of toleration within the church but ended up looking to the state for answers in general, losing their spiritual moorings, and promoting the secular domination of the state over the church in the process. The Jews also followed this path by wanting the state to grant them the rights of citizenship and the same opportunities as the rest of the French people. They were given a problematic choice between accepting their current status and remaining in their present miserable condition, as a "state within a state," or leaving their individual communities behind for a process of integration, enculturalization, and a new life of *régénération* within the state, with most choosing the latter alternative and becoming secular in the course of time. The National Assembly revealed this dark side of etatism in a most direct way by launching an open assault upon the old religious way of life, attempting to destroy the Judeo-Christian tradition during the Reign of Terror with the nationalization of church property, the desecration of churches and synagogues, the promotion of a new language game and patriotic identity, and the secularization of the clergy through the Civil Constitution and oath of allegiance to the state. This direct assault was a strategic mistake for the Revolution, as it brought civil war throughout the country by trying to change the culture overnight and not recognizing the tenacity of cultural beliefs and the religious convictions of the people. The Revolution experienced more success over a longer period of time in the nineteenth and twentieth centuries as the state increased its power over education, intelligentsia adopted the attitudes of the Enlightenment, and the Revolution became a sacred/secular symbol of the future, slowly changing French culture into the uniform image of the state and leaving the religious heritage behind.

Notes

1. Katz, *From Prejudice to Destruction*, 58; *An die Hohe Deutsche Bundes versammlung* (Frankfurt: Andreä, 1817) 39–40.
2. Herzog, *Intimacy & Exclusion*, 56.

3. Zosa Szajkowski, *Jews and the French Revolutions of 1789, 1830, and 1848* (New York: KTAV Publishing House, INC., 1970) xiv–xvi; Shmuel Trigano, "The French Enlightenment and the Jews," *Modern Judaism* 10/2 (May 1990): 171–77, 181; Hertzberg, *The French Enlightenment and the Jews*, 119–22, 328. Cf. Grégoire, *Essai sur le régénération physique, morale et politique des Juifs*, 44, 171; Zalind-Hourwitz, *Apologie en Réponse de la Question; Est-il des moyens de rendre les Juifs plus heureux & plus utiles en France?*, 77; Thiéry, *Dissertation sur cette Question: Est-IL des moyens de rendre les Juifs plus heureux et plus utiles en France?*, 7, 41, 57, 71, 82. All references from *La Révolution Française et l'emancipation des Juifs* (Paris: EDHIS, 1958).
4. Jay R. Berkovitz, "The French Revolution and the Jews," *AJS Review* 20/1 (1995): 44–47. Many prerevolutionary advocates of Jewish emancipation only wanted to convert the Jews to Christianity. Szajkowski, *Jews and the Revolutions*, xvii–xviii, 372–73. Of course, others felt usury and cheating was an indelible trait of the Jews. Cf. Katz, *From Prejudice to Destruction*, 352–53. Much of anti-Semitic feeling centered on the selling of usury, and the Jews were expelled from many major cities in Europe because of this practice, as late as 1789 in the city of Strasbourg in Alsace. See, for example, Szajkowski, *Jews and the Revolutions*, 299, 302, 310, 337. Alsace resisted the emancipation of Jews in September 1991. Professor Christian-Guillaume Koch, a Protestant leader and deputy from Alsace, produced a memorandum the previous year, arguing against assimilation of the Jews, based on their existence as a separate nation. Its title is *Reflexions sur les Juifs* and is reproduced in Szajkowski's *Jews and the Revolutions*, 385–87. See also pp. 337, 382.
5. Grégoire, *Essai sur le régénération*, 134, 158; "Motion en faveur des Juifs," in *La Révolution Francaise et l'emancipation des Juifs*," 13, 40–41; Trigano, "The French Revolution and the Jews," 172, 178; Herzog, *Intimacy & Expulsion*, 55–56. Pierre Baudin, a deputy from Ardennes, summarizes the plan with more irony later on, saying it allows Jews or Muslims to maintain their identity as long as they no longer follow the religious practices and teachings of Moses and Muhammad! Szajkowski, *Jews and the Revolutions*, 425.
6. Szajkowski, *Jews and the Revolutions*, 789–99; Katz, *From Prejudice to Destruction*, 193; Berkovitz, "French Revolution and the Jews," 26–28; Thiéry, *Dissertation sur cette Question*, 79; [Berr (Berr-Isaac)], "Lettre d'une citoyen, member de la cidevant Communauté des Juifs de Lorraine, à ses confrères, à l'occasion du droit de Citoyen actif, rendu aux Juifs par le décret du 28 Septembre 1791," in *La Révolution Française et l'emancipation des Juifs*, 8.11ff. Jews were losing jurisdiction over their people in regard to civil cases and the power of excommunication. Before this time, Jews could choose to settle matters among themselves in their own courts or appeal to a general court. Katz, *From Prejudice to Destruction*, 241–42.
7. Berkovitz, "French Revolution and Jews," 50, 81. Eventually the Jews become secular. The Pew Forum and Gallup polls indicate only 10 percent of Jews in America attend the synagogue on a weekly basis.
8. Pierre Birnbaum, "Is the French Model in Decline?," in *Jewry between Tradition and Secularism*, Eliezer Ben-Rafael, Yosef Gorny, and Thomas Gergely (ed.) (Leiden and Boston: Brill, 2006) 14–15; Berkovitz, "French Revolution and Jews," 75.

9. Hertzberg, *French Revolution and the Jews*, 7–8. Cf. Katz, *From Prejudice to Destruction*, 318–19; Szajkowski, *Jews and the Revolutions*, xxiv– xxv.
10. Ibid., 85–88.
11. Le Comte de Mirabeau, *Sur Moses Mendelssohn, Sur la Reforme Politique des Juifs*, in *La Révolution Française et l'emancipation des Juifs* (Paris EDHIS, 1968) 57, 62–67, 78–81, 85–88; 110ff., 119–20, 126–27. For example, one could make Mennonites bad citizens because they refuse to take oaths. Ibid., 124.
12. M. Thiéry, *Dissertation sur cette Question: Est- IL des moyens de rendre les Juifs plus heureux et plus utiles en France?*, in *La Révolution Française et l'emancipation des Juifs*, 2, 3, 9, 13, 21, 25ff., 29, 32–45, 58–62, 66, 69, 70, 75 76–78, 80–81, 85, 94–96. He thinks Voltaire prostituted his genius by denigrating the Jews and becoming one of their principle enemies. He feels the edict of Nantes should apply to the Jews (or all non-Catholics), and so a new of toleration is unnecessary. Ibid., 49, 97–98.
13. Zalkind-Hourwitz, *Apologie en Réponse de la Question; Est-il des moyens de rendre les Juifs plus heureux & plus utiles en France?*, in *La Révolution Française et l'emancipation des Juifs*, 1–2, 10–14, 21–24, 27, 33–38, 48–58, 61, 84. He says borrowers often end up blaming creditors when they squander their money, but they are not cheated in the arrangement. Ibid., 15ff. He also speaks of the oppressive tolls that many Jews pay beyond the ordinary fees for protection, reception, habitation, communal access, etc. The royal administration offers to protect Jews but only by receiving bribes, special taxes, forced loans, and certain provisions. Ibid., xii–xiii, 24.
14. Grégoire, *Essai sur le régénération physique, morale et politique des Juifs*, in *La Révolution Française et l'emancipation des Juifs*, 1–13, 17–27, 49–54, 57, 103. He finds Germany a particular place of cruelty in the Middle Ages. Ibid., 5, 8.
15. Ibid., 5–7, 16–17, 20, 44, 64, 71–80, 83, 86, 145.
16. Ibid., 99–103, 108, 109, 112, 118–26, 131–32, 139, 146–50, 151–55, 160, 166–67, 179, 183–90. He recognizes the danger of toleration but believes the reform will be successful. He spends much of his time criticizing the Talmud for its exceptions to the law and petty details, and thinks rabbinic work lacks originality and inspiration. Ibid., 65ff., 171–77, 191.
17. Albert, "French Enlightenment and the Jews," 35, 40; Bernard Plongeron, "The Birth of a Republican Christianity (1789–1801): Abbé Grégoire, in *1789: The French Revolution and the Church*, 29, 30. Along with Grégoire, Comte de Clermont-Tonnerre, Mirabeau, and Rabaud Sait-Etienne helped lead the fight for Jewish rights at the National Assembly. Oliver W. Holmes, "The Debate on Jewish Emancipation and the Emancipation of Slaves during the French Revolution," *Proceedings of the Tenth World Congress of Jewish Studies*, Division B, Vol. II (Jerusalem: The World Union of Jewish Studies, 1990) 232–33. Of course, there were liberal voices before the Revolution, who called for an improvement in the Jewish status but made little headway. Szajkowski, *Jews and the French Revolutions*, 298, 319, 335. The edict of November 1787 concerning non-Catholics helped pave the way for other religious minorities to obtain their rights, but Louis XVI never granted the Jews the full rights of citizenship. Szajkowski, *Jews and the French Revolutions*, 319–21, 371ff., 379.

18. Tackett, *Religion, Revolution, and Regional Culture*, 208–10; Holmes, "Debate on Jewish Emancipation," 232; Dale K. Van Kley, *The Religious Origins of the French Revolution: From Calvin to the Civil Constitution, 1560–1791* (New Haven, CT, and London: Yale University Press, 1996) 3, 5; Lewis, *French Revolution*, 14; Kselman, "State and religion," 67. Protestants accounted for 2–3 percent of the population, while the Jews represented less than a tenth of their numbers. Tackett provides a slightly higher number of about seven hundred thousand (one-third Lutheran and two-thirds Huguenots) by combining the work of Mours and Scheidhauer. Tackett, *Religion, Revolution, and Regional Culture*, 205–6; Samuel Mours, *Les églises réformées en France* (Paris: Librairie Protestante, 1958); Marcel Scheidhauer, *Les églises luthériennes en France, 1800–1815* (Strasbourg: Oberlin, 1975). Protestants were given a modicum of toleration in November, overturning the revocation of the Edict of Nantes (1685). Kselman, "State and religion," 66–67.
19. Grégoire, "Motion en faveur des Juifs," in *La Révolution Française et l'emancipation des Juifs*, 7.8–9.
20. Ibid., 12, 16–22, 28–35, 40.
21. *Oeuvres Complètes de Robespierre* (Paris: E. Leroux, 1910–) 6.168, 169.
22. Hertzberg, *French Enlightenment and the Jews*, 355–57; Hanson, *Contesting the French Revolution*, 58.
23. Hanson, *Contesting the French Revolution*, 58; *The French Revolution and Napoleon*, 35; Szajkowski, *Jews and the French Revolutions*, xxvii; Hertzberg, *French Enlightenment and the Jews*, 138ff., 191, 192. The Sephardic Jews represented only around three thousand people. Some Jews thought it was important to distinguish the Jews of Portugal/Spain from those in Poland/Germany. *Letters of Certain Jews*, Philip Lefanu (trans.) (Paris and Covington, KY: G. G. Moore and J. L. Newby, 1845) 28, 29, 34–37.
24. "Décret de L'Assemblée Nationale de 27 Septembre 1791," in *La Révolution Française et l'emancipation des Juifs*, 7.1, 2; Baubérot, *Histoire de la laïcité en France*, 8; Berkovitz, "French Revolution and the Jews," 25; Hertzberg, *French Enlightenment and the Jews*, 53; Albert, "French Enlightenment and the Jews," 40. Paris was solidly behind Jewish emancipation.
25. Berkovitz, "French Revolution and the Jews," 74.
26. Szajkowski, *Jews and the French Revolution*, 400, 401.
27. *Discours pronounce par Balthazar Faure, . . .* (Nancy: P. Barbier, an II) 7ff. [as cited by Szajkowsli, *Jews and the French Revolutions*, 402].
28. Szajkowski, *Jews and the French Enlightenment*, 406–11, 423–25, 810ff., 1024, 1025; Berovitz, "French Revolution and the Jews," 54; Hertzberg, *French Enlightenment and the Jews*, 52.
29. Tackett, *Religion, Revolution, and Regional Culture*, 237.
30. McManners, *French Revolution and the Church*, 87–88; Ord, "The Catholic Church in the French Revolution," 63. Fouché ordered the words "Death is an eternal sleep" inscribed on the gates of cemeteries. For a discussion of Pierre Gaspard Chaumette, his associate, and the rest of his minions or dechristianizers, see McManners, *French Revolution and the Church*, 87–88.
31. Ibid., 86–97.
32. Tackett, "The Meaning of the Oath," in *The French Revolution and Intellectual History*, Jack R. Censer (ed.) (Chicago: The Dorsey Press, 1989) 152; Baubérot, *Histoire de la laïcité en France*, 9; Hanson, *Contesting the French*

Revolution, 78; McManners, *French Revolution and the Church*, 26; Lewis, *French Revolution*, 61, 95. The church was certainly entitled to this land according to conventional wisdom establishing property rights during the day. See McManners, *French Revolution and the Church*, 27.

33. Frank Tallet, "Dechristianizing France: The Year II and the Revolutionary Experience," in *Religion, Society and Politics in France since 1789*, Frank Tallet and Nicholas Atkin (ed.) (London and Rio Grande: Hambledon Press, 1991) 6–7; T. Jeremy Gunn, "Under God but Not the Scarf," *Journal of Church and State* 46/1 (Wint. 2004): 13.
34. Ibid., 10; Dale K. Van Kley, "Catholic Conciliar Reform in an Age of Anti-Catholic Revolution: France, Italy, and the Netherlands," in *Religion and Politics in Enlightenment Europe*, James E, Bradely and Dale K. Van Kley (ed.) (Notre Dame: University of Notre Dame Press, 2001) 46–47. Abbé Grégoire and the United Bishops convened councils trying to reconcile the Protestant schism and bring Protestant-like reform.
35. See, for example, *The French Revolution and Napoleon*, 87–88.
36. Michel Vovelle, *The Revolution against the Church: From Reason to Supreme Being*, Alan José (trans.) (Columbus, OH: The Ohio State University, 1991) 13, 30–31, 99ff., 119–22; Baubérot, *Histoire de la laïté en France*, 15; McManners, *The French Revolution and the Church*, 100, 101; Hampson, *Life and Opinions of Maximilien Robespierre*, 201.
37. In one infamous instance, Marat was turned into a martyr and cult-like figure during his funeral, later enshrined in the mausoleum, only to be exhumed later as an evil and bloodthirsty man on April 8, 1795. McManners, *The French Revolution and the Church*, 98; *The French Revolution and Napoleon*, 117.
38. Hanson, *Contesting the French Revolution*, 119.
39. Ord, "The Catholic Church in the French Revolution," 63; Frey and Frey, *French Revolution*, xxii, xxiii, Jack R. Censer, "Glossary," in *The French Revolution and Intellectual History*, 205; Hampson, *Life and Opinions of Maximilien Robespierre*, 201; Hanson, *Contesting the French Revolution*, 119.
40. Baubérot, *Histoire de la laïcité en France*, 12.
41. Ibid., 9; McManners, *The French Revolution and the Church*, 31, 111–113.
42. *French Revolution and Napoleon*, 45–47; Frey and Frey, *French Revolution*, 6; Hanson, *Contesting the French Revolution*, 78; Tackett, *Religion, Revolution, and Regional Culture*, 15–16. Lay elections of the clergy were not a priority of the people, judging from the paucity of *cahiers* dealing with the matter. The *cahiers* show significant respect for the *curés* and want them to receive a fair share of the church's wealth. Tackett, *Religion, Revolution, and Regional Culture*, 15–16; McManners, *The French Revolution and the Church*, 12–15. The Assembly wanted to attenuate the economic inequality among the *curé* but was never able to erase it. In fact, the promised salaries were not delivered and officially denied several years later in September 1794, even to the constitutional priests. Baubérot, *Histoire de la laïcité en France*, 15, 16; McManners, *The French Revolution and the Church*, 39, 118; Tackett, *Religion, Revolution, and Regional Culture*, 91. Gliozzo sees the hand of Voltaire in the Civil Constitution, since he advocated the secularization of priest's salaries and the closing of monasteries. "The Philosophes and Religion," 275; Gay, *Voltaire's Politics*, 269. Under the Bourbon Monarchy,

the king chose the bishops and archbishops, and the popes simply blessed the decisions. Lewis, *French Revolution*, 4.

43. Tackett, *Religion, Revolution, and Regional Culture*, 5, 6; Lewis, *French Revolution*, 95.
44. Kselman, "State and religion," 69; Tackett, "The Meaning of the Oath," 152; *Religion, Revolution, and Regional Culture*, 40–41, 44; Frey and Frey, *French Revolution*, 116–17; Baubérot, *Histoire de la laïcité en France*, 10; Hanson, *Contesting the Revolution*, 79–80. The financial position of the clerics played an important role in whether they took the oath or not. Older *curés* took the oath out of a need for security. Tackett, "The Meaning of the Oath," 154, 161; *Religion, Revolution, and Regional Culture*, 84, 140–41; McManners, *The French Revolution and the Church*, 52. Only 81 out of 263 ecclesiastics in the National Assembly took the oath—perhaps, sensing the growing tide of anticlericalism in Paris. Tackett, *Religion, Revolution, and Regional Culture*, 48–49.
45. Tackett, *Religion, Revolution, and Regional Culture*, 159ff.; McManners, *The French Revolution and the Church*, 38, 46; Lewis, *French Revolution*, 95.
46. McManners, *The French Revolution and the Church*, 63–65; *French Revolution and Napoleon*, 47, 48; Baubérot., *Histoire de la laïcité en France*, 1.
47. Daniele Menozzi, "The Significance of the Catholic Reaction to the Revolution," in *1789: The French Revolution and the Church*, 78; Baubérot, *Histoire de la laïcité en France*, 10; McManners, *The French Revolution and the Church*, 59; Hanson, *Contesting the French Revolution*, 78–79. Pius VI issued this brief entitled *Quod aliquantum* on March 10, 1791. A couple years later the pope condemned revolutionary principles in general as a Calvinist plot to destroy the Catholic Church. The papacy and the Catholic Church felt the medieval model of theocracy had a civilizing effect on society and could control the anarchy of Protestantism. Menozzi, "The Significance of the Catholic reaction," 78–85.
48. *French Revolution and Napoleon*, 65. In August of 1792, a new oath was issued that allowed refractories to swear allegiance to the principles of the Revolution (liberty, equality, and property) but not to the country, and a third of them took this restrictive oath. McManners, *The French Revolution and the Church*, 63; Tackett, *Religion, Revolution, and the Regional Culture*, 44. Eventually, the *curés* who joined the Revolution and took the oath became the object of general hostility toward the church and its hierarchy. Tallett, "Dechristianizing France," 20; Kley, *The Religious Origins of the French Revolution*," 349–52.
49. Frey and Frey, *French Revolution*, 73; Lewis, *French Revolution*, 96; McManners, *The French Revolution and the Church*, 106–7; Baubérot, *Histoire de la laïcité en France*, 14. The prison massacre of 240 nonjuring priests on Sept. 2, 1792, was the most infamous episode. *French Revolution and Napoleon*, 66; Frey and Frey, *French Revolution*, 66–67.
50. Tackett, *Religion, Revolution, and Regional Culture*, 227.
51. McManners, *The French Revolution and the Church*, 121; Kley, "Catholic Conciliar Reform," 130.
52. Gérard Colvy, "Revolution and the Church: Breaks and Continuity," in *1789: The French Revolution and the Church*, 51–59; Tallett, "Dechristianizing

France," 3–4. Gibson estimates that 82 percent of the rural community was pious before the Revolution in centering much of their life around the church. Lewis, *French Revolution*, 93; Ralph Gibson, *A Social History of French Catholicism*, 1789–1914 (London and New York: Routledge) 2.

53. Montesquieu, *L'Esprit des lois* (Paris: Garner Frères, 1961) III, xix, 18 (328–29). See Ibid., II, x, 14 (156–57); III, xix, 14–21 (326–32).
54. Tallett, "Dechristianizing France, 4, 5; McManners, *The French Revolution and the Church*, 132–39; Frey and Frey, *French Revolution*, xxiii.
55. William Doyle, *Jansenism: Catholic Resistance to Authority from the Reformation to the French Revolution* (New York: St. Martin's Press, Inc., 2000) 1, 18, 22ff.; Kley, *Religious Origins of the French Revolution*, 58–59. The spiritual headquarters was housed in a female monastery at Port Royale and included the likes of Jean du Vergier, Abbé de Saint-Cyran, Antoinme Arnauld, Pierre Nicole, and Blaise Pascal.
56. *Enchiridion Symbolorum*, Henricus Denzinger (ed.) (Freiburg: Verlag Herder, 1963) 445 (2001–2007); Doyle, *Jansenism*, 26, 91.
57. Charles H. O'Brien, "The Jansenist Campaign for the Toleration of Protestants in Late Eighteenth-Century France: Sacred or Secular?," *Journal of the History of Ideas* 46/4 (Oct.–Dec. 1985): 523–38; "Jansénisme et tolerance civile à la veille de la Révolution," *Jansénisme et Révolution* (Paris: Chroniques de Port-Royal Bibliotheque Mazarine, 1990) 31, 33ff.; "Jansenists on Civil Toleration in Mid-Eighteenth Century France," *Theologische Zeitschrift* 37 (1981): 71ff.; Dale K. Van Kley, "Protestantism, Catholicism, and the Religious Origins of the French and American Revolutions," *Fides et Historia* 23/1 (1991) 60; Kley, *Religious Origins of the French Revolution*, 155–56, 341–42.
58. Kley, *Religious Origins of the French Revolutions*, 50–53, 83–85, 227; "Protestantism, Catholicism, and the Religious Origins," 61. The Jesuits were founded by Ignatius of Loyola, who inculcated unconditional loyalty to the pope and a militant discipline of followers. They favored the ultimate power of the pope in spiritual and temporal affairs but needed to compromise their ultramontanism in France and respect the independent and divine right of the king as part of the country's long-established tradition. Doyle, *Jansenism*, 8; Kley, *Religious Origins of the French Revolution*, 50, 54–55.
59. Doyle, *Jansenism*, 73; Kley, *Religious Origins of the French Revolution*, 156–59; David Bien, "Religious Persecution in the French Revolution," *Church History* 30/3 (1961): 328–29.
60. Censer, "Glossary," 203.
61. Pasquier Quesnel, *The New Testament, with moral reflections upon every verse* . . ., Richard Russel (trans.) (London, 1719–25) xl, I/1, 38–39, 319–20, 239–41; III/2, 490–91 (Matt 5:10; 18:17, 20; 23:31, 1 Cor 5:5). Jansenists wanted sermons preached in French, and also translated the Bible and the mass to facilitate lay interpretation. Kley, *Religious Origins of the French Revolution*, 60; Michel Albaric, "Regard des jansénistes sur l'Eglise de France de 1780 à 1789 d'apres les Nouvelles Ecclésiastiques," in *Jansénisme et Révolution*, Catherine Maire (ed.) (Paris: Chronique de Port-Royal, 1990) 72.
62. Erasmus treatise *De libero arbitrio* sets the tone for the Council of Trent. In the work, Erasmus wants to strike a balance between the extremes of Pelagius and Luther, or divine grace and human volition, and uses the term *synergos*

(cooperation) to speak of this mediating position. He thinks Luther has exaggerated the divine part of the equation with the concepts of *total* depravity and grace *alone*, and subtracted the place of human beings in the process. Instead, he prefers the typical Catholic notion of addition (i.e., faith plus works, tradition plus scripture, nature plus grace, etc.). *De Libero Arbitrio*, in *Opera Omnia* (Lugduni Batavorum: Pieter van der Aa, 1703–1706) 1233(D), 1234 (D, E), 1235 (E, F), 1238 (A)-1239 (B), 1243 (F)-1244 (C), 1246 (A)-1247 (D). See *Canones et Decreta Dogmatica Concilii Tridentini*, session sexta, caput 5, in *Creeds of Christendom*, Philip Schaff (ed.) (Grand Rapids, MI: Baker Book House, 1977) 2.92. Hincmar, the archbishop of Reims and leader of the Council of Chiercy, condemned five offensive points in Gottschalk's teaching —double predestination, eternal security, total depravity, and the limitation of God's will and Christ's atonement to the elect. Hincmar, *Epistola ad Amolonem*, in C. Lambot, *Oeuvres théologiques et grammaticales de Godescalc d'Orbais* (Louvain: Spicilegium Sacrum Lovaniense, 1945) 16: "(1) quia ante Omnia saecula et antequam quidquam faceret a princio deus quos uoluit praedestinauit ad regnum et quos uoluit praedestinauit ad interitum; (2) et qui praedestinati sunt ad interitum saluari non possunt et qui praedestinati sunt ad regnum perire non possunt; (3) Et deus non uult omnes homines saluos fieri sed eos tantum qui saluantur. . . .; (4) Christus non uenit ut omnes saluaret nec passus est pro omnibus nisi solummodo pro his qui passionis eius saluantur mysterio; 5) Et Postquam primus homo libero arbitrio cecidit, nemo nostrum ad bene agendum sed tantummodo ad male agendum libero potest uti arbitrio." Gottschalk contended that God only desired the salvation of the elect, citing Augustine's interpretation of "omnes" in scripture (e.g., 1 Tim 2:4). Lambot, *Oeuvres*, 9, 40–42, 45, 248. Those elected are eternally secure (carnally secure according to Hincmar) and cannot lose their salvation—a teaching that is also consonant with Augustine, although Gottschalk goes beyond his mentor when he says that those who perish were never saved to begin with, despite receiving the benefits of the sacraments. Ibid., 8, 17ff., 40, 42, 225. Gottschalk says that not all those who were baptized receive full forgiveness from Christ, but only the elect have been forgiven of all their sins—past, present, and future. Baptism cleanses the reprobate of their former sins, but only the elect receive eternal redemption, since Christ died for their sins alone. Ibid., 224–27, 280, 345–46. However, it is really an open question whether Gottschalk taught double predestination in the fullest sense. He clearly teaches single predestination, but the destruction of the reprobate is often qualified by a reference to divine foreknowledge of their merit and divine justice. Ibid., 11, 37–38; PL 121.247–49.

In 1610, forty-six Arminian ministers assembled at Goulda to express similar concerns in their *Remonstrantia*, remonstrating five offensive points of the Calvinist position—similar to the list of Hincmar. Gerard Brandt, *History of the Reformation in the Low-Countries* (London: T. Wood, 1722) 2.74–77; A. W. Harrison, *The Beginnings of Arminianism to the Synod of Dort* (London: University Press of London, 1926) 152. See *Creeds of Christendom*, 3.545–49 for their specific statement. This statement led to the famous Synod of Dordrecht (or Dort) and the framing of the five points of Calvinism, which speak of the total depravity of humankind, the unconditional nature of God's choice of a certain few, the limitation of God's intention and Christ's work (although this article was very controversial at the synod and contains ambiguity/latitude), the irresistible nature of grace, and the perseverance of the saints/eternal security. *Acta Synodi Nationalis* (Dordrecht: Isaac Ioannid Canin, 1620) 1.279–322.

63. Quesnel, *New Testament*, xxxiii, III/2, 361 (Rom. 7:18).
64. Ibid., xxxiii, II/2, 672; III/1, 102, 197 (John 10:29, Acts 9:3; 17:11), II/2, 384, 385 (Rom 9:10, 11, 15), III/2, 579, 580, 580 (1 Cor 15:10). Like a Protestant, he thinks of faith as the root of all graces or the means of becoming a Christian, but he rejects the doctrine of justification by faith alone. Faith must be animated by love or charity to bring justification. Ibid., II/2, 508, 670; III/2, 326–27 (John 3:16; 10:26, Rom 3:22–26, Gal 5:16).
65. For limited atonement, see Ibid., III/2, 708 (Gal. 4:7). For eternal security, see Ibid., II/2, 577 (Jn. 6:40). However, he divides the elect from those who were baptized [Ibid., III/2, 382 (Rom. 9:6)], leaving us to wonder whether they lost their salvation or never really received eternal salvation, as Gottschalk contended. The Calvinists are left with a similar ambiguity in regard to their belief that children should be baptized as members of the covenant of grace, following the theology of Zwingli and Bullinger, and then grafting this concept later on when Calvin and Butzer's doctrine of eternal security is added to the staple of Reformed theology. Zwingli and Bullinger did not accept the doctrine and had no problem with a child spurning the covenant and losing its salvation, but what about a Calvinist? Was the baptized child who spurned the covenant a member of the covenant or not, saved or not, secure or not?
66. Jancourt, "Unigenitus," in *Encyclopédie* (1761–1772), U; Doyle, *Jansenism*, 45.
67. Unigenitus also condemns its Protestant-like deprecation of fear as a proper spiritual motivation (61) and its Anabaptist-like concern over oaths (101). Cf. Quesnel, *New Testament*, I/1, 48–50 (Matt 5:35).
68. Kley, *Religious Origins of the French Revolution*, 81, 112, 126–28. Bishop André-Hercule de Fleury led the task of purging Jansenists from the clergy. Doyle, *Jansenism*, 59.
69. Ibid., 131, 173–74; Journal et Mémoires Marquis Argenson (Paris: Mme Ve Jules Renouard, 1866) 8.12, 35.
70. Kley, *Religious Origins of the French Revolution*, 135ff.
71. Doyle, *Jansenism*, 64; Kley, *Religious Origins of the French Revolution*, 148.
72. Dale Van Kley, "Church, State, and the Ideological Origins of the French Revolution: The Debate over the General Assembly in 1765," in *The French Revolution and Intellectual History*, 96–97; *Religious Origins of the French Revolution*, 144–45, 149. The *parlements* represent the "supreme courts of appeals in the judicial system of the Old regime." The original *parlement* was located in Paris, but twelve others were added as extensions of royal judicial authority by 1789. Some historians think of them as protecting their own aristocratic interests, while others view them as early defenders of individual freedom. Censer, "Glossary," 204–5.
73. Kley, "Christianity, Christian Interpretation, and the Origins of the French Revolution," 23–24; "Protestantism, Catholicism, and the Religious Origins of the French and American Revolutions," 60; "Church, State, and the Ideological Origins of the French Revolution," 94, Censer, "Glossary," 203.

74. Cf. Kley, "Catholic Conciliar Reform," 108–9, 124; *Religious Origins of the French Revolution,* 195–96.
75. Saige, *Catéchisme du Citoyen,* 120–21, 157.
76. Kley, *Religious Origins of the French Revolution,* 151–53, 156, 157.
77. Catherine Maire, "Agonie Religieuse et Transfiguration Politique de Jansénisme,"in *Jansénisme et Révolution,* 104, 106. Peter Campbell also speaks of the early political struggles of Jansenism. "Les crises parlementaires et les jansénistes (1727–1740), 147.
78. Ibid., 104, 109–10.
79. Doyle, *Jansenism,* 53–53; Kley, *Religious Origins of the French Revolution,* 94ff.
80. Kley, "Christianity, Christian Interpretation, and the Origins of the French Revolution," 26–28; *Religious Origins of the French Revolution,* 268; Doyle, *Jansenism,* 88.
81. Kley, *Religious Origins of the French Revolution,* 254, 269; Doyle, *Jansenism,* 82. For a collection of Jansenist essays that exhibit this emphasis, see *Jansénisme et Révolution,* Catherine Maire (ed.) (Paris: Chroniques de Port-Royal, 1990).
82. Kley, "Du Parti Janseniste au Parti Patriote (1770–1775): L'Ultime Secularisation d'une Tradition Religieuse a l'Epoque du Chancelier Maupeou," in *Janséisme et Révolution,* 115.
83. Maire, "Agonie Religieuse et Transfiguration Politique de Jansénisme," 104.
84. Strehle, *Egalitarian Spirit of Christianity,* 141; Jean Gerson, *De Potestate Ecclesiastica,* in *Oeuvres Complètes,* Palémon Glorieux (intro., texte et notes) (Paris and New York: Desclee & Cie, 1965) 6.216–17, 228, 236–42; *De Plenitudine Potestatis Ecclesiasticae,* 250–51.
85. Gerson, *De Potestate Ecclesiastica,* 211, 214, 217, 227, 233.
86. Strehle, *Egalitarian Spirit of Christianity,* 14–23. Jean Morély wrote the major treatise of the sixteenth-century Huguenots on democracy, emphasizing the Lordship of Christ and the *liberté* and *egalité* of all believers. The same emphasis upon the priesthood of the believers is found in the early Congregationalist movement. Jean Morély, *Traicté de la discipline & police Chrestienne* (Lyon: Ian de Tournes, 1562) preface, 174, 175, 272; P. Denis et J. Rott, *Jean Morély (ca. 1524–ca. 1594) et l'utopie d'une démocratie dans l'Eglise* (Genève: Droz, 1993) 330–32; *De Ecclesiae ordine,* 1.77ff., 83ff. ; Robert Browne, "A Treatise upon 23. Of Matthew," 212, 217–20; "An Answer to Master Cartwright," 465; "A Booke which sheweth the life and manner of all true Christians," 276–77, 323, 333, 387; Strehle, *The Egalitarian Spirit of Christianity,* 3, 4,14ff. *De Ecclesione ordine* is found as no. 4361 in the Department of Manuscripts de la Bibliothèque Nationale de Paris and is summarized for our convenience by Denis and Rott. The references to Browne are taken from *The Writings of Robert Harrison and Robert Browne,* Albert Peel and L. H. Carlson (ed.) (London: George Allen and Unwin Ltd., 1953).
87. [Claude Mey], *Apologie des jugemens rendus en France contre la schism par les Tribunaux séculiers* (Paris?: s.n., 1752) 1.214–16, 225–26; "Dissertatio sur le droit de convoquer les États généraux," (S.I.: s.n., 1787) 19–20, 31; Kley, *The Religious Origins of the French Revolution,* 91, 195–96, 198; Kley, "Du Parti Janseniste au Parti Patriote (1770–1775): L'Ultime Secularization

d'une Tradition Religieuse a l'Epoque du Chancelier Maupeou," in *Jansénisme et Révolution*, 120–21. For a discussion of the Decretalists, Holland, England, and the natural rights tradition, see Strehle, *The Egalitarian Spirit of Christianity*, 137–39.

88. Ibid., 1, 36, 38, 41, 86. The emphasis upon the influence of Protestantism is more mine than Kley's. In my way of thinking, the Jansenists have a strong affinity to the Puritans in a number of areas, not just those already mentioned in theology and politics. Like the Puritans, for example, they display ethical austerity in their opposition to dancing, gaming, theatre, pomp, etc.; they advocate an early form of capitalism or free economic system; and they provide the same type of rational autonomy in science, making faith look to the authority of scripture and freeing science to study secondary causality on its own. Alexander Sedgwick, "Seventeenth Century French Jansenism and the Enlightenment," in *Church, State, and Society under the Bourbon Kings of France*, Richard M. Golden (ed.) (Lawrence, KS: Coronado Press, Inc., 1982)130; Strehle, *Egalitarian Spirit of Christianity*, chap. 5, 191–92, 226–27.
89. Saige, *Catéchisme du Citoyen*, 120–26.
90. Ibid., 117–18.
91. Kley, *Religious Origins of the French Revolution*, 354; Tackett, *Religion, Revolution, and Regional Culture*, 128–29, 132. Before 1730, as many as three-fourths of the *curés* in Paris were Jansenists. Kley, *Religious Origins of the French Revolution*, 97.
92. Doyle, *Jansenism*, 83. Doyle says the number of elected Jansenists "did not number more than 30 at the most." Among the most notable were Grégoire, Camus, Lanjuinais, Saurine, and Martineau. Yann Fauchois adds to the list those who used Jansenist vocabulary "comme Charrier de La Roche, Fréteau de Saint-Just, Goupil de Préflin, ou meme Duval d'Eprémesnil." See Tackett, *Religion, Revolution, and Regional Culture*, 7; Yann Fauchois, "Les jansénistes et la constitution civile du clerge," in *Jansénisme et Révolution*, 200–201.
93. Albaric, "Regard des janénistes sur l'Eglise de France," 67.
94. Kley, "Christianity, Christian Interpretation, and the Origins of the French Revolution," 23–24, 26; "Catholic Conciliar Reform," 105; Albaric, "Regard des jansénistes sur l'Eglise de France," 71–72.
95. Kley, *Religious Origins of the French Revolution*, 200, 339, 355; "Church, State, and the Ideological Origins of the French Revolution," 108; Tackett, *Religion, Revolution, and Regional Culture*, 6– 7. A good example of this is Étienne Mignot's *Traité des Droits de l'État et du Prince, Sur les Biens possédés par le Clergé*, 6 tomes (Amsterdam: Arkstée et Merkus, 1755). Mignot rejects the notion that the clergy are exempt from paying taxes and believes they have the same obligation to pay their fair share (xii, xiii, 1.29; 2.330–35, 389). He relates natural right/laws (*droits*) to taxes (not property) in this context, claiming it is a "natural *droit*" that obliges all those who share in the advantages of society to share in its expenses (2.336). He says, the state is prior to the church in the order of creation and has the right to "alienate" the property of the church for its needs, which include the defense of the country and the feeding of the poor (2.302–304). The state is in charge of all temporal goods, and ecclesiastical property belongs to the authority of the state for its inspection and usage (xxiii, 2.349–52). The civil magistrates

act as representatives of the whole church in managing and guarding the property, and possess the authority to remove the ecclesiastical administration whenever it seems appropriate to the needs of the faithful, or members of the church/state (1.109–12). Of course, the property of heretics is subject to confiscation (1.239–41).

96. Edmond Préclin, *Les Jansénistes du XVIIe siècle et la Constitution civile do Clergé* (Paris: Librairie Universitaire J. Gamber, 1929) 482ff., 490ff; Kley, "Church, State, and the Ideological Origins," 108; Maire, "Agonie Religieuse et Transfiguration Politique de Jansénisme," 103; Fauchois, "Les jansénistes et la constitution civile du clerge," 197. Edmond Préclin's *Les Jansénistes du XVIIIe Siècle et Constitution Civile de Clergé* (1929) opened the way for scholars to see Jansenists as a significant part of the development of the Civil Constitution. However, some of the Jansenists and Richerists opposed it, perhaps seeing the imminent danger for the culture. McManners, *French Revolution and the Church*, 52–53.

5

Laïcité

The Concordat

After the death of Robespierre, chaos continued to rule the land until the Revolution gave way to a "security state" in November of 1799 with the advent of Napoleon, a general in the French army. Napoleon staged his coup on 18 and 19 Brumaire, with the help of his brother Lucien, the president of the Council of Five Hundred, and the political intrigues of Abbé Sieyès, who turned to the military in a desperate attempt to gain power and a sense of order over the unstable situation. This event started a downward spiral toward dictatorship, negating revolutionary principles and fulfilling Burke's dire prediction when Napoleon was given extensive executive powers as "First Consul" for life (1802) and then hereditary emperor (1804).[1] In his capacity as dictator, he feigned popular support or electoral fraud through plebiscites, closed down newspapers opposing his regime, and wrote an Imperial Catechism, which inculcated submission to his will as the "Lord's anointed."[2] He established his will through a uniform law code, using/misusing much of the Revolution's rhetoric and hoping to expand its ideals and France's dominion over other nations. He told Jerome, the king of Westphalia:

> Your people need to enjoy a certain liberty, equality and a well-being unknown to the peoples of Germany, and this liberal government will produce, one way or another, the most salutary changes for the system of the Confederation and the power of your monarchy. This manner of governing will be a more powerful barrier in order to separate you from Prussia than the Elbe, the fortresses, and the protection of France. What people would wish to return to the arbitrary Prussian government when they have tasted the benefits of a wise and liberal administration? The peoples of Germany, as well as those of France, Italy and Spain, desire equality and want liberal ideas.[3]

In many ways, his wars epitomized the Revolution, only bringing the conflict to the world outside its borders, trying to impose "universal liberty" on other nations and creating even more carnage: millions of casualties, three million or so dead, hundreds of thousands of refugees, and hundreds of towns and cities looted, raped, burned, and ruined.[4]

Napoleon was fundamentally a godless man but practical enough to recognize the failure of the dechristianization program and "cruel policies of the Directory" as counterproductive to the success of the Republic, as well as his own agenda.[5] He viewed religion within the utilitarian framework of the Enlightenment as a necessary part of French society, and he thought it more sensible to incorporate the church into his government plans and patronize its leaders than continue fomenting resistance. He told a group of clergy:

> This religion [Catholicism] is the only religion which can procure true happiness for a well-ordered society. . . . I will apply myself to protect and defend it at all times and by every means. . . . Without religion, one walks constantly in darkness and the Catholic religion is the only one which gives man certain and infallible enlightenment about his beginning and final end. No society can exist without morals; there are no good morals without religion; there is nothing other than religion, to give the state a firm and lasting support. A society without religion is like a ship without a compass.[6]

In this context, he promised to "remove all the obstacles that may yet oppose the complete reconciliation of France with the head of the Church."[7]

On September 10, 1801, he fulfilled this promise and reestablished good relations with the papacy, signing a concordat and healing the deep schism in French society. A number of Organic Articles were soon enacted and added to the papal agreement, serving the society together with the Concordat as the basic framework of church/state relations for the next century, until secularity was established in 1905. The laws ended popular elections of the clergy and restored the power of investiture to the church, with the proviso that the First Consul controlled the nominating of bishops and received in exchange for the office of bishop an oath of allegiance to the state, renouncing any attempt to disturb the "public tranquility." The papacy was required to renounce all prior claims to the properties seized by the Revolution, while the state must pay the salaries of all clergy in exchange for this loss of revenue. The church was given more control over the regular clergy, who were now placed under the nomination process of bishops, the necessary approval of the state, and the same oath of allegiance. Catholicism was officially recognized as the "religion of the majority of French citizens," but ultramontanism was rejected in the name of Gallicanism, allowing the state to exercise control over the church and reject papal bulls or briefs intended for the faithful in France. The religion was also disestablished for the sake of toleration, and other expressions of faith—the Reformed, the Lutherans, and later the Jews—received the new status of "recognized cults," giving them the same privileges as Catholics, including the right to public expression and the nationalization and support of their property and clergy.[8] These and other particulars were acceptable to the Catholic Church in producing a tolerable situation for the time being, but it was clear that the state had gained the upper hand and was sure to use its power in refashioning the culture into its obedient subjects.

Through state control, the French became more worldly and indifferent to the matters of religion in the course of the nineteenth century.[9] Over 90 percent of the citizens continued to baptize their children, but only a paltry 14 percent bothered to partake of communion on a holy day like Easter—let alone the other Sundays of the year.[10] The tide of the culture was moving against the church as the state demanded more and more attention from its subjects, and the forces of the Enlightenment and the Revolution took hold of the affections of the people. Naturally the church reacted to the spiritual crisis with horror and condemned the etatism of the Revolution for attempting to secularize human beings and exorcize God from their lives,[11] but its reaction was too visceral, often proceeding to the antithesis of the Revolution and siding with the enemies of liberalism, republicanism, and some of the Revolution's positive virtues.[12] The papacy and many Catholic intellectuals proved intransigent in their ways and longed for a return to the medieval synthesis, where the church brought a civilizing and unifying effect upon society against the barbarian hordes, believing the church could restore its place of honor once again by establishing the old authoritarian structure and withstanding the present chaos of Protestant/Republican forces.[13]

Ferry Laws

This hope was dashed with the collapse of the Second Empire and the establishment of the Third Republic in 1870 with its secular and anticlerical agenda.[14] When the Republicans gained full control of the government at the end of the decade, they wasted little time in working to diminish the role of the church in society as the main priority of the administration, increasingly cutting clerical salaries and ecclesiastical budgets throughout the 1880s and passing a series of anticlerical laws.[15] The battle cry was "Le cléricalisme, voilà l'ennemi."[16] Léon Gambetta, prominent left-wing Republican, considered the pope the great enemy of all modern principles of liberty and proposed scrapping the Concordat and the Organic Articles altogether. He said the pope and his agents of ultramontanism have brought a spirit of slavery to the country and continue to destroy the souls of the youth by spreading anti-French propaganda and rotting their minds with worthless dogma instead of providing sound instruction. It is essential for the future of the republic to eliminate clerical indoctrination and separate the civic and political world from religion by emphasizing reason over the "myths of religious infants" and teaching children the values of the modern world: freedom from authority, human rights, free choice, equality, truth, and an appetite for science.[17] On May 31, 1883, the Report of the Chamber of Deputies and its Commission of the Concordat endorsed much of Gambetta's analysis, finding the power structure of the Catholic Church abusive to its underlings and detrimental to the authority of the French government. It proposed ending the monetary advantages of the Catholic Church at the present time and creating a separation between church and state in the future, while recognizing the difficulty of taking this final step, thus recommending a delay in its enactment for practical and theoretical reasons.[18]

The secularization of education was the most urgent matter of business for the government in implementing the *idée laïque* during the first two decades of its existence. A series of laws were enacted in the 1880s encouraging the layification of the teaching profession and helping remove around half of the "nuns and brothers who taught in the nation's primary schools by the early 1990s." Legislation in 1881 and 1882 provided for free and obligatory public education, which excluded religious instruction from the classroom and inculcated moral and civic responsibilities in its place. The Act of 1885 eliminated the Catholic theological faculty from the Sorbonne and substituted a "scientific" approach to studying "religious phenomena"—sure to undermine the faith with its "objective" analysis.[19] The following year the Goblet law forbad clerics from teaching in the public schools.

The one name associated with these series of laws was Jules Ferry, a Republican and twice prime minister of France in the 1880s.[20] Ferry believed that the "state must be secular" and called for a complete "separation of temporal and spiritual powers," rejecting the notion of a civil religion and the need to talk of God in public. He thought it necessary to make the "social organisms of society exclusively secular (laïque)," considering it "the key accomplishment, the major concern, the great passion and service of the French Revolution."[21] He called his society to reconsider the religious policies that developed in the meantime and overturned the process of secularization, hoping to "reconstruct the great work of the French Revolution, which was destroyed by Napoleon I" and his Concordat.[22] In order to insure success this time, he was determined to seize power away from the teaching office of the Catholic Church in society and make it "the first duty of a democratic government" to keep "incessant, powerful, vigilant, and efficient control over public education," as belonging to "no other authority than that of the state."[23] Ferry and the Republicans wanted to use public education to create a unified Republican culture in France, instilling devotion to the Revolution and substituting "democratic civic loyalty for religious and traditional allegiance."[24] But this policy involved a difficult balancing act. Ferry invoked the public powers in this last statement because he knew that the "first things no one can fail to know" were not really so evident to everyone. Here he faced his greatest challenge in trying to replace the traditional role of the Catholic Church in providing a clear metaphysical foundation for ethical values with the new civic ethics, as if they were secular or neutral in regard to religious matters.[25] This problem led him to speak of ethical, political, and civil norms as a positivist, trying (or pretending?) to start "from below" and follow the rational/scientific epistemology of Descartes and

Bacon in developing all human knowledge. Through this secular method, he could maintain "confessional neutrality" in the schools and preach his metaphysical values all at the same time.[26]

> It is our faith, it is our secular instinct, and it is precisely all the foundation of positivism. For positivism, morality is essentially a human fact (*fait*) and distinct from all belief about the beginning and end of things. Morality is a social fact, which bears in itself its own beginning and end.[27]

With these comments, Ferry tried to speak of morality as a simple empirical fact of scientific inquiry and was somewhat convincing to a nineteenth-century, post-Enlightenment French audience in following a belief in the all-sufficient power of reason. Today he might seem less than sincere in failing to recognize the serious tensions and insurmountable difficulties in avoiding transcendent categories in his secular view of the state. He might appear less than rigorous to a modern professional philosopher in failing to acknowledge the limits of reason in discussing metaphysical matters like ethics and merely feigning neutrality, while preaching the unsubstantiated virtues of Republican dogma, as if the church was the only institution inculcating a catechism, but he certainly worked within an acceptable philosophical matrix of the time; even within the postmodern world, many still follow his line of reasoning in defending the possibility of a secular state developing its agenda through dispassionate scientific and rational categories, above and beyond religious or metaphysical concerns.

Law of 1905

The process of secularization continued until the Concordat and the Organic Articles were scrapped on December 9, 1905 with the enactment of a law "Concerning the Separation of the Churches and the State," passing the two chambers by a substantial margin and signed by the president of the Republic, Émile Loubet. The title displayed the basic intent of the legislature to reject any compromise with the Concordat or civil religious expressions of the past, and it was an important aspect of the law, since the legislature voted on this specific title and rejected any attempt to mitigate its force with more accommodating language like "New Relations of the Churches and the State."[28] The four-month discussion preceding the vote revealed the considerable animosity of the left toward Christianity in general, not just the clergy. Maurice Alfred said, "Every religious person is sick." Jean Jaurès said, "We are fighting the church and Christianity because they are the negation of human right and contain the source of intellectual bondage."[29] The clear intent of these left-wing legislators was to create a "new man" by undoing the place of religion in society, rather than regulate the domain of religion or negotiate its relation to the public sphere.[30]

The original law of 1905 contained forty-four articles. The first article "insures the freedom of conscience" and free exercise of worship (*culte*), as long as these rights are exercised "within the interests of public order"—the old caveat that allows for broader and narrower interpretations. The second article scraps the Concordat and the system of recognized cults, creating a new policy, where the "Republic does not recognize, pay the salaries, or subsidize any *culte*."[31] The law proceeds from this point to wall off the church from influencing the public sphere, limiting its space of operation and making religion a private matter of no social utility.[32] Religious signs or symbols are not permitted in "any public place," with the exception of "houses of worship, burial grounds, funeral monuments, and certain museums or expositions." Public manifestations of worship, such as processions, ceremonies, or the ringing of church bells, are subject to local jurisdiction and censorship (a.27). The nationalization of church property remains in effect as fully justified, but the church is made responsible for maintaining the buildings that are used for worship (a.12–17).[33] Its Ministers are supported by the respective associations and confined to their specific religious duties; they cannot deprecate a political official or encourage resistance to a civil law within the church; they cannot enter a classroom and provide religious instruction for young impressionable students in the public schools.[34] No political meetings are allowed in church, and no religious instruction is allowed in the public classroom (a.26, 30, 34, 35).

The Law of 1905 ended the battle raging in the land between the "two Frances." Hereafter the identity of France was *laïque*, bringing victory to the secular camp and ending the country's former identification with Catholicism. The law placed religion under suspicion as a divisive element in society and made the state supreme as the enlightened agent of social unity and rational progress.[35] The term most associated with the decision and the new national identity was *laïcité* and its cognates. It was first coined in the 1870s and gained currency at the time in describing French policies that reached their fulfillment in this law, and it is still used today in describing the French Republic, making an appearance for the first time in the Constitution of 1946 as a cornerstone of the society.[36] The term is impossible to define succinctly, but the typical scholastic analysis finds within it certain negative attitudes toward the religious community: the desire to eliminate religious influence on the state, the superiority of secularity, the hubris of enlightened reason, the suspicion of clergy and religion, the preference for a secular *fraternité*, the hostility toward religious pluralism, and the mania of etatism and ethnocentricity.[37] Some of the antireligious attitudes are understandable and based upon the real historical concern of ending the domination of priests in French culture and empowering the laity to participate in all realms of society with an equal voice, but the genuine concerns soon display a darker side and turn into a visceral, irrational, and overexercised reaction against the Catholic faith and religion, in general, based upon the mythic views of the Enlightenment with its fabricated history and exaggerated deprecation of the church and its leaders.[38]

Today's constitution continues to describe the country as *laïque.*[39] The use of the term means that France consciously establishes a-theism as the modus operandi of the state and rejects any seepage of religion into the public square as detrimental to society, preferring to keep its influence down below the surface at the bottom and edges of society. Of course, the atheistic establishment has considerable difficulty in denuding religion from a culture steeped in its traditions and develops cracks all the time in its attempt to wall off its influence,[40] but the fundamental power of the government continues to plod along in establishing secularity and exorcizing religious categories and meaning from the culture—sometimes implementing what other Western cultures consider draconian policies to insure this ultimate goal.[41]

A good example of a harsh measure is the 2004 French law that banned public school students from wearing clothing or insignia that "conspicuously manifest a religious affiliation." The law was passed by an overwhelming margin (494–36 in the National Assembly and 276–20 in the Senate), reflecting the strong popular support that was found across the country. The decision was based on the seventy-eight page Stasi Commission's report in December of 2003, which extolled the concept of *laïcité* and applied it to the issue at hand as the fundamental determining principle (2).[42]

At the beginning of the report, France is described as a "République laïque," and reference is made to the law of 1905 and the constitutions of 1946 and 1958, which "separate church and state" and provide a "guarantee of neutrality" in regard to religious matters (2, 11, 13, 19). *Laïcité* is understood as a unique feature of the French Constitution and touted as the foundation of national cohesion, the very "cornerstone of the Republican pact" (3–4, 9, 32). It provides the reason for giving the "political power a dominating influence over every spiritual or religious alternative, so we can live together" in harmony as one people (9). The report refers to the general will of the people supporting this concept of secularity and wants to ensure its place among the constituency in the future by encouraging the development of courses upon the philosophy of *laïcité,* making teachers sign a charter of commitment to its principles and displaying the charter at important public places and special occasions (6, 50–51, 67). The goal is to create enlightened citizens in public schools, who appreciate the origins of secularization in the French Revolution and understand its ongoing importance in developing the freedom of conscience and delivering the people from authoritarian rule, sponsored by the church and its doctrine of the divine right of kings (10–11).[43]

In this way, the report continues the Revolution's war against the *Ancien Régime* and its hierarchical order, but it fails to appreciate how the general will of the people can oppress specific religious communities, or the problem of reconciling majority rule/large government/totalitarianism with the freedom of the individual conscience. Its concept of freedom accommodates the propensity of the French Revolution to forge individuals into a unified mass of citizens and suppress local communities,[44] allowing the report to accent in its decision unity over diversity, *fraternité* over *liberté*, without collapsing under the strain of the obvious tension of considering their reconciliation a significant problem.[45] In fact, the report leaves freedom of conscience far behind when it focuses upon "extremist groups," who threaten to tear apart the national unity by spurning common French values, or when it expresses concern about the tribalism (*communautaisme*) of the Netherlands, which accents the rights of separate communities and provides equal funding for public and sectarian schools (32–35). This "drift toward community sentiment" is considered a real threat to the unity and "common values of societies," and the report thinks something must be done to prevent the fragmenting influence of diverse cultures from further eroding the sanctity of historic French identity, not restoring liberty as an important principle (15, 18).

In this context, the report rules against permitting conspicuous religious signs in public schools as disturbing the public order (41).[46] It says that Christian crosses, Jewish kippot, and Muslim headscarves put undue pressure upon other students to adopt a sectarian viewpoint, impinging upon the individual conscience and destroying the public space, which provides freedom from coercion or proselytizing (29–30).[47]

> [The *laïque* state] protects everyone against every pressure, physical or moral, exercised under the cover of various spiritual or religious prescriptions. The defense of liberty of individual conscience goes against proselyting today fulfilling the central concepts of separation and neutrality in the law of 1905. . . .
>
> Every manifestation of religious convictions in the setting of service is interdicted and the bearing of a religious sign also, even when the personnel are not in contact with the public. Even in regard to access for public employment, the administration is able to consider the behavior of the candidate in considering admittance to public service, if it reveals unfitness to exercise certain functions which demand full respect for republican principles (14, 22).

In this particular case, the principle of *laïcité* is enacted to protect the public schools, and the pretext is the controversy over the growth of Islam in the country, particularly the presence of the Muslim headscarf (*hijab*) in the public schools. The report justifies its ban, expressing concern about the pressure from the Muslim community upon their girls to adopt sectarian standards of dress, or else be treated like "whores," "infidels," or "immodest women" (46–47). It speaks of the need to promote equality among the sexes within this community and protect the rights of all women, especially these young women against the abuse of sectarian religious ideologues like the Islamists (47, 51, 58).[48] Of course, no similar concern is expressed to protect religious people against secular conformity and its more subtle and pervasive ridicule.[49]

The report reflects the burgeoning power of the state and its ultimate authority in the modern world, coercing all citizens to reflect its image. The report looks back to the dechristianization program of the French Revolution and the establishment of *laïcité* during the Third Republic, which sought to diminish the church's role in society and education, consciously trying to replace its values with a republican agenda and professing the neutrality or non-metaphysical nature of the new set of beliefs. The law of 1905 makes the establishment of secularity official, ending the Napoleonic system of "recognized cults," separating the churches from the state, and claiming that religion has no public role to fulfill in the future of the culture; the future is found in etatism. The goal of the state is to create a unified French citizenry and make all individual communities conform to *laïcité* in their inward and outward devotion—a commission the Stasi Report follows with utmost devotion—body, soul, and spirit. Any direct relation with the anti-Semitic and anti-Christian feelings of the French Revolution are disavowed in stating the policy, although one must wonder whether its problematic origin still clings to its present expression as an indelible aspect of this severe form of church/state separation.

Notes

1. *Correspondance de Napoléon I*[er], Henri Plon et J. Dumaine (ed.) (Paris, 1858–) 6.5–6; Frey and Frey, *French Revolution,* 15; Hanson , *Contesting the French Revolution,* 147, 148, 151, 1534; *French Revolution and Napoleon,* 136–139, 152–54. Napoleon justified his coup as a representative of the conservative wing of the Revolution, wanting to restore a sense of order and moderation. He blamed the Council of Five Hundred for plotting his assassination, giving him a pretext for action.
2. Buchez et Roux, *Histoire Parlementaire de la Révolution Française,* 38.332; André Latreille, *Le Catéchisme Imperial de 1806* (Paris: Société d'édition Les Belles Lettres, 1935) 81; Crook, "The French Revolution and Napoleon, 1788–1814," 30.
3. *Correspondance de Napoléon I*[er], 16.166. See *French Revolution and Napoleon,* 133–35.
4. Alan Schom, *Napoleon Bonaparte* (New York: Harper Collins Publishers, 1997) 789; Hanson, *Contesting the French Revolution,* 157, 158.
5. *Correspondance de Napoléon I*[er], 6.339. The civil code from 1800–1804 made no mention of religion and attributed natural rights to reason. One would think that if religion was an essential foundation for a moral society, it should receive some mention, and its absence belies Napoleon's patronizing rhetoric in the above statement. Elsewhere, he speaks of his willingness to accommodate whatever form the majority religion might take in a country as a necessary expedient. In France, he works to emancipate the universities from religious control. Baubérot, *Histoire de la laïcité en France,* 24–26; McManners, *French Revolution and the Church,* 142.

6. Ibid., 6.338, 339. See McManners, *French Revolution and the Church*, 140–42.
7. Ibid., 6.430.
8. Buchez et Roux, *Histoire Parlementaire de la Révolution Française*, 38.465–70 (Concordat de 1801), 470–486 (Articles Organiques de la Convention du 28 Messidor an IX); Crook, "The French Revolution and Napoleon," 31–32; Kselman, "State and religion," 71; Frey and Frey, *French Revolution*, 7; Hanson, *Contesting the French Revolution*, 151–52; Steven C. Hause, "French Protestants, Laicization, and the Separation of the Churches and the State," in *Religious Differences in France*, 138–39, 141; Baubérot, *Histoire de la laïcité en France*, 22–23; "La Construction d'une Société Pluraliste en France (XIXe–XXe Siècle)," *Foi et Vie* 86/6 (Dec. 1987): 43, 5; McManners, *French Revolution and the Church*, 142; Joan L. Coffey, "Of Catechisms and Sermons: Church-State Relations in France, 1890–1905," *Church History* 66/1 (Mr 1997): 57–58; Jean-François Zorn, "La Division dans la Separation," *Études théologiques et religieuse* 82/1 (2007): 106; Émile Poulet, "La laïcité en France au vingtième siècle," in *Catholicism, Politics and Society in Twentieth-Century France*, Kay Chadwick (ed.) (Liverpool: Liverpool University Press, 2000) 21. The Concordat was officially adopted and promulgated on April 8, 1802. In a series of codes, beginning in 1810 and ending in 1905, all non-authorized gatherings above twenty were deemed illegal. Zorn, "La Division dans la separation," 106.
9. Talett, "Dechristianizing France," 12–13.
10. Kselman, "State and religion," 74. The census of 1866 counted the population of France at 38 million with 37,100,000 Catholics, 850,000 Protestants, and 90,000 Jews. Baubérot, *Histoire de la laïcité en France*, 76.
11. J. Gaume, *La Révolution, Recherches Historiques* (Paris: Gaume Frères, 1856) 1.15–16; Menozzi, "The Significance of the Catholic Reaction to the Revolution," 76.
12. James F. McMillan, "Catholic Christianity in France from the Restoration to the Separation of Church and State, 1815–1905," in *The Cambridge History of Christianity: World Christianities: c. 1815–c. 1914*, Sheridan Gilley and Brian Stanley (ed.) (Cambridge: Cambridge University Press, 2006) 224.
13. Menozzi, "The Significance of the Catholic Reaction to the Revolution," 78–85. A couple years after his condemnation of the Civil Constitution, Pius VI unequivocally condemned the principles of the Revolution as a Calvinist plot. The popes of the nineteenth century followed his example. Ibid., 78–79.
14. Jean Baubérot, "The Evolution of Secularism in France: Between Two Civil Religions," Pavitra Puri (trans.), in *Comparative Secularisms in a Global Age*, Linell E. Cady and Elizabeth Shakman Hurd (ed.) (New York: Pargave Macmillan, 2010) 58; Kselman, "State and religion," 89–90.
15. Jan Goldstein and John W. Boyer, *Nineteenth-Century Europe* (Chicago and London: The University of Chicago Press, 1988) 357; Hause, "French Protestants, Laicization, and the Separation," 155; James F. MacMillan, "France," in *Political Catholicism in Europe, 1918–1965*, Tom Buchanan and Martin Conway (ed.) (Oxford: Clarendon Press, 1996) 35; Kselman, "State and religion," 63–64.
16. "Clericalism, that is the enemy." "Discours de Gambetta" (May 4, 1877), in *Les Fondateurs de la Troisième République*, Pierre Barral (ed.) (Paris: Armand Colin, 1968) 176.

17. "Discours de Gambetta" (Sept. 18, 1878, and Nov. 16, 1871), in *Les Fondateurs*, 178–80, 193–95. He and the subsequent report try to distance their criticisms of the church hierarchy from the "humble" and "impoverished" priests, who serve the local parish, since these priests have the affection of the local communities. Ibid. (Sept. 18, 1878) 180–81; "Rapport fait au nom de la commission du Concordat" (May, 31, 1883), in *Les Fondateurs*, 185.
18. "Rapport fait au nom de la commission du Concordat" (May 31, 1883), 184–87. The Chamber of Deputies agreed with the report and recognized the need for delay. "Chambre des députés" (June 8, 1889), 191, 192.
19. Jean-Paul Barquon, "La laïcité en France, cent ans après," Conscience et Liberté 66 (2005): 44, 45; McMillan, "Catholic Christianity in France," 228; Baubérot, *Histoire de la laïcité en France*, 49–53, 63–65; Kselman, "State and religion," 91; Goldstein and Boyer, *Nineteenth-Century Europe*, 357. Around 20 percent still opted to send their children to Catholic private schools, and around 50 percent to private secondary schools (mainly Catholic). McMillan, "Catholic Christianity in France," 228. Other *laïque* laws included the authorization of divorce, allowing businesses to open on Sunday, and ending public prayers during the sessions of parlement. Goldstein and Boyer, *Nineteenth-Century Europe*, 357.
20. Hause, "French Protestants, Laicization, and the Separation," 151–53. Ferry was a lapsed Catholic. Many Protestants supported him, but others warned against allying their cause with the *prêtophobes*. Most Protestants supported the separation of church and state, but others feared it, especially the reductions of budgets for the "recognized cults." Alexandre Vinet (1797–1847) was the chief Protestant spokesman for the separation of church and state in the nineteenth century. Zorn, "La Division dans la Separation," 108, 112–13; Hause, "French Protestants, Laicization, and the Separation," 145ff.
21. "Discours de Ferry" (June 3, 1876), in *Les Fondateurs*, 173; Baubérot, *Histoire de la laïcité en France*, 52–53. Ferry recognized the political and pragmatic need to delay the complete enactment of church/state separation. To keep the peace he would compromise his principles (e.g., leave crucifixes hanging in classrooms). "Chambre des deputes" (June 8, 1889), in *Les Fondateurs*, 192; Baubérot, *Histoire de la laïcité en France*, 54–55.
22. "Chambre des députés" (June 8, 1889); "Discours de Gambetta" (Nov. 16, 1871), 195; Hause, "French Protestants, Laicization, and the Separation," 144–45.
23. "Discours de Ferry" (June 3, 1876), 174.
24. "Discours de Ferry" (Nov. 17, 1883) in *Les Fondateurs*, 200; Baubérot, *Histoire de laïcité en France*, 60; "Leçons, discours et conférences" (March 21, 1880), in *Les Foundateurs*, 169.
25. "Discours de Ferry (Dec. 23, 1880), in *Les Fondateurs*, 195–96; Carmen Bernand, "The Right to Be Different: Some Questions about the 'French Exception,'" in *Religious Difference in France*, 209.
26. Ibid., 195; Baubérot, *Histoire de laïcité en France*," 63; Jocelyne Césari, "Islam in a Secular Context: Catalyst of the 'French Exception,'" in *Religious Difference in France*, 235–36.
27. "Discours de Ferry" (July 9, 1876), in *Les Fondateurs*, 172.
28. Zorn, "La Division dans la separation," 105–107.
29. Jean Jaurés was particularly instrumental in developing the law of 1905 and constructing the French notion of *laïcité*. He viewed the Protestants as

schismatics and wanted France to develop an organic unity in accordance with the designs of the French Revolution, not the pluralism/fragmentation of the sixteenth-century Reformation. Francis de Pressensé was also instrumental in developing the law. He was son of Edmund de Pressensé, who argued for church/state separation as a Protestant, and looked to the United States and Scotland on the issue. Baubérot, *Histoire de laïcité en France*, 4, 87; "1905–2005: La Laïcité Française et les Minorités Religieuses," *Études théologiques et religieuses* 82/1 (2007) 73; Hause, "French Protestants, Laicization, and the Separation," 149–50, 159. Aristide Briand, who served eleven times as prime minister, was also instrumental in developing the law, helping to defend it and nurture it through the political process. Émile Combe set the stage for the law as a radical Freemason and prime minister from 1902–1905. He wanted to emancipate public schools from religious influence and was instrumental in the law of July 7, 1904, barring religious orders from teaching. He closed thousands of religious schools, and thousands of priests and nuns left France. Baubérot, *Histoire de laïcité en France*, 78–80. His anticlericalism was fueled by the Dreyfus Affair (1894–1906), where a Jewish army officer was falsely accused and punished for selling French military secrets to the German government. Combe and others blamed Catholics for this act of anti-Semitism, basically because of the high-profile of the Assumptionist Order and its anti-Semitic newspaper *La Croix*. The pope denounced anti-Semitism within France, ending any connection between the church and this type of bigotry. Hannah Arendt, *The Origins of Totalitarianism* (New York: Harcourt, Brace & World, Inc., 1966) 116–17.

30. Césari, "Islam in a Secular Context," 233–34.
31. Zorn, "La Division dans la Separation," 105; Baubérot, *Histoire de laïcité en France*, 88. Also article 44. Of course, Pius X condemned the law as "fatal to religion in society." Zorn, "La Division dans la Separation," 116; Barquon, "La laïcité en France, cent ans après," 31. The law encourages the formation of religious associations or unions in the place of the former establishments. Article 2 makes an exception for the service of chaplains in hospitals, prisons, schools, and the army when it comes to government pay and sponsorship. For historical reasons, Alsace-Moselle, French Guiana, and a few other colonies are exempted from the law. Poulat, "La laïcité en France vingtième siècle," 23; Asad, "Trying to Understand French Secularism," 505–6.
32. Baubérot, "La Construction d'une Société Pluriste en France," 14; Danièle Hervieu-Léger, "France's Obsession with the 'Sectarian Threat,'" *Nova Religio* 4/2 (April 2001): 252–53.
33. Poulat, "La laïcité en France vingtième siècle," 23. Article 19 allows the government to subsidize the repair of historic buildings. In recent years (1998 and 2011), the government has changed this law to include non-historic buildings and also the possibility of assuming some of the maintenance costs. Articles 3–10 talk about taking inventory and determining what belongs to the new associations and what belongs to the state.
34. Articles 2 and 14 of the March 28, 1882 law are specifically cited. Article 30 of the 1905 law was abrogated in June of 2000, which forbids religious instruction and ministers in the classroom.
35. Baubérot, "The Evolution of Secularism in France," 59; *Histoire de laïcité en France*, 67, 91; Jean-Paul Willaime, "1905 et la pratique d'une laïcité de

reconnaissance sociale des religions," *Archives de sciences sociales des religions* 50/129 (Jan.–Mar. 2005): 67, 75.

36. Nathalie Caron, "Laïcité and Secular Attitudes in France," *Religion in the News* 9/2 (Fall 2006): 8; Gunn, "Under God but Not the Scarf," 10.
37. Barquon, "La laïcité en France, cent ans après," 35; Bernand, "The Right to be Different," 202, 234–36; Gunn, "Under God but Not the Scarf," 10; Caron, "Laïcité and Secular Attitudes in France," 8.
38. Jean Faury, *Cléricalisme et Anticléricalisme dans la Tarn* (1848–1900) (Toulouse: L'Université de Toulouse-Le Mirail, 1980) 436–37; McMillan, "Catholic Christianity in France," 224.
39. The 1946 preamble used the term *laïque* to describe the educational system, and article 1 of the 1946 and 1958 Constitutions refer to the country in this way. The 1958 version is still in effect today.
40. The 1905 law continued to recognize Sunday as the day of rest and a number of other religious holidays, which are still in effect today—Easter Monday, Ascension Thursday, Pentecost Monday, Assumption day, All Saints' Day, and Christmas. Caron, "Laïcité and Secular Attitudes in France," 19. In 1948, 1951, 1959, and subsequent years, financial aid was given to parents and students of private schools , and many private schools were heavily subsidized. Barquon, "La laïcité en France, cent ans après," 45; Barbérot, "The Evolution of Secularism in France," 59, 60. However, there was a backlash to this type of funding in the name of *laïcité* from 1960 to 1984. Yolande Jansen, "Laïcité, or the Politics of Republican Secularism," in *Political Theologies,* Hent de Vries and Lawrence E. Sullivan (ed.) (New York: Fordham University press, 2006) 476, 505; Baubérot, *Histoire de laïcité en France,* 109; *Christian Century* (July 21, 1948), 723–24.
41. The Republic shows a preference for the great historical religious expressions. In 2001, a law was enacted trying to reinforce the prevention and suppression of sectarian groups. Barquon, "La laïcité en France, cent ans après," 32–33, 46; Pourat, "La laïcité en France au vingtième siècle," 24. Barquon cites some recent instances of oppressive governmental action in local jurisdictions on pages 35ff.
42. Gunn, "Under God but Not the Scarf," 7, 9, 17; Jansen, "Laïcité," 481. The commission consisted of prominent philosophers, sociologists, jurists, and other intellectuals, and was led by Bernard Stasi, a Christian-Democratic politician. The report can be found online under the title *Rapport au President de la Republique* (www.ladocumentationfrancaise.fr/var/storage/rapports-publics/034000725/0000.pdf). The text references the page numbers in parentheses.
43. Jansen, "Laïcité," 486. The report contrasts the evolution of European countries toward secularity with the deeply religious character of America (33).
44. There is a broad consensus in France that the government should fight against sectarian groups as damaging the people's liberty. In 2000, the MILS (*Mission Interministérielle de Lutte contre les Sectes*) sought to suppress groups like the Church of Scientology, and the members of parlement followed its lead. Hervieu-Léger, "France's Obsession with the 'Sectarian Threat,'" 249–51.
45. The report recognizes the criticisms and tries to accommodate diversity or respect for the individual community, but the pervasive influence and emphasis upon *laïcité* tends to overturn most of the good intensions.

Willaime, "1905 et la pratique d'une laïcité," 75. The report particularly highlights the funding of religious schools (under certain conditions), tax relief, the accommodation given to sectarian groups for major feasts, and the presence of chaplains (23, 27, 28, 65, 69).

46. Baubérot, "The Evolution of Secularism in France," 60; Yolonde Jansen, "Secularism and Secularity: France, Islam, and Europe," in *Comparative Secularisms in a Global Age*, 77.
47. Willaime, "1905 et la pratique d'une laïcité," 76; Talal Asad, "Trying to Understand French Secularism," in *Political Theologies*, 500–501. The concern is with large, not small or discreet symbols (58–59).
48. Jansen, "Laïcité," 482; Asad, "Trying to Understand French Secularism," 516. The report expresses concern and bases its decision on what lies "behind the veil," although the reading of symbols is subject to much interpretation. Jansen, "Secularism and Secularity," 78. Vincent Geisser records some of the answers found in the French media, from the victimization of relatives to the voluntary choice to accept submissive Islamic culture. The interpretations are largely negative. *La nouvelle islamophobie* (Paris: La Découverte, 2003) 31–33.
49. The report wants the Muslim community to adapt its theology to *laïcité*, not vice versa (16), but finds the process difficult because Islam has no professional or educated clergy, making the religion less accommodating to liberal changes. Cf. Césari, "Islam in a Secular Context," 229–30.

II

Nazi Germany

6

The Rise of the Third Reich

Adolf Hitler was born on April 20, 1889, in Braunau am Inn, Austria. When he was young, he wanted to become an artist and moved to Vienna with this goal in mind, after leaving secondary school and floundering a couple years in Linz. He continued to flounder in his new environment, failing to gain admission into the Academy of Fine Arts, but the years in Vienna proved crucial to his later interest in politics, awakening his social consciousness and shaping the course of his political thinking.[1] As a starving artist, he experienced the suffering of the poor and the disparity of wealth in the city, which helped move him toward socialism.[2] As a German, he experienced the "slavization" of this "giant city," where Czechs, Poles, Hungarians, Serbs, Croats, and Jews mixed together, "corroding" German culture and creating a "racial desecration."[3] He experienced the Jewish question for the first time and developed a vehement hatred for this people as a fundamental source of German social problems, even if they represented a very small segment of the total population. He thought of them as a clandestine group, controlling the press, art, and literature and using these institutions to destroy Germanic culture with a cosmopolitan, egalitarian, and democratic point of view.[4] Because of this, he "distinguished [them] from the rest of humanity" and "grew sick to [his] stomach" at the very sight and smell of them.[5] He completely altered his early opinion, which included some sympathy toward the plight of the Jews in the Middle Ages, and embraced the pan-Germanic and anti-Semitic policies of Karl Lueger, the mayor and fiery orator of the Vienna.[6]

After serving in WWI, he joined the German Workers Party in September 1919, a small political group meeting in Munich, which was renamed the *Nationalsozialistische Deutsche Arbeiterpartei* or Nazis the following year.[7] Hitler decided to join the group after reading *My Political Awakenings*,[8] a short book written by one of its leaders, Anton Dexler. The book looks at recent world events in terms of a massive conspiracy theory involving international groups like the Jews, the Freemasons, capitalists, and Communists, who instigate wars and foment revolutions for the sake of their own materialistic advantage.[9] The author argues that these groups are responsible for the humiliating defeat of Germany in the war, the unjust provisions of Versailles, the suppression of blue-collar workers, and the raping of all cultures.[10] All these groups play a significant role in the plight of Germanic society, but Dexler reserves most of his wrath for the Jews, focusing special attention upon the Jewish question as the most significant matter of concern in society because their tentacles represent the most maniacal and omnipresent force throughout central Europe, controlling the press, literature, politics, and economics.[11] He blames their financial dealings and pacifist leanings for leaving his nation unprepared to defend itself in the war.[12] The Jews have no particular loyalty to Germany or any other nation; their only loyalty is to themselves as a supranational people, who spurn cultural identity and dominate all others through international finance.[13]

Hitler became a zealous leader of this ideology, ascending through the ranks to become the Führer of the party within the brief span of a year and eventually the chancellor of the whole nation and its Third Reich just over a decade later.[14] His meteoric rise to power was facilitated in the early days by the financial support and political connections of Dietrich Eckart, who inspired the nascent movement and met his young protégé when Hitler started attending the meetings. Eckart helped nurture the future leader in nationalism, anti-Semitism, and a mystical form of Aryanism, and as a successful playwright and publisher, he possessed the means to promote a political career and manage its public image.[15] Through his help, Hitler became the Führer of the party and drew some wider attention as a fiery orator, but it was not until his *Putsch* or attempt to seize power from the Bavarian government in Munich that he attracted the interest of the public at large. He embodied much of the people's frustrations with the Weimar Republic in his unsuccessful coup d'état and gained further sympathy for the cause during the ordeal of the subsequent trial, which he manipulated with great skill. After serving only nine months of a five-year sentence, Hitler and the Nazis began to dominate Weimar politics and grew into such a substantial political force that they gained 6.4 million votes or 18.3 percent of the electorate on September 4, 1930, making them the second largest party on the national scene. This number only increased in the next year and a half until they became the most powerful party, capturing 230 seats when 14 million or 37.3 percent of German voters cast their lot with Hitler on July 31, 1932. A short six months later, the president of the republic asked Hitler to become the chancellor and form a new government, which he quickly transformed into an absolute dictatorship, enslaving all of Germany to his will and power.[16]

As chancellor, Hitler was able to implement his anti-Semitic program, which was softened in his campaign rhetoric of 1928, 1930, and 1932 in order to gain popular support. Hitler was willing to bide his time and implement politics in a gradual but escalating manner, as he reconditioned the German people to his more zealous and militant way of thinking. He started with a party-led boycott of Jewish businesses in April 1933, but the tactic was abandoned after four days when it failed to gain enough popular support at home and abroad. For the next few years, he implemented a series of measures that restricted attendance at universities, membership in organizations, and employment through a plethora of professions and occupations like teachers, lawyers, and doctors. All this was accompanied by continuous harassment from members of the party, paramilitary organizations like the SA (*Sturmabteilung*) and SS (*Schutzstaffel*), the Hitler Youth, and a public who was becoming more and more militant and anti-Semitic through the reconditioning of their society, although Hitler was concerned about losing control over unorganized programs and found it necessary to reign in the terror at times. In 1935, the infamous Nuremberg Laws were enacted, stripping the Jews of civil rights as citizens and alienating them socially by proscribing marriage and sexual contact between Aryans and non-Aryans (*Rasenschande*). On November 9, 1938, a nationwide pogrom was organized, known as *Kristallnacht* or the "night of the broken glass," which vandalized Jewish businesses, burned over two hundred synagogues, murdered ninety-one people, and arrested twenty-six thousand, sending most of them to concentration camps for a few months—all purportedly in retaliation for the murder of a German diplomat by Polish Jews. The next few years saw the escalation of numerous laws forbidding everyday conveniences like automobiles, public transportation, shopping, pets, restaurants, and publications, severely restricting and denigrating their lives, making it impossible for many to continue under the present circumstances. Many Jews left Germany in the 1930s, but by the fall of 1941, emigration was banned and most of the ones who remained in Germany were sent to concentration camps and died there. This final solution began on a large scale in Russia with the systematic shooting of somewhere around a million Jews, led by the soulless brutality of the *Einsatzgruppen*, who followed the German army on the eastern front, and culminated with the industrialized gassing of millions more in Polish death camps.[17]

By the time of the Holocaust in 1941, Hitler had conditioned his people to accept and enact such evil. Hitler had devoted much of his energies to education and was able to produce a generation of students willing to carry out an atrocity on this massive scale.[18] Hitler saw education as the domain of the state and a means of inculcating a common set of values.[19] He was able to create an army of executioners by impressing his ideology upon the students, dedicating them to *Deutschland über alles*, and toughening them up to be thugs like the Nazis through special training in willpower, determination, physical fitness, and military service.[20]

> The crown of the folkish state's entire work of education and training must be to burn the racial sense and racial feeling into the instinct and the intellect, the heat and brain of the youth entrusted to it. No boy and no girl must leave school without having been led to an ultimate realization of the necessity and essence of blood purity. . . . His whole education and training must be so ordered as to give him

> the conviction that he is absolutely superior to others. Through his physical strength and dexterity, he must recover his faith in the invincibility of his whole people.[21]
>
> If only we can succeed in inculcating into the German people, and above all into the German youth, both a fanatical team spirit and a fanatical devotion to the Reich, then the German Reich will once again become the most powerful State in Europe, as it was a thousand years after the collapse of the Roman Empire.[22]

No program exemplified the lengths to which Hitler and the Nazis went, in their attempts to produce citizen-warriors, more than the organization known as the Hitler Youth. It was founded in 1926 out of previous groups and encompassed the vast majority of German children at the height of the Third Reich when the state mandated participation for ten to eighteen year olds in 1936.[23] The organization was largely successful in its mission to separate the youth from any alien influence in the home, church, and other societies, and to make them godless, obsequious wards of the state and its ideology.[24]

This brazen purpose is manifest in the *Nazi Primer: Official Handbook for Schooling Hitler Youth,* first published in 1937. On the first page of the text, national socialism is proclaimed as the new ideology of "all Germans." "The Unlikeness of Men" is brought forward as the first and foremost topic of the book since it represents the "foundation of the National Socialist outlook on life" and challenges the dogma of the Western opposition that all men are created equal. The doctrine of human inequality has great significance in understanding the social relationship between the races because it includes decisive features like "mental and spiritual" qualities, not just outward appearances or skin color. The doctrine represents the true, scientific alternative to the teachings of Freemasons, Marxists, Jews, the Christian church, and other groups, who want to bring everyone "who bears the face of man" into an egalitarian fraternity. The fossil record has demonstrated the theory of evolution, which is "associated with the name of Charles Darwin," and leads any scientifically minded individual to recognize that the human race never constitutes a stagnate unity but develops in a fluid manner out of older forms. Further scientific proof is found in the work of the botanist Gregor Mendel, whose analysis of plants applies to humans and confirms the fundamental truth of the theory. The primer thinks an enlightened people must accept the science and apply its verdict to the political realm, using the classification scheme developed by Hans Günther to fill out the details. This scheme exalts the Nordic race as "most strongly represented in Germany" and helps the student "when evaluating character and spirit, bodily structure and physical beauty" of the race by identifying its attributes—narrow and long skull, tall and slender stature, fine golden hair, blue or grey eyes, and light, rosy-white skin. This higher grade of humanity develops, as it does in all species, through genetic factors or internal mutations rather than environmental influences, the efforts of social engineering, or the hard work of the parents as Lamarck suggested long ago. The present verdict of science lends credence to a governmental policy that wants to act in a rigorous scientific manner and accent genetics or the breeding of people as a means of improving humanity, not pretending that changes in the social environment will make a definitive difference. The primer argues that a Jew living in Germany will ever remain a Jew, alienated from Germanic culture and contaminating Germanic blood through mixed breeding. Aryans must prevent this sacrilege by practicing selective breeding of their stock and preventing inferiors from procreating for the good of the species, even "wiping out hereditary defects" like the diseased and the feeble through drastic measures like an extermination program. To grow the population Germans need more room (*Lebensraum)* to breed, and this means expanding German territory and vital resources to meet the present and future needs of the program. The primer beats the cadence of war into the hearts of the Hitler Youth by pointing its finger at Versailles and the many other injustices the *Vaterland* has suffered through the centuries, robbing and reducing her arable land, raping vital resources, and crowding the people into an insufficient space.[25] Germany simply needs more room to expand and grow its superior race of people.

However crazy or psychotic this ideology might sound to the typical Western way of thinking, it also represented more than the ranting of one man's lunacy. Hitler was more zealous and determined in his convictions than others, and he was willing to use methods that seemed brutal and extreme to many of the *Volk*, but his point of view also represented a deep-seated Germanic *Geist* that was burgeoning since the times of the Enlightenment and expressed the typical anti-Semitism, anti-Christianity, Germanism, nationalism, and evolutionary racism that characterized large segments of the population and intelligentsia in varying degrees.[26] Hitler thought of himself as representing the spiritual and intellectual climate of modern times, and he appealed to a wide range of people in the electorate, including the very educated and well-to-do, not just low-life thugs or working-class bigots. Theodore Abel, Peter Merkl, and many other scholars have surveyed Nazi biographies and concluded that Hitler's support ran across the spectrum of social classes in Germany, finding fertile ground among the upper and upper-middle classes, with the very educated displaying the most virulent signs of anti-Semitic feelings.[27] Indeed, Hitler thought of himself as having a broad, intellectual appeal and often boasted of his insatiable appetite for books and learning—a boast that is corraborated by many of his acquaintances. During his early days in Linz and Vienna, he was a great patron of lending libraries and brought "reading material by the kilo" home on all sorts of nonfiction topics—history, religion, geography, technology, architecture, and art.[28] Even during the busy days of leading a country and conducting a world war, he amassed a large amount of material and spent late nights devouring it, often staying up until the wee hours of the morning to complete his reading.[29] He thought of himself as offering a coherent and learned vision of life, based upon the latest information and understanding of things, even if he employed brutal methods and compromised his ideals at times for pragmatic considerations, just like any other politician.[30]

Hitler's Rejection of the Judeo-Christian Tradition

Hitler's ideology begins with his pathological hatred of the Jews. In volume one of *Mein Kampf,* these people are described as "a maggot in a rotting corpse; . . . a plague worse than the Black Death of former times; a germ carrier of the worst sort; mankind's eternal germ of disunion; the drone that insinuates its way into the rest of mankind; the spider that slowly sucks the people's blood out of its pores; the pack of rats fighting bloodily among themselves; the parasite in the body of other peoples; the typical parasite; a sponger who, like a harmful bacillus, continues to spread; the eternal bloodsucker; the people's parasite; the people's vampire."[31] This pathology finds its deepest roots in the French Enlightenment, which blamed all the ills of society on the Judeo-Christian tradition. Like the sons of the Enlightenment, Hitler thinks of the Jewish faith as a sham because it has no necessary fear of divine judgment in a world to come and no compulsion to lead a life of moral responsibility or face the consequences. This is why the Jews have no sense of sacrificing their own interests for any spiritual or altruistic ideal and only spend time and energy promoting their own earthly or materialistic interests through the concerns of business.[32] Without a proper metaphysical foundation, there is nothing preventing them from worshipping the golden calf of the capitalistic enterprise system and seeking the meaning of life in wealth and possessions.[33] If their religion serves any purpose, it keeps them together as a race of people in the midst of the Diaspora,[34] preventing them from mixing with other people and becoming an integral part of other nations, but it never raises their lives above this base existence and develops any true spiritual longings.

Hitler's special pretext for hating the Jews developed from their distinct political point of view. The anti-Semitism of the Enlightenment had poisoned the atmosphere in Europe and could find any number of reasons to manifest its criticisms once hatred toward the group was established. In *Mein Kampf,* Hitler develops his own special brand of this animosity over the propensity of the Jewish community to promote egalitarian movements, often taking the leading role in parties that advocated social democracy.[35] He rejects the teaching that "all men are created equal" and feels the Jews are stationed at the vanguard of this horrid leveling of society, promoting a race-less class of people, denigrating aristocratic principles, and destroying the individual identity of ethnic nations, especially the character of his own elite race of people in Germany.[36] His racist attitude toward the Jews, along with his insatiable desire to denigrate almost everything about them, finds its primary impetus in their doctrine of democracy, equality, and rejection of his racism, displaying again the tendency of hatred to beget more hatred.[37] He points to Russia, where Jews helped eliminate the superior class of Nordic elements in the society and substituted a subhuman race of Slavic people, finding this same egalitarian force a matter of grave concern as it works its way through Central Europe.[38] He thinks of the Jews as the financial force behind international, egalitarian groups like the Bolsheviks, who wish to dominate and level the world into their banal image.[39]

At this point Hitler begins to demonize his political opponents as filled with extreme acts of deception and hypocrisy, conspiring to control the world and institutions of power while preaching a different message of equality for the consumption of the public. The Jews cannot be trusted; they are filled with the most diabolical trickery and deceit in their dealings with Gentiles, feigning to help workers through Communist ploys like trade unions but conspiring all along to make a capitalistic profit off of human misery through international business connections.[40] Hitler blames them and their banking interests for the current economic woes in Germany, which are destroying the livelihood of the average worker. He compares them all to parasites, who suck the economic lifeblood out of a people and refuse to engage in any productive work or labor to benefit society[41]—a criticism that connects Hitler to the age-old complaint about the Jews and usury, found in Luther and the Middle Ages.[42]

The Jews become the scapegoats for all the ills of society. Hitler proceeds to blame them for the cultural decline of Germany, accusing them of conspiring to destroy the souls of the people through their "activity in the press, art, literature, and theater."[43] They destroy the excellence of the German Reich by condemning militarism, preaching pacifism, belittling the army, sabotaging conscription, and undermining the war effort through their control of the liberal press.[44] They poison the souls of the people by producing "nine tenths of all literary filth, artistic trash, and theatrical idiocy," even though they represent "hardly one hundredth of the county's inhabitants."[45] They have no spirit; they possess no artistic or musical sense, no real creative genius; they have only an "apparent genius," which deigns to make money off the talents of others and continually lower German standards[46]—a criticism that resonated in the circles of Richard Wagner.

Hitler relates his antipathy of the Jews to a similar contempt for the church. This contempt follows the basic understanding of the Enlightenment, which blames the Jews for giving birth to the religion and the church for sponsoring bigotry in the world. Hitler praises the work of Voltaire and his disciples for trashing the church, and he employs their fundamental understanding of the church and ecclesiastical power throughout his analysis, continually referring to church leaders as priests and deprecating their abuse of authority. Christianity is held accountable for promulgating intolerance throughout history because of the abusive authority of priests and their need to inculcate theological dogmas as the only way to heaven. The Romans are considered much more tolerant than this bigoted religion for allowing each one to pray unto the god of their own choice. Christianity destroyed the virtuous and progressive spirit of the Aryans in Rome and caused "the worst of the regressions that mankind can ever have undergone."[47]

In the *Table Talk*, Hitler affords a few diatribes on the Bible that continue to follow the sons of the Enlightenment in deprecating its content and considering it nothing more than "Jewish mumbo jumbo." No one can "extract truths of these Jewish chicaneries, where in fact no truths exist."[48] Jesus is the only biblical character who seems worthy of esteem because he conducted a spiritual battle against the Jews and their materialism, but following the analysis of Houston Stewart Chamberlain, Wagner's son-in-law, Hitler concludes that Jesus was really an Aryan, not a Jew.[49] Unfortunately, Paul distorted the teachings of Jesus, paving the way toward the metaphysical dogmas of Christian orthodoxy and creating a glaring dichotomy between its teaching and those of its founder. Worst of all, Paul paved the way toward communism by emphasizing the equality of all human beings, destroying the "long reign" of "Graeco-Latin genius."[50]

> [Paul] realized that the judicious exploitation of this idea among non-Jews would give him far greater power in the world than would the promise of material profit to the Jews themselves. It was more then that the future St. Paul distorted with diabolical cunning the Christian idea. Out of this idea, which was a declaration of war on the golden calf, on the egotism and the materialism of the Jews, he created a rallying point for slaves of all kinds against the elite, the masters and those in dominant authority. The religion fabricated by Paul of Tarsus, which was later called Christianity, is nothing but the Communism of today.[51]

This point is driven home a number of times by Hitler, who seems to understand the intimate spiritual matrix from which a political system like communism arose[52]—much more than secular Western scholars, who tend to discount historical ties with the Christian faith and its metaphysical ideals like equality.

Hitler thinks an enlightened people should acknowledge the connection but severe the ties in a more consistent way than the Communists by developing an enlightened view of politics based on science. Christianity and the doctrine of egalitarianism rebel against the law of nature and its selection of those who are fit to survive its struggles. The scientific theory of evolution clearly refutes the biblical account of creation, which makes Adam and Eve the center of the universe and the progenitors of a set species, abstracted from the laws of evolutionary change and difference.[53] Eventually, Christianity will die out as scientific knowledge increases and destroys the religious superstition of the past. National Socialism leads the way to the future by appealing to reason and rejecting all dependence upon divine miracles or intervention, which only emasculates Germany's strength and will to improve the species. Aryans must follow the laws of nature and impose their stronger will on others, discounting all religious superstitions, which hamper human progress and escape the responsibilities of this life by looking for a better world.[54]

Hitler continually rejects any attempt to reconcile National Socialism with Christianity as chancellor. He believes the religion must be removed altogether in the course of time because it presents a serious obstacle to his goals and ideology.[55] He sees the Catholic Church trying to "occupy positions of temporal power" throughout its history and finds the "chief activity of [its] priests" set on "undermining National Socialist policy," but he prefers to wait and bide his time before unleashing a full reckoning.[56] Early on Hitler tried to distance his administration from Alfred Rosenberg's direct attacks upon the church as an ill-advised move from a tactical point of view.[57] In *Mein Kampf*, he refuses to condemn the church in any direct way, considering the institution much too powerful; he prefers to ignore it or separate it from the real world of politics, hoping it will die out, as he lacks a better alternative at the time.[58] He maintains a policy of church/state separation and declares that politics have "nothing to do with religious problems," as long as the church minds its own business and stays within its own sphere, not using its considerable power to assault the nation and undermine the "morals and ethics of the race,"[59] but Hitler recognizes the irreconcilable conflict. Later on he acknowledges the differences more openly, recognizing that "National Socialism and religion will no longer be able to exist together."[60] As chancellor, his policy follows the French Enlightenment and its culture, maintaining a strict separation between church and state, which ostensibly prohibited interference in each other's sphere,[61] but as a ruse to destroy the church. His real plan is to use the power of the state in educating/indoctrinating the youth and weaning them off ecclesiastical dogma.

> I envisage the future, therefore, as follows: First of all, to each man his private creed. Superstition shall not lose its rights. The Party is sheltered from the danger of competing with the religions. These latter must simply be forbidden from interfering in future with temporal matters. From the tenderest age, education will be imparted in such a way that each child will know all that is important to the maintenance of the State. As for the men close to me, who, like me, have escaped from the clutches of dogma, I've no reason to fear that the Church will get its hooks on them.
>
> We'll see to it that the Churches cannot spread abroad teachings in conflict with the interest of the State. We shall continue to preach the doctrine of National Socialism, and the young will no longer be taught anything but the truth.[62]

In his *Table Talk*, Hitler declares the concordat between Germany and the Vatican is no longer valid, since his power is able to triumph over the church in a more decisive way than the older policy that relegated the church and state to separate spheres. After the war, he plans to take on the "religious problem" as the "final task of my life" and "settle my account" with the priests. It is impossible to develop a society on a "foundation of lies," and so he must "exterminate the lie" and exact his "retribution to the last farthing," in order for his Nazi ideology to reign unimpeded by ecclesiastical superstition. "Just as the pyres for heretics have been suppressed, so all these by-products of ignorance and bad faith will have to be eliminated in their turn."[63]

Hitler's Will to Power

Hitler's rejection of the Judeo-Christian tradition reaches beyond its egalitarian spirit of equity and fairness and challenges the very heart of Western metaphysics with its belief in a moral law, founded upon the will of a transcendent deity. Hitler shakes his fist at the Almighty and defies the existence of any moral standard that presumes to judge the appetites of this life and condemn his will to power or sovereignty, making the power of life's forces an end in itself. This defiance becomes a defining force in his own life and develops into a caricature of brutal determination beyond that of his peers, explaining his willingness to defy basic standards of human decency and sponsor the most inhuman acts of cruelty imaginable.

Hitler's position represented an extreme expression of voluntaristic philosophy, but he certainly was not alone in his adherence to this fundamental way of thinking. In fact, his metaphysics works within the atheistic spirit of the times, especially as it is exemplified and embodied in the writings of Arthur Schopenhauer and Friedrich Nietzsche, important figures in German philosophy, who spurned the existence of a personal God and relegated life to immanent forces of will and power, much like Hitler. While no one knows the extent of his philosophical studies and personal examination of specific sources, there is no doubt that he was influenced by these philosophers and the basic voluntaristic spirit of the time, which permeated the culture and Hitler's ideas through the enormity of their stature, place, and influence in German life upon numerous secondary sources.[64] In the *Table Talk*, Hitler speaks of Kant, Schopenhauer, and Nietzsche as the "greatest of our thinkers"—Kant because of his destruction of the "dogmatic philosophy of the church," Schopenhauer because of his annihilation of "Hegel's pragmatism," and Nietzsche because he "surpassed . . . Schopenhauer's pessimism" with his more positive "will to life."[65] Along with this testimony, certain anecdotal evidence appears to indicate some direct interest and engagement within the tradition. In regard to Schopenhauer, Hitler says he "carried Schopenhauer's works with [him] through the whole of the first World War,"[66] and acquaintances like Enst Haufstaengl and Leni Riefenstahl say he was enamored with Schopenhauer and often referred to his ideas.[67] In fact, he makes reference to him in *Mein Kampf, Table Talk*, and his speeches on several occasions, and his study at Berkhof boasted a bust of the great philosopher. In regard to Nietzsche, it appears Hitler owned a first edition of his works and actually made the sacred pilgrimage to the center of the Nietzsche cult in Weimar, where he conversed with Nietzsche's sister at the archive, posed beside his bust, and brought home the dead philosopher's walking stick.[68] As a member of the Nazis, he was more than familiar with the cultlike status that Nietzsche and his ideas obtained within the group, starting from its earliest days, and Hitler must have experienced some of this influence from the mere association with many of his disciples, whether directly or indirectly.[69]

More than all this anecdotal evidence, there is the continual testimony of Hitler's own words, which speak of a legacy steeped in the tradition. He constantly refers to himself as following an abstract force behind nature, which he describes through a variety of voluntaristic terms like "fate," "Providence," the "innermost will of nature," and the "supreme" or "creative force."[70] It is the "will of God" or "Providence" to follow the aristocratic forces of nature and its law of strength and survival rather than destroy its appetites through a transcendent concept of a deity, which might inform the conscience and lives in contradistinction to the ways of this world.[71] The belief in God should be retained, but only as a concrete force of power that humans incarnate and experience within their innermost being.[72] People should live through their own passionate instincts and create their own myths to benefit the nation, rather than look to a universal standard of right and wrong inscribed in their conscience and supplied by a heaven of ideas.[73] "We must distrust the intelligence and the conscience, and must place our trust in our instincts. . . . Conscience is a Jewish invention. It is a blemish, like circumcision. A new age of magic interpretation of the world is coming, of interpretation in terms of the will and not of the intelligence."[74] Hitler plans on inculcating this voluntarism in the youth by instructing them in the need for willpower and determination, using the rigors of physical and military exercises to toughen them up.[75]

Hitler believes that "will" and "power" are more important to a leader in directing the masses than appealing to objective intelligence. The great leader must be a psychologist, not a theoretician, "a man of little scientific education but physically healthy, with a good, firm character, imbued with the joy of determination and will-power" rather than a "cleaver weakling." Intellectual appeals to objective truth and fairness have little effect in swaying the masses when compared to the art of propaganda, which incites emotions and stirs conviction through the constant repetition of its half-truths. Along with propaganda, the leader should use grand symbols and rites, impressive monuments of architecture, and powerful oratory as a means of inflaming "human passions and emotional sentiments," while finding the sole criterion of value in the "effect [they] exert on the people."[76]

Hitler thinks the masses are unworthy of leading a nation. They have no real concept of political or economic issues and would end up leveling society, creating a nation of mediocrity in the image of communism, if given the authority.[77] It is best for the people that a senate or small body of aristocrats select one man, who "with apodictic force will form granite principles from the wavering idea-world of the broad masses and take up the struggle for their sole correctness."[78] Once elected the leader assumes the "ultimate and heaviest responsibility" in ruling the nation and possesses "unconditional authority" over all aspects of society and government to unify the people into one will and spirit through the "genius and energy of [his] personality."[79]

This makes *rex lex*—the leader the law. Hitler rejects any objective standard, law, or morality to constrain the leader in calculating what is best for the people. The laws of society are based on their utility in producing what is good for the public welfare, and "all means used to this end are justifiable."[80] There are no eternal laws or inalienable rights given by God in nature serving as the basis of society and means of restraining the appetites of power to seize more power. There are no property rights to guarantee one's holdings against the wantonness of others or a leader who deems certain possessions essential to the ultimate welfare of a nation. "This earth is not allocated to anyone, nor is it bestowed on anyone as a gift; however, it is given as destiny's grant to those people who [possess] have the courage in their hearts to [conquer] take possession of it, the strength to preserve it, and the diligence to till it."[81] Force is "the only way to increase power," and its exercise involves acts of terror, persecution, annihilation, and extermination.[82]

Hitler believes "all means and possible ways must be employed" to implement his basic evolutionary view of life.[83] The fundamental purpose of the state corresponds to the "highest aim of human existence," which is found in the preservation of its species or its "struggle for survival," not economic or materialistic concerns.[84] Much like Schopenhauer, he sees the acts of procreation representing the will of nature and expressing the basic instinct of life that sacrifices the good of the individual for the preservation of the species.[85] This theme is understood within the framework of later Darwinian theory, where various forms or species of life appear and disappear, with humans developing late and fighting animals and each other for the emergence and preservation of their own kind.[86] In the end, the success of the state depends upon the ability of its leaders to follow this scientific understanding of life and develop policies in accordance with the laws of nature, which promote the victory of the strong over the weak. After all, there is no will of God that transcends nature or lives in contradistinction to the basic will of life, and so the state should accept the evolutionary forces around it and find its mission within whatever happens to transpire in it. The state should promote the selective breeding of the strong with each other and provide space for them to multiply rather than limit the size of its population within certain boundaries through artificial means.[87]

In this, Hitler commits the naturalistic fallacy on a massive scale, making whatever happens to transpire in nature the moral imperative of the state, and he refuses to see life through any other dimension. While Marx sees the history of the world as a struggle between socioeconomic classes, Hitler thinks this materialistic interpretation fails to grasp the more essential struggle (*Kampf*) in nature between ethnobiological races. For Marx, the struggle will end one day when perfect environmental conditions are created in a classless society; for Hitler, war is a normal condition of life and essential for the continuous development of the species, where the sky is the limit.[88]

Hitler focuses his special attention on the nation of Germany as the epicenter of the racial war. The country boasts a large segment of the Aryan race, but the very existence of this people is currently under siege by a new egalitarian wave of "de-Germanization, niggerization, and Judaization."[89] Hitler believes the old Reich fell because of its failure to stem the tide and "recognize the racial problem" as the "deepest and ultimate reason" that determines the life of a people.[90] The state serves no other purpose than the "preservation and advancement of a community of physically and psychically homogeneous people," who are united together by a common set of genes, with all else developing as a secondary by-product, including spirituality, language, and culture. No one can make a German out of another race. No one can make an intellectual out of a Hottentot or Zulu-Kaffir.[91] In fact, the German people were meant to dominate and enslave lower beings,[92] and right now they need more space to flourish (*Lebensraum*). They must make the use of force and the "acquisition of new soil" the centerpiece of foreign policy, so they can eliminate the weak and begin to prosper once again as a superior race of people.[93] Hitler lauds those who conquer others through the sheer exercise of their might and discounts any mystical notion of property rights or sacred boundaries between the nations, believing such boundaries limit the struggle for prosperity and excellence.[94] His immediate plans include an eastern expansion of the Reich into Russia, which is contaminated with a subhuman race of Slavic blood and contains eighteen times more *Lebensraum* for its inferior people than *Deutschland*, but the struggle for Hitler can never end when reaching one specific objective because of the very nature of life.[95]

Genocide

In the course of applying his philosophy, Hitler extended the *Kampf* beyond the typical conquest of new territory and the atrocities of warfare between combatants to conduct a genocidal campaign against certain segments of the civilian population. He started this campaign by developing a program of euthanasia, known as T-4, which eliminated undesirables in his own country. He decided to enact the program after listening to the pleas of a couple and allowing a dignified death for their child, who suffered from an incurable disease. He found a precedent for taking such action in the Greek city-state of Sparta, which served as the "first racialist state" by limiting the "number allowed to live," even abandoning their own frail and deformed children for the sake of breeding a healthier race of people.[96] With this pretext a directive was given to all doctors, nurses, and midwives on August 18, 1939, to report infirmed infants, so they could be placed in a special ward and put out of their misery by a lethal injection of medicine or simple starvation. In the fall of that year, Hitler decided to extend the program and "put an end to 'the shameful lives of the mentally ill,'" which included a whole spectrum of people suffering from maladies like schizophrenia, epilepsy, dementia, encephalitis, and even the criminally insane. In less than two years, the program claimed more than seventy thousand victims according to T-4's own internal calculation. The operation was suspended temporarily in August 1941 due to a mounting wave of criticism, spearheaded by the churches, but it resumed production a year later with tighter security, and the program ended up killing more than two hundred thousand in toto.[97]

Hitler's most infamous act of genocide was the slaughter or "holocaust" of six millions Jews. Hitler and the Nazis staked much of their political careers on resolving the Jewish problem (*Judenfrage*),[98] which plagued Europe for centuries and found only limited answers in satisfying Jews and Gentiles alike. Upon taking power, the Nazis offered their own set of solutions and implemented them with escalating cruelty, starting with alienation and discrimination, proceeding to expulsion, and ending with total annihilation.[99] The process took some time to unfold, however; at the beginning of the war, Hitler was still biding his time and expressing uncertainty about the options—what to do and where to "put these several million Jews," who lived in the conquered territories.[100] The Nazi administration even considered sending them to Madagascar at one point, but this option was ruled out as much too dangerous since the British ruled the seas.[101] In December 1939, Hitler began to drive Polish Jews into restricted confines, or ghettoes, where thousands starved to death and others endured the horrid conditions, only waiting for the Nazis to develop a "final solution" and remove most of them to death camps beginning in the spring of 1941.[102] Extermination became the final solution after many debates and halfway measures, but it was no surprise. It probably was the goal all along, considering the fact that Hitler had no limits to his cruelty and often spoke of biding his time with the enemy before unleashing the final blow.[103] Indeed, early on in *Mein Kampf*, there are ominous comments about employing "constantly increasing" tactics of extermination and annihilation toward one's enemies; about removing the Jewish stranglehold on nations through the use of the "sword"; and how using "poison gas" on twelve thousand "Hebrew corrupters, . . . traitors, profiteers, usurers, and swindlers . . . might have saved the lives of a million real Germans" in the last world war.[104] These ominous words came to the forefront of public knowledge on January 30, 1939, when Hitler declared in a dramatic prophecy before the Greater German Reichstag,

"If international-finance Jewry inside and outside Europe should succeed once more in plunging nations into another world war, the consequence will not be the Bolshevization of the earth and thereby the victory of Jewry, but the annihilation of the Jewish race in Europe."[105]

It is hard to say when the precise order was issued to fulfill this prophecy and exterminate the Jews. Eberhard Jäckel thinks it was first initiated on a large scale early in the summer of 1941, after Hitler invaded Russia and was bringing his foreign and racial policy to fulfillment.[106] Phillippe Burrin thinks the order for the total extermination of all Jews only occurred sometime later in mid-August or September when the massacre of Russian Jews reached genocidal proportions.[107] These scholars provide an interesting and detailed analysis of the data, but one wonders whether Hitler was vacillating in his policy to begin with and needed to settle the issue once and for all at a precise moment in time. It seems more likely that he was implementing his terror step-by-step until his full fury reached a crescendo. The final solution probably represented a whole series of decisions, escalating over a period of time from an intension that was present and recognized by many Nazis, soldiers, and special units from the beginning.

Perhaps, more interesting than the decision making of the Nazi hierarchy is the overall complicity of the German people in the process. During the 1930s, the Nazis actually tested specific policies through a series of plebiscites or national referenda, and even assuming a certain amount of corruption in the process, the plebiscites indicate overwhelming popularity for Hitler's policies on some crucial issues. With over 95 percent of registered voters participating, the electorate approved of Hitler's decision to withdraw from the Geneva Disarmament Conference and League of Nations (95 percent), the usurpation of his dictatorial powers (90 percent), the occupation of the Rhineland (98.8 percent), and the annexation of Austria (99 percent).

What is more difficult to define and quantify is the breadth of anti-Semitism in Nazi Germany, which tends to subsist without a simple means to identify its degree or extent, much like racism in US culture. All one can do is point to indirect evidence, but even with this caveat the indications are strong enough to suspect that the vast majority of Germans were steeped in anti-Semitic bigotry. After all, what else can one conclude about a country when it endorses an openly and rabidly anti-Semitic group like the Nazis and provides them with the unlimited power to do their damndest? Even after the fall of the Third Reich, a full 61 percent of Germans were so hardened in their bigotry that they were willing to express racist and anti-Semitic feelings to occupational forces during the denazification process—at least according to one unscientific poll taken by the military government in 1946.[108] This is not to say that the average German was on the level of Hitler in bigotry and active evil, especially during the early years of the regime, before years of propaganda and censorship hardened most of the citizens into active agents or passive observers, indifferent to his crimes. Early on, the majority of Germans approved of the Nuremberg laws (1935), stripping Jews of civil rights and bringing law and order to anti-Semitic measures, but they failed to boycott businesses in sufficient numbers and expressed much horror in certain quarters over deportations or pogroms like *Kristallnacht.* The Nazi regime reacted by suppressing news about overt persecutions and cracking down on any protests, leaving few with the courage to speak against these tactics after 1938. Of course, rumors persisted and historians believe that most Germans understood what was going on and possessed at least some level of knowledge about the Holocaust,[109] considering the size of the operation and the many possible sources of dissemination, but few considered it an outrage or dared to speak out if they did. The church, which was so vocal about "Operation Euthanasia," remained silent for the most part. By 1941, years of Nazi propaganda had radicalized a culture that was already anti-Semitic before its reign of terror and created a whole generation of students, ready to follow its agenda and willing to execute the enemy. Anti-Semitic ideology had permeated the soul of Germany and created a people that accepted or participated in the most horrid acts of inhumanity, even apart from the psychological pressure that ever exerts its coercive power in a totalitarian state and remains a factor.[110]

The German people were prepared to follow a man like Hitler because of the ideological currents that already swept through their society for over a century. Hitler's war against the Judeo-Christian tradition developed out of the animosity that permeated intelligentsia after the Enlightenment and proceeded to assault its priestly authority; metaphysical dogmas; miraculous, biblical narrative; and almost everything else about it, except Jesus. Hitler followed this atmosphere of hate and developed a special antagonism toward the egalitarian teachings of Paul and the subsequent church, which was blamed for bastardizing the Aryan race and for preventing Western culture from maturing into a more scientific view of life and finding its proper role in the evolutionary scheme of things. For this reason he joined the sons of the Enlightenment and their hatred of the Jews, going after them for giving birth to Christianity, for accepting its doctrine of equality with extreme legalistic rigor, and for using their considerable power in culture to inculcate the dogma and destroy the German people. He launched his most destructive attacks against them as a small and vulnerable target but bided his time with the church because of its strength in society. Here he prefered to play a game of duplicity for the meantime and to follow the strategy of enlightened France and its tactic of church/state separation, hoping to marginate the place of the church in society, using the state to reeducate the people, and waiting until after the war to engineer the most complete destruction of the religion. The animosity exploded into a full-blown rejection of any personal God or transcendent authority to judge human conduct and led to a decided emphasis upon the autonomous will of human beings, following the voluntaristic philosophy of Schopenhauer and

Nietzsche. This atheistic philosophy taught Hitler to reject any basis for ethics within the realm of human consciousness or transcendent ideas and provided him with the permission to create his own version of reality through the exercise of a will to power that recognized no inalienable rights and no objective standard in any law. Hitler chose to create his own reality by following the dictates of modern science, but in this he committed the naturalistic fallacy on a massive scale, by making a simple equation between a moral imperative and whatever happens to transpire in nature. Modern German science emphasized Darwinism and racism, and Hitler saw his commission within this enlightened point of view through fulfilling its purposes and destroying those who impeded progress, even though the theory was unable to find any purpose or progress in life.

Notes

1. Adolf Hitler, *Mein Kampf*, Ralph Manheim (Boston and New York: Houghton Mifflin Co., 1999) 125; *Mein Kampf* (München: Zentralverlag der NSDAP, F. Eher Nachf., 1941) 137. Hereafter the English version is designated MK, and the German is placed in the parentheses.
2. MK 21–25 (20–24).
3. MK 123 (135).
4. MK 52ff. (55ff.); William Montgomery McGovern, *From Luther to Hitler: The History of Fascist-Nazi Political Philosophy* (London: George G. Harrap & Co. LTD, 1946) 601.
5. MK 56–57 (60–61).
6. *Hitler's Table Talk 1941–1944: His Private Conversations*, Norman Cameron and R. H. Stevens (trans.), G. L. Weinberg (ed.) (New York: Enigma Books, 2008) 113 (Dec. 17, 1941); *Monologe im Führer-Hauptquartier 1941–1944: Die Aufzeichnung Heinrich Heims herausgegeben Werner Jochmann* (Hamburg: Albrecht Knaus, 1980) 153; MK 12–13, 16 (10–11, 15).
7. MK 219ff. (238ff.).
8. Anton Dexler, *Mein politisches Erwachen: Aus dem Tagesbuch eines deutschen sozialistischen Arbeiters*, 4. Aufgabe (München: Deutscher Volksverlag GmbH, 1937) 2; Lawrence Birken, *Hitler as Philosophe: Remnants of the Enlightenment in National Socialism* (Westport, CT, and London: Praeger, 1995) 31–33.
9. Ibid., 9, 17, 20–27, 42, 44, 50–51.
10. Ibid., 10–11, 15, 50.
11. Ibid., 23–24, 28, 50; Birken, *Hitler as Philosophe*, 32. Like Hitler, he can use terms like "eradication" (*Ausrottung*) and "extermination" (*Vernichtung*) as a way of dealing with the Jews, leaving the audience wondering about the literal force of the words.
12. Ibid., 31–32, 40.
13. Ibid., 7, 29–30. Jews cannot assimilate with others because they act in accordance with their own Asian blood.
14. The "Third Reich" goes back to the prophetic words of Joachim of Fiore, who divided history into three parts, based on the doctrine of the Trinity, and spoke of the coming of a third age. The first was the age of the Father

and the OT law, the second the age of the Son and the gospel of grace, and the third will be the age of the Spirit and freedom. Ernst Benz, "Die Kategorien der religiösen Geschichtsdeutung Joachims," *Zeitschrift für Kirchengeschichte* 3/1 (1931): 30, 83; Henry Bett, *Joachim of Flora* (Merrick, NY: Richwood Pub. Co., 1976) 44–45. For the Nazis, the Third Reich succeeds the Holy Roman Empire and the United German Empire under the Hollenzollerns (1871–1918), and will last a thousand years. John Gray, *Black Mass: Apocalyptic Religion and the Death of Utopia* (Canada: Doubleday, 2007) 67–68.

15. Birken, *Hitler as Philosophe*, 20ff., 30, 36–37, 40–41.
16. Ian Kershaw, *Hitler* (London and New York: Longman, 1991) 54–55; Sarah Gordon, *Hitler, Germans, and the "Jewish Question"* (Princeton, NJ: Princeton University Press, 1984) 72; Theodore Abel, *Why Hitler Came into Power* (Cambridge, MA, and London: Harvard University Press, 1986) 309–11; Daniel Jonah Goldhagen, *Hitler's Willing Executioners* (New York: Vintage Press, 1997) 86, 87. The actual numbers were down 4 percent for the Nazis from the previous election.
17. Gordon, *Hitler, Germans, and the "Jewish Question,"* 120–128; Weinberg, *Because They Were Jews*, 104–10, 172; Kershaw, *Hitler*, 149.
18. Goldhagen, *Hitler's Willing Executioners*, 27.
19. MK 73–74, 246 (79–80, 269).
20. MK 409ff., 426–27 (453ff., 474–75).
21. MK 411, 427 (456, 475–76).
22. *Table Talk*, May 20, 1942, 372.
23. The group was considered a part of the SA and generally consisted of boys ages fourteen to eighteen, although a younger group was formed later on, called the *Jungvolk*, and girls were included as well. By the end of 1935, there were over four million members (about half of the nation's youth); by the end of 1939, seven million. Kershaw, *Hitler*, 100.
24. *The Nazi Primer: Official Handbook for the Schooling of the Hitler Youth*, Harwood L. Childs, Fritz Brennecke (ed.) (New York and London: Harper & Brothers Publishers, 1938) 268.
25. Ibid., 5, 9–16, 33ff., 48–59, 68–78, 84, 94ff., 147–51, 195–206, 211–12, 243. Mixing is said to produce the worst combinations of both races (8). Races should breed and develop their own natures separately (82). Of course, the primer talks incessantly about the Jews and discusses measures to ostracize them or exclude them from the rights of citizenship (78ff.). It also maintains that the great cultures of Europe come from Norsemen, not from the east (113–16).
26. Birken, *Hitler as Philosophe*, 5; Peter Viereck, *Metapolitics: From Wagner and the German Romantics to Hitler* (New Brunswick, NJ, and London: Transaction Publishers, 2004) lxvii; P. G. J. Pulzer, *The Rise of Political Anti-Semitism in Germany and Austria* (New York, London, and Sydney: John Wiley & Sons, Inc., 1964) 325.
27. Peter Merkl, *Political Violence under the Swastika: 581 Early Nazis* (Princeton, NJ: Princeton University Press, 1975); Michael Kater, *The Nazi Party: A Social Profile of Members and Leaders, 1919–1945* (Cambridge, MA: Harvard University Press, 1983); Richard Hamilton, *Who Voted for Hitler?* (Princeton, NJ: Princeton University Press, 1982); Gordon, *Hitler, Germans,*

and the "Jewish Question," 61–62, 79; Abel, *Why Hitler Came to Power,* xv–xvii, 6, 164.

28. *Table Talk,* xxxvii, Kershaw, *Hitler,* 17; MK 34ff. This is also the testimony of one his roommates, August Kubziek. Richard Weikart, *From Darwin to Hitler: Evolutionary Ethics, Eugenics, and Racism in Germany* (New York: Palgrave Macmillan, 2004) 216.
29. Timothy W. Rybach, *Hitler's Private Library: The Books that Shaped his Life* (New York: Alfred A. Knopf, 2008) 115, 116.
30. MK 171, 212ff., 380ff. (188, 231ff., 418ff.); Jäckel, *Hitler's World View,* 13, 24. Jäckel thinks Hermann Rauschning's book *Revolution of Nihilism* (1939) is wrong when it alleges that Nazis had no ideals they would not cede for the sake of gaining power.
31. Jäckel, *Hitler's World View,* 58.
32. *Table Talk,* Nov. 5, 1941, 91 (*Monologe,* 130); MK 303, 305ff., 320 (332ff., 351). The Jews are divided over their belief concerning an afterlife. The Torah has little reference to this issue, and most of the verses that speak of an afterlife are found in the later writings (e.g., Dan 12:2–3). Hitler mocked the doctrine of hell. *Table Talk,* April 9, 1942, 315–16.
33. *Hitler's Second Book,* 30; *Hitlers Zweites Buch: Ein Dokument aus der Jahr 1928,* Gerhard Weinberg (Hrsg.) (Stuttgart: Deutsche Verlags-Anstalt, 1961) 63; *Table Talk,* Oct. 21, 1941, 61 (*Monologe,* 97–98).
34. Gereon Wolters, "Der 'Führer' und seine Denker: Zur Philosophie des 'Dritte Reichs,'" *Deutsche Zeitschrift für Philosophie* 47/2 (1999): 227.
35. MK 51, 60–61 (54, 64–65); P. G. L. Pulzer, *The Rise of Political Anti-Semitism in Germany and Austria* (New York, London, and Sydney: John Wiley & Sons, Inc., 1964) 260, 270.
36. MK 60–61, 449, 639 (64–65, 500–501, 723); Gordon, *Hitler, Germans, and the "Jewish Question,"* 94, 95.
37. Cf. Jacob Katz, *From Prejudice to Destruction: Anti-Semitism, 1700–1933* (Cambridge, MA, and London: Harvard University Press, 1980) 314.
38. *Hitler's Second Book,* 149–51, 232 (*Hitlers Zweites Buch,* 157–58, 222); Gordon, *Hitler, Germans, and the "Jewish Question,"* 100.
39. Wolters, "Der 'Führer' und seine Denker," 226–27. Marx is described as a "Jew" throughout *Mein Kampf* (e.g., 219).
40. MK 300–329, 351–52 (329–62, 386–87). The terms "Jewish" and "international" are associated innumerable times in his works. Jäckel, *Hitler's World View,* 54. See, for example, *Table Talk,* Sept. 25, 1941, 33 (*Monologe,* 70); MK 562 (629).
41. *Hitler's Second Book,* 230 (*Hitlers Zweites Buch,* 220–21); Birken, *Hitler as Philosophe,* 51, 70, 73. Jews were blamed for the economic woes in Germany. Abel, *Why Hitler Came Into Power,* 123ff.
42. Hitler tries to distance himself from the persecution of Jews in the Middle Ages and base his anti-Semitism on "racial knowledge," not "religious ideas," but he clearly has some contact with former complaints, especially in his distaste for Jewish finance. MK 51–52, 119–20 (55–56, 130–31).
43. MK 57–58 (61–62).
44. MK 143, 242–43, 272, 638 (157–58, 264–65, 298, 722–23); Birken, *Hitler as Philosophe,* 38. Jews also stir up hatred toward Germany on the international scene. MK 61, 148, 623 (65–66, 163, 702–3).

45. MK 58 (62).
46. *Table Talk*, Feb. 20/21, 1942, March 27, 1942, 246, 280 (*Monologe*, 288); MK 302–3 (331–32).
47. Ibid., Oct, 21, 1941, 61; Oct. 24–25, 1941, 67–69; Feb. 20–21, 1942, 244 (*Monologe*, 97, 103, 106, 286).
48. Ibid., June 5, 1942, 387. Nazi rhetoric vacillates between patronizing the church and attacking it. Hitler's speeches contain a number of citations and allusions to scripture, but this is all a sham. McGovern, *From Luther to Hitler*, 652; Ryback, *Hitler's Private Library*, 142. Hitler thinks that Christianity is void of true spirituality; it is pure "humbug," fit for "old women, who have given up everything because life has withdrawn from them." *Table Talk*, Feb. 27, 1942, 258 (*Monologe*, 302).
49. Ibid., Oct. 21, 1941, 60, (*Monologe*, 96–97). Hitler explains that "a large number of the descendents of the Roman Legionaries, mostly Gauls, were living in Galilee, and Jesus was probably one of them."
50. Ibid., Dec. 13, 1941, 110 (*Monologe*, 150).
51. Ibid., Nov. 29–30, 1944, 548.
52. Ibid., July 11–12 and Oct. 21, 1941, 8, 62 (*Monologe*, 41, 98–99). Hitler understands that Christianity produced the doctrine of egalitarianism in the West, but Judaism shares its culpability for two reasons: one, the Jews produced the religion; and two, they adopted the teaching of equality in an extreme form after it was developed by the church and permeated modern culture. Again, they have no creative genius.
53. Ibid., Oct. 10 and 24, 1941, 41, 66, 68 (*Monologe*, 76, 103, 105). Hitler extends the theory of evolution and thinks life exists on other planets.
54. Ibid., Sept. 23, Oct. 14 and 24, and Nov. 11, 1941, 32, 47–49, 67, 95–96 (*Monologe*, 67, 82–85, 103–4, 137–39).
55. Ibid., Dec. 14, 1941, 112 (*Monologe*, 152).
56. Ibid., Oct. 25, 1941, and April 7, 1942, 71, 309 (*Monologe*, 108).
57. Ibid., July 4, 1942, 418–19.
58. MK 115, 267 (125, 126, 293); *Table Talk*, Oct. 14, 1941, 47–49 (*Monologe*, 82–85).
59. MK 116 (126).
60. *Table Talk*, July 11–12, Nov. 11, and Dec. 13, 1941, 8, 95, 110 (*Monologe*, 41, 134, 150).
61. Ibid., Dec. 13, 1941, 110 (*Monologe*, 150).
62. Ibid., Oct. 14, 1941, 49–50 (*Monologe*, 85).
63. Ibid., Dec. 13, 1941, 110, Feb. 8 and July 4, 1942, 230–31, 415, 419 (*Monologe*, 150, 272). See Ibid., xxxii, 310; Gordon, *Hitler, Germans, and the "Jewish Question,"* 109.
64. Ryback, *Hitler's Private Library*, 104.
65. *Table Talk*, May 16, 1944, 546, 547.
66. Ibid., 547. One of his confidants confirms this account. Ryback, *Hitler's Private Library*, 106, 107.
67. Ibid., xxxvii; Ryback, *Hitler's Private Library*, 106–7.
68. Ryback, *Hitler's Private Library*, 104–7.
69. Abel, *Why Hitler Came to Power*, 134–35; Monika Leske, *Philosophen im 'Dritte Reich'* (Berlin: Dietz Verlag, 1990) 97. Nazis like Rudolf Buttman saw a direct connection between Hitler and Nietzsche.

70. See, for example, MK 29, 258–59, 383 (29, 283, 421); *Table Talk*, Oct. 24, 1941, 68 (*Monologe*, 105).
71. *Table Talk*, Nov. 19, 1941, 104 (*Monologe*, 143); MK 65, 562–63 (69–70, 630).
72. Ibid., Oct. 14, 1941, 49 (*Monologe*, 85).
73. MK 431–32 (480–81); McGovern, *From Luther to Hitler*, 625, 630. Rosenberg's work, *The Myth of the Twentieth Century*, is a good example of Nazi myth-making. Rudolf Bultmann, the NT scholar, laid the foundation for the positive use of myth by refusing to eliminate the miraculous content or myths from the NT account of Jesus but preferring to demythologize or reinterpret these passages and find a positive message within them.
74. Hermann Rauschning, *The Voice of Destruction* (New York: G. P. Putnum's Sons, 1940) 184, 222–24; Leonard Peikoff, "Nazism versus Reason," *The Objectivist* 8/10 (Oct. 1969): 3–4, 7–8; Viereck, *Metapolitics*, 9. The authenticity of the citations from Rauschning might be questioned, but they certainly summarize Hitler's basic view on the subject.
75. MK 409–14 (454–60).
76. MK 49, 107, 176ff., 182–86, 264ff., 338, 341–43, 349, 408, 468ff., 477, 494ff., 580 (52, 193ff., 199–204, 290ff., 371–72, 375–77, 384, 452–53, 524ff., 553ff., 650–51). Will is central to Nazi ideology. Leske, *Philosophen im 'Dritte Reich,'* 120–24.
77. *Hitler's Second Book*, 34–36 (*Hitlers Zweites Buch*, 66–68); MK 85–88, 446–49 (92–97, 497–501); Wolters, "Der 'Führer' und seine Denker," 227.
78. MK 381 (419); *Table Talk*, 403. The NSDAP became the "Führer Party" in the late 1920s, and "Heil Hitler" became mandatory in the 1930s. Kershaw, *Hitler*, 46–47, 99, 101.
79. MK 91, 344–45 (99–100, 378–79).
80. *Table Talk*, Aug. 20, 1942, 484; Weikart, *From Darwin to Hitler*, 210–11, 275.
81. *Hitler's Second Book*, 18–19 (*Hitlers Zweites Buch*, 54–55).
82. Ibid., 108, 125 (*Hitlers Zweites Buch*, 124, 138); MK 44, 170–71 (46, 187). It is Hitler's concept of will that produces the emphasis on terror. Leske, *Philosophen im 'Dritte Reich,'* 124.
83. Ibid., 10–11 (*Hitlers Zweites Buch*, 48–49). War was a fact of life for the Nazis. Lenske, *Philosophen im 'Dritte Reich,'* 75.
84. MK 96, 150–51, 327–28, 436–37 (104, 164–66, 359–60, 486–87).
85. *Hitler's Second Book*, 7–8 (*Hitlers Zweites Buch*, 46–47); *Table Talk*, Dec. 13, 1941, 111–12 (*Monologe*, 151); Jäckel, *Hitler's World View*, 90.
86. Ibid., 9 (*Hitlers Zweites Buch*, 47). This Darwinian view of struggle (Kampf) and victory of the strong preoccupied his thought at least as early as 1914–1918. Werner Maser, *Adolf Hitler: Legende, Mythos, Wirklichkeit* (München: Bechtle, 1971) 166; Kershaw, *Hitler*, 21.
87. Ibid., 8–9 (*Hitlers Zweites Buch*, 46–47); MK 132–33, 286, 383, 676 (145, 313–14, 420–21, 769). Mendel's law of differentiation explains that mixed or crossbred individuals are not all alike, and so Hitler thinks Germany needs more people to insure that enough of the stronger race is born and able to prevail. Ibid., 110–11, 264 (n. 227).
88. Jäckel, *Hitler's World View*, 88, 94–96; Leske, *Phjlosophen im 'Dritte Reich,'* 128–31, 141–43; Kershaw, *Hitler*, 28. The Nazis preferred the biological unity of the German people, rather than dividing them up between classes.

They also tended to unite spirit and matter together into one reality, rather than create a chasm like the Idealists or eliminate the one for the other like the Communists.

89. *Hitler's Second Book*, 112, 205 (*Hitlers Zweites Buch*, 127, 200–201); McGovern, *From Luther to Hitler*, 640; Wolters, "Der 'Führer' und seine Denker," 225ff. Generally, Hitler disapproves of mixing Aryan and Nordic blood with other races. MK 296, 401–3 (324, 443–44). However, he needed to unite the German people together and left the notion of Aryanism in a vague, mystical state, vacillating between the Nordic ideal and the acceptable reality. He even recognized that a homogeneous population like Sweden needed inequality to distinguish the truly excellent, as well as some heterogeneity to allow for the emergence of different talents. Birken, *Hitler as Philosophe*, 58–59; Wolters, "Der 'Führer' und seine Denker," 225ff.
90. MK 283 (310).
91. MK 389, 393, 395, 430 (428–29, 433–34, 436, 478–79).
92. MK 296; McGovern, *From Luther to Hitler*, 633.
93. *Hitler's Second Book*, 23, 27–28, 49, 224 (*Hitlers Zweites Buch*, 58–59, 61–62, 78–79, 216); MK 134–39, 642ff., 646, 649 (147–53, 727ff., 731, 735–36). Hitler equivocates in his rhetoric about certain races like the Japanese, whom he calls inferior at times and not inferior at other times. MK 290–91 (317–19); Birken, *Hitler as Philosophe*, 88.
94. MK 652–54 (739–41).
95. *Table Talk*, Aug. 8–11, Sept. 17–18, and Oct. 17, 1941, 20–21, 28, 55 (*Monologe*, 54–55, 62–63, 91); *Hitler's Second Book*, 149–51 (*Hitlers Zweites Buch*, 157–58); MK 140, 654 (153–54, 742); Jäckel, *Hitler's World View*, 33, 37. The classic and popular work on pan-Germanism was Hans Grimm's *Volk ohne Raum* (1926). Hitler covets America's spacious plains and believes that a simple restoration of the pre-1914 *Lebensraum* will not produce the kind of prosperity found in that country. He shows much concern over the German immigration to America, which is creating a superior society, and mentions the US immigration Act of 1924, which is "motivated by the theories of its own racial researchers." Viereck, *Metapoloitics*, 173; *Hitler's Second Book*, 105, 108–9 (*Hitlers Zweites Buch*, 121, 124–25).
96. *Hitler's Second Book*, 21 (*Hitlers Zweites Buch*, 56–57); Weikart, *From Darwin to Hitler*, 215. Sparta was Ernst Haeckel's favorite example for defending this practice. Hitler also approved of practicing abortion on the inferior, although not on "healthy women."
97. Phillippe Burrin, *Hitler and the Jews: The Genesis of the Holocaust*, Patsy Southgate (trans.), Saul Friedländer (ed.) (London, Melbourne, and Auckland: Edward Arnold, 1994) 66–67; Jäckel, *Hitler*, 123. In August of 1942, German medical professionals resumed the killing in a more concealed manner with the typical estimate running around two hundred thousand more victims.
98. MK 561 (628).
99. Burrin, *Hitler and the Jews*, 32ff., 46, 49, 60, 77.
100. Ibid., 85, 100.
101. Ibid., 77–79, 85; Gordon, *Hitler, Germans, and the "Jewish Question,"* 125. Eichmann was in charge of emigration in the late 1930s. He accepted the Zionist aversion to assimilation and felt that finding the Jews a permanent

home would be acceptable to Nazis and Zionists. Hannah Arendt, *Eichmann in Jerusalem: A Report on the Banality of Evil* (New York: Penguin Books, 1979) 33–35, 40–41, 56–60.

102. Gordon, *Hitler, Germans, and the "Jewish Question,"* 126–27; Goldhagen, *Hitler's Willing Executioners*, 145. In his political speeches, he often spoke of "removal" of the Jews. Hitler, *Sämtliche Aufzeichnungen*: *1905–1924*, Eberhard Jäckel and Axel Kuhn (Hrsg.) (Stuttgart: Deutsche Verlags-Anstalt, 1980) 119–20, 127–29, 140–41, 163, 176–77, 201, 238 [Docs 91 (April 6, 1920), 96 (April 27, 1920), 106 (June, 6, 1920), 121 (July21, 1920), 129 (August 7, 1920), 136 (August 13, 1920), 148 (September 24, 1920)]; Kershaw, *Hitler*, 24–26.
103. *Table Talk*, Oct. 25, 1941, 69, 71 (*Monologe*, 106–8); Gordon, *Hitler, Germans, and the "Jewish Question,"* 130–31. The phrase "final solution" does not refer to the Holocaust in its original intendment but any solution proposed to resolve the Jewish problem. See, for example, Burrin, *Hitler and the Jews*, 98. Goldhagen thinks that death was always Hitler's solution to the problem. *Hitler's Willing Executioners*, 423–25.
104. MK 170–71, 651, 679–80 (187, 739, 771–773).
105. Max Domarus, *Hitler: Reden und Proklamationen 1932–1945* (Würzburg: Gesamtherstellung und Auslieferung; Schmidt, Neustadt a.d Aisch, 1962–63) 2.1058; Weinberg, *Because They Were Jews*, 109–10; Jäckel, *Hitler's World View*, 61; Kershaw, *Hitler*, 150. Hitler threatens the lives of the Jews in Europe, hoping to prevent the Jews living elsewhere from inciting the United States and Britain into joining the conflict. Gordon, *Hitler, Germans, and the "Jewish Question,'* 133. Hitler repeated and referred to the original prophecy during public addresses in 1942 (Feb. 24, Sept. 30, and Nov. 8), boasting of its fulfillment after the mass murders were under way. He believed the Jews provoked the war and must be punished, particularly after the situation deteriorated in Russia for the Germans. *Table Talk*, Jan. 23, 1942, 180; Goldhagen, *Hitler's Willing Executioners*, 404–5, 424.
106. Jäckel, *Hitler's World View*, 61–62. Hitler invaded Russia in the spring of 1941, and a half million of its Jews were shot to death by November. Gordon, *Hitler, Germans, and the "Jewish Question,"* 127.
107. Burrin, *Hitler and the Jews*, 9, 133. See Kershaw, *Hitler*, 157. Burrin admits that the decision matured over a period of time. He believes the *Einsatzgruppen* acted on its own in exterminating Jews in mass, but they must have perceived the Führer's intention (8–9, 20, 22, 44). Gassing became the preferred method a year later, maybe to ease the psychological burden of killing, but it also stood as a symbolic *lex talionis* for the atrocities committed against German soldiers in WWI. Gordon, *Hitler, Germans, and the "Jewish Question,"* 127; Golhagen, *Hitler's Willing Executioners*, 157; Weinberg, *Because They Were* Jews, 109–10. The generals and the SS leaders were informed of the mass killings by 1943/1944 at the very latest. Kershaw, *Hitler*, 182.
108. Frank Stern, *The Whitewashing of the Yellow Badge: Antisemitism and Philosemitism in Postwar Germany*, William Templer (trans.) (Oxford: Pergamon Press, 1992) 111ff.; Anna and Richard Merritt, *Public Opinion in Occupied Germany: The OMGUS Surveys, 1945–1949* (Urbana, IL: University of Illinois Press, 1970) 146–48; Goldhagen, *Hitler's Willing Executioners*, 419, 605 (n. 53).

109. Helmut Krausnik, et al., *Anatomy of the SS State*, Richard Barry, et al. (trans.) (New York: Walker and Company, 1968) 388ff.; Karl Bracher, *The German Dictatorship: The Origins, Structure, and Effects of National Socialism* (New York and Washington, DC: Praeger Publishers, 1970) 63, 365, 384, 385; George Mosse, "Die deutsche Rechte und die Juden," in *Entscheidungsjahr 1932*, Werner Mosse (Hrsg.) (Tübingen: Mohr, 1966) 243 (n. 219); Gordon, *Hitler, Germans, and the "Jewish Question,"* 157, 166. One survey indicates that 37 percent of the Germans approved of the annihilation of foreigners like Jews, Poles, and non-Aryans as threatening Germany's existence, although the question is poorly phrased. Ibid., 208.
110. Goldhagen, *Hitler's Willing Executioners*, 9; Arendt, *Eichmann in Jerusalem*, 91. Goldhagen rejects the conventional explanation that the killings were coerced. One, there is no verified case, vetted in court, where refusing to kill resulted in injury to life and limb or imprisonment in a concentration camp (379). Two, ordinary German executioners thought the Jews were worthy of death (14). Three, the Order Police consisted of ordinary Germans for the most part, and they conducted atrocities against the Jews, helping *Einsatzgruppen* kill a million of them, even burning some alive (185ff.). Four, keepsake photos show the pride that German battalions took in the massacres. Five, ordinary Germans went beyond Himmler's orders in abusing, starving, and continuing to kill Jews during the death marches at the end of the war (357, 403).

7

The Immediate Sources of Hitler's Ideology

The specific sources of Hitler's worldview are difficult to enumerate or identify in most cases. He worked within concepts that were pervasive within the culture of the day and representative of a significant aspect of the German *Geist.* His theories of evolution, racism, eugenics, and euthanasia were not idiosyncratic, pseudoscientific, or radical aberrations of a counterculture. They were respectable, reputable mainstream beliefs, shared by many leading authorities within the academic, scientific, and medical communities, even if he received much of his information from secondhand or popular sources and developed the ideology in radical directions.[1] During his formative years in Vienna, he looked to Karl Lueger, the longtime mayor of the city, and Georg von Schönerer, an Austrian politician and founder of the Pan-German Party, which advocated biological racism, eugenics, and anti-Semitism.[2] Hitler read lots of books at this time dealing with his newfound political interests, including Jörg Lanz von Liebenfel's *Ostara,* a periodical exalting Aryan superiority, and Theodor Fritsch's book on anti-Semitism, *The Handbook on the Jewish Question.*[3] Between 1919–1921, he borrowed a number of books from the National Socialist Institute in Munich, displaying some breadth and depth of intellectual interests in reading the likes of Montesquieu, Rousseau, Kant, and Spengler, but also showing an obsession with anti-Semitism in reading classical works like Chamberlain's *Foundations of the Nineteenth Century* and Ford's *The International Jew,* as well as other works relating Luther, Goethe, Schopenhauer, and Wagner to the subject.[4] As leader of the Nazi party, he provided a reading list that included books from Fritsch, Ford, Rosenberg, and Günther, and while in prison he read Lenz's pamphlet on "Race as a Principle Value," Günther's *Racial Typology of the German People* on Nordic racial theory, Ratzel's *Political Geography* on racial struggle and *Lebensraum,* and the second edition of Baur-Fischer-Lenz on human genetics and eugenics, which was well-respected in the scientific community.[5]

The Wagner Circle

Of all the immediate sources, none provided a more visible and significant inspiration for Hitler and his fellow Nazis than the circle of Richard Wagner. Hitler, Eckart, Rosenberg, and Goebbels developed an intimate and reciprocal friendship with many of his disciples and relatives, including Cosima, his widow; Siegfried, his son; and Chamberlain, his son-in-law—all recognizing a link between Bayreuth and National Socialism. Many in the Nazi hierarchy were artistic and literary types, who venerated the genius of the master and found a powerful voice in him, expressing many similar frustrations about the Jews and their control of the arts.[6] Hitler had a particular reverence for the music and acumen of the master, which started early on in his life, after he attended a production of *Reinzi* during his time in Linz and developed from that time on into a lifelong obsession.[7] In his *Table Talk*, he speaks like a devotee, offering rave reviews of Wagner's work and extolling *Tristan und Isolde* as his masterpiece; he reminisces about pilgrimages to Bayreuth as a highlight of his life, the warmth and genuine friendship of Cosima and Siegfried Wagner, the letters to Chamberlain while he was in prison, and their endorsement of his movement early on.[8] The Wagners certainly shared much in common with Hitler and the Nazis, including an emphasis upon Schopenhauer and voluntarism, a revolt against rationalism and legalism, racial supremacy, Nordic primitivism in the myths of Siegfried and Nibelungen, pan-Germanism, nationalism, a loathing of the Jews, and a hatred of international capitalism.[9]

Wagner brought his circle into the matrix of proto-Nazi thinking by falling under the spell of Schopenhauer's metaphysics in the 1850s and remaining a faithful disciple of its voluntarism thereafter. He describes Schopenhauer's work in his writings as the "most lucid of all philosophical systems" and commends it as the "basis of all further mental and moral culture . . . in its every walk of life." Wagner exalts the system because of its basic insight into the true, voluntaristic essence of the world and follows its subsequent demand to negate the blind or irrational impulses of life through works of art. Like Schopenhauer, he thinks music should express the appetites of life and then turn around and find liberation from the "headstrong blindness" of the will by transporting people to a timeless, spaceless realm of peace, which expresses faith, hope, and love.[10] In this way, Wagner expresses an understanding of the Christian gospel and its mandate to deny the things of this world and the desires of the flesh (1 John 2:15–16). He wishes to deny the will-to-live, which makes individuals sacrifice their personal lives for the mere continuation of the species, nullify the phenomenal world and its appetites, and find release through Christ's "will-to-redeem," interpreting true Christianity as the ultimate act of asceticism or nihilism, much like Schopenhauer. This dialectical movement produces a tension in his music, which Friedrich Nietzsche, the most eloquent disciple and interpreter, sees as a contest between Dionysus and Apollo, the two divine forces of Greek mythology that produced the same tension in their music and tragedies. The former represents the formless and intangible essence of life, and the latter represents the longing for clarity, order, and reason, which produces the tension of all great art, even though Nietzsche (and Hitler) end up reducing the strain in their own respective ways by negating the Apollonarian element and deifying the will to power.[11]

Wagner finds a similar connection between Hellenic and German culture in his work. He sees a revival of this spiritual force arising among the people, which began after the Thirty Years' War and kept working its way through Germanic culture, finding vital expressions in poetry, music, and philosophy, and flourishing in spite of the political and cultural dominance of French culture. Its essence withstands foreign intrusion and international attempts to uproot the intimate relationship it has with a concrete, provincial location. Its spirit arises from a people, soil, and language, which are bound together within an indelible unity, having no independent existence outside the specific context it finds in Greece and Germany.[12]

Wagner says this is why the Jews remain an alien force in Germany. They exist outside of the German people in a separate community and speak a foreign language coming from an alien culture. They cannot speak German naturally and express the poetic and artistic feelings of a people rooted in the *Vaterland* when they have no real connection to it. They cannot act or sing or create great works of arts in sculpture and architecture if they have no cultural roots. They can only hear the "barest surface" of the culture and try to mimic its overt form, not express the passions of its soul or "life-bestowing inner organism." Even Felix Mendelssohn-Bartholdy with all his talent and cultural background could not awaken within the German people "that deep, that heart-searching effect which we await from Art."[13]

Wagner thinks this inability to appreciate the Germanic spirit has negative ramifications throughout the entire realm because of the position Jews enjoy in society. The Jews represent a powerful organization that is able to suppress Germanic expression in the arts, and it looks as if the utter destruction of Germanic culture is at hand. He believes the Jews are nothing but materialistic pigs, using capitalism as a steering mechanism to guide all their endeavors, developing performances in the arts for commercial, not "supernal ends," and so bastardizing the culture by consuming all of life. This materialism is permeating everyone's lives because the Jews control much of the money supply and constantly scheme to gain more through consuming vital forces, even turning a profit out of poetry, music, and the arts—something that was born from the German spirit, out of a pure love for what is "Beautiful and Noble." By controlling the money, as well as the press, they are able to ostracize good art and cheapen German lives through their poor taste, populist tripe, and materialistic interests; and for Wagner, this is intolerable. The Jews are destroying "our highest culture-tendencies," and it is time to think about using force and inducing a "violent ejection of the destructive foreign element" from the land.[14]

Houston Stewart Chamberlain wrote the magnum opus of the Bayreuth School on anti-Semitism and racism—*The Foundations of the Nineteenth Century*. He was born on September 9, 1855, in Southsea, Hampshire, England, but suffering from poor health, he went to Europe in 1870 with his Prussian tutor, visiting its many spas and eventually adopting Germany as his new home. He wrote a number of books and essays on Wagner and his work from 1892 to 1895 and developed a close relationship with Cosima through the years, starting with his first visit to the annual festival in 1882, where he met the master. He ended up marrying their daughter in 1908 and moving to Bayreuth, the "home of his soul," where he spent the last couple decades of his life before dying on January 9, 1927. In 1899, he published *The Foundations of the Nineteenth Century* under the constant encouragement of Cosima and the Wagner Circle. It sold over one hundred thousand copies by the end of the First World War and went on to more than double its sales, undergoing twenty-eight editions and a number of translations by the middle of the next war.[15] Its admirers included Kaiser Wilhelm II, who corresponded with the author and promoted the work by circulating copies among the soldiers and all popular libraries.[16] Adolf Hitler was also a fan, who probably read the book while in prison and mentions it in *Mein Kampf*, which was written at the time. Hitler even met the author a couple of time in Bayreuth and conducted a limited correspondence with him. Chamberlain greeted Hitler with a number of accolades, hailing him as a coming savior of Germany, and many Nazi writers appreciated his imprimatur and returned the favor, christening him the "spiritual founder" of Nazism.[17]

Chamberlain's work is the product of evolutionary thinking, which was so much a part of German culture during his day. He wrote his book at the end of a century that was dominated by German Idealism and its view of life as an evolutionary process. He refers to Herder, Kant, Goethe, and other German intellectuals as providing a fundamental inspiration for the theory and considers the more celebrated work of Darwin a mere flower of this overall way of thinking in the *Vaterland*, not its root. Nonetheless, Chamberlain retains important elements of the Darwinian understanding of evolution, including the emphasis on gradual development, the struggle for existence, the selection of the environment, and the importance of isolated breeding. He even uses Darwinian theory to criticize Count Gobineu's theory of race, which was so popular in Wagnerian circles, rejecting the claim that the world was "peopled by [races developing from] Shem, Ham and Japhet. . . . A noble race does not fall from Heaven, it becomes noble gradually, just like fruit-trees, and this gradual process can begin anew at any moment, as soon as accident of geography and history or a fixed plan (as in the case of the Jews) creates conditions." Gobineau's theory had its day, exerting its greatest influence upon Richard Wagner and enjoying "widespread acceptance in Germany's literacy and musical circles" through this influence, but Chamberlain is willing to criticize the Count's work on a number of points, while acknowledging the importance of his early contribution upon the development of racial theory.[18]

Chamberlain follows the Darwinian understanding that humans are no different from dogs and develop the same variety of breeds. He considers the Teutonic (or Germanic) race superior to the other forms of humanity and thinks the future of civilization depends upon them. They are related to the Hellenes of old, who possessed superior creative genius, as well as the nobles of ancient Rome and the masters of the Italian Renaissance—all possessing Teutonic blood and producing an advanced civilization. Other races of people are just not capable of producing this kind of civilization, and so the Teutons have a sacred duty to promote the dominance of their superior culture and advance the species. Teutons have slaughtered whole tribes and races of people—"as for instance, the Anglo-Saxon of England, the German order in Prussia, the French and English in North America"—in order to lay "by this very means the surest foundation of what is highest and most moral." Violence is not always necessary when peaceable means prove just as effective, but no "humanitarian chatter" can evade the fundamental struggle of racial competition that fuels the Darwinian concept of evolution and the imperative to advance the species.[19]

Chamberlain thinks people must pay particular attention to breeding in fulfilling their duty toward the perfection of the race. A natural inequality exists between human beings, relating to both physical and intellectual abilities, just like there is in the animal kingdom. People cannot produce an extraordinary race of people unless they reject promiscuous relationships between different types of individuals and practice selective breeding. While the idea of a pure race is mythical and unscientific, mixing leads to the degeneration of a race and should be avoided in most circumstances as having a detrimental effect. One can see this negative impact in the Teutonic race, which Chamberlain believes is diminishing through the promiscuous practice of mixing with "mongrel Italians," causing its narrow "dolichocephli" and blue/gray eyes to become round and dark, respectively, thus losing its superior attributes. Some crossbreeding can be helpful and even produce a certain level of greatness, and he sees no problem with Celts, Slavs, and Teutons mixing their blood together. It might have some further benefit, preventing the sterility and degeneration that comes with incest, but mixing should be practiced with great caution and for the explicit purpose of elevating the race by creating a superior mix of attributes. Germans certainly should not diminish the race by mixing it with Jewish blood, which is "alien" and "inferior" to the Indo-European lineage and way of life. Jews have tried to keep themselves pure ever since the Babylonian captivity by marrying their sons exclusively to their own kind, while letting their daughters marry Indo-Europeans and corrupting the set of superior Aryan blood.[20]

Chamberlain's anti-Semitism finds its roots within the sons of the Enlightenment and their analysis of Judaism. He looks to Voltaire as one of his patron saints and cites him in an extensive manner as a fundamental authority in establishing his anti-Semitic point of view. "Voltaire is one of the authors whom I know best, because I prefer interesting books to wearisome ones, and I think I could easily collect a hundred quotations of a most aggressive nature against the Jews."[21] His analysis hardly differs from the typical outline of intelligentsia, which deprecates the origin of Judaism in the OT, following the excoriating analysis of Voltaire and the Enlightenment, and creates a much more sophisticated prejudice through the higher critical methods of German scholarship. Chamberlain is intimately familiar with advanced scholars like Julius Wellhausen (and his JEDP theory) and agrees with the "scientific" results of the scholarship, showing the complicity of priests in all social and religious evil, just as the Enlightenment had suspected.[22] Chamberlain simply repeats the theory of the day, blaming the priests of Jerusalem for bastardizing the religion and culture of ancient Israel, destroying its freedom and multicultural affections, and creating the new religion of Judaism, based on the "priestly caste," "priestly legislation," and "priestly faith." Thus, Judaism finds its origin in the power play of priests, who advocate "one God, one altar, [and] one High Priest." These priests were able to centralize worship in Jerusalem, tear down alternative altars and gods around the country, and enslave the people to their system of laws and sacrifices. To feign their allegiance with the past, the priests pretended to find an ancient book of the law in the temple during the days of Josiah's Revival in 622 BCE, which the theory identifies with the book of Deuteronomy, but they actually wrote the book at the time in order to establish their own authority and religion. Once they completed this work and read it to the people, they continued to consolidate their power over the course of time, composing the priestly code, which consists of the "whole book of Leviticus, three-fourths of Numbers, the half of Exodus, and about eleven chapters of Genesis." They also proceeded to doctor the ancient history of Israel as found in the historical books of the OT in order to mask the actual development of the religion and pretend the "new law," "new faith," and "new hierocracy" existed from the very beginning, leaving a few salvific passages in the text of scripture from the earlier, more liberal way of thinking. Because of the priesthood in Jerusalem, Judaism became a religion of an angry God, who needed blood atonement and punctilious obedience, and proceeded to inculcate a narrow dogmatism, which accepted only certain ways to speak and act in serving Jehovah—the one, true, and only God. Jehovah became the specific God of the Jews and hated all other people on the earth, who refused to follow the specific, concrete, and literal understanding of their priests.[23]

Unfortunately, the Jews started to think and act much like their priests as a people, displaying no ability to grasp the power of myth. Unlike Indo-Europeans, they lack a creative or mystical impulse to interpret their scripture in an allegorical manner and transcend the crass materialism that finds the message of passages like Genesis 3 on a literal level. They lack a deeper, spiritual sense that allows a people to create philosophical or metaphysical abstractions and contribute to the knowledge and progress of a culture beyond economic concerns. Their one appetite leads them to search for god in the here and now, in the things of the world, in objects of silver and gold, in the rewards of the present life, not higher, spiritual values. Even their prophets saw the sin of idolatry as a constant source of temptation for the Jewish soul and often looked at the nation as more stiff-necked and wicked than others, considering the nature of this sin and its consequences. As a result, the Jew is "alien [and] everlastingly alien" to Indo-European culture and will continue to leaven the entire Germanic way of life—"our governments, our law, our science, our commerce, our literature, our art . . ."—unless something is done.[24]

In contrast to this harsh portrait, Chamberlain provides for his audience a more favorable review of Christianity, the offspring of the Jewish faith. His concept of Christianity is consonant with the Wagner Circle, which paid its respect to the conversion of Richard and Cosima Wagner to the faith in their later years, but it contradicts the basic course of the Enlightenment, which promoted anti-Semitic and anti-Christian sentiment with consistent vehemence, and the position of Hitler, who spurned Chamberlain's belief in the spirituality of Christianity as a lapse in judgment.[25] Chamberlain can speak of Christ as the most sublime revelation of God, the "absolute religious genius," the "one foundation of all moral culture," and the true negation of the Jewish religion. He can laud Jesus as bringing a new concept of God and law, which emphasizes love and mercy in contrast to the Jewish religion of hate. He thinks of those nations who fail to adopt the moral greatness of Jesus as barbaric and exalts him to a position of authority beyond the typical Nazi account.[26] But he still provides inspiration for the Nazi interpretation by understanding his teachings in terms of Aryan supremacy. Jesus was able to preach these sublime truths because he was an Aryan, not a Jew—a position the Nazis adopt from him. Jesus came from Galilee (*Gelil hayyoyim*), which means the "district of the heathen" in the Hebrew language. The area was a mixture of various ethnicities ever since the invasion of Assyria in the eighth century BCE, and it became more Greek during the times of the Seleucids and Simon Tharsi's removal of the Jews from the region. "The probability that Christ was no Jew, that He had not a drop of genuinely Jewish blood in his veins, is so great that it is almost equivalent to a certainty."[27]

Even so, Jesus and Christianity remained tainted with vestiges of Jewish elements, which need exorcism or reinterpretation to find the deeper, spiritual essence. Jesus "brought a new message," but he "lived in the Jewish intellectual world" and remained "chained to the fundamental ideas of Judaism." Paul conveyed the message to the church, but it was a mixed message because Paul was half Jewish and half Greek. He had a number of pernicious elements corrupting his Aryan side, and this explains why the history of the church is checkered with so much depravity. These negative elements might have extinguished the light, but through the process of Hellenization, the religion was sublimated, absorbing important aspects of Indo-European culture and reinterpreting the faith through pre-Christian myths of Aryan metaphysics, including the Trinity, incarnation, original sin, and vicarious redemption.[28] In this way, Chamberlain reinterprets the cardinal doctrine of the faith, rejecting an orthodox or literal understanding, finding a symbolic meaning behind its teachings, and citing liberal theologians like Friedrich Schleiermacher and Adolf Harnack to establish his point of view a number of times in the discussion. Like these liberals, he prefers to reinterpret the religion in a nonliteral or non-Jewish manner, looking for the kernel underneath the husk and finding God within the soul, not outside of human subjectivity in a world of miracles.[29] "Religion cannot find God in a mechanistic universe, superstitious history, or literal doctrine; it must find the numinous or ideal world within the experience of the heart." If there is any relationship to this world, it is found in the typical liberal tendency of post-Kantian times, which reduces religion to morality and Jesus to a simple moral teacher.[30]

Günther

Along with the liberal and literacy influence of the Wagner Circle, the Nazis received an important impetus toward their view of life from the scientific community in Germany. There were many scientists who advocated the importance of race, breeding, and eugenics in elevating a people, but few exerted a more direct influence upon the Nazi way of thinking in its early maturation than Hans F. K. Günther, who was known as *Rassengünther* or Race Günther, a professor of biology, ethnography, and racial theory, as well as an author of numerous books and essays on the subject. He offered a more sophisticated approach to the question of race than literary figures like Gobineau and Chamberlain, giving the Nazis instant credentials to forward what they considered the most scientifically sound approach to politics.[31] Günther certainly had much help in producing his scientific work and even expressed appreciation for the contributions of Gobineau and Chamberlain in helping to exhibit the importance of race and the "Nordic ideal,"[32] but there was nothing like his more exacting measurements and detailed analysis in lending credence to the theory.[33] Hitler longed for this kind of credibility, recommending Günther's works to his fellow party members and reading other academically respected works like Baur-Fischer-Lenz upon Günther's recommendation.[34] Günther helped and encouraged Hitler in his rise to power and received many academic awards for his role in the ascendancy of Nazi ideals during the time of the Third Reich, including the Rudolf Virchow plaque and the Goethe Medal for arts and science.

Günther defines race as a "group of human beings" who share the "same physical and mental picture," based on his measurements of height, limbs, skull, hair, eyes, and skin color. He sees five basic races representing the people of Europe—Nordic, Mediterranean, Dinaric, Alpine, and East Baltic—and provides a list of their physical and psychological characteristics. Of course, the Nordic race is considered superior to all the others and responsible for all the great achievements of human civilization. Its physical characteristics are "tall, long-headed, narrow-faced, with prominent chin; narrow nose with high bridge; soft, smooth or wavy light (golden-fair) hair; deep-sunk light (blue or grey) eyes; rosy-white skin." Its psychological gifts include an intense commitment to freedom; a strong sense of justice and truth; a stern and steadfast character, marked with resolve, gravitas, and *virtus*; a gift for creativity and narrative language; a passion for adventure; and a warlike spirit, punctuated with a ruthless taste for blood. Günther develops this portrait by analyzing the descriptions, figures, and busts of the past and finding Nordic blood flowing through the great civilizations, the cultural icons of European history, and the great rulers of empires in Persia, Greece, and Rome.[35]

Günther wants to resurrect the importance of race against the current wave of individualism that is ruining his Germanic people. Christianity brought the current practice of intermingling races to Germany in the Middle Ages, representing the egalitarian interests of the lower class and destroying the racial purity of an elite society. Before this time, blood was considered sacred among the Germanic tribes, and the death penalty was visited upon those who demeaned their noble heritage by having sexual intercourse with inferiors. These tribes were serious about protecting their blood against foreign contamination and even practiced "traditional eugenic customs" among themselves, including infanticide on the sickly and deformed, in order to create a more "beautiful Nordic race" of people. Günther believes it is unfortunate that these practices are no longer used, that the purity of the Nordic race is degenerating every day, and that the consequences are grave for the culture. He says it is imperative to act now before it is too late. The mighty Greek and Roman Empires fell because of the "mental and physical degeneracy of race." France has ruined its blood through the egalitarian policies of the French Revolution, giving equal rights to all its citizens and destroying the nobility it once possessed as late as the Middle Ages and the Renaissance. This country and so many others appear lost because the "denordification" process has gone too far, beyond any possibility of reversing the momentum. The only hope seems to lie within the realm of German-speaking people in Central Europe, who still have the potential to protect and promote the future of the Nordic race.[36]

Rosenberg

Among Hitler's associates, Alfred Rosenberg exercised as much influence as anyone in shaping the direction of the party's ideology. He was born in the Baltic town of Reval, a part of the Russian Empire, but he left during the times of the Russian Revolution in 1918, protesting the Bolshevik usurpation of power and believing, along with many White Russians, that Jewish finance played a major role in the coup d'état.[37] He then settled in Munich, where he joined the German Workers Party, helping to mold its ideology in the early days before it became the party of Hitler and the Nazis. He soon gained a reputation as the official trustee of Nazi ideology, editing the *Völkischer Beobachter* as Eckart's successor, nurturing young Hitler in the faith along with Eckart, introducing him to Chamberlain and the Wagner Circle, and accepting the leadership role of the party while Hitler served time in prison.[38] When the Nazis arose to power, he was awarded several posts in the course of the administration, including an appointment as head of the Reich Ministry for the Occupied Eastern Territories, after the invasion of the Soviet Union, where he challenged the SS and their criminal treatment of the Slavic people, but not in regard to the Jews. In Germany, he was mainly responsible for educating the people in Nazi ideology, much like his role in the early stages of the party. He was anointed by Hitler as the head of the Office for the Supervision of the Total Intellectual and Ideological Schooling and Education of the NSDAP (Nazi Party) on January 24, 1934, and later served as the supervisor of the *Hohe Schule*, the Center of the National Socialist Ideological and Educational Research. In this capacity, he was able to promote his great work, *The Myth of the Twentieth Century*, making it a staple in German life and selling over two million copies.[39] All schools were required by government decree to make continuous mention and use of it, along with the works of Hitler and Günther.[40]

In the work, Rosenberg follows the same metaphysical propensities that inspired Wagner, Nietzsche, and Hitler to accentuate the will and its appetites. He considers Leibniz an "intuitive and brightly conscious herald" of this voluntaristic point of view, in which being is understood in the process of becoming and the soul strives toward self-realization rather than searches for some goal outside of itself.[41] Of course, Schopenhauer is honored as a leading spokesman of the tradition and a favorite author of Rosenberg in general. Schopenhauer captured "our fundamental outlook on the world" in *The World as Will and Representation*, which depicts the will as the thing-in-itself and life as a universal struggle for existence.[42] Rosenberg takes this monistic vision of the will in the pitiless direction of Nietzsche, who is lauded for developing the concept in the nineteenth century, along with Wagner and Lagarde.[43] Like Nietzsche, he rejects the Christian emphasis upon love, sympathy, sin, and grace as destructive to the self-confident will of a superior people and indicative of the inferior mentality of plebes from which the religion arose in the first few centuries. He prefers the heroes of German legend with their courage, pride, honor, and freedom to the martyrs of Christendom, who passively submit to the principalities and powers of this world and die out of pity on the cross for others. He believes the German race should forge a "new mythos" out of its will to power, rather than look to the authority of the church or strive for fidelity to some eternal or heavenly truth existing outside one's own "creative strength."[44]

Rosenberg considers the will and struggle for human existence as a necessary product of race, both physically and spiritually, and rejects the Marxist analysis that attributes everything to class division. He says, "Race is the image of the soul"; it produces the customs, morals, and attitudes of a people, not religion or social conditions. The future of a people depends upon following the aristocratic laws of nature and its selection of the strong through the "practices of conscious selection guided by the strength of will." He exhorts his people to replace the older religious mysticism of Christianity with a new spiritual reality, which finds the sacraments, the *mysteria*, and the new *mythos* within Nordic blood. The time is approaching when the Nordic race will reach a point of no return and find regeneration impossible if it fails to act quickly and decisively.[45] The state must develop programs of "racial protection, racial breeding and racial hygiene" as necessary measures for the current times. It must eliminate "Blacks, . . . Yellow men, Mullatoes [*sic*] or Jews" from the state, the immigration of non-Nordic blood, the propagation of the infirmed, miscegenated offspring, mixed marriages, equal rights, and citizenship for inferiors. It must strengthen the army, training and educating the youth in the Nordic virtues of honor and duty to the state, and use its forces to create more *Lebensraum* for the German race to grow and develop. Right now Rosenberg wants to expel non-Germans from Central Europe and create a mono-racial society within that realm, but his plans for the future include a push to the east, the Nordification of Europe, and the continuous expansion of a will that has no a priori boundary.[46]

Rosenberg reserves most of his venom for those who oppose his racial conception of life and preach a message of human equality. The Apostle Paul incurs much of the vitriol for laying the foundation of egalitarianism in the West, exhibited in his famous words to the Galatians, "In Christ there is neither Jew nor Gentile, slave nor free, male nor female" (Gal 3:28). "This constituted a total rejection of all the cultural values of Greece and Rome" and led to the complete disintegration of the empire as Christianity began to overrun it. In the second century, Marcus Aurelius was "enervated by Christian influences" and proceeded to enact all types of egalitarian policies, disenfranchising the paterfamilias, protecting slaves, emancipating women, and providing for the poor through the public dole. This "love for humanity" eroded the strength of character in the palace and the will to power among the noble, facilitating a spiritual decline among the people and the inevitable collapse of the empire. The Catholic Church carried the banner of the effeminate doctrine through the Middle Ages and modern times, welcoming all nations, classes, and races into its "ecumenical conformism" and destroying the connection of the *Volk* to their own "space, blood, and soil" in the West. The European states eventually embraced the doctrine and proceeded to expand it in the radical direction of the French Revolution, teaching that "every Jew, Negro, and Mulatto can become a citizen of equal rights" and "marry into the Nordic race."[47]

Rosenberg's animosity toward this position is central to all his passions and erupts on many occasions into the same *ad hominem* campaign that Hitler displayed toward the proponents of egalitarianism, demonizing them with every imaginable epithet, racial slur, conspiratorial intrigue, and outright distortion.

The Jews are subject to his intense anger because they willingly embraced more than others the modern spirit of equality, after centuries of marginal living on the outside of society. Rosenberg deprecates the Jews with the typical slurs of the time, except inflating the peril and making it the continual obsession of his thought and the party. Like the sons of the Enlightenment, he considers the Jews a materialistic people from their very beginnings in OT times, possessing no real ethical or spiritual values beyond their singular fixation on the things of this world, seeking their own material well-being and advantage at the expense of others.[48] They have become "parasites" (*Schmarotzen*) ever since, living off the constructive labor of others, preferring commerce and usury to productive work, making the rest of the people slaves to their banking interests, manipulating states and current affairs through high finance, dreaming of world domination, producing no creative or intellectual achievements, and destroying the culture and general welfare of the German people though their manipulation and control of the press. Germans should eliminate this "alien" race of people, not mix with them or grant them the rights of equal citizenship. Usurers are worthy of death, not the privileges of responsible and productive citizens.[49]

As horrible as these words might be, they were not limited to the Jews. Christians received the same type of animosity from Rosenberg because of their intimate connection with the doctrine of egalitarianism. After all, it is their religion that was responsible for destroying racial divisions and laying the spiritual matrix for human equality to flourish in Western civilization.[50] The Jews were the easier and more visible targets of the Nazis, considering their minority status in society, but they were not the root of the problem and only came to the doctrine under the inspiration of Christian culture in modern times, after years of wandering in second-class citizenship, experiencing much the opposite. In many ways, the real enemy was Christianity, and Rosenberg stridently contended with the faith at certain times in his public life. The artless rhetoric and brazen attack caused political headaches for Hitler, who was much more cunning, recognizing the size and power of the church and preferring to bide his time, reeducate the people, and undermine the religion slowly until he could spring his trap. The church reacted strongly against Rosenberg when his *Myth* was first published and became even more incensed when he was made ideological instructor of the Nazis and his book a part of school curricula. Hitler tried to distance the regime from the anti-Christian rhetoric and ideology of the book, claiming it expressed a private opinion and discounting the work as unintelligible, but he was annoyed because of the unwelcomed controversy surrounding the publication of ideas that he preferred to leave unexpressed for the time being.[51] He refrained from placing his imprimatur on the book and explains his motives quite clearly in *Table Talk.*

> During the years of our struggle Rosenberg once submitted to me the draft of a leading article he proposed publishing in reply to the attacks of the Catholic Church. I forbade him to publish it; and I still think it was a great mistake that Rosenberg ever let himself be drawn into a battle of words with the Church. He had absolutely nothing to gain from it; the hesitant Catholics of their own free will regarded the Church with a critical eye, and from the truly devout not only could he expect no fair hearing for his "heretical outpourings," but he must also have realized that the opposition propaganda would condemn him for his meddling in matters of faith and successfully point to him as a man guilty of mortal sin.
>
> The fact that I remain silent in public over Church affairs is not in the least misunderstood by the sly foxes of the Catholic Church, and I am quite sure that a man like the Bishop von Galen knows full well that after the war I shall extract retribution to the last farthing.[52]

Rosenberg will play the same game as Hitler during the course of the administration, advocating church/state separation, distinguishing religious and political struggles, and calling for a "positive Christianity," which speaks to German aspirations, but all of this nonsense is a ruse meant to replace the religion with pure Nordic paganism.[53] Rosenberg knows that the church and Nazism can never live together in the same *Sitz im Leben.*[54]

Like the sons of the Enlightenment, Rosenberg tries to differentiate his animosity toward the church from an ongoing respect for Jesus of Nazareth. He follows the standard outline of the times, which sees the church corrupting the simple carpenter with superstitious stories, transforming him into a wonder-worker and divine savior, and then focuses much of the blame on Paul for adulterating the message with his dogma. Of course, he adds his own Nazi accents to the account, depicting Jesus as a descendent of Nordic blood and blaming Paul for bringing the OT and Jewish theology into the religion, but this kind of anti-Semitism was always a part of the standard treatment in post-Enlightenment intelligentsia and differed only in the degree of animosity, not in the fundamental disdain for the Jews and their religion. Rosenberg finds the real message of Christianity reawakened in Luther's rebellion against the priests of Rome and his "Germanizing" the religion, which led to "Goethe, Kant, Schopenhauer, Nietzsche, and Lagarde and today approaches its full flowering." He is hoping the future will bring a new "German Volk Church," which will reject the superstitious dogma of the past and inculcate "values of honor, pride, inward freedom, aristocracy of the soul and faith in the indestructibility of the soul of man." This new church must reconstruct the old image of Jesus as a "soft and pitying" pacifist, suffering a vicarious death on a cross, and create a new image of a "self-conscious master," who preached powerful words of spiritual exhortation to the multitudes and flogged the Jewish priests in the temple for their materialism. It must create an image of Jesus in non-Jewish terms as a "slim, tall, blond, high browed and long-headed Aryan" and excise all the former references to anything Jewish in the religion, including Jehovah and the Torah. The new theology, music, art, and architecture must arise from the soul of Germanic forces, using the inspiration of its great artists, intellects, and literary figures from the past.[55] Rosenberg is most enamored with the spiritual energy of Meister Eckhart in the thirteenth and fourteenth centuries, certainly more than the halfway measures of Luther and the Reformation, which were unable to rid the people of "permanently fixed dogmas." He thinks of Eckhart as making a more complete break with the Pauline, Augustinian church and its emphasis upon nothingness and dependence upon divine grace.[56] He considers Eckhart the founder of a "new religion—our religion," which releases the German people from the "Jewish-Roman" tradition and proclaims the "God-identity of the human Aryan soul.... The sacred union of God and nature is the primal ground of our being.... The nobility of the self-reliant soul is the highest of all values." In developing this new theology, Rosenberg is creating a new myth. He is not concerned about its truth in any Platonic sense of the term or whether it is "logically correct or false." He is not concerned about eternal or absolute truth, but only whether his myth resonates in the personal and intuitive life of the *Volk*, creating for them a new and fruitful reality.[57]

Ford and the United States

On the international scene, Hitler and the Nazis found precedent for many of their beliefs and activities in the United States. At the turn of the century, America began to develop a similar philosophy and practice of eugenics based on the same intellectual justification, using Darwin, Mendel, and other leading scientists of the day. Many states wrote laws prohibiting the marriage and procreation of "imbeciles," mandating compulsory sterilization for thousands of these unfortunate human beings, and found a willing accomplice in the Supreme Court, which upheld the laws as consistent with the US Constitution and its values in 1927 (*Buck v. Bell*). Some states added antimiscegenation laws, as in the infamous case of Virginia's Racial Integrity Act (1924), which prohibited interracial marriage and represented the accepted legal opinion of the day until the court finally overturned it in 1967 (*Loving v. Virginia*). Even the federal government produced its own version of racial profiling that same year and passed the National Origins Quota and Immigration Act of 1924, which restricted inferior stock from southern and eastern Europe entering the country, limited the number of Yiddish-speaking Jews, and preferred the Nordic descendents from the northern and western parts of Europe—all without expressly stating these motives in so many words. Racism and anti-Semitism tended to subsist in a more clandestine way in the culture, seldom resorting to legislative measures like the Nazis, but most Germans understood the general drift and identified their own beliefs with American attitudes.[58] Hitler particularly admired the America of the 1920s for its racial and immigration policies, which were creating a superior people in his mind, but he felt Roosevelt and his "Jew Deal" would ruin the evolutionary development by taking the country into a Communist direction.[59] The one American he admired the most was Henry Ford, the great industrialist, who understood the problems of the country and published an anti-Semitic book entitled *The International Jew*. Hitler read the *International Jew* during his early and formative years, hung a portrait of its "author" on the wall in his private office, and hailed Ford in the first edition of *Mein Kampf* as the "single great man" in America withstanding the Jewish threat.[60]

The International Jew is a reprint of articles that first appeared in the *Dearborn Independent*, an official organ of the Ford Motor Company, published under Ford's name.[61] Most chapters of the book open with an excerpt from the *Protocols of the Learned Elders of Zion*, which purports to reveal secret meetings of Jewish conspirators, plotting to take over and dominate the world.[62] Ford and Hitler were familiar with the work and accepted its value as representative of Jewish activity, even though they possessed enough good sense to question its literal, historical veracity.[63] According to the *International Jew*, the *Protocols* cannot be dismissed on either level. Most Jews try to dismiss it on a historical and symbolic level, but more honest Jews like Benjamin Disraeli, the British Prime Minister, admit that these types of power plays take place behind the scenes in the community, just as they are revealed in the book. At least no one can deny that the "International Jewish system" controls much of the social and economic life through their financial power. Jewish finance was responsible for the victory of Bolshevism in Russia and the defeat of Germany in the First World War, shutting down their industry, cutting off their supply of food, and controlling the press with pacifist, proletariat propaganda. In America, these financial leaders support trade unions, while professing to love the "American way of life" and its institutions. In New York, they control the political machinery through the Kehillah and the American Jewish Committee, which gave birth to Leon Trotsky, an East-Sider, and his worldwide Communist revolution.[64]

The *International Jew* thinks this power represents a clear and present danger in America for several reasons. One, its tentacles are destroying the culture. Jews have a monopoly on the theater and cinema and have turned them into a vulgar commercial enterprise, focusing on the box office to "give the public what they want." American theater has degenerated under Jewish control into a horrid spectacle of "frivolity, sensuality, indecency, appalling illiteracy, and endless platitude(s)." American cinema "brutalizes tastes and demoralizes morals" under the "Jewish manipulators of the public mind."

These Jews act like parasites, living off the hard work and creativity of others. In the music industry, they have a virtual monopoly, where they peddle popular music like jazz with its "mush, slush, . . . abandoned sensuousness of sliding notes, . . . money talk, jungle squeals and gasps suggestive of calf love, [all] camouflaged by a few feverish notes." These "Jews do not create; they take what others have done, give it a clever twist, and exploit it." They do not "make money"; they "get money."[65]

Two, their power is making people secular materialists. They have abandoned a spiritual mission of service, substituted the "grossest materialism of the day," and work to transform everyone else into their secular image. They want to denude all references to Christianity from the public consciousness. Their idea of "Jewish rights" consists of protesting *The Merchant of Venice*; calling passion plays anti-Semitic; throwing a spasm every time the name of Christ is mentioned; agitating against Bible reading, hymns, Christmas celebrations, or carols in the schools; modifying blue laws; and working to import "undesirable aliens" under the pretext that these individuals suffer persecution. They work to silence Christians and sever the identity of this country from its religious moorings, making people secular like them, but they have no problem turning around and infecting churches and schools with their "red" political philosophy and "free love" social life.[66]

Three, their power is used for their own communal benefit—much in contrast to their outward profession of democracy, equality, and integration. Jews think of themselves as a separate people and treat the influence of others as if it was harmful to their community. They live as a "nation within a nation"—working together, loyal to each other—and scoff at developing any true relationship or friendship with their fellow Americans. They insist on living in a separate reality, like the ghetto, and then have the temerity to protest the conditions and blame the *Goyim* for creating their own hell hole.[67] Democracy is used as a tool when they wish to "raise themselves to the ordinary level in places where they are oppressed below it," but there is no heartfelt devotion to any system embracing all of humanity. Aristocracy is their natural propensity whenever they are able to inflict their will on others. They certainly have no moral scruples about stealing the land of Palestine from the native inhabitants and denying them a modicum of decency and rights.[68] And if anyone should offer an objection, criticizing their hypocrisies in this way or another, or even raising the "Jewish Question," the person is smeared with the automatic charge of "anti-Semitism."[69] This tactic of victimization refuses to acknowledge in their community what Ford and his staff think are clear problems with the way Jews conduct their business: manipulating political events through powerful financial institutions; worrying only about profits; pandering to the prurient, sensual, and base desires of the audience; destroying the spiritual lives of the people, making them materialists and secularists; and showing considerable hypocrisy in advocating egalitarian values while working for their own economics and aristocratic interest. These type of criticisms certainly resonated with many on a worldwide scale for centuries and found a willing audience in Ford and Hitler to use them and forward them with much prejudice.

Ford deserves mention as a prominent figure in forwarding these criticisms and serving as a significant influence upon Hitler and the development of his ideology, but the overall development is complex and involves many other individuals and factors. Along with Ford, Richard Wagner and his circle stand out as exerting an immediate influence for inciting Hitler's disdain of the Jews as an alien and materialistic force in German culture, withstanding the spiritual and native *Geist* of the *Volk*. Houston Stewart Chamberlain, the son-in-law, helped him develop a modern or enlightened approach to thinking about social and cultural matters. Chamberlain followed the liberal, post-Enlightenment approach to religion in intelligentsia, which condemned the Jewish faith and reinterpreted Christianity in a nonliteral, nondogmatic, non-legalistic, and non-Jewish manner. He championed the current evolutionary science of Charles Darwin as a solid theoretical basis for understanding history through racial types and justifying the selective breeding of a superior race of people as sound social policy—all of which were important to Hitler. Hans Günther helped Hitler and Chamberlain by providing serious scientific credentials and research in exalting the Nordic race as the superior people and discrediting the egalitarian teachings of the church as the main opponent to the theory. Alfred Rosenberg served as the mentor of Nazi ideology and helped cultivate and crystallize Hitler's thinking on a panorama of Nazi issues: the concern about Jewish conspiracy and financial power, the emphasis upon Nietzschean voluntarism and the disdain for the weak, the rejection of Christianity and its doctrine of equality, the importance of German mythmaking, and the exaltation of Nordic blood. America served Hitler early on as the leader of a brave new world with its anti-immigration laws and eugenics program, although he found the developments in the 1930s with Roosevelt and the "Jew deal" disconcerting. He found special inspiration in the American industrialist Henry Ford, who recognized the danger of Jewish finance and materialism corrupting the spiritual values of a culture and the duplicity of this "nation within a nation," preaching a "red" political philosophy, while conspiring to control markets and caring little for social integration. Ford and these other individuals provided significant inspiration in developing certain elements of Hitler's philosophy. Of course, the overall number of influences is much more extensive and ends up including all the circumstances that converge together to make up his entire life, but what is more important than identifying and listing the precise number of influences is the simple recognition that Hitler was born into a society where Nazi-like ideas permeated all levels of society. It was not just Hitler who entertained these ideas in a handful of works that were read by a few zealots on the fringe of society but the entire culture who experienced them as dominate political, philosophical, religious, and scientific ideas, taught by the greatest minds in academia and entertained by all levels of the society on a daily basis. It was not just Hitler but many segments of the culture that moved toward Nazism in varying degrees of commitment, and eventually merged together to become his follower.

Notes

1. Klaus Fischer, *The History of an Obsession: German Judeophobia and the Holocaust* (New York: Continuum, 1998) 117–18; Weikart, *From Darwin to Hitler*, 216, 225, 232.
2. MK 98ff. (106ff.); Katz, *From Prejudice to Destruction*, 314; Weikart, *From Darwin to Hitler*, 219–20; Kershaw, *Hitler*, 20.
3. Weikart, *From Darwin to Hitler*, 217–19, 244. Hitler wrote a blurb for the thirteenth edition of the book, published in 1931.
4. Ryback, *Hitler's Private Library*, 50–51, 69. Hitler had a portrait of Ford in his office and owned a number of translations of his work.
5. Ibid., 57, 69; Friedrich Ratzel and Karl Haushofer, *Erdenmacht und Völkerschicksal* (Stuttgart: A. Kröner, 1940) xxvi; Weikart, *From Darwin to Hitler*, 223–25. Haushofer claims that Hitler studied Ratzel's work in the Landsberg prison. Günther and Lenz claim Hitler read the second edition in prison. Hitler's library contained the third edition (1927–1931). "Ratzel derived this idea from his friend, Moritz Wagner, whom he considered second only to Haeckel in contributing to evolutionary theory among German scientists." Weikart, *From Darwin to Hitler*, 193.
6. Ibid., 91, 154–57, 161.
7. Kubizel, a teenage friend from 1904–1908, speaks of Hitler's ecstatic outburst after listening to *Reinzi* and his desire to become the "future Reinzi-tribune of the Volk." Hitler described that evening to Cosima Wagner years later as the beginning of the Nazi vision. Viereck, *Metapolitics*, 125.
8. *Hitler's Table Talk*, Jan. 24/25, Feb. 3/4, and Feb. 28/Mar. 1, 1942, 184–85, 215–16, 264 (*Monologe*, 224–25, 258–59, 308).
9. Ibid., Jan. 3/4, 1942, 134 (*Monologe*, 173–74). Hitler was greatly inspired by Wagner's *Siefried*, the legendary Nibelung warrior and first Nordic superman. Much of Hitler's stage-managing ("torchlight parades, the mob choruses, the grand gestures of the Nordic heroes," and so forth) are reproductions of Wagner's showmanship at Bayreuth and the opera house.
10. Ibid., 4.14; 6.245–46, 250; Viereck, *Metaphysics*, 123.
11. Friedrich Nietzsche, *The Birth of Tragedy*, William Haussman (trans.), Oscar Levy (ed.), Rick Anthony Furtak (intro.) (New York: Barnes and Noble, 2006) ix, 3–4, 16, 40, 65, 95 (1, 5, 10, 16, 22).
12. Ibid., 4.39–44, 152, 154; 6.235; 7.87–88, 91.
13. Ibid., 3.83–87, 92– 94; Katz, *From Prejudice to Destruction*, 187, 188. He makes the same type of comment about the Jewish "poet" Heinrich Heine. "He was the conscience of Judaism, just as Judaism is the evil conscience of modern civilization." Ibid., 3.99–100. Cosima also is filled with this anti-Semitism. There is little evidence of Wagner's anti-Semitism before he wrote "Der Judenthum in der Musik." Joachim Köhler, *Nietzsche and Wagner: A Lesson in Subjugation*, Ronald Taylor (trans.) (New Haven, CT, and

London: Yale University Press, 1998) 89; Katz, *From Prejudice to Destruction*, 184, 185. Wagner finds the Jewish music of his day cold and trivial, fixed and dead—much in contrast to the traditional music of the synagogue, which was connected to its roots and inspirational. Ibid., 3.89–90, 92.

14. Ibid., 3.108–111, 118–19, 121; 4.88, 133–39, 159, 163, 165; Köhler, *Nietzsche and Wagner*, 71–72. He can speak in racist terms at times, exclaiming that Germans have a "natural repugnance" for Jews in spite of recent cries for equality and social justice. Ibid., 3.80. He expresses doubt whether Jesus was a Jew. Ibid., 6.233. "Before 1881 Wagner's anti-Semitism was more cultural than racial. In 1881, he steeped himself in Gobineau's Essay on the Inequality of the Human Races." Viereck, *Metapolitics*, 116. He follows Arthur de Gobineau's racial theory, dividing human beings into three classes (white, black, and yellow), relating the lower races to animals, connecting the white race with the gods as the architects of civilization, and expressing concerns about diluting Aryan blood through mixed breeding. *Prose Works*, 6.276–78. Unlike Hitler, he finds the violence in present day society repulsive and blames it on the tribal god of the OT corrupting Christianity. Ibid., 6, 232–35. This causes him to reject the desire to eat animals as an unnecessary blood lust. He becomes a vegetarian and favors temperance in drink, much like Hitler. He sees Jesus as trying to deliver his future church from the blood lust of Jewry and hopes the mystery of Parisal will bring full redemption. Ibid., 6.238–41, 275; Léon Poliakov, *The Aryan Myth: A History of Racist and Nationalist Ideas in Europe*, Edmund Howard (trans.) (New York: Basic Books, Inc., Publishers, 1974) 312.
15. Houston Stewart Chamberlain, *Foundations of the Nineteenth Century*, John Lees (trans.), George Mosse (ed.) (New York: Howard Fertig, 1968) ix–xv; Katz, *From Prejudice to Destruction*, 309. Hereafter Chamberlain's *Foundations* is designated FNC.
16. Poliakov, *Aryan Myth*, 319; McGovern, *From Luther to Hitler*, 504; FNC, xiv. The Kaiser praised it for awakening the German Aryanism (*das Urarische-Germanische*) in his soul.
17. Weikart, *From Darwin to Hitler*, 220; Hitler, *Table Talk*, xxviii; FNC, xv–xvii. He was strident in his rejection of the Judeo-Christian tradition. He criticizes Chamberlain in *Table Talk* for thinking that Christianity could present a positive spiritual reality.
18. FNC, xxv, xlix, 1.262–63, 276ff.; Weikart, *From Darwin to Hitler*, 124; McGovern, *From Luther to Hitler*, 504. Ultimately, he rejects speculation over human descent, as well as the prospects for progress. FNC 2.200–201, 214–22.
19. Weikart, *From Darwin to Hitler*, 124; FNC 1.26, 34–36, 188, 190, 223, 229, 252, 255, 263, 290, 542, 578; 2.227–28. He prefers to use the term Teutonic rather than Aryan, although he admits these terms and even the basic concept of race are nebulous in the present research. FNC 1.264–65.
20. FNC 1.260–61, 278–284, 290–91, 317, 331–33, 367, 516, 522. Many racists found inspiration in Tacitus's comment that Germans are a "race unmixed by intermarriage with other races, a peculiar people and pure, like no one but themselves." *Germania*, M. Hutton and E. H. Warmington (trans.) (Cambridge, MA: Harvard University Press, 2000) 4 (1); Poliakov, *Aryan Myth*, 80.

21. FNC 1.346–48.
22. See, for example, FNC 1.367, 418, 445–46; Katz, *From Prejudice to Destruction*, 308. He also makes reference to Ernest Renan in a number of places. See chapter 9 for a discussion of Wellhausen's theory.
23. FNC 1.120–21, 231–33, 358–59, 451–53, 460, 464–72; McGovern, *From Luther to Hitler*, 506.
24. FNC 1.214–16, 226, 330–31, 337–40, 411–13, 422–25; 2.38–39, 235, 246, 413; McGovern, *From Luther to Hitler*, 507–8. He mentions usury often and connects all wars in the nineteenth century with Jewish finance. See, for example, FNC 1.344. However, he thinks some individuals exaggerate Jewish influence and make them the "scapegoats" for all the problems in Europe. FNC xl. He mentions *on one line* of the work their crucifixion of Jesus—a reason much exaggerated in the literature by those who condemn anti-Semitism. FNC 1.352.
25. *Hitler's Table Talk*, Dec. 13, 1941 and Feb. 27, 1942, 111, 258 (*Monologe*, 151, 301–2). See note 28.
26. FNC 1.5–6, 196, 197, 221, 222–24, 227, 251, 258.
27. FNC 1.202ff., 206, 211–212; McGovern, *From Luther to Hitler*, 506. Chamberlain is not alone and follows the speculations of Wagner on this issue. Fichte is a good example of another early scholar who questioned the Jewish origin of Jesus. Poliakov, *Aryan Myth*, 101, 305, 312. Chamberlain expresses his disappointment over Renan's flip-flop on this issue. Early on Renan asserted in his *Life of Jesus* (1863) that it was impossible to know the race of Jesus, but then he turned around and caved in to Jewish pressure and said he was Jewish. FNC 211. Nevertheless, Renan is used as a constant source of authority and has a decided influence on Chamberlain, particularly in regard to his portrait of Jesus as anti-Semitic. *Life of Jesus*, Joseph Henry Allen (ed.) (Boston: little, Brown, and Company, 1929) 418.
28. FNC 1.246–50, 439; 2.21, 24, 26, 27, 41–47, 57, 63, 68–71, 122. Paul receives a better review from Chamberlain than he receives from Hitler and the sons of the Enlightenment. He appreciates Paul's mythical/mystical side more than the others as a true revelation from his inner, Aryan nature. FNC 2.60–61. He follows Harnack's emphasis upon the process of Hellenization in the church but sees it as more positive than Harnack. Adolf Harnack, *What Is Christianity?*, Thomas Saunders (trans.) (New York: Harper & Row, 1957) 192ff., 201.
29. FNC 2.291. Friedrich Schleiermacher, *On Religion: Speeches to Its Cultured Despisers*, 3, 15–18, 53, 141, 188; Harnack, *What Is Christianity?*, 12–13, 26, 103, 301.
30. FNC 2.484, 486, 491, 495, 500, 501.
31. McGovern, *From Luther to Hitler*, 512ff.
32. Hans F. K. Günther, *The Racial Elements of European History*, G.C. Wheeler (trans.) (Port Washington, NY, and London: Kennikat Press, 1970) 135–37, 146. Hereafter designated as RE.
33. See, for example, RE 8–9.
34. Ryback, *Hitler's Private Library*, 110; Weikart, *From Darwin to Hitler*, 223, 234.
35. RE 1–4, 51ff., 116–17, 130, 157, 172, 176, 187–88, 206, 215ff. He does not identify the hoi polloi or plebes in these kingdoms as possessing the same royal blood.

36. RE 89, 164, 166, 178, 190–94, 205–6, 234, 240–47, 254, 264; Hans Günther, *Rassenkunde des deutschen Volkes* (München: L. F. Lehmans Verlag, 1928) 394; McGovern, *From Luther to Hitler*, 521. The Jews are not a distinct race of people. They are a mixture of Asian, Nordic, and other ethnicities, although this mixture has some uniformity to it. They are a grave danger because of their economic power in society, and they can impose their spirit on the rest of us. He considers the *Judenfrage* from an ethnological and racial point of view in some detail within the appendix of the *Rassenkunde des deutschen Volkes.* Günther decries mixing in this work as *Rassenschande* (race disgrace)—a term the Nazis used in their anti-Semitic program. RE 74–79, 84, 128–29; Weikart, *From Darwin to Hitler*, 224. With the twelfth addition (1928), he makes this appendix a separate book. *Rassenkunde*, 499. Günther rejects the effeminate attributes of "philanthropy," "pity," and "sympathy" as a basis of lawmaking when dealing with inferiors and wants his Nordic race to become the *Übermenschen* of Zarathustra's philosophy. Nietzsche exerts a great impact on Günther, the Nazis, and the German society in general, creating a pitiless nation of henchmen. RE 243–45, 263.
37. Alfred Rosenberg, *Race and Race History and Other Essays*, Robert Pois (intro. and ed.) (New York: Harper & Row, Publishers, 1970) 16; *The Myth of the Twentieth Century*, Vivian Bird (trans.) (Newport Beach, CA: Noontide Press, 1982) xvii. Hereafter designated as MTC. The White Russian's claim that Kuhn, Loeb, and Co. financed the Revolution is found in Rosenberg's *Pest in Russland.* Walter Laqueur's *Russia and Germany* (Boston: Little Brown, 1965) also points to the "Berlin Letters" (1919) of Fyodor Viktorovich Vinberg, a former colonel in the tsarist army, as containing similar ideas about Jewish control of the press and finance. Rosenberg helped acquaint Hitler with the Jewish nature of the Russian Revolution and the Jewish world conspiracy as it was developed in the *Protocols of the Elders of Zion.* Kershaw, *Hitler*, 23. He also converted millions of Germans to his theory that communism was the "mask" of Jewish international finance through a series of pamphlets: *Die Internationale Hochfinaz* (n.d.), *Pest in Russland, der Bolschewismus* (1937), and *Die Spur des Juden im Wandel der Zeiten* (1920). Of course, he also championed the *Protocols of the Elders of Zion* in a number of pamphlets: *Der Weltverschwörerkongress zu Basel* (n.d.), *Unmoral im Talmud* (n.d.), *Der staatsfeindliche Zionismus* (n.d.), *Internationale Hochfinaz*, and *Der Jude* (a trans. by Rossenberg of Gougenot des Mousseaux's work, 1921). All his pamphlets were published in Munich. Viereck, *Metapolitics*, 220, 267.
38. Viereck, *Metapolitics*, 252.
39. Leske, *Philosophen im 'Dritte Reich,'* 44–45; FNC v, vi; Ryback, *Hitler's Private Library*, 127. He saw his work as a sequel to Chamberlain's *Foundations of the Nineteenth Century.* Chamberlain served as a source of great inspiration for Rosenberg, and his work is cited throughout MTC (e.g., 40, 60, 333, 347, 393, 432). Paul Lagarde, professor of Oriental Languages at Göttingen, also served as an important influence upon him. MTC lvi–lviii, 76, 141, 146, 172, 283, 285, 330–31, 371. He places Lagarde right next to Meister Eckhardt as a "great German dreamer". MTC 285. He is hoping the "iron broom" of the Third Reich will sweep away the "plague bacilli" (the Jews), fulfilling the prophecy of Lagarde concerning them. MTC 371.

40. McGovern, *From Luther to Hitler*, 654; MTC lxi; Viereck, *Metapolitics*, 216, 257. Of course, Rosenberg's philosophy was taught to the Hitler Youth, which included most children during the times of the Third Reich.
41. MTC 435–36.
42. MTC xv, 197, 200. Despite the obvious influence, Rosenberg, Nietzsche, and the many other disciples have their own specific interpretation and criticisms of Schopenhauer. MTC 196–210.
43. MTC 332.
44. MTC 33, 81, 83, 125–26, 176, 242, 246, 252–53, 442. He also rejects the "Jewish-Syrian-Roman" concept of fatalism or predestination in favor of his mystical concept of freedom. The strength of the will is central to Rosenberg's philosophy. Rosenberg, *Das Wesensgefüge des Nationalsozialismus*, 6. Auflage (München: Verlag Frz. Eher Nachf., G.m.b.H. 1933) 56–58, 69; Leske, *Philosophen im 'Dritte Reich,'* 123.
45. MTC xxxvi.
46. Ibid., 16–17, 25, 54; *Race and Race History*, 222; MTC 221, 405. He emphasizes *Volkstum* and cites Father Jahn on a number of occasions to confirm this ideal. He sees the rural, small town setting as the epicenter of what is genuinely spiritual or *volkisch*. The purpose of the state is to promote the *Volk*. MTC xliii, 329, 349. Rosenberg is more like the Nazis than Hitler in emphasizing the Nordic ideal of white skin, blond hair, and blue eyes. It is worth noting that Hitler's appearance fit more within the stereotype of the Alpine race than the Nordic ideal. MTC 175; McGovern, *From Luther to Hitler*, 640–43. Rosenberg is more mystical and less scientific than Hitler's approach—thus, his emphasis upon mythos and the Nordic soul. He speaks of a "prehistoric Nordic cultural center" of creation, something like Atlantis, as the origin of the race. He refers to ancient cave drawings and descriptions from Greece that venerate the white-skinned, blond ideal. MTC 4–6; Viereck, *Metapolitics*, 233, 234. See MTC 7–11, 24, 44ff., 58.
47. MTC 25, 44, 37, 89, 118, 119, 89, 290, 381; Rosenberg, *Das Parteiprogramm*, 26–27. Like most Nazis, Rosenberg fumed over giving women equal political rights, distorting their roles by introducing them into the workforce, pretending that women have the same creative powers, the same objective point of view, and the same abstract concepts as men, and granting them the right to an abortion in the name of female liberation. Women find their basic purpose in the propagation of the race. MTC 301, 306–309. 315–16.
48. MTC 158, 162, 379.
49. MTC 158, 162, 273–74, 283, 287, 331, 371, 379; Rosenberg, *Das Parteiprogramm*, 10–11, 21, 28–32, 37, 48, 55–57; *Race and Race History*, 175–77, 186–90.
50. MTC xv, Ryback, *Hitler's Private Library*, 121; Viereck, *Metapolitics*, 282–84.
51. J. S. Conway, *The Nazi Persecution of the Churches 1933–45* (New York: Basic Books, 1968) 6; Ryback, *Hitler's Private Library*, 121–23, 127, 136, 138, 159; *Hitler's Table Talk*, xxxviii, 318; MTC liii, liv.
52. *Hitler's Table Talk*, July 4, 1942, 418–19.
53. MTC 383, 384; Viereck, *Metapolitics*, 286–87, 290–91, 298. Of course, Rosenberg is training the German youth all along in anti-Christian hate.

54. *Nazi Conspiracy and Aggression: Office of the United States Chief Counsel For Prosecution of Axis Criminality* (Washington, DC: United States Printing Office, 1946) 3.152–57 (098-PS) [A letter from Martin Bormann to Alfred Rosenberg (Feb. 22/24, 1940)]; Conway, *The Nazi Persecution of the Churches*, 188–89; MTC 126.
55. MTC xv, xxxviii, liv–lviii, 6, 35–37, 100, 283, 307, 377–82 Viereck, *Metapolitics*, 235, 282–85. Art should weave together racial and spiritual matters. Great artists like Michelangelo, Rembrandt, and Raphael used Nordic racial models to depict biblical characters. MTC 65, 179–81.
56. MTC 71, 128–35, 140. The Nazis tended to revere German mystics. Leske, *Philosophen im 'Dritten Reich,'* 156.
57. MTC 137, 140, 142, 146, 150, 436–38, 442.
58. In March of 1938, a national poll indicated that 49 percent of Americans thought of the Jews as partly responsible for their plight, while another 12 percent thought they were entirely responsible. Weinberg, *Because They Were Jews*, 220.
59. *Hitler's Second Book*, 108, 109, 116 (*Hitlers Zweites Buch*, 124–25, 130–31); Birken, *Hitler as Philosophe*, 83, 89. He is upset about Nordic blood leaving Germany for America.
60. MK 639 (First Edition); Weinberg, *Because They Were Jews*, 212–13; Ryback, *Hitler's Private Library*, 69–71.
61. Henry Ford, *The International Jew: The World's Foremost Problem*, Gerald L. K. Smith (s.l.: s.n., 1958) 5–6; Ryback, *Hitler's Private Library*, 70. Hereafter the *International Jew* is designated IJ. The articles of the book are written by researchers associated with Ford. Later on June 30, 1927, he apologizes for the book under considerable pressure, but according to Gerald Smith, he never actually signed the apology and rescinded it in private. IJ 6–7, 9; Binjamin Segel, *A Lie and Libel: The History of the Protocols of the Elders of Zion*, Richard S. Levy (trans. and ed.) (Lincoln, NE and London: University of Nebraska, 1995) xiii. Of course, Ford fought trade unions and thought Jewish financiers were trying to steal his business. IJ 5.
62. IJ 5; Weinberg, *Because They Were Jews*, 192; Segel, *A Lie and Libel*, 11. According to Richard Levy, the *Protocols* was most likely fabricated in Paris between 1897 and 1899 by Pyotr Ivanovich Rachkovsky, the head of the Russian secret police in foreign countries. The work first appeared in a Russian newspaper, *Znamia*, in an abbreviated form from Aug. 26 to Sept. 3, 1903. Segel, *A Lie and Libel*, xi.
63. IJ 9, *Hitler's Table Talk*, xxxviii; Ryback, *Hitler's Private Library*, 71. There is a long chapter in the *International Jew* promoting the complete veracity of the *Protocols*. IJ 66, 69–92. Hitler read the *Protocols* according to the testimony of a former Nazi, first quoted it on Aug. of 1921, and mentions it in *Mein Kampf*. Hermann Rauschning, *Hitler Speaks: A Series of Political Conversations with Adolf Hitler on his Real Aims* (London: Thornton Butterworth LTD, 1939) 235–36; MK 307 (337); Segel, *A Lie and Libel*, 29–30, 46. Rosenberg published an extensive commentary on it and aided in its German publication and distribution, making it a part of the classroom and training of the Hitler Youth. A German version first appeared in the Fall of 1919. Segel, *A Lie and Libel*, 23, 27–28, 30, 60. Ford helped disseminate the work in the United States. Ibid., 24. This mythological work

is meant to display the power of the Jews, particularly controlling world affairs through the banking industry. The main contemporary example was the power of the Rothschilds' international finance of European nations in the nineteenth and twentieth century. Even Benjamin Disraeli, the Jewish Prime Minister of England, thought of Jewish money controlling the destiny of nations. Arendt, *Origins of Totalitarianism*, 27–28, 75–77, 97.

64. IJ 64–65, 84–85, 92, 95, 100–101, 128, 135, 155–57, 204–5, 209ff., 282.
65. IJ 22–25, 128, 135, 148–53, 163, 167, 201–2. Another example is sports. Jews do not participate in sports; they exploit them, especially through gambling. IJ 181–82.
66. IJ 22, 26ff., 29–32, 47–48, 104–10. Jews also want to drive patriotism out of the schools. IJ 31.
67. IJ 17, 35–36, 39, 52.
68. IJ 63, 141. The same duplicity is found in their espousal of capitalism and communism. IJ 96.
69. IJ 40, 188. There is some Aryan racism in the book, but this is atypical. See, for example, IJ 30. The book rejects the claim that Jewish rights are imperiled and considers anti-Goyism more of a problem. IJ 92, 100, 112.

8

The Metaphysics of Voluntarism

National Socialism arose out of a philosophical climate, which was induced and directed by its intellectual life at the highest level. Germany developed the finest universities in the world during the nineteenth and twentieth centuries. The universities ascended to the center of culture in central Europe with the opinion of the *Herr Professor Doctor* receiving exaggerated respect and influence throughout society and their students obtaining roles of leadership in the government bureaucracy and professional services.[1] More than any other sector the universities grew in influence and prestige, often providing the primary impetus for social change and creating a cultural climate for movements like National Socialism to germinate among the people. In fact, far from opposing Nazi ideology, many professors and student organizations laid the foundation for its development by showing early and strong support for Pan-German nationalism, connecting the people to primitive forces in nature, developing atheistic and voluntaristic philosophies, undermining the church through radical criticism of the Bible, and preaching antipathy toward the Jews, following the Enlightenment.[2]

Of special significance was the philosophical community in providing a metaphysical framework for a movement like the Nazis to develop among the people. Even if the Nazis showed little interest in the rigors of professional philosophy, there existed a climate in academia that was compatible with their ideas and sufficient enough to inspire the possibility of proceeding in this direction through popular forums. Even if no specific philosophy of Nazism existed in any literal sense before 1933, it was unnecessary for the success of the movement since a pervasive mind-set or view of life existed in academia, containing important elements that were just as potent in stimulating others to fill out the more specific and pragmatic details of a political agenda. In fact, there was enough compatibility that only a few philosophers actively resisted National Socialism, and none of them resisted to the point of imprisonment or death. A number of the philosophers joined the party or teachers union supporting Hitler, and no significant countermovement developed among the community to protest the policies.[3]

George Santayana, a one-time Harvard professor, understood the trends of German philosophy and wrote a book originally entitled *Egotism in Germany* (1915), trying to warn others about the dangers lurking in its ideas for the sake of world peace. The work expresses his concern about the spirit of self-assertion and the metaphysical conceit that induces philosophers like Fichte and Hegel to exalt the German nation and its *Volk* and find no higher tribunal of right and wrong beyond the egotistic prejudices of their state. He sees danger in the post-Kantian tendency to reduce everything in life to the prejudices of pure subjectivity or exertion of force and lose all sense of external authority beyond the ego, whether it is found in an objective world, a heaven of ideas, or the revelation of God. He calls Gottfried Leibniz the first German philosopher because he followed this egoistic voluntarism and saw each individual enclosed within a self-contained circle of experience and driven by inward forces. Arthur Schopenhauer developed the theme farther, discounting Leibniz's belief in a rational or divine plan and emphasizing the will to life as the one metaphysical truth. Friedrich Nietzsche soon converted Schopenhauer's idea into the will to power, living beyond reason and morality, throwing childish tantrums throughout his life, and showing the end result of an egoistic, voluntaristic philosophy, led by ceaseless and capricious cravings. Santayana thinks these philosophers have oversimplified the multifaceted nature of humanity and have provided a pretext for German militarism in their egotism and will to power.[4] Martin Heidegger certainly agrees for the most part when he finds the metaphysical essence of the German spirit in voluntarism and joins the Nazis through his own personal belief in this emphasis upon power.[5]

The debate over voluntarism came to the forefront in Western civilization during the Middle Ages. A number of Muslim scholars rejected the freedom of the divine will and adopted an intellectualist position, which binds the activity of God to the simple exegesis or dictates of the divine nature. Avicenna thought of God in Neo-Platonic terms as generating a totem pole of beings, emanating from the divine nature on top and expressing all that is found in God—completely, immediately, and eternally.[6] Averroes agreed with this position and found creation so necessary and eternal that God could not change anything in the slightest.[7] The moral law was an expression of the divine essence; even the natural law expressed a necessary causal connection, allowing no room to violate its nexus through divine intervention or a miracle in the normal sense of the term.[8]

The medieval church found great inspiration in the Aristotelian commentaries of Avicenna and Averroes[9] but rejected their theory of emanation as placing too many restrictions upon God, and preferred a theology that allowed for more freedom within the decisions of the divine will. Thomas Aquinas started the process by finding some latitude for the will to act on its own, even if he limited its expressions to the possibilities presented in the divine essence. God acted freely in deciding to create the world *ex nihilo* and had the power to make a different or better world if the will decided to do so.[10] The creation was an expression of God but never a simple product of the eternal essence. The creative act involved the interjection of some freedom and deliberation in choosing between a variety of options—all of which expressed some aspect of God but none of which was necessary to enact. The Schoolmen followed the Thomistic understanding and expressed this latitude by forging a distinction between the *potentia Dei absoluta* (the absolute power of God) and the *potentia Dei ordinata* (the ordained power of God). The former referred to the many possible things God can do, and the latter to what was enacted de facto, even if none of it was necessary and other ways and means were possible. Duns Scotus brought this distinction to the forefront in his theology,[11] expanding the number of possibilities beyond the simple matter of creating a different or better world and believing that God could do almost anything except violate the Aristotelian law of contradiction.[12] In regard to the law, God's options now included the possibility of dispensing with the second table of the Ten Commandments and demanding much the opposite, just as in the biblical account of Abraham's sacrifice of Isaac (Gen 22) and the Israelites' pillaging the land of Egypt (Exod 11–12)—all under the direction of the divine will.[13] In regard to salvation, the incarnation of God and the work of Christ were reduced to a *possible* way and means of effecting atonement, and they were considered ultimately unnecessary in the grand scheme of things *de potentia absoluta*; the merit of an angel, a pure man, or even Adam himself might have brought redemption just as well.[14] In fact, *nihil creatum formaliter a Deo acceptandam*. Duns found no necessary connection or nexus between a deed and its reward beyond the mere decision of God to develop a relationship; not even the work of God or the deeds offered in a state of infused grace can demand any specific reward before the throne of grace. All must submit to the acceptance of God, who rewards finite human deeds beyond the consideration of merit as a free act of the divine will.[15] This voluntarism will continue to develop among the Nominalists in the next century, where Scholastics, like William Ockham, created an exhaustive "Als-ob" theology filled with unrestrained speculation about the many possibilities within the absolute power of God.[16] For Ockham, God could damn the righteous and exonerate the guilty, overturn the entire Decalogue and demand the opposite, accept or reject people's merit, justify or condemn them, with or without Christ, with or without atonement, and with or without grace, even created grace.[17] The real fullness of God stood *behind* the singular activity of revelation in Christ and needed philosophical exploration to discover the why and wherefore behind what was ordained, unlocking the many other possibilities. Life no longer contained a direct and simple revelation of divine purposes in Christ, making Ockham question a fortiori whether life in general contains any reason or purpose or evidence of God at all. This is why the work of Ockham became so enthralled with these many options, creating an elaborate "theology of glory" in the words of Luther, because he could no longer trust the revelation of God in Christ or nature to contain the divine will. His position might represent an extreme case at the time, but it also exemplified the lengths to which Western metaphysics and its greatest scholars became dominated by this type of thinking, and displayed an atheistic or agnostic tendency within those who emphasize the voluntaristic side of the debate and abandon the knowledge of God in this world.[18]

Leibniz provided the particular pretext for this type of voluntaristic thinking in modern philosophical discourse within the land of Germany. In his work, he accepts the idea that human reason reflects the eternal wisdom of God in an immediate, a priori manner like Plato.[19] He thinks the world reflects divine wisdom and represents the best of all possible choices presented to the will of God,[20] with all things working unto the perfection of the created order, even extraordinary events like miracles.[21] But what distinguishes Leibniz's treatment most of all is the way in which he tries to establish that order through his famous doctrine of "monads." God establishes the order by synchronizing each individual substance or monad to act according to a preestablished harmony, inscribing the whole in each particular unit and making it blind or independent to what transpires in everything else.[22] This concept is much different from the typical view of theism, where God relates to the creation through ongoing, providential dealings—holding, sustaining, and perfecting its existence as the one true power of life. Here Leibniz speaks more like a Deist in letting God withdraw from creation and give each monad its own autonomy or force (entelechy), but with one important exception: God establishes a harmony before leaving the world by making each monad fit within the experience of all others and act according to the best possible plan for all involved.[23] "Every individual substance of this universe expresses in its concept the universe into which it has entered."[24] Thus, the universe develops its harmony and purpose, without receiving any outside interference to violate the internal principle of power, without God intervening, without objects pushing or pulling, interacting or influencing each other.[25] Leibniz remains committed to theism and rationalism throughout his presentation, but it does not take a great deal of imagination to see how an atheist might take the forces of nature in Leibniz's system and allow their innate forces to interact with one another in an autonomous and secular state of affairs, letting God withdraw completely from the process and developing a voluntaristic view of life as a power play between irrational forces. This Nazi-like concept could develop from Leibniz, given the right set of circumstances and a few necessary changes to the theistic ideology, just like atheism or secularism developed out of Deism in the Enlightenment as the philosophes began to lose the need for God in explaining the universe or living their lives in the state.

Schopenhauer

The most noteworthy philosopher in making the transition was Arthur Schopenhauer. He was born in Danzig (Gdańsk, Poland) on February 22, 1788, to Heinrich Floris and Johanna Schopenhauer, a wealthy merchant and a famous novelist and essayist, respectively. In the fall of 1809, he went to study at the University of Göttingen, starting in medicine and natural science and then proceeding toward the abstract world of philosophy. After a couple of years, he left Göttingen to attend classes at Berlin, where he sat under Johann Fichte and Friedrich Schleiermacher, two of the most famous philosophers/theologians of the day. Eventually, he completed his studies by obtaining a doctoral degree at Jena in 1813 and published the crowning achievement of those days, *The World as Will and Representation* in December of 1818, which became the most celebrated work of his life and one of the great books of the era. A year later he conducted a triumphant debate with Hegel and then tried an unsuccessful career as a lecturer in Berlin from 1820 to 1825, scheduling lectures to compete with Hegel's large and growing audience and failing to stem the tide of Idealism and gain enough popular support to satisfy an enormous ego. After the bitter experience, he renounced his career as a university professor, and for the last twenty-seven years of his life, he lived as a recluse in Frankfort, where he died in September 21, 1860.

During his time in exile, he continued working, writing, and fomenting vitriolic attacks upon Fichte, Hegel, and German Idealism, even after he received his own measure of acclaim and warranted a third edition of *The World as Will and Representation* (1859). He felt German Idealism was dangerous because it distorts the positive strides of Kant by forsaking the impetus of all knowledge in the things of this world and takes flights of conceptual fantasy into another realm. Philosophy should remain a discipline of immanence as Kant conceived it, leaving extramundane questions unanswered and working out its concepts in strict contact with the empirical world. The purpose of philosophy is to reflect *on the world* with abstract concepts, not create a system of concepts that have no grounding in reality. Any person living in the rich experience of the world is much better off than a scholar who produces concept out of concept in deducing a grand metaphysical structure of unsubstantiated ideas.[26]

If there exists a major difference between Schopenhauer and Kant, it concerns the possibility of knowing the thing-in-itself (or Being). Schopenhauer argues for the possibility of some knowledge because people possess a relation to the thing-in-itself, unlike all other beings in this world and much like Heidegger's later concept of *Dasein* and Being. This knowledge arises from the intimate connection to what lies within and consists most specifically of an immediate consciousness of each one's inward drives, impulses, and motives. The will, more than anything else, is known through the imperfect lens or experience of one's actions. This awareness provides the way of knowing the real inner nature of things in general. Since a person is the thing-in-itself, one comes into contact with the essence of the universe, because of the immediate relationship to self, and recognition of what exists within the person in terms of will. All other ways of speaking about the world remain subject to the limitation of perceptions or a human way of conceiving objects in accordance with the Kantian understanding of the matter.[27]

Thus, the will is the key to understanding the innermost mechanism of one's being, and through this understanding the innermost nature of the world. This will is found outside perception. It is outside of time and change, beyond the principle of sufficient reason and individuation, without knowledge or conscience in its essence and origin, without any rhyme, reason, or purpose—at least according to a person's inability to ascertain any ultimate direction. The will is the original and metaphysical; the intellect only a secondary and visible manifestation of it. There is no ability or justification to find some order, law, or purpose within the struggles of life, for nature exists prior to intellect. Its foundation comes from the irrational forces of a will-without-knowledge, which might give birth to organs like the brain and its thoughts but exists all by itself without *nous* or *logos*, mind or reason, in the beginning. Even in humans, who are most related to thought, the will remains prior to intellect and subdues all of its rivals, including knowledge: it is found throughout the body unlike the brain and its knowledge; its perturbations or passions eschew judgment through love, hatred, and other motives; its malice, spite, envy, patience, and diligence remain intact throughout the struggles of life, even when the intellect degenerates with age.[28]

In all this, Schopenhauer is following the basic concept of Leibniz by seeing an invisible will or force acting in all of nature, except acting apart from the rational orchestration of God or a heaven of ideals. He assumes that all other objects act like the human body through a determined and irrational will or motivation in their innermost being. They serve as a mirror of the will, which only provides a limited manifestation within people and reveals itself to exist outside of reason. The world is reduced to nothing more than a gradation of groundless and endless struggles engendered by the will and its blind impulses, encompassing organic and inorganic objects and reaching an apex in the rational striving of humankind. While the will remains a mysterious force, its motivations are manifested in certain instances: when its hunger becomes teeth and gullet; its lusts, genitalia; its will to walk, feet; and its will to know, the brain. In humans, the will often works outside of a person's own consciousness through functions like digestion, secretion, circulation, and reproduction. In animals, pure instinct drives them to build nests and webs apart from any understanding or foresight into the basic purposes and underlying principles. In plants, creative powers work incessantly throughout their lives apart from any knowledge or perception whatsoever.[29]

Schopenhauer seeks solace from the endless struggle of the will through a number of ways. He thinks of art as a primary way of achieving liberation from service to the will, giving people a Sabbath by painting still life or contemplating eternal ideas, which lie outside the continual flux of individual objects. Art reflects a most human capacity to formulate universal and abstract ideas through the special gift of reason, making people "will-less subjects of knowing," rather than all wrapped up in the throes and vicissitudes of the environment. The one great exception is music. Unlike the other arts, it does not escape the real world or contemplate Platonic ideas but presents "a copy of the will itself," making this form of art "much more powerful and penetrating than the other arts," since it speaks to the essence of existence and not the mere shadow. Music is designed to stir up the passions and emotions more than the rest because it speaks to the inner spirit or heart of things[30]—an interpretation that proves consequential to the works of Wagner and Nietzsche.

His view of the will and its insatiable appetites turns dark at many moments. He sees life as a "struggle of competing forces" with animals eating each other and men warring against their own species. He speaks of the incessant and irrational "will-to-life" as nature's innermost being, driving individuals to procreate and maintain the species, often at the expensive of their own personal welfare. This "will-to-life" makes sexual relationships the central point of all action, causing individuals to develop maternal instincts and sacrifice their own well-being for the health and vitality of the offspring. The constant struggle finds little proportion between effort and reward; even a temporary relief produces little more than boredom and a desire to get back to the drudgery. Whatever happiness is achieved lasts only for a brief moment and typically involves a reprieve from the aimless and endless struggle of the will and nothing positive to truly cherish and enjoy.[31]

In accordance with this view, Schopenhauer finds "the great fundamental truth" or solution in the simple exhortation to oppose nature and deny the will, since life is not worth preserving.[32] This negative philosophical lesson finds its counterpart in the ascetic practices of true Christians, like Ann Lee and the Shakers, who extinguish the "will-to-life" by committing their people to celibacy and refusing to procreate a wretched existence.[33] It also finds an efficacious example in eastern mysticism—"Brahmanism and Buddhism"—with its emphasis upon the misery of life and the preference for nonexistence.[34] In this, Schopenhauer has proceeded to the antithesis of Hegel and the liberal optimism of the nineteenth century, rejecting all belief in the rational unfolding of events toward a bigger and brighter future. He extols Voltaire and his *Candide*, rejects Leibniz's claim that this is the best of all possible worlds, and finds all reason for optimism shallow.[35] Life is empty and tragic, a continual endurance of torment in the pits of hell.[36]

This nihilistic conclusion comes from the metaphysics of voluntarism, which denies the sacred or rational nature of life and finds no reason to continue the meaningless toil. Even a medieval theologian like Ockham was forced to reject all evidence of God's existence in nature and question whether natural bodies act for any reason or purpose because of his emphasis upon the divine will and its absolute power. Life contains no reason or revelation of eternal truth if it comes from the capricious or irrational act of absolute freedom. The metaphysics of voluntarism will lead many in Germany to conceive of life as a power play, which lies outside the traditional boundaries of rational ideals and moral standards. This philosophy finds its most faithful disciple in Friedrich Nietzsche, who represents and forwards the Germanic spirit like no other philosopher. He will take the basic ideas of Schopenhauer and develop the dominant themes that embody the philosophical and political attitudes of the Third Reich.

Nietzsche

Friedrich Nietzsche was born in Rocken, Saxony, on October 15, 1844. His father became ill just four years later and died from what was diagnosed at the time as "softening of the brain." Nietzsche tried following the steps of his father, who was a Lutheran pastor, and studied theology for a couple of semesters at the University of Bonn, but he soon turned to classical philology when he matriculated into the University of Leipzig and ended up teaching the subject for ten years as a professor in Basel. During this time, he began to suffer, much like his father, from bouts of mental and physical illness, which included severe eye problems, intense migraine headaches, chronic insomnia, and excruciating stomach and intestinal problems that induced incessant fits of vomiting. His poor health brought an early retirement, forcing him to live off a modest income, yet providing an opportunity to travel throughout Germany, Switzerland, Italy, and southern France, as well as the chance to pursue his new interest in philosophy and to produce most of his great philosophical works.[37] The years of productivity ended suddenly in January 1889 when he suffered a complete mental breakdown after staging Dionysian orgies and naked dances and proclaiming his deity to crowds in the streets of Turin, Italy.[38] Glimmers of the madness were already flickering in his later works, especially *Ecce Homo*, where Nietzsche recognized his descent into a deep "melancholy" and "distress without equal," protesting against the illness, maintaining that pain and suffering engender insight into life.[39]

Many commentators identify syphilis as the underlying cause of the condition, but no one can discount other possibilities and factors. Elisabeth, his sister, blamed the abuse of medications for exacerbating his condition, and Lou Salomé, his one-time female companion, saw the collapse in terms of his philosophy, the ineluctable result of worshipping Dionysus, the god driven by frenzy and madness.[40] Whatever the cause, Nietzsche spent the last eleven years of his life in a zombie-like state within asylums or under the care of his sister.

Elisabeth Forster-Nietzsche had returned from an Aryan colony in Paraguay after the death of her anti-Semitic husband and made it her lifelong mission to help her brother and promote his work. In 1894, she founded the Nietzsche-Archiv, which moved to Weimar a couple years later and became a rival to the Wagner cult in Bayreuth, building monuments, composing liturgy, organizing rituals, and serving as the official editor and disseminator of his works. Through her efforts the Nietzschean legacy exploded into a cultlike following in the 1890s among the German masses, with a plethora of magazine and journal articles, the manufacture of statuettes and visual symbols representing his famous moustache, and phrases like "will to power" and "beyond good and evil," reaching the everyday parlance and imagination of the public. In the First World War, Elisabeth promoted her brother as a patriotic, militaristic Prussian, who represented the determination and heroism of the people. A durable version of his great work *Zarathustra* was produced during the war and carried right next to the New Testament and Goethe's *Faust* within the rucksack of German soldiers. During the Nazi era, Elisabeth and the Archiv enthusiastically supported the regime and promoted Nietzsche as a proto-Nazi.[41] Indeed, the dominant popular view of the Nazis equated their ideology with Nietzsche, and many leading figures in the Third Reich, including Alfred Rosenberg and Joseph Goebbels, became a part of the Nietzsche cult.[42] Even the Führer paid respect to the legacy of Nietzsche, making a visit to the Archiv in 1931, reflecting before his marble image, and conversing with his sister.[43] Some Nazis dismissed Nietzsche for making a few questionable comments about Germanism and anti-Semitism, but most seemed to identify with his overall *Weltanschauung* as embodying the true Germanic *Geist* and reinterpreted or ignored any questionable passages that proved less than orthodox.[44]

Like most commentators, these Nazis recognized that any claim to the mantle of Nietzsche must deal with the tensions, the contradictions, and the complex nature of his thought. As Nietzsche would say, "the will to a system [is] a disease of character," preventing the mind from experiencing genuine openness toward the future and the willingness to contradict "previous opinion"; and so, placing his thought into a system or simple linear development would destroy the very self-critical nature of the work. His writings are filled with excess and passion, not system and dogma. They present a complex "mosaic of independent monads" or self-sufficient aphorisms,[45] which are told over the course of a lifetime pilgrimage. Nietzsche believes the truth will change over time, depending on the heat of the moment. Living means dying to a former self, recognizing the chaos of becoming, and holding to the "rich ambiguity" of the life, which cannot be captured through scientific or mathematical calculations. But even these comments are subject to change, if change is subject to change. He can reject the erection of static buildings or the devotion to eternal truth, then turn around, denounce the chaos of constant change, and extol the program of Socrates, reason, science, and utilitarian calculations.[46] Jacques Derrida would say that Nietzsche destroys all truth and metaphysics, then forgets what he says, puts his comments under an erasure, and then proceeds to speak truth with much boldness. His opposites end up playing off each other, as they do in so many other authors, and give rise to multiple readings of the text.[47]

In spite of all these problems with interpretation, the Nazi reading of Nietzsche clearly represents dominant themes or a significant side of his work. There might be room for more ambiguity and self-criticism in Nietzsche than what Nazis could appreciate in their overall system and monolithic view of life, but their reading does not involve a serious distortion or exaggeration, taking a few footnotes out of context in developing their ideology or overall concept of his fundamental ideas. Their reading is not based on some absurd comments, equivocations, or marginal notes, as Derrida suggests,[48] giving rise to a possible dissemination or manipulation of the text, but finds a fidelity to a fundamental aspect of the author's view of life. Maybe, Nietzsche never developed a stomach for the kind of brutality that a genuine Nazi or real "blond beast" could exhibit in the real world of *Realpolitik*, but he sure possesses in his literary world much the same spirit on basic issues like the need to destroy the Judeo-Christian tradition and create a new humanity of passion and power.

In 1872, Nietzsche published his first important work, *The Birth of Tragedy*, while serving as a professor of classical philosophy in Basel. The book speaks of two Greek deities, Apollo and Dionysus, who coexist in Greek tragedies and serve as a productive and vital force of tension in all great artistic endeavors. Apollo represents the form of the individual, the *principium individuationis* in Schopenhauer, associated with clarity, order, and reason. Dionysus represents the deeper state, which collapses the "symbolic dream picture" of the Apollonian form and its apotheosis of individuality, and opens up to the Primordial Unity, which is the formless and intangible essence of things. The true Dionysian artist lives without a picture in a visceral world of ecstasy, frenzy, darkness, and chaos, while Homer and the gods represent the "complete triumph of the Apollonian illusion" with its victory over the throes and vicissitudes of life.[49]

In the rest of Nietzsche's writings, the Dionysian element slowly gains the upper hand in his affections. Kaufmann seeks to defend Nietzsche as a rational philosopher, who maintains a balance between Apollonian and Dionysian forces throughout his works,[50] but most commentators portray him as a devotee of the irrational forces of Dionysus. Most often Nietzsche finds his sense of nobility in those who act with passionate instincts that rise above reason and the petty understanding of the masses. He finds more life within the sovereign instincts of an earthly existence that contain real blood flowing through its veins than the old idealism and its contemplation of eternal truth or *amor intelletualis dei* (Spinoza). He prefers to affirm this world in all its profundity and mystery than crucify its life-giving energies for the sake of some higher reality.[51] In the *Birth of Tragedy*, he credits Schopenhauer for resurrecting this Greek spirit among the German people, overcoming the boundaries that would dissolve all riddles of life through an optimistic rationality or triumph of science, but elsewhere he criticizes him for speaking too pessimistically about Greek tragedy and not providing a "strong enough" affirmation to life that could constitute a "new yes." Nietzsche rejects Schopenhauer's pessimistic attempt to negate the appetites of life through ascetic and nihilistic practices, although the overall voluntaristic philosophy of Schopenhauer has a major impact upon his belief that a blind, driving force constitutes the essence of reality.[52]

Socrates is the real villain in Nietzsche's account. He provided the spiritual matrix for a degenerate form of art to arise in Euripides and the New Comedy, replacing Aeschylean and Sophoclean tragedy with a non-Dionysian art form and creating order and understanding in its place. His abstract rationality condemned Greek tragedy by destroying the instinctive and creative forces of real life. He made no room for the tragic sense of life, placing knowledge, virtue, and happiness into a simple equation, and faced death with a cavalier attitude of comprehension and triumphant optimism. Reason and conscience replaced the sensual world of passionate and instinctive existence that marked the essence of the Greek spirit in former times. Reason became a polemical weapon, wielded to destroy the deeper intuitions of Dionysian existence as witless and unphilosophical tripe.[53]

Nietzsche denounces Socratic dialectics and metaphysics in the name of his god, Dionysus. He prefers the stupidity of the skeptical mind to the rational, metaphysical tradition of Socrates and the whole Western tradition, which finds answers in a heaven of ideas.[54] The whole metaphysical question of truth is called into question because God does not exist and life has no intelligent origin. The world is not a machine with a purpose; it is completely lacking in "order, arrangement, form, beauty, wisdom, and whatever other names there are for our aesthetic anthropomorphisms. . . . None of our aesthetic and moral judgments apply to it." The world is aimless. It does not obey laws. There is no necessity in "the shape of an overreaching, dominating total force or that of a prime mover," providing it with a final intention or meaning. In a world of chaos, no static entity or thing-in-itself exists to provide a knowledge-in-itself or a semblance of unity for comprehension. The Dionysian world of becoming only permits what the imagination creates through its powers of interpretation.[55]

This leads Nietzsche to make a startling announcement, mentioned in the *Gay Science* for the first time that "God is dead!" Intellectuals have undermined the credibility of religious faith in recent days and have come to grips with the implications of their findings in the new atheistic world, but it is time to reach out and make a public proclamation, destroying whatever remnants remain of this superstition among the ignorant masses. The gravediggers have done the deed and buried the transcendent tyrant of old, performing the greatest service ever in the history of humankind, yet the news takes some time to travel throughout the kingdom.[56] With the death of God, humankind can rid the world of old categories like "good and evil," "true and false," and finally look to themselves and their own resources to determine whatever they want to pursue in the future.[57]

In moments of extreme candor, Nietzsche can face the new reality head-on and speak of himself as a thorough-going nihilist,[58] erasing his deprecation of the term in discussing Schopenhauer. This version of nihilism expresses the stark truth of a consistent atheism, which denies any meaning to life or moral interpretation of the world, since "Becoming aims at nothing and achieves nothing [*nihil*]."[59] Nietzsche wants his audience to live beyond moral judgment, "beyond good and evil," and to challenge the absolute ideals of former days, calling for a "revaluation of values," which questions all talk of ethics in an atheist universe—at least in his more consistent moments. His consistency is compromised only when he feels compelled to turn around and reevaluate the "revaluation of values," leaving room for ethical exhortation and truth. In these moments, the "revaluation of values" becomes a means of undermining the old values by replacing them with a new set of values, which sees life in a more complicated way, often accepting as valuable what was condemned in a categorical way during the former days of theism.[60] In this way, Nietzsche mitigates his former position that would eliminate ethics in toto. What remains constant is the repeated exhortation to follow one's own creative path and no longer search for one simple way within the gods above or masses below. There is no answer to discover through a rational quest or exploration of secret messages within the conscience. One must subjugate all these avenues of inquest and simply create value as a "commander" and "law-giver" through the will to power.[61]

Nietzsche goes on to develop a method of using genealogy as a means of criticizing the current understanding of moral consciousness, inspiring later generations of authors to engage in this type of historical, critical methodology.[62] He thinks values must "be viewed from the most diverse perspectives" of various disciplines to show the range of meaning, and he advances historical studies in particular as a means of showing how values change their meaning, utility, and purpose along the way. Life has many angles and develops through a series of twists and contradictions in the long process of history, sometimes setting the original and current purpose of its many elements at odds with one another. In regard to morality, Nietzsche sets up the contradiction by pointing to its strange origin within the power of a former aristocracy, who labeled the common or lowly of society as bad (*Schlecht*) and asserted their "godlike race" (*göttlichen Geschlechts*) as good (*Gut*) in accordance with the German etymology. The concept of guilt or conscience developed from a similar power play—this time between a debtor and a creditor—where the debtor was unable to fulfill the terms of conscience and the creditor received a counterbalancing pleasure or propitiation in some form of punishment, satisfying the cruelty of primitive human instincts. A "bad conscience" developed when humans entered the more peaceful world of civilization, denying their old animalistic instincts and turned the older forms of punitive torture inwardly. This guilt found its highest expression within the concept of God, whose wrath fell upon the former self—taming, emasculating, and weakening the animal nature. Nietzsche uses this genealogy to question the "value of these values" or moral understanding of life. He hopes that "morality will gradually perish" in the future as "the will to truth gains self-consciousness," often identifying the natural dispositions (and depravity) of old with what is truly human and so committing what critics of his method call the "naturalistic fallacy" on a massive scale, just like Hitler.[63]

Nietzsche follows the sons of the Enlightenment in this genealogy by focusing much of the discussion upon the nefarious role of priests and blaming them for all the evils of society in Europe. Priests exercise their own will to power by creating concepts like sin and a moral conscience, which provide the means of assigning guilt to the people and explaining the reason for human suffering and the need for punishment. They develop the "metaphysics of a hangmen" to judge what is "human, all too human," producing a judgmental and resentful society of moralism, submissive to their will and lust for power.[64] The mysterious force of "free will" is added as a corollary, so the priest can hold people responsible and condemn whatever remains outside their power to punish and forgive.[65]

Nietzsche also follows the sons of the Enlightenment (and the analysis of Julius Wellhausen) by focusing his wrath upon the Jewish priesthood in Jerusalem. This priesthood transformed the Jewish faith into what people understand today as Judaism by emasculating the "great human beings" and "heroic landscape" of OT times and transforming it into a Torah-based religion of laws and morals. The second temple priests only needed to repaint OT history with the new religious terms of guilt, punishment, and atoning sacrifice, paid to Yahweh and the priesthood, in order to provide some continuity with the former tradition. They overturned the "natural value" of the former life in this way and laid the foundation of the new Judeo-Christian tradition and its morality of revenge and resentment among the poor and base of society.[66] "Precisely on this account the Jews are the most fatal people in the history of the world: their ultimate influence has falsified mankind to such an extent, that even to this day the Christian can be anti-Semitic in spirit, without comprehending that he himself is the final consequence of Judaism."[67] The Jews developed into a "priestly people," who embody the "most deeply repressed priestly vengefulness" against aristocratic values and exalt everything that is base, "the suffering, deprived, [and] sick," as blessed before God. The Jews possess more contempt for what is truly excellent and noble than any other people in this world.[68]

There is a plethora of literature that discusses whether Nietzsche was an anti-Semite or a philo-Semite, as if there exists a real dilemma over his essential orientation.[69] Those who wish to defend Nietzsche can look around and find material within his many writings that appear to exonerate him from any bigotry in regard to the Jews. They can point to his personal rejection of anti-Semitism in some of his acquaintances, including Richard and Cosima Wagner, Elisabeth and her husband, along with a few others, as "something alien to my whole nature."[70] They can point to some passages that speak of Jews in a positive way as a people who achieved great strength through a life of difficult circumstances in the Diaspora, making them a true blessing to European society.[71] In most of these passages, he is withstanding the intense nationalism and racism of the day, which deprecated the intellectual achievements and tenacity of the Jewish people, making them the scapegoats for whatever problems plagued German society at the time, and thinks a mixture of Jewish blood might be useful and desirable in creating the "strongest possible European mixed race."[72] But all these comments are directed at specific expressions of anti-Semitism in the 1870s and 1880s and do not exonerate him from other forms of prejudice against the Jews.[73] Often the criticisms deteriorate into *ad hominem* diatribes more directed at the specific person or group who espouse some form of anti-Semitism than an objective discussion of the issues. In his Wagner period, when he patronized and idolized everything about the master of Bayreuth, he also followed Wagner's anti-Semitism as a devoted disciple, joining the criticism about Jewish decadence in music, but soon after the relationship ended, everything about Wagner and his music developed the stench of depravity, including his anti-Semitism, due to the emotive and acrimonious nature of two massive egos parting ways.[74] Nietzsche can attack the views of individual anti-Semites and then turn around and share their hatred of the Jews, even repeating the stereotypical prejudices of the day about the Jews and their control of finance, lack of creative ability, and nonproductive work ethic.[75] But more than this he shares and forwards the more virulent pretext for anti-Semitism after the Enlightenment, which understands the problems of modern society in terms of its cultural roots in Judaism and wants the complete destruction (*Vernichtung*, not *Aufhebung*) of the religion, in order to create a new humanity. The main enemy of humanity is viewed as the Judeo-Christian tradition.

The contempt for Judaism and Christianity goes together in Nietzsche's understanding of history, although Christianity receives the brunt of his anger. Christianity is the "final consequence of Judaism," the "final mastership" of its lies "three times" over.[76] The religion deserves special contempt because it "judaized" (*verjudeln*) the world, perfecting the priestly faith of moral resentment beyond the limits of its genetrix. Thus, it deserves to be cursed as the "one great curse, the one enormous and innermost perversion, the one great instinct of revenge, . . . the one immortal blemish of mankind," the "greatest of all conceivable corruptions," "humanity's greatest misfortune," and the "most fatal kind of megalomania there has ever been on earth." Nietzsche can only find the truth by negating its theologians, turning *everything* they say topsy-turvy, and holding to the opposite opinion. In *Ecce Homo*, he expresses admiration for Voltaire as a "grandseigneur of the spirit" and ends with the familiar battle cry against Christianity "Ecrasez l'infâme," pitting "Dionysus versus the Crucified" and finding "joy in destroying" the religion.[77] In *Will to Power*, he says,

> I regard Christianity as the most fatal seductive lie that has yet existed, as the great unholy lie: I draw out the after-growth and sprouting of its ideal from beneath every form of disguise, I reject every compromise position with respect to it—I force a war against it.[78]

He sees the church living in contradistinction to the historical Jesus. Like the sons of the Enlightenment (and David Strauss), he sees the early church corrupting the message of Jesus, reading their own gospel into his lips, and overturning the very origin of the faith.[79] "The church is precisely that against which Jesus preached—and against which he taught his disciples to fight."[80] "That which thence forward was called 'gospel' was the reverse of that 'gospel' that Christ had lived: it was 'evil tidings,' a *dysangel*." Jesus rejected the entire system of sin and guilt, reward and punishment in Judaism, seeing all people as the children of God and finding the kingdom of heaven within the hearts of each and every one.[81] He rejected a belief in divine judgment coming from outside the human condition or arriving sometime in the future. It is the church that resurrected the Jewish concept of sin, turning the death of Jesus into an atoning sacrifice and waiting for the Savior to come again and judge the world. Of course, Paul receives much of the blame for this perversion of the original teaching of Jesus, just as he did among the sons of the Enlightenment. He was the "eternal Jew par excellence"—a man gifted with a "genius in hatred" and "sacerdotal instinct." He preached a "blood-drinking" God, who demanded a bloody sacrifice to propitiate divine wrath in an attempt to justify the tragic death of Jesus and annulled the teachings of his Savior by setting up a "new priesthood and theology."[82]

Nietzsche's main concern about the religion centers upon its promotion of egalitarianism and destruction of excellence, foreshadowing the same type of sentiments in Hitler and the Nazis. He (and Hitler) clearly understands more about the intimate relationship historically and philosophically between Christianity and the modern political world than most secular scholars in the West, who disregard religious influence in general. He recognizes the importance of the Reformation and Luther's priesthood of the believers in promoting the "plebeanism of [the modern] spirit;" and he knows that the "French revolution [was merely] the daughter and continuation of Christianity—its instincts against caste, against the noble, against the last privileges." He knows that Christianity laid the spiritual matrix for egalitarianism and democratic polity in the modern world, but rather than celebrating the new, inclusive ideology like scholars in France and the English-speaking world, he rejects this modern point of view as embracing what he calls the *vulgus* (common), not uplifting people with *virtus* (strength/virtue). He denounces Christianity and its "equal rights for all" as creating a ghetto-empire in the lowly image of Judaism and destroying the virtue and strength of aristocratic excellence. He says Christianity is fundamentally about "resentment" (*ressentiment*) and the "rancor" of the underprivileged, who want to blame their suffering on others.[83] It is a "religion of pity," which fights for the disinherited and drains the strength out of society. The God of Christianity destroys the natural and sovereign instincts of humanity and one day will die from its feminine qualities of pity and compassion. The God of the OT with *his* anger, revenge, envy, violence, and will to power is much more vital than the effeminate and emasculated "good God" of Christian theologians. The law code of Manu with its Aryan racism is superior to a religion of weakness that levels the castes of humanity into an amalgam of mediocrity. The Christian virtue of pity is the "greatest danger" to the natural order of life; it destroys the power of the noble and creates victims of the rest, who are no longer capable of overcoming their circumstances through the will to power, no longer able to embrace suffering as a growing edge. Zarathustra prefers to extol the "lust for power," "sensual pleasure," and the "glorious selfishness" of a "mighty soul" than yield to the altruistic propensities of pity, which only serve to weaken the human condition. He despises the cries for equality as a mandate for impotence, a destruction of the solitary, and an ignoble lie against all sense of justice, since it is more than obvious that "men are not equal."[84]

Zarathustra despises the type of herd instincts that seeks the applause of the multitude and lives according to the same standards of good and evil. Like Søren Kierkegaard, he wants radical individuals, who live above the petty virtues of the masses and develop their own authentic existence.[85] He wants supermen (*Übermenschen*), those who overcome the present stagnation of humanity and create a new humanity with a new set of values.[86] The *Übermensch* has no specific form or determination in the work of Nietzsche and ever remains an act of creation, but the image becomes most Nazi-like when it assumes the form of a "blond beast" or master—images used throughout his works.[87] According to *Twilight of the Idols*, Christianity hunted down the blond beast and caged this noble German in monasteries in the early Middle Ages out of its contempt for "intellect, pride, courage, freedom, [and] intellectual libertinage," but it is time to let strength express itself. "Great birds of prey" find nothing "more tasty than a tender lamb." When the blond beasts obtain freedom from their protracted confinement in social constraints, they can fulfill their monstrous nature with innocence, conducting murder, torture, and rape as if these deeds involved no more than a childish prank. The blond beasts of prey should possess no guilt or thought in subduing others and imposing their form of freedom and instinct upon the plebes. The Darwinian forces of life dictate the destruction of the "ill-constituted, weak, [and] degenerate" at the hands of the strong. A healthy aristocracy should follow the dictates of its "will to life" and suppress, enslave, sacrifice, and exploit a whole legion of weak individuals as instruments belonging to its will. They should "do unto others" as it seems good to themselves, the "creators of values."[88] In *Beyond Good and Evil,* Nietzsche expresses this philosophy in detail and introduces the famous distinction between a "master-morality" and a "slave-morality" to encourage his blond beasts in their war with inferiors.[89] In *Will to Power,* he encourages "pride, pathos of distance, great responsibility, exuberance, splendid animality, the instincts that delight in war and conquest, the deification of passion, or revenge, of cunning, of anger, of voluptuousness, of adventure, of knowledge." He wants Europeans to destroy "morality as the instinct to deny life" and live by the forces and drives that liberate life and its growth. He wants them to embrace their unconditional naturalness, even its darker side, instead of creating an artificial moral nature like Rousseau's "Noble Savage." This might lead to a more complex set of virtues, which include love and hate, gratitude and revenge, existing together, living without scruples, and using unholy means;[90] and it clearly leads Nietzsche in the chapter titles of *Ecce Homo* to celebrate his own hubris against conventional etiquette and ask such probing questions as "Why I am so Wise," "Why I am so Clever," "Why I write such Good Books," and "Why I am Destiny"—displaying all his egotism and audacity, frankness and madness.[91]

To obtain the noble end of blond beasts Nietzsche is willing to extol the unholy means of politics and war—at least on certain occasions in his writings. He believes in these passages that might makes right. He commends the Teutonic spirit of old, which created an aristocratic/hierarchical society and sought to dominate Europe through the will to power, before "liberal progressives" emasculated its strength through false doctrines like equal or natural rights. Nietzsche prefers the vitality of war to the "advent of democracy, international courts, . . . equal rights for women, the religion of pity, and whatever other symptoms of declining life there are."[92] War might be harsh and tyrannical, but it is also a biological necessity in developing the future well-being of the race.[93] The human species demands the elimination of the weak so a higher form of life might find space to emerge and expand its life forces. Nietzsche says, "The great majority of men have no right to existence [and] are a misfortune to higher men,"[94] but he seldom goes beyond the terror of these abstract philosophical statements. He seldom lists specific measures to enact a specific policy, preferring to leave the precise manner of fulfillment to others, but when he does, his measures can remind people of the horrific days of Nazi Germany. In the *Twilight of the Idols,* Nietzsche favors the elimination of the "sick man" as a "parasite of society" through enacting a program of active euthanasia.[95] In *Will to Power,* he provides an important pretext for the Nazi program of eugenics, considering it a social imperative to prevent degenerates and decadents from disseminating their inferior seed and corrupting the race.[96] A breeding program follows later on in the work, where he advocates the development of a strong race exhibiting preferable traits like "beauty, bravery, culture, [and] manners to the highest peak of the spirit."[97] In the *Genealogy of Morals,* he speaks of the blond-headed, Aryan race as the "good, noble, and pure" conquerors of the black-headed, short-skulled aboriginal inhabitants of Europe, and so representing his version of the master race,[98] although he never proceeds farther in this direction nor identifies certain nations or ethnicities with the concept. In fact, unlike the Nazis, he continually rejects the German nationalism of his day with its *Deutschland über alles,* sometimes thinking of Germany as a declining culture in comparison to other countries like France, and he prefers to present himself as just a "good European."[99] Whatever form the master race might assume in the future, the herd-breeding mentality of the communal spirit in the *Vaterland* is unable to comprehend the more complex and multifaceted nature of his blond beast.

Above all, the basic theme and texture that connects Nietzsche with the *Geist* of Nazism and German metaphysics are embodied in his overall emphasis upon the will to power. It is no surprise that Elisabeth and many of the Nazis peddled the posthumous book, collected under the title *Will to Power,* as Nietzsche's crowning systematic representation of his ideas.[100] This dominate, Nazi-like theme first comes to the forefront in Zarathustra's speech "On the Thousand and One Goals," where he hopes to overcome the table of virtues that hang over the head of the masses. Zarathustra is striving against a life of submission, which looks outside oneself to a transcendent power and thereby weakens one's own will to overcome and command. Life consists of "dynamis quanta" that struggle with each other's power (*dynamis*), striving to exert their force and master one another, serving as the source of change or becoming in the world. There is nothing outside the tension of will upon will, nothing more than the will to incorporate, expand, grow, and dominate. "The world is the will power—and nothing besides! And you yourselves are also this power—and nothing besides!" It underlies all human activities, reducing thoughts, feelings, and purposes to a mere reflection of what is transpiring on a deeper level as the fundamental force of nature. Even the will to life or the attempt to preserve and enhance its pleasures serve as little more than an epiphenomenal effect of a more essential struggle to increase and overcome one's self and one's neighbor.[101] All of life is reduced to voluntarism or the will to power as the one metaphysical truth.

Arthur Schopenhauer and Richard Wagner appear to exert a most direct and visible influence upon Nietzsche in leading him toward a philosophy of voluntarism. Nietzsche displays "equal reverence" for both of these mentors and considers them "Spiritual brother(s)."[102] "All that is best and most beautiful is associated with the names of Schopenhauer and Wagner."[103] At an early age, he venerated Schopenhauer as a demigod from the very day he picked up a copy of *The World as Will and Representation* at a secondhand bookstore in Leipzig and began to believe that a blind, driving force constitutes the real essence of things.[104] Early letters express a total devotion to his atheistic and voluntaristic ideas, finding "no more edifying philosopher than our Schopenhauer."[105] In the *Birth of Tragedy*, Wagner is exalted as the most significant philosophical force in resurrecting the genuine Greek spirit of Dionysian voluntarism within present day music in Germany. "Music . . . is the direct copy of the will itself, and therefore represents the metaphysical of everything physical, and the thing-in-itself of every phenomenon." Wagner's music provides the greatest inspiration in following the Dionysian spirit. Wagner thinks of himself as a disciple of Schopenhauer, and Nietzsche is enamored with the "ceaseless, blind, and passionately striving will" in *Tristan* and his other great works as expressing the genuine spirit of Schopenhauer's philosophy.[106]

Nietzsche developed an "indescribably intimate" relationship with Richard and Cosima Wagner beginning in November of 1868 when they were living on an estate at Tribschen, near Lucerne.[107] He considered Wagner his dearest friend at the time, and Wagner thought of Nietzsche as his greatest interpreter. Unfortunately, their relationship soured over the course of time, with Nietzsche leaving for good in "the summer of 1876, in the middle of the first Festspiel."[108] A number of reasons probably contributed to the decision. Nietzsche's longing to free himself from simple obeisance to Wagner,[109] Nietzsche's disappointment with the growing popularism and nationalism of the Bayreuth festival,[110] Wagner's disparaging comments about Nietzsche's opera,[111] and Wagner's conversion to Christianity, which served as the last straw.[112] Their breakup was acrimonious but all so predictable when considering the nature of their correspondence, which is filled with egotism, narcissism, and emotional outbursts, both being primarily concerned with their own personal greatness and exalted place in human history. After the breakup, their wounded egos display little more than a predictable vitriol that trashes each other's work with childish tantrums, hardly acknowledging the deep-felt respect and mutual influence of former days.[113] Nietzsche will proceed beyond his venom for Wagner and begin to undermine other great figures, including Schopenhauer—all on his way to the top of Mount Olympus and his attempt to become the one, unique messenger of the gods.[114]

He achieved much of his goal through the efforts of Elisabeth and the Nazis, who turned him into a cultlike figure and national icon. His overall *Weltanschauung* appealed to the fundamental *Geist* of many Germans and helped forward the mission of the Nazis through many of its dominant themes, even if he was more complex in his thinking than most could appreciate and less than orthodox on issues like anti-Semitism and Germanism than some could tolerate in their view of the world. The Nazis found inspiration in his appeal to immanent forces in nature, along with his rejection of transcendent and rational authority and preference for animalistic and sovereign instincts. They followed him in attacking the old sense of values and decency with a new vision of the world through the commission to revaluate values and extol strength, power, and hubris. They envisioned life in the same metaphysical way as a voluntaristic exercise in expanding, growing, and dominating through the will to power, and absolutely despised in like manner the egalitarian philosophy of the Judeo-Christian tradition, which sought to prop up the weak and the down-and-out. They became the *Übermenschen* in their attempt to create a new humanity; they became "blond beasts," who exhibited the monstrous nature of Nietzsche's exhortations in propagating war without pity and using whatever unholy means available to create a new world—including euthanasia, eugenics, racial breeding, and genocide. All this represented an essential side of Nietzsche's thinking on a number of issues, which only scholars can miss when they try to allegorize, intellectualize, and overcomplicate what is plainly before the average German reader.

Bäumler

Just a few weeks after Hitler rose to power, Alfred Bäumler was appointed as a professorship of philosophy at the University of Berlin and chair of the new Institute for Political Pedagogy, which opened on July 13, 1933.[115] His fundamental academic credential was an apologetic work, entitled *Nietzsche: der Philosoph und Politiker* (1931), which he wrote promoting the subject of his book as a central figure in developing an early form of the new Nazi ideology. Official organs of the Nazi party portrayed Nietzsche as a significant forerunner of their movement well before 1933, but now they possessed the political power to propagate their Nietzschean philosophy, and Bäumler was just their man to do it. He became the leading authority on Nietzsche during the Nazi era and helped disseminate the message to the students and public alike, inside and outside of Germany.[116] Today he is subject to much ridicule due to the general dislike of Nazis in the postwar era and the hope of rescuing Nietzsche from their clutches,[117] but he clearly does not misrepresent the fundamental doctrines of his subject in any serious or perverted way. In fact, he understands the complex nature of Nietzsche's writings and ideas,[118] even if he proceeds like many of his detractors to undermine much of the complexity, and presents a more unified portrait of Nietzsche under the concept of will, which he rightly sees as the dominant metaphysical theme, both in Nietzsche and the Nazis.

According to Bäumler, Nietzsche wants to abandon all beliefs in a transcendent God for the sake of human beings, so they can trust once more in their own power, pride, strength, and decisiveness. "God is dead" was the original *Geist* of the Germanic people before Christianity invaded and destroyed their simple way of life through a transcendent, outside commentary, bringing condemnation and guilt to an innocent form of becoming and emasculating their efforts on Earth as human beings.[119] Truth is not a consciousness of something that resides outside a people in a permanent realm of heavenly ideals but remains within them as a deeply felt human experience, related to their own creative powers. They are the ones who create laws and purpose out of a world of flux and struggle, and life merely consists of a continuous state of war with its victories and defeats, masters and slaves, without any hope of resolving the conflict, assigning guilt or responsibility, and securing an everlasting peace. This view of life is captured by Nietzsche's expression "will to power"—a phrase that illuminates his entire thought and serves as the basic metaphysical truth of the world. It serves as the title of his magnum opus, which is cited by Bäumler throughout the study, and serves to describe the essence of the Germanic spirit, as well as human beings in general. The will to power represents a decided break with the Christian philosophical tradition in Descartes, Leibniz, Kant, and Hegel, with its concept of the soul or conscious spirit within each individual, as well as the rational metaphysics of the tradition, which reached its zenith in the Enlightenment. Nietzsche views life as a game of chance, or a contest between individual forces (monads) struggling for existence and subject to their will to power, played without a determined chain of events or outcome. He hopes the *Übermenschen* will bring excellence to society one day and defeat the "last men," who corrupted the world with the Christian faith and its democratic, egalitarian values, but there is no determined course of events or purpose in life to insure a favorable outcome.[120]

Of course, Bäumler hopes to relate the *Übermenschen* to his own Germanic people and their aspirations to become a new master race, but he clearly finds difficulty at this point in the apologia since Nietzsche attacks Germanism throughout his writings. Bäumler tries to reconcile Nietzsche with Nazi ideology as much as possible, but here he goes too far and spends large portions of his book trying to rationalize the anti-Germanism of Nietzsche as an understandable point of view given the context and times of his writings. According to Bäumler, Nietzsche rejects the nationalism of his German people only because it was so corrupted with the egalitarian spirit of Christianity and failed to promote the true excellence of their society. Nietzsche is exhorting his people to wake up and discover the pristine nature of their fundamental *Geist* as a means of preparing the way for a true German state to develop in the future. He attacks the etatism of his day only because of its close identification with the Christian principles of egalitarianism and democracy, enslaving the freedom of the *Volk* and destroying their deeper essence—or, so it seems to Bäumler.[121] This explanation provides the apologist with a means of reconciling his philosopher and party with each other and explaining the embarrassment of some anti-German comments, but Bäumler struggles at this point; he has difficulty simply dismissing Nietzsche's rejection of nationalism and etatism in loud and clear terms, as well as the refusal to make a simple identification between Germans, Aryans, and the master race. Bäumler's analysis does a credible job of showing the fundamental affinity of Nietzsche with the voluntaristic spirit of Nazism, but he carries the relationship beyond its proper boundary when trying to answer Nietzsche's critics within his own party on the subject of nationalism.

Heidegger

No one exhibits this general influence of Nazi and Nietzschean ideology on German thought more than Martin Heidegger, the most renowned intellectual of the time. He was born on September 26, 1889, in Messkirch, a city in Baden, where feelings of nationalism and anti-Semitism ran high during the period and once wrote a paper in 1910 celebrating the life and work of Abraham a Sancta Clara, a pan-Germanic and anti-Semitic Austrian.[122] Heidegger experienced a Catholic upbringing and studied for the priesthood a couple of years at Freiburg, but he eventually turned away from the faith in the course of the next decade. He became a student of phenomenology under Edmund Husserl and then a frustrated theology professor for a few years afterwards.[123] In 1923, he left theology for good to teach at Marburg, an early bastion of German existentialism, and then returned to Freiburg as a full professor six years later. Heidegger assumed the prestigious chair of his mentor, having written *Being and Time* (1927), one of the great books of the twentieth century.[124]

In his new environment, he received a renewed sense of inspiration from the students and their exuberance over National Socialism, and he exerted his own forceful personality in turn by promoting the cause.[125] He extolled the movement out of his own personal choice and conviction, long before the Nazi ascension to power, expressing his sympathy as early as 1931 and becoming an official member of the party and Teacher's Union supporting Hitler a couple years later.[126] On May 1, 1933, he became rector of the university, hoping to arrogate full administrative power to himself as the new *Führer-Rektor*, and he proceeded to denounce colleagues and students who withheld their unconditioned loyalty to him and the movement.[127] His brief tenure began with a rectoral address on May 27, entitled "Self-Assertion of the German University," where he speaks of himself as the spiritual leader of the university. He wants the students to find their true spiritual essence within a Nazi-like resolve and will to fulfill and create their Germanic destiny; he exhorts his colleagues, especially the scientists, to do likewise and develop their will out of the same spiritual essence and historical mission/determination of the German people.[128] On November 3, 1933, he writes an article in the student newspaper, telling the "German students,"

> The National Socialist revolution rings in the total collapse of our German existence [*Dasein*].
>
> It is incumbent on you to stay with the process [*Geschehen*], those of you who always want to press on further, those who are always ready, those who are hardened, those who never cease developing....

> Do not let principles and "ideas" be the rules of your existence.
> The Führer himself, and he alone, is the German reality of today, and of the future, and of its law. Learn to know always more deeply. Starting now each thing demands decision and every action, responsibility.
> Heil Hitler! Rector Martin Heidegger.[129]

During the summer of that year, he planned to create an ideological boot camp with communal meals, dialogue, music, and campfires, and succeeded in part when one of these camps actually transpired from October 4–10, with Heidegger providing an anti-Christian harangue to his select circle of students and faculty, who were dressed in SA or SS uniforms.[130] The next summer he developed overall plans about the academy, sending them to Stuckart on August 26 and emphasizing his desire to create a vital Nazi ambience and reshape the science and the school through spiritual forces,[131] but eventually he was disillusioned with the lack of zeal in the Nazi leadership and resigned his rectorship and political activity, unable to seize enough power and enforce his more radical agenda.[132] He felt the Nazis never appreciated his role in the spiritual renewal or his prophetic voice in announcing a new ontological viewpoint about the ultimate reality of "Being."[133] He was unhappy with Nazis corrupting the original vision of the movement, losing the spiritual impetus of science and transforming it into mere technology—a mechanical means outside of "its Greek metaphysical moorings in Being." He wanted the entities or beings of this world restored to their deeper ontological weight, rather than reducing them to a simple means of production, losing their fundamental meaning.[134] And yet, despite the philosophical criticisms, Heidegger remained a Nazi, defending Hitler's foreign and domestic agenda until the end of the war, hoping his party would rediscover its deeper, spiritual essence.[135] The most zealous Nazis found him impure and even put him under surveillance in 1936, but he continued to be identified with the movement as an important cultural icon and never wavered in his loyalty to its basic policies during those years.[136]

The question that is most intriguing about this relationship is whether the Nazis were justified in appealing to this great mind and finding a philosophical basis for their political ideas. Ever since the days of Plato and his *Republic*, many philosophers exhibited an intimate relationship between their ideas and politics, and Heidegger clearly wanted to cultivate the relationship during his time as rector in Freiburg and become the philosopher-king of the Nazi movement. Even if he failed in his mission, it is difficult to divide Heidegger the man and Heidegger the thinker in a manner that is foreign to the way he interpreted his own role at the time.[137] It is more likely to postulate some relation between his metaphysical musings over the nature of Being and his subsequent political convictions, even if the very ethereal and esoteric nature of his thought prevents a simplistic identification with anything so practical and concrete as a specific political position. In *An Introduction to Metaphysics*, he thinks of philosophy as an esoteric discipline for a limited few, which takes a longer and indirect path toward the transformation of cultural values, much less direct than the typical process. He is disillusioned with his inability to gain immediate success and notoriety, but he never discounts the ultimate political connection of his ideas or the intention to perfect Nazi ideology.

> This might suggest that philosophy can and must provide a foundation in which a nation will build its historical life and culture. But this is beyond the power of philosophy. As a rule such excessive demands take the form of belittling philosophy. It is said, for example: Because metaphysics did nothing to pave the way for the revolution it should be rejected. This is no cleverer than saying that because the carpenter's bench is useless for flying it should be abolished. Philosophy can never *directly* supply the energies and create the opportunities and methods that bring about a historical change; for one thing, because philosophy is always the concern of the few. Which few? The creators, those who initiate profound transformations. It spreads out indirectly, by devious paths that can never be laid in advance, until at last, at some future date, it sinks to the level of a commonplace; but by then it has long been forgotten as original philosophy.
>
> What philosophy essentially can and must be is this: a thinking that breaks the path and opens the perspectives of the knowledge that set the norms and hierarchies, of the knowledge in which and by which a people fulfills itself historically and culturally, the knowledge that kindles and necessitates all inquiries and thereby threatens all values.[138]

There might be few in the Nazi hierarchy who could understand or appreciate the depth and intricacy of his brilliant discussions, but some of his thoughts contain a Nazi texture and represent an important element in the Germanic metaphysical *Geist* that finds a fulfillment in this direction.

At first glance, it is difficult to discern any political application of his ideas when reading his great work, *Being and Time* (1927). One cannot deduce a specific political program or find a clear Nazi message without supplying sufficient hinges and foresight into a possible or later deconstruction.[139] The work finds its mission in raising once again the ancient Greek question concerning the nature of Being, which serves Heidegger as the most fundamental theme of philosophy, the most universal and transcendent category,[140] but unlike the Nazis, he finds the presence of Being constantly deferred and confesses his inability to grasp its essential nature in any specific form.[141]

This lack of specificity does not mean that his discussion is free from providing the groundwork or matrix for a more specific development in the direction of his later political tendencies. In fact, the seeds of Nazi and Nietzschean ideas begin to germinate within the work as he tries to relate Being and time—the basic theme of the work and one that clearly proceeds toward the voluntaristic notion of life and its duties, so essential to the Nazi worldview. Heidegger takes the inspiration for his discussion and view from the ancient Greeks. He understands the Greek concept of Being, in voluntaristic terms, as possessing a generative power, which is ever arising or Becoming.[142] He prefers this Greek concept of Being and Becoming to what is found in the scientific community of the day, which attempts to eliminate temporality in life and to treat entities, especially a human being or *Dasein*, as a static object.[143] Time is the horizon in which Being is understood; this temporality finds its locus of revelation in *Dasein*, which is most related to Being, and reveals its essence.[144] *Dasein* has a potentiality for Becoming;[145] it lives and moves within the ecstasies of a temporal horizon, uniting the past, present, and future in its existential structure and recognizing through its anxiety over death the possibility and freedom of choosing, which makes the future present.[146] *Dasein* provides the call to its own potentiality—for-Being or resoluteness (*Entschlossenheit*)—apart from any specific injunctions or universal conscience that would dictate a specific course of action.[147] The call is indefinite, "solely absorbed in summoning us to something," without any foundation within a heaven of ideas,[148] containing no specific exhortation to become a part of a cause—only the recognition of discovering human potential or the will to power, which lives just like the Nazis—beyond good and evil.

During the Nazi era, Heidegger brings this theme to the forefront and emphasizes the metaphysics of voluntarism as the basic object and interest of the Western philosophical tradition in general and the Germanic spirit in particular. In his lectures on Nietzsche, he traces the voluntarism back to Aristotle and his usage of terms like *potentia*, *actus*, and *energia* (entelechy), then he discovers it anew in Leibniz's *vis primitiva activa*, and also finds a reflection in the rational will (*Vernunftwille*) of Kant, Fichte, Hegel, and Schelling. Of course, Schopenhauer is mentioned as a part of the history and finds special honor for extending the program farther in his great work, *The World as Will and Representation*, and exerting a special influence in the latter half of the nineteenth century on figures like Nietzsche and Wagner, but Nietzsche is exalted above all others as the one who brings the process to a consummation or final result.[149]

Nietzsche serves Heidegger's purposes in the 1930s and 1940s as a means of promoting the basic philosophical orientation of the leading Nazi thinker and promoting his own deconstruction of the ideology, often blurring their ideas together, ingesting Nietzsche into his own heady metaphysics.[150] Heidegger depicts Nietzsche as understanding the legacy of Western metaphysics better than anyone else and reaching the zenith of the development through his famous phrase "will to power," which Nietzsche first develops as his leading concept in 1884.[151] Like Heidegger, he understands Being as the guiding concern of all philosophy and offers the phrase "will to power" in answering the question of Being as the closest approximation he can afford in broaching its essence.[152] For Nietzsche (and Heidegger), "being is in its very ground perpetual creation (becoming)"; "it becomes being and is becoming," ever existing as "creative transfiguration." This will to power permeates and enhances all beings, creating a higher culture through exerting force and making each one move out of the present realm of current stagnation and fight to gain strength, power, dominion, and mastery. Even if these struggles contain no ultimate meaning, values arise when creating the intended configuration out of the will to power as "constructs of dominion." It is a people's valuation that decides to preserve certain things and so posit what lasts as necessary or essential to the preservation of their lives. Truth is merely an estimation of value, which sees what is valuable for life's preservation and growth. It represents something as stable, "holding [it]-to-be true," "making something useful and permanent for its own sake." Knowledge does not copy a preexisting form of reality, but actively subsumes, stabilizes, and commands the chaotic world in forwarding utilitarian perspectives and practical needs. History is manufactured in the midst of propaganda wars, where victory reverses the old set of values and establishes a new order of truth.[153] A new sense of justice arises as it "constructs, excludes, and annihilates" what is defeated through the will to power in estimating the advantage of the victor and opening up a new vista or image of humanity.

> Justice is a passage *beyond* previous perspectives, a passage that posits viewpoints. In what horizon does this "constructive way of thought" posit its points of view? It has a "broader horizon of *advantage*." We are startled. A justice that looks out for advantage points shamelessly and crudely enough to the regions of utility, avidity, and expedience. Furthermore, Nietzsche even underlines the word *advantage* in his note, so as to leave no doubt that the justice meant here refers essentially to it. . . .
>
> Justice looks beyond to that sort of mankind which is to be forged and bred into a type, a type that possesses essential aptitude for establishing absolute dominion over the earth.[154]

For Nietzsche (and Heidegger) "the struggle for world domination" is conducted in the "name of fundamental philosophical doctrines."[155] In the *Introduction of Metaphysics*, Heidegger follows the same general understanding of the *Kampf* or struggle—this time speaking of the Spirit as a principle of domination, which spurns all appeals to world-reason and mobilizes the power of Being through its resoluteness and decisiveness. Here he disparages the egalitarian principles of American and Russian culture for producing a dreary sameness among the people and destroying "all rank and world-creating impulse of the Spirit."[156] As rector he would go on and use his authority to persecute Americanized professors, such as Adolf Lampe and Eduard Baumgarten, declaring his contempt for the mediocrity of democratic ideals and those who follow its teachings, while expressing loyalty to National Socialism and the decisive measures of the Nazi regime during times of economic hardship.[157] Just before the war, he represents the imminent conflict as a struggle to reach beyond the present course of Western culture and its history, or remain mired within the status quo of its mediocre policies, decadent tastes, and bourgeois economics.[158] Of course, after hostilities ended, Heidegger's elitist and authoritarian attitudes draw intense criticism during the denazification process; even Karl Jaspars feels compelled to testify that the "mode of thinking" in his longtime friend is "fundamentally unfree, dictatorial," and unfit for educating a new generation of students, who are still vulnerable and impressionable in post-Nazi Germany.[159]

Heidegger extends the will to power beyond the authentic existence of isolated individuals and judges the "rank and law" of an entire people and nation by "their power to command" and secure "absolute dominion."[160] This focus develops a foothold during the zenith of his Nazi involvement in the 1930s and tends to replace the earlier emphasis of *Being and Time* upon the individual failing to be "one-self" and losing its unique identity in the "they-self."[161] Now the accent falls upon "we-ourselves" finding an authentic existence within the spirit and unity of a nation.[162] This new emphasis is found in his rectoral address and continues in his writings and lectures during the period, which speak about the current upsurge of German nationalism with great enthusiasm.[163] He speaks of the "new will," the "new spiritual energies" arising from the Germanic community. He speaks of the historic gathering together of the German people as the "most metaphysical of nations" and finding a total realization of their authentic self through the state.[164] He wants this gathering to develop a new type of humanity for world domination,[165] although his emphasis lies upon the spirit or metaphysical will of the nation to power, not a special biological breeding program. He can question the official version of Nietzsche, which reads Nazi "biologism" or racial theories into the text, but still remains committed to Germanism in a deeper, spiritual sense. He remains a "metaphysical racist," as Derrida puts it, ever committed to the ontological elevation of his own people and their tradition.[166]

He hopes the struggle for National Socialism "will not be drowned by Christian and humanist notions."[167] Along with his fellow Nazis, he connects Christianity with its Jewish origins and then conflates its doctrine of egalitarianism with the later and more radical manifestation in Judaism and Bolshevism, which he considers the ultimate religiopolitical expression of the cowardly and the weak.[168] In his lectures on Nietzsche, he relates his subject's negation of the Judeo-Christian tradition and the desire for the *Übermensch* to create a new humanity, which no longer looks to the supersensuous world for a religious, rational, and moral explanation.[169] It is time to bite off the head of the serpent, severing Germany's former history in a supreme act of nihilism, and not comprise or try to lift up and improve (*Aufhebung*) in an evolutionary, Hegelian manner what must be overcome and completely destroyed.[170] Neitzsche's nihilism is the denial of reason and revelation, the rejection of the transcendent, the murder of the Christian god, the final act of annihilation, necessary to affirm the hidden potential of human nature and allow it to live by its social and sovereign instincts.[171]

Beyond the desire to overcome Judaism and Christianity, there is little direct evidence that Heidegger approved the literal means of Nazis to achieve this goal. Much suspicion develops because of his wife, Elfride Heidegger-Petri, who was a zealous party member, even before her husband, and endorsed racial and anti-Semitic measures in unequivocal terms.[172] Heidegger probably possessed some sympathy for his wife's position, but he remained more equivocal, circumspect, and discreet, never broadcasting anti-Semitic feelings in public lectures, philosophical writings, pamphlets, or speeches, and only making some off-color comments in a few private letters, leaving critics with no direct proof and wondering about his silence—a silence that continued throughout his life.[173] Even after the war, he never expressed any outrage over the brutalization of Jews and refused to condemn or even comment on the atrocities of the Holocaust, leaving people to speculate whether the sound of his silence is more damning or deafening than words of direct incrimination.[174]

After the war, he tried to manufacture a sophisticated cover-up, claiming that he only joined the party *pro forma* in 1933, that he sought to defend the university against Nazi intrusions as a rector, that he resigned his position in protest, and that he continued to present a confrontation (*Auseinandersetzung*) with the regime in his lectures on Höderlin and Nietzsche.[175] Of course, all these claims are false or misleading according to the facts as they are known today—the most significant being his massive lecture series and apologia of Nietzsche during the period. Far from confronting National Socialism, the lectures patronize Nazi interest in the philosopher, extol his brilliance, laud *Thus Spoke Zarathustra* as above everyone in its "fundamental thought" (will to power), cling to Elisabeth's *Will to Power* as the chief text, emphasize voluntarism (and resoluteness) as the fundamental impulse of Nietzsche, Heidegger, and all Western metaphysics in accordance with the revealing title of that work, and offer a salute to Hitler at the beginning and end of each lecture, even before it was mandatory.[176] During this time, he continued to embrace the typical Nazi staple of elitism, nationalism, and Germanism against the egalitarian and democratic culture of the Judeo-Christian tradition as a product of his intense voluntarism.[177]

Heidegger was at the very least an integral part of a metaphysical tradition that resonated in the *Geist* of his nation and led to the atrocities of the Nazis as an expression of its will. The emphasis upon voluntarism began with the medieval scholastics and reached a theological apex in Wilhelm Ockham denying any reason or purpose behind the divine decrees in creation. The voluntarism continued to develop in modern times with Leibniz removing the presence of God from the world and Schopenhauer, Nietzsche, and Heidegger rejecting the existence of God all together. Schopenhauer displayed the atheistic ramifications of voluntarism by depicting this world as a groundless and irrational struggle of competing forces, which exist outside of any human or divine intelligence, and inspiring Nietzsche to reject the Socratic program of rational inquiry and moral living once and for all. Life was reduced to an exertion of power, which no longer possessed a code to inhibit its will or defend its victims. The pure, groundless leadership of Adolf Hitler was a fulfillment of German self-assertion (*Selbstbehauptung*), based on the voluntaristic tradition of their leading philosophers and the zealous exercise of their will to power. Heidegger chose this term in the title of his famous address to embody the historical mission/determination of the German people in his prospective role as *Führer-Rektor* of his university and philosopher-king of the Nazi party.

Notes

1. P. G. J. Pulzer, *The Rise of Political Anti-Semitism in Germany and Austria* (New York, London, and Sydney: John Wiley & Sons, Inc., 1964) 247–48. This chapter and the previous two use some of the material and research already printed in an article on "The Nazis and the German Metaphysical Tradition of Voluntarism" (Sept. 1, 2011), with the permission of the *Review of Metaphysics*.
2. Ibid., 281; Viereck, *Metapolitics*, 6–8; *Der Berliner Antisemitismusstreit*, Walter Boehlich (Hrsg.) (Frankfurt am Main: Insel-Verlag, 1965) 16–17, 155–56, 173–74, 176; Goldhagen, *Hitler's Willing Executioners*, 83. Max Weber described the academic atmosphere in 1920 as "extremely reactionary" and "radically anti-Semitic." Uwe Lohalm, "Völkisch Origins of Early Nazism," in *Hostages of Modernism*, Herbert Arthur Strauss (ed.) (Berlin and New York: W. de Gruyter, 1993) 186–89. The Academic Day of 1925 and 1927 denounced Jewish and international influence as destructive to the German *Geist*. Student organizations were ready to embrace Hitler before he came to power and were exploited by the Nazis when they came to power as a means of controlling the universities. Leske, *Philosophen im 'Dritte Reich,'* 26, 28–29, 106–7.
3. Wolters, Der 'Führer' und seine Denker," 223–24, 228, 233–34; Rockmore, *On Heidegger's Nazism and Philosophy*, 33–34. The Deutschen Philosophen Gesellschaft met in October of 1933 and saw itself working with the new regime; later on, the Nazis were less interested or alienated from the group, and the meetings were not held. Leske, *Philosophen im 'Dritte Reich,'* 96–97, 108–9. Gereon Wolters provides a list of party members, and then identifies Alfred Baeumler, Oskar Becker, Arnold Gehlen, Martin Heidegger, Ernst Krieck, Erich Rothacker, and Helmut Schelski as some of the most prominent Nazi ideologues. Monika Leske adds the following names: Th. Kohn, Theodor Litt, Bruno Bauch, Hugo Dingler, Carl August Emge, Hans Günther, Karlfried v. Dürckheim, Hans Volkelt, Hans Georg Gadamer, Werner Schingnitz, Arnold Gehlen, Theodor Haering, Hans Freyer, Hans Heyse, Otto Dietrich, Ferdinand Weinhandl, and Paul Wolfgang Junker.

Nicolai Hartmann, Heinrich Dannenbauer, and Theodor Litt (later on) were among the few to oppose the regime. Of course, the Nazis purged or replaced many professors using political/ideological grounds in the 1930s (as many as 45 percent), although the precise statistics vary. Leske, *Philosophen im 'Dritte Reich,'* 8, 23–24, 43, 54, 110, 225–27; Hans-Peter Bleuel, *Deutschlands Bekenner: Professoren zwischen Kaiserreich und Diktatur* (Bern, München, und Wien: Scherz Verlag, 1968) 219–20.

4. George Santayana, *The German Mind: A Philosophical Diagnosis* (New York: Thomas Y. Crowell Co., 1968) xv, 12–13, 20, 33, 74, 85, 88, 92–96, 103, 108–9, 114–15, 124, 141–42, 156–57, 165.
5. Martin Heidegger, *Nietzsche*, David Farrell Krell (trans. and ed.), 4 vols. in 2 (San Francisco: HarperSanFrancisco, 1991) 1.62–64, 87, 120–21, 128; 2.222–23; 4.108ff., 147, 237.
6. A.M. Goichom, *The Philosophy of Avicenna and Its Influence on Medieval Europe*, M. S. Khan (trans.) (Dehli: Motilal Banarsidass, 1969) 14, 20. In his *First Principles*, Origen follows a similar line of thinking. There is no potential in God lurking behind the activity. Since God is almighty, the divine power must always be at work creating worlds in the past, present, and future. Something must always subsist under the divine sway, but this power is finite. Since all these created worlds are finite, and there exists no potency in God, this means that God is finite. *On First Principles*, G. W. Butterworth (trans.), Henri de Lubac (intro.) (Gloucester, MA: Peter Smith, 1973) 24, 42, 129, 238–39.
7. Oliver Leaman, *Averroes and His Philosophy* (Oxford: Clarendon Press, 1988) 16–21, 27, 37, 41, 68, 114–15. For Averroes (Aristotle), human concepts relate to how the world really is, and so possibilities must relate to actualities. One cannot have the possibility to exist or not exist. If something is possible, it must happen at some time, given the fact that time is infinite. Ibid., 29–31, 35, 38–39.
8. Ibid., 51–52, 154. Because of this teaching, the Muslim and Christian world thought of Avicenna and Averroes as heretics. Goichman, *The Philosophy of Avicenna*, 24; Leaman, *Averroes and His Philosophy*, 4–5. Ghazali (1085–1111) thought the world could have a different structure from what it has presently. God created the world from a pure fiat, *ex nihilo*, and could have created other possibilities. In fact, there is no causal nexus between discrete events, as if some force could compete and bind God's causal power. God could make someone satisfied with eating a mere morsel of food. Leaman, *Averroes and His Philosophy*, 20, 38–39, 51, 55, 61–62.
9. Goichom, *The Philosophy of Avicenna*, 73, 75, 83, 91ff., 97, 104; Leaman, *Averroes and His Philosophy*, 164.
10. Thomas Aquinas, *Summa Theologiae* (New York: McGraw-Hill, 1964–76) I, q.14, a.7; q.15, a.1–2; q.19, a.10; q. 25, a.5–6; q.45, a.3.
11. *Ordinatio* (Ed. Vat.) I, d.44, q.1; *Report. Paris.* (Ed Paris) IV, d.1, q.5, n.5; Heiko Oberman, *The Harvest of Medieval Theology* (Cambridge, MA: Harvard University Press, 1963) 36; Gordon Leff, *Gregory of Rimini: Tradition and Innovation in Fourteenth Century Thought* (Manchester, UK: Manchester University Press, 1961) 91. Leff finds an early usage of the distinction in Peter Damian during the eleventh century. The works cited from Duns Scotus are in *Opera Omnia* (Paris: L. Virès, 1891–95); *Opera*

Omnia (Civitas Vaticana: Typis Polyglottis Vaticanis, 1950–); *Opera Omnia* (Hildesheim: Georg Olms Verlagsbuchhandlung, 1968–).

12. *Ordinatio* (Ed. Vat.) I, d.44, q.1, n.7.
13. *Opus Ox.* III, d.37, q.1, n.1–3, 5, 6, 8, 12–13, 15; *Report. Paris.* (Ed. Paris) IV, d.1, q.5, n.2; *Ordinatio* (Ed. Vat.) I, d.44, q.1, n.1–2; d.47, q.1; Oberman, *Harvest*, 91; Efrem Bettoni, *Duns Scotus: The Basic Principles of his Philosophy*, Bernardine Bonansea (trans.) (Washington, DC: Catholic University of America Press, 1961) 174–75; Paul Vignaux, *Justification et Prédestination au XIVe Siècle* (Paris: E. Leroux, 1934) 11–12.
14. *Opus Ox.* (Ed. Paris) III, d.18, q.1, n.4; d.19, q.1, n.4, 6, 14; d.20, q.1, n. 8–9; Vignaux, *Justification et Prédestination*, 19–20; Stephen Strehle, "The Extent of the Atonement within the Theological Systems of the Sixteenth and Seventeenth Centuries" (ThD dissertation, Dallas theological Seminary, 1980) 42ff., 66.
15. Ordinatio (Ed. Vat.) I, d.17, q.1, n.3, 5, 9, 12; W. Dettloff, *Die Entwicklung Der Akzeptionslehre- und Verdienstlehre von Duns Scotus bis Martin Luther* (Münster, Westfalen: Aschendorfische Verlagsbuchhandlung, 1963), 73, 74, 106; Vignaux, *Justification et Préstination*, 38.
16. Berndt Hamm, *Promissio, Pactum, Ordinatio: Freiheit u. Selbstbindung Gottes, in d. Scholast. Gnadenlehre* (Tübingen: Mohr, 1977) 359; Erwin Iserloh, *Gnade und Eucharistie in der philosophische Theologien des Wihlelm von Ockham* (Wiesbaden: F. Steiner, 1956) 77; William Ockham, *Sent.*, III, q. 1, U. The works cited from Ockham are in *Opera Plurima* (Lugdini, 1494–96, Reprinted in London: Gregg Press, 1962); *Opera Philosophica et Theologica* (St. Bonaventure: St. Bonaventure University Press, 1967–82).
17. *Sent.*, I, d.17, q.1, E, T; q.5, E, F; d.47, q.1, D; II, q.19, O, P; IV, q.3, F, Q; *Quodl.*, VI, q.1, a.2, c.1–2. At one point, Ockham thinks God could command someone to hate the God-self, but later on, he overturns this possibility, saying it would involve a contradiction to fulfill a command to hate because it takes love to do God's will. *Sent.* II, q.19, O; III, q.5, G.
18. Oberman supplies a list of right- , middle- , and left-wing factions among the voluntarists. There were scholastics more extreme than Ockham (e.g., Johannes de Bassolis). Dettlof, *Die Entwicklung*, 159–62, 265, 363–65.
19. *Discourse on Metaphysics*, in *Leibniz: Discourse on Metaphysics/Correspondence with Arnauld/Monadology*, George Montgomery (trans.) (La Salle, IL: The Open Court Publishing Co., 1973) 44–47 (XXVI–XXVIII). The parentheses indicate the standard chapters/sections.
20. Ibid.,, 4–5, 22 (II, III, XIII); "Leibniz to Arnauld" (X, July 14, 1686), 131. Leibniz likes to think of God as having some choice in what was created, even if the final choice is the best option.
21. Ibid., 10 (VI); "Leibniz to Count Ernst von Hessen-Rheinfels" (Feb. 1686), 68–69; "Leibniz to Arnauld" (April 30, 1687) 184–85. He thinks of miracles as unusual occurrences, where God is acting above the powers he gave in creation, but they still must conform to the general order.
22. *Leibniz*, vii, xiii; *Discourse on Metaphyisics*, 24–25 (XIV); "Draft of the letter of Nov. 28–Dec. 8 [1686] to Arnauld," 151; "Leibniz to Arnauld" (Nov. 28–Dec. 8, 1686), 158; *Monadology*, 251–53 (1–11).
23. *Discourse on Metaphysics*, 14, 27, 33 (IX, XVI, XVIII); "Leibniz to Count Ernst von Hessen-Rheinfels" (Feb., 1686) 69; "Arnauld to Leibniz" (May 13,

1686), 93. Every individual is a microcosm expressing the entire universe. God can look at Adam and Eve and predict the incarnation. God can look at Alexander the Great and predict his entire history.

24. "Remarks upon Mr. Arnauld's letter . . ." (May 1686), 109–10.
25. *Leibniz*, vii, xi, xii; *Discourse on Metaphysics*, 30–36 (XVII–XXI); "Leibniz to Arnauld" (Oct. 6, 1687), 214, 217; *Monadology*, 262 (51–52). He does not want to reduce life to extension and motion but prefers to see the impetus or force of life in each individual. He is not sure whether plants have substantial forms, but he wants to believe that everything is fully animated (i.e., possesses soul or entelechy). "Leibniz to Arnauld" (April 30, 1687), 183, 193; Leibniz to Arnauld" (Oct. 6, 1687), 221, 224–25. He rejects the Cartesian or Occasionalist solution to the soul/body dichotomy, which posits the intervention of God harmonizing the two parts together, and prefers to think of the soul as originally created to synchronize with the body. "Leibniz to Arnauld" (July 14, 1686), 135; "Draft of the letter of Nov. 28–Dec. 8 to Arnauld," 152–53; "Leibniz to Arnauld" (Oct. 6, 1687), 214.
26. Arthur Schopenhauer, *The World as Will and Representation*, E. F. J. Payne (trans.), 2 vols. (New York: Dover Publications, Inc., 1969) xxiv, xxviii; 1.28, 83, 224; 2.69–70, 72, 76, 83; *Sämtliche Werke* (Leipzig: F. A. Brockhaus, 1938) xxv, xxxi; 1.33, 98, 99, 264; 2.74, 75, 77, 82, 90. Hereafter the English version is cited as WWR, and the German is placed in parentheses.
27. WWR 1.103, 112; 2.196–97, 210, 247, 494 (1.123, 133–34; 2.219–20, 235–36, 280, 566).
28. WWR 1.82–83, 100, 120, 128, 162–63, 274, 296; 2.277, 530, 642 (1.98–99, 119, 143, 152, 193–94; 313–14, 607, 738–39); 2.197, 198, 210–17, 234–37, 246, 250, 269, 278, 327 (219–21, 235–44, 265–68, 278–83, 304, 315, 373). There is ambiguity in Schopenhauer's discussion whether this lack of purpose is found in the way things happen to be or comes from the inability of humans to perceive any purpose, although fundamentally Schopenhauer seems to go with the former.
29. WWR 1.105, 108, 110, 114–15, 160 (1.125, 126, 129, 131, 136–37, 191); 2.259, 290–91, 295, 310–11 (292–93, 329–30, 333–34, 352–54, 382, 390, 394).
30. WWR 1.36–40, 184–85, 196, 257, 263; 2.448 (1.43–45, 217–18, 231–32, 304, 311; 2.512), . Tragedy also displays the conflict within the will itself. In discussing tragedy, he rejects the Judeo-Christian demand for poetic justice. WWR 1.254–55 (1.300–301).
31. WWR 2. (2.).
32. WWR 1.147, 276; 2.335, 345–46, 351–54, 512–14 (1.175, 325; 2.382, 394, 400–405, 587–89); 2.312–13, 318–21, 357–59, 491–92, 628 (2.354–56, 361–65, 407–9, 562–63, 722).
33. Of course, he rejects Judeo-Christian culture and prefers Indian and Greco-Roman culture. WWR 1.232 (1.274–75). He finds Christianity to be fundamentally evil and blames it for all the wars in Europe from the eighth to the eighteenth centuries. WWR 2.187 (2.208, 209). He finds Jews to be little more than parasites with their emphasis upon equal rights. Katz, *From Prejudice to Destruction*, 73. He hates the religious dogma of the West as an impediment to serious philosophical thinking and resting on faith, superstition, and bigotry. WWR 2.164–65, 186 (2.180–82).

34. WWR 1.388–90; 2.615ff., 620, 627, 633, 643 (1.459–60; 2.707ff. 712, 721, 728–29, 740). He finds death a real inspiration to philosophy. His concept of immortality is like the polygenesis of Buddhism, which rejects the transmigration of the soul. Only the will lives on, not the intellect. WWR 1.355–56, 365; 2.200, 488, 502–3, 508 (1.419–21, 431–32; 2.224, 559, 575–76, 582–83). The attachment to individual life comes from the irrational will-to-life. WWR 2.465–67 (2.531–34). At one point, he suggests carrying out a eugenics program much like Plato. WWR 2.527, 528 (2.604–5).
35. WWR 2.581–84 (2.666–71).
36. WWR 2.322, 574, 581 (2.364, 658, 666–67).
37. Friedrich Nietzsche, *Twilight of the Idols*, Anthony Ludovici (trans.), Dennis Sweet (intro.) (New York: Barnes & Noble, 2008) viii–x; *The Birth of Tragedy*, Oscar Levy (ed.), William Haussman (trans.), Rick Furtak (intro.) (New York: Barnes & Noble, 2006) viii; Walter Kaufmann, *Nietzsche: Philosopher, Psychologist, Antichrist* (Princeton, NJ: Princeton University Press, 1974) 22, 26; *On the Genealogy of Morals and Ecce Homo*, Walter Kaufmann and R. J. Hollindsdale (trans.), Kaufmann (intro.) (New York: Vintage Books, 1989) 286–87. Hereafter abbreviated as TI (*Twilight of the Idols*), BT (*Birth of Tragedy*), WKN (*Kaufmann's Nietzsche*), GM (*Genealogy of Morals*), and EH (*Ecce Home*).
38. Köhler, *Nietzsche and Wagner*, 6–7.
39. EH 202, 222ff., 224, 287, 301–3; *The Case of Wagner: A Musician's Problem*, in *The Anti-Christ, . . . and Other Writings*, Judith Norman (trans.), Aaron Ridley and Judith Norman (ed.) (Cambridge: Cambridge University Press, 2005) 271–72; WKN, 66–67. See *The Gay Science*, Walter Kaufman (trans. and intro.) (New York: Vintage Books, 1974) 34–36, 252–53 (318), 364–67. Hereafter abbreviated as CW (*The Case of Wagner*) and GS (*Gay Science*).
40. Nietzsche, *The Antichrist: A Criticism of Christianity*, Anthony Ludovici, Dennis Sweet (intro.) (New York: Barnes & Noble, 2006) viii–ix, xviii; BT, viii. Hereafter abbreviated as A (*Antichrist*).
41. Aschheim, *Nietzsche Legacy*, 18, 30–33, 45–46, 135, 142–45, 239–40; A xiv–xv; GS 103 (note 26); WKN 4–5, 8–9, 22; Köhler, *Nietzsche and Wagner*, 66. Nietzsche hailed *Zarathustra* as his "greatest present" to humankind, much greater than any work of Dante, Goethe, or Shakespeare. EH 304–6.
42. Viereck, *Metapolitics*, 183; A xv–xvi; Aschheim, *Nietzsche Legacy*, 305. Mussolini also was influenced by the works of Nietzsche, writing and lecturing on him at an early age and interpreting his political activities as the fulfillment of the philosopher's ideology. Konrad Algermissen, *Nietzsche und das Dritte Reich* (Celle: Joseph Giesel, 1947) 3; McGovern, *From Luther to Hitler*, 415, 539–40; Aschheim, *Nietzsche Legacy*, 133.
43. Aschheim, *Nietzsche Legacy*, 234–37, 242–44, 247–53. Kurt Kassler's *Nietzsche und das Recht* (Müchen: Ernst Reinhardt, 1941) uses Nietzsche's less than orthodox opinions to justify Nazi measures like racial breeding programs, but he did not dismiss the difficulties and inconsistencies in his writings. *Nietzsche und das Recht*, 70–78.
44. Köhler, *Nietzsche und Wagner*, 13; Rüdiger Safranski, *Martin Heidegger: Between Good and Evil*, Ewald Oser (trans.) (Cambridge, MA, and London: Harvard University Press, 1999) 300–301; Heidegger, *Nietzsche*, 1.241.

According to a couple of his confidants, August Kubizek and Hermann Rauschning, Hitler read Nietzsche at a young age and developed a Nietzschean worldview. Rauschning, *Hitler Speaks*, 220; August Kubizek, *The Young Hitler I Knew*, E. V. Anderson (trans.), H. R. Trevor-Roper (intro.) (Boston: Houghton Mifflin Co., 1955) 183; Steven Aschheim, "Nietzsche, Anti-Semitism and the Holocaust," in *Nietzsche and Jewish Culture*, Jacob Golomb (ed.) (London and New York: Routeldge, 1997) 18 (note 29); *Nietzsche Legacy*, 281.

45. Aschheim, *Nietzsche Legacy*, 2–3, 8, 14; WKN 75, 80, 85; TI 4, 79 (26, 51); *Thus Spoke Zarathustra: A Book for Everyone and No One*, R. J. Hollingdale (trans.) (Middlesex, UK, and New York: Penguin Books, 1978) 11, 13; *The Will To Power*, Walter Kaufmann and R. J. Hollingdale (trans.), Kaufmann (ed.) (New York: Vintage books, 1968) 91 (142); WKN 117. Hereafter *Zarathustra* is Z and *Will to Power* is WP.
46. GS 138, 168, 236, 245–46, 253, 255, 272, 335 (84, 109, 294, 304–5, 319, 324, 340, 373).
47. Jacques Derrida, *Of Grammatology*, Gayatri Chakravorty Spivak (trans.) (Baltimore and London: The John Hopkins University Press, 1976) xxxi–xxxii, xxxvii–xxxviii, xli.
48. Jacques Derrida, *The Ear of the Other: Otobiography, Transference, Translation*, Avital Ronell and Peggy Kamuf (trans.), Christie MacDonald (ed.) (New York: Schocken Books, 1985) 30–31; Aschheim, "Nietzsche, Anti-Semitism and the Holocaust," 11, 19.
49. BT ix, 1, 3–4, 14–16, 40, 65, 91, 94–95 (1, 3–5, 10, 16, 22).
50. WKN 177, 230–31, 236, 399–400.
51. GS 78, 236, 333 (3, 294, 372); Z 67, 102; WP 542–43 (1052); TI xxxi; WKN 223.
52. BT x, 75–76, 84, 87, 102, 105–6 (18–20, 23–24); WP 521 (1005); TI 52.
53. BT xi, 42–62 (11–15); WP 234ff., 244 (430ff., 437); TI xvi– xvii, 7–12, 82.
54. A 56–58, 63 (51–52, 55). In *Beyond Good and Evil*, he thinks falsehood and stupidity can serve the human condition better than truth. *Beyond Good and Evil*, Helen Zimmern (trans.), Willard Wright (intro.) (New York: The Modern Library, 1917) 4, 41, 80 (4, 34, 107). Of course, the *truth* that God does not exist presents Nietzsche with a paradox. He announces both the beginning and end of truth, often in the same work. EH 236–37, 244, 314, 326. Hereafter *Beyond Good and Evil* is designated BGE.
55. GM 151–53 (III, 24); GS 167–69, 258 (note 54) (108–9, 327–28; WP 46–47, 267, 270, 272, 280–81, 297–98, 302, 330, 337, 377–78 (69, 481, 489, 495, 516–20, 552, 556–59, 616, 634, 552, 708).
56. GS 167, 181–82, 279 (108, 125, 343); Z 14. Zarathustra uses this phrase to mock the God of Christianity, who suffocated on his own excessive pity, suffering from his own compassion on the cross for the lowly. Z 249, –73. God perishes for loving those who suffer. BGE, 68–70 (61–62).
57. WP 140 (244); GS 280, 289 (343, 347).
58. WP 18 (25).
59. WP 7, 12–13, 18 (3, 12, 25). Of course, he can turn the term on its head and accuse moralists of nihilism since they negate the natural world as it exists, while he affirms it. See, for example, WP 318 (585).

60. EH 258, 261, 270, 283; BGE 40, 87–88 (34, 149, 154); TI 33; Z 218–19; WKN 110–112.
61. Z 85, 111, 139, 213; A 10 (11); BGE 36, 117, 135–36, 146, 155 (30, 203, 211, 221, 228).
62. Michel Foucault provides one of the most scintillating and caustic examples of this type of analysis.
63. GM 3, 20, 25–31, 55–56, 72–73, 77–78, 84–85, 92, 142, 161(preface, 6; I, 2–5, 17; II, 10, 12, 16, 22; III, 21, 27); Gary Gutting, *Foucault: A Very Short Introduction* (Oxford and New York: Oxford University Press, 2005) 49.
64. WP 88–90, 202 (139–41, 375); GM 128, 140 (III, 15–16, 20); A 53–54 (48–49).
65. TI 31–32 (7). Nietzsche rejects the concept of free will. He finds concepts like ego, spirit, and will to be imaginary causes—much like subject, object, and attribute. He cites the work of David Hume and says the division between subject and object depends on the erroneous belief in cause and effect. There is no one to blame or hold responsible. TI 27–28 (3–4); GS 169 (110); WP 294–96, 352, 402 (549–51, 667, 765).
66. GM 123–24, 144 (III, 14, 22); Ashheim, "Nietzsche, Anti-Semitism and Holocaust," 7; Sander L. Gilman, "Heine, Nietzsche and the Idea of the Jews," in *Nietzsche and Jewish Culture*, 94; A 24–27, 46 (25–26, 44); Yirmiyah Yovel, "Nietzsche and the Jews: The Structure of Ambivalence," in *Nietzsche and Jewish Culture*, 124–28.
67. A 22–23 (24).
68. GM 33–36 (I, 7–9); GS 188 (136); WP 35–36 (55).
69. A xiii. See Sander Gilman, "Heine, Nietzsche and the Jewish idea," 97–98 (note 3) for a long list of the literature on both sides. Kaufmann says Nietzsche went out of his way to distance himself from anti-Semitism and proto-Nazism. WKN 298. See A 62 (55); GS 22; Weaver Santaniello, "Post-Holocaust Re-examination of Nietzsche and the Jews: Vis-à-vis Christendom and Nazism," in *Nietzsche and Jewish Culture*, 37–38. Franz Overbeck, his close friend, probably characterizes the situation best when he speaks of Nietzsche as a "convinced enemy of anti-Semitism," and then immediately turns around and says his sharp opinions about the Jews "surpassed by far every anti-Semitism." "To Franziska and Elisabeth Nietzsche" (March 31, 1885) and "Franz Overbeck" (Oct. 1885), in *Selected Letters of Friedrich Nietzsche*, Christopher Middleton (ed. and trans.) (Chicago and London: Chicago University Press, 1969) 238, 246, 346–48; Ashheim, "Nietzsche, Anti-Semitism and the Holocaust," 8.
70. *Nietzsche contra Wagner*, in CW 276; *Briefwechsel: Kritische Gesamtausgabe*, Gorgio Colli und Mazzino Montinari (Hrsg.) (Berlin: Walter de Gruyter, 1975) 3.503; Viereck, *Metapolitics*, lxxxii–lxxxiii; Santaniello, "Post-Holocaust Re-examination," 37–38; Yovel, "Nietzsche and the Jews," 120–21.
71. BGE 184–86 (251); A 23 (24); WP 31 (49); Aschheim, "Nietzsche, and Anti-Semitism and the Holocaust," 6–7; Gilman, "Heine, Nietzsche and the Idea of the Jews," 77–78.
72. Nietzsche, *Human, All Too Human*, R. J. Hollingdale (trans.) (Cambridge, UK: Cambridge University Press, 1996) 175 (475). He rejects any depiction of Jews as "diseased" and "decadent" because of racial incest or the Jewish

policy of breeding with each other. Gilman, "Heine, Nietzsche and the Jewish Idea," 78.

73. Hubert Canck, "Mongols, Semites and the Pure-Bred Greeks," in *Nietzsche and Jewish Culture*, 67–68.
74. Köhler, *Nietzsche and Wagner*, 39, 79, 87–88.
75. GS 317 (361); WP 462 (864); *Selected Letters of Nietzsche*, 58, 80, 86, 102, 273, 298, 301, 338.
76. A 22–23, 46 (24, 44); WP 102 (169); *The Nietzsche-Wagner Correspondence*, Elizabeth Foerster-Nietzsche (ed.), Caroline Kerr (trans.), H. L. Menden (intro.) (New York: Liverright, 1921) 172; WKN 136. He prefers the Arab and Muslim to the Jew and Christian. A 72 (60).
77. GS 187–88 (135–36); Santaniello, "Post-Holocaust Re-examination," 31–32; EH 283, 309, 335; A 8–9 (9), 57, 74–75 (51, 62); WP, 118 (202).
78. WP 117 (200).
79. A 32, 36–37 (31, 36–37); WP 97–98 (158). He speaks of David Strauss on a number of occasions. He read *Leben Jesu* as a young scholar and relished every word, clearly appreciating the cynicism of the work, although he considers it impossible to explore the "contradictions" of legends with scientific precision. He criticizes Strauss's more positive statement in *The Old Faith and the New* as dull and wonders how Strauss can embrace Darwin, reject Christianity, and leave ethics untouched. A 28–29 (28); *Nietzsche-Wagner Correspondence*, 172; WKN 136.
80. WP 101 (168).
81. A 35–36, 39 (34–35, 39); WP 98–100 (160–61). Nietzsche finds some major errors in Jesus's teachings: Jesus saw sin as the cause of human suffering; he epitomizes the slave morality of the Jews with its revolt of the lowly against the "higher man"; and his pacifism leads to the destruction of the state. GS 189, 296–97 (138, 353,); GM (8); WP 123 (207).
82. WP 101–3, 116 (167–71, 198); A 42–46 (40–44).
83. GS 311–12 (358); A 5, 16, 41, 45, 57 (5, 17–18, 40, 43, 51); TI 62 (34); WP 58, 108, 111, 117, 120, 144–46 (94, 179, 184, 199, 204, 249–52). He finds "all religions are at the deepest level systems of cruelties." For example, Tertullian and Thomas Aquinas believed the damnation of the reprobate would add comfort to the church triumphant in heaven. GM 48–49, 61 (I, 15; II, 3).
84. A 4–7, 14–17 (2–7, 16–19); Z 14, 42, 90, 123, 149, 206–8; 249, 272–73, 277; TI 34–36; GM 125 (III, 14–15); GS 220, 269–71 (271, 338); WP 199 (368); WKN 369, 389.
85. Z 229, 298; GS 175, 238 (117, 258); WKN 162–63.
86. Z 41ff., 52, 297, 302; BGE 201 (260); WKN 307–9. Kaufmann finds antecedents to the *Übermensch* in the *hyperanthropos* of Lucian's works from the second century and the use of the term in Heirich Müller, J. G. Herder, Jean Paul, and Goethe, whose usage in *Zueignung* (a poem) and *Faust* closely parallels Nietzsche's.
87. Z 196. Kaufmann says *blonde Bestie* does not refer to the Nordic race, and *Übermenschen* refers to artists, philosophers, and saints. It is the "highest specimens" like Shakespeare that judge the rest of humanity and make most people look like beasts in comparison. WKN 150–52, 162, 225, 285. But Kaufmann is trying to purify the account. Nietzsche might have a more expansive meaning than the Nazi concept of the Supermen, but his meaning

certainly includes their notion. In the context of GM 42–44 (I, 11–12), Nietzsche uses the image of gold in reference to a golden era of heroes and demigods, which might offer a clue to his concept of blond beast. Nietzsche even speaks of rearing or breeding (*heraufzüchten*) a master race at one point, although he lacks specificity. WP 504 (960).

88. GM 39–45, 86 (I, 11–13; II, 17); WP 142, 389 (246, 734); BGE 198–200 (258–59).
89. BGE 202–4 (260).
90. WP 74, 129, 189–90, 198 (120, 221, 343, 347, 365–66).
91. See EH 257–59 for other unseemly comments, which might signal a portent of his final madness. Above all, he hails *Zarathustra* as the world's greatest work, much greater than anything Goethe or Shakespeare ever produced. EH 304–6.
92. WP 74, 493–94 (120, 936); BT xxiv; GS 338 (377); GM 154 (III, 25). He approves of the militarism growing in Europe and thinks military and physical education as an essential aspect of schools. WP 75, 482–83 (123, 912); TI 2 (8). "That which does not kill me, makes me stronger." TI 2 (8). The Nazis quoted Nietzsche continuously on the salvific nature of war. Leske, *Philosophen im 'Dritte Reich,'* 171–72; Hans Günther, "Der Fall Nietzsche," *Unter dem Banner des Marzismus* 11 (1935): 280.
93. WP 33, 356 (53, 674–75); TI 68. His first sustained treatment of Darwinism is found in *Unzeitgemässe Betrachtung: David Strauss der Bekenner und der Scriftsteller* (1873), where he criticizes Strauss for continuing to preach morality, purpose, and meaning in life without considering the impact of Darwin on this view of life. Unlike many of his contemporaries, he recognizes that Darwinism questions the nineteenth century's belief in moral and upward progress. Dirk Robert Johnson, "Nietzsche's Early Darwinism: The 'David' Strauss Essay of 1873," in *Nietzsche Studien* 30 (2001): 63–71.
94. WP 142, 458, 467 (246, 859–61, 872).
95. TI 63 (36).
96. WP 389 (734); Aschheim, *Nietzschean Legacy*, 48–49. Nazi advocates of eugenics like Alexander Tille and Kurt Kassler understood Nietzsche in this way. Weikart, *From Darwin to Hitler*, 46; Aschheim, *Nietzschean Legacy*, 244.
97. WP 477–78 (898). Cf. WKN 304ff.
98. GM 30 (I, 5); Canck, "Mongols, Semites and the Pure-Bred Greeks," 60–61.
99. EH 243–44, 248, 276, 318–22; GS 308–10 (357–58); WP 41 (60); A 73–74 (61); Viereck, *Metapolitics*, 48, 183; TI 37–40; GM 158–59 (III, 26). He prefers a mixture of race and thinks of himself as a mixture, which included some Polish blood. Yovel, "Nietzsche and the Jews," 123; WKN 288.
100. A xvi; WP xiii. The *Will to Power* is a collection of notes, assembled by editors, which Nietzsche scribbled down from 1883–1888 but never brought together into a polished or final product. Nietzsche considered using this title at one time with the subtitle "Attempt at a Revaluation of All Values," then started to write another four-part work entitled *Revaluation of All Values* with only the first part, *The Antichrist*, appearing in the fall of 1888. The first edition of the *Will to Power* appeared in 1901, and the most scholarly form in 1911. WP xvii, xxvii–xxviii; WKN 405.

101. Z 84, 136ff.; 190–91; WP 339–40, 346–47, 350, 354, 356, 550 (635–36, 656–58, 664–65, 671, 675, 1067); GS 292 (349); WP 373 (702); WKN 189, 193, 211, 255, 261–62.
102. "To Richard Wagner" (May 22, 1869), in *Selected Letters of Friedrich Nietzsche*, 53; Heidegger, *Nietzsche*, 1.62; WKN 30–31.
103. "To Carl von Gersdorff" (March 11, 1870), in *Selected Letters*, 65; Köhler, *Nietzsche and Wagner*, 20; *Nietzsche-Wagner Correspondence*, 219.
104. WKN 24; BT x, 62; Heidegger, *Nietzsche*, 1.7.
105. "To Carl von Gersdorff" (April 7, 1866), in *Selected Letters*, 11–13; "To Carl von Gersdorff" (Aug. 1866), in *Selected Letters*, 18. According to Nietzsche, "Schopenhauer was the first admitted and inexorable atheist among us Germans," and he receives much praise for defeating Christianity as a "good European." GS 307–10 (357).
106. BT 66–68, 87, 102, 105–6 (16, 20, 23–24); GM 103 (III, 5); WKN 30–31.
107. Köhler, *Nietzsche and Wagner*, 18–21, 59–60; *Selected Letters*, 244.
108. CW 276; *Selected Letters*, ix–x, 299; Köhler, *Nietzsche and Wagner*, 84; EH 247; Safranski, *Martin Heidegger*, 48.
109. *Nietzsche-Wagner Correspondence*, xi–xiv, 225, 294–95.
110. Ibid., 222, 269, 276; WKN 38; EH 248. Nietzsche's rejection of anti-Semitism comes from the time of his break with Wagner. WKN 42.
111. Ibid., 224.
112. Ibid., 294–96; CW 276; Köhler, *Nietzsche and Wagner*, 140. According to Bäumler, Nietzsche broke with Wagner over *Parisal*, a Christian work. Alfred Baeumler, *Nietzsche der Philosoph und Politiker* (Leipzig: Philipp Recam jun., 1931) 990.
113. Ibid., 236–37, 286, 322, 331; EH 247, 249, 263. Nietzsche now says that his interpretation of Wagner in terms of Dionysus was more his own wishful thinking in the *Birth of Tragedy*. Wagner's music is a great corruption of the modern spirit. CW 241–42, 257; EH 274.
114. Ibid. Now Schopenhauer's "metaphysics are wrong" or "nearly always" wrong, "To Carl Fuchs" (July 1877), in *Selected Letters*, 162; "To Peter Gast" (July 18, 1880), in *Selected Letters*, 173. He has some genuine disagreements with Schopenhauer, even if he remains a disciple of voluntarism. He particularly dislikes the pessimism and asceticism of Schopenhauer in his attempt to extinguish the will-in-itself. Nietzsche wants to embrace Becoming and tragedy as a more life-affirming philosopher. TI 85 (5); WP 205–6, 369, 521 (382, 692, 1005); CW 271–72.
115. Leske, *Philosophen im 'Dritte Reich,'* 213–14. Bäumler was commissioned to propagate Nazi ideology and particularly worked under the auspices of Rosenberg throughout his career, participating in a number of congresses and receiving various commissions. His zealotry was displayed most infamously by instigating a book-burning episode at the university, with Marx's works being the first to go, even if he typically encouraged the reading of other ideologies. National Socialism was clearly exalted at the institute above all other possibilities, and Bäumler became the number one Nazi philosopher. Leske, *Philosophen im 'Dritte Reich,'* 93–95, 203–4, 217–18, 228–29, 232–33. Jon Krieck was a distant second. He also wanted to formulate a coherent Nazi philosophy, but was less orthodox than Bäumler.

116. Aschheim, *Nietzsche Legacy*, 234–35; WP xiii. Of course, not all Nazis were so enamored with Nietzsche. Ibid., 253; Safranski, *Martin Heidegger*, 42.
117. Kaufmann describes Bäumler as "one of the worst Nazi hacks." *Basic Writing of Nietzsche* (New York: Modern Library, 2000) 604–5, note 2.
118. Alfred Baeumler, *Nietzsche der Philosoph und Politiker* (Leipzig: Philipp Reclam jun., 1931) 7–9. Hereafter designated as NPP.
119. NPP 17–19, 54–57, 98, 105.
120. NPP 5, 12–13, 16, 20, 23–26, 31, 36–37, 44–49, 52, 56, 64–74, 114–15, 172–73. Each monad has its own power, but there is no pre-set harmony as Leibniz believed in his *Monadology*. Bäumler was a strong advocate of "total war" in his writings, as an indelible aspect of human nature. Leske, *Philosophen im 'Dritte Reich,'* 176–77.
121. NPP 13, 91, 104–5, 120, 132, 160–61, 165, 179–83; Heidegger, *Nietzsche*, 4.270; Cf. Safranski, *Martin Heidegger*, 39–41; WK 163–64. Nietzsche has equivocal feelings about Bismarck, depending on how much he identifies the great leader with the Christian state or Schopenhauer's philosophy. NPP 120, 140.
122. Victor Farías, *Heidegger and Nazism*, Paul Burrell and Gabriel Ricci (trans.), Joseph Margolis and Tom Rockmore (ed.) (Philadelphia: Temple University Press, 1989) 4, 292–93. His appreciation for Abraham a Sancta Clara will continue throughout his life.
123. Michael Inwood, *Heidegger* (Oxford: Oxford University Press, 1997) 1, 2; Safranski, *Martin Heidegger*, 9, 14ff., 90. At Freiberg, Heidegger sat under a couple of history professors, Heinrich Finke and Georg von Below, with Nazi-like ideas. Farías, *Heidegger and Nazism*, 21–22.
124. Ibid., 2; Safranski, *Martin Heidegger*, 143,189. At this time, he makes a clear dichotomy between philosophy and theology, rejecting the Catholic tradition of integration between the two disciplines. "Phänomenologie und Theologie (1927)," in *Wegmarken* [*Gesamtausgabe*] (Frankfurt am Main: Klostermann, 1976) 9.66–67; Safranski, *Martin Heidegger*, 144.
125. Farías, *Heidegger and Nazism*, 75–76, 79–80, 84.
126. Carl Fiedrich Weizsäcker, "Begegnung in vier Jahrzehnten," in *Erinnerung an Martin Heidegger*, Günther Neske (Hrsg.) (Pfullingen: Neske, 1977) 245–46; Farías, *Heidegger and Nazism*, 4, 79; Rockmore, *On Heidegger's Nazism and Philosophy*, 71, 112; Safranski, *Martin Heidegger*, 226ff., 231, 235, 244.
127. Heiddeger, *Nietzsche*, x–xi; Farías, *Heidegger and Nazism*, 86–87.
128. Heidegger, "The Self-Assertion of the German University," Karsten Harries (trans.), in *Review of Metaphysics* 38 (1984/85): 470–80; Ashheim, *Nietzsche Legacy*, 262; Farías, *Heidegger and Nazism*, 96ff., 99–100, 103, 134, 140; Rockmore, *On Heidegger's Nazism and Philosophy*, 57ff., 65, 69. He later claims that his rectoral address was merely a defense of the university, but the Germanism and voluntarism are more than apparent. Rockmore, *On Heidegger's Nazism and Philosophy*, 118. In the address, he mentions his concern that science is losing its moorings in Greek philosophy and its vision of the totality. "The Self-Assertion," 471–73.
129. Farías, *Heidegger and Nazism*, 118–19; Safranski, *Martin Heidegger*, 232–33. Farías provides a summary of the Nazi policies during his rectorship: "the expulsion of all Jews on the teaching staff; a questionnaire for each teacher showing racial origin; the new rights of students; the obligatory oath for

all teachers concerning the pure race; the obligation to use the Nazi salute at the beginning and end of each class; the organization of the University Department of Racial Matters, to be directed by the SS, who were responsible for organizing courses to be taught by a specialist from the Institute of Racial Purity in Berlin, directed by Professor Eugen Fischer; obligatory work service; economic help for student members of the SA and the SS, or other military groups, and refusal of aid to Jewish and Marxist students; the obligation to attend classes on racial theory, military science, and German culture." *Heidegger and Nazism*, 119; Guido Schneeberger, *Nachlese zu Heidegger: Dokumente zu seinem Leben und Denken* (Bern: [s.n.], 1962) 18, 60, 63, 66, 90–91, 118, 135ff., 166–67.

130. Safranski, *Martin Heidegger*, 261–62. He wanted a radical change in the university's relation between professor and student, modeled on the SA. Leske, *Philosophen im 'Dritte Reich,'* 105–6.
131. Farías, *Heidegger and Nazism*, 197–98.
132. Heidegger, *Nietzsche*, xix–xx, 4.264; Safanski, *Martin Heidegger*, 271–72.
133. Heidegger, *Beiträge zur Philosophie: Von Ereignis*, Friedrich-Wilhelm von Herrman (ed.) (Frankfurt am Main: V. Klostermann, 1989); Rockmore, *On Heidegger's Nazism and Philosophy*, 178, 193, 200–201, 243.
134. Heidegger, *An Introduction to Metaphysics*, Ralph Manheim (trans.) (New Haven, CT, and London: Yale University Press, 1987) 37–39; Rockmore, *On Heidegger's Nazism and Philosophy*, 115, 221; Michael Zimmerman, "Philosophy and Politics: The Case of Heidegger," *Philosophy Today* 33/1 (Spring 1989): 9; Safranski, *Martin Heidegger*, 318, 321. In *Introduction to Metaphysics* (1935), he speaks of Germany as the "most metaphysical nation," its need to bring about "new spiritual energies," and his rejection of the "technological frenzy" in America and Russia. The Greek concepts of *technē* and *eidos* (idea) involved the disclosure of Being (i.e., where a being like a house comes to appear or reveal its house-likeness or universal nature). A craftsman is closer to the idea than a painter, who merely copies an image from one angle. Heidegger, *Nietzsche*, 1.174–76; 4.162; Rockmore, *On Heidegger's Nazism and Philosophy*, 223. He also says that Being-ness is not malleable. He rejects the machine-ization of modern times, where humans take dominion over the earth through the power of the machine and everything is "do-able," all is "one-upmanship," and humans are losing their quest for meaning. Heidegger, Nietzsche, 3.175, 180–82. Heidegger makes this claim concerning technology after the war in his famous *Der Spiegel* interview, trying to distance himself from the Nazis. "Nur noch ein Gott kann uns retten: Spiegel-Gespräch mit Martin Heidegger am 23. September 1966," *Der Spiegel* 23 (May 31, 1976): 206, 209, 214. See also Farías, *Heidegger and Nazism*, 298; Zimmerman, "Philosophy and Politics," 7. His *Introduction to Metaphysics* and lectures on Nietzsche partially corroborate this claim. Cf. Farías, *Heidegger and Nazism*, 226–28.
135. Safranski, *Martin Heidegger*, 318, 321; Farías, *Heidegger and Nazism*, 5, 191, 277–78. Heidegger is clearly a part of the Germanic spirit of the times, not an international spirit, and does not defend the place of the university against it, like he would claim later. Leske, *Philosophen im 'Dritte Reich,'* 99–100. His *Introduction to Metaphysics* and Nietzsche lectures show traces of the continued commitment. Farías, *Heidegger and Nazism*, xi. Karl Löwith speaks

of meeting Heidegger in 1936 at Rome with his mentor wearing a swastika pin and affirming his commitment to National Socialism as consonant with the movement of history. Karl Löwith, *Mein Leben in Deutschland vor und nach 1933: Ein Bericht* (Stuttgart: J. B. Metzlersche Verlagsbuchhandlung, 1986) 56–58; Zimmerman, "Philosophy and Politics," 6.

136. Ibid., 269, 318, 321–22: Farías, *Heidegger and Nazism*, 252, 260–61. Ernst Kriek and Alfred Rosenberg were among the Nazis who opposed him.
137. Philippe Lacoue-Labarthe, *La fiction du politique: Heidegger, l'art et la politique* (Paris: Christian Bourgois, 1987) 34–38; Rockmore, *On Heidegger's Nazism and Philosophy*, 4–5, 41, 283, 284, 295; Jean-François Lyotard, *Heidegger and the "jews,"* Andreas Michel and Mark Roberts (trans.) (Minneapolis, Minn.: University of Minneapolis Press, 1990) xvi.
138. Heidegger, *Introduction to Metaphysics*, 10.
139. Lyotard, *Heidegger and the "jews,"* 67–68; Heidegger, *Introduction to Metaphysics*, 12.
140. Martin Heidegger, *Being and Time*, John Macquarrie and Edward Robinson (trans.) (New York and Evanston: SCM Press, 1962) 22, 31, 62 (3, 11, 38).
141. Lyotard, *Heidegger and the "jews,"* 79.
142. See Heidegger, *Introduction to Metaphysics*, 63–64, 96–98.
143. Safranski, *Martin Heidegger*, 150.
144. Heidegger, *Being and Time*, 19, 402, 428 (1, 351, 376); Rockmore, *On Heidegger's Nazism and Philosophy*, 148.
145. Ibid., 287 (243); Leske, *Philosophen im 'Dritte Reich,'* 101.
146. Ibid., 41, 185–86, 232, 236, 393–94, 401–2, 416, 426–27, 479 (19–20, 145–46, 187–88, 191–92, 342–44, 350–51, 365, 374–75, 426–27); Lyotard, *Heidegger and the "jews,"* 69. *Dasein* is not a victim of fate but makes and constitutes time. Farías, *Heidegger and Nazism*, 64.
147. Ibid., 318, 322, 333–34, 340, 345 (274–75, 278, 287–88, 294, 298–99); Rockmore, *On Heidegger's Nazism and Philosophy*, 44–46.
148. Ibid., 319–20 (274–75); Safranski, *Martin Heidegger*, 166–67, 219. If there is an exhortation in all of this, it concerns the need to respect this freedom to choose in others, as well as oneself.
149. Heidegger, *Nietszche*, 1.62–64, 87, 120–21, 128; 2.222–23; 4.108ff., 147, 237; Dietmar Köhler, "Von Schelling zu Hitler? Heideggers Schelling-Interpretation von 1936 und 1941," in *Schelling: Zwischen Fichte und Hegel*, Christopher Asmuth, Alfred Denker, and Michael Vater (Hrsg.) (Amsterdam and Philadelphia: B. R. Grüner, 2000) 313–15. Köhler is correct in seeing Heidegger as having more affinity with Nietzsche's voluntarism than Schelling's position. Heidegger's use of Schelling is more *via negativa* and doubtful. Ibid., 316.
150. Aschheim, *Nietzsche Legacy*, 267.
151. Ibid., 3.6, 8, 10, 18–19, 105, 259; 4.71–72, 205. Hereafter Heidegger's *Nietzsche* is designated as N. Heidegger finds Nietzsche's eternal recurrence of the same the "fundamental doctrine" of his philosophy. The doctrine finds an eternal displacement of any goal in life and accepts the inescapable and inevitable fact of suffering. (Nietzsche is never able to replace the "last man.") The present moment is the collision of the past and present, determining how everything recurs. It recognizes that the idiocy of the last man will recur over and over; he will constantly turn one's philosophy into

a trite ditty. N 2.6, 30–32, 57, 60, 75, 245–46. With this doctrine, Heidegger injects permanence (Being) into alteration (Becoming), making the infinite process of Heraclitus periodic. N 2.147; 3.173, 213. This doctrine goes along with the will to power and the revaluation of values, forming a fundamental unity as the final word of metaphysics. The eternal return "constitutes the ground and essence of the will to power," and the will to power "alone allows us to recognize what eternal return of the same means." N 1.18; 2.81, 165, 168, 199; 3.171.

152. N 1.4, 233; 2.190. In the essay "Nihilism as Determined by the History of Being" (written between 1944 and 1946, although not published until 1961), Heidegger begins his own denazification process by distancing himself from Nietzsche and his metaphysics. Heidegger says, metaphysics does not speak of the "truth of Being in a decisive way" or even raise the question of Being. In metaphysics, humans turn away from Being itself to onto-theology, which discusses the whatness of beings as such. Now Nietzsche's will to power represents the most extreme omission of Being itself, leaving Being completely outside (*ausbleiben*), withdrawn, and un-thought. N 4. 208, 211, 216, 220, 231, 238–39, 242–43, 261; Rockmore, *On Heidegger's Nazism and Philosophy*, 93–95. In his later work, he becomes more interested in the miracle of the naked experience of existence that "lets Being be" than providing a definitive explanation. Safranski, *Martin Heidegger*, 368, 427, 430.
153. N 1.60–61, 234; 3.152, 173–74, 194–99; 2.200; 3.52, 56, 60–64, 88–89, 116, 120, 235; 4.66. See N 1. 241–43.
154. N 3.245. See N 3.143–45.
155. N 3.190.
156. Heidegger, *Introduction to Metaphysics*, 46–50.
157. Safranski, *Martin Heidegger*, 226ff., 336ff., 341–42, 373; Kurt Sontheimer, *Antidemokratisches Denken in der Weimarer Republik* (München: Deutscher Taschenbuch-Verlag, 1978) 53, 262; Farías, *Heidegger and Nazism*, 210–11, 327 (n. 23).
158. N 3.91.
159. Hugo Otto, *Martin Heidegger: A Political Life*, Allan Blunden (trans.) (London: Basic Books, 1994) 338–39; Safranski, *Martin Heidegger*, 340–41, 373. Heidegger was not able to lecture until 1951.
160. N 3.333.
161. Heidegger, *Being and Time*, 163–66, 220, 224. There are times in *Being and Time* that he speaks of authenticity developing from a common heritage in the community. Heidegger, *Being and Time*, 436 (384); Rockmore, *On Heidegger's Nazism and Philosophy*, 48.
162. Safranski, *Martin Heidegger*, 66.
163. In his lecture series on Höderlin (1934/35, 1941/42) and Nietzsche, he strongly emphasizes this theme. Heidegger und Susan Ziegler, *Höderlins Hymnen "Germanien" und "Der Rhein"* (Frankfurt am Main: Vittorio Klostermann, 1980) 51; Rockmore, *On Heidegger's Nazism and Philosophy*, 129–30. The poet Höderlin was a favorite of the German people. Like Heidegger, he traces German roots and ideas back to Greece and hopes to accentuate the majesty of this tradition. Farías, *Heidegger and Nazism*, 268–75. Heidegger, *Introduction to Metaphysics*, 56–64.

164. Heidegger, *Introduction to Metaphysics*, 38–39; Jacques Derrida, *Of Spirit: Heidegger and the Question*, Geoffrey Bennington and Rachel Bowlby (trans.) (Chicago and London: Chicago University Press, 1989) 69–71; Farías, *Heidegger and Nazism*, 159; Lyotard, *Heidegger and the "jews,"* 71–72.
165. N 3.245.
166. N xxi–xxii; 3.46–47, 230–31; 4.269; Zimmerman, "Philosophy and Politics," 6–7, 14; Rockmore, *On Heidegger's Nazism and Philosophy*, 9; Farías, *Heidegger and Nazism*, 219–223. Heidegger seldom comments on Nietzsche's anti-Germanism, although he criticizes him one time as *undeutsch*. N xiii. His wife seems to follow a more literal Germanism. Heidegger-Petri, "Gedanken einer Mutter über Höhere Mädchenbildung" (1935), in *Heiddegger und der Nationalsozialismus I: Dokumente*, Alfred Denker and Holger Zaborowski (Hrsg.) (Freiburg und München: Karl Alber GmbH, 2002) 2–3; Farías, *Heidegger and Nazism*, 230ff. Sometimes he saw European thought and culture destined to dominate the world. N 250–51.
167. Schneeberger, *Nachlese zu Heidegger*, 74.
168. Safranski, *Martin Heidegger*, 272; N xxix.
169. N 1.208; 3.217, 226.
170. N 2.182.
171. N 2. 127–28, 175, 215; 3.202–3, 229, 239–40; 4.4, 80–81, 98–99.
172. Safranski, *Martin Heidegger*, 140, 378; Farías, *Heidegger and Nazism*, 230–33.
173. Ibid., 254; Zimmerman, "Philosophy and Politics," 214; Rockmore, *On Heidegger's Nazism and Philosophy*, 111. Karl Jaspers and many others find his actions equivocal in regard to individual Jewish students and colleagues. Heidegger will reject the expulsion of Jews from the university and posting the "Jewish notice," yet express concern over the increased number of Jews at the university and generally shun them after 1933. *Notizen zu Martin Heidegger*, Hans Saner (Hrsg.) (München und Zurich: R. Piper & Co., 1978) 46 (18) with 273 (note 18); 257 (241) with 324 (note 241); "Nur noch ein Gott kann uns retten," 196; Rockmore, *On Heidegger's Nazism and Philosophy*, 82, 111.
174. Ibid., 257; Farías, *Heidegger and Nazism*, xi. There is only one exception, found in an obscure lecture, where he compares extermination and agrarian technology in the modern world. Lyotard tries to make an elaborate excuse for Heidegger's silence, saying the event was caught in his subconscious level and could not be represented in his "existential-ontological approach," which makes Auschwitz and the Jews impossible to name. *Heidegger and the "jews,"* 12, 19, 22, 39, 76–77.
175. "Nur noch ein Gott kann uns retten," 196, 198, 201, 204; N ix; Rockmore, *On Heidegger's Nazism and Philosophy*, 25–26, 82, 118, 172, 284; Zimmerman, "Philosophy and Politics," 4–5; Farías, *Heidegger and Nazism*, 251; Aschheim, *Nietzsche Legacy*, 255. Some scholars like Arendt, Aubenque, and Krell think Heidegger turned from Nazism in these lectures, but there is no clear evidence of this turning beyond a few comments on technology, "biologism," etc. Hannah Arendt, *The Life of the Mind: Willing* (New York and London: Harcourt Brace Jovanovich, 1978) 172ff.; Pierre Aubenque, "Encore Heidegger et le nazisme," *Le Débat* 48 (Jan./Feb.): 121.

176. N 1.245; 2.87, 211; Rockmore, *On Heidegger's Nazism and Philosophy*, 151. The content of the work *Nietzsche* includes lectures on "The Will to Power as Art" (1936/37); "The Eternal Recurrence of the Same" and "Who is Zarathustra" (1937); "The Will to Power as Knowledge," "The Eternal Recurrence of the Same and the Will to Power," and "Nietzsche's Metaphysics" (1939/40); "European Nihilism" and "Nihilism as Determined by the History of Being" (1940, 1944–46).
177. Rockmore, *On Heidegger's Nazism and Philosophy*, 35, 284–85.

9

Biblical Criticism and Liberal Theology

The modern era brought much criticism to the traditional understanding of the Christian faith. Some of the criticism proved helpful in withstanding the biblicism of orthodoxy and providing a more sober analysis of the human fingerprints within the text of scripture, but the positive results of the research were overshadowed by the anti-Semitic and anti-Christian agenda in too many instances and often brought little more than rancor to society. Deists arose in England and France, bringing an unrelenting criticism to the Bible, exhibiting for the most part a desire to undermine the historical integrity of the revelation and replace its specific teachings on salvation with an eternal message of universal morality.[1] This attack upon the historic faith permeated much of intelligentsia and found academic credence in Germany among the universities, which served as the standard-bearers of this type of excessive criticism for the rest of culture.[2] Eventually most of the Protestant churches became liberal, following the verdict of modern scholarship, and found it necessary to compromise their message at the beginning of the twentieth century.[3] Groups like the Nazis only followed and extended the scholarship in a more extreme direction, hoping to bastardize the religion or completely destroy and replace it with something anti-Christian.[4]

Immanuel Kant (1724–1804), the greatest of all modern philosophers, represented and instilled this new concept of religion in German academia at the end of the eighteenth century. He followed the spirit of the Enlightenment and moved away from the traditional understanding of the faith toward Deism, discounting the historical content of scripture, rejecting its miraculous account of the past, and repudiating the need for divine assistance or grace in the present. He felt that true religion had no need to wait for a special moment of divine intervention, in answer to pray, or trust in a blood atonement and "pious plays things" like the "means of grace." True religion is always, generally, and readily available to all of humankind through the use of "universal reason" and demands repentance and an "improved life" to find salvation, not the bestowal of cheap grace from a source outside of one's own God-given abilities. In this way Kant makes moral improvement the real end of religion and reduces the Christian faith to moral concern like many of his contemporaries. He exhorts the interpreters of scripture to search the text for its essential message of eternal, universal, and moral value, and discard all else as the wood, hay, and stubble of temporal, ephemeral concern.[5]

Liberal Theology

This spirit began to permeate much of academia and the church at the turn of the century. Friedrich Schleiermacher (1768–1834) represented the new intellectual climate more than any other theologian, serving as a midwife in bringing much of the church into the modern world and helping to answer the many enlightened criticisms by making the doctrine of the church more defensible and acceptable to the "cultured despisers."[6] He thought it was unfair to discount the Christian faith as many of the sons of the Enlightenment because of the outward shell of orthodox confessions. No system of propositional statements can express the kernel of true religious affection, as its object lies beyond the adequacy of any outward form or expression.[7] Theology is an expression of faith, not the faith itself. Even the words of scripture have no independent authority and infallibility as if serving in place of Christ as the basis of the Christian faith. Christ is the real revelation of God. The scripture serves as an expression of faith in him, but its authority can never replace Christ and ever remains subject to certain imperfections and the scrutiny of scientific analysis. This means that certain parts of scripture are less valuable than others in expressing the essence of the faith and should be criticized, if not purged from the text. The OT should be excised in its entirety from the canon of the church because it is farthest removed from the immediate experience of God's revelation in Christ and subject to much error.[8] The church needs to rid the taint of Judaism from its confessions.

> If we consider the Church during the Apostolic Age as a unity, its thinking as a whole cannot supply a norm for that of later ages. For owing to its naturally most unequal distribution of the divine Spirit, as well as to the further fact that not everyone was equally productive in religious ideas even in the measure of his participation in the common spirit, it was very easily possible (since Jewish and pagan views and maxims were still uneradicated and their antagonism to the Christian spirit could only be recognized gradually) that expositions of religion might be produced which, strictly speaking, were rather Judaism or paganism coloured by Christianity than Christianity itself, *i.e.* were, if considered as Christian, in the highest degree impure. Contemporary with all this very imperfect material, however, were the presentations given in preaching by the immediate disciples of Christ. In their case, the danger of an unconsciously debasing influence from their previous Jewish forms of thought and life on the presentation of Christianity by word and act was averted, in proportion as they had stood near to Christ, by the purifying influence of their living memory of Christ as a whole.[9]

Christ's teaching was an "absolutely original revelation of God," which neither fulfilled nor purified the Mosaic law.[10]

Schleiermacher goes on to find the source of religion within the innermost wellspring of our being. The outward profession of faith only represents a fallible witness to what arises deep within us and consists of heartfelt dispositions and feelings of "being absolutely dependent" upon God.[11] This emphasis upon religious feelings allows Schleiermacher to insulate the substance of the faith and spare it from any decisive criticism affecting its validity. The cultural despisers can deprecate all of its overt forms in word and deed as much as they wish, but their assault can never touch what is most essential because true religion remains within the chambers of the heart and its secret messages. "The heart knows its reason, which reason does not know."[12] Faith is a simple development of human nature, which remains unaltered from its original orientation by the sin of the first parents and functions undiminished as a continuous aspect of life.[13] Humans are able to find God at any moment through this capacity because divine revelation is always and everywhere present throughout the world. All is miracle; all is divine. Life becomes miraculous once the religious view becomes dominant and recognizes the God who was present all along in the perfection of the world.[14] This means that God-consciousness is excited by world-consciousness, as it apprehends God in the ordinary course of life, not just a few miraculous events, sacred sources, or prophetic heroes.[15]

The most significant summary of the liberal theological position was delivered by the great church historian Adolf Harnack in a series of lectures, entitled *Das Wesen des Christentums*, from 1899–1900.[16] This series follows much of Schleiermacher's liberal understanding of the faith and its emphasis upon pure inward devotion as the most essential element of true religion. Harnack rejects the traditional understanding of orthodox theology because it clings to the outward forms of the faith, which are limited to the times and conditions of their expression. It is better to recognize the problematic nature of all theological systems and try to remove the kernel from the temporal husk than remain stagnant within the expressions of the past.[17]

Even the words of Jesus are subject to this type of analysis. They are limited to the conditions of his time and must be cleansed from the depravity of his Jewish background in order to find the inward message. By separating the wheat from the chaff, Harnack believes Christians can cleanse the church of destructive elements and find what is essential in three basic thrusts of Jesus's gospel. The first thrust involves Jesus's belief in an inward, present kingdom among all people, laying claim to souls, ruling in hearts, and dominating the whole of existence. Jesus might share some of the eudaemonic expectations of the Jews, who longed for a mundane kingdom of external rule in the future, but the thrust of his message is directed toward spiritual matters of eternal concern. The second thrust concerns his exaltation of God as Father and the infinite value of people's souls as children of God. This concept thinks of all humans as precious in the eyes of God and spurns the OT image of the Almighty as a cruel and capricious despot, choosing Israel as a unique possession and condemning all those who exist outside the camp to divine wrath. Even Jesus is no longer the focus of worship, since his gospel centers upon the exaltation of the Father and not his own person as if possessing a divine nature or unique relationship to God in any ontological sense. The third and final thrust concerns his emphasis in the Sermon on the Mount upon a higher righteousness and love command, where acts of mercy replace the harmful effect of Jewish ritualism, legalism, and justice. This emphasis continues in NT times with Paul's attempt to deliver Christianity from Judaism and so separate the gospel from the law.[18] Harnack hopes the church continues the process of de-Judafication and considers eliminating the OT from its sacred canon in light of the crippling effect this remnant of Judaism exerts upon the fellowship. One must dig through mountains of Jewish material before finding anything interesting or valuable for the edification of the church.[19]

OT Criticism

Julius Wellhausen provided Harnack and other liberal scholars with the most impressive and influential statement concerning the nature of the OT scripture within their cultural milieu. Wellhausen admits his strong aversion to Judaism, the priestly caste, and its emphasis upon law, antecedent to his own specific studies in the OT—an aversion he shared with many Enlightenment and post-Enlightenment scholars, who provided him with crucial elements of his theory.[20] Wellhausen provides his own testimony to some of these scholars—Karl Heinrich Graf, Eduard Reuss, J. F. L. George, Wilhelm Vatke, Abraham Kuenen, and Martin Lebrecht deWette—as pioneers in the field,[21] but it is his name that remains most associated with the theory for providing it with unprecedented academic credence and status.

Much of Wellhausen's work is predicated upon his obsession with deprecating Judaism, hoping to contrast its legalistic adulteration of true religion with the real history of ancient Israel, which he sees as more profane, free, and individualistic in its religious affections.[22] Like Nietzsche, he prefers a more natural image of human beings, connected to the concrete elements of this world, and accuses Jewish priests of rewriting the history of ancient Israel and denaturalizing its people through later religious themes of reward and punishment, sin and atonement, salvation and moral judgment.[23] The old layer of scripture relates disjointed stories of passionate individuals, who breathed the free air of their own natural impulses and acted outside the well-ordered lives, accounts, and moralistic judgments of priestly narratives. Their feasts grew out of the same agrarian interests of their neighbors in Canaan, asking God for good weather and fertility, dedicating the first fruits in return for divine blessing. Their sacrifices were considered festive occasions of joy and merriment, where a local family or clan celebrated a meal with Jehovah and established a covenant bond, with little mention of propitiation or guilt. There was no priestly code to moralize the proceedings or offer a detailed list of rules and regulations to bind the consciousness of a worshipper under a centralized authority. The patriarchs worshipped Jehovah wherever "I cause my name to be honored" (Exod 20:24), erecting their own spontaneous altars, memorial stones, tamarisk trees, and high places (*bamoth*) at the site of the epiphany. There was no tabernacle or resting place for the ark, providing a prescribed location for worship prior to the building of the temple, and it was not until the fall of the Northern Kingdom that the prophets spoke of God's dwelling place on Mt. Zion. Any condemnation of the high places (*bamoth*) before this time is a fictitious interpolation of postexilic Judaism, looking back at the past in terms of its present religious understanding (1 Kgs 14:22ff.).[24]

The most radical change took place during the times of Josiah's revival in 621 BCE. It was at this time that the call for the centralization of worship rang out to the countryside, and the first destruction of local altars took place (2 Kgs 23). The pretext for this desecration was the "discovery" of the "Book of the Law in the temple of the Lord," which demanded the destruction of these idolatrous shrines and the consecration of one, true, and monotheistic place to worship in Jerusalem (2 Kgs 22; Deut 12). Wellhausen thinks the book in question was Deuteronomy and believes most of it was actually written at the time to justify the measures of the reform. The book represents a significant change in the religion of the people, being the first important attempt at written Torah, bringing an end to religious freedom and charismatic prophecy, and so halting the spiritual development of ancient Israel. This new emphasis severed Judaism from its sacred roots in ancient Israel and provided Wellhausen with the pretext to say that the "law of Moses" is the starting point for the history of Judaism, not the history of Israel.[25]

After the Jews returned from exile in the sixth century BCE, the transformation was completed, and they became the "people of the book." In 444 BCE, Ezra and the postexilic community added the priestly code to the previous strata of the emerging canon and completed the first five books of the Bible, or Pentateuch. Moses was made the author of these books and transformed from his image in the earliest stratum of the Pentateuch as a priest and prophet into the greatest of all legislators, in order to provide the work with the requisite historical authority. According to Wellhausen, "there never have been more audacious history-makers than the Rabbins. . . . [T]his evil propensity goes back to a very early time, its root the dominating influence of the Law, being the root of Judaism itself."[26] The priests and rabbis of the postexilic community are most responsible for doctoring the OT and repainting its history with legalistic religion, zealous monotheism, miraculous stories, redemptive events, sacred festivals, and a sacrificial system of sin and atonement. Their priestly code adds this material and purifies the legends of old to create an artificial harmony with the newfangled religion. Thereafter, the people become slaves to the "clergy." The priests receive their sacrifices and tithes in Jerusalem. The scribes gain dominion over the people by continuing to expand the law, making it cover every aspect of their lives.[27] The leaders of the religious community are deprecated for their will to power and made the scapegoat for all the ills of the society—a theme that resonated throughout Europe after the times of the Enlightenment.

It is difficult to say whether these prejudices against Judaism deserve a pejorative term like anti-Semitism. In defending Wellhausen, one should mention that he never identified with Heinrich von Treitschke, Adolf Stoecker, or any of the anti-Semitic activists during his lifetime; he questions the hatred of Jews in a couple of his letters; he never uttered any specific anti-Semitic comments as far as we know; and he treated students and colleagues from the Jewish community with personal respect and dignity.[28] However, his outward decorum is not sufficient to dismiss concerns about his deep-seated prejudices, which skew his own scholarly assessment of the religion and influence others to act upon it. His antagonism toward Judaism develops from an intense dislike for legalism, and it fails to appreciate the breadth of the Jewish tradition outside the law.[29] His obsession with the Jews rewriting their own history fails to appreciate his own post-Enlightenment religious prejudices in rewriting the history of Israel and Judaism in terms of the current obsession with priests, laws, and the Jewish faith. Maybe, Wellhausen can contain his prejudices and divide between the sin and sinner as a "good" Christian by continuing to love Jews in spite of everything they represent in their religion, but he clearly influences others like the Nazis, who use his theory and find it more difficult to preserve a simple distinction between a person's worth and their way of living.[30] He might not approve of specific acts of anti-Semitism, but his work helps create a climate of hatred toward the Jewish faith that is growing and leading toward a more personal hatred of its people.[31]

NT Criticism

German intellectuals also began to undermine the authority of the church and NT through a fastidious analysis of the canonical Gospels. This process of "higher criticism" began like a thunderclap in the Promethean work of Hermann Samuel Reimarus (1694–1768), a professor of Oriental Languages in the Hamburg Gymnasium. Reimarus fell under the spell of English Deism and became one of the first to bring their rationalism, skepticism, and many doubts about the Christian faith to German soil.[32] He wrote a number of works during his lifetime, defending the claims of rational religion, but his notoriety resides elsewhere in a more negative work, which spends its time attacking the historical integrity of the Christian faith—a work that was so problematic and perilous that it was circulated as an anonymous manuscript among only a few acquaintances at first. It was only after his death that a significant portion of it was published by Gotthold Lessing in a series of fragments (1774–1778), causing an instant outcry in many quarters and incurring the special attention and wrath of Johann Melchior Goetze, the chief pastor of Hamburg.[33] The magnum opus of the collection was entitled *The Goal of Jesus and His Disciples*, a fragment that went beyond other Deists and rationalists in attacking Jesus of Nazareth as a materialistic, power-hungry Jew.[34]

In this fragment, Reimarus presents Jesus first and foremost as a product of Jewish culture. Jesus's teachings were consonant with the fundamental understanding of the OT and its laws among his people. He never attempted to dispel the customs and ceremonies of the Jewish faith nor establish new ones in their place, like Paul and the other apostles. He based his whole ministry upon fulfilling the law and the prophets (Matt 5:17–19), not destroying the scripture and substituting another religion of "new and unknown articles of faith and mysteries." When Jesus preached the dawning of the kingdom of God, the Jews understood him in the customary manner of their culture, and Jesus sought to fulfill their very expectations as a Jewish and worldly Messiah. He had no plans of developing a mission to the Gentiles and grafting them into a spiritual kingdom. He appealed to the base materialistic appetites of the Jewish people, offering them deliverance from bondage to the Romans and dominance over other nations in the coming political order. He offered to his disciples the same type of worldly treasures, including a glorious throne to judge the twelve tribes of Israel and an opulent table of food and drink at the messianic banquet.[35] In all this, Reimarus depicts the Jews, in the typical manner of Voltaire, Bolingbroke, and the sons of the Enlightenment, as having insatiable material and temporal appetites with no interest in genuine spirituality and no fear of facing moral judgment in another world.

It is only after his death that the disciples reject the image of a worldly deliverer and transform Jesus into a spiritual Savior. The historical Jesus had no thought of suffering to bind the hand of God or offering himself as a sacrifice for sin, but he died on a cross all alone, blaming God for his own failure to lead a successful messianic revolt against the Romans. This tragic end made it necessary for the disciples to fabricate a new system for understanding their fallen leader if they still wanted to partake of the secular exaltation that Jesus promised and failed to deliver. This time the disciples hoped to receive the same type of honor and riches that Jesus promised through their own cunning and wits. Their scheme involved a plot to dupe others into believing in a joyous salvation of heavenly bliss, asking them to sacrifice their possessions for admission, and then skimming the proceeds. This scam started immediately after the death of Jesus, as a massive, behind-closed-door conspiracy to steal the body of Jesus, keep it secret for fifty days, and then claim the disciples saw him alive during that period, when no one could prove otherwise. After this, they can read back into the life of Jesus stories confirming their new spiritual system with predictions of the death and resurrection, the fulfillment of messianic prophecy, and the proclamation of a spiritual kingdom—all now exemplified in the words, actions, and events of his life.[36] And yet, Reimarus finds the conspiracy easy to unravel. Like many liberal scholars after him, he enjoys enumerating the many different contradictions in the alleged witnesses; he finds the claims about the divine nature of Jesus and his ability to perform miraculous feats inflated by the later tradition, if not completely incredulous;[37] and he likes to deprecate the NT's nonliteral use of the OT, wrenching passages out of context and forcing them into the life of Jesus.[38]

The most celebrated work of this new genre of liberal literature was David Strauss's *The Life of Jesus* (1835). This book brought instant notoriety and earned him a reputation in the course of time as the most significant NT scholar of the nineteenth century, but it was not without some personal hardship in an era that was less than tolerant toward his radical ideas.[39] He suffered continual attacks from the ecclesiastical establishment and was unable to sustain a professional career, even losing an appointment to a vacant chair at the University of Zurich because of the protests.[40] After the episode, he made a pitiful attempt to amend his work and reconcile it to a more acceptable left-wing piety of the day, but none of the concessions proved sufficient to silence the critics. His third edition (1838) displays the groveling at its worst, where he claims to have learned much from his opponents' criticisms and now possesses a new found respect for the "historical, personal Christ," who is more than a myth or symbol. He can even stoop low enough to express his appreciation for the portrait of Jesus in the Gospel of John and exalt this Son of God in terms reminiscent of Schleiermacher and liberalism, professing his unique relationship to God and development as a religious individual. But none of this ingratiated him to the church, and so he returned to his former, more cynical position in the fourth and final edition (1839–40), believing he was too compliant with his opponents and needed to restore the unity and integrity of what he presented in the original work. At the end of his life, he remained a controversial figure in the church, but he helped move much of it toward a more critical position and garnered considerable respect from the academic establishment, which tended to accept many of the ideas presented in the great work.[41]

According to his own testimony, the fundamental purpose and result of his work is largely negative. He believes that his critical analysis destroys the possibility of finding any grace or salvation in Jesus Christ and reduces humankind to the dust of the ground, without any hope of receiving consolations or ailments from the heavens above.

> The results of the inquiry which we have now brought to a close, have apparently annihilated the greatest and most valuable part of that which the Christian has been wont to believe concerning his Savior Jesus, have uprooted all the animating motives which he has gathered

> from his faith, and withered all his consolations. The boundless store of truth and life which for eighteen centuries has been the aliment of humanity, seems irretrievably dissipated; the most sublime leveled with the dust, God divested of his grace, man of his dignity, and the tie between heaven and earth broken.[42]

He never offers any positive portrait of Jesus to understand who exactly he was in history and spends much of his time developing as many contradictions as possible—real or imaginary—between the different accounts in the Gospels to undermine their authority and history, even finding contradictions in the same Evangelist, like the description of Jesus's raised body in corporeal and incorporeal terms, appearing and disappearing, eating with the disciples and yet passing through walls. He emphasizes the contradictions to display the unreliability of the accounts, discredit their historicity, and underscore the Evangelists' active imagination in developing the stories. According to Strauss, the Gospel accounts are little more than mythological stories, concocted over a hundred years after the death of Jesus and designed to exalt him as the founder of a later community in their own theological terms. The most reliable of the Synoptic Gospels is Matthew, and then comes Luke and Mark, respectively, although none of them are based on eyewitness testimony or apostolic authority. The Gospel of John is mainly a "free composition" in the style of its author's words, not those of Jesus, and based upon Alexandrian categories and dichotomies like father/son, light/darkness, life/death, and spirit/flesh.[43]

Strauss brings forth the term *mythus* as the fundamental means of understanding the nature of the Gospel account. *Mythus* is the means that older civilizations used to explain phenomena in its prescientific world, but this type of explanation no longer resonates as a plausible alternative for an enlightened culture. Any talk of divine intervention is an antiquated product of ancient mythology and lacks credibility in today's modern way of thinking. The miraculous stories of scripture cannot be accepted at face value and must be understood as *mythus*. Interpreting them in a supernatural or natural manner, as if they possess a real basis in historical fact, fails to appreciate the true mythological origin of the account. Because of this, Strauss goes on to reject the enlightened works of Heinrich Paulus and other rationalists, who try to reconcile the Gospels with modern scientific reasoning by discounting the miraculous elements in the accounts but sparing the basic history. This school of thought sees the Gospels as relating a basic core of facts from eyewitnesses, who were unfamiliar with secondary causality and mistook certain natural events as supernatural or miraculous interventions from metaphysical forces. Thus, the story of the virgin birth is not pure *mythus* but has a real historical basis in the pious imagination of a young woman, who thought God was working with her during the pregnancy. The star of Bethlehem comes from the conjunction of planets; the feeding of the multitudes from the secret provisions of Jesus; and the resurrection transpires after Jesus swoons on the cross, only to revive later on through careful medical attention, or just the cool of the cave. Of course, Strauss ridicules all these explanations, finding them just as implausible as the brute miracle, and he prefers to reduce the miraculous episodes to the pure mythological imagination of the later church. He is heartened that some scholars now admit the concept of *mythus* into the infancy and ascension narratives, but he wants the program extended to include the events in between the beginning and end of the story.[44] He claims this method will not damage the eternal truth of the Gospels, just the historical truth, and points to the work of Origen and Kant as looking for what is universal beyond the literal sense,[45] but Strauss never proceeds in developing this deeper insight out of the text, leaving the reader with just a plethora of negative criticisms.

Strauss excludes the supernatural explanation of the account a priori. He refuses to consider the possibility of real miracles transpiring in the life of Jesus as worthy of historical investigation, based upon the fundamental scientific paradigm of his day, which saw the universe running like a machine with mechanical, interrelated, and inviolable laws.[46] Any talk of divine intervention must be excluded from the outset as unhistorical, since the laws of causality are a fixed tissue withstanding any possibility of an intrusion from without.[47] Even if some of the biblical miracles have a historical basis, these events are embellished beyond recognition by legendary superstition.[48] For example, the story about the resurrection might have some antecedent basis in the actual experiences of the disciples, who fled the city of Jerusalem after the death of Jesus and could create some fantasies about him coming back to life in the distant region of Galilee, where no corpse existed to contradict this type of enthusiasm. Other disciples like Paul, might have experienced internal visions that were embellished much later into palpable external appearances of the risen Christ.[49]

Strauss also excludes the prophetic material in the Gospels as soothsaying after the event (*vaticinium post eventum*). Jesus's predictions concerning his resurrection are placed into his mouth by zealous followers trying to establish their inflated estimation of him as Risen Lord. In fact, all the fulfillments of prophecy, as recorded in the NT, are soothsaying after the event and typically based on the "groundless arbitrariness of Jewish exegesis," which finds types from OT passages to match whatever blinds their eyes in the present with messianic enthusiasm. There is absolutely no evidence that Jesus was born in Bethlehem, but in order to fulfill the messianic prophecy in Micah 5:2, the Gospel of Luke creates the need for a census and brings Mary and Joseph to the town. The star of Bethlehem is invented in the Gospel of Matthew to fulfill the prophecy of Balaam (Num 24:17) and couple it with the birth of other great leaders in ancient times—all accompanied by astral phenomena. The temptation story is concocted from prefigured stories about Israel's forty years in the wilderness, Elijah's forty days fleeing to Mt. Sinai, and other tales of old. Miracles like feeding the multitudes, curing the afflicted by a word, and raising the dead all have a prototype in the ministry of Elijah and Elisha. The Passion narratives bring together a number of passages out of the OT, including Psalms 22, Isaiah 53, and Zechariah 9:9, and demonstrate the need for the Messiah to "suffer many things" (Matt 16:21).[50]

Strauss certainly accepts that the historical Jesus was a part of the messianic and apocalyptic expectations of the day, just not as he was portrayed by the later church. All the miracles of his ministry resulted from the popular expectations concerning the messianic age and have some reference to the historical Jesus, even if they were multiplied and inflated into supernatural events through the faith of his later followers. Jesus seemed to follow the popular expectation and gradually adopted the role of Messiah, but he preferred to let God or a supernatural apocalypse usher in any political kingdom and limited his own participation to the moral and spiritual sphere. Eventually his principles led him to suffer for the sake of the kingdom and die a tragic death on a cross, believing he would come back in glory during the lifetime of his disciples, but he was wrong and perished along with his many promises, just like any other false Messiah. This tragic ending completed the story of all Jewish/messianic attempts to withstand the power of Rome in the first century, and would complete the story of Jesus if not for the vivid imagination of his disciples. Following the analysis of Reimarus, Strauss blames the disciples for turning the death of Jesus into a redemptive event and envisioning him seated at the right hand of the Father in glory as both Lord and Savior of a spiritual kingdom. Strauss refuses to accept this image as a faithful representation of the historical Jesus and refuses to venerate him in any other way as worthy of special accolades. He even refuses to pay homage unto Jesus as a great human teacher and ends up devoting only one chapter to this subject—much in contrast to the liberals and rationalists of the day, who also rejected the image of a wonder-worker and Savior but still continued to follow him as the greatest of all moral philosophers.[51]

In his final work, *The Old Faith & the New* (1872), he spends much of his time casting aspersions on the Christian faith. He is hoping to develop a new vision for the future in this work, which makes room for modern science and finds as much acceptance as his critical work of Jesus,[52] but he spends most of his time disparaging Christianity and offers little of substance as a positive alternative. He rejects the many compromises that rationalism has made with Christianity in the country and extols Voltaire and Reimarus as the pillars of the modern era for their uncompromising assault upon the religion.[53] Strauss continues the barrage, maintaining that Christianity is built on a foundation of wood, hay, and stubble. We know practically nothing about the founder of the faith, beyond the fantastic reports of the second-century church, and what we know about him is filled with questionable tendencies toward apocalyptic "fanaticism and self-glorification."[54] Jesus might not be so ambitious as Reimarus portrayed him, "eager to thrust himself forward as an earthy Messiah," but he certainly was "no son of God as the Christian dogma has it."[55] Strauss also continues his polemic against Schleiermacher's Christology and his own compromise with that position in the third edition of the *Life of Jesus*, maintaining that Jesus is circumscribed within the limits of his own time and cannot speak for the whole human race as a single individual. In the fourth edition, Strauss recognized this problem and developed a Hegelian solution by believing the incarnation or unity of God and man envelops all of humanity, not just an isolated individual.[56] There he preferred the Hegelian *Aufhebung* of Christ, which treats the incarnation, crucifixion, and resurrection not so much as historical facts or past events, but rather it lifts them up into a present, eternal, and spiritual reality.[57] But in the *Old Faith & the New*, he no longer possesses this kind of faith and begins to disparage religion in general as the ignorance of infancy in a race of people, hoping to replace it with a more sober philosophical acumen. Today the origin of life is explained through the Darwinian theory of evolution and no longer needs the magic of metaphysical mumbo jumbo to fill in the gaps of knowledge with a *deus ex machina*. Life no longer has any room for divine intervention. It no longer serves any purpose or goal, as if created with any specific intendment or value, and yet, Strauss hesitates in reaching a final, nihilistic conclusion. He tries to rescue the necessity of moral value in life and engages in extensive political discussions, as if they make an important moral difference. He approves of nationalism as a proper response to Napoleon's invasion of Germany, the cultivation of great spirits through a monarchical system against the cosmopolitan melting pot of America, the rights of family and property against egalitarian movements, and war as an inevitable part of natural selection and growth.[58] Nietzsche finds this all amusing and chastens him for inconsistency, trying to retain the idea of a moral universe, while holding to a Darwinian view of nature,[59] but the problems also plague the work of this self-proclaimed "Antichrist" and all those who follow the same course. Both Strauss and Nietzsche end up preaching anti-Christianity and have difficulty finding a positive message for their audience to escape the dark consequences of criticizing everything and believing nothing.

Strauss's work helped to spawn a popular genre of literature about the life of Jesus, written from a liberal perspective and intended to reach the culture at large with the latest scholarship.[60] Among the most popular of these works was Ernest Renan's *Life of Jesus* (1863), which generated eleven editions and a number of translations during the first five months of its release! The book was written for a popular audience, with a simple style, sentimental appeal, and aesthetic texture, often neglecting the rigors and details of professional scholarship, but it was respected by Strauss and other academicians in spite of its pitfalls and enjoyed a wide influence throughout Europe well into the twentieth century. Its author was born at Tréguier, Brittany, in 1823 and studied for the priesthood in Paris, where he fell under the influence of German higher criticism and developed considerable doubts about the orthodox faith. He later became a professor of Semitic Languages at the Collège de France in 1862, only to be removed when his book appeared the following year. In 1871 he was restored to his previous position as his skepticism gained him the type of infamy and respect that the French tended to adore in their persecuted celebrities. A couple decades later, when he died in 1892, he was "already half-forgotten by the public; until his imposing funeral and interment in the Panthéon recalled him to its memory."[61]

Renan's work received these accolades because it was a product of its times, representing all that post-Enlightenment society adored about its author and subject. Toward the end of the century, scholars like Albert Schweitzer and Wolfgang Kirchbach began to criticize this intimate relationship, accusing Renan and so many other authors of adapting their studies to the "needs of the men in the street" and "making a Jesus after [their] image." In the absence of objective criteria, even the best of scholars used Jesus as a "receptacle into which every theologian pours his own ideas."[62] The nineteenth century never developed a simple way to discern what was historical and unhistorical in the Gospels, and the visceral prejudices of the authors and audience too often ruled the day in manufacturing a portrait of Jesus that matched their own cultural tastes. In Renan's account, Jesus sounds much like a nineteenth-century post-Enlightenment figure, not an actual Jew living in the first century, reducing religion to morality, advocating an inward spiritual kingdom as the most essential kernel of the message, and denouncing Jewish legalism and materialism all together. In certain passages, Renan presents Jesus as the complete antithesis of Judaism, maintaining that "the special task of Jesus was to break with the Jewish spirit," like Socrates broke with the Sophists and Luther with the Middle Ages.[63] The Jews are depicted as having a fanatical attachment to their own narrow institutions, people, and materialistic advantage as if they had the only true religion worthy of divine blessing, and Christianity becomes "more and more" like Jesus in separating itself from the Jewish past.[64] Like Chamberlain and the Nazis, Renan entertains the real possibility that Jesus was not Jewish at all, since he comes from Galilee of the Gentiles, where the population was very mixed during his lifetime, with "Phoenicians, Syrians, Arabs, and even Greeks" existing in the region.[65] Like any son of the Enlightenment, Renan focuses special attention upon Jewish priests as the greatest enemies of religious liberty and sees Jesus as laying the "eternal-foundation" of true religion by attacking these hypocrites and treating them as his greatest enemies.[66] Like a nineteenth-century liberal, Jesus withstood the sacrificial system and its many ceremonies by emphasizing moral values and preaching an inward, present, and spiritual kingdom. Jesus was the greatest moral teacher in human history, preaching the love of all humankind, the universal

Fatherhood of God, and the spiritual kingdom of the heart.[67] "He feels himself close to God, and draws from his own heart all that he says of his Father." He might think of himself as having a unique relationship to God and entertain titles like "Messiah," "Son of David," and "Son of God" later on in his ministry, but he never claimed a special divine sonship in any ontological sense that would deify his person and remove others from the possibility of experiencing this unique relationship with the Father. He might try to perform miracles, submitting to the expectation of the people and recognizing that many great religious movements were started with a certain amount of chicanery, but these instances are multiplied and transfigured by the later legend. The vivid imagination of Mary Magdalene probably played an important role in creating the myth of his resurrection from the dead. Paul and the church transformed his death and resurrection even farther by turning them into a cosmic event of redemption, converting the simple carpenter into a divine Savior and diminishing his true divine mission.[68] The Jesus of history remains a simple moral teacher of spiritual values, despite all the metaphysical dogma of the church, just like any English Deist, German liberal, and son of the French Enlightenment would have him.

The Jewish Question

Some of the German biblical scholars used their historical, critical understanding of Judaism to address the *Judenfrage* (Jewish question) in European society. Heinrich Paulus, the polemical opponent of Strauss, was one of these theologians who used an enlightened or rational understanding of religion to address the issue. Like many other scholars of the day, he applied his knowledge to this and a wide variety of topics during his long career as a professor at Jena, Würzburg, and Meidelberg, which included a famous two-volume work on the *Life of Jesus* in 1828 that explained the miracles of Jesus as the delusions of his disciples and drew much criticism from Strauss.[69] In 1831, he published a book entitled *Die jüdische Nationalabsonderung*, which tackles one of the most difficult political questions of the day: how can Jews become citizens in the emerging states of Europe when they typically live as a separate people with their own set of customs and laws?

Paulus follows the basic direction of the French Revolution in answering this question and finds it unwise to provide the Jews with full citizenship (*Staatsbürgerschaft*) unless they give up their peculiar customs and adopt the ways of the state. People cannot expect to become full citizens of a country and obtain the right to rule over others when they belong to another nation or subsist like the Jews in Europe as a nation within a nation. A Christian land cannot tolerate a Jew or Turk ruling over it and prescribing laws that oppose the basic traditions and customs of the land. It cannot have rulers who think of their own Jewish people as elected above all others and pray for a Messiah to come and smite their gentile neighbors. Jews are not worthy of the privileges that come with citizenship in this land, as long as they continue to follow divisive attitudes and customs. They may enjoy the protection of the state (*Schutzbürgerschaft*). They may enjoy the protection of their property and freedom of religious expression, as long as they pay their taxes and fulfill certain obligations that come with it, but these privileges cannot translate into full citizenship until they decide to merge with the state's traditions and become a people of the land, not just the people of the book.[70]

Paulus sees Judaism as the basic stumbling block in this process because it serves as a means of keeping its people segregated from others, making it impossible for them to unite or mix with another nation. The rabbinic traditions developed this mind-set by viewing the Gentiles as totally unclean and creating a labyrinth of procedures to keep the chosen people holy or separate from the contamination of their presence. Jesus and Paul tried to liberate the Jewish people from this bigotry and preached a universal religion of inward spirituality, but to no avail. The Jews preferred to remain within the structures of their legalistic, separatistic, and materialistic religion and to wait for a different Messiah, who would grant them an earthly paradise over the rest of the world.[71]

To make progress toward citizenship, the Jews must stop identifying their religion with the law. The state can tolerate different religious beliefs, but it cannot allow unlawful behavior or forward a different set of rules for a different group of people. The Jews are more than capable of fulfilling this necessary requirement and distinguishing religion from the law since the real foundation and origin of their religion goes back to Abraham, not Moses and the law. The Mosaic economy provided a temporal law that related to the circumstances of the people at the time of its enactment, with only the Decalogue offering an eternal message for all times and places. The legalization of the religion was a much later development, during the times of Josiah's revival and Ezra's reform, separating the people and the true worship of God into a provincial and prescribed form, and now it is time for the Jews to reject this degenerate form of faith if they wish to become integrated into another nation of a different legal heritage. They must recognize that celebrating a different day of rest is a matter of indifference if they wish to become united with a different people. They must reject their sectarian schools, support the public schools, and learn the same laws as everyone else if they wish to become a full member of society. They must learn and perform their duties as good citizens, including participation in military service. They must learn to be productive citizens and work hard with their own hands rather than wheeling and dealing through the unscrupulous business practices of middlemen and other harmful or worthless professions.[72]

A more vehement anti-Semite and anti-Christian was Bruno Bauer (1809–1882), a German theologian, biblical critic, philosopher, and historian. His overt atheism and radical criticism of the Bible caused him to lose his teaching license in the spring of 1842 and spend much of his remaining days living as an author and writing articles and books on a wide range of topics. He hated the church for provoking his dismissal from a position in theology and wanted an absolute destruction of religion and its bigotries. He felt the French solution was inadequate because it eliminated religion from the state without destroying its presence in society. Religion petrifies the human race into certain traditional forms and hinders the Hegelian development and transformation of self-consciousness as individuals and a society.[73] He admits that Christianity is higher than Judaism and other religious forms in emancipating the people from legalistic and transcendent authority, but he develops a deep-seated hatred for it, spending much of his time spewing acrimonious venom at its theologians, because they are unable to proceed one step farther in rejecting the existence of God and Jewish particularism and end up hindering a more universal, free, and autonomous form of immanent self-consciousness.[74]

From 1840 to 1842, Bauer completed a series of works criticizing the Gospels: *Kritik des evangelischen Geschichte des Johannes* (May 1840), *Kritik der evangelischen Geschichte der Synoptiker, Zwei Bänder* (July 1841), and *Kritik der evangelischen Geschichte der Synoptiker und des Johannes, Dritter und Letzter Band* (May 1842). He interprets the Gospels in a Kantian/Hegelian manner as displaying the self-consciousness of the authors and their community, and not so much the object of their account.[75] John is a work of Christian art, using the *logos* doctrine and philosophical categories of Philo, Neo-Platonism, and the Greco-Roman world to weave a creative reflection, which has no historical value whatsoever. The Synoptic Gospels are different only in degree, not kind, displaying the same type of literary stream of consciousness that developed during the second century in the church, even if their reflection is more primitive than what one finds in John.[76] Bauer assumes from the outset that a real, unique personality impressed his character upon the authors, but he begins to question this supposition in the third volume and later develops the concept of subjectivity (and animus toward the church) to such a degree that he denies the actual historical existence of Jesus in 1850–1851. He develops such a pathological hatred toward theologians that any semblance of reality in their confessions disappears as a simple product of an overzealous imagination.[77] He hopes this type of "scientific criticism" will continue into the future and bring about the destruction of the faith and its emasculation of the human race. The Judeo-Christian tradition has sucked the lifeblood out of humanity with its incredulous and miraculous stories of the supernatural and must be eliminated to restore once again all trust and reliance in the people's own powers.[78]

The animosity toward the church leads Bauer, like most sons of the Enlightenment, to deprecate the culture that produced the religion and the scripture in the first place. Just like Paulus, he writes a work on the *Jewish Question* (1843), which casts aspersions upon Judaism and calls for the exorcism of its people from civil society. The Jews are worthy of contempt because they are bigoted and inflexible, unable to adapt their way to a malleable society like Europe, and much less evolved in their religious sensibilities than Christians. They insist on clinging to the despotic god of the OT, who wars against the enemies of Israel and postpones the rights of all other peoples into the future.[79] At least Christianity makes some historical, Hegelian progress toward the universal love of all humankind, but only by breaking away from Jewish exclusiveness.[80] Bauer believes the Jews exhausted their role in the evolutionary process of society a long time ago and cannot move forward while clinging to their old Talmudic traditions and remaining bigoted and obstinate to the bitter end. Their laws prevent them from making progress, obtaining true freedom, and conceding any points to the government.[81] Even in times of old, the Mosaic economy was an impractical foundation for society and only ended up creating a nation of hypocrites, who hired Gentile servants to work on the Sabbath day and never kept the Sabbatical year, except in their fantasies.[82] The Jews like to complain about their suffering through the ages, but much of it finds a provocation within their own adherence to obstinate and impractical ways of life, which refuse to mix or compromise with the real world around them. They like to think of themselves as peculiar and different, even in the way they suffer like no one else, but they are hardly the innocent people of God, and they often suffer from the same exclusiveness, which Christianity learned from its parent religion and inflicts upon them.[83]

Because of these problems, Bauer thinks it is necessary to deny Jews the rights of citizenship within the state. The Jews are incapable of respecting others as moral equals and incapable of serving a law in the state, when it conflicts with their own national/religious laws, which are written in stone.[84] Therefore, it is impossible for them to become citizens in a modern state unless they cease being Jews. Bauer points to a committee in Baden that demanded the Jews adopt the national language, cease teaching their children Hebrew, stop circumcising their sons, and renounce their dietary laws and other measures of segregation as a good start on the road toward citizenships, although he wants to use these types of measures against Christians as well and totally abolish all religion from the state and society, much like his young disciple Karl Marx. He mentions a report that some Jews are making concessions for the sake of peace—no longer wanting a national homeland and renouncing the messianic hope of dominion—but he is skeptical about their genuine desire to renounce their particularity. He thinks the price for emancipation will mean the total destruction of Judaism in the future, as religion in general gives way to secularity through the burgeoning power of the modern states.[85]

A couple decades later he extends his venom in *Das Judenthum in der Fremde* (1863) to include an emphasis upon race. He now describes Jews in biological and physiological terms as a cursed race, possessing immutable differences in body and soul from others and making them irredeemable or impossible to merge with other cultures. He provides the Jewish race with a detailed physical description and believes the outward form bears witness to important differences in their innermost nature and behavior. Because of this, the Jews are lost forever. They have no hope of redemption. They have an innate and indelible propensity toward their many vices, which are legion: hardness to change, incapability of development, lack of creativity, inability to contribute, unwillingness to labor, dependency upon others, living like leeches, stealing money, preying on human misery, complaining about their misfortune, spewing hatred, working for their own material advantage, exploiting warfare for profit, and fomenting revolution to gain dominion. All of these vices constitute a necessary aspect of Jewish existence and threaten the very existence of Western civilization. Bauer sees Jews involved in a massive and covert plot to gain world dominion and believes it is either us or them. There is no redeeming the Jews and reconciling their immoral ways with German/Christian civilization, and so it is necessary to eliminate them. This will prevent the corruption of German culture from continuing to escalate and help assume the rightful place once again of the *Volk* in leading the *Vaterland* to a brighter future.[86]

One of the most vehement and influential opponents of the Judeo-Christian tradition was Paul de Lagarde, a philologist and historian of religion and culture. He was born on November 2, 1827, in a patriarchal home of strict orthodox beliefs and discipline, which banned the reading of Shakespeare and Goethe from the household, but he rebelled against the upbringing at a young age and become much the opposite. He obtained a doctoral degree in philosophy from the University of Berlin in 1849 and taught at a Berlin gymnasium upon graduation. Eventually, after years of hard work and scholarship, he was awarded a position in Semitic and Near Eastern Languages at the University of Göttingen in 1860. Like Nietzsche, he filled his chair with distinction and acquired a reputation as a competent philologist, but his heart summoned him to engage in a broad spectrum of subjects and fulfill a number of roles as a philosopher, theologian, historian, and political pundit.[87] Out of this wider interest he published his most important and influential work, the *Deutsche Schriften* (rev. edit. 1886), a collection of his political and religious writings from 1853 to 1883.[88] This work exerted a decided influence on many anti-Semitic figures and groups in the nineteenth century, including Friedrich Nietzsche and the Basel Circle, Ludwig Schemann and the Wagner Circle, Adolf Stoecker, Heinrich von Treitschke, Theodor Fritsche, and other leaders of the many proto-Nazi movements of the time.[89] During World War I, the work became a part of the war effort and continued to exert a marked and direct influence afterwards in recruiting the German intelligentsia, inspiring the Pan-German movement, and developing conservative groups like the National Socialists, along with their leaders—Chamberlain, Rosenberg, and Hitler.[90] The library of the *Führer* contained a copy of the 1934 edition, which he read and studied, marking up over one hundred pages in pencil, including comments that spoke of the Jews as a "pestilence" and "serious affront to the authenticity of our German identity" with its suggestions about "transporting" or even "eradicating" them from the land.[91] Like the Nazis, Lagarde promoted anti-Semitism, anti-Christianity, a new spiritual foundation, a new *Volk* religion, expansion of German territory, and the use of force by an elite leadership.[92]

Lagarde's anti-Semitism develops from the liberal and higher critical understanding of the Hebrew scripture and the Mosaic law developed in post-Enlightenment times. The Bible is deprecated as a book filled with errors and contradictions, incredulous stories of miraculous events, and continuous examples of moral turpitude, where patriarchs like Abraham and Jacob (Israel) practice deception to obtain their designs. The Mosaic law is subject to special reproach for mandating evil practices like polygamy, and responsible people of conscious are called to denounce this material and remove it, along with the rest of the OT from the Christian Bible. Lagarde thinks of the Mosaic law as developing later on in the history of its people during the times of the Babylonian captivity and corrupting whatever piety existed in Ancient Israel, much like Wellhausen and the standard liberal theory of post-Enlightenment scholars. At this time, the Jews became an arrogant people (*Rassenhochmuth*)—uniquely elected by God and separated from other nations through a labyrinth of legal procedures. Ezra and the Pharisees completed the process and made segregation the chief commandment of the Jewish faith, beyond the scope of any other religious creed. Thereafter, the Jews lost all affection for their fellow human beings, standing aloof from others as if they were unclean and refusing to merge with any other nation of people.[93]

Lagarde believes the Jews can never embrace any culture or become a part of any foreign land in which they subsist as pilgrims. They are "Undeutsches und Widerdeutsches," subsisting in the Diaspora as a "nation within a nation" and never able to embrace the genuine German *Geist* in the depths of the soul. Their very existence is an affront to any other culture because they relate to the international scene and work to destroy the particular character and interests of their national place of temporary residence. Their politics work at leveling the world and opposing the special concerns of the German people, while they endeavor all along to rule over them by controlling the money supply, slanting the news through financial power, dominating higher education and the dissemination of knowledge, and exercising power over all the stereotypical institutions of proto-Nazi concern.[94]

Lagarde thinks of the Jews as inferior to their Gentile neighbors and subject to a special measure of depravity. They receive no particular credit for developing any significant ideas, not even the concept of monotheism, which they borrowed from the work of Platonic philosophers in the ancient world. They carried no real innovations into modern European society and produced only a few men like Spinoza and Maimonides who are worthy of any real distinction. If anything, they are a negative influence, filled with a unique depravity, obstinacy, and moral turpitude that exceeds the measure of other people, even as the prophets of old testify in their own sacred writings. Jews only love this material world and its riches, not true spiritual values. They hate other people and receive hatred in return as parasites, sucking the lifeblood and sustenance out of their neighbors. Lagarde believes the problems of the *Judenfrage* are vital to the continual existence of Europe and demands, as a necessary resolution the destruction of Judaism (*das Judenthum zu zerstören*), either through their departure to another place of residence or their complete assimilation into society, where Jews cease to be Jews (*die Jüden aufhören Juden zu sein*)—a typical answer of post-Enlightenment times.[95]

Like most sons of the Enlightenment, his hatred of Judaism develops in concert with a fervent animosity toward the Christian faith as another decrepit form of religion.[96] He particularly rejects the early adoption of Jewish elements into the faith and hopes the church can cleanse the "Jewish poison" from its laws and rituals in the future.[97] He thinks people know little about the historical Jesus outside the mythological impact he exerted upon his followers, but it seems that the message of Jesus was formulated in direct opposition to Judaism from what can be verified in the Gospel account. Jesus opposed rabbinic legalism and preached a gospel of spiritual rebirth, which offered the living presence of God in a free and vital communion.[98] Christianity moved away from this emphasis during the time of Paul by adopting his Pharisaical doctrines concerning original sin and blood atonement as the new focus of attention in the faith. Paul transformed the death of Jesus into a sacrifice for sin, causing the church to focus on the past and forget the ongoing relationship with God in the present.[99] Thereafter, Christianity lost much of its vitality and developed into a set of theological dogmas, inculcating a great mythology about Jesus as a cosmic Savior.[100] Luther failed to deliver the church from this dogma and sentenced all of Protestantism to live in the past by emphasizing the sole authority of the scripture and making it a dead letter.[101] Catholicism was actually closer to a living faith, with its ability to formulate new post-Apostolic teachings and its power to renew Christ's presence in the sacraments,[102] but both traditions are dead and far removed from the fresh vision of Jesus, which promoted unlimited development of faith through the continual regeneration of God's living Spirit.[103]

Lagarde follows the typical Romantic and Hegelian understanding, which thinks of religion as evolving out of past forms toward a higher expression of spiritual reality. Because the church inhibits the progressive unfolding of the historical process when it clings to confessions of old, Lagarde wants to replace its traditions with a new religious form that is open and able to transform the people, not simply adjust what is ossified through the moderate approach of Hegel's *Aufhebung*. The new religion provides a radical departure from the antedated message of the church and speaks to the time and conditions of a specific people and their contemporary needs. The new message offers a cadence to each and every people, calling them to summon their essential resources as a nation and live in accordance with their *Sitz im Leben*. It calls the people of Germany to develop their own unified, national religion, expressing their soul in its cultural identity and rejecting the Christian need to address humanity *in abstracto*. Lagarde hopes German universities can take the lead in spreading the new type of spiritual message and eliminate specific theological instruction in divisive creeds and miraculous lore.[104]

By eliminating the universal and transcendent aspect of the old message, Lagarde transposes his new religious imperative into an immanent exaltation of the *Volksgeist* of Germany. Throughout his work, the *Volk* community receives the highest praise as the locus of true greatness and spiritual development within its historical, cultural, and inward power (*Innerlichkeit*);[105] and all else is secondary, including the precise conformation of the state and the specific makeup of the genetic pool.[106] Lagarde wants a *German* nation, derived from the ethical, spiritual, and intellectual passions of a culture, not the prospects of social or genetic engineering. He hopes to inflame the life of the nation on the grassroots level through using education to inculcate German values of duty and love for the fatherland.[107] *Deutschland über alles*!

Because of this his religious message soon devolves into an ethnocentric imperative to promote and expand the dominion of German culture in the future. All of life must develop and cultivate German soil. This causes him to reject the revolutions of 1517, 1789, and 1848 because they found their inspiration in the egalitarian and liberal ideology of the international scene and neglected the primal genius of German cultural roots.[108] This causes him to reject all forms of parliamentary government as developing outside the land and to prefer a strong monarchy and noble aristocracy as a proper German establishment, promoting the excellence of German society.[109] He provides no specific emphasis upon racial superiority, but his work contains Nazi-like attitudes that speak of the German people as a dominating race and promotes their will to grow and expand eastward at the expense of others. He proposes carving up a strong position for Germany in Central Europe (*Mitteleuropa*) by dominating Austria, expelling the Jews, and colonizing Slavic lands as far east as the Black Sea. He recognizes that creating these borders and Germanizing the territories will bring war with France and Russia, but war builds character and Germanic *Wanderlust* cannot be impeded through the fear of conflict.[110] *Deutschland über alles*!

Lagarde's sentiments on these and other issues represent the type of Nazi ideology that developed in varying degrees among the liberal theologians and critical scholars of the nineteenth century. These religious liberals attacked the Judeo-Christian tradition of Western civilization as a remnant of the unenlightened past and hoped to create a new *Volksgeist*, which eliminated the legalism and dogma of the old-time religion and allowed the Spirit to develop freely within the emerging nation of the brave new world. Their point of view began to permeate German society at the end of the nineteenth century and led to the emergence of anti-Jewish and anti-Christian groups like the Nazis, who wanted to destroy the faith once and for all as the main obstacle in their designs for creating a different type of society. Houston Stewart Chamberlain clearly found the stimulus for his proto-Nazi beliefs in the works of Voltaire, Schleiermacher, Harnack, Wellhausen, and other biblical critics. He followed the JEDP theory in claiming that Jewish priests bastardized the ancient faith of Israel through the introduction of an angry, materialistic god, who demanded propitiatory sacrifices and legalistic performance from the people. He followed liberal theologians in wanting Jewish elements, miraculous stories, and metaphysical dogmas eliminated from the Christian faith and a deeper kernel of spirituality to replace the literal superstition. In all this, he exemplified the power of the latest biblical scholarship in formulating the Nazi point of view on Judaism and Christianity, setting a precedent for many of its most important leaders and intellectuals to follow. Alfred Rosenberg, the leading Nazi ideologue, followed the liberal pattern by demanding the exorcism of the OT and all Jewish elements from the Christian faith and trying to rescue the historical Jesus from the superstitious musings of Paul and the church, hoping to start a new church free from the metaphysical dogmas of the past. Hitler thought of the Bible in the same enlightened terms, dismissing it as "Jewish mumbo jumbo," calling the priests the fundamental enemy, finding Jesus the only character worth preserving, and venting his anger on Paul for distorting the message of the historical Jesus and turning the simple carpenter into a cosmic Savior and wonder-worker. In all this, the Nazis praised the work of Voltaire and his disciples in developing the new scientific view of the Judeo-Christian tradition and couched their own point of view within its matrix, displaying the importance of this pervasive, intellectual attitude in stimulating the movement. In fact, the connection went beyond mere theory to include practical measures, as some of these nineteenth-century scholars reflected and inspired the extreme solutions of the later Nazis calling for the state to recognize problems with the old tradition and use its power to expatriate the Jews, separate the church from the state, and create a new religious order.

Notes

1. Jacob Katz, *From Prejudice to Destruction: Anti-Semitism, 1700–1933* (Cambridge, MA, and London: Harvard University Press, 1980) 27–31. Among the early Deists/biblical critics were John Toland, the Earl of Shaftesburg, Athony Collins, Thomas Woolston, Matthew Tindal, Thomas Cubb, and Viscount Bolingbroke. See chap. 1.
2. *Der Berliner Antisemitismusstreit*, Walter Boehlich (Hrsg.) (Frankfurt am Main: Insel-Verlag, 1965) 173–76.

3. Ernst Christian Helmreich, *The German Churches under Hitler: Background, Struggle, and Epilogue* (Detroit: Wayne State University Press, 1979) 41.
4. The Nazis and proto-Nazis certainly found much inspiration in biblical criticism. Katz, *From Prejudice to Destruction*, 308. See the end of the chapter, for a summary, or the previous sections on Hitler, Chamberlain, and Rosenberg.
5. Immanuel Kant, *Religion within the Limits of Reason Alone*, Theordore Meyer Greene and Hoyt H. Hudson (trans.) (New York: Harper & Row, Publishers, 1960) 47–49, 69, 79, 102, 106–9, 113–15, 182–83, 190.
6. C. W. Christian, *Friedrich Schleiermacher*, in *Makers of the Modern Theological Mind*, Bob Patterson (ed.) (Waco, TX: Word Books, Publishers, 1979) 11–12, 28, 42, 46, 58, 138.
7. Friedrich Schleiermacher, *On Religion: Speeches to Its Cultured Despisers*, John Oman (trans.), Rudolf Otto (intro.) (New York: Harper & Row, Publishers, 1958) 15–16, 87. In his *Christian Faith*, H. R. Mackintosh and J. S. Stewart (ed.) (Philadelphia: Fortress Press, 1976), he rejects belief in the Trinity (738ff.), angels (156–59), Satan (161–63), hell (549, 560, 720ff.), virgin birth (405–6), deity of Christ (122–23, 381–82, 392), and the Second Coming (708).
8. Schleiermacher, *Christian Faith*, 76–78, 89, 591–94, 598, 605–10 (15, 19, 128–32); Christian, *Schleiermacher*, 52–53, 89.
9. Ibid., 595 (129).
10. Ibid., 443 (103); Peggy Cosmann, "Neubelebung und Überbietung socianischer and deistischer Interpretamente im 'geistlichen Antisenitismus,'" ZRGG 53/3 (2000), 231.
11. Schleiermacher, *Speeches*, 3, 17–18; *Christian Faith*, 8–11, 26 (3, 6); Christian, *Schleiermacher*, 36, 47, 81. Schleiermacher's emphasis upon "feeling" (*Gefühl*) found inspiration in his Moravian, pietistic background.
12. *Pascal's Pensées*, T. S. Eliot (intro.) (New York: E. P. Dutton & Co., Inc., 1958) 78 (277).
13. Schleiermacher, *Christian Faith*, 244, 247, 296–98 (60, 72); *Speeches*, 124. Karl Barth is the most excoriating opponent of Schleiermacher and liberal theology on this point. Barth does not believe that humans are generally capable of a religious experience. There is nothing in their experience that corresponds to the Word of God. *Church Dogmatics*, G. W. Bromiley and T. F. Torrance (eds.) (Edinburgh: T. & T. Clark, 1975–) I/1, 193, 203–4, 220, 237–38; I/2, 7. Barth sees Schleiermacher's theology proceeding toward the subjective atheism of Ludwig Feuerbach, where human beings are the real God, since what they declare of God they are really declaring of themselves. Feuerbach, *The Essence of Christianity*, Karl Barth (intro.), H. Richard Niebuhr (foreword), George Eliot (trans.) (New York: Harper & Row, Publishers, 1957) vii, xxii, 29, 230. Feuerbach thinks that true theology is anthropology. If feeling is the subject, it also must be the object of faith. *The Essence of Christianity*, xxxvii, 10–11, 14–15. God's miraculous activity satisfies the subjective wishes of humans for escaping the limits of the natural world. Ibid., 31, 129, 131, 135–36. Judaism and the God of the Jews are an expression of their egotism. They regard themselves as the sole people of God and think the universe acts for their benefit. In Joshua 10, the sun stands still in the heavens, so they

can continue a slaughter of their fellow human beings. Ibid., 114ff., 119; Katz, *From Prejudice to Destruction*, 163.

14. Schleiermacher, *Speeches*, 36, 49, 88, 101, 180.
15. Ibid., 237; *Christian Faith*, 100, 234–36 (22, 57). Special miracles would erode away on the interdependence of nature and its rational order. *Christian Faith*, 179–82, 192 (47, 49).
16. The sixteen lectures were published in 1905. The English version is entitled *What Is Christianity?* [Thomas Bailey Saunders (trans.), Rudolf Bultmann (intro.) (New York: Harper & Row, Publishers, 1957)]. See Joseph B. Tyson, "Anti-Judaism in the Critical Study of the Gospels," in *Anti-Judaism and the Gospels*, William Farmer (ed.) (Harrisonburg, PA: Trinity Press International, 1999) 229.
17. Harnack, *What Is Christianity?*, 14, 146ff., 188, 301.
18. Ibid., 12–13, 47, 52–65, 125–30, 176ff.; Tyson, "Anti-Judaism in the Critical Study of the Gospels," 229–30.
19. Adolf von Harnack, *Marcion: The Gospel of the Alien God*, John E. Steely and Lyle D. Bierma (trans.) (Durham, NC: Labyrinth Press, 1990) 21–22, 133ff.; Tyson, "Anti-Judaism in the Critical Study of the Gospels," 232–33. He also thinks we need to deliver ourselves from the process of Hellenism/Platonism that turned Jesus into the *Logos*. *What Is Christianity?*, 201–3. In the second century, the "living faith" was transformed into a creed, theology, Christology, hierarchical structure, and legalistic institutions. Ibid., 193. He sees the Reformation as a positive movement, restoring the pristine purity of the church, eliminating priestly authority and its ordinances, and emphasizing "inwardness and spirituality" and the freedom of the soul. Ibid., 275, 282–84.
20. Lou Siberman, "Wellhausen and Judaism," *Semeia* 25 (1983): 75; Julius Wellhausen, *Prolegomena to the History of Ancient Israel*, W. Robertson Smith (intro.) (Gloucester, MA: Peter Smith, 1973) 3; Daniel Weidner, "Geschichte gegen den 'Strich bürsten': Julius Wellhausen und die jüdische 'Gegengeschichte'," *Zeitschrift für Religions- and Geistesgeschichte* 54/1 (2002): 40. Hereafter designated as PH. Scholars no longer think of these methods as yielding objective results, free from contextual/ideological commitments, and recognize Wellhausen's biases against second-temple Judaism. Walter Brueggemann, *Theology of the Old Testament: Testimony, Dispute, Advocacy* (Minneapolis, MN: Fortress Press, 1997) xvi, 12, 108.
21. Rudolf Smend, "Wellhausen und das Judentum," *Zeitschrift für Theologie und Kirche* 79/3 (Sept. 1982): 259; PH 3–5.
22. PH 245, 412.
23. Weidner, "Geschichte," 35–37, 40. Nietzsche read and studied the third edition of Wellhausen's *Prolegomena*. He also uses and cites other works from him. Ibid., 37.
24. PH 18, 19, 24, 30, 41ff., 54, 59, 71ff., 80ff., 91, 94, 277, 278; Weidner, "Geschichte," 35–37, 40–44, 47. Prolegomena represents his most famous and most anti-Semitic work, especially the closing two chapters, which contrast Israel and Judaism. In other works, he sees Judaism as more connected with the Israelites of old, as well as the Christian faith. Smend, "Wellhausen und das Judentum," 253–54, 258–59.
25. PH 1, 27, 32ff., 402, 410; Silberman, "Wellhausen and Judaism," 75, 79. Of course, Voltaire, the philosophes, and English Deists questioned the Mosaic

authorship as well. *Letters of Certain Jews to Monsieur Voltaire*, Philip Lefanu (Covington, KY: G. G. Moore, 1845) 70, 150–51.

26. PH 5, 111, 161, 346ff., 405; Silberman, "Wellhausen and Judaism," 76.
27. PH 72ff., 77ff., 88, 101–103, 115, 232–35, 293–94, 332, 336–37, 341, 423–24; Julius Wellhausen, *The Pharisees and the Sadducees: An Examination of Internal Jewish History*, Mark Biddle (trans.) (Macon, GA: Mercer University Press, 2001) 11.
28. Smend, "Wellhausen und das Judentum," 250–51, 268–72. As proof, Smend cites his "Letter to H. Usener" (Feb. 22, 1886), his "Letter to E. Limpricht" (Dec. 28, 1915), and other material.
29. Wellhausen, *Pharisees and Sadducees*, 112; Tyson, "Anti-Judaism in the Critical Study of the Gospels," 221–22; Smend, "Wellhausen und das Judentum," 282. He thinks of the Talmud as destroying the previous history of diversity but admits his own ignorance of post-biblical Judaism. Of course, the depiction of the Jewish faith as legalistic is the dominant stereotype of his time. See Wilhelm Bousset, *Die Religion des Judentum im späthellenistischen Zeitalter* (Tübingen: Mohr, 1926); Emil Schürer, *History of the Jewish People at the Time of Jesus Christ* (New York: Schoken Books, 1961); Rudolf Bultmann, *Primitive Christianity in Its Contemporary Setting*, R. H. Fuller (trans.) (London and New York: Thames and Huson, 1956) 59–71; Tyson, "Anti-Judaism in the Critical Study of the Gospels," 223ff.
30. Smend, "Wellhausen and das Judentum," 273. Chamberlain's *Foundations of the Nineteenth Century* is a good example of the pervasive influence. See chap. 7, p. 114.
31. Weidner, "Geschichte," 40–41.
32. David Friedrich Strauss, *Voltaire sechs Vorträge* (Leipzig: G. Hirzel, 1870) 258; Albert Schweitzer, *The Quest for the Historical Jesus: A Critical Study of Its Progress from Reimarus to Wrede*, James Robinson (intro.) (New York: Macmillan Publishing Co., Inc., 1975) 14–15, 26; Hermann Samuel Reimarus, *The Goal of Jesus and His Disciples*, George Wesley Buchanan (intro. and trans.) (Leiden: E. J. Brill, 1970) 2–3, 7, 17–18; *Reimarus: Fragments*, in *Lives of Jesus Series*, Ralph Fraser (trans.), Charles Talbert (ed.) (Philadelphia: Fortress Press, 1970) 11, 17. Hereafter Reimarus' *Goal of Jesus and His Disciples* is designated GJD. Barthold Heinrich Broches, his friend, and Johann Albert Fabricus, his father-in-law, helped influence him in this direction.
33. GJD 9, 10, 15–16: Schweitzer, *The Quest for the Historical Jesus*, 14–15; *Reimarus: Fragments*, 8–9, 18ff., 24. Schweitzer admires Lessing for disregarding the objections of Nicolai, Mendelssohn, Reimarus' family, and even his own scruples in allowing this significant type of criticism to receive a public airing.
34. GJD 18.
35. GJD 29–31, 36, 41–42 (VIII), 59–65, 74–76, 78–80, 91; Schweitzer, *Quest for the Historical Jesus*, 16–18, 23. *Reimarus: Fragments*, 40. Anthony Collins, the English Deist, argued in his *Discourse of the Grounds and Reasons of the Christian Faith* (London: [s.n.], 1724) that the disciples understood Jesus as a temporal Savior. *Reimarus: Fragments*, 17.
36. GJD 19–20, 80–84, 95, 104, 126–33.
37. Reimarus thinks of Jesus as a moral teacher and recognizes the historicity of his claim to be the Messiah, but he rejects any attempt to inflate the rhetoric

of the Gospels (even in John) and deify his person. GJD 39–40, 45, 50–53, 58–59. Jesus might have wrought some cures that some eyewitnesses perceived as miracles with their limited understanding of science, but there was never a public display of these phenomena to provide sufficient credibility and warrant belief. Reimarus has grave reservations about the miracles in the OT and NT. He has the typical dualism of Voltaire and English Deists in regard to the relationship between God and the world. GJD 53, 56, 88, 118–20; Schweitzer, *Quest for the Historical Jesus*, 19; Strauss, *Voltaire*, 240.

38. *Reimarus: Fragments*, 17; GJD 102–7, 121. In his *Discourse*, Collins denounces the NT's use of the OT. He denounces typology as a proper method of interpretation, following the Reformation's emphasis on literal interpretation, its desire to go back to the "fountains" and create a NT church, and the limitation of language to a spatiotemporal, contextual context reference in Puritan England and John Locke. Liberals like Schleiermacher tended to interpret the Bible as literal and historical, just like the later Fundamentalists; only the former cut out what they found to be incredulous on a literal level and the latter retained it all. Literal interpretation reigned in Protestantism from the sixteenth to the early part of the twentieth century. Hans Frei, *The Eclipse of the Biblical Narrative* (New Haven, CT: Yale University Press, 1974) 76ff., 81–83; Hans-Georg Gadamer, *Truth and Method*, Joel Weinsheimer and Donald G. Marshall (trans.) (New York: Continuum, 1994) 166–67, 297, 373.
39. Schweitzer, *Quest for the Historical Jesus*, 71. Heinrich Paulus supported Strauss' candidacy—much to the credit of his longtime polemical opponent.
40. Ibid., 72, 103; David Friedrich Strauss, *The Life of Jesus Critically Examined*, George Eliot (trans.), Peter Hodgson (ed.) (Philadelphia: Fortress Press, 1972) xvi, xxiv. Hereafter designated as LJ. Even F. C. Bauer criticized his former student as much too harsh in his analysis. Bauer saw mythical embellishments in the Gospels but tended to provide a natural explanation for the myths, whereas Strauss rejected any natural solution in toto. LJ, xx, xxxvii–xxxviii, 57–60 (9). Paulus and Schweitzer also think Strauss carries his use of myth too far; many of the Gospel stories have peculiar elements and a substratum of history, which cannot be explained through mythological embellishments or OT interpolations. Schweitzer, *Quest for the Historical Jesus*, 84; LJ lii.
41. LJ xxvi, xxxvii–xxxviii, xl, xlvi, lvii–lviii; Schweitzer, *Quest for the Historical Jesus*, 72; David Friedrich Strauss, *The Old & New Faith*, G. A. Wells (intro.) (Amherst, NY, and Oxford: Prometheus, 1997) xxv, xxviii.
42. LJ 757 (144). This account is based on the fourth edition.
43. LJ xxx–xxxi, 58–59, 71–73 (9–10, 13), 90 (16), 255–57, 277, 402–3, 477, 677, 735 (139).
44. LJ xxviii, lii, 39 (1), 49–50, 63–64 (11), 138–39 (28), 170 (35), 475 (99), 513 (102), 540–41 (107), 737 (140).
45. LJ lii, 40–43, 51 (2–4, 7).
46. Today's Third Quest for the historical Jesus believes that miracle stories go back to the life of Jesus based on historical investigation. There are too many first century, independent sources to think otherwise—Mark Q, M, L, John, and Josephus. Even if it is difficult to believe in miracles, Jesus and his audience thought they were transpiring during

his ministry. This material is not the product of the second-century church's embellishment. John P. Meier, *A Marginal Jew: Rethinking the Historical Jesus* (New York and London: Double Day, 1991–) 2.618, 619.

47. LJ 78, 316, 515 (14, 71, 102).
48. Schweitzer, *Quest for the Historical Jesus*, 82.
49. LJ 739–41 (140).
50. LJ 129, 156, 167ff., 189, 259–63, 470, 492, 517–18, 554, 582, 688–89 (25, 32, 35–36, 39, 56, 98, 100, 102, 110–11, 115, 132).
51. LJ xxxi–xxxiii, 43, 84–85, 287, 296, 591, 742, 767–68 (4, 14, 62, 66, 116, 140, 147); Schweitzer, *Quest for the Historical Jesus*, 94. Strauss uses the work of Reimarus often in this work.
52. Strauss, *The Old Faith & the New*, xlix–li, 1.10.
53. Ibid., 1.39–41; 2.116–18.
54. Ibid., xliv, 1.46, 87.
55. Ibid., 1.41. At one point he refers to Jewish culture as base, having no artistic or scientific achievement, but this type of anti-Semitic comment is rare in his writings. Ibid., 75–76.
56. Ibid., xlv, 1.48–53; LJ 770–72, 777 (148, 150).
57. LJ xx, xxi, xxxiv, xxxv, 780–84 (151–52).
58. Strauss, *The Old Faith & the New*, xvi, xvii, xxxviii, xli, 1.108ff., 126–27, 133, 158–61, 202, 205; 2.4, 54, 74–85, 97–104, 110–11; Schweitzer, *Quest for the Historical Jesus*, 75. He is a complete materialist and rejects the existence of the soul. Ibid., xl, 1.141, 142; 2.19.
59. Johnson, "Nietzsche's Early Darwinism," 66–67.
60. Strauss also published a popular book, *Das Leben Jesu für das deutsche Volk bearbeitet* (Leipzig: F. A. Brockhaus, 1864).
61. Schweitzer, *Quest for the Historical Jesus*, 180–83, 188–92; Santaniello, "Post Holocaust Re-examination," 35.
62. Albert Kalthoff, *Das Christus-Problem: Grundlinien zu einer Sozialtheologie* (Leipzig: Eugen Diederichs, 1903) 23; Schweitzer, *Quest for the Historical Jesus*, 309, 311, 316, 324–25. Schweitzer thinks that Jesus is an apocalyptic enthusiast and would be a stranger in the modern world. Schweitzer, *Quest for the Historical Jesus*, 252, 401–2.
63. Ernest Renan, *Life of Jesus*, Joseph Henry Allen (ed.) (Boston: Little, Brown, and Company, 1929) 418; Santiello, "Post-Holocaust and Re-examination," 34. Hereafter Renan's *Life of Jesus* is designated RLJ.
64. RLJ 84–87. In the present, Renan sees the Jews living as a separate people without any nationality or fatherland, having lost all hope in any terrestrial kingdom. RLJ 84.
65. RLJ 93. Jesus was "exempt from almost all the defects of his race." The only notable exception was his hot polemical temper in attacking his Jewish opponents. RLJ 319–20. Renan was one of the first champions of Indo-European origins and Aryanism on an international scale. Poliakov, *Aryan Myth*, 206ff.; Hannah Arendt, *The Origins of Totalitarianism* (New York: Harcourt, Brace & World, Inc., 1966) 174.
66. RLJ 139–43.
67. RLJ 132– 34, 139, 243. Like Harnack, Renan thinks of Jesus sharing the notion of a material kingdom with the Jews, but "this was, doubtless, not his first idea." RLJ 135.

68. RLJ 132, 254, 258, 260, 262, 270, 277, 402, 414, 447, 451–52.
69. Schweitzer, *Quest for the Historical Jesus*, 48–57.
70. H. E. G. Paulus, *Die Jüdische Nationalabsonderung nach Ursprung, Folgen und Besserungsmitteln* (Heidelberg: C. F. Winter, 1831) 4–5, 8–9, 102–4, 145–48. Hereafter designated as JN. He is very pessimistic about the prospects. Even Jews like Spinoza had difficulty leaving Judaism behind and participating in society after his conversion to Christianity because of his previous education in Judaism. JN 18.
71. JN 2–3, 9–10, 22–23, 28, 44–53, 57–58, 62, 82, 117–18; Katz, *From Prejudice to Destruction*, 156.
72. JN 3, 21, 28–31, 34, 41–42, 65–69, 72, 80–81, 92–93, 100–101, 123, 148–49; Katz, *From Prejudice to Destruction*, 157. He traces the Jewish involvement in business to the Babylonian Captivity. He thinks the Jews actually prefer living in the Diaspora, so they can live as middlemen. JN 40–41, 92–93.
73. David Leopold, "The Hegelian antisemitism of Bruno Bauer," *History of European Ideas* 25 (1999): 200; Katz, *From Prejudice to Destruction*, 167–68; Schweitzer, *Quest for the Historical Jesus*, 153–54.
74. Yoad Peled, "From Theology to Sociology: Bruno Bauer and Karl Marx on the Question of Jewish Emancipation," *History of Political Thought* 13/3 (Autumn 1992): 469; Douglas Moggach, *The Philosophy and Politics of Bruno Bauer* (Cambridge: Cambridge University Press, 2003) 67; Leopold, "The Hegelian antisemitism of Bruno Bauer," 193. In *Herr Dr. Hengstenberg* (1939), he draws humanity and divinity together and rejects the concept of a transcendent will. Peled, "From Theology to Sociology," 64–65.
75. Moggach, *Philosophy and Politics*, 76.
76. Schweitzer, *Quest for the Historical Jesus*, 138–41, 144.
77. Moggach, *Philosophy and Politics*, 72; Schweitzer, *Quest for the Historical Jesus*, 144, 157. Bauer accepts the thesis of Christian Gottlob Wilke and Wilhelm Wrede that Mark is the first Gospel. Bauer makes this first Gospel stand alone as a complete literary fiction and says that Matthew and Luke are literary expansions of the work. In 1851, he looks for an "Ur-Mark" to explain the two feedings of the multitudes. Schweitzer, *Quest for the Historical Jesus*, 141, 148.
78. Bruno Bauer, "The Jewish Problem," Helen Lederer (trans.), in *Readings in Modern Jewish History*, Ellis Rivikin (ed.) (Cincinnati, OH: Hebrew Union College—Jewish Institute of Religion, 1958) 25, 50; Moggah, *Philosophy and Politics*, 76–77; Schweitzer, *Quest for the Historical Jesus*, 154–56.
79. Ibid., 12, 36–37, 41–42.
80. Leopold, "The Hegelian antisemitism of Bruno Bauer," 182–83.
81. Bauer, "The Jewish Problem," 12, 14, 26; Leopold, "The Hegelian antisemitism of Bruno Bauer," 186–87.
82. Ibid., 28–29, 44–45; Peled, "From Theology to Sociology," 466–68; Leopold, "The Hegelian antisemitism of Bruno Bauer," 183–84. In regard to the Temple, no one could leave their home three times a year to attend the prescribed festivals. Today the Jews do not even pretend to honor the Temple or keep the sacrificial system.
83. Leopold, "The Hegelian antisemitism of Bruno Bauer," 204; Bauer, *The Jewish Problem*, 4–5, 20–21, 47.
84. Ibid., 198, 201; Katz, *From Prejudice to Destruction*, 218.

85. Bauer, "The Jewish Problem," 25, 31–32, 61–62, 110–12; Peled, "From Theology to Sociology," 484. Karl Marx, Bauer's pupil, rejects the solution of his mentor as extreme but thought it necessary for the Jews to renounce their religion.
86. Bruno Bauer, *Das Judenthum in der Fremde* (Berlin: F. Heincke, 1863) iv, 2, 5, 7–10, 12, 15–18, 21–25, 28, 48–53, 64–69, 77; Katz, *From Prejudice to Destruction*, 217; Leopold, "The Hegelian antisemitism of Bruno Bauer," 188. He describes the Jew as a "white negro" (*weissen Neger*), although the Jews lack the robust nature to work like Africans.
87. Vincent Viaene, "Paul de Lagarde: A Nineteenth Century Radical 'Conservative'—and precursor to National Socialism?," European History Quarterly 26/4 (1996): 527; Pulzer, *The Rise of Political Anti-Semtism in Germany and Austria*, 82; Robert Lougee, *Paul de Lagarde 1827–1891: A Study of Radical Conservatism in Germany* (Cambridge, MA: Harvard University Press, 1962) 49, 59–60, 65, 97–98. His lifetime project was to produce a critical version of the Septuagint.
88. Ibid., 529; Lougee, *Paul de Lagarde*, 220ff.
89. Wilhelm Rott, "Nationale Religion and Entstaatliche der Kirche bei Paul de Lagarde," *Evangelische Theologie* 5/2 (1938): 58; Lougee, *Paul de Lagarde*, 7, 220, 227, 230–33, 235, 246–50.
90. Lougee, *Paul de Lagarde*, 6–7, 268ff., 283, 288–90; Viaene, "Paul de Lagarde," 528, 550; Viereck, *Metapolitics*, 168–69.
91. Ryback, *Hitler's Private Library*, xvii, 117–18.
92. Arno Koselleck, "Die Entfaltung des Volkischen Bewusstseins bei Paul de Lagarde," *Historische Vierteljahrschrift* 30/2 (Nov. 1935) 320; Lougee, *Paul de Lagarde*, 289.
93. Paul de Lagarde, *Deutsche Schriften* (Göttingen: Lüder Horstmann, 1903) 22, 148, 151, 184, 225, 229, 250–52; Viaene, "Paul de Lagarde," 532; Lougee, *Paul de Lagarde*, 211. Hereafter *Deutsche Schriften* is designated as DS.
94. DS 24, 35, 211, 213, 242, 255, 320–22, 368, 388; Viaene, "Paul de Lagarde," 545.
95. DS 23–24, 184, 218, 253–56, 321, 365–68, 366, 411; Viaene, "Paul de Lagarde," 545–46; Pulzer, *The Rise of Political Anti-Semitism*, 86. He suggests sending them to Madagascar in his *Deutsche Schriften*—a plan that was seriously entertained by the Nazis as a final solution, but Lagarde never settles on a definitive solution or takes action. He never joins any anti-Semitic group or even endorses their work, mainly because he thinks of himself as a pure academician. He refuses to engage with any popular political organization. He appears to enjoy good personal relations with a number of Jewish scholars, even if he was involved in an acrimonious dispute with one Jewish scholar, defending a student who attacked his work. Poliakov, *Aryan Myth*, 309; Lougee, *Paul de Lagarde*, 94–96, 112–13, 214–15, 247, 251–52.
96. DS 60, 362; Viereck, *Metapolitics*, 227; Lougee, *Paul de Lagarde*, 41.
97. DS 130, 229, 231, 234; Viereck, *Metapolitics*, 169.
98. DS 54–56, 60, 62, 226–27, 319; Viaene, "Paul de Lagarde," 533; Poliakov, *Aryan Myth*, 308.
99. *Ueber das verhältnis des deutschen staates zu theologie, kirche und religion* (Göttingen: Dieterichische Verlagsbuchhandling, 1873) 32–35, 40–41; Lougee, *Paul de Lagarde*, 152–54, 156; DS 61, 229; Viaene, "Paul de Lagarde," 533; Rott, "Nationale Religion," 59.

100. DS 228. See DS 12, 45, 59, 84, 129, 146; Lougee, *Paul de Lagarde*, 92–93. He despised theologians and engendered a longstanding feud with Albrecht Ritschl, his colleague.
101. DS 399; Lougee, "Paul de Lagarde," 159–60; Viaene, "Paul de Lagarde," 534. He credits the new politics as coming from "die Hohenzollern in Brandenburg und Preussen," not the Reformation. DS 46.
102. Lougee, *Paul de Lagarde*," 156–57; Rott, "Nationale Religion," 59. He thinks of the Catholic Church as a political power and enemy of Germany. DS 89, 261.
103. DS 62; Rott, "Nationale Religion," 66. Lagarde follows Schleiermacher, pietism, and the liberal understanding of the religion as an inward experience, not tied so much to a historical person or specific orthodox creed about him. Religion is a personal relationship, not a metaphysical, theological proposition. Lagarde considers himself driven by a religious instinct more than reason. DS 60–62; *Ueber das verhältnis des deutschen*, 36–39; Viaene, "Paul de Lagarde," 537; Rott, "Nationale Religion," 59–60; Lougee, *Paul de Lagarde*, 119, 132–34.
104. DS 25, 66–70, 76, 96–97, 144–45, 220, 232, 277; Lougee, *Paul de Lagarde*, 5, 14–15, 19, 66–67, 120–22; Rott, "Nationale Religion," 58, 60, 64; Viaene, "Paul de Lagarde," 530–31.
105. Viaene, "Paul de Lagarde," 538–39; DS 127. Lagarde is influenced by Herder and the Romantics when he exalts the *Volksgeist* as the basis of the state. Lougee, *Paul de Lagarde*, 18, 129–30. He identifies himself as a conservative throughout his career and sees his party combating the left-wing notion that the state is the highest form of life. DS 381; Lougee, *Paul de Lagarde*, 162–63, 198–99.
106. DS 24, 124, 322; Pulzer, *The Rise of Political Anti-Semitism*, 85; Viaene, "Paul de Lagarde," 535; Lougee, *Paul de Lagarde*, 129–30. Lagarde says there is no pure German blood today. Leibniz and Lessing were Slavic, and Kant had a Scottish father, but they are still considered Germans. DS 124.
107. DS 127, 164–67, 193, 216, 323. He prefers Fichte's call for renewal among the German people to the cosmopolitan spirit of Hegel's work. DS 239–40.
108. Lougee, *Paul de Lagarde*, 142; DS 12, 245–46, 311, 369; Pulzer, *The Rise of Political Anti-Semitism*, 84. He rejects a social welfare system. Lougee, *Paul de Lagarde*, 181.
109. DS 120–22; Lougee, *Paul de Lagarde*, 172–74. See DS 333, 370, 394, 418; Lougee, *Paul de Lagarde*, 104–5.
110. DS 31, 83, 86, 110–114, 308–310, 391, 397, 406–7, 414; Viaene, "Paul de Lagarde," 548; Lougee, *Paul de Lagarde*, 184–89.

10

The Growth of Anti-Semitism and Anti-Christianity: Inside and Outside the Church

Christian Anti-Semitism

The roots of anti-Semitism have no real pretext in the fundamental teachings of the church. Beginning with Paul's letter to the Romans, the church emphasized the sinfulness of all human beings and never thought of the Jews as worse than others in their proclivity toward evil (Rom 1–3). Within the tomes and tomes of theological writings down through the ages, it is difficult to find comments or discussions among its major teachers that contradict this emphasis and exhibit clear and unequivocal anti-Semitic hatred, much in contrast to the sons of the Enlightenment, who develop a whole tradition of anti-Semitism and continuously deprecate the Jewish people and their religion without much equivocation. Usually, the accusation of anti-Semitism against the church is lodged by scholars who rummage through mountains of evidence to the contrary, find a few isolated passages or works, and develop a generalization about the church's teachings on the subject without considering the basic nuances of it confessions.

A favorite example of these scholars is John Chrysostom (ca. 344–407), the bishop of Antioch, who delivered a series of *Homilies against the Jews* in his youth, which are filled with extreme and hateful rhetoric toward the Jewish people and their faith.[1] In this series of sermons, he speaks of hating the Jews and the synagogue, comparing his animosity to YHWH's hatred of their feasts during the times of the prophets (Isa 1:13; Amos 5:21, 23). He considers the synagogue a "dwelling place of demons," similar in spirituality to a theater, brothel, and drinking hall. Jews are described as "demon-possessed" and the "most wretched of all human beings" (πάντων ἀνθρώπων ἀθλιώτεροι) because they rejected the Messiah and killed him as the "crowning act of [their] wickedness." He calls them "Christ-killers" (Χριστοκτόνοι) and finds within this act of total apostasy the fundamental rationale behind the severity of their present plight in the world. The Jews want to blame their many woes upon the evil deeds of others, but Chrysostom prefers to follow the

OT tradition of the prophets and find a higher, divine reason behind the suffering of the people, rooted within divine judgment upon their sins. He believes the sin of crucifying the Messiah led to the destruction of Jerusalem and the inauspicious state of its people, scattered among the nations and living without a home. This event also provided a divine commentary on the Jewish faith, destroying any future possibility of continuing its practice according to the prescriptions of the law. YHWH designated one place to celebrate the Jewish cult in the Mosaic law (Deut 12), and no Jew can ignore this commandment and practice the ancient customs in the *Diaspora*. The destruction of Jerusalem meant the destruction of the religion. While some have tried to rebuild the temple in the times of Hadrian, Constantine, and Julian the Apostate, Chrysostom believes that God confounded these efforts and reaffirmed the finality of the destruction.[2]

With these and other comments, Chrysostom earns the label of anti-Semitism to a certain degree, but it is important not to cherry-pick a few ideas or statements out of the overall context and exaggerate his bigotry. In all these harsh statements, Chrysostom finds his main concern as a pastor in preventing members of his own flock from returning to the ways of the synagogue and celebrating Jewish festivals, not in condemning the Jewish faith.[3] He might think of the Jews as enemies of God and "marked for slaughter" because of their iniquities,[4] but he simply wants his people to remain aloof from them and never proceeds any farther in this direction by using or even describing the church as an instrument of divine wrath or sponsoring specific measures of persecution.

Scholars often cite Chrysostom in particular and use his statements, along with some others, to provide a wholesale condemnation of NT Christianity.

> For much of western history, it was virtually impossible to be a Christian without being an anti-Semite of some stripe, without thinking ill of the people who rejected and reject Jesus and thus the moral order of the world derived from his teachings, from his revealed words. This is especially the case since Christians held the Jews responsible for Jesus' death. . . . The underlying need to think ill of Jews, to hate them, to derive meaning from this emotional state, woven into the fabric of Christianity itself, together with the derivative notion that Jews stand in opposition to the Christian defined moral order, create a readiness, an openness, if not a disposition, to believe that the Jews are capable of all heinous acts. . . . European antisemitism is a corollary of Christianity.[5]
>
> For the Tradition of Christianity, as embodied in the central text, the New Testament, is one which labels the Jew (at least in the later Gospels) as the antithesis of the healthy, sound, perfect world of the communion. The Jews are the "natural" locus for the origin of all senses of dissolution. Even in those Western situations

> where a "Philo-Semitic" image of the Jews seems to dominate (as in the fundamentalism of American evangelical Protestantism or of Cromwell's Puritans) the covert image of the Jew is that shaped by the New Testament. Christianity carries the virus of anti-Semitism, not necessarily in its institutions, which can and often are beneficient (*sic*) towards the Jews (because the function the Jews and their conversion are thought to play in bringing about the second coming of Christ), but in its central text.... Anti-Semitism is central to Western culture as the rhetoric of European culture is Christianized, even in its most secular form. This made the negative image of difference of the Jew found in the Gospel into the central referent for all definitions of difference in the West.[6]
>
> The thesis that the real roots of anti-Semitism are to be sought in the early Christian church was pioneered before the war by the English Christian James Parkes. In the face of the rise of Hitlerism, Parkes was asked by the International Student Service to investigate the history of anti-Semitism. In the preface of his seminal book, *The Conflict of the Church and the Synagogue,* dated May 1934, he explains "as the collection of the material progressed, I became more and more convinced that it was in the conflict of the Church and Synagogue that the real roots of the problem lay." At the time this was a revolutionary thesis. Now it has become almost banal, thanks to the work of Marcel Simon, whose *Verus Israël* was published in first 1948, and Jules Isaac, whose *Genèse de l'antisémitisme* appeared in 1956.... The "Christian anti-Semitism" has received its strongest statement in Rosemary Ruether's influential book *Faith and Fratricide,* published in 1974. Ruether traces what she calls the "anti-Judaic myth" right back to the foundation documents of Christianity, the New Testament writings, and she insists repeatedly that this anti-Judaism is "neither a superficial nor a secondary element in Christian thought" (p. 226), but an " intrinsic Christian need of self-affirmation (p. 181).[7]

These scholars find the basic pretext for Christian anti-Semitism in the NT teaching that the Jews murdered God and must find condemnation as "Christ-killers."[8] This belief first develops in the Gospel account, where Pilate (and the Romans) wash their hands of any complicity in the crucifixion of Jesus, while the Jews cry for his blood and accept whatever punishment comes from the hand of God (Matt 27:24–25; John 19:15–16). Jesus adds his authority to the interpretation by predicting the total destruction of the temple and the holy city in the Olivet Discourse as a fitting punishment for rejecting his messianic office (Luke 21:6, 20–24). The NT clearly blames the Jews for the crucifixion in these and other verses, but it never goes on and presents them as more depraved than other people because of their role in the event and only emphasizes their participation in the murder for a good apologetic reason. It is beyond question that Jews persecuted Christians during the first few centuries of their existence,[9] and Christians found it necessary to write a number of apologetic works, like the Gospels, pleading their case for a modicum of toleration. Christians wanted to enjoy the same toleration that Romans afforded Jews as a *religio licita* and found it necessary to persuade the magistrates of the empire that their belief in Christ represented no real threat to the authority of Rome and its laws; it is the Jews who find Christians guilty of transgressing their religious customs and stir up trouble against them (Acts 18:12–16); it is the Jews who crucified their Messiah, not Pilate or Rome, and must bear the punishment of their own sins at the hand of God. A modern mind might find this interpretation as self-serving or sanctimonious and prefer to understand the death of Jesus and the fall of Jerusalem in secular terms, discounting any moral commentary or divine activity in explaining these tragic events, but the early church lived within the same Jewish *Weltanschauung* that saw all events in life as an exercise of the divine will, bringing judgment upon those who transgress the covenant and its laws. The interpretation of the Gospels fits within the fundamental understanding of the OT, which saw the previous destruction of Jerusalem by Nebuchadnezzar as a fulfillment of divine retribution upon the sins of the Jews and devoted a number of prophetic books to the subject, not just a few verses. The scholars who denounce the NT at this point show considerable duplicity in their treatment of the two testaments, for none of them would think of deprecating the OT as engaging in anti-Semitism for providing this type of historical/moralistic commentary, and most would recognize the salvific nature of suffering as a means of sanctification in scripture, rather than follow the interpretation of Job's friends and demean the people of God as worse than others because of their many tribulations (Amos 3:2; Heb 12:6; 1 Pet 4:13–17). Indeed, these scholars stand justified in denouncing the church as anti-Semitic only if they can show that the church thought of Jews as the worst of all sinners or depicted Jews as Christ-killers with the pretext of stirring up trouble against them, but where is the evidence that makes this gospel of hate a pervasive teaching in the church? Or, has this charge become more of an urban legend that anti-Christian writers perpetuate against the church out of their own prejudice, just like a number of hate-filled Christians spoke of Jews poisoning wells or conducting ritual murders of Gentiles during the Middle Ages, all in an attempt to find a scapegoat or easy target? After all, these scholars present little evidence that the church sponsored anti-Semitism down through the ages and often know little about the overall teachings of the religion, or they choose to ignore what speaks to the contrary.[10] Even during the height of persecutions in the Middle Ages, the papacy remained the best friend of Jews in Europe and provided them with a felicitous lifestyle in Italy and Rome.[11] The hierarchy of the church rejected the false accusations that circulated throughout the era, with only a few exceptions, and condemned whatever atrocities befell the Jews in the strongest terms, including the pogroms of crusaders and the expulsions from various regions of Europe during the late medieval period.[12]

The most notable exception to the general trend is Martin Luther. At the end of his life, he abandoned an early policy of cordial and accommodating behavior toward the Jews, after reading one of their pamphlets in May 1542, and he responded in a tirade with his most infamous anti-Semitic treatise, *On the Jews and their Lies* (1543).[13] In the treatise, Luther vents considerable frustration over Jewish obstinacy in failing to accept the message of Christ and lists a number of sins that prevent them from finding redemption. One, Luther accuses them of developing lies about the messianic prophesies of scripture, showing no heartfelt interest in searching the texts for their genuine meaning. To Luther, it is clear that all hope for their fulfillment has lapsed long ago, probably during the reign of Herod, and any Jew who is open to the truth of God must reconsider the rejection of Jesus as the Messiah by his people as overlooking the only possible realization of serious moment (Gen 49:10; 2 Sam 23:2; Hag 2: 6–9; Dan 9:24ff.). Two, Luther chastens them for desiring a kingdom like Bar Kochba and Muhammad, which will subjugate, destroy, and mutilate their Christian neighbors. He believes Jews teach their children to hate and treat the *Goyim* as the enemy and pray for the Messiah to come and kill them.[14]

> That is what I have in mind when I said earlier that, next to the devil, a Christian has no more bitter and galling foe than a Jew. There is no other to whom we accord so many benefactions and from whom we suffer as much as we do from these base children of the devil, this brood of vipers. . . . [T]hey have to look into the devil's black, dark, lying behind, and worship his stench.[15]

Three, Luther creates a strong dichotomy between the law and the gospel, following Paul's concept in Galatians and Romans, and accuses the Jews of boasting about their righteousness and fulfillment of the law. (In this emphasis, he provides a theological impetus for the later German liberals to proceed farther and renounce Judaism and legalism altogether in the Christian faith.) Four, Luther chides the Jews for trusting in the flesh, boasting in their lineage, and exalting males in their daily prayers. He finds all races and sexes equal before God and thinks the Jews should circumcise their hearts, rather than trust in their own outward form or physical makeup (Rom 2:28–29). Five, Luther repeats the accusations concerning ritual murders and poisoning wells, although he expresses reservation about the truth of these charges but not the willingness of Jews to act accordingly. Six, he reflects the medieval attitude toward the evils of Jewish usury and their general lack of industry. "They let us work in the sweat to our brow to earn money and property while they sit behind the stove, idle away the time, fart, and roast pears. They stuff themselves, guzzle, and live in luxury and ease from our hard-earned goods.

With their accursed usury they hold us and our property captive." (This medieval attitude has a most direct influence on Hitler and the Nazis.) Seven, Luther thinks their deprecation of the name of Christ is unforgiveable. He mentions an incident involving three Jews, where he granted them safe passage but came to regret the decision when he heard later on that "they called Christ a *tola*, that is, a hanged highwayman." He speaks of other Jews spitting at the name of Jesus, calling him a "false teacher," making him a "tool of the devil," and referring to his mother as a whore, who committed adultery and conceived him during the uncleanness of her menstrual period. He leaves room for a private conscience to question the faith, but "to parade such unbelief so freely in churches and before our very noses, eyes, and ears, to boast of it, to sing it, teach it, and defend it, to revile and curse the true faith, and in this way lure others to them and hinder our people—that is a far, far different story."[16]

This type of public blasphemy receives no tolerance during the sixteenth century,[17] and Luther seems to make it the fundamental reason for his decision to proceed against the Jews with measures that rival the animus of Nazis.[18] He feels the German Christians can no longer tolerate the cursing of Christ in their midst, and so they must send the Jews on their way by burning down the houses, synagogues, and schools of these blasphemers. He believes all neighborly acts of charity, food, shelter, and "safe-conduct" must cease, and all the gold and silver, stolen through the vice of usury, must be "taken from them and put aside for safekeeping." All the Jewish literature, the prayer books and the Talmudic writings, that contain blasphemous utterances must be confiscated, and the rabbis forbidden from teaching altogether "on pain of loss of life and limb." It is best to say "good riddance" to these blasphemers and thieves, expel them from the land, just like the rest of Europe did in the past, and send them packing back to Jerusalem, where they can teach and believe whatever they want without corrupting the people—*cuius regio eius religio*.[19] This advice represents Luther's final solution to the Jewish problem, which he will continue to forward until the end of his life. (Fortunately, few magistrates accepted or enacted even a moderated form of his suggestions, and the Protestant community, including Melanchthon, Osiander, Jonas, Eberlin, Bullinger, and the Zurich churches, all condemned the treatise as the tirade of an old and sick man.[20] Anti-Semites might quote him in the centuries to come, but most of them find their basic inspiration elsewhere, and Hitler specially distances his own anti-Semitism from the religious concerns of the past, preferring a non-egalitarian, anti-Christian, and post-Enlightenment approach to the Jewish problem.)

In the vast domain of the church, it is easy to find some individuals or groups who take an aspect of Christian teaching and employ it outside the tensions of the faith to justify their own bigotries. After Luther, there arose other Christian anti-Semites who combined the rhetoric of the church with their own phobia about the Jews and developed a potent weapon against them.

Johann Andreas Eisenmenger, a devout Christian and Oriental scholar, was scandalized like Luther upon hearing rabbinic attacks upon the faith, and he spent twenty years researching and writing a prodigious 2,120-page tome of massive erudition, *Entdecktes Judenthum*, criticizing the Jewish tradition as perverse and hoping to restrict their economic and cultural freedom.[21] Abraham a Sancta Clara (1644–1709), an Augustinian monk and official Austrian preacher, thought of the Jews as the mortal enemies of Christians, accused them of causing the plague, sacrificing baptized children, and the typical staple of medieval crimes in the hope of purifying his Teutonic culture from the Jews and other alien influences; and Vienna later erected a statue to him on August 15, 1910, in honor of his struggle for nationalism, anti-Semitism, and xenophobia.[22] But of all these and other examples probably the most infamous of these Christians was Adolf Stoecker (1835–1909), a Lutheran pastor, who served as an army chaplain and court preacher at the cathedral in Berlin after the Franco-Prussian war. He developed political interests over the course of time and preached a "social gospel" like many Christian liberals in the last of the nineteenth and beginning of the twentieth centuries, wanting to develop a Christian state based on the egalitarian principles of the church and the economic welfare of all people. He spent much of his time attacking the capitalist banking interests of the Jews as perverting the German *Geist* and dominating its economy, and he felt it was imperative for the Jews to renounce their materialistic religion and develop spiritual values. His personal popularity soared in September of 1879 and throughout the 1880s, helping to make anti-Semitism an acceptable moral issue, although his Christian Social Workers' Party never gained sufficient support to make it a serious political force or alternative.[23] Other groups followed in the early twentieth century like the *Bund für eine Deutsche Kirche*, a group of nationalist pastors, who hoped to restore German glory and eliminate the corrupting influence of the Jews.[24] Of course, the Nazis empathized with these groups at first and spoke of them as representing a "positive Christianity" in their platform, as long as they continued to promote the German race's sense of moral decency and condemn Jewish materialism.[25]

Nazi Anti-Christianity

At the beginning of 1934, Nazi leaders like Goebbels, Rosenberg, Goering, and Schirach began a public campaign expressing open hostility toward the church.[26] Many ministers were arrested, and important theologians and philosophers were dismissed from their professorships, including Paul Tillich, Martin Buber, K. L. Schmidt, and Karl Barth. Theological faculties were placed under constant surveillance, since they served as mentors for the future leaders of the church, and enrollment among their student bodies plummeted accordingly.[27] Christian literature was suppressed everywhere and anti-Christian material circulated freely and widely among the masses, including

Rosenberg's *Myth of the Twentieth Century*, which the Central Gazette of the Curriculum Administration for Prussian Schools proposed to use in all classrooms.[28] Hitler let others handle the specific anti-Christian measures, while trying to distance his public persona from all those groups who would "destroy the church,"[29] but his general policy of *Gleichschaltung* was designed to align everything in Germany with the aspirations of National Socialism and could lead in no other direction or result than the complete elimination of all opposing forces, including the church.[30] To affect this policy, Hitler and the Nazis followed and emphasized the clandestine approach of the French Enlightenment, calling for a separation between church and state as if creating a sacred boundary,[31] hoping to limit the church to a private sphere, which will recede before the increasing power of the state. To destroy the church, the Nazis only needed to emphasize the separation of the two spheres, just like Luther and the Reformers, and then use the godless power of the state to reeducate the people into a different system of belief. Wilhelm Frick, the Minister of the Interior, said, "We do not want Protestant or Catholic civil servants, we want German civil servants."[32]

The Nazis proceeded to focus much of their attention upon the youth of Germany, hoping to make them obedient subjects of the state. Goebbels said, "The youth belong to us, and we will yield them to no one."[33] The Nazis harassed Christian youth movements and worked to absorb them into the Hitler Youth by holding meetings of the Hitler Youth on Sundays, banning double membership in other organizations, and restricting any other rallies or retreats of different groups.[34] On May 1, 1937, Hitler said,

> There is but one German people, and there can therefore be but one German youth. And there can be but one German Youth Movement, because there is but one way in which German youth can be educated and trained. The handful of people, who perhaps still cherish within themselves the thought that, beginning with the youth, they will be able to divide the German nation again, will be disappointed. This Reich stands, and is building itself up anew, upon its youth. And this Reich will hand over its youth to no one, but will take its education and its formation upon itself.[35]

By the summer of 1939, the Nazis succeeded in establishing an interdenominational German school system, staffed by people of all religious and nonreligious backgrounds, diluting serious religious confession in the classroom, ending specific denominational influence on education, and eliminating all "denominational schools or monastic or conventual schools."[36]

With the advent of war, Hitler decided to suspend further operations against the church for the sake of national unity, but he clearly planned on destroying all remaining elements of Christianity once the crisis ended.[37] In the spring of 1941, members of the party hierarchy began to speak out at public occasions, "bluntly advocating the liquidation of Christianity."[38] Friedrich Schmidt, a member of Rosenberg's staff, summarized the intention as follows:

> What about the church? Through its bishops the church is now trying to provoke the state. The Party is silent, since the Führer has given a strong directive that nothing should be undertaken against the church at the moment. They can speak and write freely. We are not going to make any martyrs. After the war will come the reckoning. For we are dealing here with an Either-Or. Christianity is a doctrine from the Near East; it is Jewish through and through. There can be no reconciliation here, such as the German Christians . . . are still trying to propagate.[39]

During the war, Hitler lived within the confines of the Concordat for the most part and left the German church to its restricted business. He escalated the program against the church only in non-German territories, particularly in the east, where he imprisoned, exiled, and murdered the Catholic priests by the thousands, leaving only a small handful of pastors to minister in a few local parishes.[40] Himmler rejoiced over the carnage and boasted, "We shall not rest until we have rooted out Christianity."[41] Hitler was more circumspect in public, but his private conversations expressed this plan to "exterminate the lie" and exact his "retribution to the last farthing," leaving no doubt that Hitler would destroy the church, just like the Jews, once his army successfully concluded the war.[42]

Gleichschaltung

The vast majority of Germans remained official members of the churches during the twelve years of Nazi tyranny. According to the last poll in May 17, 1939, 95 percent of the population, including a majority of the three million Nazis, still had an official, tax-paying affiliation with some church—54 percent Protestant and 40 percent Catholic.[43] One might think that so many Christians might serve as a significant determent to the moral corruption around them, but the people had lost much of their faith through years of biblical criticism, liberal theology, and compromise with Enlightenment ideology. Whatever Christianity was left in Protestant churches followed the basic exhortation of Luther to find their mission in a spiritual world of moral purity, away from the temptations of this world and the power of the state, and they accepted the cynical bastardization of this concept by the sons of the Enlightenment and the Nazis, who wished to destroy the church in the name of church/state separation. The churches submitted and lost their moral witness in the world, remaining largely silent about *Kristallnacht*, the Nuremberg Laws, and even the Holocaust.[44]

The Catholic Church was less compromised by the ideology of the Enlightenment than the Protestants and formed a stronger and more coherent opposition to Hitler in the early days of his ascendancy. The church recognized the danger as early as 1930, when Nazis began to make significant electoral gains and Rosenberg published his offensive book attacking the Judeo-Christian tradition.[45] On August 17–19, 1932, the Catholic bishops of Germany met at a conference in Fulda and took a firm position against the Nazis: forbidding members of the church from joining the party, pointing to its hostility toward fundamental doctrines of the faith, and recognizing the "gloomy" prospects for the church if the "party were to gain a monopoly on power."[46] The Nazis reacted harshly to this type of interference when they first came to power, and on June 30, 1934, they seized and murdered a number of Catholic leaders in a kind of wholesale massacre that was unknown in Europe since the slaughter of Huguenots on St. Bartholomew's Day three and a half centuries earlier. They hoped to silence the opposition without creating martyrs or undue publicity and continued this policy at strategic times over the next few years.[47] The church hierarchy tried to abate the tribulation and compromise with Hitler once he rose to power, recognizing that protest was futile in a highly organized police state and hoping to protect the institutions of the church from the Nazification process, but the church found only limited success in the end.[48] On July 30, 1933, the church signed the infamous Concordat, feeling there were no good options, promising obedience to the government in exchange for its self-preservation. The bishops swore allegiance to the Third Reich, the clergy agreed to refrain from political activities, and Hitler promised noninterference in the ministry of the Word and Sacrament, freedom of youth groups, along with their ecclesiastical commitments on Sundays and feast days, and pledged to inculcate "nothing incompatible with their religious and moral convictions" within the state.[49] Of course, neither side fully lived up to their part of the agreement, but the Concordat remained intact throughout the Nazi period as a metaphor or restraining force, which defined the basic relationship between the church and the state.[50] The church felt it was the only way to preserve the faith from *Gleichschaltung* or complete apostasy, but even if it found much justification for its action as the only possible recourse, the integrity of the institution as a beacon of divine truth in a dark world was compromised through this bargain with the devil. As a result, the church spent much of its time raising concerns about protecting its own kind, as in the case of the treatment of baptized Jews, but it fell silent for the most part when it came to the enormous and perspicuous affliction of other Jews outside its personal jurisdiction—at least in its public witness.[51]

No religious group compromised more with the Nazi regime than the "German Christians" (*Glaubensbewegung Deutsche Christen*), a loosely affiliated organization consisting of several subgroups that tended to merge together as Hitler rose in power.[52] In its manifesto of May 26, 1932, the German Christians called for the creation of one Evangelical Church developed out of the twenty-eight churches of the German Evangelical Church Confederation and representing the cultural and national aspirations of the German people. In this way, they rejected the international spirit of European Jewry and wanted to create a Germanic religion or *Gleichschaltung* of God and country, Lutheranism, and *Volkstum*. The manifesto spoke of the Jews as an alien and cosmopolitan race of people, who bastardize the culture, and called for the audience to stop this process by refusing to mix with them in marriage or even convert them as long as they remain citizens.[53] On December 17, 1941, the leaders of the movement lent their full support to Nazi policies against the Jews, even baptized Jews, denominating them as the "born enemies of the world and the Reich," based on their racial complexion, blaming them for the present conflict, and approving the dire measures of the regime to safeguard German life against this depraved people.[54]

Their religion tended to gravitate toward the anti-doctrinal, ecumenical framework of the post-Enlightenment world. They followed liberal theologians like Schleiermacher, Harnack, and Lagarde by considering the confessions of the church insignificant next to the inward feelings and simple spiritual piety of the *Volk* hoping to merge all denominations together and confess "one state, one people, one church."[55] They rejected conservative theologians, especially Karl Barth, who emphasized the transcendence of God, the authority of the Word, and the historic confessions of the church, and preferred to understand religion as the immanent self-development of their present cultural spirit.[56] They preferred to find the divine presence and will within themselves and cleanse Christianity from the legalistic forces of Judaism and the theological dogmas of the past, but sometimes the radical nature of the program proved too extreme for certain members and led to serious rifts and divisions within the movement. This problem all came to a head when Reinhold Krause, the leader of Berlin's German Christians, proceeded to denounce the canonicity of the OT and its "Jewish morality of rewards," "the worthless theology of the Rabbi Paul," and all things Jewish in the faith at a Sports Palace rally on November 13, 1933, with twenty thousand members in attendance, receiving thunderous applause from many in the audience but precipitating in a wave of departure from others who felt the speech was much too radical in tone.[57] After the episode, a number of individual pastors and theologians withdrew from the movement, Krause was removed from all offices in the church, and Joachim Hassenfelder, the overall leader, was forced to resign.[58]

On April 25, 1933, Hitler named Ludwig Müller, a German Christian leader of the East Prussian movement, his special advisor and plenipotentiary minister in establishing an Evangelical Reich Church.[59] During a synod of the Evangelical Church of the Old Prussian Union, meeting in Berlin on September 5–6, 1933, Müller was elevated to the position of Reich Bishop with the approval of Hitler, his longtime friend since the 1920s. The synod also enacted a law to make the clergy swear allegiance to the national government, and it added the infamous "Aryan Paragraph," which stated that no clergyman or official of the church may come from non-Aryan descent or marry an individual from that lineage, causing even a professed anti-Semite like Martin Niemöller some difficulty.[60] After the synod, Müller wielded his new Nazi powers with reckless abandon in an attempt to assimilate the church into the state, even incorporating the Evangelical Youth Organization into the Hitler Youth without authorization.[61] At first, the majority of the Evangelical clergy had difficulty submitting to the arbitrary power of Müller and his mixing of politics and religion together in this extreme manner, but through a process of necessity and intimidation, they ended up supporting or accepting the new situation as the indefeasible reality for the time being.[62] Müller successfully incorporated most churches into his leadership and all seemed to go as planned, but he failed in the end to close the deal and bring the churches of Württemberg and Bavaria into the one Reich's Church, eventually losing power and relevance due to the controversy, which was generated at home and abroad. While he continued in his office as a titular head of the church, Hitler lost confidence in him, and Hanns Kerl usurped his role as leader of Church Affairs, where he continued the attempt to unite Protestant churches until his death on December 14, 1941.[63]

The German Christians were a pro-Nazi group by conviction but spent a considerable amount of energy trying to convince the Nazi hierarchy that they were not an oxymoron. "The Swastika on our breast and the Cross in our hearts" was their sincere and faithful slogan, but many Nazis rejected them, believing that Christianity was a product of Judaism and must be eliminated just like the Jews. The German Christians persisted in trying to convince the regime of the intimate relation between a "positive Christianity" and the designs of National Socialism and presented their movement as anti-Jewish and consonant with Nazi ideals.[64] In the spirit of liberal criticism, they turned Jesus into a fabrication of their own image, making him an Aryan from Galilee of the Gentiles and a vicious opponent of all things Jewish.[65] They turned him into a *Führer* and *Kämpfer*, rejecting the "soft, weakly sentimental pictures of Jesus" and preferring to accent "his anger, his inexorable nature, his decisiveness, his strong will, his heroic nature," willing to conduct war against the enemy, but all to no avail.[66] The Nazis never supported the dream of merging church and state together, believing that Christianity was inimical to their national purposes, and continually advocated the separation of church and state as their basic tactical move and means of destroying the religion.[67] In 1937, they forbad the display of Nazi symbols in religious organizations, and in 1940, Hitler formally came out against the notion of creating an Evangelical Reich Church that would merge together Nazism and Christianity.[68]

Within the Evangelical Church, there was significant opposition to the German Christians and Reich Church. The opponents began to form a loose association at the First Confessing Synod of the Evangelical Church, which convened in the town of Barmen on May 29, 1934, and consisted of representatives from Lutheran, Reformed, and United Churches. The synod rejected the Reich Church for usurping the authority of Jesus Christ in the church, as well as his witness in scripture and the historic confessions of the faith. It confessed Jesus Christ as the one and only revelation of God, following the Neo-Orthodox theology of Karl Barth, and rejected the liberal notion that the "church can and must recognize any other events, powers, personalities, and truths apart from and in addition to this one word of God as sources of its proclamation." The church cannot and must not allow the "ideological or political views" of a certain time to dictate its message and polity—a typical vice of liberalism.[69] Following this declaration, the line was drawn in the sand, and the Evangelical Church splintered into two basic factions—the highly organized Reich Church and the less-structured Confessing Church, which subsisted as a loose conglomeration of churches and councils without a formal constitution.[70] The fission spilled over into education, with the Confessing Church forming their own illegal seminaries and the German Christians controlling state-sponsored education, which was already conducting a destructive polemic against the Judeo-Christian tradition before the Third Reich and now had the power of Hitler to exorcise all remnants of the traditional faith.[71] On June 4, 1936, the Confessing Church sent a pointed memorandum to Hitler, which was later printed in the New York Times and widely distributed in Germany, condemning the dechristianization of German culture, the hatred of the Jews (*Judenhass*), and the deification of the *Volk*, the *Staat*, and the *Führer*.[72] While their opposition was not always so courageous,[73] their group engendered some acts of outright bravery and certain individuals of great heroism, who opposed Nazi activities at the risk of their own personal freedom and lives. Bishop Theophil Wurm stood out for his particular courage in providing a forthright and continuous witness against the hatred of Jews and the "liquidation" of these and other undesirables, even though he was never arrested or executed—much to his surprise—probably because of his stature in the church and the Nazi fear of creating martyrs.[74] On October 17, 1943, the Twelfth Confessing Synod of the Old Prussian Union met in Breslau and issued their boldest declaration during a time of great peril, condemning the "liquidation" of the Jewish people and the infirmed as a direct violation of the Fifth Commandment, "Thou shalt not kill," and circulating the statement in pulpits throughout the land.[75] Of course, the Nazis tried to intimidate the church into submission and silence during its reign of terror and succeeded in many instances. In the summer of 1937, the Gestapo conducted its most brutal operation by arresting many leaders of the church, including Martin Niemöller, who first led the charge against the "Aryan Paragraph" and served as chief spokesman for the movement. Niemöller was detained on July 1, sent to concentration camps in Sachenhausen and Dachau, and remained incarcerated throughout the war, narrowly escaping execution.[76] With the threat of persecutions growing and escalating all the time, the Confessing Church lost much of its ability and willingness to withstand the many atrocities, probably recognizing the danger and futility of the effort.

Non-Christian Anti-Semitism

The impetus of modern anti-Semitism came mainly from sources outside the church. There were a number of anti-Semites who emphasized some aspect of Christianity and used it as a pretext for developing their bigotry, but they usually found their basic source of inspiration from some other source. If they were Christians, their tendency was to follow the modern world and promote its ideology through practicing biblical criticism, denouncing the orthodox traditions, and moving toward a new ecumenical religion, which retained Christian symbols and rhetoric without accepting its dogma.[77] These Christians walked within the spirit of the times, not bygone traditions, and followed the same type of anti-Semitism that characterized the sons of the French Enlightenment and the liberal theologians of Germany. This type of anti-Semitism represented a constant theme in the post-Enlightenment world and has its roots in those who wished to overcome the Judeo-Christian tradition as the fundamental obstacle in making progress toward a better society—Voltaire, Bolingbroke, Diderot, Holbach, Rousseau, Marx, and Jefferson.[78] The anti-Semites of modern times demonized Jewish culture and its effect upon modern society, demanding that Jews renounce their religion if they wish to become citizens within the new states.[79] This type of anti-Semitism arose at the end of the eighteenth century, just when these states were emerging, and it became difficult for Jews to remain a "state within a state" or alienated from the process of becoming a part of the modern world.[80] The racial component of anti-Semitism arose in the nineteenth century when Germans began to think of Jews as possessing an innate disposition toward alienation, which made assimilation impossible and cast doubts upon the traditional Christian doctrine of egalitarianism.[81]

Anti-Semitism began to fill the land of Germany in the nineteenth century, especially among those who expressed concern over the emancipation and the fear of economic and cultural domination.[82] The equality of the Jews was first proclaimed in the revolutionary years of 1848 and 1849, and it was later achieved under the leadership of Bismarck during the creation of the Reich and the new German Constitution in 1871, extending equal rights of citizenship to all people.[83] The great majority of Jews had entered the middle class at the beginning of the Second Reich, after living in poverty only a few decades earlier,[84] and now their equal footing in the constitution brought additional concern over their meteoric rise, bringing a new wave of anti-Semitism, which included all segments of German society, even among the intellectuals.[85] Nietzsche testifies to the pervasive nature of the bigotry, claiming he never "met a German yet who was well disposed toward the Jews."[86] This anti-Semitism permeated Germanic culture in varying degrees and consisted in the form of subtle discriminations, denying access to organizations, boycotting businesses, and refusing to hire, but no specific legislation was enacted between 1871 and 1931 that sanctioned the prejudice or qualified the liberty and equality of Jews in any way.[87] The number of anti-Semitic parties remained small and secured little political power before and after World War I, and yet a sizeable bloc of the Reichstag became more and more explicit in voicing concerns and creating platforms aimed at the Jewish populace, beginning in the 1890s and offering a portent of things to come.[88]

Heinrich Treitschke (1834–1896), a famous professor and historian from Berlin, helped spearhead the controversy in the last half of the nineteenth century when he published an anti-Semitic article, entitled "Unsere Aussichten," in the *Preussische Jaherbücher* on November 15, 1879. This article was the first in a series of nine articles, published between November 1879 and January 1881, which championed the necessity of a programmatic and political anti-Semitism, providing the movement with an important academic credential.[89] After the stock market collapsed in 1873, many articles appeared blaming Jewish economic interests and raising the Jewish question once again. Treitschke noticed the outrage growing among the people and expressed his own concern about the increasing power of the Jews in the stock exchange, banking industry, and the press. "The Jews are Germany's misfortune [*die Juden seien Deutschlands Unglück*]," he exclaimed, believing that Germany suffers more than other countries from the rapidly expanding size and power of these people. However, the special pretext for much of his anti-Semitism came from a strong political interest in national unity and rejection of the Jewish emphasis upon internationalism and parliamentarianism. He supported the designs of Bismarck for the most part, in creating German unity under Prussian leadership, and rejected the culture and politics of the Jews as representing chaos and fragmentation and destroying the uniform tradition of the German/Christian culture. Jews must recognize that Germany is a Christian nation and not confuse tolerance with religious indifference. Treitschke could hope for full emancipation, but only if the Jews became full Germans, abandoning their ceremonial days, rituals like circumcision, special dietary laws, and peculiar status as a nation within a nation.[90]

After Treitschke, anti-Semitism became more public, more organized, more strident, and more Nazi-like in ideology, with much of the emphasis falling upon *Volkstum* and nationalism. Eugen Dühring (1833–1921), a lecturer in economics and philosophy at the University of Berlin, accented the *Volk* ideal, promoted the purity of German blood, rejected any mixing with Jews in marriage (*Racenschädenlichkeit*), and advanced national socialism as the best form of government. He was an atheist and positivist, an extreme anti-Semite, and bitter opponent of Christianity, which he denounced as a by-product of Hebrew culture and incompatible with the Germanic spirit.[91] Georg Ritter von Schönerer (1842–1921) also promoted the same type of nationalism and emphasis upon German culture as the leader of the *Deutschnationaler Verein* and member of the Austrian Parliament (*Reichsrat*). He expressed the typical concerns about the Jewish problem and also fought political Catholicism in the ongoing *Kulturkampf* as a sympathetic proponent of Protestant national feelings.[92] Karl Lueger (1884–1910) followed much of Schönerer's agenda as a fellow member of the Austrian Parliament. His party gained control of the Vienna city council in 1895, where he served as mayor of the city from 1897 to1910, causing the Austrian bishops to express concern over the rise of pan-Germanism, anti-Semitism, anti-Slavism, and anticlericalism in the city and state but inspiring a young Hitler with great admiration for Lueger and his political agenda.[93] By 1911, this type of agenda was receiving support from more than two-thirds of the German electorate in Austria. The sentiment only escalated after the First World War in Austria and Germany, where the Jews became scapegoats, subject to mob attacks, and blamed for all social ills by a growing number of anti-Semitic clubs and associations cropping up all over the landscape.[94]

Most often the pretext for anti-Semitism was developed by taking some aspect of Jewish life out of balance with other considerations and exaggerating its place in understanding a people, but even the stereotypes were based on some notion of reality and contained a modicum of truth.[95] Sociologists have studied the available data and developed the following types of comments about the lifestyle of Jews during the time in question. According to their studies, 70 percent of Jews lived in urban centers and seldom produced their own food through the rigors of an agrarian lifestyle.[96] Furthermore,

> Jews were never the powerful "captains of industry" who produced the bulk of Germany's manufactured goods: rather, their roles were predominately those of middlemen, financiers, and members of the free professions and culture fields. . . .
>
> They were overrepresented in business, commerce, and public and private service; they were underrepresented in agriculture, industry, and domestic service. These characteristics were already evident in the Middle Ages and appeared in the census data as early as 1843. In 1933 business and commerce occupied 61 percent of all Jews in the labor force, as compared to 18 percent of all working Germans; and whereas 22 percent of Jews were employed in industry, 40 percent of Germans were similarly employed. Most striking, however, was the fact that only 2 percent of Jews were engaged in agriculture, in contrast to 29 percent among their German counterparts; this was true for both German and immigrant Jews. Immigrant Jews tended to enter the industrial labor market more than did German Jews, and this reflected their weaker financial position and lesser assimilation. In Prussia, where three-fourths of the Jews lived, by 1925 the percentage of Jewish executives in commerce and trade was over eight times that of non-Jews, and in industry it was over two times higher.

> These characteristics also held true at middle levels of management. Some cities, particularly Berlin, Frankfurt am Main, Cologne, and Breslau, had even higher percentages of Jews in high and middle-level positions.[97]

They were also preeminent in the banking industry, which often receives criticism during times of economic hardship. During the Middle Ages, Jews became involved in fulfilling this problematic service because of strictures placed upon Christian subjects and the selling of usury in canon law. The Jews suffered considerable persecution over the practice from those experiencing its pitfalls but continued their association with it as a lucrative source of income. "The two leading banking houses of Berlin were Bleichöfer and the *Disconto-Gesellschaft* of Hansemann—both Jewish. In Vienna all the major houses were Jewish except that of the Greek Sina."[98] The Jews were very wealthy, paying four times the taxes of the average German.[99]

> [A]s late as November 1938, after five years of anti-Jewish legislation, Jews still owned about one-third of all real property in the Reich, most of it acquired during the disastrous inflation of 1923 with foreign funds obtained through their international connections. . . . More than 50% of the members of the Berlin Chamber of Commerce were Jews, as were 1,200 of the 1,474 member of the Stock Exchange. . . . Major Francis Yeats-Brown (*European Jungle*) . . . tells us that in Berlin 1,925 out of 3,450 lawyers were Jews and in Frankfort, 432 out of 659. Fifteen Jewish bankers held 718 directorships. In Vienna, 85% of the lawyers, 70% of the dentists, more than 50% of the physicians, were Jews. The boot and shoe industry was 80% Jewish, as were the newspapers; the banks, 75%; the wine trade, 73%; the cinema, 70%; lumber and paper, 70%; fur and furriers, 87%; bakeries and laundries, 60%.[100]

All of this was quite remarkable for a small minority of people representing less than one percent of the total population between 1870 and 1933,[101] but it also became a pretext for resentment, especially when their financial position provided them leverage in creating public opinion and shaping the culture.

> Most of the leading organs of opinion, the *National-Zeitung* of Berlin, the *Frankfurter Zeitung*, the *Neue Freie Presse* of Vienna, were owned and edited by Jews. The same applied to the independent weeklies such as Karl Kraus' *Die Fackel* and Maximilian Harden's *Zukunft*. Of the twenty-one dailies published in Berlin during the 1870's, thirteen were owned by Jews, four had important Jewish contributors, and only four had no connection with Jews.[102]

Jews were also highly active in the theater, the arts, film, and journalism. For example, in 1931, 50 percent of the 234 theater directors

> in Germany were Jewish, and in Berlin the number was 80 percent; 75 percent of the plays produced in 1930 were written by Jews; the leading theater critics were Jewish; and a large number of prominent actors were Jewish.[103]

Unfortunately, many of them used these various media to criticize the Reich and the culture, inviting a reaction from those who rejected their left-wing politics and considered their power a threat to the traditions of the land.

The Germans had a pretext for criticizing the Jewish community on certain issues. The Jews might be the chosen people of God, but they were never the innocent people of God, beyond all reproach in their testimony to the truth of divine revelation in the world. The problem with anti-Semitism was not the willingness to question the Jewish faith and its community on specific issues of polemical concern, but the obsessive nature of the criticism in treating the Jews as the locus of social ills and creating stereotypes of their activity and beliefs, out of balance with the rest of its traditions and the entire life of its people. German Christians might have a pretext for criticizing the legalism of Judaism and following Luther's dichotomy between the law and the gospel, but even Luther rejected the extreme statements of Johannes Agricola and the antinomian movement in the 1530s, which disparaged the place of the Torah altogether. The modern type of anti-Semitism had no pretext in the overall teachings of the church and found most of its inspiration from the obsessive hate that the sons of the Enlightenment spewed at the entire Judeo-Christian tradition, blaming it for all the ills of society and hoping to replace it with a new ecumenical religion. The German Christians who developed the most anti-Semitic points of view were compromised this way by the prejudices of the Enlightenment, not the basic teachings of the church. It was the Confessing or Neo-Orthodox faction of the church that repudiated anti-Semitism, clinging to the traditional theology of the church and rejecting any serious compromises of its principles with the Enlightenment.

Notes

1. Marcel Simon, "Christian Anti-Semitism," in *Essential Papers on Judaism and Christianity in Conflict: From Late Antiquity to the Reformation*, Jeremy Cohen (ed.) (New York and London: New York University Press, 1991) 147; Moshe Lazar, "The Lamb and the Scapegoat," in *Anti-Semitism in Times of Crisis*, Sander L. Gilman and Steven T. Katz (ed.) (New York and London: New York University Press, 1991) 47. Hereafter the former book is abbreviated EPJC, and the latter ATC.
2. Chrysostom, *Homilies against the Jews*, C. Mervyn Maxwell (trans.) (Ph.D.. dissertation, University of Chicago, 1966) lvii, 5, 9–10, 16, 20–21, 26–32, 80, 93, 97, 149, 160–61, 170–71, 175–77; 181, 193, 199–201 (PG 48.845–54, 853, 871, 877–79, 898, 901, 904–7, 909, 913–16); Paul Lawrence Rose, *German Question/Jewish Question: Revolutionary Anitsemitism from Kant*

to *Wagner* (Princeton, NJ: Princeton University Press, 1990) 3; Goldhagen, *Hitler's Willing Executioners*, 50–51.

3. Ibid., xlixff., 1–2, 11–12, 19, 23, 27, 60ff., 102, 106 (PG 48.844, 847–51, 853, 864ff., 881–82). Chrysostom battles with pagans, not just Jews, and also calls their altar a "table of demons." He says the "impiety of the Jews is *equal* (ἴσα) to that of the Greeks, even if the temptation or "deception of the Jews is far worse for Christians." Ibid., xliii, 26, 58 (PG 48.852, 863).
4. Ibid., 8, 253 (PG 48.846, 937). Some Christians were going to Jews for the purpose of receiving a healing, and Chrysostom thinks it is better to die than participate in their arts. Ibid., 35–36 (PG 48.855). His special focus questions those Christians who celebrate Passover and confuse it with Lent. Ibid., 67 (PG 48.867). He constantly cites the admonition of Paul in Galatians 5:2 that if anyone receives circumcision, Christ will be of no value.
5. Golhagen, *Hitler's Willing Executioners*, 42, 49.
6. ATC, "Introduction," 14–15, 18.
7. Nicolas de Lange, "The Origins of Anti-Semitism," in ATC, 26–27. See EPJC, "Introduction," 12. Jeremy Cohen says the "most important Church fathers" conducted anti-Jewish polemics (*Adversus Judeos*) and finds the practice unseemly, if not anti-Semitic, but one wonders at this point whether anti-Semitism is becoming a label for anyone who disagrees with the Jews or Judaism. "Traditional Prejudice and Religious Reform," in ATC, 85; EPJC, "Introduction," 13.
8. Ibid., 52; Katz, *From Prejudice to Destruction*, 116, 323. This charge will continue among the church fathers, although it is hardly the single basis or even an important reason for anti-Semitism in the church's history. Simon, "Christian Anti-Semitism," 138, 167 (note 24).
9. Edward Flannery, *The Anguish of the Jews: Twenty-Three centuries of Anti-semitism* (New York/Mahwah: Paulist Press, 1985) 30–37; Justin Martyr, *Dial. With Trypho*, 110, 133 (PG 6.730–31); Tertullian, *Ad Nationes*, 1.14 (CC 1.33, 34).
10. Anti-Jewish diatribes are rare in liturgical texts. Few church historians discuss the issue because there are few documents or theologians that deal with the subject. Simon, "Christian Anti-Semitism," 153; Heiko Oberman, *The Roots of Anti-Semitism: In the Age of Renaissance and Reformation*, James I. Porter (trans.) (Philadelphia: Fortress Press, 1984) 66, 68. Of course, there are instances of anti-Semitic remarks among the church fathers in the fourth and fifth centuries. Cyril helped instigate the confiscation of Jewish property and their expulsion in 414. Ambrose defended the burning of synagogues and reproved Theodosius II for intervening on behalf of the Jews. However, the most important church father, Augustine, expressly forbad the persecution of the Jews, setting the fundamental precedent for the church due to the enormity of his stature in the Middle Ages. The Theodosian Code set the most important legal precedent and made it illegal to harass the Jews. Simon, "Christian Anti-Semitism," 155–61; Flannery, *The Anguish of the Jews*, 56–58.
11. Ibid., 73–74, 102–3, 122–23; Bruno Bauer, *Das Judenthum in der Fremde*, 38. From 430–1096, the relations between Jews and Christians were relatively good, except for some temporary, sporadic, and topical problems. In 1096, the First Crusade brought with it the persecution of the Jews like a

thunderclap, although the hierarchy of the church denounced this activity. The Jews were resented at this time for the practice of usury, which was an unseemly practice in Christendom and condemned early on by the church at the councils of Nicea (325), Carthage (345), and Aix-la-Chapelle (789). Canon law forbad Christians to sell usury, but its measures did not apply to Jews. Bernard of Clairvaux connected the Jews with usury, and Philip Augustus cancelled the debts of Christians to Jews shortly after his coronation in 1180. Pope Innocent III, who presided over Lateran Council IV (1215), found it necessary to put a moratorium on the crusaders' debt in order to stop the bloodshed. He imposed a number of regulations, including a dress code and living quarters, and became one of the few popes to diminish the social standing of the Jewish community in a serious way. Flannery, *The Anguish of the Jews*, 83, 88, 91–93, 98, 102–3, 112, 142–43; Bauer, *Das Judenthum* in *der Fremde*, 42; Lester K. Little, "The Jews in Christian Europe," in EPJC, 284, 293; Strehle, *The Egalitarian Spirit of Christianity*, 186; R. M. Mitchell, *Calvin's and the Puritan's View of the Protestant Ethic* (Washington, DC: University Press of America, 1979) 20; T. Wilson, *A Discourse upon Usury* [1572] (New York: Augustus M. Kelley, 1963) 232, 283; Simon, "Christian Anti-Semitism," 144; David Ruderman, "Champion of Jewish Economic Interests," in EPJC, 519. The church fathers were against the practice of usury. Wilson, *A Discourse upon Usury*, 217ff., 280–83; R. Bolton, *A Short and Private Discourse* (London: George Miller, 1637) 2–5. Many scholars discount explicit theological factors in the expulsions of the Jews and consider the matter of usury the leading cause of the hardship. The sixteenth century saw a marked decrease in the expulsions. Grégoire and the Jewish emancipators of the eighteenth century generally blame European nations for the persecution of the Jews in the Middle Ages through policies that denied them certain occupations and forced them into the practice of usury, while exonerating the church from culpability in this matter. See chap. 4, pp. 74–75; EPJC, "Introduction," 16–17; R. Po-chia Hsia, "Jews as Magicians in Reformation Germany," in ATC, 127–28; Oberman, *Roots of Anti-Semitism*, 43.

12. Bauer, *Das Judenthum in der Fremde*, 38–39; Flannery, *The Anguish of the Jews*, 108–10; Solomon Grayzel, "The Papal Bull *Sicut Judeis*," in EPJC, 236, 269, 270; Little, "The Jews in Christian Europe," 283–84. Even Bernard of Clairvaux opposed the pogroms. Beginning in 1480, the Inquisition persecuted the Marronos (Jewish Christians) because they were considered heretical and hypocritical by Jews and Christians alike. Heretics had no protection in the late medieval period and were treated more harshly than Jews. Flannery, *The Jewish Anguish*, 64, 137. Pope Gregory I (590–604) set the precedent for the benevolent treatment of the Jews in the Middle Ages, whose *Sicut Judeis* had a long history before its first official issuance under Calixtus II (1119–1124). Gregory's statement provided general guidance for the church and was periodically issued as a papal bull, beginning in the twelfth century, to protect the Jews as an onus of Christian piety whenever their rights were in peril. *Decretalia Gregorii* , "De Iudaeis, Sarracenis, et eorum servis," in *Corpus Iuris Canonici*, pars secunda (Lipsiae: ex officina Bernhardi Tauchnitz, 1881) IX, Lib. V, tit. vi, c. ix; EPJC, "Introduction," 15–16; Grayzel, "The Papal Bull *Sicut Judeis*," 231–39, 242. Augustine and

Gregory I serve as the two most important sources of authority in the Middle Ages. Of course, there was some inconsistency in the general policy, particularly in attempts to convert Jews by eliminating the major stumbling block, the Talmud. Some popes and certain theologians encouraged the burning of this sacred text. B. Brumenkranz, "The Roman Catholic Church and the Jews," in EPJC, 200; Granzyl, "The Papal Bull," 248; Kenneth R. Stow, "The Burning of the Talmud in 1553," in EPJC, 401–2, 409; Oberman, *Roots of Anti-Semitism*, 31–32.

13. LW 47.123–24, 133; Flannery, *The Anguish of the Jews*, 152. The content of the pamphlet remains unknown. Luther's first anti-Semitic treatise was *Against the Sabbatarians* (1538), and he added a couple of other treatises to his most infamous work as appendages, entitled *On the Ineffable Name and the Lineage of Christ* and *On the Last Words of David*. He consulted medieval authors like Margaritha, Porchetus, Nicholas of Lytra, and Paul of Burgos in his research on the Jews. LW 47. 217, 256 (note 159); WA 53.482; Mark U. Edwards, "Against the Jews," in EPJC, 357; Flannery, *The Anguish of the Jews*, 352–53. LW stands for *Luther's Works*, Jaroslav Pelikan (St. Louis: Concordia Publishing House, 1958–), and WA stands for *D. Martin Luthers Werke* (Weimar: H. Böhlau, 1883–).
14. LW 47.156–57, 176ff., 183, 192ff., 209ff., 228, 253, 263–64, 292–93; WA 53.433, 449ff., 455, 462ff., 475ff., 491ff., 510, 519–20, 542.
15. LW 47.256, 278; WA 53.513, 530.
16. LW 47.140–42, 149ff., 164ff., 169, 191–92, 211, 217, 240, 256–67, 277, 279; WA 53.420, 421, 427ff., 439–43, 461–62, 477–82, 500, 513–22, 530–32. *Tol ᵉdot Yeshu*, a life of Jesus that was used in the Middle Ages, used this scandalous story about an affair between Mary and Pandara. Jews did refer to Mary as a promiscuous women and Jesus as her illegitimate son.
17. Calvin calls for the separation of church and state in his *Institutes*, but he refuses to accept public blasphemy. *Inst.* 4.11.11–14; 20.3 (CO 2.899–903, 1094). This policy will lead to the most infamous episode in his career—the execution of Michael Servetus , the apostle of Anti-Trinitarianism. This act found approval among the cantons of Switzerland, Lutherans in Germany, and even among some of the greatest spokesmen for toleration in the era, like John Jewel and John Owen. Strehle, *The Egalitarian Spirit of Christianity*, 242–43.
18. Wilhelm Maurer, "Die Zeit der Reformation," in *Kirche und Synagogue*, Karl Heinrich Rengstorf und Siegfried von Kortzfleisch (Stuttgart: Ernst Klett Verlag, 1968) 1.397–400; Rose, *German Question/Jewish Question*, 7–8; Edwards, "Against the Jews," 367–68. The charge of blasphemy seems uppermost in his thinking when he wrote *On the Ineffable Name and On the Lineage of Christ.* WA 53.587–609; Edwards, "Against the Jews," 362.
19. LW 47.265–76, 284–88; WA 53.520–29, 535–38.
20. Hsia, "Jews as Magicians," 119–25; Gottfried Seebass, *Das reformatorische Werk des Andreas Osiander* (Nürnberg: Verein für Bayerische Kirchengeschichte, 1967) 82 (note 60); CR 5.728–29 (*Philippi Melancthonis Opera quae supersunt omnia*); Johann Eberlin von Günzburg, *Sämtilche Schriften*, Ludwig Enders (ed.) (Halle a. S.: Max Niemeyer, 1896–1902) 3.113–15; Oberman, *Roots of Anti-Semitism*, 35, 47, 73; LW 47.123, 135–36; Flannery, *The Anguish of the Jews*, 353; Edwards, "Against the Jews," 364–65.

21. Katz, *From Prejudice to Destruction*, 14–15, 19, 20.
22. Farías, *Heidegger and Nazism*, 24–26, 29.
23. Pulzer, *The Rise of Political Anti-Semitism*, 45–46, 48, 90–91, 97–102; Adolf Stoecker, "Zur Begründung einer christlich-sozialen Arbeiterpartei" (Jan. 3, 1881), "Notwehr gegen das moderne Judentum" (Sept. 26, 1879), "Principien, Thatsachen und Ziele in der Judenfrage" (May 27, 1881) in *Christlich-Sozial.: Reden und Aufsätze* (Bielefeld und Leipzig: Velhagen & Klasing, 1885) 3–6, 163, 167–68, 193–94, 197; *Der Berliner Antisemitismusstreit*, 237; Richard S. Levy, *Antisemitism: A Historical Encyclopedia of Prejudice and Persecution* (Santa Clara, Calif.: ABC-CLIO, 2005) 1.66–67. See Stoecker, *Christlich-Sozial.*, 21–23 for his party's platform.
24. J. S. Conway, *The Nazi Persecution of the Churches 1933–45* (New York: Basic books, 1968) 10. Katz thinks that Christianity and its bigotries served as a catalyst for modern anti-Semitism. He lists a number of anti-Semites who used Christianity in this way. Katz, *From Prejudice to Destruction*, 318–19.
25. Rosenberg, *Das Parteiprogramm*, 18 (art. 24); Peter Matheson, *The Third Reich and the Christian Churches* (Edinburgh: T. & T. Clark LTD., 1981) 1.
26. Conway, *Nazi Persecution of the Churches*, 78.
27. Matheson, *Third Reich and the Christian Churches*, 41; *Nazi Primer*, 276; Conway, *Nazi Persecution of the Churches*, 191, 194.
28. *Kirchliches Jahrbuch*, 431; Helmreich, *The German Churches under Hitler*, 319; Conway, *Nazi Persecution of the Churches*, 56.
29. *Dokumente zur Kirchenpolitik des Dritten Reiches*, Georg Kretschmar und Carsten Nicolaisen (Hrsg.) (München: C. Kaiser, 1971–2008) 1.8–9; Helmreich, *German Churches under Hitler*, 129, 309.
30. Helmreich, *German Churches under Hitler*, 132.
31. Conway, *Nazi Persecution of the Churches*, 67–69, 77, 104, 230. Church/state separation was a slogan among the Nazis, but many other groups, like the Social Democrats, were hostile to religion and wanted to privatize it as well. Following Luther's doctrine of church/state separation, German Protestants meekly submitted to the government for the most part. Luther felt this arrangement would cleanse the church of worldly temptations; secular Socialists like Hitler used it to preserve the state from ecclesiastical power and corruption.
32. Wilhelm Niemöller, *Kampf und Zeugnis der Bekenneden Kirche* (Bielefeld: L. Bechauf, 1948) 261.
33. *Völkische Beobachter* (Aug. 5, 1935).
34. Müller, *Katholische Kirche und Nationalsozialismus*, 190–93; Friedrich Zipfel, *Kirchenkampf in Deutschland 1933–45* (Berlin: Walter de Gruyter, 1965) 294; "Ratification of the Concordat" (Sept. 10, 1933) and "SS Report on Catholic Clergy" (May/June 1934), in Matheson, *The Third Reich and the Christian Churches*, 35, 48; Friedrich Zipfel, *Kirchenkampf in Deutschland 1933–45* (Berlin: De Gruter, 1965) 294; Nathaniel Micklem, *National Socialism and the Roman Catholic Church* (London: Oxford University Press, 1939) 223–24; Conway, *Nazi Persecution of the Churches*, 177–78, 216, 290, 293; Helmreich, *German Persecutionunder Hitler*, 221, 330.
35. *The Persecution of the Catholic Church: Facts and Documents* (London: Burnes Oates, 1940) 118.

36. Nazi Party Directive No. 79/39 (April 12, 1939) and Nazi Party Directive No. 132/39 (June 9, 1939), in Conway, *Nazi Persecution of the Churches*, 366–69 (Appendix 10). See also Ibid., 178–82; Helmreich, *German Churches under Hitler*, 319–20.
37. Conway, *Nazi persecution of the Churches*, 232.
38. Matheson, *The Third Reich and the German Churches*, 95.
39. Ibid., 90, or Gerhard Schäfer, *Landesbischof D. Wurm und der NS Staat 1940–45* (Stuttgart: Calwer Verlag, 1968) 22.
40. Conway, *Nazi Persecution of the Churches*, 296–300, 308, 309.
41. *Memoirs of Ernst von Weizsäcker*, John Andrews (trans.) (London: Victor Gollancz LTD, 1951) 281.
42. *Hitler's Table Talk*, Dec. 13, 1941, Feb. 8, 1942, July 4, 1942, 110, 230–31, 419 (*Monologe*, 150, 272); Conway, *Nazi Persecution of the Churches*, 331; Gordon, *Hitler, Germans and the "Jewish Question,"* 109. See chap. 6, p. 124 in this book.
43. Hubert Mohr, *Katholische Orden und Deutscher Imperialismus*, M. M. Šejmann (Vorwart) (Berlin: Akadamie-Verlag, 1965) 336–40; Matheson, *The Reich and the Christian Churches*, 99; Doris Bergen, "Nazism and Christianity," Journal of Contemporary History 42/1 (Jan. 2007): 29; Helmreich, *German Churches under Hitler*, 36–37, 92; Conway, *Nazi Persecution of the Churches*, 232; James Zabel, *Nazism and the Pastors: A Study of the Ideas of Three Deutsche Christen Groups* (Missoula, MT: Scholars Press, 1976) xii.
44. Helmreich, *German Churches under Hitler*, 190, 332; Conway, *Nazi Persecution of the Churches*, 223, 261.
45. Joseph Prud'homme, "The Churches and National Socialism in the Thought of Eric Voegelin," *Journal of Religion & Society* 13 (2011):11–14; Kershaw, *Hitler*, 94; Conway, *Nazi Persecution of the Churches*, 6.
46. Matheson, *The Reich and the Christian Churches*, 6–7 or Müller, *Katholische Kirche und Nationalsozialismus*, 62–63. Hannah Arendt considers the Jewish Germans all-too-passive in trying to cooperate with the Nazis and accepting their fate. *Eichmann in Jerusalem*, 10–12, 122–23.
47. Conway, *Nazi Persecution of the Churches*, 92–93, 158–60.
48. Ibid., xxii–xxiii, 69, 332.
49. Matheson, *Third Reich and the German Churches*, 30–33 (art. 32); Werner Weber, *Die deutschen Koncordate und Kirchenverträge der Gegenwart* (Göttingen: Vandenhoeck & Ruprecht, 1962–1971) 15–32; Helmreich, *German Churches under Hitler*, 245, 364–65; Conway, *Nazi Persecution of the Churches*, 20–26, 30.
50. Conway, *Nazi Persecution of the Churches*, 63–64, 165.
51. Gordon, Hitler, *Germans and the "Jewish Question,"* 248–49; Helmreich, *German Churches under Hitler*, 254, 277, 328. German Catholics did not elect anti-Semitic candidates in the early part of the twentieth century. Pulzer, *Rise of Political Anti-Semitism*, 174–77. It was Protestants that supported Hitler early on. Kershaw, *Hitler*, 94.
52. Doris Bergen, *Twisted Cross: The German Christian Movement in the Third Reich* (Chapel Hill, NC, and London: University of North Carolina Press, 1996) 1–2, 5–6; Zabel, *Nazism and the Pastors*, xiii, 27; Helmreich, *German Churches under Hitler*, 78–80, 127.

53. "Manifesto of the 'German Christians'" (May 26, 1932), in Matheson, *Third Reich and the German Churches*, 5–6 or *Kirchliches Janrbuch*, 4–6; Helmreich, *German Churches under Hitler*, 127; Zabel, *Nazism and the Pastors*, 140–45.
54. *Kirchliches Jahrbuch*, 481; Helmreich, *German Churches under Hitler*, 329–30.
55. Wenner, "Monatsbericht der Regierung (Sept. 1934)," and Ziegler, "Monatsbericht (Oct. 1937)," in *Die kirchlichen Lage in Bayern nach den Regierungspräsidentenberichten 1933–* (Mainz: Matthias-Grünewald Verlag, 1966–) 44, 212; Bergen, *Twisted Cross*, 103–4, 109; Zabel, *Nazism and the Pastors*, 51, 144, 204–5.
56. Bergen, *Twisted Cross*, 173, 175–76.
57. Ibid., 143–45; Zabel, *Nazism and the Pastors*, 32–33; Conway, *Nazi Persecution of the Churches*, 52–53; Helmreich, *German Churches under Hitler*, 149–51. There was a variety of opinions among the German Christians about the status of the OT. Many spoke of eliminating it; others spoke of the NT superseding it; and some actually liked the OT, especially the Prophets, because they found it anti-Semitic. Zabel, *Nazism and the Pastors*, 162, 211–12; Bergen, *Twisted Cross*, 145, 153; Peggy Cosmann, "Neubelebung and Überbietung socianischer und deistischer Interpretamente im 'geistlichen Antisemitismus'," *ZRGG* 52/3 (2000): 214–16. Their attitude toward Paul varied widely, although most chose to ignore him and spend time rescuing Jesus. Bergen, *Twisted Cross*, 158.
58. Helmreich, *German Churches under Hitler*, 150–52. They lost prestige when some important theologians quit the movement after this incident, including Karl Fezer, Paul Rückert, Heinrich Bornkamm, Friedrich Gogarten, Hermann Beyer, and Gerhard and Helmut Kittel.
59. Ibid., 134.
60. Bergen, *Twisted Cross*, 13, 35; Helmreich, *German Churches under Hitler*, 144, 147–48. In 1933, there were only thirty-seven Jewish pastors out of a total of eighteen thousand.
61. Helmreich, *German Churches under Hitler*, 153.
62. Conway, *Nazi Persecution of the Churches*, 71, 74–75.
63. Matheson, *The Third Reich and the Christian Churches*, 54–55; Helmreich, *German Churches under Hitler*, 185ff., 325–26.
64. Zabel, *Nazism and the Pastors*, 26ff., 124, 128–29, 139; Bergen, *Twisted Cross*, 3, 36–38, 42, 115; Conway, *Nazi Persecution of the Churches*, 45.
65. Bergen, *Twisted Cross*, 154ff.
66. Martin Wagner, "Heidische Frömmigkeit," *Das Evangelium im dritten Reich* 2/6 (Feb. 5, 1933): 45; Ludwig Müller and Christian Kinder, *Der Reichsbischof die Deutschen Christen* (Berlin: Gesellschaft für Zeitungsdienst G.m.b.H., 1934) 14; Joachim Hossenfelder, "Die Kirche und die Reaktion," *Das Evangelium im dritten Reich* 1/1 (Oct. 16, 1932): 2; Zabel, *Nazism and the Pastors*, 116–18, 138. All references come from Zabel's work.
67. Conway, *Nazi Persecution of the Churches*, 39, 54–59; Bergen, *Twisted Cross*, 3; Rauschning, *Hitler Speaks*, 57–63; Aschheim, *The Nietzsche Legacy in Germany*, 226.
68. Bergen, *Twisted Cross*, 117, Conway, *Nazi Persecution of the Churches*, 252.
69. *Die erste Bekenntnissynode der Deutschen Evangelischen Kirche zu Barmen: Text—Documente—Berichte*, Gerhard Niemöller (Hrsg.) (Göttingen:

Vandenhoeck & Ruprecht, 1959) 2.196–202; Helmreich, *German Churches under Hitler*, 161; Karl Barth, *Church Dogmatics*, I/1, 43, 255–56; II/1, 4–5, 10. Barth saw the emphasis on *Volkstum* as the basic impetus behind the German Christian heresy. Barth, *Community, State, and Church; three essays*, Will Herberg (intro.) (Gloucester, MA: Peter Smith, 1968) 38.

70. Helmreich, *German Churches under Hitler*, 163, 167. "After its foundation, nine thousand clergymen joined the Confessing Church; in contrast, five thousand joined the anti-Semitic German Christians." Gordon, *Hitler, Germans and the "Jewish Question"*, 255.
71. Matheson, *Third Reich and the Christian Churches*, 26, 51; Bergen, *Twisted Cross*, 13. The Gestapo censored the Confessing Church from printing material on Nov. 12, 1934, and May 6, 1935.
72. Helmreich, *German Churches under Hitler*, 199–201; Matheson, *Third Reich and the Christian Churches*, 58.
73. Conway, *Nazi Persecution of the Churches*, xx–xxi.
74. Helmreich, *German Churches under Hitler*, 330–31, 336, 346.
75. *Kirchliches Jahrbuch*, 403.
76. *Nazi Primer*, 275–76; Matheson, *Third Reich and the Christian Churches*, 36–38; Gordon, *Hitler, Germans and the "Jewish Question,"* 254–55; Conway, *Nazi persecution of the Churches*, 212.
77. Pulzer, *Rise of Political Anti-Semitism*, 314.
78. Flannery, *The Anguish of the Jews*, 176.
79. Pulzer, *Rise of Political Anti-Semitism*, 226–27; Herzog, *Intimacy & Exclusion*, 53–56; Goldhagen, *Hitler's Willing Executioners*, 58.
80. *An die Hohe Deutsche Bundesversammlung* (Frankfurt: Andreä, 1817) 39–40; Katz, *From Prejudice to Destruction*, 58, 87, 236–37; Segel, *A Lie and Libel*, 8. Katz says the expression "a state within a state" came into vogue in the 1780s. Johann Heinrich Schultz was the first to apply it to the Jews.
81. Eleonore Sterling, *Judenhass: Die Anfänge des politischen Antisemitismus in Deutschland (1815–1850)* (Frankfurt a. M.: Europäische Verlagsanstalt, 1969) 120, 125–28; Klemens Felden, "Die Übernahme des antisemitischen Stereotyps als soziale Norm durch bürgerliche Gesellschaft Deutschlands, 1875–1900" (Ruprecht-Karl–Univeresität zu Heidelberg, 1963) 51; Goldhagen, *Hitler's Willing Executioners*, 66, 68–69; Pulzer, *Rise of Political Anti-Semitism*, 295.
82. Werner Jochmann, "Structure and Functions of German Anti-Semitism, 1878–1914," in *Hostages of Modernzation: Studies on Modern Antisemitism, 1870–1933/39*, Herbert Strauss (ed.) (Berlin and New York: Walter de Gruyter, 1993) 52–53; Goldhagen, *Hitler's Willing Executioners*, 61–62, 73; Weinberg, *Because They Were Jews*, 99.
83. Katz, *From Prejudice to Destruction*, 2–3, 210; Gordon, *Hitler, Germans, and the "Jewish Question,"* 7.
84. Heinz Holeczek, "The Jews and the German Liberals," in *Leo Baeck Institute Year Book* XXVIII (London: Secker and Warburg, 1983) 79; Weinberg, *Because They Were Jews*, 92.
85. *Der Berliner Antisemitismusstreit*, 30, 155–56; Flannery, *Anguish of the Jews*, 165, 176–81. Cf. Gordon, *Hitler, Germans and the "Jewish Question,"* 26–27.
86. BGE 184 (251).

87. Gordon, *Hitler, Germans and the "Jewish Question,"* 27; Weinberg, *Because They Were Jews*, 99.
88. Weinberg, *Because They Were Jews*, 98; Gordon, *Hitler, Germans and the "Jewish Question,"* 32.
89. *Der Berliner Antisemitismusstreit*, 77, 238, 240.
90. Ibid., 6–11, 35–38, 55–57, 86–90, 151–52, 209–10, 227–29, 242, 248, 254–58; Wenberg, *Because They Were Jews*, 93; Katz, *From Prejudice to Destruction*, 263.
91. E. C. Dühring, *Die Judenfrage als Rassen- Sitten-, und Culturfrage* (Karlsruhe and Leipzig: H. Reuther, 1881) 21–29; Pulzer, *Rise of Political Anti-Semitism*, 52, 54–55; Cosmann, *Neubelebung und Überbietung*, 210; Santaniello, "Post-Holocaust Re-Examination," 27.
92. Pulzer, *Rise of Political Anti-Semitism*, 151–54.
93. MK 121 (132–33); Pulzer, *Rise of Political Anti-Semitism*, 164–68, 180, 204–5, 216. Lueger was the head of the Christian Social party, but he was not a religious man.
94. Theodore Abel, *Why Hitler Came into Power* (Cambridge, MA, and London: Harvard University Press, 1986) 156; Birken, *Hitler as Philosophe*, 38; Pulzer, *Rise of Political Anti-Semitism*, 214. There were more than seventy of these anti-Semitic/racist groups in 1919. Kershaw, *Hitler*, 38.
95. Pulzer, *Rise of Political Anti-Semitism*, 75.
96. Goldhagen, *Hitler's Willing Executioners*, 42. In 1910, they were 3.6 percent of the population in Berlin and 8.6 percent of the population in Vienna.
97. Gordon, *Hitler, Germans and the "Jewish Question,"* 10–11, 16; Helmut Genschel, *Die Verdrängung der Juden aus der Wirtschaft im Dritten Reich* (Göttingen: Musterschmidt-Verlag, 1966) 21–22; *Statistik des Deutschen Reichs* (Berlin: Verl. für Sozialpolitik, Wirtschaft und Statistik P. Schmidt, 1927–1941) vol. 451 (1933): 5.23. They were overrepresented in the gymnasia and universities as teachers and students. Pulzer, *Rise of Political Anti-Semitism*, 12; Gordon, *Hitler, Germans and the "Jewish Question,"* 14.
98. Pulzer, *Rise of Political Anti-Semitism*, 11.
99. Gordon, *Hitler, Germans and the "Jewish Question,"* 15–16.
100. Rosenberg, *Myth of the Twentieth Century*, xx–xxiii. See Hannah Arendt, *The Origins of Totalitarianism* (New York: Harcourt, Brace & World, Inc., 1966) 52.
101. Goldhagen, *Hitler's Willing Executioners*, 42; Pulzer, *Rise of Political Anti-Semitism*, 8, 41.
102. Pulzer, *Rise of Political Anti-Semitism*, 13.
103. Gordon, *Hitler, Germans and the "Jewish Question"*, 14. See Segel, *A Lie and Libel*, 17–18, 22.

11

German Etatism, Racism, and Ethnocentrism

The war against the Judeo-Christian tradition escalated in Germany as the culture became more and more ethnocentric and rejected the egalitarian and cosmopolitan vision that had been so central to the church since its inception. The Germans developed intense national feelings at the beginning of the nineteenth century, reacting to the dominance of France in the region, reeling from the Napoleonic wars, and cultivating its own desire to create a large secular state. The result was a reduction of the 360 states to 39 (Napoleon), 25 (Bismarck), 17 (Weimar), and finally one all-encompassing Socialist state under Hitler, which essentially destroyed all meaningful relations with the non-German world.[1]

Many German nationalists credited the great German philosopher Johann Gottlieb Fichte (1762–1814) with providing the fundamental spiritual impetus of their cause.[2] Early on, Fichte embraced the revolutionary spirit of liberty and democracy, but he renounced it during the French occupation of Berlin in 1807 and gave voice to the sense of alienation and longing for a separate German identity in his *Addresses to the German Nation*, which began as a series of public lectures that year on December 13.[3] This resentment toward France was burgeoning among the German people and producing a considerable reaction in the form of nationalistic publications and pronouncements. In Fichte's *Addresses*, he tells the audience that foreign elements are destroying their culture, and they must rise above the alien invaders in order to preserve and defend their way of life. Napoleon might facilitate the resurrection of our nation if he is such a "great soul," but the primary impetus must come from the freedom and creativity of the German people. And so, he calls the people to create their own future through a voluntaristic act of self-determination, not sit back passively and accept whatever destiny lies ahead. This resurrection can come only if Germans help themselves, rather than wait for blind chance or destiny to unfold its unpredictable course. Germans must summons the creative power of the Spirit within them and fight once again for their freedom, rediscovering their historical roots in resisting the status quo of oppression, just as they ransacked Rome in the Middle Ages and revolted against its religion during the times of the Protestant Reformation.[4]

He wants a government that arises out of the native instincts of the German people and resists interference from the international community in the process. He resents the international image of Germans as a horde of barbarians ransacking classical culture in the past and possessing no intellectual or spiritual value, and he reacts to the antithesis by claiming a privileged status for his people in leading all of humanity toward a better age.[5] This vision of the future carries with it a demand for self-respect and a growing distaste for any international group, especially the Jews, who threaten ethnocentric claims.[6] In other writings, he says the Jews can never be Germans in the full sense of the term, and they should be denied civil rights or deported back to their native land of Palestine if at all possible.[7] "The only way to give them citizenship would be to cut off their heads on the same night in order to replace them with those containing no Jewish ideas."[8] Fichte focuses much of his ire against the Jews, the church, the guilds, the nobility, and any other cohesive group that acts like a state within a state and uses its international connections to undermine national unity.[9]

He sees his fellow Germans as a branch of the Teutonic race but prefers to find their common "organic unity" in language, not racial theory, as the primary vehicle of forging a people and differentiating them from others.[10] Language is a product of a natural and social environment, which deposits its image within the words of a people, and not an arbitrary construct, developed from nominalistic signs, and distinct from their life and thought. The external boundaries that separate the human race into geographical regions develop in accordance with internal and spiritual boundaries, which are set within a language or a common way of thinking. The knowledge of the natural and supernatural world finds its expression within the language of a people.[11]

This common life he hopes to subsume under the state as the unified expression of their will. He supports a heredity monarchy as the most efficient means of producing a united people, without placing any system of checks and balances upon the government to limit its power. In fact, he sees the citizens deriving their rights from the state and all cultural endeavors placed under its control. Later on, he hopes to create a national church, which will unfurl the flag in the sanctuary, stock cannons and muskets at the altar, honor the fallen in battle, and inculcate good citizenship among the parishioners.[12] In his *Addresses*, his primary interest centers upon the need for public education, or extending the power of the state in the realm of education, to create a "universal and national self." The purpose of the new education is to mold the "vital actions and impulses of its pupils" into a "corporate body" with nationalistic characteristics, acting for the "common interests" and producing as its essential feature "love of the fatherland," and "from that love there spring of themselves the courageous leader of his country and the peaceful and honest citizen." This education would become compulsory for all children, taking them away from their parents and taking them away from the church, which obstructs the opportunity for good education by providing a mere "nursery [school] for heaven." The children would become wards of the state and receive a useful education in matters of temporal concern.[13]

Much of Fichte's ideology is reflected in the ideas of Georg Hegel (1770–1831), the greatest philosopher of the nineteenth century. Hegel found inspiration in the works of Fichte, Schelling, and the German Idealists, providing the most systematic presentation of their ideology, and he ended up succeeding Fichte at the University of Berlin, receiving the chair, the most prestigious chair in all of philosophy, after Fichte's death. The stature, popularity, and influence of Hegel was enormous at the time and grew to encompass the entire culture of the nineteenth century, including a wide spectrum of political thought, ranging from the nation-state ideas of Bismarck to the totalitarian visions of Marx, Engels, and Lasalle, all directly and decidedly inspired by his all-encompassing philosophy. The left-wing could take heart in his emphasis upon the whole community, public education, and the welfare state; his criticism of greed, reifying and reducing individuals to a commodity, bought and sold; and his conception of history, involving a dialectical process of alienation and liberal progress toward a brighter future. The right-wing could find inspiration in his call to patriotic allegiance, his emphasis upon personal responsibility and punitive justice, his acceptance of inequality as a part of nature, his belief in property rights as an idealized possession, and his recognition of the self-interests of capitalism. His influence covered all sides of the political landscape, in which no one could capture the essence of his thought with a simple creedal statement, or claim his authority with a simple label like left-wing or right-wing, liberal or conservative—words that contain considerable ambiguity, even among his followers. His ideas certainly provided a pretext for the culture to develop some Nazi-like tendencies in deconstructing his work, although it is impossible to assign a specific label or monolithic influence to the overall system and its complexities, which defy any simple "ism."[14]

With this proviso, one can find significant tendencies toward a National Socialist perspective in certain areas of his thought, especially in his attempt to subsume each concrete moment and individual member into the whole. For Hegel, an individual only exists in the imagination as a nonessential element or mere moment of what is universal, beyond perception and impossible to describe in language as a specific object. True consciousness develops through a process that recognizes itself in all of reality, "of being both itself and the object" of its encounter, not living in isolation from one another. This self-consciousness becomes the primary end of life and makes communal living the necessary means and substantive groundwork for discovering individual identity. In moral living, the law becomes the "pure will of all," found in every heart, where the individual no longer sees itself in isolation and longs for accolades from all others as establishing the validity of an individual action and subsuming its duty under the universal expectations that are found in everyone.[15]

Hegel wants to place all individuals under the concrete authority of the state as the "absolute power on earth." The state is higher than civil society and the family, serving as the most perfect manifestation of the divine will in its present immanent form. The individual must look unto the state in order to discover its "destiny" and "universal objective thinghood" in the "customs and laws of its nation." The state is not "laid down as the security and protection of property and personal freedom," guaranteeing the individual rights of citizens, as if there exists an external life or moral tribunal outside the national interests. The state contains the real, absolute will of God on earth, fulfilling the moral purpose of each and every individual member in its dominion. Hegel proceeds along these lines by dismissing the modern political emphasis upon social contract, the sovereignty of the people, and the separation and balance of powers, wanting in its stead a real person or personality to forge a rational unity in the country, without the chaos of competing forces. He models his concept of the government after the Old Prussian system, with its bureaucracy of aristocrats, who are appointed by the monarch and not the people. The monarch receives his authority from heredity and acts with masterful independence, waging war at his discretion, proposing legislation on his own, and exercising absolute veto power over the parliament. Hegel expresses great admiration for world leaders like Napoleon and looks for this type of leadership coming from a single nation as the vehicle of the divine Spirit in leading the world into a higher stage.[16] In the present era, he thinks of Germany as receiving a special call from divine providence to serve as the highest point in an ever-evolving history,[17] helping to provide a philosophical matrix for the ethnocentric mania and fetish over the nation-state that will envelop German culture and eventually lead to the Third Reich.

Along with Fichte and Hegel, Friedrich Ludwig Jahn (1778–1852) was a significant academic leader in promoting national unity during the times of the French occupation, attacking its version of liberty, equality, and the European mentality. He established the first gymnastic society (*Turnverein*) at Berlin in 1811, which combined physical and *völkisch* education together, and received the nickname "Father Jahn" from his young disciples as their venerated mentor and founder of an important youth movement. In 1840, Jahn was awarded the Iron Cross for his bravery during the Napoleonic wars, stirring up nationalistic sentiment and leading a volunteer force of the Prussian army, and he was elected to the German National Parliament eight years later. After his passing, a parliamentary committee of the German Diet cited Jahn's *Deutsches Volkstum* (1810) and Fichte's *Speeches* as crucial works in creating the nation and hailed the two authors as "the spiritual godfathers" of the new Germany.[18]

In his great work, Father Jahn emphasizes the *Volk* as the essence and foundation of the state. Those who conquer a people learn this lesson the hard way and end up submitting to the language, religion, and culture of the ones they conquered. The people serve as a powerful force in society, independent of the government, and yet it is important to wield them together into a unified whole through the state for the sake of preserving the past and insuring the future. In this cause, he follows Kant, Hegel, and the basic penchant of German philosophy to seek and create unity as the fundamental and ultimate human endeavor. He states, "The striving for unity is the sublime offering of humanity, One God, One Vaterland, One house, One love." He admits that the concept of *Volkstum* is esoteric and understood only through an inner feeling, thinking, passion, and history, but he still finds it necessary to bring all the detail and experiences together into a unity and to justify the creation of one people. He says the "Volk, Deutschheit und Vaterland" still live but need awakening and strengthening at present through a variety of specific measures. Of course, the first step is to forge the people together into one state, making loyalty to the state their fundamental duty. "A Volk without a state is nothing but a vaporous phantom, much like the gypsies and the Jews. Only the state and Volk together can make a Reich." Second, he wants to eliminate all "unGermanized" aliens and all mixing with them as destructive to the German way of life. He believes that a purer race is better for the nation and uses the example of America and Vienna to demonstrate how a mixture can bastardize a culture. Third, he considers the mother tongue an essential aspect of a people and rejects mixing it with other languages or creating a multilingual society. Fourth, he wants to create one German church out of the various denominations, which will encourage the *Volkstum* as its essential service. The original gospel of Jesus found its most receptive audience within the German spirit, which helped bring reformation in the past when the church fell into corruption, and remains the only hope for much-needed change in the present. Fifth, he wants to place education into the hands of the state and use it to produce the prototype of an ideal citizen, making each student belong to the people. He wants all children to receive a uniform, public education and rejects the modern tendency toward specialized education as creating a fragmented people, who can no longer converse with each other. The purpose of education is to inculcate a common way of life in Germany, which enjoys the greatest culture, history and literary figures in all of Europe, and to censor whatever materials become unprofitable to the souls of the people and their devotion to the *Vaterland*. Along with the steady course of German ideology, a proper education must include physical exercise, military training, and a strong emphasis upon practical work and activity, making the students productive citizens, fit for service to their country.[19] In all this, Father Jahn provides a matrix for an education that was distinctly German, exerting a considerable influence on the school system and inspiring others, like the Nazis, to proceed in further, more militant directions.

Perhaps, the most influential professor in promoting etatism, racism, and ethnocentricity was Heinrich Treitschke, an instigator of Berlin's *Bewegung gegen das Judentum* at the end of the nineteenth century.[20] According to Friedrich Meinecke, a professor at the University of Berlin (1914–1928), Treitschke shaped the historical and political opinions of Germany from the early 1860s to the late 1930s like no other scholar and writer, serving as the editor of the *Preussische Jahrbücher* and the *Historische Zeitschrift*, important and prestigious publications.[21] He used his position and influence in society to promote the cause of nationalism against the international spirit of the French Revolution. He particularly disliked Napoleon for trying to create the "empty form of a single world," destroying the national identity of the German people, and liberating the Jews, who served as the agents of internationalism. His heroes were those who stood up for Germany: Luther for withstanding the power of Rome, Frederick the Great for establishing the military might of Prussia, and Bismarck for founding the new Reich in 1871.[22]

In his work on *Politics*, Treitschke speaks of the state as the revelation of the divine will here on earth. Treitschke demands the people submit to the will of the state as the "source of all authority." The state cannot tolerate the destructive behavior of dissidents, who practice polygamy (Mormons), refuse military service (Mennonites), and spurn their duty as citizens to follow its will with "unconditional obedience." Treitschke believes one has an obligation to accept the authority of the state and follow its decrees, regardless of individual conscience or the erroneous nature of its policies. The people have no pretext for rebelling against the government in natural laws, personal ethics, or religious scruples. Treitschke cites Machiavelli and separates the church and any other moral standard from prejudging the state and condemning its activities. In fact, he proceeds toward a voluntaristic explanation that sees "will" as "the essence of the state" and exalts in the capricious use of power as a sign of true greatness. He says that great nations seldom justify their activity by appealing to the intellect or rational order of things, but they exercise force, much like Sparta, Rome, and Venice—nations not "rich in mental endowment." War and conquest are absolutely essential to the vitality of a nation and its people. A nation is born when an individual or group imposes its will on the whole body politic, and finds its true greatness by expanding the dominion over others. Treitschke rejects the notion of establishing a nation through a social contract and has little use for international rules that inhibit the expansion of imperialistic power. His concept of power leads him to exalt leaders that are filled with "will-power, strong ambition, and a passionate desire for success" as a necessary means of accomplishing the mission of the state.[23] It also makes him prefer a monarch as the best form of government to unify the will to power.

> In the state the contrary is the case. It represents power first and foremost, and its ideal is incontestably a monarchy, because in this

> form of government the power of the state is most clearly defined and finds its logical expression.[24]

Of course, he follows the typical ethnocentric analysis of German authors, comparing Germany to the Ancient Greeks and exalting them as the "two noblest nations in the world's history." Like Aristotle he recognizes a "natural inequality among men" that tends to exalt his own kind and disparages the basis for egalitarianism in the Judeo-Christian myth about Adam and Eve, believing that nature has made real differences in species and reaps vengeance upon those who mix them together and produce "less noble" creatures as a result. He divides the human race into four basic classes—white, black, red, and yellow. The yellow race is despotic, servile, and lacks genuine aesthetic ability; the black is obsequious, athletic, and inferior in culture; the red has fallen into decay since the zenith of Peruvian civilization; and the white is divided between the Aryan and Semite. He hopes Germany will follow the manifest destiny of American expansionism and British imperialism and take a leading role in the colonization of the world by the white race.[25]

Treitschke and most Germans were looking for their own identity and ascension among the developing states during the nineteenth century. They reacted against the dominance of France in the region by longing for their own powerful state and rejecting the burgeoning international mentality of the Enlightenment and the subsequent revolution for the sake of cultural and ethnic expression. Many of their great intellectuals expressed this longing and showed the extreme lengths of the reaction by dispensing with individual rights and subsuming personal identity under the community and the concrete authority of the state as the "absolute moral ideal and power on earth." The state became their identity, and the egalitarian spirit of Christianity the enemy. Etatism was soon transformed into a racist doctrine of Germanism, as the doctrine of Adam and Eve was challenged in the name of cultural and ethnic superiority.

Racism

This type of racism has existed throughout the long annals of human history. Hinduism starts its version of history with a racial war between Aryan invaders and the dark-skinned, thick-lipped people of Northwest India, seeking to justify the present caste system or bigotries in the society. Shintoism starts with the *Kojiki* or "Records of Ancient Matters" describing the descent of the Japanese people from the Kami or godlike beings and exalting the sacred nature and divine origin of their inviolable shores. The West follows the same pattern when it exalts the Greco-Roman world and deprecates the ransacking of this classical culture by the barbarians and the dark ages—a history that Germans came to resent. Aristotle helps inflame the Western attitude by considering

Hellenic people more intelligent and masterful than others, destined to rule and enslave the barbaric populations of Europe and Asia.

Racism found a special "scientific" basis in modern Western civilization during its critical, formative years in the seventeenth and eighteenth centuries. The interest over race was excited by tales of explorers who were reaching distant lands and observing strange people of varying appearance, custom, and development. Abbé Prévost published fifteen volumes of *Histoire général des voyages* (1746–1759) based on John Green's *New Collection of Voyages and Travels* (1745–1747), describing contact with these primitive people, and found a popular audience among curious Europeans. Count Buffon followed with another collection of stories in his *Historie naturelle* (1749), which proved even more popular and proceeded to explain the variety of life around the globe by extending the age of the earth, challenging the book of Genesis and its six thousand years of history, thinking of humans as sharing a common origin with apes, and considering the white race superior to other degenerate forms. François Bernier tried to wrestle with the new discoveries in a Parisian article (1684) by developing a new method of classifying humans into Europeans, Far Easterners, Blacks, and Lapps, although Leibniz objected to the scheme in the name of human decency, holding to the typical monogenetic theory of the day in order to preserve basic equality and rejecting any division of humans into separate races because of physical differences. The egalitarian belief in Adam and Eve prevailed for the time being, serving as the basis of human dignity, but it was confronted with a disturbing reality that human beings were not a simple monolith, stamped out of the same mold.[26]

Many intellectuals began to question the religious dogma of monogenism, beginning with the Enlightenment, and felt free to express definitive racist opinions now that the religious strictures of the past were no longer binding, including those who still emphasized that "all men are created equal."[27] The philosophes led the way in attacking the book of Genesis and undermining the biblical belief in a fundamental unity among the species.[28] Voltaire makes reference in his writings to the first voyages around the continent of Africa as presenting a shock to the basic beliefs of many travelers, who experienced the lack of progress among the inhabitants, and he proceeds to relate his own firsthand experiences of their inferiority. He finds the people of Africa "hardly a degree above some brutes," utterly lacking in intelligence, and thinks it incredulous to believe they were made in the image of God. These people love music and dance, and yet they lack the requisite intelligence to create European instruments like violins or bagpipes. It makes one wonder whether they evolved from apes or monkeys, or maybe vice versa. He seems to accept the stories of the day about mixed monstrosities developing out of the union between humans and apes and couples it with a belief that human-like beings existed in the past, given the many ancient stories of satyrs and the current accounts of certain Filipinos possessing tails, but there is too much uncertainty about the specific details to obtain a more precise picture or speculate about the overall historical process. The evidence only allows him to assert that a different principle exists today in each species of human beings, explaining the different degrees of intelligence and corporeal features, and these differences are not a product of the environment or climate. He believes, for example, that Blacks have round eyes, flat noses, woolly hair, and a general lack of intelligence, no matter where they are born and live in this world. Voltaire ends his analysis by dividing human beings as they exist today into the following groups: Whites, Negroes, Albinos, Hottentots, Laplanders, Chinese, and [Native] Americans.[29]

Immanuel Kant helps bring the concept of race to the forefront of German society with an essay entitled "Von den verschiedenen Racen der Menschen" (1775). Kant speaks in the essay of four different races: the White, the Negro, the Hindu, and the Hun or Mongol race.[30] He thinks all of them evolved from a common stock (*Stamme*) and rejects a polygenetic model as threatening the metaphysical understanding of humankind, even if the original form no longer exists intact.[31] He explains the unity and diversity by conceiving of the original pair of humans as possessing the potential to change into a specific race, given certain environmental factors. Nature planted within them numerous seeds (*Keime*) and dispositions (*Anlagen*), triggering some seeds and suppressing others when humans first entered a specific set of circumstances, permanently fixing the races as a onetime event.[32] Each race is best suited for its original environment, which might lead to a certain relativism or appreciation for the differences between the various races, but Kant discredits this ecumenical direction elsewhere. Instead, he develops his racial theory into the typical racist doctrine of the day, extolling the white race for obtaining the "greatest perfection" of all human beings and expressing contempt for Indians, Negroes, and Americans as lacking talent, vitality, and culture.[33] The white race possesses the greatest balance and perfection of the original mixture with its *Keime, Triebfedern,* and *Anlagen* and exhibits its most phlegmatic form in the German national character.[34]

Johann Blumenbach deserves credit for bringing a significant amount of scientific rigor to the study of race.[35] He thinks of Carl Linnaeus as the first author of natural history to attempt a classification of human beings, but Blumenbach develops a more scientific approach by examining and measuring skulls as the first line of evidence, along with anatomical discussions of many other body parts—ears, breasts, genitals, legs, feet, and stature.[36] His method and interpretation are first presented to the faculty at Göttingen on September of 1775 in the form of a dissertation entitled "On the Variety of Mankind," which soon became the major work in the field. He obtains a professorship in medicine just a few years later at the school and gains an international reputation during his career, earning membership and honor from every important scientific body of his day.[37]

Unlike many others, Blumenbach finds it necessary to struggle against the racist tendencies that taint the field in the eyes of its retractors. He tries to establish the uniqueness and dignity of each and every human being against Linnaeus, creating as much distance as possible between primitive people and animals and finding much difference between humans and apes in regard to their speech, reason, posture, pelvis, dental structure, cranial capacity, and internal organs. He also promotes the human genus as possessing a fundamental unity, differing only in variable or secondary features, and accuses those who develop more racist opinions, including Tyssot and Voltaire, of lacking scientific rigor, pronouncing differences based on superficial impressions, and championing a novel opinion about human pluralism mainly out of contempt for the scripture. Blumbenbach attributes racial differences to a "degeneration" that transpires through the influence of external factors like the climate, the soil, the diet, and the "mode of life and art," changing the "color, structure, proportion, and stature" in an accidental way. He considers the climate to exert the "greatest and most permanent" influence in determining the outward appearance or color of skin in the course of a long period, allowing for its continuous reproduction in future generations.[38]

Beginning with the second edition (1781), Blumenbach lists five "varieties" (*Varietäten*) of human beings—Caucasian, Mongolian, Ethiopian, American, and Malay—and provides a detailed description of each.[39] The first place is assigned to the Caucasian as the "primeval" form, which degenerates into two extreme forms (Ethiopian and Mongolian) and two intermediate forms (American and Malay).[40] Some racism develops here in his concept of Caucasians as the archetype of humanity, as well as his description of them as the "most handsome and becoming" of varieties according to the original form and color of the race and "our opinion of symmetry." He explains that white people probably came from the area around Mount Caucasus, the "autochthones of mankind" and the present source of the "most beautiful race of men today," judging from his analysis of a single skull, and all other forms involve degeneration.[41] In spite of these comments, his overall penchant tends to proceed in another direction, and he ends the account with a more typical note: "That no doubt can any longer remain but that we are with great probability right in referring all and singular as many varieties of man as are at present known to one and the same species."[42]

With Blumenbach, science entered the field with its many experiments trying to establish whatever racial theory was present at hand. Physiognomists and phrenologists thought that outward appearance was a means of revealing inward intelligence and found the key to European intellectual superiority in an oval face, straight hair, and a distinguished nose. Others, like Cesare Lombroso, believed they could discern criminal propensities by investigating certain external, anatomical features like "enormous jaws, high cheek bones, prominent superciliary arches, solitary line in the palms, extreme size of the orbits, handle-shaped ears found in criminals, savages, and apes," giving a new twist to the concept of depravity, limiting the doctrine to certain types of people, and promoting the worst kind of racial profiling. Some scientists, like Paul Broca, believed that intelligence related to the size of the brain and found this organ significantly larger in superior races. Samuel George Morton tried to establish his belief in polygenism by taking cranial cavities and filling them with mustard seeds or lead shots to gauge the size of the various races and rank them accordingly. Americans took IQ tests, invented by Alfred Binet, to identify children with special educational needs, and used them as a weapon to justify segregation, eugenics, and restricting immigration for undesirable people.[43]

Arthur de Gobineau brought the science of racism to a whole new level by making it the most important concern of social policy and disseminating that concern among a wide audience through a popular work entitled *The Inequality of the Human Races* (1853). This book made a lasting impression on Wagner, Chamberlain, Hitler, and all those who shared his more extensive racial agenda.[44] In its preface, Gobineau maintains that the "racial question overshadows all other problems, that it holds the key to them all, and that the inequality of races from whose fusion a people is formed is enough to explain the whole course of its destiny." He expands on this thesis throughout the book, producing many examples of how a culture degenerates when its "primordial race-unit" deteriorates through the "influx of foreign elements" and loses the purity of its blood. This is precisely what happened to the great empires of ancient time; they bastardized their racial stock. Their decline had little to do with any military defeat, which has no ability to alter the "irresistible instincts of a race," no matter how brutal the conquest or oppressive the subsequent regime. It has little to do with the outward matters of culture like religion, law, and style of government, which remain secondary or symptomatic of a deeper problem, only representing the varnish of a people or covering what is more essential. For this reason, Gobineau assails the call for egalitarianism, which is inundating continental Europe in the wake of the French Revolution and diluting the superior blood of the Aryan race, leading to the destruction of the culture. The Aryans are responsible for building the great civilizations of the past, but whatever remains of their work will collapse if current trends continue to incorporate other races, elevating those who have no ability to produce this type of society to equal status and mixing our stock with their inferior blood.[45]

Gobineau refuses to accept any egalitarian explanation of the differences in terms of environmental or cultural conditions. Even the "most complete change of environment has no power to overturn . . . the permanence of racial types." Similar races live throughout the world in a wide variety of conditions, and great civilizations develop "independent of soil and climate." Gobineau offers no alternative theory to explain the origin of different races, finding current hypotheses that emphasize the climate, mutations, or hybrids totally inadequate and thinking it may be impossible to speculate about the "primal and generating causes" of the past starting from our present knowledge of natural forces. Some anthropologists like to speak of multiple origins, but these original stocks have vanished, along with the original qualities through crossbreeding, leaving us with much difficulty in reconstructing the past. The scripture provides us with the story of Adam as an explanation that is worthy of our pious devotion, but this man represents a mere "ancestor of the white race"—a race that no longer exists in its original form.[46]

Because of this, Gobineau limits his discussion to our observations about the races as they exist today in a secondary or derivative form. These races he groups into three basic categories, starting with the superior whites, descending to the mediocre yellows, and ending with the inferior blacks. He believes the white race had a monopoly on "beauty, strength, and intelligence" at one time, although they have fallen from their pristine glory and exhibit different and lesser degrees of their original qualities as Italians, Germans, Slavs, Semites, and so many other ethnic subgroups. The other two races recede from the white prototype in a more dramatic fashion and receive an unflattering portrait in general that renders them incapable of creative achievement and advanced civilization. Gobineau advocates a policy of segregation, reflecting the natural repulsion that exists between the races, and discourages mixed breeding in general, even if mixture can produce favorable characteristics in some instances.[47]

Charles Darwin offered a grand explanation for the origin of humankind and the various races of people, beginning with his *Origin of the Species* (1859), that Gobineau never envisioned or even thought possible, and yet resonated as a definitive answer for most naturalists in the years to come. Darwin's solution saw humans evolving from lower forms of life over a long period of time and differing from these forms and their own kind only in a matter of degree within a continuum, which contains no qualitative leaps into something completely different. The higher animals and lower races are versions of civilized humanity in this evolutionary scheme of things and share many of the same traits, including the use of language, tools, mental powers, and moral or social instincts—only in a less developed way.[48] This theory certainly had antecedents in the speculations of ancient Greeks, medieval theologians, Diderot, Goethe, Maillet, Buffon, Maupertuis, and Lamarck,[49] but Darwin provided it with a substantial apologetic witness, assembling definitive evidence from nature, finding a coherent mechanism to explain the process, and making the concept more credible to the scientific community. His proof was manifold: (1) the breeding of domestic animals in society as analogous to nature, (2) the thirteen species of finches, adapted to different conditions on the Galapagos Islands, (3) the nonuse of certain anatomical features, (4) the resemblance between creatures, and (5) the science of embryology or ontogeny, which displays a recapitulation of the evolutionary past within the development of individuals.[50] All this evidence provided a compelling case for the theory of evolution and helped make it the emerging theory of science—but only because Darwin added to his observations an efficient cause as a plausible means of explaining the dynamics of the process. What past theoreticians lacked was a coherent mechanism to explain how the evolutionary changes took place over a period of time, and Darwin solved this perplexing problem in the eyes of many naturalists by proposing the concept of "natural selection." Darwin proposed that nature favored certain offspring because of their ability to survive in the environment of their specific birth. Favorable variations will tend to accumulate in a population over a period of time among those who survive and propagate whatever fortuitous attribute allowed them to adapt and prosper.[51] People develop dark complexions in certain areas, not as a direct result of the climate, but as a means of surviving in it by escaping deadly diseases like miasma or yellow fever.[52]

Darwin's mechanism found an auspicious matrix within the economic thinking of the day. Darwin was fascinated with the economic philosophy of Adam Smith and its conception of individual struggle as a means of producing general advancement and thought this view of capitalism had lessons for us in the world of biology.[53] Later disciples will refer to Darwin's mechanism as "survival of the fittest" and the merger of this biological and economic theory as "Social Darwinism."

No person better illustrates this early relationship between the two fields than the Reverend Thomas Malthus, who first published a version of Social Darwinian thinking in *An Essay on the Principle of Population* (London, 1798). In this work, Malthus underscores his relation to Adam Smith and follows his laissez-faire economic policy when discussing the problem of hunger, letting nature check the excessive population rather than appeal to a heavy-handed government solution to mitigate the misery.[54] He thinks it is better for the long-term health of a population to let it struggle within the tough circumstances of life and evolve into a stronger people. The process of struggling is the "gracious design of Providence," preventing the population from increasing beyond the food supply and creating massive starvation. If the government decides to intervene in a specific circumstance, it only exacerbates the horrid conditions and extends the scope and duration of the misery. Increasing the wages drives up the cost of living for everyone and causes those who receive no raise to suffer even more. Enacting "poor-laws" grants a benefit without receiving any labor or increase of production in return and "spreads the general evil over a much larger surface" without alleviating the plight of those most affected.[55]

These and other arguments appealed to the young Darwin and exerted a decisive influence upon him when formulating his biological/economic philosophy and its concept, natural selection or survival of the fittest.[56]

> In October 1838, that is, fifteen months after I had begun my systematic inquiry, I happened to read for amusement Malthus on *Population*, and being well prepared to appreciate the struggle for existence which everywhere goes on from long-continued observation of the habits of animals and plants, it at once struck me that under these circumstances favourable variations would tend to be preserved, and unfavourable ones to be destroyed. The result of this would be the formation of new species. Here, then, I had at last got a theory by which to work; but I was not so anxious to avoid prejudice, that I determined not for some time to write even the briefest sketch of it.[57]

Darwin sees a future where "civilized races of man will almost certainly exterminate, and replace, the savage races throughout the world,"[58] but he expresses some concern about the dysgenics practiced in the West and its future.

> We civilized men, on the other hand, do our utmost to check the process of elimination; we build asylums for the imbecile, the maimed, and the sick; we institute poor-laws; and our medical men exert their utmost skill to save the life of every one to the last moment. There is reason to believe that vaccination has preserved thousands, who from weak constitution would formerly have succumbed to small-pox. Thus the weak members of civilized societies propagate their own kind. No one who has attended to the breeding of domestic animals will doubt that this must be highly injurious to the race of man.[59]

Following this comment, he can proceed even farther and encourage the preservation of the strong and extermination of the weak.

> In the case of corporeal structures, it is the selection of the slightly better-endowed and the elimination of the slightly less well-endowed individuals, and not the preservation of strongly-marked and rare anomalies, that leads to the advancement of a species. So it will be with the intellectual faculties, since the somewhat abler men in each grade of society succeed rather better than the less able, and consequently increase in number, if not otherwise prevented. When in any nation the standard of intellect and the number of intellectual men have increased, we might expect from the law of the deviation from an average, that prodigies of genius will, as shewn by Mr. Galton, appear somewhat more frequently than before.[60]

These inauspicious words find no concrete application or expansion within the rest of his writings, but they leave the door open for Social Darwinians, eugenicists, and Nazis to express and enact a more specific agenda that works with the fundamental spirit of the new biology.[61] Darwin's theory develops and establishes its veracity based on the analogy of what transpires in domestic breeding and provides a rationale for escalating the practice as sound scientific policy.

Darwin also shares some of the racist sentiments of these groups, although his position and opinions are much less offensive or extreme than most of them. He recognizes that the "various races, when carefully compared and measured, differ much from each other,—as in the texture of the hair, the relative proportions of all parts of the body, the capacity of the lungs, the form and capacity of the skull, and even in the convolution of the brain,"[62] but he never dwells on this point as if it contains the most significant area of interest. He finds no clear distinctions between the races to justify a system of classification and observes only the "finest gradation . . . between the highest men of the highest races and the lowest savages,"[63] even if natural selection shows a preference for civilized people. In fact, he prefers to use the term "sub-species," instead of race, because of the great similarities between humans in "tastes, dispositions, and habits," preferring to accent their unity over any diversity. The great "majority of rising men" in the field see "all races of man" evolving from a "single primitive stock," even if "they designate the races as distinct species." The best guess is that all humans evolved from "Old World monkeys," and the best place to look for these "extinct apes" is on the Continent of Africa, where gorillas, chimpanzees, and the rest of our closest cousins live today.[64]

The concepts of Darwin became popular in Germany through the work of Ernst Haeckel, the eminent professor of biology at the University of Jena from 1862 to 1909. In his popular work, *The History of Creation* (1868), Haeckel extols Darwin as "the greatest naturalist of our century," believing his theory of evolution explains "all biological phenomena" and makes "all botanical and zoological series of phenomena intelligible in their relation to one another."[65] He believes the theory is comprehensive in scope and will transform our entire political, religious, and philosophical view of life in the future as its ramifications are experienced throughout all of society.[66] He acknowledges and discusses at length the work of many precursors, who expressed an incipient version of evolutionary theory[67] and reserves special honor for the work of Lamarck, who was first to say that "all animals and vegetable species are descended from common, most simple, and spontaneously generated prototypes." He even accepts Lamarck's belief that the personal effort of an organism transforms its anatomy and generates new and improved offspring in the process, but Lamarck's work provides only a partial explanation and lacks the comprehensive power of Darwin's empirical evidence and mechanistic explanation in the survival of the fittest.[68] Life is a "struggle of All against All."[69] Natural selection is the overarching truth. If anything, it owes a great debt to Thomas Malthus's work in the area of economics and population control for directly inspiring the idea in Darwin, along with Adam Smith's underlying economic philosophy, where competition creates a complex diversity or division of labor and fuels progress, without the intervention of government.

Just like capitalism, Darwinism provides the complete explanation for the rich abundance of life in all its diversity, complexity, and variety of species without resorting to metaphysical intervention or unnatural and unnecessary postulates.[70]

Unlike many of its early proponents, Haeckel recognizes the ramifications of the theory and no longer believes in a personal God or a universe that serves an ultimate intention. Darwin's theory refutes this way of thinking by showing "how arrangements serving a purpose can arise mechanically without causes acting for a purpose."[71] Natural selection depends upon the fortuitous combination of genes that happen to survive in a given circumstance and has no antecedent design or purpose to serve. It has no need of supernatural causes or interference when all is explained through the "spontaneous generation" of life out of inorganic material and the "gradual development of all organisms."[72] Maybe, it is plausible to identify God with the forces of nature and become a pantheist, but this new religion of Nature must replace the dark ages of superstition and its miraculous deity with truth and knowledge; and the theory of evolution is the "irrefutable testimony of truth."[73] It is no longer plausible to believe in a geocentric or anthropocentric universe. Human beings are no different from animals. They are controlled by the same external and internal forces, deriving from a "common ape-like" form and reaching back in a long chain of events through countless transformations, and have no special or unique origin in a single pair. The "recognition of the animal origin and pedigree of the human race" implodes the Judeo-Christian tradition and begins a new era of development, challenging and changing the "views we form of all human relations."[74]

The new human relation is predicated upon racial divisions. Haeckel groups humanity into four genera, twelve species, and thirty-six races, based on three fundamental characteristics—the form of skull, the color of skin, and the type of hair. He says the differences between the races are greater than the differences between animal and vegetable species in general and provides an extensive description of each category to impress the point. His racial tree starts with the Nigritos, living in Malacca and the Philippine Islands, and ascends to the Indo-Germanic tribes of Northwest Europe and North America. All wooly-haired and dark-skinned people exist in a "much lower stage of development, and [are] more like apes, than most of the Lissotrichi or straight-haired men." They are "incapable of a true inner culture and of a higher mental development, even under favorable conditions now offered to them in the United States." The "rudest savages" are closer to animals in their mental abilities, unable to receive instruction from "civilized men," even though many have tried to enculturate them in the past. The "Caucasian or Mediterranean man" stands at the "head of all races" in corporeal and cerebral capability, "most highly developed and perfect," creating the great civilizations of the world from time immemorial. Haeckel divides this race into two principal parts—the Hamo-Semitic and the

Indo-Germanic, which separated a long time ago, and centers his affections on the Indo-Germanic tribes, which he further divides into the Romanic branch (the Greco-Italo-Celtic) and Germanic branch. During the classical and medieval period, the Romanic branch outstripped the rest of humanity in developing their civilization and dominating others; now it is the Germanic branch that is "spreading the network of civilization over the whole globe" and "laying the foundation for a new era of higher mental culture." Haeckel sees the imminent future much like Hitler, with inferior races succumbing to their superiors as the inevitable march of history, dominated by the process of Darwinian evolution and biological determinism.[75]

Darwinism exerted a greater impact on Germany during the nineteenth and early twentieth century than any other country in the Western world. Darwin saw Germany as the "chief ground for hoping that our views will ultimately prevail" in academia and culture.[76] As early as the 1860s and 1870s many German intellectuals were "appealing to Darwinism to support their political and social theories" and using the theory to challenge the West with scientific, anti-Christian positions.[77] Karl Vogt, an early advocate of Darwinism, continually challenged the Christian spirit of egalitarianism in his *Lectures on Man*, stressing the inferiority of non-European races and becoming the first German biologist to relativize the killing of the weak, the disabled, and the mentally ill.[78] Robby Kossman, a German zoologist, wrote an essay in 1880, where he outlined the typical Darwinian attitude of the day, rejecting the value of individual human life for the sake of the species and hoping humanity will evolve as a whole into a "higher level of perfection . . . through the destruction of the less well-endowed individuals."[79] Almost all Darwinists renounced the Christian faith and repudiated the principle of equality and love for the downtrodden as so much religious dogma from the past. The new era of eugenics was proclaimed and protruded to a place of prominence within the scientific and medical community in the first decade of the twentieth century, judging from the large quantity of material written on the subject in articles and books.[80] Alfred Ploetz founded the first eugenics society in the world, the German Society of Racial Hygiene (1905), as a disciple of Haeckel, and he established a journal devoted to the field, where Ludwig Plate, the successor of Haeckel at Jena, served as a coeditor. In 1911, a prestigious scientific journal like *Umschau* joined the burgeoning interest in Social Darwinism by offering a large cash prize of 1,200 marks for the best essay on the burning topic of the day: "What do the bad racial elements cost the state and society?" Two eugenicists were used as judges, and they awarded the prize to an essay that "calculated the cost of institutionalizing 'inferior' people in the city of Hamburg alone at 31,617,823 marks annually"—a considerable sum meant to draw the ire of fiscally responsible citizens.[81]

Of course, German eugenicists had a decided interest in race, which they saw as the leading indicator of evolutionary theory in the first place.[82]

Fritz Lenz, a professor of eugenics in Munich, wrote an article about this racial and ethical ideal in 1917, demanding that "we place our entire life in its service; . . . that we really can live according to it. With every deed and with every inaction, we have to ask ourselves: does it benefit our race? And then make our decision accordingly."[83] Almost all Darwinists followed Haeckel and treated racism as a leading political and philosophical ideal, which demanded immediate action for the sake of their superior race of people, and a number of them viewed racial struggle (*Kampf*) and extermination as a positive step in the evolutionary scheme of things like Rudolf Cronau, Alfred Kirchhoff, Friedrich Hellwald, Oscar Peschel, Oscar Schmidt, Friederich Rolle, and Friedrich Ratzel, just to name a few.[84] Beginning in the 1890s there was a proliferation of books and articles from these and other authors discussing the racial struggle and viewing this Darwinian perspective as the "universal key to interpreting history, society, and culture." Jews were not connected with this struggle or deprecated as racial inferiors like other non-European people, but they incurred the wrath of Darwinists because of their political position, which centered upon the doctrine of equality.[85] Social Darwinists like Hans Günther, Alfred Rosenberg, and Adolf Hitler hated the Jews mainly because of their rejection of the new biology and its political ramifications, not because of any innate or significant defect found in their branch of the evolutionary tree. Anti-Semitism added racial epithets to their political opponents and forced this hateful analysis upon an evolutionary doctrine of race, which had no original intention of degrading the Jews in any significant way and aimed its malicious scientific scale at other groups of people. Modern anti-Semitism was ultimately born from the atmosphere of hatred growing out of the Enlightenment toward the Judeo-Christian tradition and developed all sorts of anachronistic justifications along the way.[86]

Notes

1. Viereck, *Metapolitics*, 55, 126; McGovern, *From Luther to Hitler*, 211. Nazis wanted *German* science, *German* economics, *German* history, and *German* myths to benefit the nation, not universal truths in various fields of a general human culture. McGovern, *From Luther to Hitler*, 628–30.
2. Fichte thinks of himself as a herald, or the first one to step forward and proclaim these things. His address might have exerted little immediate influence upon the audience, but it clearly had a major impact on the Nazis and proto-Nazis of later generations. Johann Gottlieb Fichte, *Addresses to the German Nation*, George Armstrong Kelly (ed. And intro.) (New York and Evanston, IL: Harper & Row, 1968) 214; McGovern, *From Luther to Hitler*, 216; Lagarde, *Deutsche Schriften*, 240, 248. Hereafter the *Addresses* are designated AGN. Hitler was certainly familiar with the great philosopher and received a copy of Fichte's *German Beliefs*, written by Maria Grunewald, just before he wrote his second book. Hitler's overall ideals are close to Fichte's philosophy, maybe closer to it than ideas of any other major intellectual figure. Ryback, *Hitler's Private Library*, 91, 107–8.

3. AGN xv–xviii.
4. AGN xv–xvii, xxiv, xxviii, 2, 4, 38, 80–81, 86, 107–8, 121, 123; Viereck, *Metapolitics*, 68; McGovern, *From Luther to Hitler*, 211–12, 219, 229–30, 236; Lougee, *Paul de Lagarde*, 42, 47.
5. AGN 204–5, 228; Santayana, *The German Mind*, 67, 74.
6. Rosenberg, *Race and Race History and Other Essays*, 19.
7. McGovern, *From Luther to Hitler*, 239, 259.
8. Johann Gottleib Fichte, *Beitrag zu Berichtigung der Urteile des Publikums über die fränzösische Revolution* (Leipzig: Felix Meiner, 1922) 115 [*Sämtliche Werke*, J. H. Fichte (Hrsg.) (Berlin: Veit, 1845) 6.149–50]; Katz, *From Prejudice to Destruction*, 57.
9. Ibid., 114–15; Katz, *From Prejudice to Destruction*, 60.
10. AGN 3, 45–48; McGovern, *From Luther to Hitler*, 238. Many authors after this time spoke of the primitive authenticity of the German language. Philologists began to connect the language with Sanskrit as a mother tongue and helped forward the Indian/Aryan theory of origins, which Herder, Schlegel, Hegel, and a host of Enlightenment and post-Enlightenment figures advocated as a means of replacing Adam and Eve. The linguistic category of Indo-European or Indo-European languages grows out of this passion for Aryanism. Poliakov, *Aryan Myth*, 90ff., 186–92, 195ff., 256, 259, 327–28.
11. AGN 49–52, 190–191. He thinks of German as a living language, not dead like other Teutonic languages that come from Latin, a dead and foreign language. People with a dead language lack creativity and ingenuity. Unlike other Teutonic peoples, Germans have remained connected to the "uninterrupted flow of a primitive language," which developed out of real life and allowed for new possible combinations, expressing deep-seated spiritual concerns, and genuine ongoing experience. AGN 59, 62, 66, 72–73, 76.
12. McGovern, *From Luther to Hitler*, 222–23, 234–36, 251–53.
13. AGN 10–13, 16, 29, 134, 162–72.
14. Georg Hegel, *The Philosophy of Right*, T. M. Knox (trans.), in *Great Books of the Western World*, Mortimer Adler (ed.) (Chicago: Encyclopaedia Britannica, Inc., 1977) 23–28, 37–38, 42–3, 67, 76–77 (44–64, 99–101, 115–18, 200, 240–45); Hegel, *Phenomenology of the Spirit*, A. V. Miller (trans.), J. N. Findlay (foreword and analysis) (Oxford: Oxford University Press, 1977) 19–23, 306–9, 320–21 (32–39, 504–9, 526). Hereafter designated as HPR and HPS, respectively. Hegel is not always popular with the orthodox Nazis. For example, Baeumler had much sympathy for him, feeling those rejecting him were simplistic, whereas Rosenberg condemned him because of his influence on Marxism. Leske, *Philosophen im 'Dritte Reich,'* 162–65, 234–35. He is also problematic because of his rejection of physiognomy, phrenology, and the reading of skulls as signs of inward spiritual activity. HPS 192–93, 201ff. (320, 333ff.), 537, 539, 540 (314, 320, 333, 343); McGovern, *From Luther to Hitler*, 619–20. However, Heidegger was anti–Semitic, and Nazis looked to him for support on this vital issue. Theodor Haering, *Fichte, Schelling, Hegel* (Stuttgart und Berlin: Kohlhammer, 1941) 419; Eberhard Fahrenhorst, *Geist und Freiheit im System Hegels* (Leipzig und Berlin: B. G. Teubner, 1934) 97–98; Herbert Franz, *Von Herder bis Hegel: Eine bildungsgeschichtliche Ideenvergleichung* (Frankfurt am Main: M. Diesterweg, 1938) 284; Leske, *Philosophe im 'Dritte Reich,'* 160–61.

15. HPS 17, 45, 60–61, 77–78, 217, 221, 224, 244, 247, 260, 277, 298 (29, 72, 98–99, 130–31, 360, 367–69, 373–74, 406, 411, 434–36, 461, 489); HPR 84 (264–65). The individual object is beyond perception. A sugar cube is white, "also" sweet, "also" cubical, and so on, living in the midst of the "also" as its essential "determateness." HPS 73 (120–21).
16. HPR v, 80–83, 92–95, 108–11, 231 (257–261, 275–81, 329–31, 342–43, 347, 351); HPS 267–70 (447–52); Santayana, *The German Mind,* 85, 96; McGovern, *From Luther to Hitler,* 260, 272, 285, 289, 299–302, 326, 329–34. He does not proceed as far as many Communists and supports the sacred place of the family in society. HPS 286–87 (474).
17. HPR 113 (358); Viereck, *Metapolitics,* 201; Santayana, *The German Mind,* 20, 88; Poliakov, *Aryan Myth,* 242–43. Montesquieu finds the myth of Germanic/Frankish origins and supremacy ruling the ideology of France during the Enlightenment. The German word *Frank* pushed itself into the land (France) and stood for liberation (enfranchisement). Poliakov, *Aryan Myth,* 17, 25–27.
18. Johann Friedrich, *Jahn als Erzieher* (München: Eduard Pohl, 1895) 48; Viereck, *Metapolitics,* 62ff., 68–71. Alfred Bäumler would later write a monograph entitled *Friedrich Ludwig Jahns Stellung in der deutschen Geistesgeschichte* (Leipzig: H. Eichblatt [Max Zedler], 1940).
19. Friedrich Ludwig Jahn, *Deutsches Volkstum* (Berlin: Aufbau-Verlag, 1991) 13–14, 21–23, 29–34, 38, 61–68, 71, 77–79, 87, 111, 116–19, 133–34, 147–48, 160–61, 175, 177, 188, 229, 253ff., 264–67, 314. Viereck, *Metapolitics,* 70, 82–83. Viereck finds his gymnast movement the basis of the "Storm Troopers." Certainly, Hitler's strong interest in the youth of the country has a strong precedent in Father Jahn's work.
20. Katz, *From Prejudice to Destruction,* 245–47.
21. Heinrich von Treitschke, *Politics,* Hans Kohn (ed. and intro.) (New York and Burlingame, CA: Harcourt, Brace & Word, Inc., 1963) xii. Hereafter designated as HTP.
22. HTP xi, xxi, 54, 132–34, 176, 196.
23. HTP 8–16, 33, 46–47, 51, 55–58, 62–65, 123, 139, 145. McGovern, *From Luther to Hitler,* 372, 375.
24. HTP 144. Like Hegel, he thinks it is a mistake to divide sovereignty. HTP 73–74, 169. Many predict that all of Europe will follow Britain's parliamentary system, but Treitschke does not find this inevitable. The accidents of heredity are no less wise in selecting a ruler than a democracy. HTP 177, 186–88.
25. HTP 6–7, 64–65, 89–90, 105–108, 125–26, 131; McGovern, *From Luther to Hitler,* 368–69.
26. Scott David Foutz, "Ignorant Science: The Eighteenth Century's Development of Scientific Racism," *Quodlibet Journal* 1/8 (Dec. 1999): 1–3 [pages from online edition]; Poliakov, *Aryan Myth,* 165–68; Daniel Mornet, "Les Enseignements des bibliotèques privées (1750–1780)," *Revue d'histoire littéraire de la France* 17 (1910): 460; D'Souza, *The End of Racism,* 51ff.; Peter Fenves, "What 'Progresses' Has Race-Theory Made Since the Times of Leibniz and Wolff?," in *The German Invention of Race,* Sara Eigen and Mark Larrimore (ed.) (Albany, NY: State University of New York Press, 2006) 16–17. Color of skin was particularly important in dividing the human race in the seventeenth century. Poliakov, *Aryan Myth,* 142–43.

27. D'Sousa, *The End of Racism*, 125–26, 132ff.; Stephen Jay Gould, *The Mismeasure of Man* (New York and London: W. W. Norton, 1996) 63–66, 422. Jefferson and Lincoln thought Blacks deserved civil rights or equal protection under the law, even if they were inferior to Whites. Their interpretation of the phrase, "all men are created equal," differs somewhat from the original intendment in the seventeenth century. The Puritan John Wise said we should treat all people alike since we all come from one stock. *A Vindication of the Government of New England Churches* (Gainesville, FL: Scholars' Facsimiles & Reprints, 1958) 40–45.
28. Birken, *Hitler as Philosophe*, 28; Poliakov, *The Aryan Myth*, 133–34, 169, 176–77.
29. *Oeuvres Complètes* (Paris: Garnier Frères, Libraires-Éditeurs, 1877–85) 11.5, 7; 12.237, 380; 21.462; 27.484–87 (WV 27.167, 200); D'Sousa, *The End of Racism*, 61–62. Voltaire discounts any place the monstrous offspring of humans and apes might have in the story of human evolution since they are unlikely to produce further offspring, much like mules. Comparing Blacks and apes and discussing the possibilities of their copulation with each other afforded wide-spread interest in the eighteenth and nineteenth centuries. Poliakov, *Aryan Myth*, 176–81.
30. Immanuel Kant, "Von den verschiedenen Racen der Menschen," in Kant's *gesammelte Schriften* (Berlin: George Reimar, 1902–1923) 2.432, 441. He defines a species (*Gattung*) by its ability to produce offspring with its members, and so unites all human beings together. Ibid., 2.429–30.
31. Ibid., 2.429, 430, 440–41; John Zammito, "Policing Polygeneticism in Germany, 1775: (Kames,) Kant, and Blumenbach," in *German Invention of Race*, 39–43, 58.
32. Ibid., 2.434–42; "The Natural Principle of the Political Order," in *Eternal Peace, and Other International Essays*, W. Hastle (trans.), Edwin Mead (intro.) (Boston: The World Peace Foundation, 1914) 3–5; Susan Shell, "Kant's Conception of a Human Race," in *German Invention of Race*, 59; Robert Bernasconi, "Kant and Blumenbach's Polyps," in *German Invention of Race*, 73–75; Mark Larrimore, "Race, Freedom and the Fall in Steffens and Kant," in *German Invention of Race*, 103–4; McGovern, *From Luther to Hitler*, 151–53. His account emphasizes the importance of climate in shaping the varieties of human races, but he admits it is a problem for the system to explain why the process of change stops working after awhile. In fact, he considers the entire account to be little more than speculative musings. Ibid., 2.429, 436, 442–43.
33. Kant's *gesammelte Schriften*, 8.174 note, 358–59; 9.316–18; Schell, "Kant's Conception," 56, 66; Larrimore, "Race, Freedom and the Fall," 105.
34. Larrimore, "Race, Freedom and the Fall," 113–15. He speaks of spiritual temperaments among the races (Phlegmatic, Melancholy, Choleric, and Sanguine), following Linnaeus's treatment in the 1758 edition of *Systema Natura*.
35. Bernasconi, "Kant and Blumenbach's Polyps," 74; Johann Friedrich Blumenbach, *On the Natural Varieties of Mankind*, Thomas Bendyshe (trans. and ed.) (New York: Bergman Publishers, 1969) ix–x. Hereafter Blumenbach's work is designated NVM. The work translates the first and third editions.

36. NVM 150, 234ff., 246ff. He points to the work of Petrus Camper and Governor Pownall with skulls, but he criticizes Camper's techniques in measuring skulls. NVM 55–56, 235, 267; Poliakov, *Aryan Myth*, 162.
37. Zammito, "Policing Polygeneticism," 43; NVM vi–viii, 31–32. In 1775, Blumenbach speaks of "polygeneticism" as "much discussed in these days," and his meteoric rise and immense reputation speak of this burgeoning interest. Kant and Blumenbach worked independently in 1775 but developed a cordial correspondence in the 1790s. Zammito, "Policing Polygeneticism," 35, 39, 43.
38. NVM 8–9, 56–57, 83, 95, 98–99, 104–7, 110, 121, 163–64, 175ff., 191–92, 198, 207–9, 215, 263, 270–71; Zammito, "Policing Polygeneticism," 46. He saw Blacks as superior to animals and entitled to basic human rights when many others thought differently.
39. NVM vii–x, 264–66. He recognizes the arbitrary nature of these classifications. Zammito, "Policing Polygeneticism," 47–48. He lists the racial divisions found in many other authors, including Leibniz, Linnaeus, Buffon, Abbé Prévost, and Kant. He abandoned Linnaeus's list after a three-year journey around the world. NVM 99, 150, 267–68. He lists varieties of skin color: white (European), yellow (Mongolian), copper (American), tawny (Malay), and black (Ethiopian). The proximate cause of blackness is the abundance of carbon in the body, which is excreted through the blood vessels of the corium and embedded in the Malpighian mucus in the external integument of the skin. NVM 209–11. See NVM 227–29 for the five types of faces. Climate once again is the principal factor.
40. NVM vii–xi, 264–65. He has difficulty classifying Jews. He thinks of them as Caucasian but also as an Eastern racial group. Jonathan Hess, "Jewish Emancipation and the Politics of Race," in *German Invention of Race*, 206–7.
41. NVM xi, 264–66, 269; Hess, "Jewish Emancipation," 206; Gould, *The Mismeasure of Man*, 401; Poliakov, *Aryan Myth*, 173; D'Souza, *The End of Racism*, 124; Foulz, "Ignorant Science," 4.
42. NVM 276.
43. Gould, *The Mismeasure of Man*, 85, 87, 115, 119, 153, 176ff., 182–83, 260–62; D'Souza, *The End of Racism*, 126–27; Foulz, "Ignorant Science," 6. For a discussion of craniology and phrenology in the nineteenth century, see Poliakov, *Aryan Myth*, 264.
44. Arthur de Gobineau, *The Inequality of the Human Race*, Adrian Collins (trans.) (New York: Howard Fertig, 1967) vii; Poliakov, *Aryan Myth*, 238; D'Souza, *The End of Racism*, 63; McGovern, *From Luther to Hitler*, 500, 504.
45. Ibid., xiv, 5–11, 13, 19–25, 33, 40, 44–45, 69, 93, 97, 211–12; McGovern, *From Luther to Hitler*, 502–3; D'Souza, *End of Racism*, 63.
46. Ibid., 38–39, 56, 59–60, 106ff., 117–21, 118, 133–39, 145–46, 208; Poliakov, *Aryan Myth*, 234.
47. Ibid., 27–28, 74–75, 145–46, 151–153, 174, 179, 205–9, 211; McGovern, *From Luther to Hitler*, 501–2. However, he rejects those who find only a slight difference between some races and the higher apes. He admits that some Blacks are smarter than "our peasants or even . . . the average specimens of our half-educated middle class." IHR 73, 180
48. Charles Darwin, *The Descent of Man*, in *Great Books of the Western World*, Robert Maynard Hutchins (ed.) (Chicago: Encyclopaedia Britannica, Inc., 1978) 294–95.

49. According to Aëtius, Anaximander, a pre-Socratic philosopher, thought life evolved from the sea. Creatures changed form as they hit dry land. *The First Philosophers: The Presocratics and Sophists*, Robin Waterfield (trans.) (Oxford: Oxford University Press, 2000) 17; Frederick Copleston, *A History of Philosophy* (Garden City, NY: Image books, 1962) I/1.41–42. Augustine thinks Genesis 1 expresses the order of nature, not the precise time of events, and speaks of plants and animals produced "potentially" in the act of creation. Augustine, Gen. ad lit., I, 1, 3–4, 9, 15; IV, 26, 33, 34; V, 3, 5, 25; VIII, 3 (PL 34.247–49, 252, 257, 314, 318–19, 323, 326, 338, 374). Thomas Aquinas speaks of the development of new species after the initial act of creation. *Summa Theologiae* (New York: McGraw-Hill, 1964–76) I, q. 68, a. 1; q. 69, a. 1; q. 72, a. 1; q. 74, a. 2. A few speculated over the existence of a race before Adam and/or the existence of several races in medieval times. Edward Tyson (1650–1703) observed structural analogies between humans and chimpanzees in his *Orang-Outang*, and many followed his lead, especially comparing apes/monkeys to the "basest" level of the human species. Poliakov, *Aryan Myth*, 131–33.
50. *Descent of Man*, 331–32, 590; Michael Ruse, *Darwinism Defended: A Guide to the Evolution Controversies* (London: Addison-Wesley Publishing Co., 1982) 48–49; Peter Bowler, *Darwinism* (New York: Twayne publishers, 1993) 85; Stephen Jay Gould, *The Panda's Thumb* (New York: W. W. Norton, 1980) 29, 246–47; *Ever Since Darwin* (New York: W. W. Norton, 1977) 216. Of course, ontogeny is disputed these days as a sufficient proof, even if Darwin and his early disciples emphasized it as most essential.
51. Ibid., 340; Gould, *Panda's Thumb*, 11. Darwin's theory rejects the mechanism of Jean-Baptiste Lamarck, even if many early Darwinians embraced it. Lamarck thought evolution was fueled by the inheritance of characteristics that parents acquired through a lifetime of work; that is, an organism can somehow genetically pass its reaction toward the environment to its posterity. Bowler, *Darwinism*, 4; Gould, *Panda's Thumb*, 77. Even if Darwin rejects this possibility, he still recognized that other factors, such as isolation, mutation, and chance, enter into the evolutionary mechanism. Gabriel Lasker, *Human Evolution* (New York: Holt, Reinhardt, and Winston, Inc., 1963) 41; Gould, *Ever Since Darwin*, 11.
52. Ibid., 356–57.
53. Gould, *Panda's Thumb*, 66–68; *Ever Since Darwin*, 100.
54. Thomas Robert Malthus, *An Essay on the Principle of Population*, Philip Appleman (ed.) (New York and London: W. W. Norton and Company, 1976) xiv, 18, 44–45, 97. In the *Wealth of Nations*, Smith talks about the relation between population and the means of subsistence among animals and humans. Adam Smith, *An Inquiry into the Nature and Causes of the Wealth of Nations* (New York: Modern Library, 1937) 79.
55. Ibid., 37–39, 47, 52–54, 99, 102–3, 118–22, 134–35; Ruse, *Darwinism Defended*, 26. While the poor have no right to free public support, Malthus supports some ways of alleviating poverty like workhouses, where people receive jobs. EPP 43, 135.
56. EPP xv; Gould, *Panda's Thumb*, 66–68.
57. *The Autobiography of Charles Darwin, 1809–1882*, Nora Barlow (ed.) (New York: W. W. Norton and Company, 1969) 120.

58. Darwin, *The Descent of Man*, 336.
59. Ibid., 323. See D'Souza, *The End of Racism*, 130.
60. Ibid., 325.
61. Lothrop Stoddard, *The Revolt against Civilization: The Menace of the Under Man* (New York: Charles Scribner's Sons, 1923) 242.
62. Darwin, *The Descent of Man*, 342.
63. Ibid., 287, 346.
64. Ibid., 336, 341, 347–50, 591; Bowler, *Darwinism*, 100. Christoph Meiners (1745–1810) was a predecessor of Darwin in this regard. He thought of humans progressing step-by-step from the beasts and having an African origin. Like Darwin, he saw the importance of breeding in understanding the development of human beings and warned against the dangers of racial mingling and crossbreeding. *Untersuchungen über der Verschiedenheiten der Menschennaturen* (Tuebingen, J. G. Gotta'schen, 1815) 3.74–77, 129, 312ff.; Poliakov, *Aryan Myth*, 179–80.
65. Ernst Haeckel, *The History of Creation*, 2 vols., E. Ray Lankester (trans.) (New York: D. Appleton and Company, 1901) xv, xvi; 1.7, 362. Hereafter designated as HC. Haeckel compares the theory to Newton's law of gravitation, considering it "one of the greatest achievements of the human mind." HC 1.26.
66. HC 1.7; 2.496–97.
67. He lists and discusses the ancient Greeks, Lamarck, Geoffroy Saint-Hilaire, William Charles Wells, Alfred Wallace, Goethe, Kant, Lorenz Oken, Gottfried Treviranus, Leopold von Buch, and many other German developmentalists. HC 1.4–5, 78–80, 83, 88–95, 104ff., 109ff., 111ff., 114ff., 121–22, 173–75. Charles Lyell paved the way for Darwin, pointing to the slow transformation of the earth's crust over a long and uniform period. Of course, Wallace worked independently from Darwin on the concept of natural selection. HC 1.129.
68. HC 1.117–18, 124, 138, 161–62, 172, 220, 252–53; 2.458.
69. HC 1.20.
70. HC 1.138, 300–3, 387.
71. HC 1.296.
72. HC 1.18–21, 77. Like many Darwinians, he points to useless organs to show the lack of wisdom in how creatures are constructed. HC 1.13–16. He explains the evolution of a complicated organism like the eye by pointing to a "simple spot of pigment in the lowest animal." HC 2.454–55.
73. HC 1.72, 74; 2.472, 498. His most (in)famous, oft-repeated, and irrefutable proof for the theory of evolution is ontogeny, where "the embryonic development of the individual is completely parallel to the paleontological development of the whole tribe to which it belongs." That is, "ontogenesis, or the development of the individual, is a short and quick repetition (recapitulation) of phylogenesis, or the development of the tribe to which it belongs." This proof is accompanied by equally (in)famous drawings of embryos illustrating the process. HC 1.10–11, 334, 350–57; 2.32ff., 148, 462, 470.
74. HC 1.40, 256; 2.364, 411.
75. HC 2.412–23, 429–38, 445–46, 490–93; Weikart, *From Darwin to Hitler*, 106–8. Haeckel had a major impact on German thinking in the nineteenth

and twentieth centuries and probably exerted some influence on Hitler and his ideas. Hitler read a number of scholarly works in his youth, but it is likely that most of his Social Darwinism was secondhand, given the fact that few people read scientific theories in the original sources. Weikart, *From Darwin to Hitler*, 216–17.

76. *The Life and Letters of Charles Darwin*, Francis Darwin (ed.) (New York: Basic Books, Inc., 1959) 2.270; Arendt, *Origins of Totalitarianism*, 179.
77. Weikart, *From Darwin to Hitler*, 10–11.
78. Karl Vogt, *Lectures on Man: His Place in Creation, and in the History of the Earth*, James Hunt (ed.) (London: Longman, etc., 1864) 222–24, 422–23; Weikart, *From Darwin to Hitler*, 95, 110.
79. Robby Kossmann, "Bedeutung des Einzellebens in der Darwinistischen Weltanschauung," *Nord und Süd* 12 (1880): 420–21. Many Darwinists expressed this exact sentiment. Weikart, *From Darwin to Hitler*, 2, 80–83, 92; Arnold Dodel, *Moses or Darwin?: A School Problem for All Friends of Truth and Progress* (New York: The Truth Seeker Company, 1891); Alexander Tille, *Volksdienst von einem Socialaristokraten* (Berlin: Weiner'sche Verlagsbuchhandlung, 1893); August Forel, *The Sexual Question: A Scientific, Psychological, Hygenic and Sociological Study*, C. F. Marshall (trans.) (New York: Medical Art Agency, 1925); Friedrich Hellwald, *Culturgeschichte in ihrer natürlichen Entwicklung bis zur Gegenwart* (Augsburg: Lambart & Comp., 1875).
80. Weikart, *From Darwin to Hitler*, 52, 55; Poliakov, *Aryan Myth*, 298.
81. Ibid., 15, 99, 117–18; Poliakov, *Aryan Myth*, 297. The Krupp family offered a prize of 50,000 marks in 1900 for the best essay questioning "old theories of equality" and composing its own political policies based upon present evolutionary theories and hereditary facts. The jury consisted of six famous scientists, including Ernst Haeckel. Poliakov, *Aryan Myth*, 294–95.
82. Ibid., 114–17.
83. Fritz Lenz, "Race as a Principle of Value: On a Renewal of Ethics," 1917; Weikart, *From Darwin to Hitler*, 7. See Fritz Lenz, *Die Rasse als Wertprinzip: Zur Erneuerung der Ethik* (München: J. F. Lehmann, 1933) for a reproduction of this article.
84. Alfred Kirchhoff, *Darwinismus, angewandt auf Völker und Staaten* (Frankfurt a. M.: Keller, 1910) 73–74, 86–87; Oscar Peschel, "Ursprung and Verschiedenheit der Menschenrassen," *Das Ausland* 33 (1860): 393; Oscar Schmidt, *The Doctrine of Descent and Darwinism* (New York: D. Appelton and Company, 1895) 297–98; Weikart, *From Darwin to Hitler*, 184, 187–90. Weikart deserves credit for developing the material and sources used in this last section.
85. Weikart, *From Darwin to Hitler*, 195, 204. August Forel (1848–1931), a prominent Swiss psychologist, implied that inferior races should be exterminated, and he may be considered the father of German eugenics. Margaret Sanger, the founder of Planned Parenthood, believed in the elimination of Blacks. D'Souza, *The End of Racism*, 118; Weikart, *From Darwin to Hitler*, 201. Johann Peter Frank (1745–1821), a German physician, provided a proto-eugenics program for racial breeding in his *System of Complete Medical Police*. Frank felt we should supply the same techniques to humans as we use in breeding animals. Those described as "bad seed," "sickly and

miserable people," "all crippled, maimed, very stunted, dwarfish persons" should be prohibited to marry, and we should "leave procreation to healthier citizens." *A System of Complete Medical Police*, Erna Leskey (intro. and ed.) (Baltimore, MD: Johns Hopkins University Press, 1976) 47–51; Sara Eigen, "Policing the Menschen=Racen," in *German Invention of Race*, 186–88.

86. Schopenhauer sees fundamental appetites as more important in explaining human conduct than the intellect and provides excellent testimony to the power of hatred to skew our judgment. *The World as Will and Representation*, 2.212–17, 229–37, 255.

III

International Communism

12

The First International: Karl Marx and Friedrich Engels

On the other side of the political spectrum, there arose another form of socialism in the nineteenth century that served as the chief political rival of the Nazis during their rise to power but also represented the same type of enlightened animus toward the Judeo-Christian tradition. This form of socialism thought of religion as a type of "opium" that prevented people from fulfilling or controlling their own destiny as social beings and called for the complete elimination of this dangerous narcotic from all realms of society. The group developed this analysis and prescription out of the work and writings of Karl Marx, an atheist and member of the Young Hegelians in Berlin, and they proudly took on the name of Marxism, as if following the legacy of this one man.[1]

Karl Marx was born in the Prussian city of Tier on May 5, 1818. His parents were of Jewish descent and came from a devout family of rabbinic learning, but his father was only a nominal believer, imbibing the liberal spirit of the Enlightenment, and he eventually converted to the Evangelical Church of Prussia for professional reasons as a prominent lawyer. In the autumn of 1835, a young Marx followed his father's footsteps and studied law at the University of Bonn and then the University of Berlin, where he learned Hegelian philosophy from teachers like Eduard Gans and joined the *Doktorklub*, a radical group that consisted of "Young Hegelians."[2] During this time, Marx became a thoroughgoing materialist and later wrote a dissertation in philosophy at the University of Jena, which bound the human conscious to the material world and its natural development and criticized the inconsistencies in the atheist/materialistic thought of Epicurus.[3] The Young Hegelians helped push Marx in this radical direction and brought, along with the cynical view of metaphysics a Promethean critique of the present order of religion and politics. They used the dialectical method of Hegel to criticize and negate the present form of church and state in Prussian society, rather than submit to a Germanic self-understanding of spiritual and public life as the embodiment of an absolute Ideal, based on the former presuppositions of the old

Hegelianism. All of them called for democratic reform and political liberties, many of them attacked religious concepts as the chains enslaving humankind to another world, and a few of them, like Moses Hess, proceeded to a more radical, Communist position by emphasizing total equality and eliminating property rights altogether.[4]

The one member of the Young Hegelians who directly influenced and promoted the career of Marx above all the rest was Friedrich Engels. He was born on November 29, 1820, in the town of Barmen to a factory owner, who moved his family over a decade and a half later to Manchester, England, and founded a cotton-spinning business there and then later again in Barmen and nearby Engelkirchen.[5] The business was prosperous and made the family well-to-do, but the working and living conditions of the poor workers deeply affected the social consciousness of the young Engels and found continuous remembrance and reference throughout his life in many books, letters, and essays relating the horrid and wretched detail.[6] This experience brought with it a critical and sometimes cynical attitude toward the type of political/social system that could justify these conditions and the disingenuous nature of a Christian piety that could treat human beings in this way, leading eventually to a complete rejection of the faith. His religious background included an orthodox family upbringing and the evangelical fervor of the Pietist tradition in the Rhineland of Germany,[7] but he responded harshly to the hypocrisies of Christians and eventually developed scholastic support for his discontent through reading the trenchant criticisms of Strauss's *Life of Jesus* concerning the many contradictions in the scripture. On October 8, 1839, he announced to his older brother that he was a "Straussian" and compared the NT critic to a "young God," who "brings the chaos [of scripture] out into the light of day," and bids, "Adios Faith! It is as full of holes as a sponge."[8] In 1841 and 1842, he decided to pursue a liberal education as a nonmatriculated student at the University of Berlin, the bastion of Hegelian ideology, and developed a relation with the Young Hegelians there, just like Marx before him, proceeding to the radical left-wing of the movement. A few years later, he (and Marx) criticized the group in the *German Ideology* (1845/46) as laboring too much within the old metaphysical abstractions and neglecting a more concrete connection with practical and material reality.[9]

Influences

There were a number of influences that shaped the basic orientation of Marx's and Engel's philosophy, but none of them proved more decisive than the work of Georg Hegel, the most celebrated philosopher of the era. Marx even refers to his dialectic method at one point as the "last word of all philosophy."[10] This method depicts life much like Marx, as a process that is moving or evolving into a higher state of unity. The method views each being as unfolding its own immanent content in becoming other than itself and then proceeding to take back this unfolding as a means of continuous growth toward a higher stage.[11] An object or thing-in-itself does not remain extraneous to a subject or being, as it does in the philosophy of Kant, but finds its purpose as a means of subjective expression, even if it takes time to transform or internalize the external object and make it one's own. The goal of the process is to bring all concrete moments into the unity of the whole and eliminate the "alienation" (*Entfremdung* or *Entäusserung*) between the subject and object by tarrying with the "negative" and bringing about content or meaning to being.[12] The purpose of history is to bring about a higher stage of development and unity.[13] This leads Hegel to subsume each and every individual under the unity of the whole until individuality vanishes before the universal,[14] and translates into a totalitarian view of politics that sounds much like Marx and Engels, where the individual finds definition within the whole and develops their ethical life only in serving the community. Hegel follows this Communist direction by wanting the state to take the place of civil society and the family in providing education for everyone and sustenance for the poor and rejecting the notion of individual or civil rights existing outside the needs of the nation as a whole, even if he never proceeds as far as the later Marxists.[15]

The most important difference between Hegel and the Marxists concerns the emphasis in his philosophy upon the Absolute Idea or Spirit. Hegel follows the ontological tradition of Plato in believing that abstract human attributes possess ultimate reality, and so he proceeds to project human reason or spirit into the heavens, creating a separate, individual, and absolute Being.[16] Marx and Engels hope to eliminate the need for this type of ideal "mystification" in their philosophy and preserve the positive results of Hegel's work by applying it to the one and only world of material reality. The dialectic method remains an important tool and significant achievement as long as its application is fitting or limited to understanding the things of this natural world as "transforming itself endlessly in a constant process of becoming and passing away."[17] They wish to use the method within the "materialist conception of nature and history" and transform it into a force of practical activity (*Tätigkeit*) in the world, rather than escape into a fanciful contemplation upon ultimate or pure subjectivity. They see the dialectic method as a revolutionary force that calls for endless development, deconstructing and demythologizing present existence, treating nothing as "final, absolute, [or] sacred," and dissolving all "stable time-honored institutions" for the sake of creating a higher form.

> All successive historical systems are only transitory stages in the endless course of development of human society from the lower to the higher. Each stage is necessary, and therefore justified for the time and conditions to which it owes its origin. But in the face of new higher conditions which gradually develop in its own womb, it loses its validity and justification. It must give way to a higher stage which will also in its turn decay and perish. Just as the bourgeoisie

> by large-scale industry, competition and the world market dissolves in practice all stable time-honored institutions, so this dialectical philosophy dissolves all conceptions of final, absolute truth and of absolute states of humanity corresponding to it. For it [dialectical philosophy] nothing is final, absolute sacred.[18]

Ludwig Feuerbach provided the most scintillating and incisive criticism of Hegelian idealism for atheists in the mid-nineteenth century. His major work, *The Essence of Christianity* (1841), came out the same year Marx received his doctoral degree in philosophy and crystallized for him and his fellow atheists the most telling arguments for their position against Platonic and Hegelian mystification, considering it a fanciful product of the human imagination.[19] Engels said that this work "exploded" Hegel's system, making "[us] all Feuerbachians at once."[20] In the work, Feuerbach attacks idealism and wants to develop a materialistic philosophy that embraces the entire human being in all its carnality and earthiness—body, soul, and spirit, rather than cut a person into different parts or "tear him out of his nature." *Der Mensch ist was er isst.*[21] The object of philosophy is to promote the *Ens realissimum*, "not the Substance of Spinoza, the ego of Kant and Fichte, the Absolute Identity of Schelling, [or] the Absolute Mind of Hegel." In religion, human beings go outside their own nature, representing their inner being in the heavens, only to return once again unto themselves through this circuitous path, as if receiving a revelation from on high. "God" is only the highest projection of subjectivity, or the consciousness of a person's own perfection, abstracted, glorified, and placed outside of oneself in a heavenly realm. Theology is only a form of anthropology, which testifies to what a person considers sacred in one's being. "The beginning, middle, and end of religion is MAN."[22]

Marx and Engels work within the fundamental matrix of this analysis, although they afford some criticism of the approach in wanting to present a more radical statement of atheism. They prefer a consistent materialistic point of view, which continually deprecates religion as nothing more than a source that alienates the human race from its true and only existence in the world,[23] but this time their criticism goes too far. It seems to exaggerate the differences between the two positions on the issue since both sides depict religion in much the same way as a "false consciousness" debasing humankind and a form of "self-alienation" that separates humankind from its true nature.[24] Feuerbach continually criticizes Hegelianism for creating a spiritual realm, which "externalizes" (entäussert) and "alienates" (*entfremdet*) human beings from controlling their own destiny and leaves them impoverished before an external and almighty power.[25] He also speaks of religion as a specious and illusive attempt to satisfy the "self-flattering wishes" of the heart, and spends much of his account like any other Marxist, deprecating the desire to find miraculous deliverance from death and disease, the need for a divine justification to establish human society and law, and the audacity of exalting a particular people above others, even making the universe serve its end, as in the case of Israel (Josh10), but other religions as well.[26]

The more militant form of atheism was represented at the time by Bruno Bauer.[27] He was the clear ideological leader of the Young Hegelians and exerted a special influence upon the young Marx in particular, first as a teacher in Bonn and then as a close personal friend, beginning with their first encounter in 1836 and continuing during the next seven years through a number of meetings and an active correspondence until the very end of 1842. At one time they even planned on editing a journal together entitled the *Archiv des Atheismus*, and they probably joined forces to produce the *locus classicus* of the Young Hegelians, *The Trumpet of the Last Judgment against Hegel the Atheist and Antichrist* (1841), although scholars generally attribute most of it to Bauer because of the extensive nature of the biblical and theological erudition on display in most of its pages. *The Trumpet of the Last Judgment* served as a clarion call for the Young Hegelians to rescue the legacy of Hegel from idealistic interpretation and recognize the real atheistic and militant ramifications of Hegel's revolutionary philosophy.[28]

The Last Trumpet was written under the anonymity of a conservative Christian preacher, who displays throughout the work all the narrow-minded, Bible-thumping, and unctuous preachments of his stereotypical position. Bauer wishes to parody and mock the preacher, and yet he gives him enough philosophical insight to recognize the fallacious nature of interpreting Hegel in a spiritual manner and to reject the many liberal Protestants who compromise with a philosophy that is clearly anti-Christian and atheistic on its most fundamental level—the exact point that Bauer wants to inculcate and convey to his audience as the proper understanding of the philosopher. Of course, the preacher has no interest in following the results of Hegel's system and wants to warn a different audience about the dangers of making any compromise with it, as a present and powerful source of temptation for true believers. According to his analysis, the philosophy has a tendency to feign compatibility with Christian truth by employing the doctrinal language of the orthodox faith, but all of this is a Trojan horse meant to deceive believers and undermine the true confession through satanic tricks as seen in the case of liberal Protestants. These "Christians" have succumbed to the ruse of Hegelianism, following the liberal compromises of Friedrich Schleiermacher, and forsaken the orthodox confession of an objective revelation in Christ for a religion founded upon inward subjectivity. This emphasis upon subjectivity in Hegel and Schleiermacher only leads in one direction away from the belief in an external revelation or personal, transcendent God to an objectified image of the human self-consciousness, making the separation between the finite and infinite an illusion and "God" a "duplication of myself" in this inward relationship. Hegel and his disciples "know that atheism is consequent upon the system, . . . as the necessary result of the pure comprehending self-consciousness." He might play "mirror-tricks" to deceive the faithful into recognizing some piety in his thought, but he knows full well that the "Ego has only to deal with itself in religion," that the Ego represents "both combatants" (the finite and infinite) in his system, that no transcendent or personal God can exist given his presuppositions. Of course, he employs orthodox language by speaking of doctrines like the Trinity and the divine incarnation, but he only overturns their true meaning in the end by reinterpreting them in terms of the inward relationship of self-consciousness. "The Trinity is the abstract nature of self-consciousness placed in Heaven." The incarnation speaks of the human nature of religion, as people try to live outside of themselves in another realm. Even the scripture is deprecated in light of the new religion of subjectivity; as the literal, outward meaning of its miracles gives way to their "inner significance," appealing to the "inner man." This new "religion" of subjectivity has brought the same compromises to the followers of Schleiermacher, who deny the Trinity, the incarnation, and the miracles of scripture, and must serve as a warning against forsaking the faith for a mess of pottage.[29]

In fact, it should be obvious that Hegel actually hates the Judeo-Christian tradition and wants to destroy it. His ultimate design is for the church to collapse before the rational and scientific progress of a new age and the growing power of an absolute state. This hope is not relegated to the outcome of a scholastic debate or the prophetic insight of idle speculation about the course of this world but involves a more practical and radical call to arms. "His theory is praxis. . . . It is the revolution itself." Hegel finds the French Revolution to be the greatest event of world history and wants Germans to employ its atheistic and destructive philosophy as a paradigm for overthrowing both God and country in the fatherland. He clearly exhorts philosophers to be "active in politics" by negating the "state, the church and religion" and proceeding to the "opposite" in his dialectic method, making it a necessity of logic to "overthrow the established order."[30] The antithetical nature of Hegelian logic provides the pretext for revolutionary activity—a point not lost on the preacher (or Bauer and Marx) but often neglected today in the world of Marxist scholarship.

The radical forces in France exerted a strong influence upon the Young Hegelians and future Marxists in developing their antithetical attitude toward bourgeois culture. Engels thought of modern socialism as a product of the French philosophes and their left-wing, avant-garde rejection of the established order. "They recognized no external authority of any kind whatever, . . . subject[ing] everything to the most unsparing criticism—religion, natural science, society, [and] political institutions." They turned "the world upon its head," negating "every form of society and government then existing, every old traditional notion," as an irrational social convention based upon by-gone prejudice.[31] In the *Holy Family* (1844/45), Marx and Engels extol the French materialists for putting an end to the metaphysical prejudices of the past during the eighteenth century and particularly name Pierre Bayle, Claude Adrien Helvétius, Étienne Bonnot de Condillac, and Julian Offray de la Mettrie, among others, as pivotal figures in the final transition. French materialism led directly to socialism and communism as it came to recognize the "influence of the environment on man" and need to arrange this empirical world through social engineering, rather than continue the metaphysical tradition of blaming an individual for his or her behavior as if one could act in another way outside the material and inhuman conditions that create bad behavior in the first place.[32] The French Revolution provided the modern impetus toward socialism by assaulting the private property of the aristocrats and created a whole generation of Socialists—Comte de Saint-Simon, Gracchus Babeuf, Charles Fourier, Pierre-Joseph Proudhon, Auguste Blanqui, Louis Blanc, Étienne Cabet, Wilhelm Weitling, Robert Owen, Charles Kingsley, and Frederick Maurice—all providing an early inspiration for the later Marxists.[33] After the Revolution, the country of France experienced a number of birth pangs along the way in its eventual and inevitable move toward socialism. The revolutionary spirit was quelled by certain events, including the Reign of Terror, the coronation of Napoleon in 1804, and the restoration of the monarchy under Louis XVIII, but it was resurrected once again through other events that provided great hope to the Communists: the proletarian revolution of 1848 and the Paris Commune of 1871, where workers seized power for a few months and pushed the country in a Communist direction.[34]

Marxism

Eventually the radical forces of left-wing revolutionary ideals were forged into a coherent system through the work of Marx and Engels, losing much of its early antithetical nature for the sake of establishing a new thesis. Marx and Engels forged the system through a collaboration of ideas in the 1840s, which began during September 1844, at a ten-day meeting in Paris, and continued in earnest for the next several years. Before this time Engels had gained the greater reputation as a writer, and he wrote an article entitled "Outlines of a Critique of Political Economy" in February of 1844, which Marx devoured and praised as a "brilliant sketch on the criticism of the economic categories" from a Communist viewpoint,[35] but the relationship soon changed. Engels decided to take the backseat and began to extol the work of Marx above his own, consciously settling for the role of a junior partner in the relationship. Even their first book, *The Holy Family*, Engels cared little about maintaining his superior position as a noted author and wanted the name of Marx placed first as the fundamental author of the treatise—an attitude that continued to mark the relationship for the years to come.[36] Engels considered Marx the real genius of the movement and felt that his colleague "stood higher, saw further, and took a wider and quicker view than all the rest of us" in providing Marxism with "the greater part of its leading basic principles, especially in the realm of economics and history" and its "final trenchant form," which "rightly bears his name."[37] He proceeded to give him credit for developing the "materialistic conception of history" and the "secret capitalistic production" through the concept of surplus value, even if it is clear that the former concept had a much greater development in his own writings.[38] Marx became the infallible witness of a truth revealed once and for all; so much so that even the world of academia bought into the inflated image and produced a number of scholars who tended to exaggerate the differences between the two men's approaches and liked to blame Engels for whatever went wrong with communism, particularly in regard to the Soviet Union.[39] Marx, not Engels, was the source of true communism according to these scholars, belying the importance of Engel's contribution to the movement and the testimony of their writings, which develop the same fundamental theses and outline the same, basic political philosophy.

Marx and Engels developed their ideology as a monolith in order to forge the emerging Socialist factions into a united front. Their most famous collaborative effort was the *Communist Manifesto*, written for the Communist League Second Congress—an international meeting of Socialists held in London from November 29 to December 8, 1847. Engels wrote the early versions, Marx added the finishing touches, and the work was published in February 1848. Its purpose was to present a platform for the meeting, providing a coherent theoretical and scientific basis for socialism and forging the disparate mixture of different nationalities and ideological commitments into one new group, or Communist League. Later on, Marx performed the same service for the International Working Men's Association, which was founded by French and English activists in 1863 and held its first conference a couple years later in London. Early on, the International expressed a wide range of political points of view and forced Marx once again to reenter the realm of politics as an active participate, molding the group into his own ideological image, gaining control over the General Council, and placing himself "firmly and visibly at the helm" of what became a powerful force of labor throughout all of Europe. The First International represented proletarian interests as a whole, rejecting all national and ethnocentric commitments, and turned Marxism into a worldwide phenomenon, which threatened the world order of allegiance to the many state governments.[40] Marxism was now the one, true dogma.

Marx's Theory of Economics

The starting point for the system is the dehumanization of the workforce in the present capitalistic economy, not the actual misery of poverty per se. In 1843/44, Marx began to use the term "alienation" (*Enfremdung/Entäusserung*) to describe the degrading condition of the factory workers and returned to the term in *Grundrisse*, *Kapital*, and elsewhere, making it a significant concept in his thought and movement.[41] While the term remains vague and contains many possible facets worth deconstructing, its general meaning revolves around Marx's intention to deprecate a process where the individual or group loses control of what it produces, where the subject creates a product or object of self-expression and ends up subjected to it in the course of time.[42] Humans lose control when the entities of their own creation become independent and return to exercise power over their creators, enslaving them as an object and making them serve what was originally an expression of their own subjectivity. Marx wants to reverse this relationship once again by helping society unleash their "human essential powers" and recapture the upper hand in shaping their own reality.[43]

Marx finds the answer to human alienation in a new social and economic order. Humans suffer from "disillusion" and turn to nonsensical answers like religion because of their miserable conditions in society, but this "holy form of self-estrangement" only prevents them from finding true happiness in the real world. The disillusion will disappear only when humans assume radical responsibility for their own happiness through the use of scientific reason and destroy the root cause of their problems, found in the "self-estrangement in its unholy form."[44] Society needs to abolish certain unholy entities of its own creation, such as "property, capital, money [and] wage-labor" as "objective products of self-estrangement," in order for "man to become man" once again and finally dispense with out-of-body experiences within a heavenly realm. In capitalism, workers are alienated by the means of producing commodities over which they have no control and become objectified as a cog in a machine or a commodity for the market—bought, sold, and exploited by the few who own the economic system.[45] The workers have no dignity here. They labor to subsist and subsist to labor. They are left "unpaid" for their real value by the theft and robbery of the capitalist, who deigns to make a profit off of human misery through this means of exploitation (*Ausbeutung*)—a term that Marx uses in his later work as a substitute for alienation, indicating through this provocative word considerable moral indignation with the capitalist means of production.[46]

Marx wants humans to find fulfillment in the workplace. Labor should be an expression of their essential nature as human beings, not a force that alienates and robs them of their dignity. Like Benjamin Franklin, Marx thinks of human beings in terms of tools (*homo faber*), who first distinguished "themselves from animals in the past as soon as they [began] to produce their means of subsistence . . . producing their actual material life." The development of tools and the means of production define what is most essential about the human race by determining "the ensemble of social relations" and creating individuals "as they really are; i.e. as they operate, produce materially and hence as they work under definite material limits, presuppositions and conditions independent of their will." And so, labor must be considered in any social structure as the most essential function of humans in fulfilling themselves and made rewarding by those who wish to reconfigure society.[47] Marx goes on to measure the value of a product by the amount of labor-time necessary to produce it, based on the belief that commodities tend to "exchange in proportion to the relative amounts of labor required to produce them"—at least in the long run, regardless of their use or the quality of work that went into their production.[48] In all this, Marx wants to offer all workers a sense of dignity, fulfillment, and self-expression, which the capitalist system has denied them, through identifying the importance of labor for society, the economy, and the fulfillment of each and every individual. If he has a problem at this point, it is not found in his penetrating analysis of a disquieting fact about the nature of capitalism and its treatment of labor but in offering a solution to a genuine problem. How do you make the drudgery of many jobs that seem necessary for society any more fulfilling in a different scheme of things? Even he clearly has difficulty in making factory work fulfilling in any system and seems to admit so in his later works. As early as *Grundrisse*, he makes a passionate plea for a shorter workday, recognizing that he cannot cure the monotony of labor and prefers to offer fulfillment in a call for liberation from it.[49] This implicit admission reveals a critical weakness in his system, which sought to eliminate alienation as its basic concern and was unable to do so according to the testimony of its own author.

He criticizes the fundamental motive of capitalists in his analysis, complaining about their desire to maximize profit and reduce the value of workers to a commodity—cheap and expendable.[50] Capitalism produces a "commodity fetishism," where everything is reduced to an economic calculation of cash and trade, reifying the workers and destroying their personal worth as wage laborers.[51] A system of capital controls the workers as a civilized way of exploitation, allowing the capitalists to calculate the worth of their laborers and receive much more for their service than what they pay laborers when selling the product of their hard work on the market. The capitalists hope to make a profit, or create surplus-value through the motive of "buying under and selling over the value" of the product. The rate of surplus-value depends mainly upon the cost of labor, not so much upon the expense of the instruments and material used as a means of production, and gives the capitalists every incentive to work the employees to death and pay them as little as possible, giving them a mere subsistence, so they can continue the drudgery of meaningless and continuous toil.[52] There is nothing unjust about this arrangement within the capitalistic modus operandi, but the workers are clearly vulnerable in the system to much abuse, and their social and economic needs are not a part of the equation.[53]

This fact alone contains an imperative to try and reshape the social environment if Marx wants to make a real and effective change in the lives of his constituency. "If man is shaped by environment, his environment must be made human."[54] The commodity fetishism arises out of an objective set of social circumstances, which need serious social engineering in order to end the oppressive order. The modes of production condition the way people think about life and need changing in order to create a different ideology.[55] "It is not consciousness that determines life, but life that determines consciousness." German philosophy confounds the process by starting outside "the material activity and the material intercourse of men" in the ivory tower of a heavenly realm and then descending to earth with a spiritual message, reversing the *ordo essendi* and the *ordo cognoscendi*. Religion comes from "the entire hitherto mode of production and intercourse," not from heaven. Moral concerns have "real, materialistic causes," based upon a certain set of social conditions, not an absolute foundation in the "predicates of God," "the essence of man," or universal law; Kant's "good will" represents "the impotence, depression, and wretchedness of the German burghers, whose petty interests were never capable of developing the common national interest of a class" and were "constantly exploited by the bourgeois of all other nations," especially France.[56] All ideology depends upon social interests and class conflicts arising from an economic condition; all religious, legal, political, and social structures are built upon the mode of production as their material condition.[57] Marx and Engels might back down and admit the interaction of other elements on occasion, but their persistent tendency is for material production to dominate all other factors and serve as the "ultimately determining element," prevailing over other "accidental causes."[58] It is this emphasis/overemphasis that leaves them vulnerable to much criticism from sociologists like Max Weber for reducing the multifaceted reasons behind human behavior to a monocausal dogma, but they obstinately insist upon the explanatory value of this one persistent theme and probably deserve most of the criticism for a plethora of oversimplified and categorical statements, which contain no proviso or caveat to mitigate the absolute rhetoric.[59]

The emphasis upon the mode of production causes Marx and Engels to view history as a struggle between economic classes—"freeman and slave, patrician and plebeian, lord and serf, guild-master and journeyman, . . . oppressor and oppressed." The first line of the *Communist Manifesto* says, "The history of all hitherto existing society is the history of class struggles."[60] The current classes that are struggling with each other are the bourgeoisie and the proletariat. The former grew out of the burghers or petty bourgeoisie of the Middle Ages—the producers and traders in commodities, who were restricted in their businesses to provincial settings and eventually gave way to modern industry as commerce expanded beyond the towns and manufacturing grew through technological advance.[61] The feudal system of industry no longer served the needs of the growing market and was absorbed for the most part by the centralization of giant industrial production, which caused the masses to become factory workers or proletariat and enslaved them to the "industrial millionaires, the leaders of whole industrial armies, the modern bourgeois."[62] This modern mode of production brought significant advantages with it in a number of areas: reducing nationalism through world markets and bringing "the most barbarian nations" into the civilized world; improving "all instruments of production" and developing technological wonders far beyond the "Egyptian pyramids, Roman aqueducts, and Gothic cathedrals" through "more massive and colossal productive forces than all preceding generations together"; but it also concentrated power into hands that are "constantly decreasing in number and growing richer," while the wage-workers increase in size and deteriorate more and more into a state of poverty. This circumstance cannot continue for long. Marx and Engels see a crisis brewing as the gap between the bourgeoisie and proletariat widens, as the profit margin shrinks, as the bourgeoisie put more capital into machines and less into labor-power, as they demand more menial tasks and give less pay, as they overproduce for their markets and create a mass of people who can no longer afford their goods.[63] In the *Communist Manifesto*, they predict the coming of an "open revolution" and the "violent overthrow of the bourgeoisie," with the proletariat leading the revolt, arresting the private property of the few, and establishing a new order of socialism. This move toward socialism might seem a qualitative leap into the unknown, but it only recognizes the preexistent "social nature of the modes of production" and merely brings the basic character of production into harmony with itself. In certain positive ways, the bourgeoisie have prepared the world for socialism by enhancing its social nature, bringing the workforce together, replacing the spinning wheel with the spinning machine, supplanting the individual workshop with the factory, and making yarn a joint project, but the contradiction between socialized production and capitalistic appropriation cannot stand and must lead to the demise of the bourgeois.[64]

Dialectic Materialism

Marx and Engels can predict the outcome of the present struggle because it operates, like all of history, according to certain material and dialectical laws. They both speak of this process, but Engels provides the first expansive treatment of the laws in *Anti-Dühring* (1878) and generally receives credit as the father of dialectical materialism—a doctrine that was practically synonymous with communism during the Stalin era.[65] Engels certainly talks more about these "driving forces" standing behind the conscious motivations of people than Marx, who generally operates on the human plane in resolving its own unique problems with reference to human agency.[66] Engels was interested in expanding the dialectical understanding of life to encompass the entire realm of nature, reducing the gulf between organic and inorganic matter, rejecting hard-and-fast classifications, dissolving any sense of rigid objects, and viewing all of life as a continuum of evolutionary flux.[67] Engels sees this concept of life going back to ancient Greek philosophy and receiving its first clear formulation in Heraclitus who saw everything as fluid, "constantly coming into being and passing away"—much like Darwin and Hegel, who set the modern paradigm and provided Engels with his greatest inspiration early on. The dialectic understands motion as the fundamental cause of events in nature. It rejects any occult investigation into mysterious chemical or mechanical forces and any rigid system that investigates fixed objects like the old metaphysical categories or the Aristotelian law of contradiction with its "absolutely irreconcilable antithesis," as if one can separate being and non-being, the positive and the negative, the cause and effect, the true and false, the good and evil.[68] Everything has an antithetical nature and lives in "contradiction to itself," giving it potency in developing a new form. Engels develops the dialectical impetus for motion in three laws: the law of the transformation of quantity into quality and vice versa, the law of the interpenetration of opposites, and the negation of the negation. Through these ways and means, progress is made throughout history as life evolves into "higher forms."[69]

Of course, both Engels and Marx make sure to distance their account from the metaphysical ideas of Hegel, or any other a priori categories that start before and outside of the lived experience of real human beings in this world. They believe that ideology is driven by worldly matters or basic materialistic interests like food, shelter, and clothing. Even the longing for human liberation is not fulfilled through the ideological discussions of self-conscious individuals, outside the proper historical conditions necessary for its realization. "Slavery cannot be abolished without the steam engine and the mule jenny, serfdom cannot be abolished without improved agriculture, and that, in general, people cannot be liberated as long as they are unable to obtain food and drink, housing and clothing in adequate quality and quantity." All ideas relate to this sensuous world and are "directly interwoven with the material activity and material intercourse of men."[70] Marx and Engels even reject any talk of forms or categories in the mind providing a priori ways in which human beings appropriate the world, although they offer no alternative epistemology or counter to Kant's monumental *Critique of Pure Reason*. Both speak much like a positivist in identifying appearance and reality in many of their statements and only qualify the view on a few occasions when they are forced to meet obvious objections, just like they do with other extreme and absolute statements in their work.[71] Engels too often speaks in the simplistic way of a positivist asserting that "our perceptions of an [object] and its qualities . . . agree with reality outside ourselves."[72] Marx says that "the world is the world of the head," that philosophy "stands on the world with its feet," promising "nothing but truth," "that his practical philosophy and social reasoning develops out of an objective, scientific analysis of the material world."[73] In fact, Engels lauds Marx on a number of occasions for placing social studies on a "firm, unshakeable foundation," making it a science and developing the one comprehensive theory of the discipline.[74] This assessment displays little of the temperament associated with scientific skepticism or objectivity and reveals more a legacy in the "scientism" of the contemporary culture, as well as the Hegelian and German propensity toward *Gründlichkeit*, which professes to explain it all through a "system of totality."[75] This belief in the scientific and comprehensive nature of Marx's work led to continuous bombastic rants against critics and demands for "personal submission" from those who afforded even the slightest variance from the truth, creating a cultlike following.[76] Moses Hess, a fellow editor at the *Rheinische Zeitung*, said, "Dr. Marx . . . is the name of my idol. . . . Imagine Rousseau, Voltaire, Lessing, Heine and Hegel united in one person—I say united, not simply thrown together—then you have Dr. Marx." Disciples like Engels and Kautsky turned the Communist Party into a confession of faith, honoring Marx as the one, true prophet and author of the one worldview.[77]

Religion

The new religion of communism scoffed at religion in its more customary form. Marx and Engels see the progress of science and socialism making religion irrelevant in meeting the expressed needs of humankind in the future.[78] Marx devotes only a few dozen pages to its discussion in his early works and ignores it later on, mentioning it only by way of illustration once he discovered the fundamental laws that envelop and explain all things.[79] Marx sees religion as nothing other than a product of changes within the social conditions of the world like everything else.[80] It is not a genuine philosophical meditation upon the meaning of life, nor even the self-serving illusions of individual longing for clerical power or personal immortality, but the practical consciousness of the masses reifying a social relation into a supernatural form and expressing its weakness in coping with the brute realities of the natural world.[81] In his *Contribution to the Critique of Hegel's Philosophy of Law* (1843/1844), he makes his most celebrated pronouncement and says that religion is "the opium of the people," not individuals. It represents the *people's* way of coping with a heartless world but only weakens any impulse or resistance to change their real conditions by substituting an illusory form of happiness and contentment.[82] Marx wants the people to resist all efforts to cover up the maelstroms of concrete reality with transcendent and alienating images of a peaceful state and seize control of their lives by working to recreate this one and only world into a more human existence.[83]

His ire particularly falls upon the Judeo-Christian tradition as the main force of religious alienation in Western civilization. He describes the Jewish faith with special contempt, claiming it arose from the "practical need/egoism of a civil society," and quickly proceeds to equate this "self-interest" and "the jealous god of Israel" with money, like any other son of the Enlightenment. In spite of its outward form, the Jewish faith is all about "commercial and industrial practice," and the real Jew is basically secular, selling "usury" and "huckstering," putting "egoism and selfish need in place of species-ties," turning everything into the "alien entity of money," and leavening the entire Christian world with "atomistic individuals who are inimically opposed to one another," filled with "egotistic need and trading." The Christian world became Jewish to the core by adopting its money system and corrupting civil society with its values.[84] The Christian faith must be destroyed along with Judaism, and Bauer is wrong to separate the two and consider the former less inimical to society than the religion of its origin. Christianity bears special responsibility for anesthetizing the world with its emphasis upon heaven, creating social apathy among the oppressed, by its talk of an ultimate day of judgment in the world to come and exhortation to submit unto oppressors in the meantime, since God will take care of them in the hereafter. "The social principles of Christianity justified the slavery of Antiquity, glorified the serfdom of the Middle Ages," and served the interests of the bourgeoisie in its Protestant form after the Reformation, degrading legions of the proletariat to inactivity in changing the here and now.[85] Marx wants to resolve the problem by extending the anti-Semitic program of Bauer and eliminating Jews, Christians, and all religious people from society, not just Jews from the state.[86]

Engels certainly agrees with the general sentiments of Marx on religion, but he shows a much greater interest in discussing and criticizing its many facets and develops a more eclectic range of comments as a result.[87] For example, his discussion of its origin is more eclectic than Marx's fixation upon the sociomorphic model, predicated on the different modes of production, as the universal explanation of all things. He sees animism or the personification of natural forces as developing out of a universal urge of primitive people and makes this element the initial step toward creating a more concrete concept of the gods, before leaving this timeless dimension and speaking of social factors or abstract philosophical meditations.[88] Of course, he continues to place at the forefront of his discussions the economic and historical conditions in developing religious ideals as a decisive aspect of the Socialist agenda and especially accents the ability of the dominate class to justify its exploitation of the masses through "religious shibboleths,"[89] but he sometimes leaves the predictable party line and provides a more nuanced and even favorable review of religious influence. Engels even finds a number of parallels between present socialism and primitive Christianity, as the religion of the oppressed.[90] He also sees positive strides in the Reformation, crediting Calvin for bringing democratic and republican ideas into the modern world, commending the Peasants' War in the 1520s as a revival of early Christian egalitarianism, and exalting its leader, Thomas Münzer, as preaching revolution and anticipating proletarian emancipation, beyond simple bourgeois equality, while Luther remained in a "cowardly servility to the princes."[91]

However, he has no interest in finding a positive place for religion in the party or the world to come and expresses concern about a number of French Communists who think of Christianity as the basis of their point of view, while excusing them for their lack of biblical, critical, and scientific knowledge.[92]

He thinks of his approach to scripture as scientific and says that a critical scholar has only two basic respectable choices when it comes to biblical studies: (1) The Tübingen School, represented by Strauss and Renan, which sees the four Gospels as written later in the church by non-witnesses, accepts no more than four of Paul's letters as authentic, strikes out all miracles and contradictions in the NT, and tries to "save what can be saved," and (2) the more skeptical position of Bauer, who provides the most unrelenting criticism of the Gospels and questions whether Christianity grew out of Palestinian Judaism by showing the "enormous influence" the "Philonic school of Alexandria and Greco-Roman vulgar philosophy—had on Christianity," making Alexandria and Rome the birthplace of the new religion, not Galilee and Jerusalem. The Tübingen School presents the "extreme maximum" that is possible to accept from a scientific point of view, and Bauer "presents the maximum that can be contested" in scripture, with the truth probably lying somewhere in between the two enlightened approaches.[93]

The Secular/Socialist State

Marx and Engels point to scholastic and scientific debate as leading toward their worldview, but they never trust the outcome of civilized discourse and really want the reign of religion and other forces of alienation to end through social coercion. They define human beings as social or "political animals" like Aristotle and want to mold them into their true essence through this way and means.[94] They engage in much claptrap and double-talk about freedom along the way, speaking of communism as fulfilling individual freedom and relating the freedom of each to the freedom of all, but all this talk seems empty in light of their desire to create a common life.[95] In their view of "total emancipation," no distinction remains between the political state and civil society, between the general will and private interests; they want to absorb all things under the common life of Marxist ideology and eliminate all vestiges of distinct institutions and separate existence.[96] The family must be "destroyed in theory and practice" as a bourgeois institution of private ownership.[97] The "rights of man" must be destroyed as promoting anarchy, sanctioning greed, privatizing civil society, and separating individuals from each other.[98] Private property falls along with civil rights because it represents the usurpation of resources and debases others to a life of poverty and alienation, want and dependence.[99] The *Communist Manifesto* calls for the seizure of all means of production by the state and has no difficulty with this type of usurpation as long as it is done in the name of the proletariat, without displaying any concern for the tyranny of the majority or the historic place of property rights in withstanding the arbitrary power of government. It reduces humanity to a socialized mode of production, discounting all other needs and expressions. Engels says "only conscious organization of social production" can raise human beings above the survival of the fittest in the animal kingdom.

This mode of production answers to the "historic activity of men" who first raised their species above the animals by producing the necessities of life and controlling their own destiny.[100]

Marx and Engels offer little practical advice, for setting up a social experiment or administrative structure, beyond expressing contempt for Prussian civil service and bureaucracy and calling for social control.[101] In the 1920s, Marx was interpreted by the Marxist-Leninist state of Russia as recognizing the need for a transitional phase of socialism with a centralized authority before proceeding to the ultimate goal of communism, and so differentiating the two terms. This interpretation was based upon his usage of the phrase "dictatorship of the proletariat" on a couple of occasions. In a letter to Joseph Weydemeyer of the New York Turn-Zeitung (published January 1, 1852), Marx spoke of a transitional period between capitalism and communism in which a "dictatorship of the proletariat" would exist before all classes were abolished.[102] In his "Critique of the Gotha Program" (1875), he spoke of a transitional period once again as the "revolutionary dictatorship of the proletariat" and thought of it as "still stamped with the birthmarks of the old [capitalist] society from whose womb it emerges,"[103] but the remaining bourgeois influence would include democracy, not exude it. In fact, it is questionable whether Marx ever intended to dispense with democracy, given his continual insistence upon it during organizational meetings, even if the logical outcome of his overall ideas might lead in the direction of Lenin.[104]

Marx wants a state that has a basis in real human existence, developed out of the modern philosophical community and its reasoning about human relations.[105] Religion provides no guidance in understanding the human condition or creating an effectual and enlightened state, which answers to the genuine needs of real human existence. The church subsists as a cosmopolitan organization under many different forms of government, unable to judge the "correctness of constitutions," teaching unconditional submission to all authorities, and advocating the separation of church and state from its very inception. Even the church supports the idea of an "atheistic state" and knows the so-called "Christian state" represents an oxymoron and really comes from a "secular, . . . human background." Marx thinks religion will disappear in the future as it recognizes its inability to address matters of serious concern and acknowledges its singular purpose in proposing the most inane stopgap fantasies, existing only from the *deus ex machina* of human ignorance and receding before the march of modern secular science.[106] Newton reduced God to a first impulse, and Laplace eliminated the rest of the divine space, declaring to Napoleon that he no longer had any "need of that hypothesis" to satisfy his equations.[107] Marx applauds the progress and wants to continue advancing the program of the Enlightenment and expand the process of exorcising divine spirits from all realms of society. In his work "On the Jewish Question" (1844), he is unsatisfied with the pace of secularization in Western civilization and considers state policies like America's First Amendment and Bauer's "political emancipation" insufficient in rooting out religion from the souls of the people. "The emancipation of the state from religion is not the emancipation of the real man from religion." Marx prefers to follow his more expansive enlightened policy of reconciling public and private interests by proposing a complete "human emancipation" and eliminating religion from civil society, making the existence of the Jew, Christian, and all religious individuals impossible by political and social coercion.[108] Engels certainly agrees with this approach and would prohibit every religious organization from his community and "declare atheism a compulsory article of faith," exceeding the strictures of the French Revolution and Bismark's *Kirchenkulturkampf* by "prohibiting religion in general."[109]

The animosity toward religion prevents Marx and Engels from acknowledging the religious nature of their own presuppositions and mission. They make a concentrated effort to hide the overall agenda in much of their work, analyzing the process and forces of history without providing moralistic commentary or optimistic reports about any progress toward social justice. They try to offer simple empirical observations, developing concepts of socialism from materialistic laws of science and providing a dispassionate account of what happens to transpire in the course of historical events, but they succeed only in part and spend much of the time concealing a deep-seated metaphysical viewpoint and prophetic mission with their call to change the world into a new egalitarian image. This imperative has no specific basis in science and no genuine interest in interpreting the world or accepting the brute realities of a Darwinian universe, predicated upon the survival of the fittest and filled with nothing more than meaningless change. This part of their system clearly makes more sense within a religious perspective, which might supply a moral imperative to create an egalitarian world of social justice or direct their actions in achieving a utopian goal, as if life contained an ultimate and antecedent purpose, but they refuse to admit it. They have enough philosophical acumen to recognize the religious nature of these concepts, but they refuse to admit their allegiance to them, preferring to push the moral and theological presuppositions underneath the surface and pretend to work in a strict scientific manner.[110]

And they live with this denial boldly, saying, "Communists do not preach morality." There is no true morality, not even a proletarian morality; "all moral theories" reflect class interest and "the economic conditions of society obtaining at the time." "There is no more reason to moralize" about horrific events like the brutal assassination of Tsar Alexander II than "there is about the earthquake in Chios."[111] And they stick to the script throughout their analytical works, developing consciousness out of a historical process through the prevailing system of production, avoiding any talk of an outside imperative, and pretending to find the call for action within a specific economic condition,[112] but all of this appears to deny the fundamental nature of their moral orientation in studying and criticizing events. Most often this perspective remains concealed from the reader, but sometimes it erupts in direct words and actions, when they attack the unscrupulous behavior of political foes and the disloyalty of former allies, when they decry the brutal conditions of European factories and living conditions of the workers, when they burn with righteous indignation against the bourgeoisie, condemning their theft and robbery, and denouncing the oppression and exploitation of the proletariat.[113] To these atrocities they respond with horror and a call to action that has nothing to do with a simple description of their opponent's behavior and much to do with justice. Like Hitler and the Nazis, they commit the naturalistic fallacy on a massive scale, pretending that a scientific description of the way things happen to transpire in life contains a moral imperative in promoting or denouncing it.

The main focus of Marx, Engels, and all left-wing politics is to spread the doctrine of equality as the fundamental moral principle of life. In their "scientific" analysis, "the idea of equality" is presented as a simple "historical product" of the way life happens to evolve, but they clearly become obsessed with its ascension and want to extend the "modern demand for equality" and make "more far-reaching demands from this bourgeois demand" in pushing for the "abolition of class."[114] This monomania involves the complete rejection of any qualitative distinction between types of labor or skills in the workplace, including the normal hierarchy between mental and physical labor, and leads to "one of the most vital principles of communism," which rejects rewarding people according to their ability and gives "to each accordingly to his need."[115] Marx and Engels do their best to distance this fundamental principle from a religious exhortation and chasten the French Communists for thinking of Christianity as the primary basis for its current status in Western civilization, but even Engels recognizes the importance of egalitarianism in primitive Christianity, that it is hard to understand the Western emphasis upon equality outside of its moorings in the writings of the NT and its ascension in the Protestant Reformation through Luther's priesthood of the believers.[116] If anything, Marxism turns Christian egalitarianism into an idol and loses the existential basis of the concept in Jesus and Paul, who rejected the legalism of their day and its tendency to create absolute godlike demands out of one side of the law.

Marx and Engels think of equality as a godlike force enveloping the future. They share the innate penchant of all left-wing ideologues or progressives to embrace the future as the basis of their agenda, as if history justifies itself, or the triumph of an idea provides its own sanction.[117] This liberal spirit dominated the nineteenth century and found its classical statement in the philosophy of Hegel, who said, "World history [is] the world court of judgment."[118] Marx may claim that Darwin brought "the death-below" to this type of theological thinking,[119] but his basic ideology proceeds in a different direction and remains solidly within the progressive spirit of the age, when he applies its optimism to the class struggle, predicting *and* rejoicing in the historical triumph of egalitarianism within a classless society. He still believes in the triumph of the good and the progressive march of history toward an ultimate end.[120] He just no longer believes in the good providence of God or the theistic foundation of the liberal spirit in Hegel, leaving his critics to wonder how life could move with such purpose toward an ideal and turn out the right way he wants it to be within a system based upon the blind and irrational forces of matter.

Of course, he like most individuals ends up tempering the concept of destiny or determinism when confronted with the human need to inculcate a personal agenda and ask others to accept moral responsibility in creating a better world. He continues to think of material circumstances as most essential in shaping human beings and often speaks of economic determinism without any noticeable qualification or pause in diction, but he turns around and has many Promethean moments that reject a passive submission to economic forces and inculcates the creative power of humans to change causal circumstances with self-conscious activity.[121] In his *Theses on Feuerbach,* he considers philosophy to have a purpose and finds it mission in changing the world, not contemplating natural forces or metaphysical realities. (*Die Philosophen haben die Welt nur verschieden interpretirt, es kommet drauf an sie zu verandern.*)[122] In the *Communist Manifesto,* he ends with the clarion call for the proletariat to unite for battle. (*Proletarier aller Lander, vereinigt euch!*)[123]

Lenin and the Russian Communists followed the fundamental thought of Marx's work in seizing power during the October Revolution in 1917, and they proceeded to enforce Marxist dogma as the new ideology of the Socialist state. They followed Marx on a number of issues, as presented in this chapter: the need for a radical revolutionary change, following the antithetical spirit of Hegelianism and the assault upon the *Ancien Régime* in French thought and action; the denial of any dichotomy between personal and general interests, wanting to absorb all levels of society into a common way of life and provide total "human emancipation"; the rejection of private property and individual rights; the accent upon social change in shaping the religion, customs, and ideology of a people; and the use of social coercion to eliminate Jews, Christians, and other religious people—all finding their precedent in the French Revolution. They also had the same faith in science and socialism in meeting the existential needs of the people and making religion irrelevant in the future; the same tendency toward materialism and positivism, believing that science provides certain knowledge about the world and a sure basis of ideology; and the same conception of life as an evolutionary, dialectical process, which progresses toward an egalitarian future and justifies their ideology in the *eschaton.* In all these matters and many more, they followed Engels and turned Marx into the one true prophet and his system into an absolute science and explanation of it all. Some of their interpretations were questionable, including the "temporary" dictatorship of Lenin, Stalin, and their successors, but few were completely heterodox and most seemed necessary in implementing and establishing a Communist-type of revolution in Russia as Marx envisioned it from a pragmatic point of view. If Russian communism took on a unique form, it was consonant with his overall thought and recognition that "real communism" must exist within a specific context and develop out of a Russian reality, not the course of western European events as Marx describes them.[124]

Notes

1. Of course, Marxism never presented a simple monolithic doctrine in its various expressions, in spite of its own image and reputation. After all, "many of what are now considered Marx's most important writings were not printed until the twenties and thirties [of the twentieth century] or even later." Leszek Kołakowski, *Main Currents of Marxism*, P. S. Falla (trans.) (New York and London: W. W. Norton & Company, 2005) 5–8.
2. Denis R. Janz, *World Christianity and Marxism* (New York and Oxford: Oxford University Press) 7–8; Richard P. Appelbaum, *Karl Marx* (Newbury Park, London, and New Delhi: Sage Publications, 1988) 21–22; Kołakowski, *Main Currents of Marxism*, 80, 83; Julius I. Loewenstein, *Marx and Marxism* (London, Boston, and Henley: Routledge & Kegan Paul, 1980) 9.
3. Delos B. McKown, *The Classical Marxist Critique of Religion: Marx, Engels, Lenin, Kautsky* (The Hague: Martinus Nijoff, 1975) 16; Kołakowski, *Main Currents of Marxism*, 85–88.
4. Marx and Engels, *The German Ideology*, in *Collected Works* (New York: International Publishers, 1975), 5.30 [*Werke* (Berlin: Dietz, 1964) 3.19, 20]; Kołakowski, *Main Currents of Marxism*, 69, 70, 77–78, 91–93, 121; Appelbaum, *Karl Marx*, 22. Hereafter, the English translation of their works is abbreviated MECW, and the German is given in parentheses. In the *Holy Family* (1844/45), Marx and Engels make their break with the Young Hegelians and attack them on a number of issues.
5. J. D. Hunley, *The Life and Thought of Friedrich Engels: A Reinterpretation* (New Haven, CT, and London: Yale University Press, 1991) 2; Loewenstein, *Marx and Marxism*, 57.
6. "The Conditions of the Working-Class in England," MECW 2.378–79; *The Conditions of the Working-Class in England*, MECW 4.363–64 (2.293–95); Terrell Carver, *Engels* (New York: Hill and Wang, 1981)11, 14–17; Hunley, *Life and Thought of Friedrich Engels*, 6.
7. MECW 1.416–23; Hunley, *Life and Thought of Friedrich Engels*, 3–4; Gustav Mayer, *Friedrich Engels: A Biography* (New York: A. A. Knopf, 1936) 4–5; McKown, *Classical Marxist Critique of Religion*, 61–62; Hunley, *Life and Thought of Friedrich Engels*, 6.
8. "To Friedrich Graeber" (July 12–27, 1839), MECW 2.457–63 "To Wilhelm Graeber" (Oct. 8, 1839), MECW 2.471; *German Ideology*, MECW 5.27 (3.17); Hunley, *Life and Thought of Friedrich Engels*, 9–11.
9. *German Ideology*, MECW 5.30 (3.20); Carver, *Engels*, 5; Hunley, *Life and Thought of Friedrich Engels*, 12–14. At this time, he read Hegel's *Phenomenology of the Spirit*, *Science of Logic*, and *Encyclopedia of the Philosophical Sciences*; Kant's *Critique of Pure Reason*, *Prolegomena to*

Any Future Metaphysics, and *Perpetual Peace*; and Feuerbach's *Essence of Christianity*.

10. "To Ferdinand Lassalle" (May 31, 1858), MECW 40.316 (29.561); Allen W. Wood, *Karl Marx* (New York: Routledge, 2004) 215.
11. *Hegel's Phenomonology of the Spirit*, A. V. Miller (trans.) (Oxford and New York: Oxford University Press, 1977) 32 (53). Hegel considers formal logic when speaking of either/or alternatives and talking about static entities like blue and non-blue as fundamentally untrue to the dynamic nature of life, where solid objects are constantly dissolving and "opposites" actually feed off of each other (e.g, black/white, north/south). Each entity has the other within it and feeds off it in forming a unity. Ibid., 97–100 (158–61), 106–8 (169–71); Wood, *Karl Marx*, 212–13. The triadic formula of "Thesis-Antithesis-Synthesis" also tends to oversimplify a more complicated dialectical reasoning presented by Hegel, Marx, and Engels in considering the interaction of all things, even if it is used on occasion as a helpful illustration of the concept. For example, see the following charts in Engels:

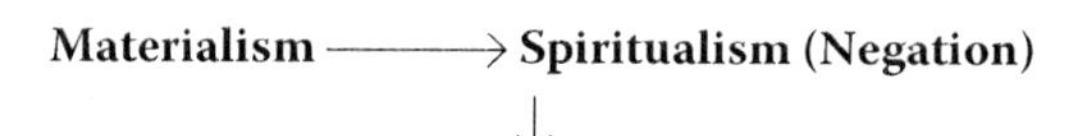

↓

New Materialism (Negation of the Negation)

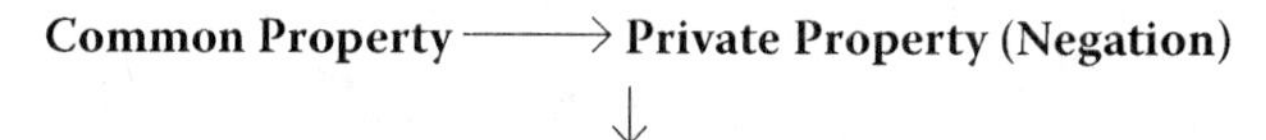

↓

Common Property (Negation of the Negation or Higher Negation)

See *Dialectics of Nature*, MECW, 25.606 (20.583); *Anti-Dühring*, MECW, 25.128–30 (20.128–30).

12. Ibid., 17 (29), 19 (32), 21 (37), 23 (39), 145 (238), 306–8 (504–8), 320–21 (526) 457 (801); 492 (808).
13. Georg Hegel, *Philosophy of Right*, in *Great Books of the Western World*, Robert Maynard Hutchins (ed.) (Chicago: Encyclopaedia Britannica, Inc., 1977) 110 (343).
14. *Phenomenology of the Spirit*, 45 (72), 60–61 (98–99), 77–78 (130–31), 298 (489).
15. See chap. 11, p. 226.
16. Van A. Harvey, "Ludwig Feuerbach and Karl Marx," in *Nineteenth Century Religious Thought in the West*, Ninian Smart, et al. (ed.) (Cambridge: Cambridge University Press, 1985) 296–97. In the *German Ideology*, Marx and Engels berate Max Stirner for making the Hegelian world of thought dominate the world and making people mere vehicles of a "holy" dimension. *German Ideology*, MECW 5.172–75, 282–84, 292–93 (3.156–59, 263–65, 273–75).
17. *Dialectics of Nature*, MECW 25.594–95 (20.18–19); Loewenstein, *Marx and Marxism*, 35.
18. *Anti-Dühring*, MECW 25.11 (20.10–11); Etienne Balibar, *The Philosophy of Marx*, Chris Turner (trans.) (London and New York: Verso, 1995) 24–26;

L. Feuerbach and the End of Classical German Philosophy, MECW 26.359–60 (21.267). Hegel seems to applaud whatever was successful in the past and provides no means for judging the present state of things. Kołakowski, *Main Currents of Marxism*, 65–66.

19. "Contribution to the Critique of Hegel's Philosophy of Right. Introduction," MECW 3.186–87 (1.390–91); *Holy Family*, MECW 4.125 (2.132); Appelbaum, *Karl Marx*, 60; Loewenstein, *Marx and Marxism*, 35; Janz, *World Christianity and Marxism*, 8–9; Kathleen Clarkson and David J. Hawkin, "Marx on Religion: The Influence of Bruno Bauer and Ludwig Feuerbach on His Thought and Its Implications for the Christian-Marxist Dialogue," in *Scottish Journal of Theology* 31/6 (1978) 542.
20. *Feuerbach and the End of Classical German Philosophy*, MECW 26.364 (21.272); Loewenstein, *Marx and Marxism*, 38.
21. "Man is what he eats." Ludwig Feuerbach, *The Essence of Christianity*, George Elliot (trans.), Karl Barth (intro.) (New York: Harper & Row Publishers, 1957) xii–xiv.
22. Ibid., xvi, xxxv–xxxvii, 12, 31, 34, 95, 184, 207– 8, 230. "What man declares of God, he in truth declares of himself." Ibid., 29.
23. *Feuerbach and the End of Classical German Philosophy*, MECW 26.382–83 (21.292); Clarkson and Hawkin, "Marx on Religion," 542.
24. Clarkson and Hawkin, "Marx on Religion," 547, 552; Kołakowski, *Main Currents of Marxism*, 95.
25. Feuerbach, *Essence of Christianity*, 26, 33; Wood, *Karl Marx*, 12.
26. Ibid., xvi, xvii, 114–116, 119, 129–36, 208, 249–50, 255–56. For the same opinion in Marx, see "Luther als Schiedsrichter zwischen Strauss und Feuerbach," in *Werke*, 1.26–27; Clarkson and Hawkin, "Marx on Religion," 542.
27. David McLellan, *The Young Hegelians and Karl Marx* (New York and Washington: Frderick A. Praeger, 1969) 79–80; Clarkson and Hawkin, "Marx on Religion," 533–34.
28. Bruno Bauer, *The Trumpet of the Last Judgment against Hegel the Atheist and Antichrist*, Lawrence Stepelevich (trans.) (Lewiston, NY: The Edwin Mellen Press, 1989) 1–2, 37–38; Kołakowski, *Main Currents of Marxism*, 75; Clarkson and Hawkin, "Marx on Religion," 536–37; "To His Father" (Nov. 10/11, 1837) MECW 1.10–21. Engels also shows specific influence from Bauer, especially in his discussion about the origins of Christianity in the "Philonic School of Alexandria and Greco-Roman vulgar philosophy." *Zur Geschichte des Urchristentums*, in *Werke*, 22.455–56.
29. Ibid., 33, 81, 93–100, 119, 122–23, 137, 171–73, 189, 192, 201; Friedrich Schleiermacher, *The Christian Faith*, H.R. MacIntosh and J. S. Stewart (ed.) (Philadelphia: Fortress Press, 1976) 120–23, 405–7, 738–51. Schleiermacher finds religion by reflecting upon the "inward emotions and dispositions" of the heart. *On Religion: Speeches to Its Cultured Despisers*, John Oman (trans.), Rudolf Otto (intro.) (New York: Harper & Row Publishers, 1958) 3, 17–18.
30. Ibid., 126–33, 140–41, 150, 163, 169–70. Marx criticizes Bauer in the autumn of 1843 for wanting to eliminate religion from the state and failing to bring complete human emancipation to all realms of society. "On the Jewish Question," MECW 3.152, 168–69 (1.353, 371). Bauer's anti-Semitism is discussed in chap. 9, pp. 223–24. In his later work, he thinks of the Jews as having

a special innate depravity that prevents them from making progress and participating in society.

31. *Anti-Dühring*, MECW 25.16, 19 (20.16–17).
32. *Holy Family*, MECW 4.124–27, 130–31 (2.131–35, 138). They also recognize a whole patriarchy of individual scholars laying the foundation of French materialism: Democritus, Epicurus, Duns Scotus, the Nominalists, Descartes, English materialists and Deists, along with their predecessors (Bacon, Hobbes, Locke, and Newton). Ibid., 124–31 (2.131–38).
33. "Juristen-Sozialismus," in *Werke*, 21.493–94; *Anti-Dühring*, MECW 25.246, 250–51 (20.241, 244–46); *Holy Family*, MECW 4.34–35 (2.35–36); Kołakowski, *Main Currents of Marxism*, 152–59, 173ff.; Loewenstein, *Marx and Marxism*, 17, 20–22.
34. Balibar, *Philosophy of Marx*, 8, 20, 21; Appelbaum, *Karl Marx*, 20. Kołakowski says, "The Babouvist movement marks the point at which liberal democracy and communism began to part company, as it came to be seen that equality was not a completion of liberty but a limitation to it." The term "Communist" was separated from "Socialist" in the 1830s, indicating a more radical agenda than the latter, demanding the abolition of property, the equality of consumption, and the use of force to change the basic structure of society by those exploited in the present system. *Main Currents of Marxism*, 153–54.
35. "Summary of Frederick Engels' Article 'Outlines of a Critique of Political Economy'," MECW 3.375–76; Loewenstein, *Marx against Marxism*, 57; Carver, *Engels*, 21–22.
36. "To Marx" (Feb. 22–26 and March 7, 1845), in *Werke*, 27.22; Carver, *Engels*, 24–26.
37. *Feuerbach and the End of Classical German Philosophy*, MECW 26.382 (n.) (21.291); Loewenstein, *Marx against Marxism*, 58.
38. *Anti-Dühring*, MEW 25.27 (20.26); Carver, *Engels*, 47, 74–75. In 1890, Engels admitted that he provided the most detailed account of "historical materialism." Marx refers/alludes to dialectics on occasion but skips it in many of his major works.
39. Ibid., ix, x, 144–45. According to Hunley, György Lukács and Karl Korsch began to drive a wedge between them. Lukács believes that Engels followed the mistaken precedent of Hegel by overextending the validity of dialectics to all of nature. George Lichtheim believes that Engels was the founder of dialectic materialism and became a natural determinist and positivist in *Anti-Dühring*, whereas Marx never followed this overexercised materialism. *Life and Thought of Friedrich Engels*, 47–50, 61–64; George Lukács, *History and Class Consciousness: Studies in Marxist Dialectics*, Rodney Livingstone (trans.) (Cambridge, MA: The MIT Press, 1971) xix–xx; Boris Nicolaievsky and Otto Maenchen-Helfen, *Karl Marx: Man and Fighter*, Gwenda David and Eric Mosbacher (trans.) (Harmondsworth, UK: Penguin Books, 1976) 92. Hunley agrees with the earlier viewpoint and finds an essential agreement between the two colleagues. See *Life and Thought*, 126. For their close relationship in life and thought from the older, Marxist perspective, see *Reminiscences of Marx and Engels* (Moscow: Foreign Languages Publishing House, 1968) 83–84, 148, 182–83.
40. "Manifest of the Communist Party," MECW 6.496 (4.475–76); *German Ideology*, MECW 5.49 (3.35); Carver, *Engels*, 27–28; Kołakowski, *Main Currents*

of Communism, 186–87, 337; Appelbaum, *Karl Marx*, 31. The first meeting was held during the summer of 1847 in London, with Engels drawing up the program, which outlined the "Principles of Communism."

41. Clarkson and Hawkin, "On Religion," 7; Kołakowski, *Main Currents of Communism*, 182, 218, 236.
42. *German Ideology*, C. J. Arthur (ed. and intro.) (New York: International Publishers, 1970) 15; Clarkson and Hawkin, "Marx on Religion," 6–10.
43. *German Ideology*, MECW 5.80 (3.70–71); "Contribution to the Critique of Hegel's Philosophy of Law. Introduction," MECW 3.176 (1.379); McKown, *Classical Marxist Critique of Religion*, 49–50; Wood, *Karl Marx*, 23–24, 51–52, 75, 79.
44. "Contribution to the Critique of Hegel's Philosopy. Introduction," MECW 3.176 (1.379); *Anti-Dühring*, MECW 25.301–2 (20.294–95).
45. *Holy Family*, MECW 4.53 (2.55–56); *Das Kapital*, MECW 35.705–6 (23.742); Appelbaum, *Karl Marx*, 73; Kołakowski, *Main Currents of Communism*, 114, 147.
46. Ibid., 35.270–71 (23.280–81); *German Ideology*, 5.87 (3.67); McKown, *Classical Marxist Critique of Religion*, 7; Wood, *Karl Marx*, 9. Marx rejects any bourgeois justification for this system in terms of the end justifying the means (Bentham and Mill) or as a form of "mutual exploitation" (Helvétius and Holbach). Like most left-wing ideologues, he believes in a social system that maintains everyone's dignity at all times.
47. *German Ideology*, MECW 5.31–32, 35–36 (3.20–21, 25–26); *German Ideology* (Arthur), 21; Balibar, *Philosophy of Marx*, 28; Wood, *Karl Marx*, 29, 35; Kołakowski, *Main Currents of Maxism*, 114–16.
48. *Das Kapital*, MECW 35.48–50, 86 (23.53–54, 90–91); *Anti-Dühring*, MECW 25.186, 190 (20.186, 189–90); Appelbaum, *Karl Marx*, 99.
49. *Grundrisse: Foundations of the Critique of Political Economy* (Rough Draft) Martin Nicolaus (trans.) (London: Pelikan Marx Library, 1973) 706, 712; *Das Kapital*, MECW 37.807 (25.828); Appelbaum, *Karl Marx*, 132; Loewenstein, *Marx against Marxism*, 83, 181.
50. *Das Kapital*, MECW 35.369, 590–91 (23.386, 620–21); Wood, *Karl Marx*, 47–48. Marx reduces everything to economics and has little concept of a person's worth outside this category.
51. "Manifesto of the Communist Party," MEW 6.487 (4.464–65); Appelbaum, *Karl Marx*, 81; Loewenstein, *Marx against Marxism*, 137; Balibar, *Philosophy of Marx*, 69. Reification (*Verdinglichung*) is Lukács term, although the concept is borrowed from Marx.
52. *Das Kapital*, MECW 35.180, 196, 207–8, 219, 370–72, 541 (23.184, 200–1, 211, 223–24, 386–89, 564); *Anti-Dühring*, MECW 25.27, 147 (20.26, 148); Loewenstein, *Marx against Marxism*, 73; Wood, *Karl Marx*, 136–38; Kołakowski, *Main Currents of Marxism*, 211, 229, 233. In *Das Kapital*, where Marx sets forth the concept of surplus-value, he feels that machines/innovation add little to surplus-value, even if more will be invested in machines and less in labor-power in the future, reducing the profit-margin of capitalists. He commends capitalism for technological innovation and progress, even if the human cost is enormous. *Das Kapital*, MECW 35.214–15, 623–24 (23.219, 657–58); Kołakowski, *Main Currents of Marxism*, 240; Wood, *Karl Marx*, 42, 48.

53. Kołakowski, *Main Currents of Marxism*, 227–33, 261; Wood, *Karl Marx*, 136. In 1817, David Ricardo, the next great economist after Smith, saw laborers being paid a mere subsistence level.
54. *Holy Family*, MECW 4.131 (2.138).
55. Balibar, *Philosophy of Marx*, 67.
56. *German Ideology*, MECW 5.36–37, 159–62, 193–95, 447 (3.26, 27, 143–45, 176–78, 432–33).
57. Ibid., 31–32, 35, 43 (3.22–23, 25, 29–30); "Manifesto," 6.503; *Feuerbach and the End of Classical German Philosophy*, MECW 26.365–66, 392 (21.274–75, 301–2); "Juristen-Sozialismus," in *Werke*, 21.494; Wood, *Karl Marx*, 74, 100; Kołakowski, *Main Currents of Marxism*, 127. Engels gives credit to Saint-Simon for discovering that "economic conditions are the basis of political institutions." *Anti-Dühring*, MECW 25.246–47 (20.241–42).
58. "To Joseph Bloch" (Sept. 21/22, 1890) MECW 49.34–36 (37.463–65); Carver, *Engels*, 66–67; Wood, *Karl Marx*, 64, 110–11; Kołakowski, *Main Currents of Marxism*, 278–80. Later in life, Engels stresses that they never intended to reduce all things to economic concerns and always recognized the significance of other material factors like region, climate, geography, and so on.
59. Loewenstein, *Marx against Marxism*, 113, 115, 117; Kołakowski, *Main Currents of Marxism*, 303. For example, the invention of the steam engine did not lead Spain but England to develop a capitalist economy, so there must be other factors.
60. "Manifesto," MECW 6.482 (4.462); Kołakowski, *Main Currents of Marxism*, 187; Wood, *Karl Marx*, 90–91.
61. *German Ideology*, MECW 5.70 (3.57); Kołakowski, *Main Currents of Marxism*, 247.
62. "Manifesto," MECW 6.485–86 (4.463–64); *Das Kapital*, MECW 35.749–50 (23.789–90); *German Ideology*, MECW 5.76 (3.58).
63. "Manifesto," 6.485–90 (4.463–67); *Anti-Dühring*, MECW 25.139–40, 261, 267 (20.139, 140, 255, 261); *Das Kapital*, MECW 35.620ff., 623 (23.653ff., 657–58); Appelbaum, *Karl Marx*, 108–9.
64. "Manifesto," MEW 6.491, 495 (4.469, 473); MCC 186; *Das Kapital*, MECW 35.751 (23.791); *Anti-Dühring*, MECW 25.256, 258, 266 (20.250–52, 260); Kołakowski, *Main Currents of Marxism*, 251. "Co-operation ever constitutes the fundamental form of capitalist mode of production." *Das Kapital*, MECW 35.430 (23.355).
65. Carver, *Engels*, 48; Balibar, *Philosophy of Marx*, 3; Hunley, *Life and Thought of Friedrich Engels*, 50; Kołakowski, *Main Currents of Marxism*, 312. Balibar says the phrase "dialectical materialism" was first coined by Joseph Dietzgen in 1887. Even Engels admits that Marx only alludes to this doctrine in *Das Kapital* while he provides "the most detailed account" in *Anti-Dühring* and *Ludwig Feuerbach*. "Joseph Bloch" (Sept. 21/22, 1890), MECW 49.36; Carver, *Engels*, 74–75.
66. Norman Levine, *The Tragic Deception: Marx contra Engels* (Oxford and Santa Barbara, Calif.: Clio Books, 1975) 108, 137; Hunley, *Life and Thought of Engels*, 59; Wood, *Karl Marx*, 88–89.
67. *Dialectics of Nature*, MEW 25.327 (20.319–20); *Anti-Dühring*, MECW 25.14 (20.14); Kołakowski, *Main Currents of Marxism*, 313.

68. *Anti-Dühring*, MECW 25. 21–22, 85–86 (20.20–21, 85–86); *Feuerbach and the End of the Classical German Philosophy*, MECW 26.384 (21.293–94). Engels accepts Kant's concept of a primordial, rarefied nebula and sees matter and motion as eternal. He expresses some doubt about Darwin's "survival of the fittest," believing there is more to life than mere subsistence, and appears to lean more toward the Lamarkian explanation of the mechanism. *Dialectics of Nature*, MECW 25.323–25, 584 (20.315–17, 565); *Anti-Dühring*, MECW 25.54–56 (20.53–55); Kołakowski, *Main Currents of Marxism*, 313; Carver, *Engels*, 57–58.
69. *Dialectics of Nature*, MECW 25.606 (20.583); *Feuerbach and the End of Classical German Philosophy*, MECW 26.386 (21.295).
70. *German Ideology*, MECW 5.36, 38, 51 (3.26, 43, 46); Balibar, *Philosophy of Marx*, 36–37, 47–48; Wood, *Karl Marx*, 168.
71. Wood, *Karl Marx*, 168–71; Cf. Hunley, *Life and Thought of Friedrich Engels*, 126.
72. "Introduction to the English Edition of Socialism: Utopian and Scientific," MECW 27.287 (22.296, 297); Carver, *Engels*, 51.
73. "The Leading Article in No. 179 of the *Kölnische Zeitung*," MECW 1.195–97 (1.97–99).
74. *Dialectics of Nature*, MECW 25.592–593 (20.18–19). Marx and Engels think of science as advancing toward a better and better tomorrow. *Anti-Dühring*, MECW 25.80 (20. 80–81); Janz, *World Christianity and Marxism*, 8. They clearly have little understanding of the problems that postmodernism has brought to this position in the work of Michel Foucault, who questions the scientific status of the so-called human sciences, and Thomas Kuhn, who wonders whether science makes any linear progress in the first place. Rudi Visker, *Michel Foucault: Genealogy as Critique*, Chris Turner (trans.) (London and New York: Verso, 1995) 3–5, 40–42; Thomas S. Kuhn, *The Structure of the Scientific Revolution* (Chicago: Chicago University Press, 1970) 2, 96, 170.
75. "Introduction to the English Edition of Socialism," MECW 27.278 (22.287); Georg Hegel, *Scientific Logic*, A. V. Miller (trans.) (London: George Allen & Unwin LTD, 1969) 840; Loewenstein, *Marx against Marxism*, 33. *Gründlichkeit* is Engel's own word in describing this phenomenon.
76. For example, *German Ideology*, MECW 5.23 (3.13) and passim; *Anti-Dühring*, MECW 25.7, 309 (20.9, 303); *The Reminiscences of Charles Schurz* (New York: The McClure Company, 1908) 1.138–39; "Konspect von Bakunins Buch 'Staatlichkeit und Anarchie'," in *Werke*, 18.626; Loewenstein, *Marx against Marxism*, 97. Mikhail Alexandrovich Bakunin (1814–1876) wanted smaller communes than Marx and warned that the emphasis upon the state would lead to a new tyranny of the "scientific" elite ruling over the ignorant masses. *Statism and Anarchy*, C. H. Plummer (trans.) (New York: Revisionist Press, 1976) 245–46 (280–81).
77. "Mose Hess an Berthold Auerbach" (Sept. 2, 1841), in MEGA, Abt. I, 1/2, 261; Loewenstein, *Marx against Marxism*, 96, 101.
78. Janz, *World Christianity and Marxism*, 8.
79. *German Ideology*, MECW 5.36–37, 45–46 (3.26–27, 37–38); McKown, *Classical Marxist Critique of Religion*, 13–14; L. N. Mitrokhin, "Marx's Concept of Religion," 22/1 (1984): 23–24; Janz, *World Christianity and Marxism*, 10–12.

80. "Reviews from the Neue Rheinische Zeitung. Politisch-Ökonomische Revue No. 2. G. Fr. Daumer," MECW 10.244 (7.201); Mitrokhin, "Marx's Concept of Religion," 33. For example, Protestantism developed from the real economic conditions of the sixteenth century. *Sola fides* expressed faith in the credit system, value of commodities, mode of production, individual agents of production, and increasing value of capital.
81. *German Ideology*, MECW 5.159–60 (3.142–43); Harvey, "Ludwig Feuerbach and Karl Marx," 291–92; Mitrokhin, Marx's Concept of Religion," 25–31.
82. *Contribution to the Critique of Hegel's Philosophy of Law*, MEW 3.175–76 (1.378–79); Kołakowski, *Main Currents of Marxism*, 106; Janz, *World Christianity and Marxism*, 13.
83. Puthenpeedikail M. John, "Religious Criticism: Fundamental Issues of Religion in the Early Writings of Karl Marx," *Religion and Society* 17/2 (1970): 62–63; James Luchte, "Marx and the Sacred," *Journal of Church and State* 51/3 (Summer 2009): 420–22, 427.
84. "On the Jewish Question," MECW 3.170–74 (1.172–77); *Holy Family*, MECW 4.109, 110 (2.116); McKown, *Classical Marxist Critique of Religion*, 38.
85. "The Communism of *Rheinischer Beobachter*," MECW 6.231 (4.200); Janz, *World Christianity and Marxism*, 13–14; McKown, *Classical Marxist Critique of Religion*, 35.
86. "On the Jewish Question," MECW 3.160, 174 (1.361, 376–77). Cf. chap. 9, pp. 222–23.
87. Jacques Bidet, "Engels et la Religion," in *Philosophie et Religion* (Paris: Editiones Sociales, 1974) 179–80; McKown, *Classical Marxist Critique of Religion*, 65, 81.
88. Bidet, "Engels et Religion," 169; "Preparatory Writings for *Anti-Dühring*," MECW 25.605 (20.582–83); McKown, *Classical Marxist Critique of Religion*, 72.
89. *The Peasant War in Germany*, MECW 10.412 (7.343); Michael Löwy, "Friedrich Engels: On Religion and Class Struggle," *Science & Society* 62/1 (Spring 1998): 81; McKown, *Classical Marxist Critique of Religion*, 79–88; Bidet, "Engels et Religion," 180.
90. "Zur Geschichte des Urchristentums," in *Werke*, 22.462; Löwy, "Friedrich Engels," 82; McKown, *Classical Marxist Critique of Religion*, 84–85.
91. "Introduction to the English Edition of Socialism," MECW 27.291 (22.300–301); *The Peasant War in Germany*, MECW 10.414ff., 419, 421–23, 427 (7.345ff., 350–54, 358); *Dialectics of Nature*, MECW 25.603 (20.580); Löwy, 82–83.
92. "Progress of Social Reform on Continent," MECW 3.399, 407 (1.487, 495); Löwy, *Friedrich Engels*, 85.
93. "The Book of Revelation," MECW 26.11 (21.9); "*Zur Geschichte des Urchristentums*," in *Werke*, 22.455–56.
94. "These on Feuerbach," MEW 5.4 (6) (3.534); *German Ideology*, MECW 5. 437–38 (3.422–24); Appelbaum, *Karl Marx*, 141; Kołakawski, *Main Currents of Marxism*, 102, 104, 148.
95. *German Ideology*, MECW 5.329–30, 342, 439 (3.70–71, 311–12, 325, 424–25); Balibar, *Philosophy of Marx*, 40.
96. *German Ideology* (Arthur), 8, 11–12; "On the Jewish Question," MECW 3.154–55 (1.355–56). In his *Contribution to the Critique of Hegel's Philosophy of Law*, he starts with a quote from Hegel that relates particular and general interests together in finding true freedom, but he then proceeds

to criticize Hegel for viewing state citizenship outside one's communal existence, separating civil society from the state. MECW 3.5, 77 (1.203, 281). Engels expresses admiration for Robert Owen and his assault upon the family, private property, and religion. *Anti-Dühring*, MECW 25.250–51 (20.245–46).

97. "Theses on Feuerbach," MEW5.4 (4) (3.534); "Manifesto," MECW 6.501 (4.478)
98. *Holy Family*, MECW 4.113, 117 (2.119–20, 124); "On the Jewish Question," MECW 3.166 (1.368–69); *German Ideology* (Arthur), 9. Marx's early works defend individual expression and freedom of the press, especially against scientific censorship in the name of religion. "The Leading Article of No. 179 of *Kölnische Zeitung*," MECW 1.187–91 (1.88–93); Kołakowski, *Main Currents of Marxism*, 99; Wood, *Karl Marx*, 52.
99. *German Ideology*, MECW 5.51, 365 (3.46, 348); "Manifesto," MECW 6.498 (4.475); *Holy Family*, MECW 4.38 (2.39–40).
100. *Dialectics of Nature*, MECW 25.331 (20.323–24); *Anti-Dühring*, MECW 25.266 (20.260).
101. *Contribution to the Critique of Hegel's Philosophy of Law*, MECW 3.44ff., 127 (1.246ff., 331); Wood, *Karl Marx*, 58.
102. "To Joseph Weydemeyer," MECW 39.62, 65 (28.507–8); Balibar, *Philosophy of Marx*, 105. Engels sees the state withering away in the future. Carver, *Engels*, 60.
103. "Critique of the Gotha Program," MECW 24.95 (19.28). Marx never tells Engels to cede his textile mills. It is not necessary for everyone to become a proletariat immediately. "The Eighteenth Brumaire of Louis Bonaparte," MECW 11.130–31 (8.141–42); Wood, *Karl Marx*, 94–95, 155.
104. Shlomo Avineri, *The Social and Political Thought of Karl Marx* (Cambridge; University Press, 1968) 47, 204ff.; Kołakowski, *Main Currents of Marxism*, 342.
105. "On the Jewish Question," MECW 3.156 (1.357–58); "The Leading Article of the *Kölnische Zeitung*," MECW 1.200–201 (1.102–3). His list of political philosophers in the Kölnische Zeitung include Machiavelli, Campanella, Hobbes, Spinoza, Grotius, Rousseau, Fichte, and Hegel.
106. "The Leading Article of the *Kölnische Zeitung*," MECW 1.198–200 (1.100–102); "On the Jewish Question," MECW 3.151, 156 (1.352, 357–58).
107. *Dialectics of Nature*, MECW 25.380, 552 (20.470, 535–36).
108. "On the Jewish Question," MECW 3.151–55,160, 174 (1.352–56, 361, 377).
109. "Refugee Literature—II," MECW 24.16 (18.352).
110. *Karl Marx and Friedrich Engels: On Religion*, Reinhold Niebuhr (intro.) (New York: Schocken Books, 1967) xi–xiv; Balibar, *Philosophy of Marx*, 98, 100, 117 Wood, *Karl Marx*, 159–60. Weber was much more honest than Marx and Engels. He had a tendency to agree with atheism but recognized the significance of religion and presented himself as a mystic or religious wannabe at times. Loewenstein, *Marx against Marxism*, 121.
111. *German Ideology*, MECW 5.247 (3.329); *Anti-Dühring*, MECW 25.87 (20.87–88); "To Jenny Longuet" (April 11, 1881), MECW 46.83 (35.179).
112. Kołakowski, *Main Currents of Communism*, 266–67; Wood, *Karl Marx*, 159–160.
113. *Das Kapital*, MECW 35.270ff. (23.279ff.); Wood, *Karl Marx*, 151, 153, 251. A term like exploitation appears to have little economic meaning, although

Wood tries to defend Marx by comparing his usage to a game, where a player "exploits" or takes advantage of another person's mistake. The problem with this defense is that the context of Marx's usage hardly fits this analogy.

114. "Preparatory Writings for *Anti-Dühring*," MECW 25.604 (20.581); *Anti-Dühring*, MECW 25.95, 98–99 (20.95–96, 98–99). Of course, there is much truth in what Marx and Engels say about the mode of production shaping ideology. Modern female equality has a distinct relation to the industrial revolution and its advanced machinery putting less of a premium upon physical strength, even if it is not the only factor. "Manifesto," MECW 6.491 (4.469); *Das Kapital*, 35.397–98 (23.416).
115. *Das Kapital*, MECW 35.199 (23.203–4); *German Ideology*, MECW 5.537 (3.529–30); Balibar, *Philosophy of Marx*, 105; Kołakowski, *Main Currents of Marxism*, 261.
116. See Stephen Strehle, *The Egalitarian Spirit of Christianity: The Sacred Roots of American and British Government* (New Brunswick, NJ and London: Transaction Publishers, 2009) 3–4, 7–10, 13–14, 83, 278–80.
117. Wood, *Karl Marx*, xv.
118. Georg Hegel, *Elements of the Philosophy of Right*, H. B. Nisbet (trans.), Allen W. Wood (ed.) (Cambridge: Cambridge University Press, 1991) 371 (340).
119. "To Ferdinand Lassalle" (Jan. 16, 1861) MECW 41.247 (30.578).
120. *Holy Family*, MECW 4.126–27 (2.134); *Feuerbach and the End of Classical German Philosophy*, MECW 26.359–60 (21.267); "To R." (Sept., 1843), MECW 3.144 (1.345–46); Balibar, *Philosophy of Marx*, 84, 91; Bidet, "Engels et Religion," 170; Kołakowski, *Main Currents of Marxism*, 105.
121. *German Ideology* (Arthur), 23; Appelbaum, *Karl Marx*, 39; Wood, *Karl Marx*, 64, 114; Kołakowski, *Main Currents of Marxism*, 130, 339. In his doctoral dissertation, "The difference between the Democitean and Epicurean Philosophy of Nature," Marx says that Epicuruc averted Democritus's determinism by introducing a random "swerve" into the movement of atoms. Appelbaum, *Karl Marx*, 23. Engels tends to subject human beings to natural laws more than Marx, but even he believes in one's ability to direct social forces through an act of the will. *Anti-Dühring*, 25.266 (20.260); Kołakowski, *Main Currents of Marxism*, 316.
122. "Theses on Feuerbach," MECW 5.5 (11) (3.535); Balibar, *Philosophy of Marx*, 13; Kołakowski, *Main Currents of Marxism*, 118–19.
123. "Manifesto," MECW 6.519 (4.494)
124. "Drafts of the Letter to Vera Zasulich," MECW 24.354; "To the Editorial Board of the Otechestvenniye Zapiski" (Nov. 1877), in Karl Marx and Frederick Engels, *Selected Correspondence*, I. Lasker (trans.) (Moscow: Foreign Languages Publishing House, 1950) 377–79.

13

The Second International: Karl Kautsky

After the death of Engels in 1895, Karl Kautsky served as the leading interpreter of Marx for the next two decades. He helped found the *Sozialdemokratische Partei Deutschlands* (SPD), which was the largest Socialist Party in the world, boasting over one million dues-paying members during his tenure and growing it from a minor party with 6.1 percent of the Reichstag vote in 1881 to 34.8 percent of the total vote in 1912.[1] He coauthored the first platform of the party, the Erfurt Program of 1891, helping to ensure the place of Marxist dogma in the group.[2] The platform included a call for the privatization of religion, secularization of schools, free public education, free health care, trade union rights, a reduction in working hours, a democratic process, the national supervision of industry, and the equal rights of all classes, races, and sexes. Kautsky also served as the virtual pope of the Second International and edited *Die Neue Zeit*, the leading international Marxist journal for a whole generation of Socialists, from its founding in 1883 until the end of the First World War. The Second International fulfilled a significant aspect of Marx's dream by bringing theory and praxis together in a loose federation of Socialist parties and trade unions representing the masses of workers.[3] Kautsky's overall contribution was not so much as a political organizer or activist but as a writer and editor, producing nearly forty books and more than eight hundred journal and newspaper articles from 1883 to 1918, during the peak of his power, and culminating in his greatest work, *Die materialistische Geschichtsauffassung* (1927), which summarized a career of study and reflection in its 1,733 pages.[4]

Kautsky consciously carried on the legacy of Marx and Engels in his work as a faithful disciple, while still leaving room for a certain amount of development and a few areas for critical analysis. He first met the two patriarchs of the movement in March 1881 and developed a close relationship with Engels over the next decade after the death of Marx.[5] He considered both of them the architects of his political agenda and followed their basic understanding of economics as the driving force of social and intellectual life,[6] but he was critical enough to recognize that Marxism must undergo constant revision to meet new historical conditions and change in accordance with its own dialectical method.[7] In regard to the class struggle, he recognized some fallacy in the predictions of Marx and Engels about the end of specific economic roles and actually observed an increase in the division of labor during his lifetime, in spite of their optimistic expectations, projecting their own desires into the future of ending the monotonous nature of proletarian work and developing the full potential of each worker at the job.[8] He even questioned the simple division of modern society into the bourgeoisie and the proletariat by observing the tendency of the division of labor to multiply classes and produce an ever-increasing number of middle-class professions, in spite of Marx's valid concern about the concentration of capital into the hands of the few.[9] Socialism remained a means of eliminating conflict between the classes by advocating the common ownership of property and production, but it hardly resolved all social ills and never was able to present a simple, monolithic vision of a more complex future.[10] The goal remained much the same in improving the life of workers, but "the forms of socialism may vary considerably in different countries, at different times, and in different branches of production" because of the "natural and traditional conditions of social life" in each culture and the constant need for development. Any form of socialism was interpreted as a means and only a means to this end.[11]

These types of criticisms were acceptable within the framework of the Second International, but Kautsky eventually had a falling out with the SPD and the international Communist community when he questioned the place of violence and revolution in their overall mission. He was not a pacifist by any means but had a distinct aversion to violence and often justified inactivity as a better alternative with an avalanche of arguments, preferring to use intellectual and moral appeals than taint the higher ground with dubious methods.[12] According to his critics, he preferred "action-less waiting" or "passive radicalism" to making a real difference in the concrete world and "built [his ships] for lakes and quiet harbors, not at all for the open sea, and not for a period of storms."[13] When Rosa Luxemburg wanted to follow the efficacious example of Russian workers in 1905 and called for massive strikes in support of universal suffrage a few years later, Kautsky balked about the use of force, expressing concern over the possibility of some workers attempting to overthrow the government and preferring a strategy of weakening the opposition through a policy of attrition (*Ermattungsstrategie*) using the current democratic process.[14] In the midst of the First World War, he left the SPD over this same issue of violence, complaining about some of its leaders supporting the German war effort and forsaking the international cause of communism for the sake of nationalism.[15] He was one of the first Marxists to consider warfare a form of imperialist exploitation, where industrial capitalists and their bourgeois states want to expand their markets, find lucrative investments, employ cheap labor, annex colonies and new territories, gather an army, and expand their interests, including the interests of his own fatherland.[16]

Kautsky's international reputation also diminished at this time due to his condemnation of the Bolshevik Revolution in Russia. Kautsky thought of democracy and human rights as an indispensable part of the Communist revolution, and ergo nonnegotiable.[17] He denounced Lenin and the Bolsheviks in the strongest terms for developing socialism without democracy in his work on the *Dictatorship of the Proletariat* (1918), and he actually called for his party to fight and overthrow them early on, before returning to his typical style and cadence of waiting for their demise and exhorting his disciples to exercise patience. He condemned Lenin for setting up a "new dictatorship in place of the old Czarist dictatorship," replacing "old exploiting classes" with "new exploiters and rulers."[18] Lenin disempowered the working class and established a dictatorship *over* the proletariat by eliminating open discussion of issues in the press, stripping the citizens of all human rights, operating a secret society with a messianic leadership, believing in its infallible hold on the truth, and setting up socialism at any cost, as if the end justified the means.[19] In this and other polemics, Kautsky displays a genuine commitment to democracy and human rights—more than his opponents—but this commitment leaves him in doubt about imposing a real Communist regime upon society as a person of moral conscience, and so threatening the individual rights of others. It leaves him with the serious problem of espousing a political philosophy that eliminates the private space of individuals to operate outside the whole and then trying to make them willing subjects of a society that is predicated upon the removal of individual life and freedom. It sentences Kautsky to a state of limbo throughout his career and causes him considerable angst in reconciling his notion of communism into a theoretical and practical unity, above and beyond any other tensions in his work.

His version of communism with a conscience makes the soul of Kautsky better suited for reformation than revolution. He likes to envision socialism evolving as an ideology and societies like Britain and Germany evolving along with it through consistent reform. In promoting this view of history, he continually points to the later writings of Marx and Engels for inspiration and underscores their recognition of the many positive changes taking place in these countries, which moderate the imminent cry for revolution as an absolute imperative.[20] Political insurrection remains a viable option if reform proves ineffective in transforming society, but the method of establishing a Socialist government is less significant and may include working with the present political system, as long as the goal of ending exploitation and oppression is accomplished.[21] Kautsky tries to maintain his orthodoxy, rejecting aberrant positions and striking a balance between revisionists like Bernstein, who form political alliances with the "progressive bourgeoisie," and revolutionaries like Lenin, who want a single violent upheaval to remake all things new,[22] but he clearly gravitates toward the position of Bernstein. He recognizes the value of slow social reform and has difficulty denouncing Bernstein and his program, even while clinging to Marxist rhetoric and maintaining the importance of the proletariat leading the way and seizing power in the class struggle.[23]

Kautsky's belief in slow social development also relates to the fact that he emphasizes the theory of evolution more than most Marxists of his generation.[24] Early on in the 1870s, he read a number of works that dealt with the theory, including Thomas Buckle's *History of Civilization in England*, Ernst Haeckel's *History of Creation*, Ludwig Büchner's *Force and Matter*, and Charles Darwin's two great books, the *Origin of the Species* and the *Descent of Man*. In his memoirs, he continually puts forth the name of Darwin in order to lend scientific credence and gravitas to his concepts, even if a whole complex of individual scholars were involved in shaping his understanding of evolutionary theory.[25] He considers Darwin's theory his starting point and merges it with Engels's positivism and dialectic materialism or any other scientism of the day, while muting any nonscientific influence or metaphysical system like Hegelian dialectics as less significant in his overall thinking.[26] He (and Engels) maintains the scientific nature of their social theory and specifically tries to relate the Darwinian concept of evolution to socialism by stressing the social nature of human origins in the theory and rejecting the typical interpretation that identifies it with capitalism. Kautsky thinks the bourgeois capitalists have adulterated the work of Darwin by limiting their analysis to the lower stages of evolution, where individuals struggle for survival against each other. The bourgeois create this image of life in order to justify their exploitation of the poor and quest for dominance over others, interpreting the theory through their own individual self-interests and making war an indelible aspect of human existence.[27] In all this, they fail to appreciate different phases of survival techniques within the theory, especially the higher phase of struggle, where ants, bees, birds, and mammals develop social instincts, sacrificing individual interests for the sake of the offspring and perpetuating the species.[28] According to Kautsky, "socialism is the higher stage of the historical development of the struggle for existence."[29] According to Darwin, "Man [is] a social being" and strives to preserve the society as a whole. Humans develop moral convictions like sympathy and altruism as survival mechanisms of the group, allowing the species to continue through mutual support and discounting the importance of the individual. "He is morally evil or unethical who seeks his own advantage at the expense of others; he is morally good and ethical who defends the others when they are in danger, even when he is himself thereby endangered. Depending on the strength or weakness of his social drives, man will incline more to good or to evil."[30] However, the basic impetus for evolution is found with the "new impulses and condition of the environment," rather than the emphasis of Darwin, Malthus, and Social Darwinians upon breeding and overpopulation.[31] Kautsky remains a committed Socialist in his analysis of Darwin but ever looks to changes within the external world to provide the basic mechanism for shaping and contouring human beings into a new image. "In other words, it is the geographical differences which produce the differences between varieties in the natural state: differences in climate, configuration of the soil, the nature of nutrition and mode of obtaining it, the species of enemies, etc."[32]

Kautsky attributes the differences between humans to their society and environment and rejects the emphasis of Darwinians upon race as an all-determining destiny of people. Nature mingles variations together in a species and is much too promiscuous in the way it operates to select certain characteristics like a breeder might do and perpetuate them in future generations creating a new permanent form of existence. Much of this obsession with race today in "Germany and its neighboring countries" is designed to promote the "race they themselves belong to . . . [as] the most eminent in the world, destined to enslave and to exploit the others," but modern anthropologists reject this type of racism and see differences between people in a constant state of flux and transition without possessing immutable boundaries based on blood. There is no significant difference between the mental abilities of civilized and primitive peoples that would establish for the scientific community a clear hierarchy in their endowments, given the high degree of sophistication in all languages and the range of talent found among all humans, making it impossible to weigh one against the other. Whatever differences remain will "disappear more and more among men" in the future, with the mixing of people through world traffic and the advance of modern technology, diminishing the struggle for existence within different environments and dissolving the "races into a single human race." Even differences between sexes will diminish in the future as technology removes the advantage of male muscles and brings egalitarianism into the realm of their economic value.[33]

Religion

Kautsky thinks of science as advancing in the future, leading the way toward an egalitarian society, and liberating humanity from the bigotry of the past, especially the nonsense of primitive religious belief. The only true religion of the future is science.[34] Kautsky often speaks of religion in the typical Marxist manner as the expression of an economic condition and oppressive instrument of the bourgeoisie, but he tends to consign this approach to a later phase or manifestation in its development and provide a more eclectic concept of its origin, even beyond the limited discussion in the work of Engels upon the issue.[35] He considers the analysis of the eighteenth century with its focus upon priestly power and exploitation of the masses passé in light of the more scientific approach of the nineteenth century, which explores the religious expressions of primitive cultures, extrapolates the roots of the phenomenon from this research, and develops a different understanding accordingly. In particular, he follows the work of Edward B. Tylor and Heinrich Cunow, who connect the origin of religion with animism or the primitive reflection of tribes upon the powers of nature and existence of the soul (*anima*).[36] Dreams serve as the particular impetus of the phenomenon in primitive people because they have no scientific sophistication and cannot differentiate the phantasms of the dream world from reality. Often in dreams the mind wanders into far-off regions outside the limitation of finite reality and engages with anyone living or deceased, providing a pretext for inventing concepts like the soul to explain this out-of-body experience. Eventually, the souls of the deceased receive divine exaltation through exaggerated accounts of the past in eulogies and help the present tribe fend off the power of nature in time of need through their own godlike powers.[37] Thus, religion arises from the belief in the soul and the reverence of ancestral spirits before it becomes a vital part of social organization in the tribe.[38] It might function in modern times as the basis of forging society together and organizing a moral way of living, but the original impetus for its development came from the dream world of primitive people and reverence for the dead, not specific social concerns.[39] Kautsky uses this genealogy as a means of critique, discrediting the place of religion in contemporary society through a study of its bizarre and incredible origin.

He also wants to undermine the value of religion in contemporary society by disavowing the need for moral ideals, so much associated with its modern expression. He believes that social goals or imperatives can develop apart from religion through the "knowledge of the given material foundation" and the practical need associated with it, although he never supplies a clear explanation of how this is possible.[40] He says humans have no need of believing in a transcendent deity or absolute guide to direct their society but are more than capable of adapting to this world and setting their own goals through their own complex set of needs and desires.[41] Morality is only useful if it addresses contemporary needs and changes with its experience in society, rather than temper into the immutable divine essence of the Judeo-Christian tradition or the rigid shackle of deontological ethics.[42] This limited concept of morality finds its imperative within the scientific analysis of social history and refuses to look elsewhere or envision some ontological or Platonic basis in the heavens above.

In general, Kautsky's review seems less hostile and more willing to find some noble aspiration in religious affections than Marx or Engels, although he deprecates specific manifestations and sees a more enlightened future without this relic from the unscientific past. He does not follow the precedent of his mentors and design direct policies to eliminate religion from civil society, but rather he allows religion to continue at the margins of society, separated from the state, in order to watch it disappear over the course of time, much like a son of the Enlightenment. Thus, religion can remain a private matter in his view and receive accommodation as a *privatus cultus*, as long as it stays on the margins of corporate life. Lenin roundly criticizes this position as much too patronizing and lenient, but Kautsky seems less anxious to employ direct methods against an anachronistic way of thinking that will die out of its own accord in the future as people become enlightened through empirical explanations and recognize the all-pervading nature of social concerns in addressing their problems, rather than wasting their blood and treasure wrangling over metaphysical nonsense. There is no need to work against religion when a passive policy proves just as effective in relegating it to oblivion. "Where religion becomes a private matter, religious ideas are already considered backward and irrelevant."[43] One can see the efficacious nature of this policy working among the Jews, who are assimilating into Western Europe through their emancipation and absorption in society and losing their culture, language, and religion through this admission policy into the state.[44]

> The disappearance of the Jews will not involve a tragic process like the disappearance of the American Indians or the Tasmanians. It will not be equivalent to a declining into stupidity and degradation, but to a rising to greater strength, to prosperity and well-being, to the opening up of an immense field of activity. It will not mean a mere shifting of domicile from one mediaeval ruin to another, not a transition from orthodox Judaism to ecclesiastical Christianity, but the creation of a new and higher type of man.[45]

Kautsky might reject the racial anti-Semitism of the Nazis,[46] but he also opposes Zionism/Jewish nationalism in the name of the Communist revolution[47] and wants the total assimilation of Jews through their complete admixture with non-Jewish blood.[48] Either way, the Jews are destined for extinction in Nazi and Communist ideology alike.

Kautsky expresses much contempt for the sacred writing of the Jews in the typical style of the French philosophes and German intelligentsia. Following the higher critical analysis of the day, the biblical account of ancient Israel is considered a later construction, fashioned within the postexilic community of the fifth century BCE, "manipulated and supplemented by fabrications, with the greatest audacity, in order to answer the requirements of the rising ancient caste." The Judean priesthood "exalted itself above the mass of people" in order to line its pockets with their tithes and offerings. It borrowed its "arrogant claims" from the Babylonian priesthood, along with many legends and customs like the myth of creation (Enuma Elish), the account of the great flood (Gilgamesh Epic), the story of the tower of Babel (ziggurat), and the observance of the Sabbath day. It also changed the ancient Hebrew doctrine of polytheism to monotheism through observing the central place of Marduk in the Babylonian cult, but this new theology brought a significant problem in reconciling the "philosophy and wisdom" of an "immense civilization" like Babylon, where all races of people were embraced and welcomed into a cosmopolitan society, with the provincial bigotries of a "little tribe of mountaineers" and its ethnic god. The Hebrews developed extreme xenophobia during OT times, "living under conditions which caused the hatred of strangers," suffering the ceaseless caprice of neighbors and continuous warfare in the land, and developing extreme hatred for foreigners and their gods as evil because of the constant threat. This extreme ethnocentricity caused a problem for the postexilic priesthood in combining the new ethical monotheism with the "ancient fetishism" of a tribal god, a chosen people, and a specific place of worship, creating an account of its ancient people, filled with capricious redactions and contradictions.[49]

Kautsky displays the same dismissive and enlightened attitude toward the writings of the NT and its history. He contends that the passages about Jesus, James, and John the Baptist in the writings of Flavius Josephus, the first-century Jewish historian, are nothing but later interpretations of the church and uses this "evidence" of forgery as proof that the early Christians had a "complete indifference to the truth" when composing the history of the NT. "The historical value of the Gospels and of the Acts of the Apostles is probably not of higher value than that of Homeric poems, or that of Nibelungenlied." While theologians still "make every effort to maintain their authority," scholars today find these writings "completely useless as sources for the biography of Jesus," with some experts like Bruno Bauer "absolutely denying the historical reality of Jesus." There is no "true historical kernel" for even a liberal theologian like Harnack to hang onto, beyond the probable facticity of Jesus's existence in Galilee and his execution later on in Jerusalem. Like the Jewish scripture, the Gospels are nothing more than a hodgepodge of "fabricated material," filled with numerous contradictions in its various accounts, written much later in the church by individuals who were unfamiliar with the historical Jesus, and forged to exalt him as Savior and Lord. Kautsky says the authors actually used mythical material from mystery cults in composing their narrative and creating the new Savior: the birth of Jesus comes from the legend surrounding the Buddha and his miraculous incarnation in the immaculate body of the Virgin Queen Maya; the Lord's Supper from one of the Mithra sacraments; and the resurrection from the Adonis feast in the springtime.[50] Kautsky draws these parallels without providing much evidence of a specific historical connection, but this criticism might hold for all of his writings, which make sweeping analogies and claims, leaving the details of rigorous scholastic research to others.

Kautsky's overall assessment of Christianity is mixed. The religion clearly brought an "absurd ignorance" and "intellectual decline" to Western civilization with its many biblical "contradictions" and "unreasonable assumptions" like the doctrine of the Trinity, which belongs to the "most stupid superstitions" of humankind. Christianity's ignorance was matched with a certain moral turpitude and degeneration as the product of Judaism and its hatred for others, only replacing the "race hatred" of the Jews with its own "fanatical form" of "class hatred."[51] This animosity went beyond any proletarian group in the modern world and deserves condemnation for stirring up rancor and turmoil in the world, but even Kautsky is forced to recognize some connection between the religion and his own political beliefs in describing the Christian faith in this way, and he must alter his assessment accordingly. The connection moves Kautsky to follow the more eclectic approach of Engels and make more positive comments in acknowledging the similarities and recognizing certain precursors to communism among its early follower and a number of marginal groups in the Middle Ages and the Reformation. Kautsky says, the Gospels and the book of Acts speak of a form of "equalizing communism" within primitive Christianity, calling for the "divisions and distribution of the rich man's superfluity among the poor"—a message that was fairly universal during the times of the Roman Empire due to the economic conditions.[52] This communism was based on consumption, not production, and transformed the early Christian fellowship into a new family with an egalitarian view of women and a renunciation of the bonds of marriage, just like the early Essenes and the later monastic movement.[53] The communism of consumption had a common meal, which expressed and sealed the firm egalitarian bond between Christians during the first three centuries of the church before it became a mere symbol of the fellowship in order to placate the rich.[54] The church of Constantine left the early proletarian spirit of Christianity, but Kautsky sees this original aspect of the gospel resurrected at certain moments in church history and commends a number of revolutionary, sectarian groups for standing at the threshold of communism, including the Waldenses, the Taborites, the Lollards, and the Anabaptists.[55] He finds Thomas Münzer "the most brilliant embodiment of heretical communism" in this history for leading the revolt of peasants against the "powers that be" during the time of the Reformation.[56] Of course, it is the economic conditions that provided him and the other Christians with the real underlying impetus behind their move toward communism and not a priori principles coming from the religion.[57]

In all this, Kautsky remains committed to the basic party line, but his overall treatment of religion is more complex than Marx's consistent antagonism. He makes more nuanced and eclectic comments, not limiting its interpretation to the means of production and recognizing a certain positive quality in some of its forms serving as a forerunner of present day communism. He also develops a less hostile policy in dealing with those who retain a remnant of the old superstition and displaying a more flexible attitude in working with them. This policy characterized his fundamental approach to politics, which prefers to use nonviolent methods, reform the present system within a democratic process, respect the dignity and freedom of the citizens, and recognize the need for change in all of us, even in Socialists. He remains firm in rejecting any need for religion and its moral ideals, but exercises some caution in political tactics and a willingness to wait patiently, as science erodes away at superstitious beliefs, and the Socialist state assumes more and more the space that religion once occupied in society. Kautsky believes German higher criticism has undermined the historical integrity of the Judeo-Christian tradition, but the news takes time to filter down to the masses, making it necessary to patronize the superstitions of religious people and certain party members, as long as the state remains separated from it. The enlightened policy of making religion a private matter serves as a sufficient means of performing a quiet euthanasia upon the religion and destroying its place over time in the souls of the people. Lenin will prefer the more direct revolutionary measures of Marx, but Kautsky wants to preserve the pretense that communism protects human rights, while working all along to eliminate the space in which those rights operate in the lives of the citizens.

Notes

1. Dick Geary, *Karl Kautsky* (New York: St. Martin's Press, 1987) 5–6; John H. Kautsky, *Karl Kautsky: Marxism, Revolution & Democracy* (New Brunswick, NJ and London: Transaction Publishers, 1994) 9. "By the early 1890s the SPD was running nineteen daily newspapers and forty-two weeklies; by 1914 it had ninety dailies." Neil Harding, *Leninism* (Durham, NC: Duke University Press, 1996) 55.
2. Karl Kautsky, *The Materialist Conception of History*, John H. Kautsky and Raymond Meyer (trans., ed., and abridged), John H. Kautsky (intro.) (New Haven, CT, and London: Yale University Press, 1988) xxv; Geary, *Karl Kautsky*, 3.
3. Kautsky, *Karl Kautsky*, 2, 208–9; Geary, *Karl Kautsky*, vii; Gary P. Steenson, *Karl Kautsky, 1854–1938: Marxism in the Classical Years* (Pittsburgh, PA: University of Pittsburgh Press, 1991) 3; Kautsky, *Materialist Conception of History*, xxv; Kołakowski, *Main Currents of Marxism*, 357.
4. Steenson, *Karl Kautsky*, 2; Kautsky, *Materialistic Conception of History*, xxii.
5. Ibid., 47–48. Both had some initial criticism of his work.
6. Karl Kautsky, "My Book on the Materialist Conception of History," in *Karl Kautsky and the Social Science of Classical Marxism*, John H. Kautsky (ed.) (Leiden: E.J. Brill, 1989) 68, 101–2; Karl Kautsky, *Thomas More and His Utopia* (New York: Russell & Russell, 1959) 160; *Materialist Conception of History*, 232–33. He particularly finds economic interests behind the theory and praxis of religious movements. See, for example, Karl Kautsky, *Communism in Central Europe in the Time of the Reformation* (New York: Russell & Russell, 1959) 54–55, 126–28, 132, 157; *Thomas More and His Utopia*, 37–39, 52–56, 69–70. Kautsky recognizes some validity in Weber's criticism of the Marxist position and acknowledges that the materialist position can be overstated. *Materialist Conception of History*, 275–76, 359–60, 370; *Thomas More and His Utopia*, 160.
7. *Materialist Conception of History*, xxvii, 460, 461; Kołakowski, *Main Currents of Marxism*, 379; Kautsky, *Karl Kautsky*, x; McKown, *Classical Marxist Critique of Religion*, 124ff.
8. Ibid., 259–62.
9. Kal Kautsky, "The Revisionist Controversy," in *Selected Political Writings*, Patrick Goode (ed. and trans.) (New York: St. Martin's Press, 1983) 21, 24; *Materialist Conception of History*, xl, 372; Kautsky, *Karl Kautsky*, 40.

10. *Materialist Conception of History*, lix, 219, 253.
11. "Capitalism and Socialism," in *Selected Political Writings*, 133–34; *Materialist Conception of History*, 418, 427.
12. Geary, *Karl Kautsky*, 69; Kautsky, *Karl Kautsky*, xii, 42.
13. "Die Neue Taktik," *Die Neue Zeit* 30/2 (1912): 694; Leon Trotsky, *Terrorism and Communism: A Reply to Karl Kautsky* (Ann Arbor, MI: University of Michigan Press, 1963) 88; Geary, *Karl Kautsky*, 71.
14. "The Mass Strike," in *Selected Political Writings*, 53–56; *Materialist Conception of History*, 376; Geary, *Karl Kautsky*, 68–69; Kautsky, *Karl Kautsky*, 110.
15. By 1915, the SPD was condemning annexation and promoting peace but still supporting the war. Geary, *Karl Kautsky*, 9–10.
16. "The Road to Power," in *Selected Political Writings*, 76–77, 82–87; *Materialist Conception of History*, 295; Kautsky, *Karl Kautsky*, 10–11, 142; Geary, *Karl Kautsky*, 46–50. Kautsky speaks of imperialism as the last desperate throe before capitalism implodes. "The Revisionist Controversy," in *Selected Political Writings*, 30; "Road to Power," 76ff. Marx and Engels had a much more positive view of colonialism and its civilizing effect. Kołakowski, *Main Currents of Marxism*, 425.
17. Kark Kautsky, *The Dictatorship of the Proletariat*, H. J. Stenning (trans.) (Ann Arbor, MI: University of Michigan Press, 1964) 6, 7, 10–11; Kautsky, *Karl Kautsky*, 111; Geary, *Kautsky*, 18–19.
18. Ibid., 1, 2, 6–7; "Gedanken über die Einheitsfront," in *Kautsky gegen Lenin*, Peter Lübbe (Hrsg.) (Berlin und Bonn: J. H. W. Dietz Nachf. GmbH, 1981) 196; Geary, *Karl Kautsky*, 9–10, 70, 78, 146, 161–62; Kautsky, *Karl Kautsky*, 35, 66–68; *Marxism and Bolshevism* (1934). Lenin responded to Kautsky's fainthearted socialism and "theoretical vulgarization of Marxism" three months later in the famous tract, *The Proletarian Revolution and the Renegade Kautsky*. Ibid., 1–2; McKown, *Classical Marxist Critique of Religion*, 122.
19. Geary, *Karl Kautsky*, 70; Kołakowski, *Main Currents of Marxism*, 142–43, 394–95. As early as *What's to Be Done?* (1902), differences develop between them. Lenin shifted his emphasis from the proletariat to intellectuals, the party, and the leaders. *What's to Be Done?*, in *Collected Works* (Moscow: Progress Publishers, 1960–) 5.375. Like Lenin, Kautsky believed that the proletariat needed intellectuals to crystallize their concerns, but he also felt that experienced workers know more about drafting specific legislation in parliament and organizing trade unions, strikes, and cooperatives than those coming from academic backgrounds. "Akademiker und Proletariat," in *Die Neue Zeit*, 19/2 (1901): 90.
20. "Capitalism and Socialism," in *Selected Political Writings*, 131–36; *Materialist Conception of History*, xlix, lxiii; Appelbaum, *Karl Marx*, 108–9.
21. "To Adler" (May 5, 1894), in *Briefwechsel mit August Bebel and Karl Kautsky*, Friedrich Adler (ed.) (Wien: Wiener Volksbuchhandlung, 1954) 152; "Die sozialistischen Kongresse und der sozialistische Minister," in *Die Neue Zeit*, 19/1 (1901): 37; "Revisionist Controversy," 30; Kautsky, *Karl Kautsky*, 5, 42–43.
22. Ibid., 15–16; Kołakowski, *Main Currents of Marxism*, 380. Kautsky rejected forging political alliances with other parties in order to preserve purity, but unlike Lenin, he would work within the trade union movement because it

expressed in his mind a genuine Socialist and proletarian class consciousness. Kautsky, *Karl Kautsky*, 59–62.

23. Karl Kautsky, *Die Soziale Revolution* (Berlin: Buchhandlung Vorwärts, 1911) 51; "Die sozialistischen Kongresse und der sozialistische Minister," 37, 44; "Allerhand Revolutionäres," in *Die Neue Zeit*, 22/1 (1904): 590; Geary, *Karl Kautsky*, 42–44, 74–76; Kautsky, *Karl Kautsky*, 2; Kołakowski, *Main Currents of Marxism*, 389–90.
24. *Materialist Conception of History*, 172–73.
25. Steenson, *Karl Kautsy*, 24–25, 28. Cf. *Materialist Conception of History*, 66–67.
26. Steenson, "Karl Kautsky: Early Assumptions, Preconceptions, and Prejudices," 33, 41; *Materialist Conception of History*, xxxii, 6, 66; Kołakowski, *Main Currents of Marxism*, 383.
27. "Der Sozialismus und der Kampf um der Dasein," *Der Volksstaat*, nr. 49 (April 28, 1876) 2 (col. B), nr. 50 (April 30, 1876) 1, (col. C), 2 (col. B); Steenson, *Karl Kautsky*, 29–32.
28. Ibid., 2 (col. A).
29. "Der Sozialismus und der Kampf um der Dasein," nr. 50 (April 30, 1876) 2 (col. A). He thinks of socialism as the goal of evolution and the end of war.
30. *Material Conception of History*, 63–69.
31. Karl Kautsky, *Are the Jews a Race?* (Westport, CT: Greenwood Press, 1972) 35ff.; *Material Conception of History*, 173–74. He rejects Darwin's emphasis upon the fortuitous superiority of an individual affecting a whole species and accepts the Lamarkian concept of acquired characteristics. Ibid., 37–38, 55; *Material Conception of History*, 46, 48.
32. Ibid., 33. He generally thinks of inventions and improvements in technology as a product of the environment and discounts the notion of original genius. Generally speaking, the inventor discerns existing needs and uses previously available implements and ideas. "The mind only has to solve problems the environment sets for it; it does not spontaneously produce problems of its own accord." *Material Conception of History*, 167–69. And yet, he hopes science, technology, and conscious activity will make humans less subservient to the environment in the future. *Are the Jews a Race?*, 54–55; *Material Conception of History*, 183; Steenson, "Karl Kaustky: Early Assumptions, Preconceptions, and Prejudices," 39–40.
33. Ibid., 20, 27–31, 62, 75, 80, 227; *Materialist Conception of History*, 90, 124–25, 135–37; "Ethics and the Materialist Concept of History," 45.
34. "Religion II," in *Die Neue Zeit*, I/10 (Dec. 5, 1913): 353, 357; *Materialist Conception of History*, 82; McKown, *Classical Marxist Critique of Religion*, 154. Of course, he does not consider religion to be scientific or philosophical because it is founded upon faith, not proof or evidence. Ibid., 354.
35. McKown, *Classical Marxist Critique of Religion*, 152–54.
36. "Religion I," in *Die Neue Zeit*, I/7 (Nov. 7, 1913): 182–84; McKown, *Classical Marxist Critique of Religion*, 123–26. Tylor (1832–1917) was a social anthropologist from Britain and wrote the book *Primitive Culture and Anthropology* (1871). Kautsky revises his position in "Religion I" through the immediate influence of Cunow—a professor of political science at Berlin, one-time editor of the *Neue Zeit*, and author of a series of articles on the subject, "Religionsgeschichtliche Streifzüge" (1913), and a book entitled *Der Ursprung der Religion und das Gottesglaubens* (1913).

37. Ibid., 186–88; McKown, *Classical Marxist Critique of Religion*, 126–28. God is just the greatest of these ancient souls.
38. "Religion II," 354. Kautsky discounts the importance of charismatic leaders in founding religion, since social organization is more significant in creating and perpetuating a mass movement than individuals.
39. McKown, *Classical Marxist Critique of Religion*, 131–33.
40. "Ethics and the Materialist Concept of History," 42–43; *Materialist Conception of History*, 494, 507–9; Kołakowski, *Main Currents of Marxism*, 385; Geary, *Karl Kautsky*, 12.
41. *Materialist Conception of History*, 11–12; "Ethics and the Materialist Concept of History," 38, 41.
42. Ibid., 25, 37, 219; "Ethics and the Materialist Concept of History," 34–35, 46–47. According to Kautsky, the concept of good and evil finds its religious origin within the friendly and not-so-friendly disposition of the spirit world; heaven and hell are the places for the noble and not-so-noble in the original meaning, not the good and the bad. "Religion II," 355–56.
43. "Religion II," 352–55, 359–60; McKown, *Classical Marxist Critique of Religion*, 153, 156–57.
44. *Are the Jews a Race?*, 153, 156, 241–44.
45. Ibid., 246.
46. Ibid., 66.
47. Ibid., 214–15, 220–21, 240–41.
48. Ibid., 66, 214–15, 220–21, 238–41, 246. Kautsky discounts the alleged physical traits of Jews and their racial uniformity. Ibid., 90–91, 112–15, 121.
49. *Foundations of Christianity: A Study of Christian Origins* (New York and London: Monthly Review Press, 1925) 187, 212, 216–17, 231, 234–40, 275–77.
50. Ibid., 325, 28, 31–33, 36–38, 42–43, 27–31, 146–47, 176–77, 363, 393, 396, 442, 471.
51. Ibid., 327–31, 379.
52. *Communism in Central Europe in the Time of the Reformation*, 8–9; *Foundations of Christianity*, 38–44. See Acts 2:44–45; 4:32.
53. *Foundations of Christianity*, 12, 335, 374–75; *Communism in Central Europe*, 15.
54. Ibid., 421–22. He personally rejects a common distribution of wealth and favors individual consumption, based upon a person's likes and dislikes. His main interest is the concentration of wealth and production in the state. Ibid., 467–68.
55. McKown, *Classical Marxist Critique of Religion*, 142–46; *Foundations of Christianity*, 422; *Communism in Central Europe*, 256. In *Communism in Central Europe*, he conducts a long and protracted defense of the Münsterites, claiming that historians have distorted their movement and cause.
56. *Communism in Central Europe*, 154; *Thomas More and His Utopia*, 1. Thomas More is the other great figure standing at the threshold of communism, and Kautsky devotes an entire book to his vision.
57. *Foundations of Christianity*, 451–52. He sees the woolen manufacture as instrumental in producing revolutionary, democratic, and Communist impulses in Bohemia, particularly in Prague, Iglau, and Pilsau. "The woollen worker became . . . a sweated workman, receiving the raw material from the

dealer and delivering to him the manufactured article, or a cloth producer turned capitalist himself, and employing a large number of journeymen." The majority of the Taborites, the most dreaded proletarian warriors in medieval Europe, were wool-weavers. The Bohemian town of Tabor was a hotbed of Communist activity and brought some victories, even though it ultimately failed because its version of communism was based upon the needs of the poor, rather than the requirements of production. *Communism in Central Europe*, 54, 59, 67, 71–76.

14

The Third International: Lenin, Stalin, and Khrushchev

Vladimir Ilyich Ulyanov was born on April 2, 1870, in the town of Simbirsk (present day Ulyanovsk). His family seemed to lead a peaceful, middle-class life, with his father working as a well-paid provincial school inspector within the tsarist bureaucracy, but for some unknown reason the children shunned the well-established order and privileges of their lifestyle for the hardship of left-wing political activity, following the example of the elder son, Alexander. As a member of a clandestine group, Alexander led an unsuccessful attempt on the life of the tsar and was hanged for his part in the plot, but this ended up arousing in his siblings, including young Vladimir, a deep-seated hatred for the regime and a passion for extreme revolutionary politics. In the course of time, Vladimir developed his own relations with circles in Kazan and Samara familiar to his brother, whose radical members followed the Jacobin tradition of Narodnaya Volya and its appetite for conspiratorial techniques, ruthless violence, and revolutionary activity on behalf of the people.[1] At the end of the decade, he became an orthodox Marxist through reading Marx, Engels, Chernyshevsky, and Plekhanov, and by the time he moved to St. Petersburg in the summer of 1893, he was a recognized expert on Marxist ideology in Socialist circles and was able to exercise his considerable political skills in organizing the movement, spreading the message to the proletariat, and working with officials toward factory legislation.[2] In the fall of 1895, he became one of the principal members of a group called the Union for the Struggle for the Liberation of the Working Class. He helped organize a strike causing considerable disturbance, but he was arrested as a threat to the established order, along with the rest of the leadership; jailed for fifteen months; and sent to Siberia for the next three years. While he was gone, there remained enough of a following to organize and convene the First Congress of the Russian Social Democratic Labor Party (RSDLP) in Minsk and lay the foundation of the future Communist Party in the country, even if it proved ineffectual without him and soon dissipated after the delegates were arrested and again sent into Siberian exile. Upon his return, Vladimir took on the pseudonym Lenin and wrote the book *What Is to Be Done?* (1902), hoping to seize control of the

Second Congress of the RSDLP and calling for a more professional, cohesive, and efficient organization, centered around a national newspaper, *Iskra*, with local agents reporting activities and receiving instructions from its editorial board—Lenin, Plekhanov, and Martov, among others.[3] Lenin eventually gained the upper hand at the congress and renamed his faction the Bolsheviks (Majority), forcing a split with Martov and the Mensheviks (Minority) a decade later at the Prague Conference, rejecting any call for moderation and breadth within the party, and exhibiting a portent of his authoritarian and dogmatic style of leadership in the years to come.[4]

The October Revolution and the Civil War

In February and March of 1917, fortune smiled upon the Bolsheviks when the industrial workers of Petrograd and the war-weary masses revolted against their miserable conditions and forced Tsar Nicholas II to abdicate on March 15, ending three hundred years of Romanov rule.[5] A provisional government was set up under George Lvov and Alexander Kerensky, with liberal and democratic leanings, which tried to please all factions and show moderation in continuing the war as a defensive measure, but it was unable to settle the unrest with its policies. Lenin returned to Russia after spending over a decade abroad and took a firm, Socialist stand in his famous "April Theses," calling for the overthrow of the government, an immediate end to the war with Germany, a new civil war against exploitation, and social control of the economy. Through a barrage of speeches, pamphlets, articles, and manifestoes, Lenin won over the party and people to his cause, making him the one indispensable figure in the Russian Revolution and the Communist seizure of power in the months to come. On July 24, Kerensky tried to form a coalition government excluding the Bolsheviks, but the tide turned against him when the Second All-Russian Congress of Soviets threw its might behind the Bolsheviks, and Lenin took control of the government on November 7.[6]

Lenin's rise to power was facilitated by a consistent and strident position opposing Russia's involvement in the war, causing some newspapers to consider his immigration a German plot.[7] In his writings at the time, he dismisses the war as a battle between "imperialist" forces, which represent the bourgeois interests of advanced countries in seeking to divide the world and plunder weaker nations, creating a "world system of colonial oppression."[8] In his mind, capitalism has degenerated into its last phase of imperialism, where the free competitive markets no longer exist for individual entrepreneurs, and companies use the power of the state to pillage the world of its resources. The petty bourgeoisie extol the virtues of free enterprise, but they live in the illusion of a former capitalist ideal, which only represents a temporary stage in a bygone era. Free competition "gives rise to the concentration of production" in the development of capitalism and must recede before an era of monopolies, where large companies collude together and form cartels, control raw materials, sign exclusive contracts with labor, close trade outlets, and sell below the market price to ruin competitors. This process finds its most critical development in the banking industry, where a financial oligarchy of fewer and larger banks controls the state and determines foreign policy through the use of capital. Lenin finds a present example of "rentier" or "usurer" states in Britain, France, and Belgium as embodying the process. These countries export capital because profits are shrinking at home, and they exploit foreign markets to sell their goods and obtain cheap labor. They let other countries do the hard work of agriculture, industry, and mining, while they reap the financial rewards as investors, following the bourgeois practice of separating ownership or money capital from the actual management of the capital. Of course, this form of exploitation requires the use of force in foreign markets to guarantee investments, and so war develops between the bourgeois states to possess and maintain the markets, making war an inevitable result of capitalism.[9] Moderates like the petty bourgeoisie and the Mensheviks fail to understand imperialism as the essential nature of the present capitalistic system when they try to justify the war in terms of national defense or accept bourgeois promises to annex no more land; but the sole interest of the bourgeois is found in promoting their own class and annexing more territory for their own financial gain, regardless of their false promises and pseudo-patriotism, and it is time to wake up the people and make war against the true enemy in the ultimate struggle between the classes.[10] Lenin calls the people to civil war and rejects any participation in the current World War as the concern of imperialists, providing the Bolsheviks with their own distinct version of history and perspective on the present conflict.[11]

In denouncing the imperialist war and promoting the civil war, Lenin finds his own unique accent or version of Marxism, which promotes revolution as the exclusive interest of the party and opposes more moderate and eclectic voices. Lenin feels the present leadership of the International has accepted the status quo and forsaken the class struggle and revolutionary fervor against bourgeois governments by supporting respective sides in the war and endorsing centrist or moderate policies. He accuses Karl Kautsky, "the most outstanding authority of the Second International (1889–1914)" of being "a model of utter bankruptcy as a Marxist, the embodiment of unheard-of spinelessness, and the most wretched vacillations and betrayals since August 1914," and calls for a "new, revolutionary, proletarian International." He wants to rename the movement the "Communist Party—just as Marx and Engels called themselves" and restore its earlier identity.[12] He wants an organization of professional revolutionaries and an "armed insurrection" to overthrow the Russian government following the call to arms in the French Revolution and the early writings of Marx and Engels.[13] He argues for a violent revolution against the bourgeoisie in order to destroy the "inhuman conditions" of the present system and obtain a meaningful victory.[14] Marxism had spread throughout Russia since the mid-1890s, but it had failed so far to gain the upper hand because many of the "legal Marxists" corrupted its consciousness by "toning down social antagonism," rejecting the "social revolution and dictatorship of the proletariat," and "restricting the labour movement to narrow trade unionism and a 'practical' struggle for petty, gradual reform." This passive policy cannot make a qualitative difference in the life of the workers and must change its approach to more radical measures. Even the SPD has rejected the attempt of Bernstein and the reformists to revise Marxism and work within a bourgeois government, trying to "convert the nascent working-class movement into an appendage of liberals." Even most German social-democrats have come to realize the ultimate need of setting aside a few successes within bourgeois politics and subordinate economic reforms to the reconstruction of society through more militant political activity.[15] In order to reach the goal of the party, it is necessary to subordinate Kautsky's desire for a "pure democracy" as a "useless and harmful toy" and grant "full power" to the Soviets in ruling the country, allowing them the "use of violence against the bourgeoisie" as a necessary means of ending oppression and giving them a "rule that is unrestricted by any laws."[16] The party serves the interests of the community best as an independent unit, consisting of a Marxist intelligentsia supplying the larger picture and a professional core of committed revolutionaries implementing the policies.[17] Lenin refuses to entrust the success of the political process to the consciousness of the masses and dismisses the moral significance of democracy, power-sharing, and listening to alternative points of views as a bourgeois justification of the status quo. In all this, he sets the precedent for dealing with political opponents in a ruthless manner, creating a policy that generates the subsequent and continuous civil war or reign of terror within the country against all "enemies" inside and outside the party.[18]

Lenin cares little for conventional ethics and thinks only in utilitarian terms, just like the revolutionary government of France, which serves as the paradigm. He rejects the need for God or an eternal standard of morality to restrain human conduct and sees his own activity as a necessary and transitional means of accomplishing the goals of the party.[19] He says, "Exploiters have no rights."[20] "Dictatorship means unlimited power based on force, and not on law."[21] This power is necessary for the party to wield in suppressing the bourgeoisie because of their desire to withstand the Soviets and continue exploiting the masses through their counterrevolutionary activities.[22] A few weeks after the October Revolution, he announced the "Red Terror" and established the Cheka or political police to execute the policy. At first it meant rounding up army officers, counterrevolutionaries, and other opponents in the civil war and executing them, but then it escalated into draconian punishments for a wide swath of people, imprisoning or executing tens of thousands if a bomb exploded at Soviet headquarters or an assassin made an attempt on the life of an official.[23] It finally came full circle and fell back upon those who shared similar Socialist convictions as a means of terrorizing and liquidating political enemies, labeling moderates, Menshiviks, social revolutionaries, and even party members with the term "bourgeois"—an ill-defined and pejorative term in Communist rhetoric, meant to intimidate and smear an opponent.[24] Stalin says,

> The history of the Party further teaches us that unless the Party of the working class wages an uncompromising struggle against the opportunists within its own ranks, unless it smashes the capitulators in its own midst, it cannot perform its role of organizer and leader of the proletarian revolution, nor its role as the builder of the new, Socialist society.[25]

As the government grew in size during the reign of Stalin, the power was exercised by a bureaucratic system of "careerists, parasites, and sycophants," who kept the entire population of the Soviet Union under constant surveillance and fear of the unknown.[26]

Both Lenin and Stalin think of individual life as expendable and are willing to purge all elements of society withstanding their rule and vision of the future. Later Communists try to manufacture a different image of Lenin, hoping to distance his name from the "aberrations" of the Stalin era, but the subsequent reign of terror was merely an extension of the institution created by Lenin and designed to produce cutthroats and butchers just like him.[27] In fact, Lenin promoted Stalin's ascension in the party early on, above and beyond the objections of others, and appointed him secretary general of the Central Committee in April 1922, even if Stalin took advantage of its power over the bureaucracy by appointing his own men and outmaneuvering others in the struggle to succeed Lenin.[28] Those who wish to defend Lenin often point to his "Letter to Congress" or "Testament" (Dec. 23/24, 1922), in which he criticizes Stalin for concentrating "unlimited power" in his own hands and hopes he will use "sufficient caution" in exercising this power. Lenin notes the discord developing on the Central Committee between factions favoring Stalin and Trotsky and thinks it best to ease the tension by doubling the size of the committee from fifty to one hundred. He thinks Trotsky has "excessive self-assurance" and a "preoccupation" with administrative details, while Stalin should be removed and replaced with another member "more tolerant, more loyal, more polite, and more considerate to compatriots, less capricious, etc."[29] However, the letter cannot change the overall assessment of a career defined by tactics of terror and brutality. It cannot change the institutionalized violence of the regime, so the letter sounds more like the cry of despair from an old man, who is terminally ill and confined to a room in the Kremlin—out of touch, losing his grip on power, living under constant surveillance, afraid, and maybe about to receive his own medicine—a lethal dose of poison from his successor. The letter was ignored by the Central Committee as containing no relevance, and the main concern about brutality is never specifically addressed in it—a point that Stalin raised years later in his own defense.[30]

Scientism and Intolerance

After all, intolerance has a firm foundation within the scientism of Marxist ideology, which finds no other alternative ideas as expressing a modicum of truth. Lenin simply follows this objective epistemology to its logical and practical conclusion. Lenin's intolerance comes from a firm belief in the objective truth of Marxism and the perspicuity of its teachings for those who practice scientific analysis and understand the results in nature, society, history, and economics.[31] He follows the basic Marxist concept of epistemology, which rejects the agnostic understanding of Kant and thinks of people as possessing "objectively" and "universally real perceptions" and knowledge of the "things-in-themselves," with the typical elements of Kantian analysis like space, time, and causality corresponding to the real relations or properties of things existing in the empirical world.[32] Lenin believes people evolve through their continuous interaction with the environment, and so it makes sense to think of their ideas as objective, adapted to the requirements of nature and growing "closer and deeper" in understanding as people evolve through their struggle with it.[33] This struggle led to the development of Hegelian logic in the course of time as the "universal truth" and law, constituting the essential fabric of the material world. Lenin follows Engels's emphasis upon dialectic materialism and expresses disdain for those who subscribe to a positivist epistemology in understanding the material world and yet question the fundamental theory of its inner workings.[34]

Following this epistemology, Lenin leaves no room for existential questions of faith and doubt, subjectivity and intuition, inconsistency and fragmentation in his comprehensive analysis. He thinks it is important to present a consistent (and extreme) doctrine of materialism, following the example of Marx and Engels in denouncing those like Feuerbach who patronize religious affections, and he hopes to expunge any remnant of fideism or idealism in developing a pure system.[35] The obsession with purity leads him to spurn the modern philosophical community and its typical recognition of a subjective human component in our knowledge of the world, considering it a dangerous step or pretext in opening the door for another reality. The Kantian concept of subjectivity provides a pretext for losing contact with the concerns of concrete existence and escaping into an ideal or metaphysical world engendered from inward fantasies. Lenin discredits the modern emphasis in epistemology by pointing to a simple fact, that the earth existed long before humans were able to experience it, making matter the origin of their ideas and the basis of their experience, and not vice versa.[36]

The realist epistemology allows Lenin to inculcate Marxism as an absolute dogma. Its truth is not a matter of opinion resulting from an inward reflection upon human subjective longings but an objective scientific certainty providing the one and only direction to objective reality and making all other positions the result of "falsehood and confusion."[37] Stalin says:

> The power of the Marxist-Leninist theory lies in the fact that it enables the party to find the right orientation in any situation, to understand the inner connection of current events, to foresee their course and to perceive not only how and in what direction they are developing in the present, but how and in what direction they are bound to develop in the future.[38]

This approach follows the fundamental program of Lenin and Engels in applying the teachings of Marx to every field of thought and judging all areas of inquiry through one comprehensive theory as the infallible guide.[39] This approach finds no room for complexities or pluralism in a "variegated medley of philosophical views" to deviate from the one exclusive truth.[40] There is one path, one prophet, and one party. Anyone who deviates in the slightest is subjected to the vitriol of Lenin in his writings and much worse in his presence.[41] This dogmatic posture led the one party, in due time, to impose its monolithic view of life on education, expelling all non-Marxist professors and permitting only one version of history in the social sciences.[42] "Philosophy was not an intellectual process but a means of justifying and inculcating the state ideology in whatever form it might assume." When Lenin died on January 21, 1924, the party decided to embalm his corpse and exhibit his remains in perpetuity within the mausoleum of Moscow, perhaps representing its steadfast and obtuse commitment to dead orthodoxy in its own inimitable way.[43] The party that was supposed to replace the *Ancien Régime* of church and state came to represent the same cultural stagnation of dogmatic and authoritarian rule.

Russian Orthodox Church

Communism succeeded in a place like Russia, since it fit within the basic mentality and texture of the culture, just replacing the old orthodox dogma with a new one. During the late medieval period, Russia experienced none of the revival in Aristotelian studies and the Scholastic disputes that brought detailed philosophical analysis to metaphysical issues and threatened to split the Catholic Church's belief in the simple unity of its traditions. In modern times, it showed little interest in movements like the Renaissance, Reformation, and Enlightenment, which provided the intellectual foundation for undermining the *Ancien Régime* with a severe form of criticism and led many to leave the church and commit total apostasy.[44] Education was controlled by the powers that be in Russia and instilled "love for the Church and loyalty to the Tsar and the Fatherland."[45]

The Orthodox Church provided the spiritual matrix for the traditional culture to prevail century after century. The Orthodox believe in a fixed tradition forming an integral unity in the one true church and refer to the maxim of St. Vincent of Lerins and the early Middle Ages—*quod ubique, quod semper, quod ab omnibus traditum est.*[46] The tradition consists of the holy scripture, the teachings of the church fathers, the seven ecumenical councils, the canons of church laws, and the customs, sacraments, icons, and worship experience of the fellowship. It directs the faithful toward the proper definition of the faith—a *fides quae creditur,* rather than emphasize a personal relationship with Christ or living in direct communion with God and seeking the divine will day-by-day. The goal of faith is to align your individual conscience with the church and its traditions, not follow your own concepts or personal judgment. The individual finds the will of God by living in communion with the church, which guarantees all other authorities, including the scripture and its interpretation.[47]

The Orthodox have no real concept of the priesthood of believers. The church professes to contain the final authority on matters of faith as a whole, but it clearly looks to the leadership as the fundamental source of inspiration and guidance. Its concept of authority begins with Christ and the Apostles, continues with their successors through the laying-on of hands, and develops into a hierarchy of bishops, priests, and deacons, descending down to the laity.[48] In theory, the bishops are chosen by the people and act *ex consensus ecclesiae,* but their decisions represent the church and must be obeyed as the external doctrinal authority and "teacher of the whole church."[49] "All the blessings of Christ come from the bishop," who appoints the parish priests, bestows the Spirit in blessing the entire fellowship, and carries within himself the supernatural power to administer the sacraments.[50]

The polity of the church proved useful to the state in establishing its rule and sustaining its autocratic nature for centuries in Russia. After Christianity was introduced to the country, the church developed an immediate and intimate relation with the state through the conversion of Princess Olga, St. Vladimir of Kiev, and many of their subjects in the tenth century. The relationship brought aspirations of making Moscow the "Third Rome" when Constantinople fell in 1453, with the see developing some independence from the Eastern Church and new prestige, and grand dukes adopting the title of tsar—a Slavic term for Caesar.[51] The unity between the religious and the secular remained intact for the next few centuries, but struggles continued within the two-headed government for power until the tsars assumed the dominant position during the time of Peter the Great and made the church a department or civil servant of the state. From 1721 to 1917, the church found much of its purpose in sustaining the authority of the state, encouraging obedience among the citizens, and performing loyal duties on behalf of the tsars. For its service, the church was given exclusive rights to propagate its dogma, control education, and sanction certain civic matters like marriage and divorce, making other denominations and religions subject to its power. Of course, those who belonged to the establishment had certain privileges associated with the structure of power, and those who chose other expressions of faith or doubt lost access to power, sometimes threatening their position and livelihood.[52] When reform came in 1905, the Orthodox hierarchy had difficulty relinquishing the hegemony and opposed the government granting freedom to other religious groups, while continuing to harass and persecute Catholics, Baptists, Muslims, and other dissidents, who numbered around twenty million according to one estimate.[53] During the civil war, the leadership wanted a return to the old system of power, with its privileges restored and the "lawful Orthodox Tsar of the House of Romanov . . . return(ed) to the Throne of all-Russia" as God's anointed ruler.[54] Even today, in post-Communist Russia, the Orthodox still have a tendency to favor authoritarian rule and limitations on democracy and religious freedom—all of which comes from their basic religious orientation to accent the authority of spiritual leadership and show a distinct obstinacy toward change in the name of tradition.[55]

Religion

Of course, Lenin would deny any connection between religion and his commitment to authoritarian rule and a monolithic tradition. He had no specific upbringing in orthodox teachings as a boy and shows little interest in discussing religious matters and questions as an author, beyond the admonition to destroy it as an anachronistic and harmful way of thinking.[56] Perhaps, he thinks there is nothing to say about religion or metaphysics as a Marxist, since it exists outside the concrete world of scientific analysis and represents only the outward form of a deeper economic reality, which explains all ideological commitments.[57] Or perhaps, he has nothing more to say in light of the scintillating criticism of the past and would lend no value to the obvious truism of Marxist analysis.

Indeed, his few comments on the subject tend to follow the party line and repeat what Communists already know from Marx, Engels, Kautsky, and the rest.[58] He speaks about the twofold origin of religion in nature and society—much like Engels and Kautsky. Religion starts off its initial phase with primitive human beings struggling with the forces of nature and hoping to find miraculous deliverance through supernatural powers, and then develops again under socioeconomic conditions, providing consolation for the downtrodden and sanctioning the status quo for the ruling class—the most important theme in Marxist analysis.[59] Here Lenin repeats Marx's dictum that religion is an "opium of the people," or a "spiritual booze, in which the slaves of capital drown their human image, their demand for a life more or less worthy of man."[60] "Those who toil and live in want all their lives are taught by religion to be submissive and patient while here on earth, and to take comfort in the hope of a heavenly reward."[61] This and other religious beliefs bring alienation to the working class and will end only when scientific explanation demythologizes the world and socialism creates a better life in the here and now, destroying religion once and for all.[62] Lenin seems to understand the egalitarian spirit of early Christianity and finds it helpful to work with progressive priests and religious dissidents, but he never conceives of religion as stimulating anything positive in society and invariably speaks of it as an instrument of exploitation.[63] "All modern religions and churches, all religious organizations, Marxism always regards as organs of *bourgeois* reaction serving to define exploitation and to stupefy the working class."[64] Any attempt to reform it would produce a "new, refined subtle poison for the oppressed masses," making it a more insidious deception than before.[65] Religion is the most dangerous foulness, the most shameful 'infection,'" and must be destroyed, not coddled through halfway measures that ignore the real danger.[66]

In this context, Lenin follows the sons of the Enlightenment in making religion a "private affair" and calling for the "complete separation of Church and State" to eliminate its corrupting influence from society. He wants to end "religious discrimination" by cutting off any support or subsidy from the government to ecclesiastical and religious organizations, while maintaining that religion consists of irrelevant metaphysical dogmas and has no relation to the state or the conduct of public affairs.[67] Lenin continues to follow the position of the Enlightenment for the most part but goes beyond the typical secular rhetoric that feigns the appearance of neutrality in the party or the state as if tolerating the ongoing existence of a dangerous narcotic. Religion is not a matter of indifference to the party, which finds its basis in materialistic values and its commission in cleansing the rank and file from nonscientific beliefs. The party cannot follow Kautsky and the liberal policy of toleration but must perform a more militant role in conducting propaganda against religion through the press and various publications to prevent the "bamboozling of the worker" with this nonsense and insuring the victory of the French Enlightenment and its atheism in society.[68]

After taking power Lenin moved immediately against the church to end its dominance in Russian society. On January 23, 1918, the Council of the People's Commissars issued a decree "Concerning Separation of Church and State, and of School and Church," which followed the antireligious agenda of Lenin and provided the basic outline for future dealings with the church in the Soviet Union.[69] The decree spoke of eliminating "all restrictions of rights" upon religious and nonreligious people alike but clearly empowered the state to replace the role of the church in society and create a godless environment for the people. Its measures gave civil authorities control over birth, death, and marriage registration; forbad religious ceremonies at state or public functions; prohibited religious instructions in public and "private educational establishments," where "general instruction is given"; ended special privileges or subsidies for all religious groups; and made church buildings and articles of worship the property of the state, subject to confiscation and removal for secular purposes.[70]

The Russian Orthodox Church responded in the summer of 1918 by becoming the epicenter of opposition to the new order. It categorically rejected all the measures in the decree and called for the reestablishment of its former privileges and the removal of the anti-Christian government.[71] Six days after the Bolsheviks came to power, the church restored the old institution of the patriarchate to reassert the authority it lost during the days of Peter the Great and named Metropolitan Tikhon of Moscow as the patriarch to lead counter-revolutionary forces against the "invasion of Antichrist and raging godlessness," sometimes openly encouraging the parishioners to join forces with the White Guard to restore the old tsarist regime.[72] In the winter of 1918, Tikhon became the leading opponent of the government and publically condemned the Soviets and their policies, denouncing them as "monsters of the human race," threatening them with the fires of hell, and excommunicating them from the church and its sacraments of grace.[73] The priests received the instructions to defend the church, along with its property, and the people were called to "martyrdom" in withstanding the assault upon its sacred institutions.[74] The hostility continued for the next five years and only abated when Tikhon was arrested in October 1922 and forced to recant his opposition to the regime and its policies as an ill and dying man.[75] After swearing allegiance, he was released from prison, and most of the clergy submitted to the authority of his example in promising civil obedience as faithful servants of the bishop and the hierarchical church. This new policy was affirmed when Metropolitan Sergius became the eventual successor of Tikhon, fulfilling the lesser role of "deputy *locum tenens*" from 1927 to 1943 and promising total loyalty and support to the government.[76]

The party responded by continuing their campaign to end religion, irrespective of the church's loyalty. It identified the struggle for socialism with atheism and called for the development of "wide-scale organization, leadership, and cooperation in the task of antireligious agitation and propaganda among the broad masses of the workers."[77]

> The All-Russian Communist Party is guided by the conviction that only the realization of conscious and systematic social and economic activity of the masses will lead to the disappearance of religious prejudices. The aim of the Party is finally to destroy the ties between the exploiting classes and the organization of religious propaganda, at the same time helping the toiling masses actually to liberate their minds from religious superstitions, and organizing on a wide scale scientific-educational and anti-religious propaganda.[78]

The party used different instruments in the campaign, including the Red Army and trade unions, but the most infamous group was the "League of the Militant Godless," which started in 1925 under the auspices of Yemelyan Yaroslavksy, Trotsky's deputy in the Department of Anti-Religious Propaganda, and the group reached its zenith in 1932 with a membership of 5.5 million.[79] The League promoted atheism by encouraging work on Sunday, sponsoring anti-Christmas and anti-Easter campaigns, disseminating antireligious literature, and establishing antireligious museums and libraries.[80] It often provoked a strong reaction by arranging tasteless stunts, like competitions between the remains of saints and mummified animals, christened and unchristened infants, and the productivity of technology and the blessings of prayer in agriculture;[81] or, producing offensive posters, like the one depicting the Virgin Mary looking at a billboard advertising the "first scientific artistic film on abortion in the U.S.S.R. [and exclaiming], 'Oh, why didn't I know that before!'"[82] Its magazine was filled with this type of vulgarity.

> No. 4 displays little artistic merit. The frontpiece represents the Jewish, Christian and Mohammedan Deities seated idly together. The former has one Cyclopean eye in the middle of the forehead and, instead of a nose, a vulgar combination of three fingers. Below, the infant Jesus is reading *Bezbozhnik* [the magazine of the group]. In another picture entitled "The Miracle of Cana at Galilee", Jesus is making home-brew with a Samovar still. The last page represents angels stealing the peasants' eggs, chickens, pigs, milk, grain, etc., and carrying them to the priests.[83]

The government's tactics went beyond its constitutional rights to spread antireligious propaganda and escalated into a more direct assault upon the church considering its power over the lives, institutions, and possessions of the people in a Socialist state. At one point, in May 1922, the Soviets thought of using the power of the state to provoke a schism in the church, dismissing undesirable bishops and priests and "reconciling the ends of the church with those of Communism and the Soviet authority." The effort was led by Bishop Antonin and a group of priests, who declared their loyalty to the Bolsheviks and the social revolution, but the so-called "Progressive" or "Living Church" (*Zhivaia Tserkov*) was never able to gain sufficient traction and usurp the place of the traditional church and its leaders in the affections of the people.[84] More typically, the Soviets used the power of the state to seize churches, closing thousands of them down, and turn them into theaters, dance halls, museums, and secular meeting places.[85] The most infamous display of this power occurred on February 23, 1922, when a decree was issued confiscating sacred objects and other treasures of the church as a means of addressing the devastating famine of 1921/22 and funding the relief effort. Tikhon tried to rescue the sacred objects from destruction by raising money through foreign relief agencies and permitting the sale of nonconsecrated objects, like ornamental jewels, for this purpose, but the government forbad the church from organizing any relief efforts and proceeded to misstate Tikhon's position on the sale of church property, wanting to paint the church as bourgeois and materialistic.

The government ended up confiscating several billion rubles worth of articles, provoking widespread protests and leading to the imprisonment of many church leaders, and the death of some, including the Metropolitan Veniamin.[86]

The clergy were a particular target of persecution in the Soviet Union. They "were for a time disenfranchised, deprived of the right to hold public office, compelled to pay higher taxes, and subjected to discrimination in the allocation of housing and rations."[87] The government justified the persecution claiming they were disloyal to the state, leaders of the counterrevolution during the civil war, and stockpiling provisions, keeping them away from the starving masses.[88] It is difficult to know the exact number of bishops and priests executed during the early years of Lenin, but it certainly ran well above a thousand, based upon conservative estimates. Archbishop Silvestr wrote a letter to the pope on February 7, 1919, and speaks of the assassination of Metropolitan Vladimir and hundreds of priests, claiming some of them were buried alive.[89] John Meyendorff says the business of seizing church property led to the death of 691 priests in just that one instance, as well as the continuous harassment of a much greater number.[90] A memorandum from the Committee of the Russian Zemstvos and Cities says the Communists had murdered thirty bishops and more than twelve hundred priests during its first five years of power and lists some of the prominent names.[91] The persecution only decreased when Tikhon swore allegiance and the government began to recognize how difficult it was to wean the peasants off religion, even in a new Socialist environment.[92] The early hooligan tactics seemed to have the opposite effect on the people, leading to the outbreak of religious revival,[93] and so the Thirteenth Congress of 1924 said, "It is necessary to cut short resolutely all attempts to combat religious prejudices by administrative means such as the closure of churches, mosques, synagogues, prayer-houses, etc. . . . Special care must be taken not to offend the religious feelings of the believer."[94] The times of active persecution decreased after this time and were replaced by more subtle approaches, which proved effective in eroding the power and place of the church in the course of time. Through this way and means, the church will lose its former glory, which boasted 100 million members, 67 dioceses, 54,174 churches, 50,105 priests, 15,210 deacons, 21,330 monks, 73,299 nuns, and 1,498 monastic institutions—all before the Communist revolution destroyed its place in society through years of persecution.[95]

Stalin Era

Joseph Vissarionovich Dzhugashvili (Stalin) was born on December 21, 1879, in the Georgian town of Gori. His mother sent him to a local church school dreaming of him entering the priesthood one day. He continued this path some years later by attending Tiflis Orthodox Theological Seminary in the capital of Georgia, but he was expelled from the school in May 1899 after reading a number of illicit books from the city library and converting to atheist/Marxist ideology—at least according to the official version.[96] He soon began to participate in left-wing political activity, joining the Social Democratic Labor Party in 1901 and fomenting demonstrations and organizing strikes for the workers. A couple years later he cast his lot with Lenin when the party split between Menshiviks and Bolsheviks and was rewarded for his service a decade later with a position on the first Central Committee of the Bolshevik Party. During the stormy days of the October Revolution, he used his position as the editor of *Pravda* to promote Lenin's cause against the provisional government, and Lenin returned the favor and promoted him within the party after the coup d'état. Eventually, Lenin named him general secretary of the Central Committee in April 1922—a position Stalin used to outmaneuver opponents, amass power, and develop a monstrous dictatorship for the next three decades over the Soviet Union and its many satellites.

The official version of ideology during the Stalin era was embodied in a work entitled *History of the Communist Party of the Soviet Union (Bolsheviks): Short Course* (1938). The work was issued in millions of copies and made prescribed reading for secondary schools, all places of higher education, and party meetings as containing the imprimatur of the dictator and resolution of all problems of history, philosophy, and social sciences once and for all. The fourth chapter on "Dialectical and Historical Materialism" was attributed to Stalin before the war and the whole book after the war, although it seems as if an anonymous commission of writers and editors worked with Stalin in producing the entire corpus.[97] The fourth chapter provides the basic philosophical orientation of the Marxist-Leninist system and focuses upon the concept of dialectic materialism as the fundamental matrix in understanding all processes of life. The chapter finds the origin of this grand interpretive scheme within the dialectics of Hegel and the materialism of Feuerbach but looks to the work of Marx and Engels as providing a more consistent expression, cleansed of all idealistic fantasies. The Marxist analysis rejects metaphysical speculations and rests upon the sure foundation of science, which provides the human subject with an objective knowledge of the world and its dialectical forces. Science develops the dialectical method by observing the constant movement of nature through the interaction of opposites and supplies Marxism with an objective guideline for its practical activity in the world. Even the imperative for social revolution finds its basis within the scientific community and its observation of qualitative leaps within the quantitative and dialectic processes of evolutionary development, as in the case of ice suddenly changing into water at a specific temperature. This type of qualitative development allows the Marxist-Leninist system to list a number of specific stages in the scientific study of social interaction: the primitive communal, the slave, the feudal, the capitalist, and the socialist. These stages represent evolutionary development "as an outward and upward movement, as a transition from an old qualitative state to a new qualitative state, as a development from the simple to the complex, from the lower to the higher," and contain an imperative to facilitate the progressive development by promoting emerging elements like the proletariat and opposing the moribund forces that inhibit the course of time.[98] The orthopraxis of Marxism rests upon its ability to predict the future through dialectical analysis and find within the progress of the world an imperative to promote whatever represents the new and eliminate whatever inhibits its emergence.

This dogmatic mentality of social progress characterized Marxism from its inception and brought with it the intellectual justification for Stalin's purging of "public enemies" on a massive scale and enslaving the entire nation to his vision of the future. Socialism was considered the economic panacea and was imposed upon the people through a series of five-year plans, beginning in 1928 during the Stalin era and ending only in 1991 with the collapse of the Soviet Union. Stalin launched these economic plans, using unprecedented measures of totalitarian force, eliminating all vestiges of small-time capitalism, dissolving the private agriculture of the Kulaks, developing collective farming, and sending untold millions who protested the policies to their death and/or the labor camps in the forest and mines of Siberia. He proceeded to place each citizen within a sector, factory, and cog of the state-run machine and use them as a means to create surplus-value for the rapid industrialization of the society.[99] Those who resisted the process of collectivism were purged—often gathered up, sent to remote regions, and told to develop the forbidden land without any aid from the government, leading to the complete liquidation of many districts within the Soviet Union.[100]

In 1935, Stalin began his infamous Great Purge, which extended Lenin's reign of terror to include members within the party, following the assassination of Sergei Kirov, the popular leader of the Leningrad party and possible successor of Stalin as general secretary.[101] This murder became the pretext for an extensive purge of the Communist Party over the next four years and claimed many of its unsuspecting members:

> . . . the party committees of whole regions . . . their own successors in office, whose hands still reeked from the execution; all the Old Bolsheviks, all Lenin's closest associates, former members of government and of the Politburo and the party secretariat, activists of every rank, scholars, artists, writers, economists, military men, lawyers, engineers, doctors, and—in due course, when they had done their stint—the agents of the purge themselves, whether senior officers of the security service or especially zealous party members.[102]

Even a large number of Stalin's own sycophants were purged for some unknown reason, gripping the whole nation with fear and paranoia over the capricious nature of the tyrant and "the fact that being arrested and sentenced to death or to an arbitrary and indefinite term of imprisonment had nothing to do with whether a man's work was good or bad, whether he did or did not belong to any kind of opposition, or even whether he did or did not love Stalin."[103] Confessions were obtained through coercion, using inhumane interrogation techniques like "physical and mental torture, deprivation of sleep, threats to close relatives and the administration of narcotic drugs," and convictions were based on specious evidence like "guilt by association, guilt by category, guilt by occupation, and guilt by admission and guilt by silence."[104] A small percentage of the "guilty" were paraded before the public and given show trials to vindicate the administrative measures against traitors. This method was used against the Old Bolsheviks, who were forced to confess their crime of plotting with Trotsky to overthrow the government, made to implicate others in demonstrating the broad nature of the conspiracy, and were taken out and shot immediately—without any material evidence, due process, or right to a defense. Stalin justified these and other measures as necessary in creating a Socialist state within a backward country and was reputed to say, "One cannot make an omelet without breaking a few eggs." The problem was his recipe called for more than just a few eggs and cost the lives of millions, maybe even tens of millions according to some estimates.[105]

The church suffered great tribulation during the first half of Stalin's reign. Religion caught the particular attention of the dictator because his positivist mentality found it impossible to tolerate subjective or metaphysical approaches to life, withstanding the march of scientific progress. On the eve of his ascension to power, Stalin said,

> The Party cannot be neutral towards religion, and it conducts anti-religious propaganda against all religious prejudices because it stands for science, whereas religious prejudices run counter to science, because all religion is the antithesis of science.[106]

With scientism as the ideology of the state, Stalin undertook a major offensive against the church when he first assumed full power in 1928, imposing high and arbitrary taxes, executing and exiling thousands of the clergy, closing places of worship, appropriating churches and seminaries for secular purposes, and seizing church bells for their metal.[107] On May 22, 1929, the fourth article of the RSFSR constitution was amended, eliminating the right of religious propaganda and leaving only the freedom for "anti-religious propaganda," which the government used with great zeal to deprecate all religious sensibilities. The government proceeded to make "acts of deceit, with the purpose of encouraging superstition among the masses of the population and with a view of deriving profit" subject to penal sanctions as an additional means of suppressing evangelical fervor.[108] By the time of the German invasion on June 22, 1941, half of the priests, monks, and nuns were gone and fewer than 500 Orthodox churches remained open.[109]

The future of the church looked bleak, but the prospects soon changed in the late 1930s and early 1940s with the Nazis posing an imminent threat to the Communist regime. Stalin desperately needed the loyalty of the church to withstand the German invasion, and the Metropolitan Sergei and his subjects responded by supporting the war effort as patriotic Russians, donating large sums of money, and calling the people to defend the "sacred frontiers of our fatherland" with their own lives.[110] The act of patriotism was critical to the survival of the regime and moved the tyrant to change his policies regarding the church in a number of areas, disbanding the League of Militant Atheists, stopping the publication of antireligious propaganda, closing atheist museums, reopening seminaries, monasteries, and thousands of churches, alleviating burdensome taxes, reinstating the patriarchate, broadcasting a religious hour on Moscow Radio, allowing for some religious publications, including the Bible, reinstituting Sunday as the legal day of rest, and permitting the celebration of Easter in public.[111] After the war, Stalin resumed the campaign against religion and disciplined members of the party who observed religious rites but never returned to the brutality of the former days, and he continued to provide some space for the exercise of religious freedom, as long as it was confined to the places of worship and had no influence on those outside the walls of the church.[112]

An important exception to the general trend was the rise of anti-Semitism during the postwar era. The war brought a strong resurgence of the nationalist feelings in Russia, and the Jews were perceived by many in the government as "stateless cosmopolitans," who possessed little fidelity to the fatherland, just like Hitler described them in Germany.[113] Stalin hoped the Jews would assimilate into the Russian landscape, following the programmatic vision of post-Enlightenment Europe,[114] but Judaism was a formidable foe, hindering the process with its ethnic beliefs and proving difficult to uproot in the mentality of its people. Too many Jews were continuing to preserve their identity with each other as the chosen people of God and looking for a homeland in Palestine to settle as a specific nation, rather than joining the aspirations of the Russian people or the worldwide revolution of workers.[115]

> Judaism has been taken over by Zionism, which is at present the official ideology of the state of Israel. Attempting to win over the masses of working Jews and to divert them from the world revolutionary labor and national liberation movements as well as to justify Israel's expansionist policies, Zionism began to use tenets of Judaism for its political aims (for example, messianism, which proposes the creation of a new, "ideal" Israel, with Jerusalem as its center, that would include the whole of Palestine). Since the second quarter of the 20th century Zionism has found support among the most reactionary Jews, especially in the USA. In its chauvinist and annexationist policy Zionism makes use of the Judaic dogma that the Jews are god's chosen people and employs Judaism to substantiate the concept of a "worldwide Jewish nation" and other reactionary positions.[116]

When the process of assimilation proved too slow, the Communists sought to cut off the culture, language, and tradition with more direct policies, forbidding instruction in Hebrew and Yiddish, suppressing Zionist associations and doctrine, arresting many of the leaders, and finally closing down all Jewish organizations in 1948.[117] Soloman Mikhoels, the leader of the Jewish community and head of their Antifacist Committee (JAC), was accused of forming a large espionage network for Western intelligence. He was murdered by Stalin and his henchmen on January 12, 1948,[118] and 110 victims soon followed—"ten were shot, 20 were sentenced to 25 years in reform camps, 3 were sentenced to 20 years in reform camps; 11 to 15 years of exile, 50 to 10 years, 2 to 8 years, 1 to 7 years, 2 to 5 years, and 1 to 10 years. As for the remaining 10 people, 5 died during the course of the examination, and the other 5 cases were closed shortly after their arrest."[119] The paranoia focused upon the Jewish community because of their international connections through family, friends, and Zionist organizations and its real or perceived possibility of undermining the regime by spreading Western ideology and installing foreign spies in their midst. The apotheosis of this paranoia came during the last couple months of the dictator's life when Jewish doctors, associated with the Leningrad All-Union Institute of Experimental Medicine, were arrested for a plot to poison Soviet leaders through their ties with the "international Jewish bourgeois nationalist organization Joint, established by American Intelligence Services." Immediately after the death of Stalin, the doctors were exonerated and released from prison, and the accusers given a slap on the wrist for inflaming anti-Semitism without sufficient evidence, but the damage was already done. With many of the Jewish leaders gone, often sent to prison, torture, and death in the Lubyanka prison, the Jewish community was unable to survive the years of secular oppression and were left to dream of a messianic resurgence one day, far off in the distant future for a people who had lost their souls.[120]

The Soviets persecuted religious groups for disloyalty and patronized those who practiced obeisance and compromised with the ideology of the regime, but they remained obstinate in the ultimate design of destroying all religions no matter how subservient or useful the groups were to the administration. The hostile attitude came from their steadfast adherence to the Marxist-Leninist tradition, which remained constant throughout the years of Communist rule without significant change in the fundamental program. It was embodied during the Stalin era in the *Great Soviet Encyclopedia*, which served as a basic source of propaganda for the administration and Communist point of view on all matters of human interest, reaching a prodigious length of sixty-five volumes and sixty-five thousand entries in its first edition (1926–1947). The massive work presents Marxist-Leninism as the only scientific philosophy that makes "full use" of scientific methods, discoveries, and its "objective knowledge of reality." This objectivist philosophy rejects all religious mythology as the "antithesis of science" and theology as the "negation of independent thought." The growth of science and its social counterpart in communism will lead to a steady and inevitable decline in the reliance of people upon matters of faith as religion struggles in vain to "find some way of reconciling its doctrine with scientific truths or even of adapting them to its own needs." Social science has shown that religion is a simple product of social conditions, often expressing the "social protest by the popular masses against class exploitation and foreign domination," and nothing more. Christianity arose as the protest of slaves, before it was corrupted by the rich and a hierarchical polity of bishops, and lost its early spirit of egalitarianism. In Russia, the Orthodox Church brought this polity to the forefront when it was established in 988/989 and aided the state in sanctifying an authoritative and submissive culture of exploitation through its hierarchical structure.[121] All in all, the church is nothing more than a source of oppression and superstition in society and must recede before the advance of science and social consciousness, liberating the people from alien principles and reconciling them with the material world in resolving their concrete problems.

Khrushchev and Beyond

After the death of Stalin, the central committee of the party reaffirmed its commitment to dialectic materialism and antireligious propaganda in its decree "On Major Shortcomings in Scientific Atheistic Propaganda and Measures for Improving It" (July 7, 1954). It called for the government to take more decisive and vigorous measures against religion, noticing a marked "increase in the number of citizens attending religious festivals and observing religious ceremonies" and rejecting the "indifferent or neutral" approach to the problem displayed by the previous administration.[122] The campaign was extensive in nature and included compulsory courses in "scientific atheism" in every school, special lectures on the subject in towns and collective farms, an expansion of the atheist museum in Leningrad, a plethora of pamphlets, journals, and books attacking religion and circulating into the millions of copies, and the constant bombardment in film, radio, and television on a daily basis.[123]

The campaign accelerated in 1958 when Nikita Khrushchev became chairman of the Council of Ministers and renewed the commitment to expunge religion.[124] He expanded previous measures and even presumed to meddle into the sacred confines of family life and prohibit parents from rearing their own children in a specific religious tradition.

> In 1961 children under the age of eighteen were forbidden to attend Baptist services, and in 1963 this was extended to the Orthodox Church as well. Other laws were now interpreted to mean that parents have no right to teach their children what will ultimately be harmful to them. Applied to religion, this meant that parental instruction or

> encouragement in the faith was illegal. Though it is doubtful that the application of this law was widespread, there were in fact cases in which children were taken away from parents for these reasons and sent to atheistic state boarding schools.[125]

The repression was less violent than the early years of communism and less direct in attacking the personal faith of loyal Russian citizens,[126] but the overall scope of the operation was much more extensive than recent efforts and brought a decisive decline in the number of religious institutions and outward symbols or expressions of faith. "During the Khrushchev period, . . . the Russian Orthodox, Baptists, Lutherans, and Catholics lost approximately half of their churches. The Jewish faith was treated even more harshly: synagogues were reduced in number from some four hundred to less than one hundred."[127] By the end of his reign in 1964, only 7,600 Orthodox churches remained open for worship, and its seminaries went from eight to four.[128]

After the fall of Khrushchev, the church was given a respite from the continuous harassment of unbelief and the barrage of antireligious propaganda. The official organs of the state still used the same Marxist rhetoric to deprecate religion as the opium of the people and its demise as the "inexorable progress of history," but renounced the more violent and caustic tactics of the past as counterproductive in achieving the ultimate goal. The church was given a relative amount of autonomy and afforded the protection of the state as long as it made no "political statements against the interests of the Soviet State" or discouraged believers from participating in society or spread superstitious rumors about the "end of the world" and "miraculous healings."[129] This form of independence was parlayed into a modicum of civil rights when religious freedom received strong and unexpected support from the Communists during the last days of their rule under the leadership of Mikhail Gorbachev and his policies of *perestroika* (reconstruction) and *glasnost* (openness). In 1990, the Executive Committee of the Communist Party granted the Russian Orthodox Church the right to spread their religion throughout the country and celebrate their liturgical services and rituals without any harassment from the government and its many officials. With the collapse of the Communist regime a year later, the new leadership opted for a Western-style "secular state," separating religious groups from the state, prohibiting the establishment of a "state-sponsored or mandatory religion," and permitting the dissemination of religious doctrine, but this arrangement did not satisfy certain elements within the Orthodox Church, who wanted to restore its former position in society and undermine the missionary activity of a burgeoning evangelical population.[130] The Orthodox Church pushed the Duma to pass and Yeltsin to sign legislation "On the Freedom of Conscience and Religious Association" (1997), which provided federal and local supervision of new religious groups and honored the Russian Orthodox Church for its "special contribution" in establishing the "state system of Russia" and the "development of its spiritual and cultural" life.[131] Ever since, the church has worked to strengthen its bond with the government and establish its dominance once again in the lives of the Russian people.[132]

Notes

1. Kołakowski, *Main Currents of Marxism*, 642; Neil Harding, *Leninism* (Durham, NC: Duke University Press, 1996) 17–18. They succeeded in assassinating Alexander II on May 1, 1881, but failed six years later in their attempt on Alexander III.
2. Harding, *Leninism*, 23ff.; Kołakowski, *Main Currents of Marxism*, 643.
3. V. I. Lenin, *What Is to Be Done?: Burning Questions of Our Movement* (New York: Progress Publishers, 1970–78) 5.485, 506, 514; Harding, *Leninism*, 28–32, 36–37; Kołakowski, *Main Currents of Marxism*, 660. Hereafter *Collected Works* is designated CW.
4. Alan Wood, *Stalin and Stalinism* (London and New York: Routledge, 2005) 13; Harding, *Leninism*, ix, 7; Kołakowski, *Main Currents of Marxism*, 671.
5. The event took the Bolsheviks and other Socialist groups by surprise. Lenin was residing in Switzerland, and Trotsky was settling into a new life in the United States.
6. *The Russian Revolution and Religion: A Collection of Documents Concerning the Suppression of Religion by the Communists 1917–25*, Boleslaw Szczesniak (ed. and trans.) (Notre Dame, IN: University of Notre Dame, 1959) 1–2; Kołakowski, *Main Currents of Marxism*, 735–37; Wood, *Stalin and Stalinism*, 8–9; Harding, *Leninism*, 49, 79–85, 90–91, 96–97, 102–6. Trotsky concluded in his own history of the revolution that "each and every participant in these events, himself included, could with impunity have been replaced by another—with the sole exception of Lenin." Harding, *Leninism*, 110.
7. Lenin, "Two Worlds" (April 6, 1917), in CW 24.30; Kołakowski, *Main Currents of Marxism*, 735. Cf. Harding, *Leninism*, 90, 97. The Germans provided Lenin and other repatriates with safe conduct on their way back to the country.
8. Lenin, *Imperialism, The Highest Stage of Capitalism*, in CW 22.191, 300; "The Task of the Proletariat in the Present Revolution" (April 7, 1917), in CW 24.21–22; "Blancism" (April 8, 1917), in CW 24.34; Harding, *Leninism*, 8, 9. *Imperialism* was written in mid-1916 and published the following year. It represents the most fundamental text of Leninism. Harding, *Leninism*, 113; Lenin, *Imperialism*, 187.
9. Ibid., 194, 197, 200, 203–7, 215–19, 227, 238, 257, 260–61, 266, 300; Harding, *Leninism*, 117–18, 123–25; 130; Lenin, "All for the Fight against Denikin!," in CW 29.436.
10. "Two Worlds," 33; "Blancism," 34–35; "The Tasks of the Proletariat in our Revolution" (Sept. 1917), in CW 24.65; *The Proletarian Revolution and the Renegade Kautsky*, in CW 28.286–87; Kołakowski, *Main Currents of Communism*, 753; Harding, *Leninism*, 66–67. The SPD was more practical than Lenin and felt it would lose its mass-base if it took a position against the war. It chose to argue that patriotism and internationalism were compatible. Harding, *Leninism*, 72–74.

11. Harding, *Leninism*, 78, 140–41. The concept of capitalist imperialism is found in Engels, Kautsky, and other Socialist leaders, but Lenin brings it to the forefront and makes it an integral part of his system.
12. "The Tasks of the Proletariat in Our Revolution," 76–77, 84, 87; *Imperialism*, 266.
13. "Conspectus of the Book The Holy Family by Marx and Engels" (ca. May/Sept. 1895), in CW 38.40; *What Is to Be Done?*, 464, 514; "The Dual Power" (April 9, 1917), in CW 24.39; "The Tasks of the Proletariat in Our Revolution," 69, 78; *The Proletarian Revolution and the Renegade Kautsky*, 238.
14. Ibid., 28; *The Proletarian Revolution and the Renegade Kautsky*, 242–43. Lenin follows the typical understanding of dialectical materialism by attributing qualitative changes to quantitative changes (e.g., H_2O reaching 100 degrees C.) This material change provides justification for revolutionary activity, as opposed to waiting around for slow evolutionary change. "Conspectus of Hegel's *Science of Logic*," in CW 38.123–24; Harding, *Leninism*, 232–33.
15. *What Is to Be Done?*, 354ff., 362–63, 405–6, 412.
16. *What Is to Be Done?*, 479–80; *The Proletarian Revolution and the Renegade Kautsky*, 236, 240; "Notes for an Article or Speech in Defence of the April Theses," 32–33; *One Step Forward, Two Steps Back*, in CW 7.225. He constantly refers to Kautsky's arguments in the *Dictatorship of the Proletariat* as absurd, stupid, monstrous, and so on. He couples Plekhov together with Kautsky as leaning toward social-democracy and vacillating over the true revolutionary spirit of Marxism. "The Dual Power," 39; "The Tasks of the Proletariat in Our Revolution," 68; *Development of Capitalism in Russia*, 32; *The Proletarian Revolution and the Renegade Kautsky*, 229. Plekhov is considered the father of Marxism in Russia and influences all the Marxists of Lenin's generation. He advocated the need for political revolution and attacked revisionists like Bernstein but felt it was necessary to wait upon capitalism to develop with its democratic institutions and let the proletariat lead the way, not a centralized party. Some of the tension that developed between Lenin and Plekhov involved personal rivalry, but there were some ideological and practical differences that eventually alienated the former colleagues. Kołakowski, *Main Currents of Marxism*, 620–25, 635–39, 660.
17. *What Is to Be Done?*, 383, 384: Kołakowski, *Main Currents of Marxism*, 665–73.
18. Harding, *Leninism*, 173, 253, 273–75. In 1921, all factions were dissolved by Lenin. Leon Trotsky, *Terrorism and Communism: A Reply to Karl Kautsky*, Max Shachtman (forward) (Ann Arbor, MI: University of Michigan Press, 1963) xvi. In the USSR, "only members of the Central Committee of the party were entitled to vote for the members of the Politburo, and they, in turn, selected the General Secretary. Ordinary members of the party played no role whatever in these crucial deliberations—their vote for the membership of their local party was four or five times removed from the leadership selection process at the national level." Harding, *Leninism*, 196.
19. "The Tasks of the Youth Leagues," in CW 31.294; Kolawski, *Main Currents of Marxism*, 769.
20. *The Proletarian Revolution and the Renegade Kautsky*, 280.

21. "The Victory of the Cadets and the Tasks of the Workers Party," in CW 10.216–17, 244–46.
22. *The Proletarian Revolution and the Renegade Kautsky*, 253, 256, 271–72.
23. Vladmir Petrov, "Aims and Methods of Soviet Terrorism," in *The Soviet Union*, 137–38.
24. "Concerning the Decree on Revolutionary Tribunals" (March 30, 1918), in CW 27.219–20; *The Proletarian Revolution and the Renegade Kautsky*, 268; Kołakowski, *Main Currents of Marxism*, 746.
25. *History of the Communist Party of the Soviet Union (Bolsheviks): A Short Course* (Toronto: Francis White Publishers, LTD., 1939) 359.
26. Kołakowski, *Main Currents of Marxism*, 748, 754–55.
27. John Gray, *Black Mass: Apocalyptic Religion and the Death of Utopia* (Toronto: Doubleday Canada, 2007) 46, 57; Harding, *Leninism*, 256, 262.
28. Wood, *Stalin and Stalinism*, 30; Harding, *Leninism*, 250; Kołakowski, *Main Currents of Communism*, 802.
29. "Letter to Congress" (Dec. 23/24, 1922), in CW 36.594–66; Kołakowski, *Main Currents of Marxism*, 748–49; Harding, *Leninism*, 245. Lenin was clearly a more polished, cosmopolitan intellectual than Stalin. He traveled abroad and knew several languages—Greek, Latin, French, German, and English, whereas Stalin had "virtually no experience of life outside of his native Georgia and adopted Russia" and "developed a strong suspicion of all things foreign." Harding, *Leninism*, 243.
30. Harding, *Leninism*, 247; Wood, *Stalin and Stalinism*, 29; Kołakowski, *Main Currents of Marxism*, 749. Payne thinks Stalin succeeded in poisoning Lenin through the assistance of his doctors. Robert Payne, *The Life and Death of Lenin* (New York: Simon and Schuster, 1964).
31. Harding, *Leninism*, 240–42.
32. "Conspectus on Hegel's Book Lectures on the History of Philosophy," in CW 38.419, 478–79, 485; *Materialism and Empirio-Criticism: Critical Notes Concerning a Reactionary Philosophy*, in CW 13.82, 283. He sees Engels as an authority in rejecting the idealism of Ernst Mach and George Berkeley. For Engels, sense-perception is the image (*Abbild*) of reality, even if it is not the identical copy. Engels sees objective reality in concepts like law, order, and causality, and accuses Kant of inconsistencies on this point—the worst of all possible sins in Lenin's mind. Kant is found in a state of limbo between materialism, idealism, and agnosticism. *Materialism and Empirio-Criticism*, 23, 163, 170, 302.
33. "Conspectus on Hegel's Book Lectures on the History of Philosophy," 417–18, 464–66.
34. "Conspectus on Hegel's Book The Science of Logic," in CW 38.99; *Materialism and Empirio-Criticism*, 1, 2; Harding, *Leninism*, 226–29. After 1914, Lenin changed his emphasis to dialectical materialism and can be understood as a disciple of Engels from this time onward. Marx referred to the concept as a useful tool but never made it a comprehensive theory embracing all of life like Engels and Lenin. *Materialism and Empirio-Criticism*, 208; Loewenstein, *Marx against Marxism*, 125; Harding, *Leninism*, 228.
35. *Materialism and Empirio-Criticism*, 98, 204, 293–94, 297–98. Lenin lost his faith around the age of fifteen or sixteen before he studied Marxism. Kołakowski, *Main Currents of Marxism*, 723. He provides the typical Marxist

history of his movement in *Philosophical Notebooks*, which speaks of its evolution in the modern world through French and British materialists and highlights the contributions of Feuerbach and Bauer. "Conspectus of the Book The Holy Family," 34, 41–45.

36. Ibid., 63, 298, 310; "Conspectus of Hegel's Book Lectures on the History of Philosophy," 446. Lenin moves closer to the Hegelian viewpoint in 1914 by emphasizing the power of human consciousness as an active agent in creating reality, rather than a passive observer reflecting its antecedent reality. As a revolutionary, he wants to promote the power of a human activity that "changes external actuality, abolishes its determinateness." "Conspectus of Hegel's Book Lectures on the History of Philosophy," 218.
37. Ibid., 114.
38. Gurian, "Development of the Soviet Regime," 1.
39. Ibid., 2; Harding, *Leninism*, 13.
40. "Notes on Shulyatikov's Book," in CW 38.486.
41. Wood, *Stalin and Stalinism*, 26–27, 33; Loewenstein, *Marx against Marxism*, 127–28; Kołakowski, *Main Currents of Marxism*, 272; Harding, *Leninism*, 169. He constantly besmirches his polemical enemies as ignorant, stupid, monstrous, not true Marxists, and so on. See, for example, *Materialism and Empirio-Criticism*, 157, 170, 270, 302; *The Proletariat Revolution and the Renegade Kautsky*," passim.
42. Michael, Karpovich, "Historical Background of Soviet Thought Control," in *The Soviet Union*, 25; Kołakowski, *Main Currents of Marxism*, 824.
43. Kołakowski, *Main Currents of Marxism*, 749, 848. Lenin's work also represents a stagnant addiction to repeating the same point *ad nauseam*.
44. Ibid., 603–5.
45. Vladimir Kuroyedov, *Church and Religion in the USSR* (Moscow: Novosti Press Agency Publishing House, 1977) 6; N. S. Timasheff, *Religion in Soviet Russia 1917–1942* (New York: Sheed & Ward, 1942) 5.
46. "What [has been believed] everywhere, always, [and] by everyone."
47. Lawrence Cross, *Eastern Christianity: The Byzantine Tradition* (Sydney and Philadelphia: E. J. Dwyer, 1989) 47–48; Sergius Bulgakov, *The Orthodox Church*, Lydia Kesich (trans.) (Crestwood, NY: St. Vladimir's Seminary Press, 1988) 12, 23–24, 27–29, 82.
48. Bulgakov, *Orthodox Church*, 38, 43–44; Cross, *Eastern Christianity*, 43.
49. Cross, *Eastern Christianity*, 50; Bulgakov, *Orthodox Church*, 47–48, 75.
50. Bulgakov, *Orthodox Church*, 43–45; Cross, *Eastern Christianity*, 41–42, 49–50.
51. John Meyendorff, *The Orthodox Church: Its Past and Its Role in the World Today*, John Chapin (trans.) (New York: Pantheon Books, 1968) 102, 107–9; Timasheff, *Religion in Soviet Russia*, 2.
52. Timasheff, *Religion in Soviet Russia*, 4–5; Sabrina P. Ramet, *Nihil Obstat: Religion, Politics, and Social Change in East-Central Europe and Russia* (Durham, NC and London: Duke University Press, 1998) 229; David E. Powell, *Antireligious Propaganda in the Soviet Union: A Study of Mass Persuasion* (Cambridge, MA, and London: The MIT Press, 1975) 3–4; Kołakowski, *Main Currents of Marxism*, 603–5.
53. Christel Lane, *Christian Religion in the Soviet Union* (Albany, NY: State University of New York Press, 1978) 26; Howard L. Parsons, *Christianity*

Today in the USSR (New York: International Publishers, 1987) 10, 11; Denis R. Janz, *World Christianity and Marxism* (New York and Oxford: Oxford University Press, 1998) 32.

54. "Resolution Taken by the Russian Church Council Abroad at Sremski Karlovtsi" (Nov. 21/Dec. 3, 1921), in *Russian Revolution and Religion*, 58–59. This is the prayer of Metropolitan Anthony, President of the Russian Church Abroad.
55. Janz, *World Christianity and Marxism*, 46–47; Ramet, *Nihil Obstat*, 243–45.
56. Georges Labica, "Lenin et la Religion," in *Philosophie et Religion* (Paris: Editions Sociales, 1974) 256–7; McKown, *Classical Marxist Critique of Religion*, 94.
57. Ibid., 258, 265, 281–82; Kołakowski, *Main Currents of Marxism*, 663.
58. McKown, *Classical Marxist Critique of Religion*, 108; Labica, "Lenin et la Religion," 268–69. Among his foremost works on religion are "Socialism and Religion" (1905), "The Attitude to the Workers Party to Religion" (1909), "Classes and Parties in Their Attitude to Religion and the Church" (1909), *Materialism and Empirio-Criticism* (1908), and two letters written to Gorky in 1913.
59. "Socialism and Religion," in CW 10.83–84; McKown, *Classical Marxist Critique of Religion*, 109–10; Labica, "Lenin et la Religion," 259. Of course, his brief discussions lack the complexity of Engels and Kautsky.
60. Labica, "Lenin et la Religion," 271–72; Lenin, "Socialism and Religion," 83–84, 87; "The Attitude of the Workers' Party to Religion," in CW 15.402–6; "Classes and Parties in Their Attitude to Religion and the Church," in CW 15.420–23; Kołakowski, *Main Currents of Marxism*, 723.
61. "Socialism and Religion," 83.
62. McKown, *Classical Marxist Critique of Religion*, 107.
63. Ibid., 103–4, 110–11; Bohdan R. Bociurkiw, "Lenin and Religion," in *Lenin: The Man, the Theorist, the Leader*, Leonard Shapiro and Peter Reddaway (ed.) (New York: Frederick A. Praeger, 1967) 125–26; Lenin, "Attitude of the Workers' Party to Religion," 403; "Socialism and Religion," 85.
64. *Religion in the U.S.S.R.*, Robert Conquest (ed.) (New York and Washington, DC: Frederick A. Praeger, 1968) 7.
65. "L. N. Trotsky," in CW 16.325; "Attitude of the Workers' Party to Religion," 411.
66. "To Maxim Gorky" (Nov. 13/14, 1913), in CW 35.122; Powell, *Antireligious Propaganda in the Soviet Union*, 15; Timasheff, *Religion in Soviet Russia*, 13; Labica, "Lenin et la Religion," 276.
67. "Socialism and Religion," 84–85; Labica, "Lenin et la Religion," 272ff.; *Religion in the U.S.S.R.*, 9.
68. Ibid., 85–86; Labica, "Lenin et Religion," 273–74; *The Russian Revolution and Religion*, 6, 15. He says you can accept Christians into the party but cannot treat their religion as a private affair and must convert them to atheism. *Religion in the U.S.S.R.*, 9; Kołakowski, *Main Currents of Marxism*, 723–24.
69. "Decree of the Soviet Commissars Concerning Separation of Church and State, and of School and Church" (Jan. 23, 1918), in *Russian Revolution and Religion*, 34–35; Kuroyedov, *Church and Religion in the USSR*, 10–11; Powell, *Antireligious Propaganda in the Soviet Union*, 24–25.

70. *The Russian Revolution and Religion*, 8–10. This provision was based on the decree of November 8, 1917, which abolished proprietorship of land. "Decree on Land Nationalization" (Nov. 8, 1917), in *Russian Revolution and Religion*, 28–29. See Lenin, "The Tasks of the Proletariat in the Present Revolution," 23. The nationalization of land was a central plank in Lenin's program and more important to him than civil rights. "Report of the Unity Congress of the R.S.D.L.P.," in CW.10.352–53; Harding, *Leninism*, 43–44. The Commissariat of Justice said that the churches maybe used for secular and antireligious purposes. It also "ordered the 'painless but complete liquidation of monasteries, as chief centres of the influence of the Churchmen.' By 1920, 673 had been 'liquidated,' their 2 ¼ million acres and 4,248,000 roubles confiscated, and their 84 factories, 436 dairy farms, 602 cattle farms, 1,112 apartment houses and 704 hostelries 'nationalised.'" *Religion in the U.S.S.R.*, 14.
71. "Resolutions of the Conference of Orthodox Clergy and Laymen" (June 1917), in *Russian Revolution and Religion*, 27–28; Kuroyedov, *Church and Religion in the USSR*, 13; *Russian Revolution and Religion*, 3.
72. Kuoyedov, *Church and Religion in the USSR*, 13–16; Meyendorff, *The Orthodox Church*, 122; *The Russian Revolution and Religion*, 3–4.
73. "Message of the Patriarch Tikhon, Anathematizing the Soviet Regime" (Feb. 1, 1918), in *Russian Revolution and Religion*, 36–37; *Russian Revolution and Religion*, 11.
74. "Instructions to the Orthodox Church against Government Acts" (Feb. 28, 1918), in *Russian Revolution and Religion*, 37–39. After submitting to the regime, the Orthodox followed the Communist spin and no longer saw those who attacked the regime as martyrs for Christ. N. S. Timasheff, "Religion in Russia 1941–1950," in *The Soviet Union*, 191; Kuoyedov, *Church and Religion in the USSR*, 17–19.
75. *Russian Revolution and Religion*, 12–13, 157; Kuoyedov, *Church and Religon in the USSR*, 18–20. The Orthodox Church became a-political during his tenure, professing no allegiance to any type of government system and accepting the most radical dichotomy and secular form of church/state separation.
76. Meyendorff, *The Orthodox Church*, 134–35.
77. Powell, *Antireligious Propaganda in the Soviet Union*, 34–35.
78. "On Religion" (March 18–23, 1919), in *Russian Revolution and Religion*, 49. In 1923, the RSFSR prohibited actions that encouraged superstitious beliefs among the masses. "Violation of the Rules on the Separation of the Church and the State," in *Russian Revolution and Religion*, 107. Article 13 of the RSFSR Constitution seemed to allow religious propaganda, but this provision was changed a decade later on May 22, 1929 to allow "freedom of religious worship and antireligious propaganda," and so eliminating the right of religious people to proselyte. *Russian Revolution and Religion*, 13, 22, 27.
79. Powell, *Antireligious Propaganda in the Soviet Union*, 34; Ramet, *Nihil Obstat*, 230; *Religion in the U.S.S.R.*, 16–18. The League was shut down three months after the Nazi invasion on June 22, 1941. Ramet, *Nihil Obstat*, 232; Timasheff, "Religion in Russia," 184.
80. *Religion in the U.S.S.R.*, 24; Powell, *Antireligious Propaganda in the Soviet Union*, 35.

81. John Shelton Curtiss, *The Russian Church and the Soviet State 1917–1950* (Gloucester, MA: Peter Smith, 1965) 211–12; Matthew Spinka, *Christianity Confronts Communism* (London: The Religious Book Club, 1938) 113; Warren Bartlett Walsh, *Russia and the Soviet Union, A Modern History* (Ann Arbor, MI: The University of Michigan Press, 1958) 425–27; Powell, *Antireligious Propaganda in the Soviet Union*, 36.
82. A. J. Mackenzie, *Propaganda Boom* (London: John Gifford Limited, 1938) 98; Powell, *Antireligious Propaganda in the Soviet Union*, 37.
83. "Religion from the U.S. Legation in Riga on Anti-Religious Propaganda in Soviet Russia" (June 8, 1923), in *Russian Revolution and Religion*, 167.
84. "Report of the U.S. Commissioner in Riga Concerning the Situation of the Church in Russia" (July 17, 1922), in *Russian Revolution and Religion*, 85–86; "Message of the Living Church 'Sobor'" (Aug. 6, 1922), in *Russian Revolution and Religion*, 92; "Memorandum from Committee of the Russian Zenstvos and Cities" (1923), in *Russian Revolution and Religion*, 158.
85. "Requisition of Church Valuables" (June 22, 1922) and "Results of the Confiscation of Church Valuables" (July 5, 1923), in *Russian Revolution and Religion*, 82–83.
86. *Russian Revolution and Religion*, 17–18; "Epistle of Patriarch Tikhon to All the Faithful of the Russian Church" (Feb. 15, 1922), in *Russian Revolution and Religion*, 67; "The *Atheist* Attacks Public Religious Processions and Teaching—'The Clergy'" (March 1922), in *Russian Revolution and Religion*, 68; "Memorandum of Conversation with Mr. Cotton of the American Y.M.C.A. (April 18, 1922), in *Russian Revolution and Religion*, 69; "Memorandum," 158–59; Donald W. Treadgold, *Twentieth Century Russia* (Chicago: Rand McNally & Company, 1964) 250–51; William C. Fletcher, *A Study of Survival: The Church in Russia 1927–1943* (New York: The Macmillan Company, 1965) 16–17; Walter Kolarz, *Religion in the Soviet Union* (London and New York: Macmillan & CO LTD/St Martin's Press, 1962) 38; Meyendorff, *The Orthodox Church*, 131; Powell, *Antireligious Propaganda in the Soviet Union*, 27–28. For a list of confiscated items and desecrated relics, see *Russian Revolution and Religion*, 249–50.
87. *Religion in the U.S.S.R.*, 14; Powell, *Antireligious Propaganda in the Soviet Union*, 25; Constitution of the RSFSR (July 10, 1918), article 65; N. S. Timasheff, *Religion in Soviet Russia* (New York: Sheed & Ward, 1942) 26–27; *Religion in the U.S.S.R.*, 14.
88. "Telegram of Chicherin to Cardinal Gasparri" (April 2, 1919), in *Russian Revolution and Religion*, 52.
89. "Letter of Archbishop Silvestr to Pope Benedict XV" (Feb. 7, 1919), in *Russian Revolution and Religion*, 50.
90. Meyendorff, *The Orthodox Church*, 128. See *Religion in the U.S.S.R.*, 15, 157. The most severe years of persecution were from 1922 to 1924. Meyendorff says some fifty bishops were shot or died following deportation between the years 1923 and 1926.
91. "Memorandum," 156–57. See the *Russian Revolution and Religion*, 247 for a list of sixty-two bishops imprisoned or exiled during this time.
92. *Russian Revolution and Religion*, 185–89; Powell, *Antireligious Propaganda in the Soviet Union*, 29. See the *Russian Revolution and Religion*, 184 for his confession.

93. "Revival of Religion in Russia" (US Ambassador in Rome, Dec. 9, 1921), in *Russian Revolution and Religion*, 62–63.
94. Kuoyedov, *Church and Religion in the USSR*, 21.
95. Curtiss, *The Russian Church and the Soviet State*, 9, 10. Cf. Nicolas Zernov, *The Russian and their Church* (Crestwood, NY: St. Vladimir's Seminary, 1978) 165; Meyendorff, *The Orthodox Church*, 117–18. The Communists sought to destroy religion in general but recognized differences in religious expressions and treated them accordingly. Ramet, *Nihil Obstat*, 35–36. The Catholic hierarchy condemned the new Communist order at first, and many of its leaders were arrested, imprisoned, exiled, and expelled. Kolarz, *Religion in the Soviet Union*, 197–200. Of the 790 Catholic priests, "138 were imprisoned, 40 were murdered, and 5 died in prison." *Russian Revolution and Religion*, 19–22, "Letter of Rev. Xavier Klimaszewski to Archbishop John Baptist Cieplak Concerning His Experiences in Saratov" (1924), in *Russian Revolution and Religion*, 225; "Memoranda from the Polish Executive Committee in Belorussia and Ukraine" (May 12, 1925, and fall of 1925), in *Russian Revolution and Religion*, 228, 231. Sectarian evangelical groups fared well when the Communists first came to power because the regime wanted to disestablish and undermine the Orthodox Church, but this policy soon changed in 1923. The Communists did not want any form of religion to flourish. Powell, *Antireligious Propaganda in the Soviet Union*, 27. On August 12, 1923, the evangelical leaders and their two million followers declared their loyalty to the government in accordance with Paul's words in Romans 13 and even lauded its efforts in feeding the poor and countering the corrosive nature of capitalism in society. "Epistle of the Supreme Council of Evangelical Christians to All Communities and All Single Brethren Evangelical Christian Residents in the Union of Soviet Socialist Soviet Republics" (Aug. 12, 1923) in *Russian Revolution and Religion*, 210. The Communists were not overtly anti-Semitic until Stalin in the 1930s and seemed to leave the Jews alone for the most part, although they sought to suppress the teaching of Yiddish and Hebrew at times. Of course, they suppressed the Zionist movement for undermining the Russian Communist dream of a utopia in their own country through an alternative nationalism. *The Russian Revolution and Religion*, 23–24; Roger N. Baldwin, *Liberty under the Soviets* (New York: Vanguard Press, 1928) 76–78. At first, the Communists were more cautious in dealing with Muslims since religion was so much a part of its culture. Powell, *Antireligious Propaganda in the Soviet Union*, 26–27; *The Russian Revolution and Religion*, 65. The Stalin era brought more oppressive measures to the community, imprisoning the *ulema* for teaching exploitive doctrines like the veiling of women, confiscating community property, destroying mosques, banning the Arabic script, and suppressing Muslim schools. Muslims were also accused of conducting counterrevolutionary activities during the Great Purge and the number of mosques dwindled from ca. 26,000 in 1917 to 1,312 in 1942. Alexandre Benningsen and Marie Broxup, *The Islamic Threat to the Soviet State* (New York: St. Martin's Press, 1983) 40–48; *Religion in the U.S.S.R.*, 73–74; Ramet, *Nihil Obstat*, 24.
96. Wood, *Stalin and Stalinism*, 11–13.
97. Kołakowski, *Main Current of Marxism*, 862.

98. Joseph Stalin, *Dialectical Materialism* (New York: International Publishers, 1940) 5–10, 13–14, 17–23, 26, 34–40. This emphasis on progress moves the Marxists away from Darwin and sounds more like the metaphysical speculations of Hegel, which they renounce in their "scientific" method. Chap. 4 rejects the idealistic claim that we cannot know the thing-in-itself.
99. Kołakowski, *Main Currents of Marxism*, 818–19, 849–50; Wood, *Stalin and Stalinism*, 30–31.
100. Petrov, "Aims and Methods of Soviet Terrorism," 140–41.
101. Gurian, "Development of the Soviet Regime," 7–9; Wood, *Stalin and Stalinism*," 38. There is significant circumstantial evidence to suggest that Stalin was involved in the death but no absolute proof.
102. Kołakowski, *Main Currents of Marxism*, 852.
103. Ibid., 853.
104. Wood, *Stalin and Stalinism*, 40, 46–47.
105. Wood, *Stalin and Stalinism*, 38–47. Wood thinks that millions contracted Stalin's paranoia—about enemies, foreigners, spies, and so on—and became his accomplice in the mass hysteria. In 1940, Stalin made Nicolai Ezhov, the head of the NKVD, the last victim and scapegoat of his Great Purge, accusing him of going too far and terrorizing the people. Trotsky, Stalin's greatest enemy, was killed the same year in Mexico, probably through one of Stalin's agents. Petrov, "Aims and Methods of Soviet Terrorism," 144–45. Modern scholars estimate the USSR casualties in WWII to be anywhere between 27 and 30 million.
106. *Bolshaya Sovetskaya Entsiklopediya* (Large Soviet Encyclopedia) (Moscow, 1926–1947) 1789; cited in *Religion in the U.S.S.R.*, 19.
107. Timasheff, *Religion in Soviet Russia*, 39–40; Treadgold, *Twentieth Century Russia*, 350; Petrov, "Aims and Methods of Soviet Terrorism," 153; Powell, *Antireligious Propaganda in the Soviet Union*, 29.
108. Curtiss, *The Russian Church and the Soviet State*, 233; Powell, *Antireligious Propaganda in the Soviet Union*, 30; Ramet, *Nihil Obstat*, 24; *Religion in the U.S.S.R.*, 13, 22, 27.
109. Nathaniel Davis, *A Long Walk to Church: A Contemporary History of Russian Orthodoxy* (Boulder, CO: Westview Press, 1995) 12–13. Cf. *Religion in the Soviet Union*, 34; Timasheff, "Religion in Russia 1941–50," 158; Meyendorff, *The Orthodox Church*, 153, 155.
110. *Religion in the U.S.S.R.*, 34; Timasheff, "Religion in Russia," 154.
111. Powell, *Antireligious Propaganda in the Soviet Union*, 32, 38; Meyendorff, *The Orthodox Church*, 155; Timasheff, "Religion in Russia," 155–57.
112. *Religion in the U.S.S.R.*, 40; Timasheff, "Religion in Russia," 156–57, 175–78.
113. Gennadi Kostyrchenko, *Out of the Red Shadows: Anti-Semitism in Stalin's Russia* (Amherst, NY: Prometheus Books, 1995) 168–70, 176. The Communists also sound much like Hitler in complaining about Jewish dominance in the arts, journalism, higher education, the medical profession, and so on.
114. Ibid., 63; Powell, *Antireligious Propaganda in the Soviet Union*, 33. The Communists often reduced Judaism to materialistic concerns, much like Hitler and the sons of the Enlightenment. Lenin rejected Bauer's analysis and found the roots of Judaism in the "money system" or in "commercial and industrial practice." "Conspectus of the Book The Holy Family," 37.

115. Due to international pressure, the USSR supported the creation of the state of Israel in 1948, hoping it would become a Socialist state. Earlier, some Jews favored the creation of a Jewish state in Crimea as an alternative to Zionism, but Stalin had a negative reaction to the proposal. On May 4, 1934, the Politburo responded to Zionism with a decision to transform the Birobidzhan district in the Far East into a Jewish region, but the project failed due to massive repression and assimilation policies. Kostyrchenko, *Out of the Red Shadows*, 50–51, 101ff., 144ff., 152.
116. *Great Soviet Encyclopedia: A Translation of the Third Edition* (New York: MacMillan Inc., 1973–1983) 11.312.
117. Powell, *Antireligious Propaganda in the Soviet Union*, 34; Baldwin, *Liberty under the Soviets*, 76–77; *The Russian Revolution and Religion*, 23; Kostyrchenko, *Out of the Red Shadows*, 133, 168. Stalin was only escalating Lenin's policies.
118. Kostyrchenko, *Out of the Shadows*, 90ff., 94, 98. Of course, the JAC was shut down. Ibid., 112–13.
119. Ibid., 132.
120. Ibid., 79ff., 86–88, 132, 177–78, 182–83, 248–49, 303, 312; Powell, *Antireligious Propaganda in the Soviet Union*, 34; Kostyrchenko, *Out of the Red Shadows*, 281; *Pravda* (Jan. 13, 1953), cited in Kostyrchenko, *Out of the Red Shadows*, 290–91.
121. *Great Soviet Encyclopedia*, 13.38; 17.668–69; 23.272–73; 25.585; 28.161, 187.
122. Meyendorff, *The Orthodox Church*, 138; *Religion in the U.S.S.R.*, 45–48, 64; Powell, *Antireligious Propaganda in the Soviet Union*, 39.
123. John Anderson, *Religion, state and politics in the Soviet Union and successor states* (Cambridge, UK: Cambridge University Press, 1994) 32–34; Ramet, *Nihil Obstat*, 234; *Religion in the U.S.S.R.*, 46; Powell, *Antireligious Propaganda in the Soviet Union*, 40–41.
124. Donald A. Lowrie and William C. Fletcher, "Khrushchev's Religious Policy, 1959–1964," in *Aspects of Religion in the Soviet Union 1917–1967*, Richard H. Marshall (ed.) (Chicago: The University of Chicago Press, 1971) 131–35; Janz, *World Christianity and Marxism*, 39–40; Meyendorff, *The Orthodox Church*, 159; *Religion in the U.S.S.R.*, 47.
125. Janz, *World Christianity and Marxism*, 41. See Ramet, *Nihil Obstat*, 234. The policy was short-lived, and the parental right to instruct children in religion and attend services together restored. Kuroyedov, *Church and Religion in the USSR*, 42–43.
126. Gavin White, "Religion and Social Control in the Soviet Union 1945–1964," in *Persecution and Toleration*, W. J. Sheils (ed.) (Oxford: Basil Blackwell, 1984) 477–79. Four months after the initial decree in 1954, the Soviet thought it necessary to curb excess antireligious activity by issuing a decree "On Mistakes in the Conduct of Scientific Atheistic Propaganda among the Population," not wanting a backlash or "intensification of religious prejudices." *Religion in the U.S.S.R.*, 45.
127. Powell, *Antireligious Propaganda in the Soviet Union*, 19. See William C. Fletcher, "Religious Dissent in the USSR in the 1960s," *Slavic Review* 30/2 (July 1971): 299–300; Ramet, *Nihil Obstat*, 234.
128. Davis, *A Long Walk to Church*, 112. Western experts estimated the number of religious people around 28 percent, and the Soviets estimated anywhere from 15 percent to 30 percent. Janz, *World Christianity and Marxism*, 41.

129. Janz, *World Christianity and Marxism*, 41–44; Kuroyedov, *Church and Religion in the USSR*, 52–53; Ramet, *Nihil Obstat*, 234; *Church and Religion in the USSR*, 44–45.
130. John D. Basil, "Church-State Relations in Russia: Orthodoxy and Federation Law, 1990–2004," *Religion, State & Society* 33/2 (June 2005): 152–53; The Constitution of the Russian Federation (Dec. 12, 1993), article 14, 28.
131. On Freedom of Conscience and Religious Associations (1997), prologue. This act refers to the Russian federation as a "secular state" and excises all religious ceremonies and rites from its activities [art.4 (4)]. However, it wants to strengthen "cooperation of the state with religious associations," so they can "enjoy public support." Article 4 (3) specifically justifies the rebuilding of 2,300 Russian churches since the fall of communism, saying the state regulates the distribution of "taxes and other privileges," and grants "financial, material, and other support to religious organizations for restoration, maintenance, and preservation of buildings and objects that are monuments of history and culture." Article 8 (and following) speaks of giving agencies within the government the authority to recognize and register religious groups and grant them a certain status. In order to receive the status of "all-Russian," a group must meet the standards of a "centralized religious organization" and operate fifty years in the Russian federation before any consideration [art. 8 (5)]. Article 13 speaks of regulating foreign organizations.
132. Basil, "Church-State Relations in Russia," 154–57.

Postscript

The doctrine of church/state separation developed out of different motivations and religious perspectives in the modern world. The Reformation first developed its concept of separation out of the growing dissidence in the church within the medieval period, which questioned the exercise of temporal powers in the papacy. The Reformers brought this discontent to the forefront of society and sought to eliminate worldly power from the church for the sake of preserving its soul. They felt the church had corrupted its ways in the Middle Ages and needed to concentrate upon the spiritual mission of the gospel and the inward purity of the fellowship, rather than risk losing its salt in a struggle to exercise a more extensive dominion and utilize more coercive means. The so-called Radical Reformation or Anabaptists often extended this aspect of the Protestant position to a more consistent extreme, decrying magistrates as infidels, rejecting any participation in government, and renouncing the use of the sword altogether.

In America, the Protestant propensity toward church/state separation was represented by a number of important groups and individuals among the early colonists. William Bradford and his Pilgrims represented the original separatist tradition of Congregationalism, which sought to reform the church outside of governmental authority and create a pure fellowship apart from the corrupting influence of temporal powers. Roger Williams followed this part of the Congregationalist tradition in his desire to create a fellowship of true believers, causing a schism within the Massachusetts Bay Colony through his sanctimonious preachments against the established authority within the church and state. He wanted to build a "wall of separation" between church and state in order to protect the two realms from corrupting each other, while allowing individuals to serve in both realms as long as the left-hand and right-hand remained unaware of their respective activities.[1] The Baptists became the strongest advocates of this position and reduced religion to a private matter between the individual and God. Their position was motivated by a heartfelt desire to promote the purity of the church and freedom of religious expression, but they often ignored the darker side in those individuals and groups who were less devoted to the mission of the church and used it as a pretext for diminishing the church and its role in society, as the study exemplified in the specific cases of the French Revolution, Nazi Germany, and Communist Russia. In Virginia, the Baptists joined with Thomas Jefferson to forward the position and gained a great victory in disestablishing the Anglican Church, or ending a priori government-sponsored privileges for any denomination of the Christian faith through the *Virginia Statute for Religious Freedom* (1786). They worked with Jefferson in commending the separation of church and state as a means of liberating the people from religious uniformity and promoting freedom of diverse expression, but often displayed a witting or unwitting tendency to ignore the darker motivations of their "Founding Father" and the total ramifications of his broader agenda, which clearly sought to end Christian influence in society a posteriori by denying a representative participation of its ideas or symbols in government and using public education to wean the citizens of Virginia off the Christian faith. The Baptist position showed its affinity to the dark side through the historical connection with Jefferson and the overexercised rhetoric ever since, which exalted his place and stance in the cause of religious liberty and glossed over many of the more disturbing details.[2]

This hagiography surrounding the name of Jefferson makes it difficult to develop a critical evaluation of his position, but the evidence linking him to the Enlightenment and the dark side is hard to miss.[3] Already his early literary notebook displays the influence through its extensive use of Viscount Bolingbroke, the mentor of Voltaire, containing "54 excerpts and over 10,000 words" from the English Deist and making him the most prominent author in the work. The many excerpts are filled with the typical vitriol of the Deists and philosophes toward the Judeo-Christian tradition and reveal Jefferson's own deep-seated animus and proclivity toward a hostile view of the faith from the very beginning of his maturation.[4] His mature works and letters only continue to confirm this enlightened tendency as Jefferson proceeds to deprecate the Jewish people and their faith with the same type of anti-Semitic comments that marked the age of reason and to denounce the church along the same line for perverting the simple moral teachings of Jesus, turning him into a wonder-worker and divine Savior, and spilling "oceans of human blood" over these types of metaphysical dogmas—just like any Deist or philosophe.[5] Toward the end of his life, he expresses his hope for the future, that it will witness a "quiet euthanasia" of the tradition and establish a more sober religion of nature, replacing the dependence of faith upon special revelation with the philosophes' confidence in the power of reason.[6] Throughout his life, Jefferson leaves this type of clear and unequivocal testimony, revealing his affinity toward the religious sensibilities of the philosophes and disdain for the faith of the *Ancien Régime.*

Of course, none of this would matter if religion was really a private affair, but Jefferson showed a willingness throughout his career to go beyond the process of private polemical debate and employ more coercive political means to perform the "quiet euthanasia." By crossing this line, he followed the example of the French Revolution in using the state to promote the program; he just moved at a slower pace by recognizing the political and religious realities of the country and the necessity of accomplishing the objective in a quieter manner, always careful not to disturb the public peace through direct and noticeable Jacobin-like acts of confrontation. His quiet program led him to promote and use public education as a more subtle means of accomplishing the same objective. Among his darker moments as the "Father of Public Education," he proposed a series of three bills in October 1776, the first two seeking to undermine the church's place in the future of educating the youth in Virginia and revealing at least a part of his motive in promoting state-sponsored education. The Bill for the More General Diffusion of Knowledge launched a plan to create an educational system that would take the Bible "out of the hands of children" and replace its moral lessons with other edifying examples from Greco-Roman and European culture[7]—clearly trying to establish a Voltairean type of historical consciousness and undermine the Judeo-Christian tradition in the minds of the students. His Bill for Amending the Constitution of William and Mary wanted to seize control of the school away from the church and eliminate theological instruction all together—a plan he enacted through his own executive powers as a visitor to the college and governor to the state, instead of using the typical legislative process.[8] In 1816, he supported the same process in New Hampshire, where the state tried to arrest Dartmouth College, a private Congregationalist institution, away from the board of trustees.[9] Later on, as rector and founder of the University of Virginia, he refused to appoint a professor of divinity to teach "theology, apologetics, and Scripture," against the typical practice of the day, but he decided to replace this type of ecclesiastical instruction with an ethics professor, who was encouraged to inculcate the tenets of natural religion.[10] The school was founded with the explicit intention to challenge the clerical and federalist stranglehold on education in the North. It certainly promoted some sense of liberty in the sense of freeing the curriculum from the dogma of priests in accordance with the French model, but it also became a pretext for advancing Jefferson's own religious sensibilities and Republican agenda by prescribing textbooks, editing others, and stacking the faculty with his own constituency, especially in the law school.[11] His concern over ecclesiastical power preoccupied his energies throughout much of his career and caused him to scheme at various times against the church and propose other measures withstanding the basic rights of typical citizenship, including a prohibition against the clergy from serving on school boards, holding public office, and preaching politics in the pulpit[12]—a policy most Americans accept today.

As president of the United States, Jefferson inscribed this policy in a famous letter to the Danbury Baptist Association (January 1, 1802). The letter was written in defense of his decision to eliminate the national day of prayer and fasting, but it also contained an outline showing his basic concept of the relationship between church and state as a means of defending the decision. Early in his career, he wrote the first draft of the *Virginia Statute for Religious Freedom* (1786), which promoted the freedom of religious expression, the disestablishment of the Anglican Church, and the right for all citizens to hold public office, regardless of their religious profession. Now in this letter to the association, he wanted to outline a more extensive policy that proceeds in a different direction and called for an end to Christian influence on the government. He says the church serves as a corrupting force in the public square, and it is necessary to relegate religion to a private "matter which lies solely between Man & his God" by erecting a "wall of separation between church & state."[13] Jefferson was still reeling from his run for the White House the previous year, when his opponents tried to warn the nation about his connection to the Enlightenment and contempt for the Christian faith.[14] Jefferson tried to keep his religious opinions quiet during the campaign and now wanted to make his silence a national policy, hoping to keep religion off the table and silence religious expression in the public square—much in contrast to the earlier emphasis upon the freedom of religion. His early statute called for the inclusion of all religious people; His "wall" called for the exclusion of the church. His Declaration of Independence made religion the basis of government, using the Lockean conception of the state as the guardian of God-given or natural rights; His wall spoke of government in much different terms, as the product of rational/secular autonomy and religion as an alien metaphysical speculation, without any practical relation to corporate life, except in a negative sense, following and exceeding the ultraisms of most philosophes. The two Jeffersons remained in tension throughout his life and produced a nation that remains deeply divided over the issue to this day; all agreeing with the disestablishment of the church or ending any place of guaranteed privilege to specific religious groups, but disagreeing over the place or space of religion in general to find representation and compete for the affections of the American people within the public square; some emphasizing the relationship of church and state, and others calling for the separation.

The Supreme Court created much of the controversy in *Everson v. the Board of Education* (1947), when it made Jefferson's letter to the Danbury Baptist Association an authoritative means of interpreting the First Amendment and erected a "wall between church and state," which is "high and impregnable." The choice of Jefferson was certainly debatable, given the simple fact that he was not at the Constitutional Convention and represented only a minority, French viewpoint among its delegates, but none of this seemed to bother Justice Hugo Black, who considered Jefferson the "number one, number two, and number three" authority when it came to understanding the First Amendment.[15] Those who defended the wall certainly distanced their position from the anti-Semitic and anti-Christian roots of Jefferson's opinion on the issue, promoting it as a means of maintaining government neutrality in regard to religion and not showing partiality by endorsing any religious practice or point of view through providing it space for a specific expression in the public domain. Most reduced the caustic rhetoric of Jefferson and the Enlightenment in defending the wall, even if traces of its original rationale arise to the surface from time-to-time in their arguments and find more explicit expression in its most zealous defenders like the ACLU. These traces certainly provide a pretext on the other side of the debate to deconstruct and psychoanalyze their opponents in an attempt to unveil darker motivations lying underneath the outward rationalizations, but this type of deconstruction might be better served by proceeding along the lines of the present study and speaking of the latent history clinging to the wall through its French origin, using genealogy as a means of criticizing values in the manner of Michel Foucault, rather than engaging in ad hominem attacks, vitriolic polemics, and casting aspersions on the other side. Those who promote the wall might not think of themselves as anti-Semitic or anti-Christian, but are they able to escape its dark history in maintaining their position?

After the watershed ruling in 1947, the court followed the Jeffersonian model and worked to eliminate the remnants of religious expression from the public square. The court continued to interpret the Establishment Clause as a broad indictment of allowing any "endorsement of religion" by the government,[16] although its decisions lacked consistency and caused the jurists at one point to reduce the wall to a "line," which was "blurred, indistinct, and variable" in *Lemon v. Kurtzman* (1971). This particular case maintained the possibility of achieving fundamental government neutrality in regard to religion and developed a threefold test to see if a statute would pass constitutional muster and further the basic objective of establishing a secular state.

> Every analysis in this area must begin with consideration of the cumulative criteria developed by the Court over many years. Three such tests may be gleaned from our cases. First, the statute must have a secular legislative purpose; second, its principal or primary effect must be one that neither advances nor inhibits religion, . . .; finally, the statute must not foster "an excessive government entanglement with religion."[17]

But one might wonder if it is ever possible for the government to remain fundamentally neutral in maintaining the Jeffersonian concept? Does the very concept demand a Voltairean skewing of history, dismissing the positive contributions of the Judeo-Christian tradition in forging the nation, in order to maintain the secular nature of the government? Does the concept marginate religion as a "private matter" and inculcate a Deist or enlightened outlook on life, which finds freedom in human autonomy, secularity, or independence from the will and presence of God? Does the concept represent the ideology of the age of reason, dismissing the subjective nature of human knowledge in the post-Kantian/post-modern world, only pretending to develop metaphysical ideas from rational, objective, and scientific analysis (Jules Ferry), making history justify itself (Marx), science provide a moral imperative (Hitler), or ethics a simple calculating sum, revolving around a utilitarian goal (Robespierre)? Does the concept retain something even more sinister and forward an indelible remnant of its dark history or the attempt to replace the Judeo-Christian tradition with a new emphasis upon allegiance to the state or etatism? At the very least these types of questions can be placed upon the concept if one follows the postmodern analysis of Foucault and finds a trace of its origin within the modern expression.

Notes

1. Roger Williams, *Mr. Cottons Letter Lately Printed, Examined and Answered* (London, 1644) 45; *The Bloudy Tenent of Persecution for Cause of Conscience*, Richard Groves (ed.) (Macon, GA: Mercer University Press, 2001) 83, 153, 239; Philip Hamburger, *Separation of Church and State* (Cambridge, MA: Harvard University Press, 2002) 43–45, 51–52, 59.
2. Strehle, *The Egalitarian Spirit of Christianity*, 257–62.
3. For a fuller discussion and documentation of Jefferson's viewpoint on the Judeo-Christian tradition and the relationship between church and state, see my article "Jefferson's Opposition to the Judeo-Christian Tradition," in *Faith and Politics in America: From Jamestown to the Civil War*, Joseph Prud'homme (ed.) (New York: Peter Lang, 2011).
4. *Jefferson's Literary Commonplace Book*, in *Papers of Thomas Jefferson*, Douglas L. Wilson (ed.) (Princeton, NJ: Princeton University Press, 1989) 5, 8, 11.
5. "To Benjamin Rush" (April 21, 1803) F 9.462, L 10.380–85; "To William Canby" (Sept. 18, 1813) L 13.377, 378; "To William Short" (Aug. 4, 1820) F 15.257, 260; "To Joseph Priestly" (April 9, 1803) F 9.458, 459; "To Edward Dowse, Esq." L 10.376, 377; "To Charles Thomson" (Jan. 9, 1816) F 11.498; "To William Short" (April 13, 1820) L 15.245; "To Samuel Kercheval [William Balwin]" (Jan. 19, 1810) L 12.345, 356; "To Rev.Thomas Whittmore" (June 5, 1822) L 15.373, 374; "To James Fishback" (Sept. 27, 1809) L 12.315–16 (along with Jefferson's missing composition draft); Robert M. Healey, "Jefferson on Judaism and the Jews," *American Jewish History* 78/4 (June, 1984) 363–66. F stands for *The Works of Thomas Jefferson*, Paul Leicester Ford (ed.) (New York and London: G. P. Putnam's Sons, 1904, and L stands for *The Writings of Thomas Jefferson*, Andrew A. Lipscomb (ed.) (Washington, DC: The Jefferson Memorial Association, 1905.
6. "To William Short" (Oct. 31, 1819) F 12.142; Robert M. Healey, *Jefferson on Religion in Public Education* (New Haven, CT, and London: Yale University Press, 1962) 157–58, 161ff., 204–5.
7. *Notes on Virginia* (1782) F 4.62; Jennings L. Wagoner, *Jefferson and Education* ([Charlottesville, VA]: Thomas Jefferson Foundation, 2004) 35.
8. *A Bill Amending the Constitution of the College of William and Mary*, in *The Papers of Thomas Jefferson*, Julian P. Boyd (ed.) (Princeton, NJ: Princeton University Press, 1950–) 2.539; *Autobiography* (1743–1790) F 1.78;

R. O. Woodburn, "An Historical Investigation of the Opposition to Jefferson's Educational Proposals in the Commonwealth of Virginia" (PhD dissertation, Washington, DC: The American University, 1974) 50–54, 145, 148; Wagoner, *Jefferson and Education*, 40; Leonard W. Levy, *Jefferson & Civil Liberties: The Darker Side* (Cambridge, MA: Harvard University Press, 1963) 9–11.

9. Edwin S. Gaustad, *Sworn on the Altar of God: A Religious Biography of Thomas Jefferson* (Grand Rapids, Mich.: William B. Eerdmans, 1996) 16–17.
10. "Report on the Commissioners for the University of Virginia" (Aug. 4, 1818), in *Writings* (New York: The Library of America, 1984) 467; Healey, *Jefferson on Religion*, 170–72, 216ff.; Gaustad, *Sworn on the Altar*, 163.
11. "To James Madison" (Feb. 17, 1826) F 12.456; "From the Minutes of the Board of Visitors" (March 4, 1825), in *Writings*, 479; *The Life and Selected Writings of Thomas Jefferson*, Adrienne Koch and William Peden (ed.) (New York: The Modern Library, 1944) 725–26; Wagoner, *Jefferson and Education*, 87, 125, 137–38; Levy, *Jefferson & Civil Liberties*, 144–53.
12. *Jefferson and Madison on Separation*, Lenni Brenner (ed.) (Fort Lee, NJ: Barricade Books, 2004) 75 ["To Marquis de Chastellux" (Sept. 2, 17850]; "To P. H. Wendover" (March 13, 1815) L 14.282–83; Leonard W. Levy, *The Establishment Clause: Religion and the First Amendment* (Chapel Hill: The University of North Carolina, 1994) 70–72; Hamburger, *The Separation of Church and State*, 81, 84–88, 135; David N. Mayer, *The Constitutional Thought of Thomas Jefferson* (Charlottesville: University Press of Virginia, 1994) 165; Healey, *Jefferson on Religion*, 136–37, 227–28. He rejects his former position of excluding the clergy from office in the face of mounting criticism but then reinstates it in his Bill for Establishing a System of Public Education (1817). "To Jeremiah Moor" (Aug. 14, 1800) F 9.142–43.
13. "To Mssrs. Nehemiah Dodge and Others, a Committee of the Danbury Baptist Association in the State of Connecticut" (Jan. 1, 1802), in *Writings* (New York: The Library of America, 1984) 510; "To the Attorney General (Levi Lincoln)" (Jan. 1, 1802), in *The Writings of Thomas Jefferson*, A. A. Lipscomb (Washington, DC: The Jefferson Memorial Association, 1905) 10.305; Daniel Dreisbach, *Thomas Jefferson and the Wall of Separation between Church and State* (New York and London: New York University Press, 2002) 17, 41ff., 46, 48, 56, 185; Hamburger, *Separation of Church and State*, 159–62; Levy, *Jefferson & Civil Liberties: The Darker Side* (Cambridge, MA: Belknap Press of Harvard University, 1963) 7. He drops a specific reference to the proclamation in an earlier draft, lest he offend the Republican constituency up north by going too far. He also strikes out the adjective "eternal" in front of the term "separation," as well as references to the role of the federal government as "merely temporal" and secular. His practice in regard to fast days is marked by political pragmatism. He calls them whenever necessary, but he wants to make them nonmandatory and nonsectarian. *Autobiography* (1743–1790), in *The Works of Thomas Jefferson*, P. L. Ford (ed.) (New York: G. P. Putnam's Sons, 1904) 1.12; Dreisbach, *Thomas Jefferson and the Wall*, 58, 59. His northern constituency is less radical than Jefferson in regard to church/state relations. Isaac Backus, the leader of Baptists in the North, does not advocate the severe, Jeffersonian position of John Lelland and the many Virginia Baptists on public religion. He never "opposed the fact that the Westminster Confession of Faith was mandatory for all Massachusetts

school children, nor did he object to laws against 'profanity, blasphemy, gambling, theater-going, and desecration of the Sabbath, which [he] accepted as within the domain of the government in its preservation of a Christian society.'" J. J. Owen, "The Struggle between Religion and Nonreligion," *American Political Science Review* 101/3 (Aug. 2007) 500; Edwin S. Gaustad, *Sworn on the Altar* (Grand Rapids, MI: W. B. Eerdmans Pub., 1996) 107; Stephen Strehle, *The Egalitarian Spirit of Christianity* (New Brunswick, NJ, and London: Transaction Publishers, 2009) 259, 260. John Adams and the Massachusetts Constitution (1780) also called for a "Publick Religion." J. Witte, "Publick Religion: Adams v. Jefferson," *First Things* 141 (March 2004) 31. The concept of a wall antedates Jefferson. It is used by a number of notable authors: Richard Hooker, Menno Simons, Roger Williams, and James Burgh. The specific source matters little in understanding Jefferson's concept, but a good guess is James Burgh, a dissenting Scottish schoolmaster, whom Jefferson read and admired. Burgh used the metaphor extensively in his works. Daniel Dreisbach, *Thomas Jefferson and the Wall of Separation*, 79–81. His severe position develops early on, as seen in his *Commonplace Book*. The excerpts reject that Christianity played a role in the common law tradition of England. He cites the work "Houard in his Coutumes Anglo-Normandes, I.87," which speaks of the "alliance between church and state" as a fraud of the clergy and refers to their falsification of Alfred's laws with "four surreptitious chapters of Exodus [20–23]." The Bible and its Decalogue are not part of the common law. *Jefferson's Literary Commonplace Book*, 351ff. (873–79), 362–63 (879).

14. Noble E. Cunningham, "Election of 1800," in *History of American Presidential Elections, 1789–1968*, Arthur M. Schlesinger (ed.) (New York: Celesea House, 1971); *The Papers of Alexander Hamilton*, Harold Coffin Syrett (ed.) (New York and London: Columbia University Press, 1974) 21.402–4; Frank Lambert, *The Founding Fathers and the Place of Religion in America* (Princeton, NJ: Princeton University Press, 2003) 274–77; Henry Wilder Foote, *The Religion of Thomas Jefferson* (Boston: Beacon Press, 1960) 3, 46; Healey, *Jefferson on Religion*, 164. Hamilton made religion a central issue in the 1800 campaign, warning the voters of Jefferson's relationship to the French Revolution and its "atheism."

15. Roger K. Newman, *Hugo Black: A Biography* (New York: Pantheon Books, 1994) 67, 141–43, 448–50. Black grew up as a Baptist but left his former religious convictions back in the Bible Belt and began to identify with the ideology of authors like John Dewey, Bertrand Russell, and Albert Camus—the leading atheists of the day. Roger Newman, his leading biographer, describes him as basically an "irreligious man," who "drifted from organized religion," except for an occasional visit to All Souls Unitarian Church. Ibid., 463, 521. The dissent only wanted to proceed further and deny Catholics the use of buses in the name of the wall. The dissent was spearheaded by Felix Frankfurter, a secular Jew, a founder of the ACLU, a left-wing Socialist, and a Harvard professor. Black's decision went through eight drafts in his attempt to please the opposition and reiterate his commitment to church/state separation. James F. Simon, *The Antagonists: Hugo Black, Felix Frankfurter, and Civil Liberties in America* (New York: Simon and Schuster, 1989) 81; Hamburg, *Separation of Church and State*, 465–68, 474–75; Newman,

Hugo Black, 361. For a discussion of Frankfurter and the ACLU, Thomas L. Krannawitter and Daniel C. Palm, *A Nation under God?* (Lanham, MD: Rowman & Littlefield Publishers, 2005) 60–63.

16. This is the phrase of Sandra Day O'Connor from *Wallace v. Jaffee* (1985). For William Rehnquist's famous rebuttal, expressing his complete frustration with the court's incoherent position and contradictory decisions, see *Wallace v. Jaffree*, 472 US 92, 106–7, 110–11.
17. *Lemon v. Kurtzman* , 403 US 612–616, 620, 625.

Index